Answers... to the Difficult Questions

for Spiritual Seekers

Answers... to the Difficult Questions

for Spiritual Seekers

Dennis Waite

MANTRA BOOKS

Winchester, UK
Washington, USA

JOHN HUNT PUBLISHING

First published by Mantra Books, 2019
Mantra Books is an imprint of John Hunt Publishing Ltd., No. 3 East Street, Alresford
Hampshire SO24 9EE, UK
office@jhpbooks.net
www.johnhuntpublishing.com
www.mantra-books.net

For distributor details and how to order please visit the 'Ordering' section on our website.

ISBN: 978 1 78904 220 7
978 1 78904 221 4 (ebook)
Library of Congress Control Number: 2018952700

A CIP catalogue record for this book is available from the British Library.

Design: Stuart Davies

Contents

Preface

All seekers encounter problems periodically. A question arises which appears to challenge the veracity of their chosen path. If an answer is not found quickly, there is a great danger that the particular teaching will be abandoned and another sought. I cannot speak for other teachings but I know that traditional Advaita has answers to *all* (seeker-related) questions. This book records the questions from hundreds of seekers over the years and the answers I gave. (I first invited questions to my website in 2005.) It would be surprising if your particular worries are not covered somewhere and it is likely that there will be many questions that have not yet occurred to you! If you have one which is not answered, contact me via the website! (http://www.advaita-vision.org/)

Special thanks go to Rick Scott, who spent many hours reviewing the material and making suggestions for improving the clarity and readability of the answers. Being a professional copy-editor in his earlier life, he also made innumerable corrections to punctuation, spelling, grammar, idiom, layout, repetition etc., thereby significantly improving the presentation and saving the publisher lots of work!

Introduction

If you do not have your own guru and are obliged to glean all of your understanding of non-duality from books and the occasional satsang, it is inevitable that there will be aspects that you do not fully understand. Dennis Waite, author of the universally acclaimed 'Back to the Truth', has been answering 'The Difficult Questions' at his website (Advaita.org.uk) for many years now. Here, he groups together over 450 of these questions into 7 sections and 57 sub-sections, providing additional introductory and clarifying material. It is very likely that this book will resolve your difficulties. (If not, send in your own question via the 'email me' link at Advaita Vision (http://www.advaita-vision.org/questions-and-answers/).)

Note on the use of Sanskrit terms

Since Advaita uses some concepts which have no direct equivalent in everyday use, and often no precise English word, it is necessary to employ some Sanskrit words. It is not expected (in the West, at any rate!) that seekers will learn the language, or even the script that was used to write it. Instead, the Roman alphabet is used to 'transliterate' the script so that you can at least pronounce words. Since the Sanskrit language has nearly twice as many letters as ours and more than three times as many vowels, it is necessary to manufacture variants of our Roman letters so that it can cope. Various methods of achieving this have been devised. This book uses one which was devised in the early days of the Internet so that words could easily be typed on a keyboard. It uses lower and upper case versions of the same Roman letter to stand for different Sanskrit letters. It is not necessary for you to learn these; the correct letters are used for those who have learned the difference (and the actual Devanagari script is only used in the Glossary). Appendix 1 contains a short description of this 'transliteration scheme' (which is called ITRANS).

Author background

It is my belief that people who are generally happy with their lives, who have plans for the future, who fill their time with pursuits (whether or not these might be deemed worthwhile) and who share these aims and endeavors with others, do not ask the sort of questions addressed in this book. They have better things to occupy their minds!

Rather it is the outsider, the loner and introvert, the one who thinks too much about life, and why he or she does not seem to be a part of it. For the first 20 years of my life, I could be described by the first three terms but did not have time to consider the questions of life, the universe and everything – I was too busy being educated. As soon as I left university and no longer had to study in my spare time, I found myself irresistibly drawn to what might be called 'philosophical musing'. What was the point of it all?

My so-called education gave me no background for this, so that I spent many years of searching without any sense of direction ... and without finding anything! I was asked about how I came to discover the truths taught by Advaita in an interview for 'Non-Duality' Ezine in 2010 and answered as follows:

I guess the first hint must have been when I was about 6-8 years old. My parents sent me to a Methodist Sunday school and I attended for maybe 6-9 months. I eventually stopped going and I recall telling my parents that it just did not make any sense – if there was a God, then he couldn't (just) be in heaven; he had to be everywhere.

But I didn't actively begin seeking until my early twenties, by which time I was convinced that I was never going to gain any lasting satisfaction from worldly pursuits and decided that I had to look to philosophy for some explanations. I began attending the School of Economic Science (SES) in response to the 'Course of Philosophy' lectures that they advertised on the London Underground. And I stayed for a couple of years until they wanted me to part with a week's salary to be initiated into

Transcendental Meditation. (I didn't really know anything about this at the time and resented the pressure. Years later, I discovered its value and even appreciate that the financial demand insures commitment.) But at that time, they were still mainly influenced by Ouspensky and their teaching was a bit weird to say the least.

After a break to get married, have a child, get divorced and re-marry, I returned to SES in the mid eighties, by which time their teaching was much more influenced by Advaita. And I stayed until around 1998, by which time I had myself been tutoring for a number of years. I left because I had realized as a result of outside reading that the school's Advaita was corrupted by other philosophies such as Sankhya, Yoga and the Grammarians. I also followed Francis Lucille (a 'Direct Path' teacher) for a while at this stage.

After being made redundant in 2000, I tried to set up my own computer consultancy for a couple of years and wrote a book on Earned Value metrics. When this didn't work out, I started the website (http://www.advaita.org.uk) and began to write about Advaita full time. It was really this process – setting down all of the aspects of the teaching, asking questions, reading lots of books until any points that I did not understand were cleared up – that consolidated my understanding. Basically, I have been doing this every day, evenings and weekends included, since 2002. And, over the period of say 2004 – 2008, I came to the realization that I had no further questions. I was totally convinced of the truth of the teaching and found, through the question and answer section of the website, that there was no question that I could not answer (to my own satisfaction!).

(Note that this does not mean I can answer all questions to other's satisfaction. A lot of this teaching is stepwise and you cannot leap to the top step without traversing the intermediate ones. Also, some seekers may require lots of quotations from scriptures to back up an answer, and I am not always able to provide these – there are hundreds, mostly written in Sanskrit! And, of course, some seekers are so entrenched in, and committed to, their existing mistaken beliefs that they cannot open up to any new ones. The parable of pouring more tea into a cup that is

already full applies here.)

But, again, I am not sure that you appreciate the significance of all of this at the transactional level. Dennis still quite definitely exists. It is a mistaken belief that the person somehow disappears on enlightenment. The person continues until death of the body, driven by prArabdha karma (the arrow continuing to its target once the bow string has been released). [Note that the Sanskrit terms used in this response are explained in answers to some of the questions later and in the Glossary.]

It should also be noted that I have often added additional comments within either question or answer, which did not appear in the original. This might be for additional clarification or to provide an English explanation of a Sanskrit term. [When I do this, the comment is contained in square brackets, in black font, as with this sentence.]

Several warnings!

All readers should take note of the following comments before delving into the book:

I have allocated each of the questions in the book to a section, and the sections are ordered in a logical manner. 'Background' material is addressed first; then we look at where the seeker initially finds him/herself as a 'person' living in a 'world'. Next, the question is asked as to what we can do to discover the 'truth' and how Advaita helps in this respect. Only at the end of the book do we look at the nature of 'reality' and what this means.

However, this book is not a presentation of the teaching of Advaita, as would be given by a qualified teacher starting with a new group of naïve seekers. Some of the questions are clearly being asked by students who already possess considerable understanding. In such cases, the answers I give acknowledge this and may not be suitable for a less qualified seeker. This, indeed, is one of the main problems that I condemn in the case of the 'satsang' style of teaching. It is simply not the case of 'one size fitting all'.

Another (potentially more serious though related) point is

this: Advaita uses a teaching methodology known as adhyAropa-apavAda. Here is how I explain it in 'Advaita Made Easy':

"First of all, it is necessary to mention one of the fundamental aspects in the teaching of Advaita, namely the practice of stating something as true and then later modifying it – attribution and rescission or retraction. The technical term for this is 'adhyAropa-apavAda'. What it means in essence is that what you're told initially may not actually be completely true! It is the intention of the teacher to address a seeker at his or her present level of understanding. By analogy, if you think of someone learning mathematics, there would be little point in teaching differential calculus to a student who has yet to learn algebra, and algebra would be of little value to someone who did not even know basic arithmetic.

Note that this does not mean that you cannot trust what the teacher tells you! In fact, many teachers will give you the bottom line right from the start, even though you will almost certainly not understand why it is so. What they will then do, however, is start from the beginning, using simple arithmetic! There is no point in being impatient. You have to take it step by step. Indeed, patience is one of the mental prerequisites for studying Advaita".

Because the questions in this book are not 'step by step', from the same student, they constantly jump between 'levels' of understanding. I have attempted to point this out if an answer is likely to mislead but cannot guarantee that this will not happen! See also my answer to Q.452 in the section on 'The Teaching of Advaita', where I address a related concern attributable to the same problem.

A second, through related, problem is what is referred to in many answers as confusion arising as a result of 'mixing levels'. The concept of 'levels' of reality is generally attributed to Shankara, who was responsible for 'systematizing' the teaching of Advaita at a time when Buddhism was in the ascendance (around the 8th Century CE).

In this scheme the absolute reality, which, of course, is the *only* reality, is called paramArtha (adjective pAramArthika).

This reality is non-dual and is also referred to as Brahman (in a general context), Atman (in a 'personal' context) or Consciousness. [Atman could be thought of as the essential, unqualified feeling of existence, which you can never doubt.]

The 'empirical' reality – the experiential level of the person living in a world of objects – is called vyavahAra (adjective vyAvahArika). Since the absolute reality is non-dual, this 'level' is not in itself real – its reality depends upon Brahman. The word that describes this state of affairs is 'mithyA'. [Note that Advaita defines 'real' as being that which exists in all three periods of time (past, present and future), or even 'beyond' (atIta) the three periods of time (trikAla)].

There is a third level, called pratibhAsa (adjective prAtibhAsika), which is the illusory state of dream for example. And, for completion, one can also consider a fourth level, called tuchCham, which means absolutely non-existent. Examples used in the scriptures are the son of a barren woman or the horn of a hare.

Thus, 'mixing up of levels' occurs when a questioner tries to talk about one level using the terminology of another. For example, one cannot talk about time or space with respect to Brahman because these concepts are rooted in the dualistic world.

Format

The format of each section in the book is that, following an introduction, the questions that have been asked, which relate to this topic, will be presented. I retain the chronological numbering of the original questions so that reference back to the original material will still be possible. This means that, now that they have been resorted into topic, numbering will no longer be chronological. In some cases, I have often reworded my answers or added additional comments in order to make them clearer.

I occasionally add introductory material at the beginning of a section or sub-section, and a summary of the key points at the end of a section or sub-section, where this is considered to be helpful.

Most seekers picking up this book will already be familiar with most of these terms so the answers (and sometimes the questions) often use these words without any explanation. For those readers who are not, however, all terms are defined in the Glossary at the end of the book.

[The questions were originally asked via my website (http://www.advaita.org.uk/) or blog (http://www.advaita-vision.org/) and the numbers correspond to those given when the Q&A was published at one of these locations. The complete set of questions, together with links to their answers, is given at http://www.advaita-vision.org/questions-and-answers/. Some of the later questions are also answered by other bloggers, but their answers are not recorded here – see the on-line material for those.

The website's invitation to ask questions warns that these may be posted to the site but that anonymity will be maintained. In transcribing these questions therefore, if a question (or answer) has used the actual name of the questioner, I have replaced this with 'Fred'.]

What Is Advaita?

The best explanation would be gained by reading my book 'Advaita Made Easy', which provides a short, readable summary of this. But of course the rest of this book effectively does this by using the teaching of Advaita to answer all of the questions.

It is an undeniable fact that the majority of people today are dissatisfied with what they perceive as being a mediocre existence. They may feel that they are limited by an unattractive and illness-prone body or by a mind that is imperfectly educated and unable to make intellectual leaps of understanding. There are very many things that we want – objects, partners, lifestyle, jobs etc. – but few that we seem to be able to obtain. (And, even when we do obtain them, their rewards are invariably ephemeral.) Western society relies upon the media advertising all of these things, and thereby continually reinforcing the desires. Being repeatedly frustrated by this materialistic lifestyle, it should be hardly surprising that many turn towards the spiritual in the hope that this might bring about peace and a durable happiness.

The problem is that all 'paths' and 'systems' can only promise you a *future* happiness, so that we need to have some sort of reassurance that the commitment of our time and effort will prove worthwhile. Unfortunately, the majority of the 'new age' techniques bring with them no reassurance at all. Frequently, these systems are quite contrary to reason and often rely upon putting one's belief into something that is totally unbelievable. Cynically, one might think that the only reason that there are *several* books upon a particular topic is that the later authors realized after the first book that there was money to be made out of a gullible public.

A 'spiritual seeker' might be defined as the person who has realized that the attaining of 'things' does not, in fact, bring about lasting happiness. All it does is trigger the beginning of the next desire. This is what leads people to seek the magical, the fantastical that will shatter our mundane existence once and for all. Whether this be foretelling our future through tea leaves or crystals, or communicating with aliens or angels hardly matters; our minds make the leap from the worldly to the unknowable, other world where we are promised something that will truly satisfy.

But of course it doesn't, because such worlds are not only unknowable but also imaginary. The fact that this cannot be proven to be so allows such ideas to exist but makes no difference to the outcome. Desiring the illusory is ultimately no more satisfying than obtaining the desirable.

We need to think about what it is that we really want and then refine our desires; evolving from wanting mere gross objects to the desire to discover our own nature and that of reality itself. It is discovered that our desires develop from the gross to the more refined. There is a natural and a necessary progression involved here. We begin with wanting simply *things* in the outside world (of course these may be people or situations etc.). Then we realize that it is not the things themselves that we want but the happiness that we believe they will bring. The objects are many but the happiness is actually only one. Moreover, there usually comes a time when the object ceases to give happiness and you want to get rid of it!

The next step follows logically from the previous. The fact that things do not always give happiness means that the happiness is not actually in the object but in our self. It is never anywhere else! And it is this fact that deserves serious investigation. Happiness is, in fact, our natural state and that this is revealed whenever a desire is removed (e.g. when we obtain something that we want and the desire for it goes away). Clearly, since we do not experience happiness all the time, this natural state must somehow be covered over. So the next startling realization is that nothing I can *do* could ever obtain happiness for me (since I cannot choose whether or not to have desires). Indeed, it seems that most of the things that I do bring unhappiness! Instead, what has to happen is that I must come to know this natural state, i.e. my true self. This true self is not something to be obtained but something I have to know. Accordingly, the penultimate refinement of my desires is from wanting to find my Self to wanting Self-knowledge.

And thus we come to Advaita. Advaita is a proven teaching methodology to give me knowledge of my Self. The knowledge is contained in the scriptures called the Upanishads, which were written down thousands of years ago, having previously been passed down by word of mouth from the ancient rishis. Since they were necessarily in fairly dense form, and written in Sanskrit, they need to be interpreted and explained by someone who both knows the Self and is familiar with the techniques, stories and metaphors used to unfold these scriptures. These techniques have themselves been passed down from guru to disciple in a structured manner. Accordingly, the last refinement is from wanting knowledge, to wanting to hear these scriptures explained by a qualified teacher. [Note: see the section of Q&As on 'Scriptures' for some discussion on why you should pay any attention to 2000+ year old material written in Sanskrit.]

So, what does Advaita actually say? Very briefly, we experience ourselves as separate persons in a universe of objects. Despite this seeming duality, according to Advaita, reality is actually non-dual. This non-dual reality is called Brahman. When we think about it, we find that we do not entirely believe that we are just a body or a mind. Many religions say that there is an immortal 'soul' in each person. Advaita calls our essential self, which is beyond body and mind, the Atman. And the fundamental message of the Upanishads is that this Atman is Brahman.

There is an oft-quoted sentence which is said to summarize Advaita. This is:

brahma satyam, jaganmithya, jivo brahmaiva naparah (this is the Romanized equivalent of that Sanskrit sentence). Translated, it means: "Brahman is the reality; the world is not in itself real; the individual self is not different from Brahman". And the purpose of the teaching is simply to bring about this realization.

Unlike religions and most other spiritual systems, you are not asked to set aside reason and accept the unprovable as truth. On the contrary, you are encouraged to question everything until all doubts are satisfied. The only 'practices' you are expected to follow are those which promote self-control of mind and senses so that discrimination may operate in a still mind. Thereafter, it is simply a matter of listening or reading, clarifying confusion and reflecting until there is 'enlightenment'.

Here is a very brief explanation of the 'source' of Advaita, from 'Advaita Made Easy':

"Advaita is best thought of as a teaching method rather than a philosophy, although pedantically it is one of the schools of one of the six branches of Hindu philosophy. This particular branch, called Uttara Mimamsa, derives its teaching from the latter part of the massive body of scriptures called the Vedas. These contain the Upanishads, which form the principal source material for Advaita. There are two other major

sources, both of which are actually based upon the Upanishads as well. One is called the Bhagavad Gita, itself part of the much larger, famous, epic poem called the Mahabharata. The other is a philosophical text, called the Brahma Sutra, which is intended to answer doubts and objections about what is said in the other two. To be strictly accurate, the Vedas themselves constitute a 'source of knowledge' which cannot be obtained from anywhere else. In order to be able truly to understand what they are telling us, however, we need a teacher who has learned the method of interpreting them from his teacher".

An extremely succinct summary of the 'purpose' of Advaita might be as follows: All the problems of life are caused by one thing – Self-ignorance. The only solution, therefore, is Self-knowledge. Swami Paramarthananda indicated that this summarizes the teaching of the Bhagavad Gita, a text that itself aims to summarize the teaching of Advaita as conveyed through all of the Upanishads.

With respect to this, the method for obtaining this Self-knowledge is to listen to someone who has it and who is able to explain it to you. In order to be able to do this, one needs a clear and receptive mind. In the answers, I invariably refer to the methods for cultivating a still mind as 'practice' as opposed to listening to, and asking questions of, a guru. It is the latter which gives the knowledge and I do not regard that as 'practice'.

Teaching

Q.7 What is the practice of Advaita Vedanta?

Q: How does one practice Advaita?

A: Advaita (Vedanta) is not really something that one practices; it is rather a particular method of *teaching* the non-dual truth.

Q.8 Does it require faith?

Q: Does the Vedanta tradition ultimately rely on faith? And if this is the case, why is Advaita not a religion rather than a philosophy?

A: As regards faith [Sanskrit shraddhA], this is required to a degree but the nature of this is similar to that of trusting someone whom you respect. If a close friend gives you instructions for traveling from A to B, you do not ask whether or not you should have faith in their directions. You trust them implicitly and follow them without question. When it comes to trusting the words of acknowledged sages, there is even less reason to question them. The ultimate authority is the shruti, the Upanishads, whose words have been validated time and again by such sages over the past several thousand years. (Note that you will encounter quite a few Sanskrit terms – here 'shruti' – in both questions and answers. If you don't know what they mean, all are explained in the Glossary!)

The literal meaning of religion is 'to bind back (to the truth)', from the Latin re-ligare. Therefore, Advaita is literally a religion. However, as with many English words, the original meaning has become distorted over time so that we now associate with the word 'religion' all of the dogma and misunderstanding that has overlaid the original statements of whichever religion you care to consider. If, therefore, you understand this 'modern' meaning of the word, then Advaita is not a religion.

Q.57 Monism

Q: What is the difference between non-dualism and monism?

A: I said the following in 'The Book of One' (2nd edition):

"Nor is Advaita the same as monism. Monists say that there is only one 'thing'. The pre-Socratic Greek philosophers, for example, suggested that this one thing might be water, fire or air. Advaita tells us that the Self is not a 'thing'; it is not any sort of object but the universal Subject. Even this is not strictly accurate because 'subject' necessarily implies the existence of at least one 'object' and Advaita denies this – ultimately, words, and concepts, are simply inadequate to comprehend reality.

"Advaita is actually more 'extreme' than monism. As John Grimes points out in Ref. 140, there are three aspects of the word 'different': two things may belong to different species; they may be different members of the same class or there may be internal differences. The definition

of monism still permits internal differences whereas Advaita does not. Accordingly, if we are to call Advaita 'monism', it has to be qualified as 'absolute monism'.

"Nor is Advaita equivalent to any branch of Idealism. The Self is not an appearance or concept (which is actually just another object, albeit a subtle one) and it exists in the mind of no one, including that of God.

"There is only the Self, aka the Absolute, Truth, Consciousness, to specify a few of the names used for this unity; there are no 'others'. When we think we see separate 'things' out there in 'the world'; when we see 'objects' or 'other people'; or when we see 'thoughts' in 'the mind' or sense 'feelings' in 'the body', we are making a mistake. Our ignorance is preventing us from seeing correctly. Once this ignorance is removed, we recognize that there is, in truth, only our (real) Self, that all the apparently separate 'things' are not truly separate. Indeed, all 'things' (whether apparently solid objects or insubstantial thoughts) are only name and form of the same, non-dual reality, as you will see shortly".

Perhaps a simpler way of putting it is that monism states that all the separate things in the world are actually made out of the same stuff. Advaita sort of agrees ('everything is Brahman' – the 'stuff' is Consciousness) but additionally states that the appearance of separateness is due to our error, as a result of ignorance.

Q.269 Why isn't everyone interested in Advaita?

Q: Why do some people have zero interest in this philosophy or, maybe more specifically, why do so many seem incapable of understanding it?

A: Why are some people not interested in classical music? Gardening? Astronomy? Why can't everyone understand quantum mechanics? Calculus?

Intellectual curiosity and capability depend upon upbringing and genetics or, if you prefer the more traditional viewpoint, karma. Also, most people believe that they can find happiness in the world of objects, status, achievement etc. Very few have realized that discovering the truth about themselves and the world is, in the final analysis, the only worthwhile pursuit. All else is ephemeral; as Shakespeare says in Macbeth: '...full of sound and fury, signifying nothing'.

Q.271 Attempt to derive Advaita logically

Q: I am making a bold attempt to boil down the teachings of Advaita to a very simple logical/definitional essence (see below). Have you ever tried something similar? If you have a chance and can have a look at what I've written below, I'd love to hear your thoughts. All suggestions are welcome.

Beginning of analysis:

Number 1

* I exist
* I know I exist
* I am therefore conscious

Number 2

* I am within existence
* Existence is therefore conscious

(Numbers 3 – 7 not included because not helpful)...

A: I did once think that I would try to set down what was effectively a 'logical proof' for non-duality but I never quite got around to trying seriously. So I would certainly agree that it is an interesting idea. But I think that it is actually not possible in the end. All our reasoning relates back to perception and Brahman cannot be perceived. (You can only think about something that you have perceived/conceived at some time in the past. And you cannot conceive of something that is not based upon something previously perceived.) This is why there is a need for shabda pramANa – scriptures and a guru to interpret them for us. These speak of Brahman and give lots of pointers and negations etc., until such time as we directly intuit the truth – but this is still not a perception, and not itself derivable by reason.

The teaching of Advaita is not inimical to reason, which is why we can (and should) always subject what we read or are told to rigorous reason in the light of our own experience. But it cannot get us there on its own.

But don't let me stop you trying! I do think, though, that for your arguments to be persuasive, they must be set down clearly step by step so that each stage in your argument may be followed. So, for example, I am OK with your 'Number 1' but you lose me at 'Number 2'. What does 'I am within existence' mean? What is this saying which is different from 'I exist'? Doesn't saying that 'something exists' simply mean that 'I am aware of it'? But is this true? Is it not simply the case that I am aware of some activity in my brain?

It's a minefield! And you have to anticipate the readers' objections and counter them before they are able to grow.

Q: Thanks for the feedback. First to your specific point regarding Number 2, the point is actually very basic. Since I am an existent, conscious entity, then we know that existence must be conscious (i.e. not inert). But this just proves your point that in this type of work, wording is critical.

I do want to take exception to your larger point about a logical proof not being possible. The way I think about it, a logical proof uses a series of assumptions that seem reasonable and then arrives at a conclusion. So what you can prove to someone logically actually has as much to do with what foundational assumptions you can get someone to agree with as much as it does being able to draw a conclusion (e.g. through deduction).

In this context, do you think the issue is more on the assumption side or on the reasoning side? I think most people would agree with what I would call key assumptions (in this framework) such as 'I exist', 'I am conscious', 'I know my thoughts, feelings, and emotions' etc. The question then becomes which (if any) of the great key statements of Advaita (e.g. thou art that) can one prove logically based on these assumptions. Perhaps you are correct that you can't prove any of them. But it is definitely fun to try!

A: I still don't follow your reasoning on that point, I'm afraid.

To substitute the nouns in your argument, I could say: "Since this ruler is a wooden, straight object, then we know that wood must be straight". Apart from which, I don't actually see 'existence' as being something that you can predicate.

But you might actually be interested in studying the third chapter of Gaudapada's kArikA on the mANDUkya upaniShad. In his introduction to this, Shankara says: *"Now it is asked whether non-duality can be established only by scriptural evidence or whether it can be proved by reasoning as well. It is said in reply that it is possible to establish non-duality by reasoning as well. How is it possible? This is shown in this chapter on Advaita".*

That is the translation by Swami Nikhilananda. Professor Jayantkrishna H. Dave translates it in much the same manner but adds in his comments: *"There is a shruti text which says that the intellect should not be led astray by uncontrolled logic but it is possible to use logic as a* corroborating and co-operative factor *…"* (my emphasis). (He doesn't mention *which* shruti text.)

Swami Satchidanandendra should have the last word, however. He points out that *"Because Atmatattva [the truth or principle of Atman] is not a prameya (object of perceptual knowledge), it cannot possibly be established by any pramANa whatsoever; because it is svataHsiddha (self-established), there is no need whatsoever for establishing it by means of any pramANa".*

[This question is from some years ago and my book 'A-U-M' now addresses this aspect directly.]

Q.319 Apparent contradictions in Advaita

Q: I read a serious critique of Advaita on the Internet, written by a philosophy professor (Prof. R. Collins at Messiah College, PA). I would like to know your thoughts about what he said.

1. He said that their view is self-contradictory: *"If the only reality is Brahman, and Brahman is pure, distinction-less consciousness, then there cannot exist any real distinctions in reality. But the claim that this world is an illusion already presupposes that there is an actual distinction*

between illusion and reality, just as the claim that something is a dream already presupposes the distinction between waking consciousness and dream consciousness. Moreover, Shankara's idea of salvation – that is, enlightenment through recognition that all is Brahman – already presupposes a distinction between living in a state of unenlightenment (ignorance) and living in a state of enlightenment".

2. If Brahman is perfect, pure, and complete Knowledge, then ignorance cannot exist in Brahman. But, since nothing exists apart from Brahman, it follows that ignorance cannot exist. Therefore, our perception of a world of distinct things cannot be the result of ignorance.

3. Finally, one could never have any experiential basis for believing Advaita. There appears to be a real world of distinct things. Even in dreams, there are innumerable distinct experiences. Thus Advaita cannot even explain the world as being an illusion or dream. Because Advaita contradicts our experience, science could never give us good reason to believe it, but rather every reason to reject it.

A: Shankara and Advaita do not claim that 'the world is an illusion'. On the contrary, the world is real – but not real 'in itself'. The world is 'name and form' of Brahman, which is the non-dual reality. The problem arises when the world is taken as actual (i.e. dualistic) reality. Shankara's word to describe the world is 'mithyA'. The apparent contradiction arises from mistranslating this word. Advaita does not deny the seeming reality of the world and its teaching, which as is noted incorporates dualistic concepts. It provides interim explanations which are rescinded once enlightenment takes place, since those (ultimately erroneous) concepts are no longer needed.

The apparent contradiction of ignorance results from a confusion of absolute and empirical reality. Brahman is the absolute reality but is beyond description by definition (there would have to be a separate subject to describe an objective Brahman). At the level of the jIva and the world, we know that there is ignorance – I do not know Chinese for example. But this is not a problem, since the jIva, world, Chinese language and ignorance are all mithyA.

Following enlightenment, the world is still seen as separate but is known not to be. Science can never be a source of knowledge for the truth of Advaita. It is necessarily dualistic, relying on an observer and observed phenomena. This is entirely within the realm of mithyA so no 'absolute' reality could ever be evidenced. Scriptures provide the pointers to the truth, which is finally 'realized' in the mind of the seeker. This is not an experience.

Q.345 How can we believe the claims of Advaita?

Q: What is the purpose of life?

If, as stated in Advaita, we are actually in a state of sat-chit-Ananda and we are this 'Self' already, why have these 'illusions' and this 'ignorance'?

How can we believe in lIlA? What could be its purpose? There is no convincing answer – I am sure you will concur.

This then raises my more fundamental query. This 'Self' on which reams have been written – what is the proof that such a 'Self' exists?

The root problem is that in the end, even Advaitic teachings finally rely on 'blind faith' to put their point across. There's nothing wrong in having faith. All religions ask for blind belief in the almighty to get you your promised 'Kingdom of God'. It's only in Advaita that folks try to push their case by saying: "No, it's not pure faith, it's by reason and discourse that we reach the truth etc.".

To quote Gaudapada in his Mandukya Upanishad kArikA, *"That which is stated in the scriptures 'and is supported by reason' is true and nothing else"*. The 'reason/discourse' argument for following Advaita is pure bunkum, in my opinion. It relies on blind faith not on a deity, but in an obscure 'Self'.

And, even if reality is non-dual, why this seeming duality? Why does this mithyA of life exist?

A: This is the perennial difficulty of asking a question about the nature of absolute reality and expecting a totally satisfactory answer at the experiential level. It cannot be done! Reality is non-dual while all your concerns are at the level of dualistic appearance. The world and all its objects are name and form only; they do not have any reality of their own. Their reality is Brahman, the non-dual Consciousness.

So the simple answer is that the question of whether life has any purpose is ultimately meaningless, because what you are calling 'life' is mithyA and the concept of 'purpose' is mithyA.

We are not 'in a state of sat-chit-Ananda'; we are Brahman, whose nature is sometimes described (for the sake of trying to talk about it) as sat-chit-Ananda. But all that this means is that there is only absolute, limitless Consciousness – and we are That.

The 'explanations' of the scriptures are *always* interim only, until we realize the truth for ourselves and no longer require those 'pointers'. The concept of lIlA is one that is unlikely to appeal to most intelligent people today but obviously satisfied some in the past.

'What is the proof that the Self exists?' Who is asking?? You can never doubt the existence of yourself – who would be doing the doubting? It is possibly the only thing that you never need any proof for! The real question is 'what is this Self?' and that leads to Self-enquiry, which is the real 'purpose' of the scriptures and the only pursuit worth following.

Also, there is no such thing as 'blind faith' in Advaita. You simply listen to someone whom you have reason to think knows what they are talking about. And you continue to listen as long as what they say continues to sound reasonable and does not contradict your own perception or reason. And eventually, you have the 'Aha!' moment of realizing that you are already that Self, which the scriptures have been trying to talk about. It's not a 'vision', blinding or otherwise.

Why are there tables and chairs and bookshelves etc.? Why isn't there just wood? There are all these different forms and we have all these various names for them and yet all is in reality Brahman. Isn't it fantastic?! But I'm afraid you will never get an answer to the question 'why?' I think someone called it the devil's question! The bottom line is that there has never been any creation; no one has ever been born. Yes, of course it appears otherwise, and that is because of our ignorance. Gain Self-knowledge and the question will disappear.

If it is the second edition of Book of One that you have just read, then you will have read the description of bhAga tyAga lakShaNa on page 250. Since I actually reference this in a number of questions, I reproduce the story below:

"We are already That – the truth, reality or whatever other word is preferred. We do not need to (nor can) do anything to bring about this already existing fact. One aspect of the value of the scriptures, therefore, is in their ability to bring about the realization of this already existing fact.

"As things stand at present, I know that I am 'I' and that Brahman is 'That' – it is unthinkable that I can be Brahman. I think I am an insignificant, limited, body-mind which is a created thing whereas Brahman is the unlimited, all-powerful, ubiquitous creator. How can we be the same? But the mahAvAkya tat tvam asi cancels out all of these contradictory elements and tells me that 'I' am 'That', i.e. Brahman. This canceling out of contradictory elements, leaving an equality of the non-contradictory parts is called bhAga tyAga lakShaNa. The oneness that is pointed to (lakShaNa) is understood by 'giving up' (tyAga) the contradictory parts (bhAga).

"There is an excellent metaphor that explains how this works. Suppose that you and a friend, A, both went to school with a third person, X. Although you were not particularly friendly with X, you knew him quite well but, since leaving school you lost touch and have forgotten all about him. Today, you happen to be walking along with A and see Y, who is a famous film star, walking by on the others side of the street. You have seen films starring Y and admire him very much. A now makes some comment

such as "Y has come a long way in the world since we knew him, hasn't he?" You are mystified since you have never even spoken to Y as far as you know and you ask A to explain himself. A then makes the revelatory statement: "Y is that X whom we knew at school".

"All of the contradictory aspects, that X is an insignificant, scruffy, spotty youth that you once knew at school, while Y is a rich, famous and talented actor, are all cancelled out, leaving the bare equation that X and Y are the same person. Furthermore, the knowledge is aparokSha – immediate. We do not have to study the reasoning or meditate upon it for a long time.

"In the example of tat tvam asi, the canceling out of body, mind etc. is possible because of what has gone before. We have investigated these beliefs and exercised our reason, negating the false impressions (neti, neti). Without this preparation, there could not have been the sudden understanding that tat and tvam are indeed the same".

The situation you are in is that you believe that you knew the spotty oik, X. But, not only do you not know the film star, Y, you even suspect that he does not exist at all. The purpose of Advaita is first to convince you that Y really does exist and then, once you really understand that, to show you that Y and X are in fact the same.

Perhaps you should use the word 'Consciousness' rather than 'Self' as being less emotive of unhelpful ideas. Consciousness is not a side-effect of an evolving mind as science claims. Rather everything, including mind and science, is an appearance in Consciousness. Consciousness is the ultimate reality; the only existing 'thing'. You can call the doubting ego the 'small self' if you like. (It is actually the 'real Self' reflecting in the mind.) And doubt itself is the result of this 'reflected Self' (which you could call the 'ego') identifying with a particular idea.

One last metaphor (which I know you will have heard before). There is only a rope here but you claim that it is a snake. Why does it look like a snake? What is the point? You tell me!

The primal question is not answered because the question

itself is a mistake. There is no duality. Why does there seem to be? Because you are not looking properly! Advaita shows you how to look properly. The only faith is the willingness to listen, and not to reject because you think that you already have the answers (or 'know' that there is no answer). This is a vast difference from organized religions, where you genuinely do have to accept things which you can never discover to be true in this lifetime.

I think perhaps you have not yet appreciated the extent of mithyAtva (the condition of being mithyA). mithyAtva itself is mithyA. You could say that the teaching of Advaita is successively to sublate anything and everything that you might think to be real until you are left with only Consciousness as the ultimate reality. The doing of this, using the scriptures together with a qualified teacher, is perfectly logical and reasonable, requiring no leaps of faith. The 'faith' is only in the commitment to follow it through. The end point is the recognition of the non-dual nature of every 'thing'; there are consequently no questions remaining to be answered. There is no 'why', only 'That'. Your 'whys' only have apparent relevance whilst you accept the appearance as real and therefore dualistic.

Q.440 Is Advaita provable?

Q: Is Advaita provable, in the Western, scientific, empirical sense of the word? I guess part of the attraction for me is that it seems to be (along with some other Eastern thought systems) a methodical and thorough exploration of consciousness; consciousness being something (along with death) that Western culture can't even define let alone explain and explore. Or is my thinking mistaken?

A: Who would prove what? Science is intrinsically empirical and could never say anything about the nature of reality. There are a couple of articles that you should read to clarify this. One by myself is in four parts, beginning (http://www.Advaita-vision.org/science-and-the-nature-of-absolute-reality-part-1/) and one by AchArya Sadananda in three parts, beginning (http://www.

Advaita-vision.org/science-and-vedanta-part-1/). Nevertheless, Advaita's explanation of the nature of Consciousness is not contrary to reason or to Western science and philosophy. See my book 'A-U-M' for this.

If you are comfortable with the language and 'explanations' of modern physics, try Amanda Gefter's book 'Trespassing on Einstein's Lawn'. (I must confess I found this a bit hard-going at times!) This shows that the 'frontiers' of science are now beginning to think along lines not altogether too distant from the Vedantic scriptures!

Scriptures

As will be seen in later sections, I recommend *only* the traditional teaching method, and for several very good reasons. It has to be admitted, however, that there are aspects of this that do not initially appeal to most Western seekers. The obvious ones are the facts that it derives from ancient scriptures and that these were written in Sanskrit. Also, teachers have to be explicitly qualified in reading and interpreting these scriptural texts – a skill that has been passed down from teacher to disciple for over a thousand years. Finally, the manner in which the knowledge is passed on requires seekers to attend regular classes for many years, something that is anathema to today's 'Internet mind'.

The Vedas act as pointers to the truth; they are not in themselves 'truth' or 'reality' – they are ultimately mithyA. A well-known metaphor used in Advaita is pointing out the house to which one wants to refer as being 'the one with the crow on the roof'. Once this is seen, it matters not at all that, by the time you reach the house, the crow is no longer there.

To extend the metaphor, assume that our reason for asking about the house was that we wanted to meet Mr. X, its owner. Suppose that, at the time that we were given the description, we did not know that Mr. X lived there. But, when we knock on the door, lo and behold, Mr. X answers. Similarly, although we may not know that, 'from the pAramArthika standpoint all are mithyA', when we actually 'get there' we find it to be so. The Vedas told us; we had faith in them and were proved to have been right in having that faith. The Vedas were real from the vyAvahArika standpoint (which is where we were) and that is what is important.

Again, it is like the dream lion that wakes us from the dream. It was real in the dream, which is where we were. The fact that it is known to be unreal once we have awoken is irrelevant. The bottom line is that the scriptures are 'valid' to the extent that they 'work'.

Q.35 Is study of the scriptures a waste of time?

Q: Is study of the scriptures a waste of time? There is a quotation from Shankara in the Vivekachudamani that states: "Study of the scriptures is fruitless as long as Brahman has not been experienced. And when Brahman has been experienced, it is useless to read the scriptures".

A: This quotation is from the vivekachUDAmaNi (verse 59), which may have been written by Shankara (though this is disputed by many). However, it highlights the danger of taking a quotation out of context. Verse 61 clarifies this statement: *"Except for the medicine of the knowledge of God, what use are Vedas, scriptures, mantras and such medicines when you have been bitten by the snake of ignorance?"* And, later still in the same work (verse 281) the author says: *"Recognizing yourself as the self of everything by the authority of scripture, by reasoning and by personal experience, see to the removal of all ideas of additions to your true self whenever they manifest themselves"*.

The way that this should be interpreted is that the scriptures alone are unlikely to be of any help when you are totally identified with ideas of separation and suffering (and especially if your teachers are telling you that reading them is a waste of time anyway!). What is needed is basic preparation of the mind (as specified by Shankara) followed by listening to the teacher, clarifying doubts and then assimilating everything (shravaNa, manana and nididhyAsana). The teacher must be well-versed in the scriptures (a shrotriya) and will unfold their meaning in a systematic manner.

Q: But these two verses appear to amplify what was said in verse 59. It is direct knowledge of the Self, of Brahman, (not 'knowledge' of the scriptures) that truly removes ignorance and is Liberation.

A: I have a problem with the concept of 'knowing the Self'. When we talk about 'knowing' something, it is invariably (outside of Advaita circles!) referring to us, as separate body-minds, objectively knowing some thing or fact etc. In this common usage of the verb 'to know', it is not possible for us to know the Self or for the Self to be known. This is because it is only by *virtue* of the Self, working through the mind, that we can know anything. The sort of metaphor which is useful here is the one of the battery in the torch. It is only by virtue of the battery that the torch is able to illuminate anything but you cannot see the battery with it.

This usual sense of the word also cannot apply to the knowing of the Self by the Self, since it doesn't have a mind with which to conduct any knowing. To stretch the metaphor, the battery on its own cannot illuminate anything.

It is in this sense of illuminating things, however, that the scriptures talk about the Self 'knowing'. In fact, the phrase that is often used is that the Self is 'self-effulgent'. The Self is its own light and there is no other light that can illuminate it (i.e. nothing else can know it). In particular, there is no process of 'knowledge' involved in self-awareness. Prior to realization, the (apparent) world is perceived, thoughts conceived etc. by virtue of the 'light' of Consciousness. Upon realization, when the body and mind are transcended, there are no longer any 'objects' to be illuminated (since all is now 'known' to be Brahman) so that Consciousness now effectively illuminates itself. We 'become' Consciousness and there is now nothing to be known and no need for a mind through which to know.

'Maha Yoga', one of the best books about the teaching of Ramana Maharshi, has this to say on the subject:

"The Sage is often loosely described as 'one that knows the Self'. But this is not intended to be taken in a literal sense. It is a tentative description, intended for those that believe ignorance to be something that exists; they are told that this ignorance is to be got rid of by winning 'Knowledge of the Self'. There are two misconceptions in this. One is that the Self is an object of knowledge. The other is that the Self is unknown, and needs to be known. The Self being the sole Reality, He cannot become an object of knowledge. Also being the Self, He is never unknown. The ancient lore tells us that He is neither known nor unknown, and the Sage confirms it.

"How can this be? The Self is the pure 'I AM', the only thing that is self-manifest; by Its light all the world is lighted up. But It seems to be unknown, and to need to be known, because It is obscured by the world and the ego. What is needed is to remove these. The Sage explains this by the analogy of a room that is encumbered with unwanted lumber. If space be wanted, all that is needful is to clear out the lumber; no space has to be brought in from outside. So too, the ego-mind and its creations have to be emptied out, and then the Self alone would remain, shining without hindrance. What is loosely called 'knowing the Self' is really being egoless, as the Self. Thus the Sage does not know the Self; he is the Self".

So, to return to your point, I suggest that what actually happens is that reading the scriptures, listening to the teacher, reflecting and meditating on what has been heard eventually succeeds in eliminating all of the ignorant ideas etc. that prevented realization of the truth. Then, the Self shines without impediment. This 'condition' is what is referred to as 'knowing the Self'. So, I would maintain that the 'knowledge of Self' (so-called) comes after the ignorance has been removed, not before.

Q.96 Characteristics of Krishna

Q: I have a query regarding the role of Krishna in the Advaita Vedanta philosophy.

As you may know Krishna devotees believe that Krishna

is the Supreme Godhead, the supreme source of energy in the Universe – an energy that manifests itself in several different ways (material, spiritual, etc.).

What do Advaitins believe about Krishna? Do they believe in the same qualities about Krishna as Krishna devotees, *except* that Krishna is a manifestation of Brahman, and not the supreme source?

A: I am not an expert on Hindu Gods, I'm afraid. As you probably know, the Bhagavad Gita is equally highly regarded by both Dvaitins and Advaitins. The 'characteristics' of Krishna are acknowledged as having provisional validity in vyavahAra by Advaita but, as with the entire apparent universe, gods too are ultimately only mithyA. (They are also only 'super' jIva-s, not gods in the sense that the Christian God is.) Since there is only the non-dual Brahman in reality, every 'thing' else is part of Self-ignorance, to be realized eventually as nothing other than name and form. If you think of the rope-snake metaphor, asking about the qualities of Krishna is equivalent to asking whether the snake is poisonous or not.

Q.109a Studying the Upanishads

Q: I've just been looking at the kena, kaTha, IshAvAsya, and mANDUkya Upanishads. All very beautiful but all are very intense. So my first question is: Does understanding these Upanishads take time or should they make sense immediately?

My second question is whether, through enough study and analysis of scripture, plus bhakti, karma and j~nAna yoga, the tamas can really fade?

A: The Upanishads are not easy material. They were always intended to be passed down by a teacher and explained bit by bit. They are very abbreviated, couched in archaic language, utilizing myths and metaphors from an ancient time. And, of course, they were written in Sanskrit so you are also relying on the ability of the translator to put them into English that is understandable by the average 21st-century westerner. So, no, you should not expect to understand them right away!

If you are looking for less tamas in your life, then karma yoga and bhakti yoga will help and probably the best practice of all is meditation – regularly for twice a day, half-an-hour each session without fail. The mind will become more peaceful, concentration will improve etc. (But not immediately – you should expect difficulty in the early days and then a gradual improvement over months and years rather than days or weeks.) If what you want is enlightenment, then these things are valuable but will not in themselves bring it about – for that, gaining knowledge is the only way.

Q.292 Do we have to read certain scriptures?

Q: Is it possible to become enlightened without reading the scriptures, for example the Upanishads? Ramana Maharshi became enlightened without studying the sacred texts and there are other examples, like the Buddha.

I am studying the tanmAtra aspects of the tattva bodha and was wondering if I have to finish it before moving on to the Gita and Upanishads. It gets very technical and I was told it was written by Shankara, although you have mentioned it probably isn't? So if it's not by Shankara, is it worth studying?

A: It is possible to become enlightened without studying the Upanishads – as you note, Ramana was an example of this. There are also other non-dual systems. However, the Vedantic scriptures are well-proven as being efficacious, providing that they are explained by somehow who genuinely understands them.

Academics can argue about it but no one can be absolutely sure whether a given text was authored by Shankara or not. There is no problem about moving on to another text if you are not benefitting from one. I myself have not studied tattva bodha. But there is a clear implication that, if you cannot follow a simpler text, then you are likely to have difficulty with a more complex one. And there are certainly texts worth studying even though they were not written by Shankara. Unless you can read Sanskrit, you are going to have to rely on someone else's translation and commentary anyway!

Q.397 Why are scriptures needed?

Q: From the blogs and articles on Advaita, it seems like Scriptures are the basis from which everything is derived. If Scriptures were also written by humans, why is it considered sacred? Why can't we independently come to the same conclusions completely disregarding scriptures?

For example, why couldn't Vivekananda or Ramana Maharishi state something original about Self without reference to scriptures? All we see is a definition of Self without knowing the process by which it has been arrived at. I feel I am no different from the guy who slaughters innocent people because something is stated in a Book.

A: Upanishadic material was passed down by word of mouth long before it was written down; from teacher to disciple; from those who knew to those who did not. The disciple trusts that the teacher will explain things until such time as the disciple realizes the truth. The seeker is specifically asked to use reason and own experience to validate what is said. If what is initially taken on trust is found to be invalid, it is rejected. If it is contrary to reason, it is rejected.

How does this process differ from science? There is nothing wrong with the method of science. It is, indeed, a good and rigorous method. The problem is that some things (empirical) are amenable to a scientific investigation and some things (nature of reality) are not. You cannot have a subject-object investigation of the non-dual.

Should you re-prove/re-derive all of the scientific laws from first principle and your own experiments before you accept them? And if something is true, and fully understood by those who have gone before, how can one state something 'original'? Moreover, why should one try? If teacher-seeker tradition over thousands of years has established an optimal way of passing on knowledge, isn't it the height of arrogance to think one could do better?

Q.242 apauruSheyatva (unauthored scriptures)

Q: What do you understand by the concept of apauruSheya – the idea that the Vedas were 'unauthored' by man (passed down from God).

A: I have to say that my preferred (reasonable) interpretation of the adjective 'unauthored' is that the words were 'originated' by Self-realized sages and subsequently passed on by word of mouth until such time as written materials became common. These sages, being Self-realized, no longer identified themselves as body-minds, as named individuals, so they had no wish whatsoever to have their bodily-assigned names associated with them. They knew that what they were conveying was non-personal, eternal truth that had nothing to do with personality. The sole purpose was to pass on this knowledge so that other minds, believing in separation, might be enlightened. Such absolute truth is beyond authorship and hence is reasonably construed as 'unauthored'. But, obviously, the words chosen are bound to be those current at the time and place in which they were originally spoken. And the method of presentation will be as learned by the speaker from parents and teachers in that then-current society.

The mythology of such words being literally passed down by Ishvara, Narayana or whoever is no different from the creation myths propounded in the various upaniShad-s. It is a ploy to make the ideas readily acceptable to minds more inclined to bhakti than j~nAna; i.e. part of the adhyAropa-apavAda method. The absolute truth is non-dual and therefore cannot be expressed in words (also there is no one to express it and no one to whom it might be expressed).

Q: What about the fact that the scriptures are in Sanskrit, and refer to India and its customs?

A: Anyone who has realized the truth of Advaita and has learned or devised a method for communicating it to others may set this down in any language, and those who understand that language may learn from it. Unquestionably, however, those methods which have been proven time and time again are best communicated verbally by one who is realized and understands them well. It is this proven history and the power of sampradAya that uniquely qualifies shruti. But someone must have authored these words, and someone must have written them down at some point in history. And it could just as well have been someone in another country in another language. It is all relative; all mithyA.

Q: The Vedas are coeval with creation – the ShvetAshvatara upaniShad (6.18) states this as much when it says:

"*yo BrahmanaM vidadhAti pUrvam yovai vedAMshcha prahiNoti tasmai.* Seeking Liberation, I take refuge in the Lord, the revealer of Self-knowledge, who in the beginning created Brahma and delivered the Vedas to Him".

This clearly implies that the eternally existent Vedas were transmitted to Chaturmukha Brahma – and that the Vedas are coeval with creation itself.

A: The scriptures should not be taken literally. They utilize the technique of adhyAropa-apavAda, which is spoken of in many of these answers. For example, they speak about creation in several ways. Initially, it is said that God *created* the universe – this is clearly dvaita. Then it is said that God *manifests* as the universe. This is the position of vishiShTAdvaita. And (finally) it is said that God *appears* as the universe – i.e. we see name and form of what is actually only Brahman. This is the position of Advaita.

Q: The absolute truth is non-dual and therefore cannot be expressed in words. If so, how do we know that it is so unless somebody/something tells us? In order for somebody/something to tell us, it has to be expressed in words, doesn't it?

A: The methods of communication of the truth are various but none are direct. Use of stories, metaphor, adhyAropa-apavAda, lakShaNa-s etc., when used skillfully, eventually enable the seeker to make the leap directly to grasp that which is itself indescribable.

Q: 'Because the Vedas say so' is a pramANa in itself, at least to the sampradAya. Could you comment on this?

A: Yes, certainly; they are pramANa for those aspects that are not accessible to pratyakSha or anumAna. Where what is said contradicts reason, however, they should not be taken literally. Shankara points out in bhagavadgItA bhAShya (18.66): *"Surely, even a hundred Vedic texts cannot become valid if they assert that fire is cold or non-luminous!"* He points out that they *"through the generation of successively newer tendencies by eliminating the successively preceding tendencies, are meant for creating the tendency to turn towards the indwelling Self... Even in the world, when it becomes necessary to make a child or a lunatic drink milk etc., it is said that it will help growth of hair etc.!"*

And there are contradictory statements in shruti too, as for example with respect to creation. Gaudapada points out (mANDUkya kArikA 3.23) that: *"That which is supported by shruti and corroborated by reason, is alone true and not the other"*. Shankara says that the creation texts *"serve other purposes"* and reiterates Gaudapada's stance.

Q: I'd be surprised if you can come up with an example wherein shruti contradicts pratyakSha or anumAna pramANa-s.

A: Choose any of the presentations on creation (including, and especially ajAtivAda). In fact, since the final teaching of Advaita is ajAtivAda, is not any teaching of a creation contradictory?

Q: There is an omnipotent God – this is a given. He has composed the Vedas. Hence the Vedas are valid. What the Vedas say is the Truth. Why? Because it is the word of God. This is a typically circular argument about scripture. The validity of the scripture rests on the inferred belief in an Almighty Lord.

However, the Advaita Vedanta position is different. Here the shruti is held both sacrosanct and coeval with creation and hence, like creation, has no discernible beginning.

Ishvara or God communicates the eternal Vedas at the beginning of each creation to the Creator of the next cycle – and this also we know only from the Vedas themselves.

A: How does this position differ from that which you have just agreed is circular? I do agree entirely that one's belief in shAstra begins with faith. But this is usually belief in the guru, who 'translates' and unfolds shAstra according to sampradAya as you have pointed out. This, then, is faith in someone who has proven themselves to be reliable and trustworthy. Initially it is faith, then later it is directly realized knowledge (hopefully!).

In the end, of course, it really does not matter what you take as an interim understanding, does it? If that adhyAropa brings you to direct intuition of the truth, it has served its purpose; it all has to be dropped in the end as having no more reality than the dream. This includes, of course, not only the authorship of the Vedas (or not) but the Vedas themselves. We really should not become hung up on the vyAvahArika.

Q.139 j~nAna yoga and the Brahma Sutras

Q: I am about to begin study of the Brahma Sutras commentary from Shankaracharya. All of the various schools are about knowledge of Brahman but they differ in their approach. As far as I can see, Shankara is leading the seeker to Brahman through a philosophical approach to Vedanta, but others were not able to follow this path (j~nAna?). Those such as Sri Ramanuja approached Vedanta through rituals (bhakti?).

Now, since I am now more attracted to the intellectual path (been trying bhakti my whole life and cannot give praise to external powers as easily as others), can I practice j~nAna solely? There is no need for bhakti as a primary but may it be a secondary?

A: Best of luck with the Brahmasutra commentary! Much of this is excellent at clarifying some of the more difficult concepts, but you need to be aware that there are parts that are quite obscure! I have never succeeded in reading any version all the way through. What I can recommend is the audio commentary of Swami Paramarthananda. Providing that you are familiar with the essential teaching of Advaita already, and also understand most of the Sanskrit terminology, this commentary can be very highly recommended.

If you prefer to read rather than listen, V. H. Date's 'Vedanta Explained', or the commentary by Swam Sivananda, are more readable than most. Ramanuja and Madhva are not non-dualists so you will not be learning about Advaita if you study works based upon their commentaries.

Certainly you may follow the path of j~nAna alone. The traditional (Advaita) view is that bhakti (upAsana) and karma yoga are 'preparatory' to j~nAna. Some will argue that all three effectively merge anyway as you progress but the bottom line is that only Self-knowledge can remove Self-ignorance.

Definitely you are making the right decision to turn away from Neo-Advaita if you want to make progress in understanding. But there is no instant solution. You may find it hard-going to begin with (especially if you try to study the Brahmasutra bhAShya!) but remember what the Bhagavad Gita says about this: *"The happiness that comes from stillness of mind is like poison in the beginning but like nectar in the end. But the happiness that comes from senses and objects, though like nectar in the beginning, turns to poison in the end"* (XVII. 37 – 8). So perseverance is the key!

Q.197 Different philosophies from same scriptures

Q: Could you explain how it can be that there are different philosophies in India that all claim to be derived from the same scriptures? How can Shankara (Advaita), Ramanuja (vishiShTAdvaita) and Madhva (dvaita) hold such widely different views? Why should we accept one rather than the others? Surely only one can be true: in which case the others are mistaken?

A: Good questions!

Enlightenment equates to Self-knowledge, which 'comes'

when Self-ignorance is eliminated. When it happens, it is direct and immediate; there is no longer any question of doubt. The best metaphor that I have come across is the one used to explain bhAga tyAga lakShaNa – see Q.345. This sort of realization can come about 'spontaneously' in one who is 'ready' but it is counter-intuitive. (After all, we can see separate things and persons out there. How could we naturally think that reality is non-dual?) This is why it is generally thought necessary that a seeker should have a qualified teacher – one who can use techniques such as this to undermine the habitual thought patterns and point towards the truth.

The reason that the scriptures are so valuable is that so many of these techniques are contained within, albeit sometimes in an archaic form that is not readily accessible. Everyday experience and the methods of science, for example, will never bring about an understanding of Self, because they are necessarily objective (and ultimately there is only the 'subject').

But yes, you are right, there are various interpretations of the scriptures – the dualism of Madhva and the qualified non-dualism of Ramanuja are just the more well-known ones. Each has to make his own decision as to which teaching to follow. If you read Shankara's bhAShya on the Brahmasutra, you will find that he takes the arguments of the alternative viewpoints and elaborately and systematically refutes them. The fourth prakaraNa of Gaudapada's kArikA-s on the Mandukya Upanishad also devotes a lot of space to proving ajAti vAda and destroying all of the alternative views that attempt to demonstrate that there are such things as creation or causality. (You can read all about this in my book 'A-U-M: Awakening to Reality'.)

All of the material is there if you want to investigate it. Or you can just take the word of others who have been through the process before you. Until realization dawns, there is always an element of faith.

Summary

Q: So is there one final or specific verse, or particular scripture that is considered the single most advanced teaching or pointer to this ultimate truth of Brahman being all there is?

A: The Muktika Upanishad (one of the later Upanishads) says that, if one is unable to study all the Upanishads (only 108 left these days) or not even the major ones (those 12 subsequently commented on by Shankara), then the Mandukya on its own is sufficient to give mokSha. You do, of course, also need Gaudapada's kArikA-s to explain the Upanishad. And you might just need my book 'A-U-M' to explain Gaudapada…

Q: So basically, your book AUM is sufficient!?

A: It covers the 'bottom line' of Advaita but ideally one would already be familiar with most aspects before reading it. As the Muktika says, one would best read all 108 Upanishads or at least the major ones! (So you should really read all my other books first! LOL!)

Seeking the Truth

Other religions/philosophies

There are a number of philosophies that conclude that reality is non-dual and clearly, if this conclusion is valid, then these philosophies are all teaching the 'same thing'. But since I am unfamiliar with these approaches, I have never attempted to address any questions relating to them. (I understand that they include Taoism, Sufism, Zen, Kabbalah, and esoteric Christianity.)

The mainstream, orthodox religions (Christianity, Islam, Hinduism, Buddhism, Taoism, Sikhism and Judaism) are not overtly non-dualistic. The philosophies-religions prevalent in India at the time of Shankara included Buddhism and Jainism. What we would now call 'Hinduism' comprised six distinct philosophies: nyAya and vaisheShika, sAMkhya and yoga, pUrva mImAMsA and uttara mImAMsA.

The last of these – uttara mImAMsA – is divided into three principal schools: dvaita, vishiShTAdvaita and Advaita. Traditional Advaita obviously does not accept any of the other teachings and Shankara (the teacher principally responsible for systematizing Advaita) explicitly refutes them in at least two places (his commentaries on the Brahmasutra and Mandukya Upanishad).

Traditional Advaita is taught by teachers whose teacher-disciple lineage stretches back hundreds of years (in principle, back to Shankara). There have been disagreements amongst scholars over some aspects and this has led to some divergence, but the essential elements of traditional teaching remain unchanged. More recently (late 19th century onwards), however, several key teachers emerged whose style of teaching (and sometimes the content as well) differed. Their disciples often distorted these even further so that, today, there are teachers claiming or claimed to be advaitins whose teaching differs significantly from mainstream traditional. There are many reasons why this is unsatisfactory from the seeker's point of view and I explain all of this in my book 'Enlightenment: the Path through the Jungle'. Questions relating to some aspects of this are addressed in this section.

There are also a number of 'approaches' which are not religions but are followed by some people who might then be tempted to equate them with Advaita. In recent times, a 'Course in Miracles' and 'Law of Attraction' have attracted (!) attention, but there are also always individuals who claim to have 'found God' or 'moved to a higher plane' and gain followers willing to pay to hear all about it! This section has a number of questions about approaches which are *not* Advaita. (Note that I am *not* claiming that no other approach has any value. I am not familiar with any other teaching so cannot really comment.)

Q.27 Similarities between Christian Science and Advaita

Q: In 'Conscious Immortality: Conversations With Ramana Maharshi' (recorded by Paul Brunton and Munagala Venkataramiah), the sage was asked: *"There is a religion called Christian Science which has a similar doctrine [to the concepts voiced by Shri Ramana]. Is it correct?"* Shri Ramana's reply was: *"Yes, but do not concern yourself with results"*. What are your thoughts on the similarities (and/or differences) between Advaita and Christian Science? In the context of his answer to the query, what do you think Shri Ramana meant by saying *"do not concern yourself with results?"*

A: My immediate reaction is to comment that I know nothing about Christian Science and to suggest that, if you tell me what you understand to be the beliefs of Christian Science, I will then tell you whether these are the same as Advaita.

As regards your final query, however, I do not think it matters whether or not there are similarities. The key point about all religions (allowing the literal meaning of this word, i.e. 'joining back' to the truth) is that they begin with 'me' wanting something, whether this is union with God, a meaning to life or simply 'happiness'. This is our starting point, as it were. All valid religions, however, must bring about the realization that there is no 'me', so that the original intent is lost and the recognition dawns that I am already that in which all of this seeming world arises. In other words, the end result that I thought I wanted is dissolved and known to have been completely misconceived. Hence, to set out on an apparent path with the attitude 'do not concern yourself with results' could help speed up the final understanding.

A quick look at 'Christian Science' at Wikipedia throws up the phrases 'spiritual healing' and 'humanity's sense of separation from God.' This implies that it has little in common with Advaita in its final sense. Advaita does cater for all levels of seeker and provides initial stages of teaching that are explicitly dualistic. In the end, however, there is only the non-dual truth expressed by the mahAvAkya-s; there is no separate humanity, and healing bodies or minds is all part of the dream.

Q.49 Is the 'Law of Attraction' a useful tool?

Q: I noticed the question on your website which asked: 'Do Thoughts Create Reality?' and I certainly understood your answer after reading your book. However, Dennis, do you feel we should ignore the 'Law of Attraction' because it will only create illusions? Or do you feel it's a useful tool as long as we realize we are only playing games with the 'unreal'.

Hardly a week goes by without a new book appearing about 'Cosmic Ordering' and we now have a well-publicized DVD called 'The Secret', about The Law of Attraction. It's certainly the hot topic of the moment.

A: This 'Law of Attraction' (which I had not heard of) immediately reminded me of 'The Power of Positive Thinking' – a book that used to be advertised on the back of newspapers decades ago.

All it seems to be saying is that those people who are optimistic are happier and more fulfilled. But it's all relative. People and the world are ultimately no different from the dream of the individual mind. All is only relatively real, which is effectively unreal. (See Q&As in the sections on 'Appearance' and 'Reality' for clarification of this.)

It is certainly true that you can live an enjoyable life or a life of suffering or anything in between and your attitude will certainly influence this. But this is not essentially any different from saying that you can have a good dream or you can have a nightmare. If you want to avoid the dream altogether, you have to wake up from the dream! If you want to 'escape' from saMsAra (the 'eternal round of birth and death' of the waking dream), you have to realize it only has dependent reality, too. (Whereas the dream depends on your mind, the world depends on Ishvara.)

Yes, following the 'law of attraction' may well help the person that you take yourself to be to achieve your ambitions but, as you saw in the book ('How to Meet Yourself'), you are then simply brought to the realization that you are still unfulfilled. This is inevitably so because you are not the person. Who-you-appear-to-be in the dream may find the buried treasure and marry the beautiful girl, but all is seen to be worthless when you wake up. And it is no different in so-called 'real' life, because that, too, is effectively a dream.

So, in answer to your question, I would advise against being taken in by such things because, quite simply, they only operate within the context of the seeming world. In using them, you tacitly take the world to be real and this can only perpetuate saMsAra instead of helping you to free the mind from its dominion.

Q.125 On happiness and choice

Q: I am curious to know how you feel about the 'Secret' and/or Neale Donald Walsh (Conversations with God), or the 'Law of Attraction' ideologies?

I guess when I posit the concept that there is no person or

individual to desire, create or to even have a life to begin with, since it is all the Life of God, how can a book such as your 'Happiness' book be written?

I guess what I am asking is: I understand (I think!) that on the mental and or human level there is the 'appearance' of choice, but *in truth* there is none. There is the appearance (if you will) that the above 3 concepts or ideologies have made people happy and abundant, but when I read my Advaita books – it's all an 'illusion', since there is no one to be happy or abundant, just 'life' being abundant or happy.

I guess I still apparently need to 'understand' (Nisargadatta word) who I really am!

Does this make sense? I am trying to reconcile these ideas by struggling with 'being in the world and not of it' as Jesus put it.

A: I know of these books but haven't read them. I haven't even read 'A Course in Miracles'.

The point that you always have to remember is that, prior to enlightenment, there *are* people, there *is* a world and these are *real*. It is only post enlightenment that we realize that these were only seeming reality, that everything is name and form of a non-dual reality. And even then, it all seems to continue as before – not as an 'illusion' but as mithyA rather than satyam.

So, the apparent duality is where we have to start from. All seeking and all teaching are at this level. "It is all the Life of God" is simply a concept in duality. You must not pretend otherwise. Apparent free will does have its part to play at this level. When you hear ideas such as these, there is an effective choice to ridicule them, ignore them or decide to pursue them. And that decision will have its karmic outcome in due course. And the truth is not about a 'happy' outcome but about transcending happiness and unhappiness altogether. There is always an 'effective' person (until death) and that person may be happy or unhappy, enlightened or unenlightened. The difference with the enlightened person is that the essential Self is known and is unaffected by any of it. It doesn't really make any sense to talk about 'life' being abundant or happy.

Q.62 Buddhism and suffering

Q: Could you please explain the following words of the Buddha:

There is suffering but no one who suffers

There is doing but no one who does

There is a path but no one who treads one

There is nirvANa but no one becomes free

A: This is Buddhism and not Advaita!

However, it can easily be explained from an Advaitin perspective. The quotation is (presumably deliberately!) mixing paramArtha and vyavahAra viewpoints. In reality (paramArtha), there is only Brahman; there are no jIva-s to suffer, act, follow a path or become free – 'we' are already complete and perfect. From the empirical viewpoint (vyavahAra), where the mind is deluded into thinking there are separate people and objects, there is bound to be suffering (for the mind), choice and action for the person and a path to lead the mind to loss of Self-ignorance. When the mind loses that Self-ignorance, it realizes that 'I am Brahman' and already free. This event is called enlightenment or nirvANa in Buddhist terms.

Q: It is indeed Buddhism, but yes I expected an Advaitin response. The point is that 'I' cannot help a suffering individual because he doesn't even exist. So why are all the Buddhists through history trying to help their suffering brothers if they know they don't exist?

A: Again, this is a paramArtha-vyavahAra problem. 'Others' do not exist in absolutely real terms but certainly do at the level of the empirical world. While there remains Self-ignorance, the mind will genuinely suffer. Having been there, the jIvanmukti has compassion and will help if at all possible, even knowing that the Self can never suffer. (Note that I said jIvanmukti and not simply j~nAnI. Only one with the fruits of Self-knowledge – peace of mind, love, fearlessness etc. – will certainly respond in this way. Those who were not sufficiently mentally prepared prior to enlightenment may not.)

Q.95 Insight and spiritual paths

Q: Having read a little of several spiritual traditions, I am under the impression that there are two main spiritual paths.

First, there is direct insight, such as Chan Buddhism. In this path, you simply dismiss all thoughts while resting in awareness. Then insights will spontaneously arise, blowing ignorance away. Usually it takes many sudden insights.

Second, there is insight through absorption, such as Vedanta. In this path, you repeatedly study several philosophical arguments. As you slowly assimilate these arguments, ignorance is replaced by insight.

My first question is, is my above assessment correct? My second question is, do you experience sudden insights in Vedanta as you do in Chan Buddhism?

Or perhaps my assessment is incorrect, and that Vedanta uses direct insight like Chan Buddhism?

A: I'm afraid my knowledge of other traditions is virtually nil so I cannot offer any comparisons. Also, the topic of Advaita epistemology is quite a large one – there are whole books on it. There is actually a section in my book 'Enlightenment: The Path Through The Jungle' addressing the question you are asking but I will try to give a brief answer here.

Advaita says that knowledge 'vRRitti-s' occur in the mind as the teaching is unfolded by a teacher who is skilled in the techniques of the scriptures. This word does not really translate as 'insight'. The point is that all of this is effectively already known, since it is our very nature. It is more in the way of recognition. The technique of bhAga tyAga lakShaNa is a good one to explain how it operates (see Q.345). So it is not a matter of 'assimilation'. There are various metaphors which attempt to illustrate how the final enlightenment comes about. These range from the sudden switching-on of a light to fog clearing slowly. Intermediate between the two might be switching on a succession of spotlights. As one bit of teaching is given, understanding dawns and pieces of the overall 'landscape' of reality are permanently illuminated. When all of the spotlights have finally been turned on, everything is clearly seen. With this metaphor, it could be said that enlightenment proceeds by sudden jumps but might be considered to be gradual overall. Hope this gives you some idea of Advaita's slant on the process.

Q.210 Enlightenment in Buddhism

You are a big advocate of 'traditional vedAnta'. I fully agree with the reasons for this (practicality & effectiveness of teaching method). But I still struggle to resolve how *non-vedAnta* 'sages' in other spiritual traditions (e.g. Buddhism), apparently attained mokSha. If vedAnta is the means of knowledge for the Self, then how can a jIva who has never employed this method ever attain mokSha on their own? Technically, without vedAnta, it should be impossible.

Leading on from the above, is Buddhism the same as Advaita Vedanta? I believe Shankara and his Guru specifically criticized Buddhism on certain teachings. What were these objections? Is the Buddhist notion of enlightenment (nirvANa) the same as Vedanta's definition of mokSha?

Every time I read snippets of Buddhist texts, I never came across anyone teaching about Non-duality. Is this even asserted within Buddhism as the nature of Self?

A: There is a great danger for confusion here. You ask whether other approaches can lead to mokSha but you are using the Advaita term 'mokSha', presumably with its Advaita meaning. Unless the other approach uses the same definition, you are not talking about the same thing. For example, the concept (realizing that Atman = Brahman, freedom from saMsAra etc.) could have no meaning at all for those branches of Buddhism that believe that shunya is the nature of reality. But Advaita is a means to an end only and is itself mithyA so there is no reason why other non-dual paths should not have their own equally valid teaching methods for leading one to the truth. My own search happened to lead me to Advaita and, in it, I found completely reasonable explanations for everything; explanations that did not conflict with my scientific upbringing.

As far as I am aware (and my knowledge of Buddhism is extremely limited!), the only branch that is close to Advaita is the yogAchAra sect. And their belief is that Consciousness is 'momentary', arising with a thought or perception etc. and dying an instant later. So even this branch is not the same as Advaita. You will find that the Mandukya kArikA-s and the Brahmasutra address (and dismiss) the other spiritual approaches that were prevalent at the time.

Q.273 nirvANa

Q: Once I went to a Buddhist Internet forum to share my theory that I thought that nirguNa Brahman and nirvANa were two different words for the same thing. I was a bit excited thinking about what this might mean for the links between Advaita (Shankara) and Buddhism, et cetera. I got a reply from an angry Buddhist telling me, No, Brahma the creator god and nirvANa were definitely not the same. I gave up trying to explain. What are the subtle differences between the two ideas of nirvANa and nirguNa Brahman?

A: nirvANa is not actually a word that is used in Advaita. What I understand to be the equivalent word is 'mokSha'. This literally means liberation (i.e. from saMsAra, the cycle of birth and death). Pedantically, the 'individual soul' or jIva is already free or liberated – it was never bound in the first place. The problem is that the mind thinks that it is separate and suffering etc., because it is ignorant of the truth – which is that 'I am Brahman', the non-dual reality. As a result of mental preparation and listening to and reflecting upon the explanations given by a qualified teacher, this truth may be realized for oneself. This realization is an event in the mind, called enlightenment, which forever removes the mistaken beliefs. But the realized person continues in that body until its death (when the prArabdha karma is exhausted). Subsequently, that 'person' is not reborn. But, pedantically, nothing is 'attained' in this process. It is just that the already-existing truth is realized by the mind.

As I say, I don't know the Buddhist definition or understanding of nirvANa. But your Buddhist informant has confused the creator god 'Brahma' with the non-dual reality 'Brahman'. If you want to talk about the saguNa aspect of Brahman, the correct term is Ishvara.

Q.435 How can we be sure?

Q: I have a friend who became a born-again Christian as a young man. I knew him before his 'conversion' experience, and he became very different afterwards. For decades, he has maintained his rock-solid belief in Jesus and evangelical Christianity. He has that 'glow' of certainty and confidence that seems to come with believing in such a system with 110% conviction. His faith is literally unshakeable, and he is dead certain that he is right. I have a back-of-the-mind concern that when someone 'gets it' in terms of Advaita after a long period of seeking, that something similar is happening. We cannot think directly about the non-dual Brahman, cannot experience non-duality, cannot even really talk about it. How can we be *sure* that we are not simply hypnotizing ourselves into this conviction after long years of painful seeking?

A: How can we be sure? I, too, encountered someone who was a 'certain' Christian. We had quite a few discussions and, as you say, the belief was unshakeable. The difference is though, in my experience, that such people are unable to back up their beliefs with reason. They will blithely quote from the Bible as though that ends the matter. As you know, in the kArikA-s, Gaudapada uses more reason than he does scriptural citations, although scriptures are traditionally the final authority. Although I included some scriptural quotations in my book 'A-U-M', this was principally for completeness and so that the related commentaries might be referenced. The intention was that all that I said was reasoned and hopefully unarguable. I cannot imagine there is any Christian text that can claim that.

The key tool and argument is probably one of the earliest – the 'neti, neti' of the Brihadaranyaka Upanishad. Rather than trying to 'find' the answer, you keep discarding all attempted explanations when you find that they do not stand up to reason. When everything has been rejected, you are still left with you, the 'rejecter'. You can use reason to reject those religions/philosophies that rely on scriptural authority alone, because you can always ask: 'Why should I accept what is written here when it can never be supported by reason or experience?' Advaita cannot be rejected in this way. It is the difference between 'belief' and 'knowledge'.

Q.458 Taoism

Q: I am just back from a vacation in Greece where I enjoyed a few days of reading Taoism: living in the spirit of Tao is the easy way of just floating with the stream of life. This means just living from our intuition instead of using our intellect performing the mental acrobatics of Advaita Vedanta. Indeed, as Wittgenstein pointed out correctly, one should remain silent instead of speaking (words are merely hindering tautologies) the unspeakable.

We lost our so-called enlightenment through our education/ conditioning which did not happen where people still live (or lived) in harmony with the 'natural flow of life'. This also means that, for us to recover enlightenment, life (Tao) is the only teacher and no so-called person should be considered a teacher.

A: It is certainly true that silence avoids the ambiguity of words! But since our problem is one of Self-ignorance, clearly knowledge is needed. I don't believe that life can bring you that knowledge. My own experience is that life tends to increase identification and sense of separation. I suggest that most people leave life with greater Self-ignorance than they had to begin with. The words of

Advaita do not, in any case, speak the truth; they merely point to it.

It is not the case that we begin our life in an enlightened state. 'Enlightenment' means Self-knowledge, not innocence. Innocence has much more in common with ignorance! In any case, are not education and conditioning an inevitable part of life? In which case, if life brought us to this condition, how should more life now remove it?

Living a life of tranquility, away from the trials of modern life at one with nature might well be very nice (though not very practicable for most people). But it would not bring about Self-knowledge!

Neo-Vedanta

This is a term that is applied specifically to teaching in the lineage of Swami Vivekananda (the disciple of Ramakrishna Paramahamsa) who 'brought' Advaita to the West and lectured extensively, especially in the US. It must not be confused with 'Neo-Advaita'. It diverges from traditional Advaita on several issues, apparently as a result of importing some elements that actually belong to the Yoga philosophy (which is dualistic). Most seekers are unaware of this and can be misled into accepting some erroneous notions.

The Ramakrishna and Vivekananda missions are still very active, and some of their monks have produced excellent written commentaries on scriptural texts and other valuable material for the seeker. See (http://www.Advaita.org.uk/teachers/ramakrishna_parampara.htm) for the lineage chart.

Q.392 Neo-Vedanta

Q: Are there major differences between the lineages of Swami Sivananda and Ramakrishna Paramahamsa? If I want to study traditional Vedanta, which teachings/teachers would you recommend?

A: If you want 'traditional', steer clear of Ramakrishna-

Vivekananda etc. – they are 'Neo-Vedantins' and diverge significantly in some respects. Sivananda I do not know so much about (except that his Brahmasutra commentary is very good). I think his lineage may also introduce elements of Yoga philosophy. I suggest you go for Swami Dayananda and disciples – you can't go far wrong there!

Q: The only real question that matters – 'Who am I?' – is also the major issue for the Ramakrishna lineage. Is their approach less truthful, and if so in what sense?

A: The bottom line of many systems may be the same. (Indeed, *must* be the same for any valid system, of course.) It is how they guide the seeker to that understanding that is important. But, for Neo-Vedanta, attaining nirvikalpa samAdhi is attaining mokSha. This cannot be true (says the traditionalist) because samAdhi is an experience in time. We are already free, perfect and complete; our problem is that we do not know it.

Q: I notice that you rarely cite any work from the swamis of the Ramakrishna Order (save a few quotes from Vivekananda). Is there any particular reason for this or is it just that your own interests have lead you to focus on other authors (Chinmayananda, Dayananda, etc.)?

A: The reason that I do not often quote from the Ramakrishna tradition is that, following Vivekananda, their teaching began to diverge from that of traditional Advaita, embodying teachings from the Yoga tradition and blurring the original clear messages. This has been so significant that their teaching is actually given a name in India – Neo-Vedanta. This is not to say that many of the books written by monks of the Ramakrishna Order are not to be recommended – some of them are excellent – but one does need to be careful if still unsure of the 'correct' teaching.

Direct Path

This is another 'offshoot' of traditional Advaita. It is called 'direct path' because it does not rely upon scriptural techniques of bringing a seeker to an understanding gradually, with intermediate explanations which are partial and might be said to be wrong and misleading (if not taught in a logical sequence as per Advaitins adhyAropa-apavAda methodology). Instead, it attempts to show how one's own perception may be explained in such a way as to lead to a direct realization of the non-dual truth.

The original proponent of this approach was Atmananda Krishna Menon and his magnum opus 'Spiritual Discourses' is probably still the best source for the teaching. A lineage chart can be found at (http://www.Advaita.org.uk/teachers/Atmananda_parampara.htm).

Q.279 Does an object exist before we see it?

Q: At the level of vyavahAra, does an object 'exist' before it is discovered and cognized by a conscious entity (i.e. person, animal etc.)? Most people would say yes, believing that, for example, a rock they just discovered in their backyard was probably there the day before. However, I understand that the teachings of Advaita that hold Consciousness/awareness as satyam point towards the opposite conclusion. As Swami Dayananda says, 'Pot is, awareness is.' What is your view?

A: The contents of your dream world are created by your mind and do not exist before (or after) the dream. But the waking world is said to be the creation of Ishvara and exists independently of any individual's perception. The very wording of your question – 'discovering' the object – contains the implicit assumption of its pre-existence. Advaita is not 'unreasonable'. Note, however, that we can only establish the existence of an object through perception. And, if we ourselves have not seen something, we must rely upon the word of someone else. To be pedantic, of course, the 'isness' of the object belongs to Brahman, the substratum; the object itself is mithyA.

The 'final' (pAramArthika) statement of Advaita is that there is no creation (ajAti vAda). The above theory – that Ishvara creates the world and we then perceive it – is called sRRiShTi dRRiShTi vAda. The contrary view, which is the one that you are suggesting, is called dRRiShTi sRRiShTi vAda. This is held by a 16th century advaitin, prakAShAnanda, and he puts forward this view in his work 'vedAnta siddhAnta muktAvalI' but it is not mainstream Advaita. See Creation Theories in Advaita: Vidyasankar Sundaresan (http://www.Advaita.org.uk/discourses/teachers/theories_vidyasankar.htm) for a good summary. If you want to read an entire book on the subject, see 'Idealistic Thought in Indian Philosophy' by Suchita Divata (D K Printworld, 1994, ISBN 812460021X).

Q: This is very helpful. Am I correct however, in thinking that this view is adopted by many Direct Path teachers? For example, Sri Atmananda in chapter 12 of 'Atma Nirvriti' states: *"Before seeing, there is no seen. The footnote to this passage reinforces the point by saying, '... with the accent on the thing that has no existence in itself, but upon the seeing as a result of which an object comes into existence".* John Levy, one of his main students in Europe, pushes the point further in 'Nature of Man According to Vedanta'.

A: I don't think this is quite how Direct Path sees things. I think that the idea is that you try to see that objects are not separate from Consciousness as a stage in the process of realizing that there is only Consciousness. But I didn't think there was any sense of 'bringing them into existence'. How could you bring something into existence by perceiving it? What would you perceive before there was something there to perceive? Traditionally, one would say that we misperceive something 'out there' as a separate object as a result of avidyA. In reality, what is out there is the same Brahman as the one that is perceiving.

But I am no expert on Direct Path. I suggest that you ask Greg Goode – he would be happy to clarify this point.

I subsequently asked Greg and his response follows:

Great summary, Dennis! As one begins with Direct Path inquiry, there seem to be many different kinds of objects. In fact, there seems to be the whole world, body and mind. That is, cars, trees, colors, sounds, aches, pains, itches and twitches, thoughts, feelings, desires, and relations such as time, space, number, causality etc.

All these things are investigated directly. It is first seen that these objects can't exist or even appear independently of awareness. Like Dennis mentioned, this is a sort of preparatory insight. This enables the shocking discovery that these things can't be found as candidates for existence or non-existence in the first place! It is realized that there's nothing available upon which you can hang the predicates 'exists' or 'doesn't exist.' The term 'Existence' comes to mean global Experience, which is another word for Awareness itself.

More specifically, the 'of' in experience drops out. That is, experience previously seemed to be of things or about things. But it comes to be your discovery that the remotest galaxy or the most sublime mental state is a sweet, seamless, part-less, clear and loving intimacy that is your very self.

Atmananda's books go into this, and my book 'Standing as Awareness' goes into it. There is also a 'sequel' or 'user guide' – 'The Direct Path' – which gives more exercises and investigations to stabilize the realization that all there is is awareness, always and already!

Q.280 Direct Path and the 'intellectual mind'

Q: An answer given to a questioner in one of your recent newsletters said in part: *"Direct Path may offer a suitable route for a certain type of mind (very intellectual!)"*. I wonder if you could explain (defend) that. The implication is that something is omitted in this approach. And what is it compared to?

Obviously the Direct Path has an appeal for me, and, yes, I am overly intellectual, and, yes, I am steeped in philosophy, but the cautions within your answer to the questioner would apply to anyone looking at the truth, by whatever means. From my reading of it, you are comfortable with Greg Goode, whom I would describe as Direct Path, and his words speak with caution (of what Consciousness is not).

A: I think I would like to rewrite the statement using a little more care! *"Direct Path offers a suitable route for a certain type of mind (intellectual), providing that the mind is suitably prepared to begin with (sAdhana chatuShTaya sampatti) and providing that the teaching is guided by a suitably qualified guru".* And the same arguments that apply to satsang teaching also apply to Direct Path, e.g. occasional visits to or by a teacher are insufficient.

As far as I am aware, most of the present-day Direct Path teachers only do 'satsang'-style teaching. Shri Atmananda says that: *"The subjective experience of the real 'I' is exclusively the subject of Vedanta. This can be gained only by personal contact, in an attitude of complete surrender, with a Jnyanin [sage] who is established in that subjective Reality" (Notes, 420).* I don't personally agree with this statement and I have gained most of my own knowledge through reading and listening to recorded talks. At the time that I originally answered this question, there were few Direct Path books around so that reading widely was not really an option to compensate for the lack of teachers. Fortunately, that has now been remedied. Jean Klein's books and Atmananda's 'Spiritual Discourses' have been republished. Francis Lucille, Rupert Spira and Greg Goode have also all published books on Direct Path.

Satsang teachers

This is my own categorization (see my book 'Enlightenment: The Path Through The Jungle') but most seekers will know what I mean. It refers to anyone who travels around the world, giving short (2 – 3 hour) question-and-answer sessions or maybe occasional, week-long 'residential' courses (although these are often so-called 'silent' retreats). Anyone can register for these or even just turn up on the day for the one-off talks. There is no particular topic, although the teacher may speak for a while on whatever subject comes to mind (or has been planned in advance).

Teachers in the 'lineages' of Ramana, Nisargadatta, Osho, Atmananda and Adyashanti all tend to teach via satsang, as well as the 'Independents' (those with no lineage at all). See my hierarchy charts at (http://www.Advaita.org.uk/teachers/lineages.htm).

Seekers ask questions on topics of particular interest to them (but perhaps no one else). They may already be very knowledgeable or may be complete beginners, serious or cynical. It matters not to the teacher because there is no continuity at all and will probably never meet again.

Problems and objections are listed much more reasonably and systematically in the 'Jungle' book.

Surprisingly perhaps, there have been few specific questions in this area. Or, to be more accurate, there have been lots of questions but they are concerned with the sub-category of satsang teachers – Neo-Advaitins.

Q: I am confused about what you mean (in the book 'Enlightenment: The Path Through The Jungle') by teachers who teach by satsang. I understood satsang to mean an occasion to gather round a master to imbue his teachings and that this has been a time honored traditional practice of Saints and Gurus in India.

In the section where this is mentioned, it seems to take for granted that the reader is aware of what you mean by this term, as well as that a 'Neo-Advaita' movement, which I can't really understand, has emerged. Since I imagine I may not be the only one perplexed and uninformed about all this, could you perhaps elaborate on this, possibly in the selfsame sections, as it certainly seems important and I am anxious to understand.

Could what is termed 'workshops' in the US, which is to imply a weekend, week-long, or even just a day or half-day seminars be the way you mean 'satsang' in the UK? Even if that is the case, I don't understand the undesirability of this, as great traditional teachers like Vivekananda traveled around conducting lectures and seminars to teach. So I am still in the dark and would implore you to shed light on this issue on behalf of those of us in ignorance about these matters.

A: What you say is correct. But the terms 'satsang teacher' and

'Neo-Advaitin teacher' are now in common usage in the West and understood by most. The book addresses the whole issue of correct traditional teaching versus the modern 'non-teaching' methods. Here are the definitions of those terms from the appendix of this book:

satsang (satsa~Nga) – (In the context of this book) the style of teaching popular in the West, whereby the teacher hosts short meetings of an hour or two or longer 'residential' courses of up to one or two weeks. The teacher may speak on a topic for a short time but, more usually, attendees ask whatever question might be on their mind and the teacher endeavors to answer this. Note that, in its traditional use, the word literally means 'association with the wise or good'. It refers to a meeting in which some teaching is given, followed by question and answer. This is essentially the same meaning; the difference is that it forms just a part of traditional teaching whereas it is the entirety of most Western teaching.

Neo-Advaita – the style of teaching that purports to express only the final, absolute truth of Advaita. It does not admit of any 'levels' of reality and does not recognize the existence of a seeker, teacher, ignorance, spiritual path etc.

Neo-Advaita

Here are a few of the 'defining' statements about Neo-Advaita from the 'Jungle' book:

157. *'Neo-Advaita' is a very recent phenomenon and its principal protagonists were unknown before the mid nineteen-nineties. It is the term used for the style of teaching that purports to express only the final, absolute truth of Advaita.*

158. *Effectively, it states the 'bottom-line' conclusions without having carried out any of the intervening stages. Instead of systematically undermining all of the seeker's pre-existing beliefs, it attempts to supplant them with a radical new belief. This new belief is contrary to everyday (i.e. dualistic) experience and there is no rationale given in justification.*

159. *Neo-Advaita has no methodology, since its teachers explicitly*

reject the scriptures as a pramANa along with everything else. This aspect is the key to the essence of traditional teaching. Just as the eyes are the means for acquiring knowledge of form and color, the ears the means for acquiring knowledge of sounds and so on, so are the scriptures (together with a teacher who understands the methods) the means for obtaining Self-knowledge.

160. *It does not admit of any 'levels' of reality and does not recognize the existence of a seeker, teacher, Self-ignorance, spiritual path etc.*

163. *Despite insisting that there is no one to become enlightened and that this word itself has no meaning, Neo-Advaitins nevertheless admit that the way that they perceive the world now differs from how they once saw it. And many speak of the (non-)event which triggered this transformation. It is never explained why there is such a reluctance to refer to this (non-)event as 'enlightenment'.*

164. *If the purpose of teaching is for 'education', i.e. the 'leading out' (Latin 'educere') from ignorance into knowledge, then traditional Advaita counts as teaching, Neo-Advaita doesn't.*

165. *Neo-Advaita is a belief-system without a system – i.e. no structure, no method, no practice; the 'bottom line' without any preceding text.*

Q.67 Don't traditional and Neo-Advaita say the same?

Q: I've just read your dialogue with Jeff Foster (http://www.Advaita.org.uk/discourses/trad_neo/jeff_dialog.htm). I think you both have something valuable to say.

It seems that both traditional and 'Neo' Advaita do the same thing: they point out to the person that there is no person! The difference is that the neos don't like to acknowledge the 'person' to whom they are pointing this out – because ultimately there isn't one ...

So the neos operate from the ultimate perspective (so to speak). The problem with this arises in the communication of it. Any attempt to point to, to describe or communicate this ultimate nature of reality, belongs by default at the level of the empirical. It involves apparent time, progression and cause and effect (the neos themselves talk of 'seeing through', 'when the penny drops', 'it can be seen' etc.).

Other than the failure to acknowledge this shuffle between the empirical and the ultimate levels, I think that the actual core 'message' of the modern non-dual 'teachers' is as sound and as powerful as some of the great Zen and Dzogchen masters.

A: The difference between the two approaches is that traditional is self-consistent, whereas the Neo-Advaitin one is not. Neo is actually hypocritical in a sense because it denies the person yet still attempts a dialog with one. Traditional positively acknowledges the person at the level at which the discussion takes place. And only the latter approach can work really because the person firmly believes that he or she *does* exist, no matter what anyone says, and education can only lead the person from where he/she is.

Furthermore, it is not possible to 'operate from the ultimate perspective' – Brahman does not act and there is no space, time or causation in reality (as you, yourself, say). I have never disputed that the 'bottom-line message' of traditional and Neo-Advaita is the same. Since the bottom-line is non-duality, this is necessarily the case. What is in dispute is whether Neo-Advaita constitutes a valid method of teaching and, having gone into this in considerable depth, the answer has to be that it does not.

Q.70 More questions on Jeff Foster dialog (see Q.67)

Q: [In the dialog with Jeff Foster] in the first four questions, you seem to be trying to establish how Jeff would describe the status of the person. You go on to say that 'Appearing to no one' is simply meaningless.

I found this comment quite jarring (I may have misunderstood something here though!).

If I'm allowed to change the wording slightly (keeping what I believe Jeff's meaning to be intact) to 'Arising for no one', I would say that this is almost a definition of non-duality. In Zen they might say something like: Firstly, there is me here and the mountain over there, then there is just the experience (it has to be said 'for no one') mountain! This is the non-dual 'moment' – one taste as the Tibetan masters say! The middle of the equation falls away and there is just IS-ness! Of course if there is an experiencer of this, we are back in duality.

Manifestation proceeds and phenomena arise, not for the person, but *as* the person, world, thought, feeling, body etc. Any claim to these arisings, is more arising.

A: Yes, I understand what you are saying but I have to stand by what I wrote. It is simply not possible to talk about seeing or experiencing reality. This must be to confuse dual and non-dual. The point is surely that all that we see, think, feel etc. is objectively perceived by the mind in vyavahAra; i.e. it is a person to whom the <whatever> is arising. From the vantage point of the absolute (if such a thing has any meaning), there is *only* the absolute; i.e. no 'arisings' whatsoever. The idea of 'manifestation' or 'creation' is just that – an idea in the mind of a person to rationalize what is perceived by the mind; i.e. all within vyavahAra.

Q: OK Dennis, I agree that there is not a major difference in opinion – it may have something to do with our different backgrounds.

My background is in Buddhism, Zen and Dzogchen, primarily the non-duality emphasis in those traditions. I don't have a great deal of knowledge of traditional Advaita but I have been influenced by Sri Ramana Maharshi, Sri Atmananda Krishna Menon and Jean Klein amongst others.

Still, I feel that there is not a problem with 'arising for no one'. Here is my take on non-duality:

(Throughout this I'm aware of the shortcomings of the word 'experience' [as with 'knowing'] and its normally dualistic implications.)

There is not me here and the computer there ... there is just the experience 'computer'. A truck rumbles by outside ... there is not 'me' hearing the truck; there is just the experience 'truck'! There is no two-ness in present experience. There is the sound of the truck, then the thought "but I am hearing the truck"; there is not a 'me' and that thought, there is just the experience 'thought'.

So, there is not me here observing the computer there – those are two sides of the same *one* experience. All there is is the self-shining display of 'reality' with no observer to be found (that would be more display). That is (as far as I'm concerned) the meaning of non-duality!

Whatever is arising *is* consciousness; not me *and* objects, just what is! No twice-ness, just what is, as it is!!

After the fact (so to speak), we can analyze that ears were needed to hear, the brain was required to process and translate information etc. I'm also not particularly knowledgeable about metaphysics, science and philosophy and I don't really know about the ontological status of 'objects' and 'events' etc. But it doesn't matter; non-duality is the 'shift' from the experience of a separate me to the experience of reality as it is – which includes the experience 'me'!

On a broader note I agree that it is meaningless to think that there could be an experience of the 'all'! How could it be known? There would be no distinctions etc. Reality presents *as* the particular, but that particular is *not separate* from the 'all'! So in that sense, every experience is an experience of oneness/Self!

I've had dialogues with Greg (Dr. Greg Goode, Philosophical Counselor and teacher of Direct Path Advaita) in the past and I love his take on all this, but I also think that he would have no problem with 'arises for no one'.

A: Yes – I recognize the sorts of statements I have heard from Greg in the past – I think he would be happy with what you say. Indeed, I have no real quibble with your full explanation. My quibbles with the neos are twofold (with respect to our discussion). Firstly, speaking like this is fine from one who is knowledgeable in non-dual philosophy to one who is also knowledgeable. It is not acceptable (or does not constitute helpful teaching) when speaking or writing to one who is unfamiliar and trapped in their dualistic problems.

Secondly, I believe that many (most?) neos do not actually understand or appreciate what you are saying here. Your explanations are, in fact, Direct Path Advaita and not Neo-Advaita. So maybe the essence of your question and comments is that Direct Path adherents would have much more sympathy with Neo-Advaita than would traditionalists – and I think I agree (although I also recall Greg criticizing the neos on lists and in private emails).

Q.75 More concerns about the teaching of Neo-Advaita

Q: I've been studying non-dual philosophy for ten years and have been a devotee of Ramana Maharshi for two, and every contact with Ramana through words, pictures, and his ashram in New York has given me peace. Indeed, this is the quality he says to look for in a guru!

I recently came across the writings of Tony Parsons and this has been anything but peaceful. Tony says that Self-enquiry is 'not possible' but he seems to imply that he has a better method – read his books and attend his seminars. I would not be troubled by Tony if he had simply said 'nothing is possible' and left it at that. But the way in which he presents his teachings seems to imply that satsang with him or one of his recommended students is the only way to realization and this has been highly disturbing to me because I see his logic:

Self-enquiry is a method that requires the illusion of free will doing the enquiry; reading or hearing Tony's lectures is passive, they can be heard 'by no-one', (as opposed to self-enquiry, which must be done by 'someone') and requires no free will, hence no ego illusion is strengthened. (These are my words.)

This implies that he and his students are the only way as yet, but this 'dream seeker' feels no attraction to Parsons and even less interest in reading him further or attending his meetings. Tony would most definitely claim that I feel disturbed by him because I have truly heard him and my ego is threatened; and this is good; but what I feel is not a sense of risk or danger, but a sense of paralysis, as his logic has taken away Ramana's way and self-enquiry and left me with another option – go see him – and I am simply not interested.

I would really appreciate any insight into this conundrum. Basically, is it true that only Tony's (or Gill's or Kersschot's) 'communications' are the only possible method of awakening (because receiving them does not involve a false sense of 'you' doing something), and that 'self-enquiry is a myth'?

A: The quandary that you describe is one, I am sure, that is shared by many seekers and it is specifically in order to resolve issues such as this that I wrote 'Enlightenment: The Path Through The Jungle'.

The key to the understanding of this problem relates to 'levels' of reality. The absolute truth is that there is no creation, there are no objects, no people, no duality of any kind. This is what the Neo-Advaitin teachers claim and this, too, is what traditional Advaita teaches. But it does not seem like this to the 'person' who is deluded by Self-ignorance into believing that they are a separate individual living in an alien world. A useful metaphor is the dream. The dream world may be endlessly complex and totally believable to the dreamer but this is not seen until the dreamer awakens, when the dream world and the dreamer are seen (by the waker) never to have existed separate from the mind.

Neo-Advaita refuses to acknowledge the validity of the empirical world of the person, whereas traditional Advaita does. Traditional teaching openly acknowledges the person and aims to remove the Self-ignorance via a series of well-proven, stepwise procedures, carefully gauged to the level and understanding of the seeker. Neo-Advaita simply restates the bottom-line reality. No matter how many times this message is repeated, it is most unlikely to have any effect (except for the negative effect that you mention). Furthermore, it is not at all helpful to deny the existence of the person since that is what the seeker believes himself to be. The belief in 'I' must not be denied since that essential 'I' is also the non-dual reality.

To most people, it does feel that we have free will and this belief creates no problem as long as we use it to 'choose' a path that is going to lead to enlightenment! Advaita is not inimical to reason. Each step of the traditional path is logical, totally comprehensible and brings immediate and unarguable Self-knowledge. When Neo-Advaitin teachers make statements such as 'heard by no-one', it does not take much discrimination to 'choose' between Neo and traditional Advaita! The ego is also not a problem, in the sense that you need not worry about it. As you progress on a traditional path, it naturally loses its dominion and ultimately is seen for what it is – a mistaken superimposition.

Q.83 Modern non-dualism teachers

Q: You really seem to have got it in for the modern non-dualism teachers. It's starting to come across as slightly obsessive! ;-)

I have two points to make:

Firstly, these communicators (why I am not going to call them Neos will become clear) have never set themselves up as being teachers of Advaita. Their message is a distillation of the pure non-dualism that is found at the esoteric core of many systems: Zen, Dzogchen, Taoism, Advaita, Sufism and others. Neo Advaita is a term only used by yourself, Möller de la Rouvière and a few others to categorize something that never purports to be a teaching of Advaita Vedanta.

Secondly, some of the criticisms that you level at them could equally be applied to the methods (non methods) of teachers in most of the systems above (even Shankara, in the main, wasn't insistent on the necessity of any practice or means for the realization of Brahman – conceding that yogic practice may have some limited value "for those of inferior intellect").

Since you readily admit to only having limited knowledge of other 'systems' of non-duality, do you think it appropriate and fair to rebuke all modern non-dual communicators in this way? (Of course many certainly do deserve criticism – purely for their lack of grasp of their subject, but this could be applied to teachers of Advaita Vedanta too.)

A: Thanks for your open and forthright comments – I appreciate it!

You are right in at least two respects. The message of the Neo-Advaita teachers *is* a distillation of non-dualism from various traditions. (I will continue to use the term 'Neo-Advaita', if that is ok. I accept your point that many of these teachers do not claim any association with Advaita but it is gaining wider usage and most of those who read my website will know what is meant.) However, the fact that it is a distillation is one of my main complaints. The teaching is distilled so much that no teaching as such is present any more. All that is left are terse statements which, though often true, do little to help those seekers who are 'new to the game'. It may also be true that the criticisms apply equally to modern teachers of any other non-dual tradition, since non-duality of any 'sort' must essentially be the same. Since, I am unfamiliar with those teachings, however, I would not presume to attempt to criticize them directly.

I cannot agree that the criticisms apply equally to Shankara or to any other traditional teacher because traditional teaching by definition incorporates proven methods. Shankara most certainly *did* insist that initial practice was needed in order to prepare the mind. He specifically stated that those without some preparation would never become enlightened; those with some might become enlightened but would not reap the associated benefits such as peace of mind etc., while those who were fully prepared could enjoy both.

Your assertion that I may be rebuking some teachers unfairly is not really justified I think because, in those essays etc. where I do criticize teachers, the precise grounds upon which the criticism is based are always made clear. So, I guess the platitude would be 'if the cap fits ...'. My book 'Enlightenment: The Path Through The Jungle' should clarify this whole subject once and for all.

Incidentally, my concern is not 'obsessive'; I simply want to help all of those seekers who feel that they are not getting anywhere or are depressed in the light of some of the messages they are hearing at satsangs or reading in books.

Q.84 'No-path' teaching and Neo-Advaita

Q: You mention the 'no path' teachings and refer to Neo-Advaita. This seems to be a sticking point for you. It is interesting, as this understanding evolves, that, for the 'person', there is definitely a path needed. Whether that be reading, writing, scriptures, whatever, there is some sort of 'polishing the stone' that seems to be needed.

I don't know what the stance of the 'Neo-Advaita' teachers is; however I agree with you that the mind must go through a process in which all possibilities are exhausted – the mind becomes frustrated and gives up, even on spiritual experiences, as these always come and go.

At this point of exhaustion, a simple looking without thought occurs. In this seeing, it may be clear that there never was a person to seek. Of course it seemed like there was, hence the search in the first place. This seems to be the path.

I also agree with you that there seems to be a period of integration – the old mental habits continue to arise and are seen in the clear space of knowing; immediately extinguished like a moth flying into a bonfire.

It all boils down to the fact that there is no separate self in the organism. The human body is not much different from a tree or a cat, other than the advanced brain capable of logic. In this logic we take what seems evident and place a belief that there must be some separate person in there. If this is clearly seen, then all paths and all seeking and all problems drop away because there is no one there to do any of this. It is only in the mind that suffering or enlightenment can occur. Our true nature is that which is seeing, not anything seen.

A: Neo-Advaita is not a 'sticking point' for me. The reason that I am particularly interested in it is that it is clear that many are confused by it. I wanted to explain to such people how it can be that what the neos say can be essentially true yet no help at all. I have accordingly spent some significant time studying the problem and writing about it.

On the specifics of what you write, I have never said that *"the mind must go through a process in which all possibilities are exhausted – the mind becomes frustrated and gives up"*. What I have said (in 'The Book of One') is that: *"Enlightenment is of the mind; the Self-knowledge that destroys the Self-ignorance takes place in the mind. There is no frustration at all when Advaita is taught correctly. On the contrary, it is a joyful process in which aspects that caused confusion are replaced by clarity. It is also the person that seeks enlightenment and the person that finds it, even though the 'finding' also includes the realization that there never was a 'person' in reality"*.

Q: Very well said. Within the dream of being a person, delusion and enlightenment can arise. Beyond both and clearly present *now* is our true nature – that in which suffering or bliss appears. Although thoughts still arise, when the belief in the separate person falls away, suffering is known as false immediately in the light of knowing.

What I take to be Neo-Advaita is the concept that there is nothing to be done and no one to do it, hence you're already enlightened. There is a false but very 'real' wall of concept built around this person. Many teachers, including Bob Adamson and Gilbert Schultz, who I'm most familiar with, spend a lot of time breaking through these concepts of a separate person in the world who suffers.

It is then possible, if this is truly looked into deeply, that this false sense of self drops away, leaving the understanding that there never was a seeker in the first place. The search was a chasing of the tail, however 'necessary', in order to see through the mind and the web of illusion of the person. This is what is meant by frustration and wearing out of the mind. In seeing that all spiritual experiences eventually pass, the expectations and false beliefs of enlightenment fall away and there seems to be just a naked looking without thought, a noticing of this silent witnessing that's always going on and is not dependent on anything that may arise, whether enlightened or suffering.

A: There is also much confusing use of language in Neo-Advaita. When the subject under discussion is so elusive (and ultimately, indeed, cannot be spoken of at all), it is extremely important to use words very precisely.

'Dream of being a person' is such a confusing usage – who is dreaming? It is not the case (for a seeker) that 'you are already enlightened'. In vyavahAra, the person is a reality and this remains the case until the person becomes enlightened. It is only then, that one might say that the person does not exist (and never did). (And even then the 'as-if' person effectively continues to exist from the empirical perspective. Otherwise there could be no enlightened teachers!) The seeker only knows the apparent reality of vyavahAra and this is the level that the teacher has to address. Neo-advaitin 'teachers' attempt only to make statements at the level of paramArtha and this is why they fail.

Q.88 Re: traditional Vs Neo-Advaita debate

Q: Reading some of the essays with respect to the above, as you have invited comments I thought to respond as follows: Maybe I have missed the point here but it strikes me that, when engaging in philosophical arguments of this nature, who is trying to prove what to whom and why bother anyway to argue the toss concerning the significance or non-significance of a bunch of concepts?

On the level of appearance, surely all is valid and has its place. So if we find it is not possible to measure perfection/imperfection, there being no one to measure it, all must come together. Therefore nothing is rejected or needs to be changed, attacked or defended. All is wonderful as it is.

A: You are employing Neo-arguments! Which means you are confusing absolute and relative realities. At the absolute level, there are no persons, no arguments, no right or wrong; indeed no descriptions at all have any relevance or meaning. There is not even any knowledge, consciousness or Advaita!

But everything in the world takes place in relative reality. Here, all this *is* valid. There are persons, with minds – and most of these are full of Self-ignorance. Self-knowledge is needed to remove this and it almost invariably comes in the way of teaching of one sort or another, along with reason and even philosophical argument. Valid teaching will successfully remove Self-ignorance; invalid teaching will not.

End of story!

Q.112 Questions on Neo-Advaita 'teaching'

Q: Not discounting your fine work and the clarity with which you present it ... the question of whether or not Neo-Advaita can 'deliver the goods' makes exactly as much sense as the question of whether or not the sound of a lark can.

A: That sounds like a typical Neo-Advaitin comment to me! The bottom line is that the problem is Self-ignorance and only Self-knowledge can dispel that. Sounds of larks (or Neo-Advaitin 'truths') will never provide Self-knowledge.

Q: I think the bottom line problem is, rather, the ineffability of it all.

That said, I'm wondering in what realm do the words 'only' and 'never', which you have so freely used, really function? The Relative? The Ultimate? The Linguistic?

Really, I am only writing out of a sense of bafflement as to the expenditure of energy being given to trying to discredit what has been tagged 'Neo-Advaita'. What's the point? Do you think traditional Advaita is threatened? Seekers will never stop seeking. Those who are exposed to Neo-Advaitic ideas and remain unsatisfied will likely run in droves toward more path-oriented teachings. Seekers of truth aren't likely to feel they've reached the end of the search when only the intellect has been convinced. If they do, then they weren't really seeking the truth in the first place. Worried about confusion? Isn't confusion one of the great motivating forces in the search for truth?

"Typical Neo-Advaitin comment" indeed! (!) It almost sounds like a dirty word!

I do not believe that the sounds of larks provide Self-knowledge. (Did you really think that's what I was saying? My point was just the opposite, the notions of sequence and cause being absent.) When there is unobstructed hearing of the lark's song, the concept of Self-knowledge is rendered nonsensical. (Does that sound too Neo-Advaitic? Too Zen? Too true?) It may be that my choice of words here is technically unsatisfying, but you get my drift.

Thanks again for all of your good work and the time you took to respond to my e-mail. Feel free to classify any of my questions here as unanswerable.

A: I can now see that you have given serious thought to the difficulties and intransigent problems inherent in talking about all of this stuff (rather than simply making clever, throw-away remarks, as many who support the Neo-Advaitins do). Now that you have revealed that you know what you are talking about, I withdraw the 'typical Neo-Advaitin comment' comment!!

I am really not trying to discredit Neo-Advaita as such. All I am trying to do is to pin it down as an attempt to achieve the impossible (namely describe the way 'it really is') and to point out to its many adherents that it is not in the remotest sense a teaching method that is likely to bring about enlightenment. There is no doubt that many seekers are severely frustrated (and even occasionally suicidal) as a result of taking on board the non-teaching of Neo-Advaita and it is to help them that I wrote the 'Jungle' book.

To answer your questions: the words 'only' and 'never' apply to the relative realm, as all words necessarily do. That is where we all find ourselves and the aim is to realize that it *is* only relative and that the (indescribable) reality is non-dual.

Traditional Advaita is not under threat. It has survived for over a thousand years because it works. Neo-Advaita is a flash-in-the-pan which will fade away when it is discovered that it doesn't.

You are right that confusion (and, even more so, suffering) is a great motivator in the search for truth. But surely you cannot be claiming that it is ok for a supposed teacher of truth to add to that confusion?

Regarding your expansion of the 'lark singing' remark, this seems to highlight the other major concern in the 'Jungle' book about what is meant by enlightenment. It is not an experience, e.g. of being totally in the present and at one with nature etc., with no concerns or thoughts and so on. Experiences begin ... and end; enlightenment is irrevocable. What it is (according to traditional Advaita) is the event in time, in the mind, when the last of Self-ignorance is cleared and there is full Self-knowledge. The mind is said to 'take on the form of the undivided reality'.

Q.143 On the arguments between traditional and Neo

Q: Since I finished reading your book 'Enlightenment: The Path Through The Jungle', I've gained deep respect for traditional teachings. Since then, I've followed some of the back and forth comments expressed on your website, particularly those involving Tony Parsons. I appreciate your concern for holding up the tried-and-true perspective of traditional Advaita and also your willingness to present both sides of the argument. However, this wrangling that's come to prominence lately is not a good sign in my opinion. It clarifies distinctions, but I'm wondering if it clarifies what truly matters.

No doubt, there are people who have discovered the more traditional approaches through an introduction to these ideas gained through the so-called Neo-Advaita point of view. And if some of the traditional folk have moved in the other direction, i.e. to the Neo approach, so be it. I don't think it's helpful for anyone to take strong positions that result in continual bickering, particularly about fine points of distinction that in the end don't really matter all that much, except in the minds of the combatants. Zen koans make far better mental gymnastics.

It reminds me of the silly arguments, often taken ever so seriously, by various Christian denominations over the past two thousand years, such as the Calvinist/Armenian debates, not to mention the various segments of Hindus, Islamists and Buddhists. Even if one gains some sort of mental conviction about these finer distinctions, what has one really gained?

Isn't it possible to hold our opinions much more lightly, with a degree of love and true respect, always open to wider views? Our insistence on being right is a troubling human quality that we seem hell-bent on perpetuating, particularly unseemly in matters deemed to be the root and essence of being.

A: I agree with you. Having made the points that I wanted to make in the book, I would now like effectively to take a 'back seat' apart from responding to 'questions' made by visitors to the site. But the book was bound to generate some strong feelings and I think it was necessary to allow some of these to be aired so that, hopefully, everyone may be better informed and eventually settle down into the attitude that you yourself have expressed. I don't think that it would have been reasonable to refuse to answer any questions that arose, or refuse to respond to any objections or publish any more articles on the subject, whether 'for' or 'against'. The site exists to disseminate views on topics in Advaita and provide links to related sites. I will not publish any articles that are merely ad hominem attacks on other teachers but, where they are part of an ongoing debate that clearly interests many readers, I do not feel that I can legitimately exclude them.

I hope and expect that the 'fuss' will die down naturally over the next few months. But I am glad that you made this point since it gives me the opportunity to make this clear.

Q.147 On the merits of Neo-Advaita (ref. Jeff Foster)

Q: I recently visited one of your listed teachers, Jeff Foster, in London. I wanted to experience a Neo-Advaita teacher to check for myself whether these guys are as misleading as you claim.

I took along a pencil and paper and made notes! Jeff was an incredibly grounded, patient and compassionate fellow, who, when I sought him out after the talk, gave me his full attention and time. I asked him about traditional versus Neo-Advaita. His answer surprised me. He said he would never reject the traditions, or tell anyone to give up their spiritual practices. This challenged my assumptions about Neo-Advaitin teachers, after all I'd read on your site!

I posed to him the dilemma: if the person is an illusion, then what is the benefit in self-inquiry? He said, to the person, it is of much benefit. As long as there is a person there, who thinks he or she can benefit from spiritual practice, then that's exactly what they should be doing. He said he didn't see himself as a teacher at all, or anything for that matter. He said he sees himself as trying to describe, as clearly as possible, the 'seeing that there is no person', the awakening from the dream, and the settling into clarity.

He also said that he didn't expect anyone to see this until they saw it. In other words, his message is not a rejection of the traditions, but merely to say that the traditions will appear to be relevant as long as there is a person. Also, he said (and this cleared so much up for me) that the only reason he doesn't give out specific spiritual practices, is that he doesn't know what's best for anyone, and does not favor any single one of them.

Crucially, I asked him whether I should keep going with my

self-enquiry, and he enthusiastically answered yes, of course. He even gave me some incredibly helpful and knowledgeable pointers and information about self-inquiry. I told him that I was very surprised, after reading everything on Advaita.org.uk, that a so-called 'Neo-Advaitin teacher' had been more helpful, compassionate, knowledgeable and more genuine than many of the other 'traditional' teachers I've met.

I told him I would contact you, Dennis, about it, and he says that you two have spoken before, and that you were very respectful to him but had very strong beliefs about what was correct and what was not, and I think he was implying (though I might be wrong) that you were coming from a place of intellectual understanding rather than direct experience, though that might be my own projection. I did get the feeling from Jeff though that he genuinely respected you and the traditions very much, but that he doesn't understand why he is referred to as 'Neo-Advaitin'. I can't remember exactly what Jeff said here, but it was something to do with the fact that maybe his earlier work had a more 'Neo' emphasis, but his expression has moved far away from that as he's been doing the public talks.

So, I am no longer sure that what you are doing by separating 'Neo-Advaitin' teachers from the others is such a great idea. For example, many people may now be put off visiting teachers like Jeff, because of what you say, and yet in some ways I find Jeff more 'traditional' (in his clarity, compassion and helpfulness) than some traditional teachers!

The point is, I think, that Jeff and teachers like him do not stick to any one lineage or tradition, so he meets people exactly where they are. In the meeting, I asked him what he thought of teachers who repeat "there is no person; there is no point to traditions, etc.". He replied with directness that ultimately it might be true (the gateless gate and so on) but that it doesn't help the person who is looking for help. Also, that it's too easy to set yourself up as a teacher by just repeating those words and having a purely intellectual understanding, and that's why he always emphasizes that it's not about intellectual understanding or repeating "there is no person", but a clear seeing, which is what the traditions are always talking about! I was very surprised at this, Dennis, as it's exactly what you say!

It seems that, in rejecting what you call 'Neo-Advaitin' teachers: You are subtly putting down teachers with something incredibly important and helpful to say.

You are putting teachers in the 'Neo-Advaitin' box without really knowing what they teach.

More worryingly you are, I think, very subtly setting yourself up as an 'authority', and potentially misleading people like me. I could have missed out on Jeff whose words have resonated more strongly than those of other teachers who have been 'endorsed' on your site.

In separating traditional from Neo, you are adding more separation into a world already full of it, and certainly there must be more mis-categorized teachers out there.

Your site in the most part has been very helpful for me, and I am sure many others. But I am sure you can understand my concern now that I've experienced Neo-Advaita for myself, and seen that it's not always everything you say it is.

A: First of all, let me assure you (though you haven't implied otherwise) that there is nothing personal in any of my criticism of Neo-Advaita. Although I have not met many teachers of any persuasion in person, I have communicated via email with many, and pretty well all of them seem genuinely to believe that they are saying useful things and they mostly seem very personable, polite and friendly.

However, being sincere and responsive does not in itself make a good teacher. Nor does it make what is said necessarily true or helpful. The ultimate mark of a good teacher is that he or she leads the seeker eventually to enlightenment. And the key requirements seem to be A. knowledge of proven methods; B. ability to convey these in such a way that the seeker also gains that knowledge. (A subsidiary requirement is that the teacher is also enlightened – and Shankara himself also puts this requirement last.)

When I have discussed Advaita and teaching methods with Jeff, he has always come across with all of the traits that you mention and, as a person, I genuinely like him. My understanding of his teaching is based upon his first book 'Life Without a Centre' and our discussions (some of which you can read at the website) were also based upon this. There is no doubt in my mind that most of what was said in there was fundamentally unhelpful. It is, however, perfectly possible that he has altered the style and content of his teaching since then so that what he now says may be more valid and useful to the seeker.

The 'bottom line' of all teaching has to be that the seeker's problem is one of Self-ignorance. He already is the non-dual Brahman but he does not know this. Accordingly, practice of any kind, experience of any kind will not in itself bring about enlightenment. Only Self-knowledge can do this.

Jeff may not call himself a Neo-Advaitin (or even a teacher). Tony Parsons also ridicules the term. But the fact remains that they advertise and hold satsangs and seekers go to these expecting to learn something useful. They write books and seekers read them, expecting to learn something useful. To my mind, this gives them the status of would-be teachers, irrespective of what terms they use. And what they say bears some resemblance to the scriptural writings about the nature of reality. So I think the reference to them as 'Neo-Advaitin teachers' is a reasonable one. Unfortunately, what they 'teach' is most unlikely to bring about Self-knowledge.

It is quite possible that what is said by such teachers appears reasonable at the time if you are not extremely well 'clued up' about the whole subject. They are successful in what they do precisely because they are personable, persuasive and usually much more knowledgeable about the subject than those to whom they speak. Most of them can 'blind with science' those less experienced. These concepts are subtle in the extreme. It is ultimately not possible to describe reality in any way. All words break down in the limit. Accordingly, any discussion is constantly playing with words at the boundary of meaninglessness. It is hardly surprising that a seeker comes away from a meeting with someone who is practiced in manipulating these concepts fully believing what they have been told.

But the proof is in the follow-up let-down, when it is later realized that nothing has changed. Nothing has been really understood and life carries on as before. All that can be done is to go back for another fix!

I'm not entirely sure what, of what was said, persuaded you that there was teaching of value. You say: *"He said he would never reject the traditions, or tell anyone to give up their spiritual practices"*. Yes – he has said much the same to me, too. His message of the first book essentially boils down to: "This is all there is". He repeats this in many ways throughout the book. And it is true (assuming that what is meant is 'sarvaM khalvidam brahma'). But the understanding of this can only come about as the end result of a systematic approach which gradually supplants all of the erroneous misconceptions with which we have lived all of our lives. Simply stating this as a fact at the outset achieves nothing. You have heard this – are you now enlightened?

You say: *"He said, as long as there is a person there, who thinks he or she can benefit from spiritual practice, then that's exactly what they should be doing"*. Not necessarily. It all depends upon how mentally prepared they are already and their present state of understanding. To repeat: practice in itself will never bring enlightenment.

"He said he sees himself as trying to describe, as clearly as possible, the seeing that there is no person, the awakening from the dream, and the settling into clarity". Describing 'how it is for me' is not providing Self-knowledge. The seeker has to gain the direct knowledge for him or herself. This is done traditionally by providing pointers etc. that enable this to take place. Read the example of bhAga tyAga

lakShaNa in Q.345 for a good example of how traditional teaching works and then quote an analogous example from Neo-Advaitin teaching.

"But what he said, which really struck a chord, was that he didn't expect anyone to see this until they saw it. In other words, his message is not a rejection of the traditions, but merely to say that the traditions will appear to be relevant as long as there is a person". Well, the first sentence is not really saying very much, is it? The second point is precisely why traditional teaching is necessary, yes! ALL teaching is for the person, including Neo-Advaita. Who else would it be for? It is the person who gains enlightenment when Self-knowledge is gained by the mind. Who else would become enlightened? And the person is not going to become enlightened as a result of the teacher repeatedly stating that there is no person!

"Also, he said (and this cleared so much up for me) that the only reason he doesn't give out specific spiritual practices, is that he doesn't know what's best for anyone, in the sense that there are some very effective practices in all the traditions, and since he is not aligned with any one tradition, he does not favor any single one of them". I'm afraid that I cannot help but see this as a cop-out. Traditional Advaita teaching is suitable for anyone who is sufficiently mentally prepared. And I am not talking here about practice of any kind, but of Self-knowledge. What, in any case, does he offer instead?

"Crucially, I asked him whether I should keep going with my self-enquiry, and he enthusiastically answered yes, of course. He even gave me some incredibly helpful and knowledgeable pointers and information about self-inquiry. I told him that I was very surprised, after reading everything on Advaita.org.uk, that a so-called 'Neo-Advaitin teacher' had been more helpful, compassionate, knowledgeable and more genuine than many of the other 'traditional' teachers I've met". As I have already said, Jeff is a genuinely sympathetic person. However, supporting your ideas (wrong or otherwise) may dispose you to think favorably of him but says nothing about his ability as a teacher. (In fact, it seems from the earlier comments that he is actually saying effectively 'I

don't want to teach you anything at all' and you are responding by saying he is a good teacher?!)

"I asked him what he thought of teachers who repeat 'there is no person; there is no point to traditions, etc.'. He replied with directness that ultimately it might be true (the gateless gate and so on) but that it doesn't help the person who is looking for help. Also, that it's too easy to set yourself up as a teacher by just repeating those words and having a purely intellectual understanding, and that's why he always emphasizes that it's not about intellectual understanding or repeating 'there is no person', but a clear seeing, which is what the traditions are always talking about!. I was very surprised at this, Dennis – as it's exactly what you say!" This would seem to suggest that he has indeed changed his emphasis somewhat (in the right direction!).

Regarding your more general points about my categorizations and 'setting myself up as an authority', have you read 'Enlightenment: The Path Through The Jungle'? This addresses in great detail all of these issues and hopefully provides evidence enough to convince anyone of the distinctions and the need for these.

Hope this resolves your concerns, which I obviously regard very seriously.

[* Note that, whilst compiling this book, I discovered this page on Jeff's website: http://www.lifewithoutacentre.com/writings/on-Neo-Advaita/. In it he states that: *"There is a strange new club called 'Neo-Advaita'... I was once a fully-paid-up member of this loveless cult. I left about six or seven years ago, sneaking off in the dead of night, ready and willing to be a living, breathing human being again with a beating heart, and ready and willing to listen deeply to my fellow humans, and the relief was so, so great"* (Copyright 2015). So this happy conclusion should hopefully satisfy everyone!]

Q.149 Was Nisargadatta a Neo-Advaitin?

Q: Why does Dr. Goode refer to Nisargadatta as 'Neo-Advaita' in the introduction to your 'Jungle' book on Enlightenment? I have been following the blog of Floyd Henderson for years and had not picked up that inference.

A: He doesn't say that Nisargadatta was a Neo-Advaitin; he says that Nisargadatta (and Ramana and Papaji) *inspired* Neo-Advaita. One of the main points is that all three of them effectively established satsang (attending occasional question and answer sessions) as a bona fide method of teaching. Those teachers who claim any of these as their inspiration mostly teach only using the satsang method. In other words, (probably) none of the teachers in these 'lineages' can now claim to be traditional teachers.

The other point about Nisargadatta in particular is that he had a habit of making 'radical' statements about self, reality etc., as if to 'shock' the listener into an intimation of the truth.

Greg is also perhaps a bit less concerned about differentiating 'satsang' from 'Neo-Advaita' as a teaching method.

Q.154 May one read books by Neo-Advaitins after realization?

Q: Once you have done the so-called work or practices and have realized the self, then it seems that both Neo and traditional teachings are talking about the same thing and there is enjoyment in reading books from both schools. That is to say: if a Neo teacher is talking about this relative existence after realization, I may relate to it or not, but I can still enjoy it because I don't expect to get anything from it other than the enjoyment one might get from reading poetry for example. There was a time when I would read books like 'I Am That', looking for answers, solutions, clarification. Now I just like the way Nisargadatta points to the truth.

What are your thoughts on chopping wood and reading Neo-Advaita?

A: Yes, of course you are right in essence, although 'practice' will never bring enlightenment. What we enjoy is determined by our vAsanA-s (nature if you like), so that some like reading poetry, some don't (though we can get the taste for it, i.e. acquire new vAsanA-s). I agree that both Neo- and traditional teachings are talking about the same thing when it comes to absolute reality. I think you will find, though, that most Neo-Advaitins deny any 'relative existence'. They also deny the existence of 'realization' so that there can be no 'after realization'.

But you will probably rightly accuse me of nit-picking here! The enjoyment or not of reading or listening to a Neo-Advaitin teacher will again depend upon one's nature. It is difficult to just sit back and enjoy if you are forever picking holes in what they say and complaining that it will not benefit the seeker in his seeking!

Q.164 How can traditional be 'better' than 'Neo'?

Q: With respect to the ongoing traditional versus Neo argument, if there are 'not two', then how can one be better than another?

A: The 'not two' refers to paramArtha; the 'better than another' refers to vyavahAra, where there are (contrary to the claim of Neo-Advaitins) seekers, paths and enlightenment at the end of those paths.

Q: You missed the subtlety of my point. As a one-time student of Western philosophy, I learnt that it's all 'horses for courses'. In other words, while some teachings or commentaries may resonate for some, they may not resonate for others. So once again, if paramArtha and vyavahAra are essentially 'not two', then why do you separate them?

A: All teaching takes place in vyavahAra. Most people need to go through a prolonged period of deconditioning of the usual dualistic beliefs before being able to take on board the bottom-line message of Advaita. A very few may be able to see the ultimate truth straight off. Others may have already spent years trying this and that and reading many books. The 'non-teaching' of Neo-Advaita is only ever going to be of any value for these latter categories. All the rest have to go the long way round.

Q.165 More questions on my criticism of Neo-Advaita

Q: Why do you claim that your method is valid and the 'method' of the so-called Neo-Advaita is not?

A: I do not have a method. I advocate the traditional Advaita path as one that has been vindicated for the past 1500+ years by many seekers. I have also satisfied myself that it is one that is in accord with reason. Neo-Advaita has no path (and denies that there is one).

Q: Could it not be that both are valid?

A: The ultimate statements of both are the same. To this extent they are both 'valid' but, as noted above, you cannot say that the 'methods' are the same. The 'non-method' of Neo-Advaita might work for someone who has already been 'traveling the traditional path' for many years and understands all of the theory.

Q: It seems a bit ridiculous: each one claiming that the other one is 'ignorant'.

A: I don't think I have ever claimed anyone is ignorant. I criticize the teaching methodology and misleading statements, never the person. Can you provide a reference please, if you think otherwise?

Q: There is no straightforward path to enlightenment. How could there be a straightforward path to nothing?

A: What is your definition of enlightenment? Your statement implies that it is different from mine.

Q: There are many paths. Each one follows his own. Setting yourself up as a teacher is in fact very dualistic and artificial and the greatest teachers aren't teachers. Both Tony Parsons and you have fallen into the teacher trap, I am afraid.

A: I have not 'set myself up as a teacher'. All my books take the stance that 'I have been looking into Advaita as a teaching that explains the nature of self and reality and this is what I have found so far'. I do not teach – hold no satsangs or residential courses. I just write books and try to help seekers by passing on what I have learned via these questions and answers.

Q.170 More criticism of the Neo-Advaitin debates

Q: I have been looking at the material on the Advaita.org website. I was interested to see all of the debate, attack and counter-attack between Dennis Waite and the so called Neo-Advaitins such as Tony Parsons, Jeff Foster etc. My question is: has full and total 'realization' occurred for any of these so called authorities on the subject, or are they all communicating from their limited experiences along with learned book knowledge i.e. from a state of ignorance?

I can't imagine Sri Nisargadatta or Ramana Maharshi engaging in this kind of behavior. Arguing about how many 'people' have been awakened by traditional Advaita versus Neo-Advaita (as if it's a competition) is nonsense. Do we actually have any fully realized being present at the empirical level (as Dennis Waite calls it) and if so why would they want to awake the 'unreal'? If the One is experiencing Itself through the dream of existence then presumably It intends the unreal to exist as Its cosmic play. Once Reality is known why would there be any need to re-enter the dream to change anything? Waking up all apparent persons surely spoils the dream? If I dreamt that my house was flooded, when I wake in the morning do I arrange for the fire service to be in attendance for when I sleep again tonight?

A: I actually make some of the same points in my books so that your criticism seems somewhat harsh!

In 'Enlightenment: the path through the jungle':

"12. *The book makes no specific claims about relative 'success rates' of the different approaches. There are no statistics available upon which any such claims might be made and views might well differ even upon whether a given teacher is 'enlightened' or not. What it will do is to present, analyze and criticize the various issues and endeavor to persuade the reader that anything other than the traditional approach is unlikely to succeed"*.

And, in Question 93 on the website, as part of the answer I said: *"Suppose you have a dream in which you find someone injured, say, and you are just about to call for an ambulance when you wake up. Having woken up, your concern for the injured person disappears completely because you now know that the entire incident was illusory. Similarly, the enlightened mind knows that the world, with its separate persons, global warming etc. is mithyA only. All is Brahman and nothing needs to be done (or can be done because Brahman does nothing). [Note that this is not to say that the realized man ignores those who are suffering around him. On the contrary, action will take place in response to the need, without any attachment, according to the nature of his body-mind.]"*

If you can point to anything I have said on the website that is unreasonable in my criticism of Neo-Advaita and that is clearly "communicating ... from a state of ignorance", then I will happily remove it.

On the topic of the 'empirical level' (this phrase is not my invention – it is a reasonable translation of the Sanskrit 'vyavahAra'), I'm not sure what you mean by 'awaking the unreal'. It is certainly pointless to talk about motives with respect to the 'cosmic play'. The bottom line is that there has never been any creation – everything is Brahman, perfect and complete. But your implication is that whatever is happening is fine (from the point of view of 'the One') so that must also include seeming arguments between traditionalists and Neo-Advaitins!

Even the enlightened will tend to continue to do whatever their nature dictates. This may well include trying to communicate what has been discovered, even to those non-existent others who are now known to be already free.

One other point: on your comment that *"I can't imagine Sri Nisargadatta or Ramana Maharshi engaging in this kind of behavior"*. According to the stories about Shankara's life (there is no 'certified' biography), he used to travel around the country specifically to engage in philosophical disputes with those who disagreed with him and a section of his commentary on the Brahmasutra specifically refutes the positions of other philosophies. Similarly, parts of Gaudapada's kArikA on the Mandukya Upanishad specifically address other views and contradicts them. Since these two can be regarded as the 'fathers' of Advaita philosophy, I think the precedent is established!

Q.186 Further objections to the criticism of Neo-Advaita

Q: I have been reading your website with great interest, however, there are a few misconceptions being put forth in your Q&A section about Neo-Advaita that should perhaps be corrected. You are no doubt a more learned person than I, yet I have run the gamut of looking into spiritual matters, grew up in a metaphysical western religion, closely studied Ramana Maharshi, Papaji and Nisargadatta and have at last found what the so-called 'I' was looking for: the non-existence of a personal 'I' and the freedom to just *be*.

The truth is always simple. If a philosophy is considered valid because it has 5000 years of practice behind it, why are there so few in those 5000 years who have found what they sought by its practice? It does not take years of practices and memorization of hundreds of scriptural verses. It takes no more than an instant of clarity to see that layering concepts over concepts only further muddies the essential and clear truth. I came to this instant of clarity through Neo-Advaita. Once you have seen the pretence of the 'me' for the illusion that it is, it can no longer be returned to.

You stated: "This idea that there is no one to act, no free will and therefore no responsibility is one of the most dangerous ideas to have been taken up by Neo-Advaitin teachers. It runs completely contrary to traditional Advaita by failing to recognize that, at the level of the world (apparent though it may be), people exist as separate individuals who act and interact. It is intrinsic to the whole process of seeking on a path and eventually becoming enlightened. This process cannot be bypassed by attempting to deny it before the mind is ready. As you say, these false ideas effectively license the ego to do whatever it wants. This is, of course, completely contrary to what Advaita is really about".

I don't know exactly from whence you take this assumption that Neo-Advaita gives anyone's ego license to do whatever it wants. Just the opposite. Losing the sense of the reality of ego eradicates any selfish desires the ego would bring with it that would give rise to acting against the desire of others. Once the individual is faced squarely with the naked truth that the individual 'me' is only a concept, an arising of form out of the great primordial soup, with which we identify, then all desires fall away.

Why would the human form named 'George' or 'Lilith', or whoever the form thinks itself to be, desire more than the All that it now knows itself to be? Once the 'me' falls away, it becomes obvious that selfish striving for power, money, fame, and other such trappings are obsolete, because you are and have nothing less than All. The only desire left is to give this wonderful freedom to others, knowing full well there are no 'others' yet for as long as we appear to be here we are to treat them with no less love and compassion than we would give ourselves because we *are* them and they *are* us, we are all the All. I know this to be true because I am living it as are many others who are seeing the simple truth through Neo-Advaita.

Nisargadatta's teacher told him 'You are That.' And it connected to Nisargadatta's truth of being. He knew it to be true the instant he heard it. He did not need 5000 years of tradition to help him know this. Neo-Advaita says to start from the standpoint that 'You are That.' And Ramana said to inquire into who 'you' are. 'You' is a false concept, just a thought or collection of thoughts that float in and out of consciousness. I AM is the Presence and Awareness that is always there with or without a concept called 'you.'

This is Neo-Advaita in a nutshell. It is beyond the direct way and is the end of the endless study and searching for who we are of which the 'me' or ego is so fond. For the ego will perpetuate the illusion of a 'me' with a past, present and future searching, on and on ad infinitum, as a survival mechanism, and it particularly enjoys using ancient religions for the purpose. The longer it keeps the 'me' hypnotized by such ideas as that considerable study and perseverance are necessary, the longer the ego will continue to survive.

Your statement "The sense that is carried by them, to those who may not be as 'enlightened' as Ramesh, is just as you say; namely that we can 'do what we want' as long as we believe that it is not really 'me' who is doing these things", carries no water. The moment the 'me' is seen through, there is an instant sense of expansiveness and awareness that only the I AM, the Oneness of everything, is real and true. And with that comes a sense of such acceptance of All and everything that there is no desire anymore to do things contrary to anything's or anyone's well being, or even to interfere in the perfect goings-on of That essence of perfect Allness. And in fact, how would that idea even arise from a sense of Oneness and completeness of All? One could never call someone enlightened who exhibited such tendencies, since those two states of mind originate from such opposite sources.

A: Thanks for your considered comments on the material – these are always appreciated.

In response to the points that you make:

1. "If a philosophy is considered valid because it has 5000 years of practice behind it, why are there so few in those 5000 years who have found what they sought by its practice?"

Do you have any statistics on this? I don't, and must admit that I don't know how one would acquire any. I think that we only tend to hear about those who subsequently went on to teach or write about what they found. But what determines that is the nature of the person involved. There is obviously no *ultimate* purpose in teaching when there is no one to become enlightened in reality. I suspect that most who become enlightened remain in obscurity.

Traditional teaching simply removes ignorance, incidentally; it doesn't 'layer concepts over concepts'.

2. "I don't know exactly from whence you take this assumption that Neo-Advaita gives anyone's ego license to do whatever it wants. Just the opposite. Losing the sense of the reality of ego eradicates any selfish desires the ego would bring with it that would give rise to acting against the desire of others".

This seems to be the central point that you are making. Let me say that first of all, I have always said that Neo-Advaitin teaching can bring about enlightenment for those who are ready. This effectively means for those who have previously been through years of more traditional enquiry 'to no avail'. But that prior teaching prepares the ground, as it were and gives considerable intellectual understanding and this, I suggest, makes all the difference when it comes to hearing the minimalist message of Neo-Advaitin teaching.

For someone new to seeking, the statements that 'there is no person', 'no one does anything', 'there is no such thing as free will' can so easily lead to the conclusion that, therefore, anything that I might do is irrelevant, hurts no one and 'I don't have any choice anyway'. Of course, the teacher may not intend that it should be taken this way but then they are no longer around after the talk has ended.

For those who do understand, and certainly for those who are 'enlightened' by the message, there is certainly no danger of subsequent licensed, unbridled behavior but then how many of those attending a particular satsang go away enlightened?

You say: "The moment the 'me' is seen through, there is an instant sense of expansiveness and awareness that only the I AM, the Oneness of everything is real and true. And with that comes a sense of such acceptance of All and everything that there is no desire anymore to do things contrary to anything's or anyone's well being".

Of course – I agree entirely but the point is that the vast majority of readers/listeners to such words do not actually see this straight away, if at all.

3. "Nisargadatta's teacher told him 'You are That.' And it connected to Nisargadatta's truth of being. He knew it to be true the instant he heard it. He did not need 5000 years of tradition to help him know this".

Yes – so the story goes. I don't know whether or not it is apocryphal but I do know that Nisargadatta attended his teacher, Siddharameshwar's (traditional) talks for many years, taking notes, before this realization came to him. (The book of translation of his notes is available if you don't believe this.)

And, regarding Ramana Maharshi, here is a quote from him about the need (or lack of it) for preparatory practice:

"The means that make one qualified for enquiry are meditation, yoga, etc. One should gain proficiency in these through graded practice, and thus secure a stream of mental modes that is natural and helpful. When the mind that has in this manner become ripe, listens to the present enquiry, it will at once realize its true nature which is the Self, and remain in perfect peace, without deviating from that state. To a mind which has not become ripe, immediate realization and peace are hard to gain through listening to enquiry. Yet, if one practices the means for mind-control for some time, peace of mind can be obtained eventually". (Excerpt from Self-Enquiry (Vicharasangraham) Of Bhagavan Sri Ramana Maharshi.)

4. "This is Neo-Advaita in a nutshell. It is the end of the endless study and searching for who we are of which the 'me' or ego is so fond".

Have you read the Mandukya Upanishad and Gaudapada's kArikA (or my own book on these, 'A-U-M: Awakening to Reality')? If you do, you will see that the simple, final statements of Neo-Advaita were being made as early as the 7th Century AD (if not long before). They are not new. But traditional teachers emphasize that this particular work should only be approached after all of the other major Upanishads have been studied with the help of a qualified teacher. If you think of the analogy with quantum mechanics, some of the formulae of higher mathematics may well have elegant simplicity… but they can only really be understood if you have learnt elementary arithmetic first.

In a discussion relating to Tony Parsons, I made the following statements:

The point is that the world *is* real at the level of the world (just as the dream world *is* real in the dream). It is certainly true that, from the standpoint of absolute reality, there is no world and no seeker; only the non-dual Consciousness or whatever you want to call it. But, from the standpoint of a seeker, all of these really do exist and a path with relevant disciplines is needed to prepare the mind for receipt of relevant Self-knowledge to dispel the ignorance. The preparation and the teaching are actual causes leading to the actual effect of enlightenment within empirical reality. They are not illusory at this level.

Even post-enlightenment the world still appears, since it is not a manifestation of our mind (as is the dream). [Note that this is discussed in a later section.] The world of seeming duality continues, so that the Neo-teacher is still obliged to 'communicate' with the seeker, even supposing he truly knows that what he says is 'right from the absolute perspective'.

It is difficult, actually to defeat the Neos' arguments while utilizing the same 'ground rules' (i.e. attempting to speak of the appearances of empirical reality from an assumed standpoint of absolute reality).

This is a tricky subject and confusion of levels is actually the most frequent cause of misunderstanding in Advaita. It is not that believing in separation makes it true. Separation is real at the transactional level – otherwise no transaction would be possible! It is only from the assumed standpoint of absolute reality that there are not 'two things'. And I say 'assumed' because, of course, one cannot actually take a stance in absolute reality and say anything at all. You could say that the Neo-Advaitin's point of view is fine until he opens his mouth but actually you cannot even think about reality since thought, too, is necessarily dualistic.

If you think about the dream situation, the dream is real for the dreamer but upon awakening, the waker now sees that the dream world was entirely in his (the waker's) mind. Note that it was not in the dreamer's mind – the dreamer too is a figment of the waker's mind.

For the dreamer, he (the dreamer) was a separate individual in a world of objects and other people. And the dream world had validity for no one else. In the case of the waking world, however, the world does have validity for others. The waking objects do not exist only in my mind. They have solidity and continuity and, significantly, they are still there post enlightenment – the waking world does not disappear as did the dream world. Of course, our senses dictate the way in which we see this world. A blind person will perceive it quite differently from a sighted one – but both will agree that there is something out there!

This difference between dream and waking worlds is explained by traditional Advaita by saying that, whereas the dream world was a creation of the individual waker's mind, the waking world is a creation of Ishvara's mind (where Ishvara = Brahman + mAyA). Again, from an absolute standpoint, Ishvara is just as much mithyA as is the world, the person and the teaching. But at the transactional level you have to accept them all in order to be able to make sense of things. You begin with this and only dismiss them when your understanding reaches the appropriate level. You have to understand arithmetic and algebra before you can take on board differential equations. You cannot simply deny the world when all of your experience, upbringing and knowledge are telling you that the world is blatantly obvious.

Q.243 The last rug

Q: I have been reading your material on traditional versus Neo-Advaita. Both sides of the issue seem valid. I for one have not studied traditional Advaita but instantly recognized what the Neo-Advaitins were saying from my own position. I think it is inevitable that any serious 'seeker' would end up on the shores of an Advaita-type outcome. It remains in the realm of the psychological and perhaps cultural make-up of the 'seeker' whether he/she gravitates toward a traditional explanation or a non-traditional one. Neo-Advaita may be what some people need to 'pull the last rug of the mind/body bastion from under their feet.' Others, as you say not having any preparation, need a structure.

I would say, there are many, many people who are very happy to be only interested in everyday living, or stay in the confines of their cultural beliefs and others who prefer to believe in creators, angels, aliens, etc. Apart from a 'New Age' type of romanticism about 'we are all one', they would probably never approach Advaita. It may be that the Advaita arguments are all 'preaching to the converted'.

A: I would define a serious seeker as someone who has genuinely decided that life is never going to provide the answer; i.e. not someone who is suffering a temporary psychological setback and is still effectively grounded in the appearance.

I don't disagree with anything you say really except to emphasize that, for the relative newcomer to serious seeking, traditional Advaita provides a clear progression which will eventually lead that seeker to realization. Neo-Advaita (as discussed extensively in this section) does not and, for this relative newcomer, is only likely to lead to confusion and frustration.

Unfortunately, what you say about everyday living and New Age romanticism is definitely true. The vast majority of authors on the list of my own publisher write books in these categories – communicating with the dead, magic crystals, palmistry etc. – and their books probably sell far better than my own! And you actually find those sorts of book in the high street bookstore, whereas you never find books on Advaita (apart from Eckhart Tolle, of course – thanks to Oprah Winfrey! – and his are not exactly traditional

Advaita).

Q.251 Neo-Advaita and meditation

Q: I think that some Advaita teachers are somewhat disingenuous in that they insist that there is no point in coming to their meetings or buying their books, etc., as there is nothing that 'you' can do. I usually roll my eyes and still buy their books and turn up at their meetings though! I know that really they mean 'you' in the 'small you' sense but it's still difficult to grasp exactly what they mean.

I have been meditating for 30 odd years so I have a feeling for the presence, and enjoy what appears to be my own awareness as it seems to be fresh and new all the time, which I've always assumed to be why we don't 'feel' any older. But my point is that it might be because I've meditated that I have come to this point, or maybe because I've just got a spiritual nature and would have been interested in Advaita anyway. I intend to buy your 'Book of One' as your approach seems to be more inclusive.

I really admire some of the Neo-Advaita teaching for the stripped-down minimalist approach but their insistence on meditation being dualistic exasperates me, as last time I looked, 'transcendence' meant going beyond (to the bigger Self).

What do you think about this? I do understand the pointlessness of an apparent person seeking to find that there is no one. It's made worse by the fact that I seem to know this already but still keep going around in circles. When I just stick to enjoyment of my own awareness all this goes away; perhaps this is where the problem lies?

A: The problem is that Neo-Advaitin teachers have no methodology for developing what they are trying to say. Thus, they are effectively speaking without any meaningful context. They tend to confuse the two levels (paramArtha and vyavahAra) so that what they say does not really make sense.

Meditation is an extremely valuable practice for many of the classical pre-requisites of sAdhana chatuShTaya sampatti. But, as with all practices, it cannot itself lead to enlightenment – only Self-knowledge can bring this about, as a result of shravaNa, manana and nididhyAsana. 'Seeking' is certainly not pointless. This is one of the Neo-Advaitin fallacies. The person is in the dualistic world and has to gain Self-knowledge to remove his ignorance. There is no way around this.

Q: What you say about levels makes immediate sense and is a good example of how knowledge destroys ignorance; I could feel a lot of 'distress' caused by attending satsangs dissolve as soon as I read this.

I tend to have the mental model (or conceptual metaphor) that meditation is like a 'portal' embedded in dualistic reality; that, if stumbled across, lets unlimited 'being' be known. I wouldn't even say 'being' being known by the 'small self' – just 'being' being known by 'being', which slowly comes to be known as all that there is.

Your concept of levels has already helped me to be able to express this a bit more eloquently than I could before, even though my underlying experience hasn't changed. So it is a bit like Nisargadatta says: 'using the mind to unpick the mind'.

A: It's not a good idea to think of the 'levels' too literally – there is only actually the non-dual reality. But the appearance of name and form is so 'realistic' that practically everyone takes it for reality itself. It's good to think of dreams in this respect. Our dreams can be extremely real, too – while we are dreaming.

Advaita is sometimes referred to as 'non-duality in spite of seeming duality'. We are always aware of the seeming duality; otherwise we would not be able to function in the world. When we gain Self-knowledge, we realize the non-dual reality, both in the sense of comprehension and fulfilling. But we never become 'directly aware of' or 'know' that reality in an objective sense – it is what we *are*. Read the section on 'Reality' for lots more on this.

Q: I have been looking at your website, especially about the Traditional Advaita versus Neo-Advaita debate. I can see how I've got into a bit of a muddle. As an example, I am 54 and have been practicing some sort of meditation since I was 23, which I have hugely enjoyed. I then stumbled across Advaita and Neo-Advaita when following up a 'lead' on Ramana Maharshi.

So of course, I've found it appealing. The only problem is that a lot of the people who turn up at these things haven't meditated for years and had that sort of empirical experience. I'm not saying it's better, just different. The problem for me was the nagging feeling of the fundamental hypocrisy of all this – none of them seem to realize that all these people who turn up think that there is a method i.e. turning up! This reminds me of the self referential sentences along the lines of 'this statement is not true', which led Bertrand Russell and co. into all sorts of morass when they were trying to 'prove' mathematics.

I think I've learnt more in a couple of days talking to you and perusing your site than I have in a while. I can't wait to get hold of your books. The problem with a lot of Neo-Advaita books is that they are just transcriptions of dialogues they've had with their students. Nothing wrong with this as far as it goes, but they don't start with fixed axioms and develop them logically, so they haven't had to think it all out.

I remember a bit of Sanskrit that always stuck with me when I heard Deepak Chopra say it: 'aham brahmAsmi' – I am the totality.

A: It is certainly difficult not to see holding satsangs as a bit hypocritical when it is claimed there is no seeker, no teacher, no path, etc.! 'Enlightenment: The Path Through The Jungle' is specifically about all of this; i.e. comparing traditional, satsang and Neo-Advaitin teaching and explaining in detail why the first works and the other two are most unlikely to do. It is set out in short points (559 of them) – inspired by Wittgenstein!

aham brahmAsmi is one of the four 'great sayings' (mahAvAkya-s) and means 'I am Brahman'. Most of the problem with Neos is that they attempt to speak as if from this level all of the time. And of course this is not possible. If you are a (would-be) teacher addressing someone who thinks they are a seeker, you are already firmly in duality so this is where you have to start. From the perspective of the world, there is clearly time, space and causality; and you, the person, are subject to these. It is only from the viewpoint of absolute reality (if there could be a 'viewpoint'!) that you can say that time, space and causality are all 'in you'. What this means is that who-you-really-are is totally unaffected by them. The universe is mithyA. In reality 'everything is Brahman'. ('sarvaM khalvidaM brahma', says the Chandogya Upanishad 3.14. This is not one of the 'four' sayings but actually there are many, many sayings in the scriptures that are mahAvAkya-s.)

Q: So what you are saying really is what I (intuitively) suspected all along; that as long as one recognizes presence/awareness/existence as the most basic level, all the other things (i.e. phenomena perceived from other levels) it pretty well doesn't matter. However, I do like the Neo-Advaita boiled down simplicity of 'you are that which knows you exist' or as Sailor Bob says 'the only thing you can't negate is your own existence'.

A: You will find that pretty much anything (accurate) that is said by Neo or satsang teachers has been said by traditional teachers well over a thousand years ago. There really is nothing new that could be said, only using more modern metaphors to express them. Thus, for example, 'the only thing you can't negate is your own existence' was said by Shankara in, I think, his commentary on the Brihadaranyaka Upanishad in the 8th century CE. The point is that you can't just come right out with many of these statements and expect the hearer to know what you are talking about. You have to start from their level of understanding and take things one step at a time.

Q.294 Suffering and Neo-Advaita

Q: I just re-read your conversation with Jeff Foster (http://www.Advaita.org.uk/discourses/trad_neo/jeff_dialog.htm) and it seems so clear to me that the two of you are like kids on a teeter totter, with the 'not-two' as the fulcrum. The apparent self and its 'suffering' are just what the real Self does in the world. The suffering is perceived as painful but cannot do any real harm, and when it stops it stops, and nothing changes. 'I' think that's actually what both of you are saying, from 'two' sides of a line in the dirt.

A: That's all fine from an assumed absolute perspective. But the average seeker has only a relative perspective – the suffering seems to be real and he/she wants to end it. When the Self-ignorance is removed, it is seen that the suffering was not real and cannot harm and, you are right, that nothing is really any different. But until the ignorance goes, the apparently real suffering remains. So, from the point of view of the seeker, Self-knowledge is required. And this is the crux of the matter – traditional Advaita provides a proven methodology for providing this; Neo-Advaita, by its own admission, has no methodology at all.

Some other points in a non-recorded Q&A

It is certainly true in part that the 'movement' is a reaction to the traditional approach. And many seekers find the basic 'ethos' of Neo-Advaita in tune with the modern outlook on life. But I think that many of the 'teachers' are capitalizing on this, seeing in it an easy way to make money, without much concern about actually passing on any knowledge.

I would not say that traditional teaching is secretive. It may be 'elusive' but this is part of the filter. A seeker with genuine mumukShutva will overcome any obstacle to uncover the truth and a significant aspect of this is looking and discarding until one finds a real source. Nowadays, with the Internet, this is really not much of a problem! There may well be some initial frustration but, if one is really serious and prepared to take as long as necessary, the teaching is always available and always free.

Ideally, one would affiliate oneself with a qualified teacher for an indefinite period. But it is difficult for someone with a typical modern lifestyle to do this, and qualified teachers are not easily come by! The fact that it may be possible to attend an occasional seminar by a Neo-Advaitin is no recommendation at all. This is like saying that one really needs a highly qualified surgeon to cure a medical problem but, instead, you can visit lots of local alternative-therapy practitioners just as well.

I have never had the opportunity of associating with a true teacher and have had to rely upon much reading and discussion for many years in order to come to my present understanding. The internet now provides the opportunity to listen to qualified teachers, or read transcriptions of their talks. You can listen to Swami Paramarthananda unfold most of the scriptures, for example, Upanishads (http://hinduonline.co/AudioLibrary/CommentaryOnUpanishads.html).

Listening to these assiduously, via mp3, is effectively the same as listening to them in the lecture hall. Thus, the shravaNa element is covered. The problem is that the mp3 player cannot answer your questions. Accordingly, you will almost certainly need to be able to direct these to someone or some forum that can provide authentic answers, manana, to clear your doubts. This might be a qualified person who is prepared to respond or it might be a discussion forum of knowledgeable people. Again, the Internet is available whereas, traditionally, you were obliged to affiliate yourself to a qualified guru.

Science

Q.47 The soul and cloning

Q: What do you think might happen if scientists cloned a person? Suppose it was me! Would that new baby have part of my soul or spirit? And if it did, suppose it died; would I be diminished in any way? And do you think it would grow up completely the same or would its obviously different environment make it a person in its own right, thinking and behaving completely differently to myself?

A: There is no such thing as 'my' soul. In reality, there is only the non-dual Self – and 'you' are That. You are not 'a part' of That, in the way that a wave is a part of the ocean. There is only That. The wave and the ocean are each only water.

In the (apparent) world, That is manifest as many forms, which are given different names. But all of these 'separate' things are still That, just as rings and necklaces are all gold, but in different forms, which are given different names. The names relate to function, not substance. The reality of the ring is always only gold. The reality of 'you' is always only the non-dual Self.

The Self does not die. Bodies are apparently born and apparently die but you are not the body.

The behavior of (apparent) persons is dictated by genetics and by environment (parents, education, society, etc.). Therefore, the behavior of a cloned person would certainly differ from that of the one from which it was cloned because the environmental factors would all be different.

Furthermore, this behavior is deterministic, following cause and effect laws; since the causes would inevitably be different, so would the effects. But none of this impacts the Self in any way whatsoever. The Self of 'you' and the Self of 'your clone' would always be the same because there are not 'two things'.

Having said that, traditional Advaita teaches that the jIva (which term is used by Advaita to refer to the individual self) accumulates saMskAra as a result of its actions. This is what is known as the law of karma – if you perform 'good' actions, you accumulate 'good' saMskAra (puNya); 'bad' accumulates 'bad' (pApa). Since it teaches reincarnation for jIva-s who are not yet enlightened, these saMskAra accumulate over *all* of your past lives, having the effect of putting you into future situations to 'account for' or 'reconcile' those past actions. (This is an extremely brief description of karma, upon which whole books have been written!)

Consequently, according to that theory, one might presume that a clone of you would also begin with your specific collection of saMskAra from your past lives and therefore have to 'meet' similar situations to you in order to deal with that. Although it would be doing so in an environment different from yours, its 'pre-programmed behavior' being identical (to begin with), it would then be very likely that it would act similarly in many ways.

However, the cloning technique really only affects the DNA, which determines how the body develops. Since this is a new body, presumably developing normally in the womb of a woman, one has to assume that it would acquire a new jIva in the same way as a naturally conceived embryo (http://www.Advaita-vision.org/between-lives/) and its follow-up in which I describe this process as defined in the Upanishads). This being the case, it would follow that the child would effectively bear no relationship to you at all. It would certainly look like you but would behave as entirely different (or not) as any other unrelated being.

At least, all of that is speculation informed by Advaita!

Q.409 Materialism and Consciousness

Q: Regarding Gaudapada Karika 4.28, what is the best argument you are aware of against the materialist position that consciousness is an emergent phenomenon? In particular do you think it is inherently illogical to say that consciousness can arise from the inert?

More generally, is it the position of Vedanta that the materialist position is inherently illogical/impossible or simply that it is incorrect because it is contrary to scripture?

A: Schopenhauer said that Materialism is *"the philosophy of the subject who forgets to take account of himself"*. And this really sums up my own view of the situation with respect to Science and its so-called 'hard problem'. Science is forever trying to discover how consciousness can 'arise' from matter and never even considers the possibility that matter might actually be name and form of Consciousness. In other words, Consciousness does not arise from matter; matter (as it were) arises from Consciousness. They view the topic 'back to front' because they ignore the significance of the observer. And this is despite the physicist's realization that the observer cannot be ignored in quantum mechanics, for example.

The term used in the scriptures for the materialist is lokAyata (worldly wise) or chArvAka, after the philosopher of that name who is associated with these beliefs. (They have also been called mAmsa-mImAMsaka-s or 'flesh philosophers' because of their belief that we should aim to maximize pleasure in life.) The beliefs are also associated with the god bRRihaspati and Shankara has sarcastically used this term in a derogatory sense to refer to 'intellectuals' who play the role of disputant in his commentaries.

I think that the problem with modern scientists is partly that they have failed to define their terms accurately and partly that they have made mistaken assumptions. They have taken this flawed starting point as axiomatic and endeavored to build their theories from there. Needless to say, they inevitably end with mistaken conclusions also!

Q: So science is entirely wrong with all of their investigations into space, the universe and evolution. In fact, everything is Consciousness! What scientists have still to discover is what Advaita Vedanta knew a long time ago!

A: Scientists are entirely wrong to the extent that they are supposedly defining the nature of absolute reality but of course they are increasingly correct to the extent that they are describing the nature of empirical reality. For the most part, they do not accept that they will never be able to achieve the former.

It is better to say that everything is name and form of Consciousness. Or Consciousness is the substrate of everything. As an analogy, our experience and perception of ice and steam are very different; yet they are each name and form of water. And the ways in which they behave scientifically are quite different. So scientists can be excused not realizing this sooner. But some recent scientific literature is sounding increasingly non-dual-like! Read Amanda Gefter's 'Trespassing on Einstein's Lawn' for example.

Q.456 The 'hard' problem

Q: Could you say something about the relationship between the 'hard problem' of consciousness in modern science and Advaita's mAyA?

A: Science's problem is trying to explain how consciousness can 'emerge' from inert matter. Advaita's problem is trying to explain how the world can emerge from Consciousness.

The concept of mAyA is an interim explanation only. If it satisfies the listener and moves them forward towards accepting non-duality, then it has served its purpose. Ultimately, it is rejected by Advaita. There is only Consciousness. There cannot be Consciousness *and* a force called mAyA.

Every(seeming)thing is non-dual Consciousness. There only seems to be separate things because our mind differentiates forms and gives them names. Just as in the clay-pot metaphor.

The concept of mithyA is better for 'explaining' the nature of the world. The world is not real 'in itself'; it depends upon Consciousness for its existence just as the pot depends upon clay.

There is an essay – 'Consciousness – not such a hard problem' – on precisely this topic in my book 'Western Philosophy Made Easy: A Personal Search for Meaning'.

Q.23b Science and quantum physics

Q: I cannot agree with you regarding science and quantum physics. The reason that science is in disarray over the very small is because it is bordering on the subjective and cannot be rationally understood, therefore it does not fit in with the 'scientific' view. Also, there are too many quantum physicists who have radically changed their view on 'how it works' to dismiss the connection out of hand.

A: I don't dispute that the study of quantum behavior and/or the mathematics involved may cause scientists to re-examine the nature of reality. It may even bring them to consider non-dualism, but I still maintain that all science is necessarily objective, therefore dualistic and consequently irrelevant when considering the nature of reality.

Art

Q.332 Creativity

Q: What happens to creativity (writing, painting, music, ...) when you awake from the dream of dualism?

A: My immediate response would be that enlightenment entails the realization that who-you-really-are is responsible for the appearance of the entire 'creation'. Man's petty attempts to write music or literature, or use pigments to make marks on paper, pale into insignificance in the vastness of this vision. Practically speaking also, one does not acquire skills that were not there before. One's body and mind were determined by prArabdha karma and this will work its way out until the death of the body. The key point about enlightenment is that all of this is now known to be so.

One mitigating factor which might influence things could be that one's mental and emotional impediments tend to diminish so that there might be more freedom of expression and consequently the appearance of an increase in creativity.

But here is a link to an extensive comment on this topic posted to NDHighlights the same day you sent the question: http://www.gornahoor.net/?p=5381&cpage=1. I suspect this might give you more of the sort of answer you were expecting (hoping?) to hear.

Q.382 Art and Vedanta

Q: As an artist and casual reader of Advaita Vedanta, I wanted to ask about Advaita Vedanta's opinion on Art (be it music, painting, dance etc.).

Personally, I have been advised by several elders to continue producing and practicing music. But does this go against the advice of Advaita Vedanta? Am I acting on desires? Will art get artists permanently stuck in the cycle of samsara?

A: Advaita's ultimate 'interest' in anything worldly is limited to the extent to which it can prepare the mind to accept the truth of non-duality. Therefore, one can certainly see how any sort of art can have the effect of stilling the mind and opening up the senses to see beyond the base material universe, as it were. Also, interest in and practicing of art does not preclude pursuit of spiritual truth and there is no reason why it should cease after the dawning of Self-knowledge.

An 'interest' or 'pre-disposition' is something inherited or inculcated and constitutes an aspect of prArabdha karma, which continues until death of the body. There is no reason why it need conflict with another interest in pursuing spiritual knowledge. But an artist may have to insure that this is the case. If he or she 'identifies' with their art, or has the strong belief that 'I am an artist', it is certainly possible for there to be conflict!

We do have to act in our lives. Creating art and music is one of the better actions! It brings joy to others and, as pointed out above, can be a potent element of karma yoga. The only proviso that occurs to me is that, if the music or art expresses passion, anger etc., take care not to become identified with it!

The State of the Person

This is where we start from – the belief that we are a separate individual in what is usually considered to be a hostile environment. We are limited in so many ways and, in the extreme, 'everyone is out to get us'! We have dreams and ambitions, desires and fears. Sometimes we achieve our goals or something totally unexpected and wonderful happens – and we are happy (for a while). Other times, illness or disappointments occur, totally outside of our control – and we are miserable. Some look for a meaning in all of this or at least a sense of purpose – what should we do with this life? My book 'How To Meet Yourself… and find true happiness' was all about this dilemma.

Can Advaita provide some explanations for all of this? What is our basic problem? How may we address this? What can it tell us about the elements of our make-up – body, mind, ego, etc.? Can we learn anything from the states of consciousness other than waking?

The questions in this section seek to answer some of the problems associated with our fundamental identifications, namely thinking that we are our emotions, body, mind or intellect.

Emotions

Q.5 Feelings

Q: What about feelings? Can they be observed in the same way as thoughts?

A: There is effectively no difference between perceptions, feelings and thoughts. All of these appear to awareness in exactly the same way. We are aware of a chair apparently 'out there', a pain or a thought apparently 'in here'. Advaita does not really differentiate between them. Francis Lucille, for example, a Direct Path teacher, calls them all 'mentations'. This is useful as a reminder *not* to differentiate.

Q.276 Who is afraid/angry?

Q: I once consulted a swami from the Chinmaya Mission about how to deal with my phobia of rats. He told me to observe and ask who's afraid of them. I can observe the fear (though sometimes being drawn to it and becoming even more fearful) but I can't find the subject feeling the fear!

If I can locate what I think is the subject feeling the fear (inside the head, near the heart, etc.), then they too are objects. In other words, there's no subject but only fear arising in awareness. Does this prove there are no objects as there's no point talking about objects if the subject can't be found? The reason the subject can't be found is logical – I am the subject, i.e. Consciousness, so there's no way to illuminate or observe my Self.

And yet I was told that whatever I can observe, feel, think, etc., is not me. But if there's no subject found (as proven above) but only awareness, then it is not meaningful to say that 'what I see, feel, etc., is not me' because there's not a me seeing, fearing or thinking. There is just plain seeing, feeling, etc. Please correct me if I am wrong.

My temper is bad and I really want to pursue knowledge and get rid of anger, hatred, tamasic energies, etc. Intellectually, I know that I cannot be any *thing* (feeling bad, deeds, etc.), so there's really nothing to get rid of from the absolute standpoint. But what is still bothering me is that I caught myself (or rather the ego) being unkind to someone and I observed myself 'pinching' the person in anger. There's no guilt, however, and this is what's bothering me as I think I should feel bad about 'my' misdeeds.

I was merely witnessing the act of anger and felt detached from the doer and in the process 'stopped' myself from continuing the act. I know there's no excuse for what I did but the act of witnessing prevents the usual guilt from arising. Am I abusing Vedanta, making excuses, or am I too tamasic, and deluded into thinking I am witnessing the angry doer, rather than genuinely being detached from the doer in this case?

A: Realizing the truth is a stepwise process, in a sense. Initially there is identification with the body and the feelings and thoughts – 'I' am angry, frightened, etc. Then there is identification with the witness – 'I' see these thoughts arising and this body doing 'bad' things. Ultimately is the understanding that there is only Consciousness. Every seeming thing else is only name and form; movement in/of the non-dual Brahman.

Everything (every 'thing') that you perceive, feel or conceive has a limited existence – a beginning and an end in time. Thus, according to Advaita, these are not 'real'. (In fact, they are mithyA, as is described and defined elsewhere.) But that which observes all of this does not come and go; it is there all of the time, even when there is nothing to observe. It, according to Advaita, is therefore 'real', or satyam. This is who-you-really-are; this is the Atman.

But you do have to continue to live in this seeming world and, at the level of the world, you are a separate entity interacting with other jIva-s and objects. Cause and effect operate here. So you need to differentiate between the reality and the appearance. Appreciate the former but act as if the latter were true. For that, all of the usual dictates of dharma, morality, karma, etc., should be taken into account.

It sounds as though you have attempted to bypass the 'preparation' stages of spiritual seeking and jump straight to the gaining of Self-knowledge. This is quite common in the West! But not only does this make the knowledge phase more difficult, it also means that you will still be buffeted by the emotions. You really need to gain a degree of mind and sense control first. It is this that will enable you to cope with tendencies to suffer fear and anger, not the discovery of your true nature. It will also mean that you are better able to listen to and assimilate the teaching. It is a myth that gaining enlightenment automatically means that you will become serene and tranquil!

Q.401 Who is the doer/enjoyer?

Q: Who is the doer and enjoyer of action if not Brahman and ego?

A: In reality (pAramArthika viewpoint), there is no doer, enjoyer, ego or action. From the point of view of the person in the world (vyAvahArika viewpoint), you can use whatever 'explanation' you feel happy with (since all 'explanations' have to be dropped in the end anyway)! The usually accepted way of explaining it is that Brahman (Ishvara) enables the action to take place through the jIva (Consciousness is 'reflected' in the mind).

Q: Nisargadatta says: "Delve deeply into the sense 'I am' and you surely discover that the perceiving centre is universal, as universal as the light that illumines the world. All that happens in the universe happens to you, the silent witness. On the other hand, whatever is done, is done by you, the universal and inexhaustible energy".

My question in two parts:

1. If my awareness is the absolute one and there is no other – then yours does not exist?

2. If they both exist as the Absolute but are separately perceived by two minds why am I not aware of your experience as well as my own?

So far as I can see, without reliance on solipsism, non-duality/Vedanta must posit a reality where the Absolute is being 'dipped into' by separate minds?

A: I suggest you read the essay I published (http://www.advaita-vision.org/chidabhasa/).

At the empirical level, there are separate people with separate minds and sensory equipment. A has A's mind and sees through A's eyes; similarly B has B's mind and eyes. A doesn't see through B's eyes or know what is in B's mind. But A functions by virtue of the non-dual Consciousness being reflected in A's mind; similarly so does B.

In the metaphor in the essay, you can imagine the sun shining onto two mirrors. The light is reflected off the first into room X and off the second into room Y. The first mirror does not illuminate room Y and the second mirror does not illuminate room X. Each mirror is illuminated by the one sun, which is the only actual source of light for all of the illumination.

At the absolute level, of course, there are no rooms, mirrors or people – all are mithyA and there is only Consciousness.

Body

Q.188 Why isn't the seat of awareness in the brain?

Q: I am playing devil's advocate here, but how can we be sure that this awareness of awareness is not seated in an area of the brain which we know nothing about? Consequently, when the mind/brain/body dies, all the 'awarenessing' would die with it?

A: The way that you phrase this question may be the cause of your problems. You say 'awareness of awareness'. If you are talking about Consciousness in the absolute sense, i.e. Brahman from the pAramArthika standpoint, it is not 'aware of' anything since there is nothing else for it to be aware of and it is not meaningful to speak of this (or anything else if it comes to that). As has been quoted (Wittgenstein) by many writers, including myself: "*whereof we cannot speak, thereof we should remain silent*".

Advaita has 'explanations' of the mechanism whereby we come to 'know' an object or thought but these are quite complex and pre-scientific, so are not amenable to the modern mind. And of course they are equally mithyA. From the standpoint of absolute reality, observer, knowledge, observed and everything else is only ever Consciousness; unchanging and eternal. Every supposedly separate entity, conscious or inert, is only name and form of that same Consciousness. Once this is truly known, then all such questions as those you pose become redundant.

Regarding your specific question, 'how can we be sure' relates to the mind and its reasoning faculties etc. 'Being sure' normally means having scientifically verifiable evidence or some such and, you will already realize the answer to this – you can't! Advaita is an Astika philosophy, which means that it derives its premises, if you like, from the scriptures. The criteria for these to be valid as a pramANa or means of knowledge is that they are not available from any other pramANa, i.e. perception, inference etc. But, for them to be acceptable, they must also not be *contradicted* by any other pramANa either.

So the bottom line is that you initially accept ideas such as 'the mind arises in Consciousness and not vice versa' on faith. You cannot get this information by looking into the brain and finding out for yourself, or by sitting down and thinking about it. But, although it may initially seem to be a weird idea, the more you find out about Advaita and verify those things that can be verified, the more convinced you become that the philosophy is sound. And there comes a time, maybe, when you realize that there is no longer any doubt whatsoever that this is how it is. This is called enlightenment.

Q.275 Status of the body

Q: Why do I (the individual) need a body?

A: In answer to your question, let me ask you a counter question: Who is this 'individual' that you refer to?

Q: The individual I refer to is named so-and-so and has a body, mind, intellect, heart and ego. Advaita (as I understand it) holds that the existence of this name and form is dependent on that of the Absolute. Is the body solely a means of manifesting the subtle body (mind, intellect, heart and ego) or does it have another purpose?

A: There is a critically wrong word in your first sentence. It should read 'The individual I refer to is named so-and-so and *is* a body, mind, intellect, heart and ego.' So your question, 'Why do I need a body?' is not valid. You neither need nor have a body in reality. At the empirical level of reality, where you believe that you are the body (even if intellectually you concede that you might be wrong), your task is to come to the realization that you are not.

In reality, world and bodies, mind, intellect, etc., are simply name and form of the non-dual reality (you).

Q: While I understand I am not my limbs and some other body parts, how can I not be depending on my heart to be conscious, I mean alive? How can we say there will be this sense of being after the heart stops? And if we cannot, is it possible that non-dualism is just another belief system?

A: You are making the same error as the scientists in concluding that Consciousness is a phenomenon that arises in the body (brain). In fact it is the other way round – the entire (apparent) universe, including bodies and minds, and including your own body and heart, are appearances arising in Consciousness. See the article I wrote for Yoga International on this (http://www.Advaita-vision.org/science-and-consciousness/).

Mind and Thinking

Q.4 Watching and thinking

Q: Do you mean it literally when you say that you just sat and watched/observed? In such cases, one must still be 'thinking', correct?

A: You imply that thinking is somehow bad. But thoughts simply arise in Consciousness. If you have ever tried to 'think' a thought, you will find that this is not possible. What actually happens is that the thought comes and *then* you say 'Hey, I just thought that!' But in fact there is never any 'thinker', in just the same way that there is no 'doer'. Every 'thing' is just the non-dual reality, partially obscured by the limiting idea that there is an 'I' somewhere involved in all of this – there isn't. In the case of thinking, there is 'identification' with the idea that there is an 'I' who thinks.

But, certainly, there can be observing without thoughts arising. This happens in meditation. Except that it is probably better to say 'seeing' rather than 'watching' or 'observing', since the latter two carry more of a sense of someone doing something consciously, whereas you can 'see' something without any intention at all.

Q.41 Does the mind exercise self-preservation?

Q: I have noticed that the deeper I go into the Advaitic mode of 'thinking', my mind becomes more 'creative' and also more 'interested' in objective information/knowledge. Do you think this is a self-preservation reflex of the mind?

A: I'm not sure what you mean by 'going into the Advaitic mode of thinking' but I think I recognize what you are getting at. Many people, when they first begin regular meditation, find that more 'interesting' or 'creative' thoughts seem to be arising, so that there is great temptation to follow these up to the detriment of the meditation. It does seem here that the mind is somehow 'rebelling against' the attempt to impose order upon it. There is a fallacy here, however, in the assumption that there is an entity called the mind, which has, so to speak, a mind of its own!

The point is that thoughts arise. Which thoughts do arise, and which are given attention, depends on your nature and upbringing etc. The 'arising' is quite automatic – an impulse arrives, either from a perceived sensory input or as part of a 'train' of thoughts – and it triggers a thought. We have no control over this arising, although we are able to train the mind such that the degree to which we react to the thought can be affected. And it is certainly true that 'creative' thoughts tend to come when the mind is still and there are no other competing thoughts, especially of the 'I want' variety. (This automatic nature is discussed further in the section on 'Free will'.)

'I am a separate entity' is a thought and 'I have a mind' is another thought. You may have noticed that, if you are trying to solve a particular problem, actively thinking about it may fail to bring any solution. If, however, you forget about it and simply get on with whatever else you have to do, you may find that, in a relaxed moment some later time, the answer will simply arise (as another thought).

So the answer to your question is that, no, there is no 'self-preservation' instinct here, because the mind is not a separately existing entity.

Q.44 Can enlightenment be in the mind if it is illusory?

Q: In Question 38 on depression you state: *"suffering stems from mistaken identification with the body and mind"*. In the second part of the same question you say: *"'Enlightenment' is effectively of the mind"*.

"Mistaken identification with the body and mind" implies that the mind is illusory. If the mind is seen through as an illusion – then how can it be used as a tool for 'Enlightenment'?

Or is that the point: The mind is the tool that is used to realize 'Enlightenment', but in that 'Enlightenment' the mind is seen for what it is – an illusion.

It seems to be a bit of a paradox, could you help me out please?

A: *"The mind is the tool that is used to realize 'Enlightenment', but in that 'Enlightenment' the mind is seen for what it is – an illusion"*.

That is very well put! This is why Taoism, for example, speaks about the gateless gate. It seems as if there is a gate to get through but, once you are 'there', you look back and see that there was no gate. It is also why Neo-Advaitins continually talk of there being no one to become enlightened, nothing to be done etc. or of everyone already being enlightened. We are already 'That' but we don't know it.

Ignorance itself is said to be anirvachanIya – not able to be categorized; literally: unutterable, indescribable, not to be mentioned; similarly as regards mAyA. We try to understand with the mind but this is not possible. Like the pole in pole-vaulting, it has to be let go of before we can pass over the bar, even though it has been the instrument by which we got there.

But, as usual, there is a danger of misunderstanding here. The problem is with the word 'illusion'. The mind (as with everything in the world, whether gross or subtle) is not an illusion; it is mithyA. This means that it is not real *in itself*. Its reality is borrowed, if you like, from Brahman or Consciousness.

There is always only Brahman. But the initial, 'unenlightened' state is that the mithyA mind does not know this. Consequently, thinking it and its associated body are separate from 'other' body-minds and from the rest of the world, it suffers. 'Enlightenment' occurs when the mind sees through this mistaken view and accepts that there is no separation, because there is only non-dual Consciousness. Thereafter, emotional and physical aches and pains continue but there is no 'suffering' because the mind now knows that 'who I really am' is totally unaffected by this.

So thinking of the mind as a 'tool' for enlightenment is a mistake. It is the mind itself that 'gains' enlightenment, which is just a fancy name for realizing the truth taught by Advaita. Nothing 'really' happens (from the perspective of absolute reality), since there is only Consciousness. See the section on 'Enlightenment' for more specific discussion on this topic.

Q.56 Is a still mind important?

Q: Moments of stillness come unannounced; without effort; where thought stops. These are then recognized.

Tony Parsons said today that these are just 'another state' of no more importance than any other. Eckhart Tolle seems to suggest an entirely different understanding of this.

Surely moments of quiet, where the mind is just aware, living in the moment, where there is a sense of balance and calm are the beginning of what Krishnamurti termed 'The Awakening of Intelligence'? Out of this come compassion and love. Once this begins to happen it has its own volition and is not dependent on the seeker.

What are your thoughts about this?

A: It is certainly true that a still mind is 'just another state' but not true that it is of no more importance than any other. If you have ever tried to solve a difficult problem, you will surely have found that it is made even more difficult by a mind in which lots of other things are going on, hopes, fears, imaginings, arguments this way and arguments the other. Discrimination and reason operate far more efficiently and effectively in a still mind.

It was not simply a whim that caused traditional Advaita and yoga to identify different 'levels' of student according to their degree of mental 'readiness' or 'preparedness' or that Shankara laid down the sAdhana chatuShTaya sampatti requirements before a seeker could become enlightened. Since the problem is the ignorance in the mind, it stands to reason that the quality of the mind is going to be instrumental in dissolving that ignorance.

I'm not sure what you mean by 'it has its own volition and is not dependent upon the seeker', though. By 'it', I presume you mean the mind? What do you mean by the 'seeker'? You see, I think I would have to say that, at the level of vyavahAra (which is what we are discussing), the seeker and the mind are effectively the same thing. It is because of identification with ideas in the mind that I think I am not Brahman and am consequently seeking to 'discover' this fact. In reality (paramArtha), I am already free and seeking has no purpose.

So yes, at the empirical level, things such as a still mind do have an effect, acting as part cause for a subsequent realization. And realization certainly affects the mind (and the seeker), though who-I-really-am remains throughout unaffected by anything (since there isn't anything else).

Q: By 'it' I certainly don't mean the mind, I refer to that quality of silence that comes without effort, without volition. The seeker being that part of the self that would try to grasp that silence or pursue it, and hold it as its own – which is of course impossible. It is only when the seeker is absent that there is the possibility of that otherness, or silence/stillness, or Being, or whatever term seems appropriate to convey that which cannot be conveyed, but only pointed to.

Hope that makes my question/statement somewhat clearer!

A: Yes, that's right. I don't know whether you have practiced meditation. I used to for many years. You initially find that, when the thoughts and distractions begin to break up leaving a complete stillness, there is a tendency to grasp this with a 'wow – this is it!' and, of course, it immediately disappears. It is only when you can witness with complete detachment that it comes (or not) and stays, often for quite some time.

Q.58 The simplicity of 'not two'

Q: Having just read your book, I'm somewhat overwhelmed by the complexity behind the simplicity of 'not two' and I truly enjoyed reading it. Isn't it somewhat masochistic to do all these mental gymnastics when stilling the mind/ego dissolves the illusion? I must be my own saboteur when yielding to the mind's thirst for ever new, ever different books – all saying the exact same thing – Advaita cannot be understood!

A: Glad you enjoyed it. You are right that essentially it is very simple. The problem is that the mind makes it complex and each of the ways in which it does this (and, by so doing, obscures the truth) has to be tackled in turn. The seemingly complex problems require carefully reasoned arguments to dissolve them. Stilling the mind may well dissolve the illusion – but only for a time. Only Self-knowledge will remove the Self-ignorance and that cannot come by any 'doing'. Practice of meditation or samAdhi is only an event in time and will never bring about the timeless. We are already free but the mind needs enlightening! Hence the need for scriptures and their interpretation (ideally by a qualified teacher).

Also Brahman (Advaita) does not need to be understood – because you are That. But this fact *is* something that has to be discovered and understood.

Q.61 What is the mind?

Q: What is the mind? I have heard many descriptions of what it does and of its qualities etc. but I have never had a satisfactory definition of what it is.

A: The mind is a term of convenience rather than an actual entity, applying to processes rather than objects. We say that thoughts arise in the mind and think that this is somewhere in the brain, just as some say that emotions arise in the heart. (It was once thought that the mind was co-located with the physical heart rather than the brain, which accounts for the references to our 'soul' being in the 'cave of the heart' and so on. Nowadays, it is probably more common for us to think that the mind is responsible for both.)

[Note that Shankara explicitly notes this in his commentary on the Brihadaranyaka Upanishad: 3.9.20 – *"Heart refers to the intellect and manas (mind) taken together"* and 4.3.22 – *"The heart is the lotus-shaped lump of flesh, but being the seat of the internal organ, intellect, it refers to that by a metonymy ..."*.]

So the mind is really just the notional 'place' where we are conscious of thoughts, emotions, perceptions etc. and where we make decisions based upon these. In Hindu philosophies, of course, there is more to it than this.

The mind as a whole (antaHkaraNa) consists of four separate functions, which are assigned to different 'organs' of mind. The part that is responsible for raw input/output of data from the senses and to the muscles etc. is called manas. The memory bank of past data is called chitta. That part that actually discriminates and makes decisions is called buddhi. Finally, the process of identifying the sense of 'I' with any of these or with the body or roles, for example, is assigned to another 'organ of mind', ahaMkAra. But they are all processes and functions rather than physical structures and no dissection of a brain is going to locate any of them. Advaita says that the mind is 'subtle', i.e. is not made of gross matter at all.

One of the things that should be appreciated about any description of anything in vyavahAra is that it is provisional only. If it satisfies the curiosity or search for understanding at this point in time, it serves its purpose. Ultimately, all descriptions or definitions about anything have to be discarded because all is Brahman and Brahman is beyond description.

Q.73 Language and reality

Q: I feel that language itself is the only entity which has the possibility to create ignorance, duality, freedom, bondage, etc. In the realm of language, the (individual) subject and object are created by language itself and its structures (nouns, names, verbs, ...). The very concept of being (existing) or not being (not existing) is given by language itself and has no power outside its frames. Time and space are created by language also. Only language has the possibility to create the division of perceiver-perceived, and so on. Is reality outside the frames of language?

A: In a sense, what you say is true. There is a famous section in the Chandogya Upanishad which deals with this. Here is what I say in 'A-U-M: Awakening to Reality':

"The Chandogya Upanishad (6.1.4-6) says that any product is only a new word: "just as, through a single clod of clay, all that is made of clay would become known, for all modification is but name based upon words and the clay alone is real ...". *(This is known as the vAchArambhaNa shruti – meaning 'depending on mere words or some merely verbal difference' – and is a very important text in Advaita.) The making of the pot is simply changing the form of the clay and giving it a new name.*

"In the same way, then, when the world and the jIva come into being, all that is happening is that Brahman is acquiring new forms and new names to go with them. But, before, during and after, all that actually exists is Brahman".

So it is certainly true to say that language helps perpetuate the illusion of duality even if it does not in itself cause it. There is no question but that language can only take place in seeming duality and its use inherently assumes another (to whom it is directed) and objects/thoughts/feelings that form the topic of the language. But the cause of our failure to realize that all there is, is Brahman and 'I am That' is Self-ignorance. Whether or not you can argue that language is the cause of Self-ignorance is rather more doubtful. And one has to admit that it is only by skilled use of language, through shravaNa and manana, that we gain the direct Self-knowledge to remove that ignorance and bring about enlightenment.

I'm not sure what you mean by your last question. As noted above, language necessarily implies dualism but reality cannot be 'outside' anything (otherwise it would not be non-dual).

Q: Language creates the illusion of the 'I' and the illusion of the 'this' or 'that'. Language creates concepts, definitions, conditions ... Language divides reality into 'I' and 'you'. Krishna Menon once said "... where there is no where ...". What is that? The words of the sage are useful in order to neutralize the illusion, and ignorance created by worldly language. Do you agree?

A: Yes. I quote Krishna Menon in 'Book of One': *"Language is the art of concealing thoughts; thoughts are the art of concealing truth"*. Nothing can affect reality, including language but I think we agree that its use can certainly confuse us in vyavahAra. And yet, as you say, the sage has to use language in order to point the way out of our confusion, towards the truth.

Q.89 Why should I be afraid of a thought?

Q: The things that I am afraid of are mostly just thoughts. Why should I be affected by a thought? How can a thought hurt me?

A: It all depends upon who you think you are! Nothing can affect who-you-really-are because there is nothing other than that in absolute reality. But, while you believe yourself to be a body-mind, those things that can affect the body-mind (such as death!) will be believed (by the mind) to affect you also. Emotions such as fear are triggered by thoughts, even when there is nothing actually present here and now that can harm the body-mind.

Therefore, to answer your specific questions, while you believe that you are a body-mind, you have no choice about whether a thought will cause fear – it is an automatic, cause-effect happening dependent upon your particular nature. Even though the thought cannot ever affect who-you-really-are, the mind will be disturbed and, being identified with the mind, you will seem to be affected also.

Q.109b Mind of a realized man

Q: several of the things you say do not tally with what I have read and been told by other teachers:

1. There is no mind – the realized don't have a mind.
2. The Self is not the ultimate goal while manifested here. If you stay in the Self, problems will eventually appear again; you must reside in Awareness.

Can you clarify?

A:

1. The realized man has a mind just like everyone else. How could he function in the world without one? The difference between the enlightened mind and the unenlightened is the presence of Self-knowledge in the former.

2. According to traditional Advaita, the ultimate goal of man is mokSha, which should be understood as the gaining of Self-knowledge. (In reality, man is already Brahman so is already 'free' but the mind of the unenlightened person does not realize this.) Whether or not a person is enlightened, the body-mind will still experience pleasure and pain; i.e. 'problems' will still arise. The difference is that the enlightened person knows that he or she is not the body-mind and so accordingly does not undergo 'suffering' as a result of whatever happens. (He knows that who-he-really-is cannot be affected by anything.)

Q.156 Consciousness and awareness

Q: Simple question: is there a (useful) distinction to be made between consciousness and awareness (capitalized or not)? They seem interchangeable to me, but some authors seem to write that one is a primordial ground and the other always has content, as in 'consciousness of' or 'awareness of'.

A: Yes, in everyday usage they are usually used interchangeably. But teachers frequently differentiate as you have indicated – some one way, some the other – which is why it is so important to define the terms that you are using very carefully. Traditionally the word sAkShI (witness) is often used in this sense but it is also pointed out that this is not the 'final' realization. As long as there is a 'subject' aware of or watching an 'object', there is duality. Whatever you want to call the 'ultimate' reality, it has to be non-dual. Best to stick to 'Brahman' or 'Atman'! In the end, no word can be adequate since language itself is dualistic. This is why, in the Mandukya Upanishad, it is the *silence* following OM that represents turIya (which can be equated with Brahman).

Q (originally Q.192): In reading several sources (Balsekar, Ramana, and others) there remains a confusion about thought and its place in Awareness/Consciousness. All seem to agree that a still mind is a necessary condition of Consciousness. (Experientially, I think I know what a 'still mind' is, but have no descriptors.) However, in functioning in everyday life, mental activities such as choosing, judging, comparing *are* necessary. What is the place of thought in Consciousness?

A: It is not possible to say that 'awareness' and 'consciousness' are either different or equivalent because it depends upon who is using them. If, for example, you are reading Nisargadatta, then they are certainly not the same and he uses these words in the opposite way to most other teachers.

Regarding thoughts and mind, a still mind is required for discrimination (viveka) and the ability to control the mind is one of the requirements of sAdhana chatuShTaya sampatti, and is needed to some degree if one is to gain Self-knowledge (enlightenment). I think this is what you were asking.

Q: A little more on the second question, if you will: what is the place of thought in Consciousness?

To clarify my own question: it seems like functional thought (i.e. getting by in daily activity) necessarily precludes a 'still mind'. The mind in thought of any kind is not a still mind (or is this incorrect?). Balsekar makes the distinction between a working mind and a thinking mind, but I don't see how they can be present at the same time. Any other understanding of this gets foggy and imaginary by giving the two a hierarchical relationship.

A: I haven't heard of Balsekar's 'categorization'. Bearing in mind that all of this relates to empirical reality only, I would differentiate on the basis of buddhi versus manas. manas is the part that frequently gets caught up in desires, fears and circling thoughts in general – i.e. unproductive and unhelpful activity. buddhi (sometimes referred to as the 'intellect'), on the other hand, is concerned with discrimination, judgment etc. and functions optimally in stillness. A 'trained' mind (i.e. in one who has gained sAdhana chatuShTaya sampatti – 'SCS') is one where manas is under control.

In one who is enlightened, both aspects still exist and all types of thought will still occur. Obviously there will be fewer of the unhelpful thoughts, to the extent that SCS was gained for enlightenment, but desires etc. are still likely as a result of prArabdha karma. They will have much less impact, however, because it is known that I am already unlimited and complete – in reality I can want for nothing.

I would call a mind 'still' when it is not clouded by the circling thoughts etc. It is still operating and, indeed, may well be processing input to a greater degree than normal, but it now does so with supreme efficiency and buddhi is able to direct the process optimally. When we are meditating, of course, the mind (should) *really* become still, with no movement of thought at all and with the attention on the mantra (or whatever other type of meditation is being used), not being diverted by any external or internal source. (When the mantra stops, leaving complete stillness, it is called samAdhi.)

Q.206 The role of the mind in enlightenment

Q: The most intriguing promise of Advaita for me is its claim that ignorance blocks knowledge. Because ignorance exists in the mind, it's the transformation of the mind which allows knowledge. Once ignorance is removed from the mind, then reality is clearly perceived.

Eckhart Tolle and Adyashanti don't seem to address this. Eckhart Tolle's view is that if one takes the position of presence regularly (e.g. as the observer), then eventually the presence will dominate. Adyashanti seems to advocate a combination of stillness meditation and self-inquiry.

Both, however, maintain that it's only when a person is, to a certain degree, fed up with the mind-created dream-world, that enlightenment becomes possible.

Ontologically, their stance and Advaita are similar, e.g. no past and future, Atman is Brahman, etc. However, Advaita's idea that the transformation of the mind allows the perception of reality makes more sense to me.

Yet, who am I to say? Tolle and Adyashanti have 'made it.' If they don't emphasize the role of discursive argumentation to transform the body-mind, maybe they know better.

Do you, as someone who has accomplished the Advaita method, still experience identification with the mind? Or do you never experience identification with the mind these days? Do you experience fearlessness?

A: Because we are already free in reality, we need not (and cannot) 'do' anything to bring it about. No amount of practicing 'being in the present' or 'meditation' will ever bring enlightenment. It is simply that we do not know that we are Brahman so the only solution is to remove the ignorance. In other words, it is not a 'claim' on the part of Advaita. Once you accept the axiom of non-duality, it necessarily follows.

The 'being fed up' aspect is what often motivates people to become seekers. This is really the understanding that things in this life are never going to bring lasting happiness.

You need to be careful with the use of words, even to yourself. The idea of 'perceiving reality', for example, is likely to mislead. Enlightenment is the realization that reality is non-dual and that 'I am That' but, afterwards, we still see the world as before, just as we still see the sunrise and sunset while knowing that this is the earth rotating. You can never 'perceive' reality. Since reality is non-dual, who would be perceiving what?

Your question regarding 'identification with mind' and 'fearlessness' relates to the often questioned distinction between the j~nAnI and the jIvanmukta – see questions 105 and 161.

Q.228 Is Advaita a cure for life?

Q: What do you think about the fact that many people (e.g. the aboriginals in Australia) have never even heard about non-duality and enlightenment? Maybe they don't suffer from the dual thinking problem of the mind (although most of them generally create a God who is different from their 'selves' or their communities). The same holds for the early years of a child: it experiences likes and dislikes where the thinking process is not yet linked to a central 'I-reference' point. Is all this just a matter of programming/ education?

A: I'm afraid I know very little about the beliefs of other cultures, and our interpretations of the thought processes of young children can only ever be speculative. You can postulate whatever beliefs you feel happy with to account for empirical reality. In the end, though, you have to come to terms with the fact that, from the absolute standpoint, there has never been any creation, no one has ever been born, etc.

Q: I started reading 'Oneness' by John Greven. Your comment on his book was the catalyst for my asking the question: "The description of how the ego-sense arises in early childhood and subsequently deludes us as to our true identity is particularly good".

What I meant is that Advaita only serves the purpose of being a cure: for people with a different education (e.g. the aboriginals) or small children (before their ego-sense arises). It is possible to live in a non-dual manner, so that they don't need an Advaita or non-dual approach to be 'cured'.

A: I don't accept that any aspects of empirical life can be 'non-dual'. All perception, thought and action are necessarily dualistic – how can anyone live without these? The purpose of Advaita is not to 'cure' them so that they can 'live in a non-dual manner'; it is to enable them to realize that, despite the continuing, empirical duality of life, the *nature* of absolute reality is non-dual. Thus, they can appreciate that life is only a seeming reality; that who-they-really-are is that non-dual reality, and that the world is only a seeming manifestation of that same reality.

Q: What do you call 'reality'? I see no difference between a seeming reality (I versus creation) and a non-dual reality (I am creation). And what is the impact or benefit of realizing the non-dual reality?

A: Reality is that which never changes; that which is the only existent, conscious 'thing', which lacks nothing and is limitless. Every, *seeming* 'thing' in creation is, on the other hand, transient and limited. The benefit of the realization is the knowledge that 'I' am that reality, and consequently need have no fear of any sort, knowing that I am perfect, complete and unlimited.

Q.235 Brahman and the mind

Q: The commentary on the Brahma Sutra by Swami Paramarthananda states that, *"We must know what we are investigating"*, and *"Have an appropriate means of acquiring data"*. Such an approach must mean that we have projected a goal (however vague or otherwise) and at some point we will achieve that goal. This is what our minds do, so whatever is 'discovered' or 'realized' in this way can only be within the 'known' that is the mind.

The main drive of what we call our mind is its own search for security and permanence; if any system can contribute to its maintenance and continuity it will latch onto it – all religious and spiritual traditions have this fatal flaw. For this reason we need to understand the mind, not through a path or prescription but through our own observations of the moment-to-moment movement of this 'self' perpetuating but amazing tool. To ask how to do this is to be back in the loop that is the mind, the known; all we can do is to 'watch' – but without becoming the 'watcher'.

All this is very unsatisfying, but only for a mind that seeks a result.

A: Of course, we have to start out believing that we are looking for something for 'me' – usually happiness. Of course, we have a goal (to become enlightened). How else could it be? Simply observing the mind may lead us to the realization that we are not the mind but how can it lead us to the knowledge that we are Brahman?

The knowledge about Brahman has to come from outside initially, trusting in what we are told by the teacher or the scriptures. Eventually, through careful guidance, we may come to the realization that who-we-really-are is, in fact, this same Brahman. There is no problem with searching for security. When the mind finally realizes that there is only Brahman and 'I am That', it finds infinite security. It seems that, like another questioner with whom I am presently in discussion, you feel that enlightenment means 'death of the mind' (manonAsha). Please read the essay from Swami Suddhananda (http://www.advaita.org.uk/discourses/teachers/blueprints_premananda.htm) and my own essay on this topic (http://www.advaita-vision.org/manonasha-not-the-literal-death-of-the-mind/).

What is 'unsatisfying' is being told simply 'This is IT' (or whatever) and 'that is all that you need to know'. Then, there is simply no way of removing the Self-ignorance; you have simply put yet another layer of ignorance in front of the stuff that was there already.

Q.238 The mind and the I-thought

Q: The mind has an important job to do, processing information about what we are continually experiencing, and using that to assess and plan our actions through the further process of reflection (thinking). To that end, the mind is as important (and as mechanical) as are the instinctive reactions of our bodies.

For us, the mind has taken on an exaggerated importance in that we tend to believe that the contents (the memories formed from our experiences) have a reality that is beyond the physical. For many, the mind has become exalted to the status of being the 'I', the real 'me'; sometimes a 'soul'. So, my point is that as necessary and important as the mind is, it has become a 'self'-centered and 'self'-maintaining tool. Therefore, whatever movement the mind makes in matters of beliefs, in pursuing goals in the fields of religion, spirituality or any other belief concept, its main pre-occupation is in maintaining its 'self' structure through identification with the belief. Further, to maintain its 'self' structure it may form a strong attachment to any concept that appears to support the sense of 'I' – whether or not the belief (concept) is true or not.

This all may seem very 'heady' but surely it is a simple matter of observing these natural processes, how they arise and how they continue to sustain the 'I' concept? It may also help to realize that the mind and its processes (thinking) are as automatic as breathing, and arise in a part of the brain. We are conditioned to think in terms of mind-body whereas it would be more helpful to talk of brain-body. Understanding the relationship between how the brain creates a 'me' as opposed to 'not me' would give a clearer picture of the dualistic situation we find ourselves in.

I realize we make huge investments in maintaining the 'I' delusion and how these investments are skillfully maintained; it is in this sense that I refer to the security the 'self' seeks through the maintenance of this belief structure. The so-called 'mind' can only be clear when uncontaminated by the 'I' concept, otherwise all our undertakings, our goals, whether spiritual or otherwise, will only serve the divisive 'I'. Most systems (and non-systems) do not seem aware of the subtlety of the mind with respect to its 'self' maintaining process.

It is the function of the ego-mind to fit the intimations we have of the non-duality of 'Life' into a framework that 'it' can manipulate into yet another 'self'-maintaining structure. Our whole, intelligent brain-body organism is continually aware of such intimations (it cannot be otherwise); then along comes the mind and tries to understand the unknown in terms of the known.

It seems we are all aware of 'intimations' (some obvious, some more subtle) arising from within ourselves and from nature, that we are not just mind and body and are not separate, isolated creatures. It may be this 'feeling' that impels us to 'search'. No doubt this 'search' can take us into all sorts of weird and wonderful ventures – perhaps spiritual or scientific. We can never 'find' the source of these 'intimations', perhaps because they are too 'close' to us; they are what we are – the very basis of life and everything. The best we can ever understand is that we are not who we have been told or believe we are, and to simply acknowledge the 'otherness'.

Perhaps a person following a particular path does realize these things – and perhaps it is incidental and could arise when cutting the grass or drinking tea!

A: I don't disagree with most of what you say – and neither does Advaita. In fact, if you study Ramana Maharshi, it is his 'Who am I?' enquiry that is intended to root out this 'I thought' and expose it for what it is, along the lines that you indicate.

However, this 'I thought' arises in Consciousness. Consciousness is prior to any thought and the mind and body themselves arise within it. It is not 'I, Dennis' or 'I, somebody or other' who is the non-dual reality but 'I, the Consciousness prior to thought'. This is where the idea of destruction of the mind or ego comes from. Their literal destruction is, of course, not possible and, if it were, there would be no realization of the truth since this realization has to occur in the mind itself. But, the 'real I' being prior to mind, what is referred to as the 'destruction of the mind' is the recognition that the mind and its 'I thought' are not who I really am.

This is very subtle stuff for most people and requires much preliminary teaching to undermine the many pre-existing misconceptions and prepare the mind for the final understanding. So it may occur spontaneously while drinking a cup of tea… but it is most unlikely to do so!

Q.281 saMskAra and memory

Q: I have been reading about memories and their being carried over into future lives. It said that all saMskAra-s are stored in the chitta, from previous lives since the beginning of time. Also, on your website and maybe also in one of your books you said that buddhi functions best out of stillness. This implies that there is a pool of knowledge which buddhi can assess. Is that pool within buddhi, in chitta or is it the causal itself?

A: saMskAra-s are not memories. It is prArabdha saMskAra that determines the sort of life into which we are born and the sort of situations we will encounter. This is so that we will reap some of the fruit from our past actions. There is no memory of those past actions; it is simply an effect from their prior cause.

The reason buddhi functions best in stillness is that, when still, it is able to see the situation neutrally. There is no accessing of a pool of knowledge. It is manas that accesses information and plays around with it, asking 'what if' questions and so on; buddhi simply 'sees' the right answer, in the present, without any of this.

Q.307 Where the mind cannot reach

Q: I am allowing life to teach me as I go through it, but I'm not finding it easy.

Most of the time I feel I don't want to even speak because I feel nothing I say is 'correct'. At the same time, however, I feel that even if I do speak, whatever I say would not be 'wrong' because 'right' and 'wrong', 'correct' and 'incorrect' do not exist. Words and concepts are a massive hindrance to my understanding, yet I cannot overcome them.

I want to say that I know that everything is Brahman, but then something says: "you can't 'know' that everything is Brahman because that cannot be known with the mind", so I'm always hitting a wall.

Even writing this email is not working out. I can't express what it is I truly mean. I'm afraid to speak because I fear I will say something that is not 'true'. But then I realize that if I did say something, it wouldn't be 'true' or 'untrue' anyway.

There is a subtleness to existence that I can't put into words. There are problems that I'm coming across as I learn more that I can't articulate.

The only purpose learning has, I'm sure, is just to take you to the realization that the 'learning' was not necessary in the first place, but, at the same time, it *was* necessary. You see how that was kind of paradoxical? Well, I'm coming across the same kind of problems 'in my mind', the same kind of paradoxes.

I guess I can articulate one question: According to Advaita, everything is Brahman but we can never know Brahman. This means that Brahman is effectively what I am aware of when I see anything, this PC for example. So this means that even this PC or the pen on the desk is Brahman. But I do 'understand' the pen on my desk. How can this be so if the pen is Brahman and Brahman cannot be understood?

I am thinking that there is a subtlety here that I'm not appreciating. I guess I understand my own concepts of the pen, e.g. it's made of plastic, it's long, it has black ink etc., but the Brahman that it really is, is what I would not understand?

I'm sorry this email has been such a mess. I have so many questions in my head that I can't put into words. I suppose some of this email has been about trying to express what I cannot express. I sometimes feel I should just completely surrender, let things be as they will be, don't try to understand things or work things out, because things will always be perfect, no matter what. But then I feel lazy, like I'm not doing what I'm 'supposed' to be doing. My mind is full of paradoxes and ironies and questions I cannot express and it's killing me.

There is much I feel I 'know', but it is nothing I can put into words. When I try, the things I feel I 'know' break down and enjoy no kind of expression. At the same time, there is much I don't understand ... but then, in reality, there is nothing to understand.

Please respond to this. Very little of what is written here in words has successfully expressed what I'm trying to get at. I hope, however, that you can read what isn't written and see my situation for what it is.

A: Language (and thought) can never describe reality. What we perceive (as separate objects) is always mistaken; we superimpose some memory or idea about what is in front of us upon what is actually there. So, inevitably, whatever we say is wrong in the final analysis.

But clearly language has utility – we would not function very well in the world without it! We just have to be aware of its limitations. And it has the ability to point us towards the truth, even if it cannot go there itself. So do not condemn words and concepts or underestimate their value.

When you start to think about Brahman, you will inevitably encounter paradoxes and places where the ideas cannot reach. It is rather like trying to investigate the self scientifically – you cannot, because in order to do this, you would have to objectify the subject and this is a contradiction in terms. You cannot 'know' Brahman as an object. But this is not ultimately a problem – because you *are* Brahman.

You say: "The only purpose learning has, I'm sure, is just to take you to the realization that the 'learning' was not necessary in the first place, but, at the same time, it was necessary". This is exactly right. Swami Paramarthananda tells a story to illustrate this. Here is how I related it in the second edition of 'Book of One':

"It is an extension of the story mentioned much earlier about the lady who is looking everywhere for her necklace but then realizes that it has been around her neck all the time. This version has the lady discovering her loss after returning from visiting a friend, to whom she had been showing the necklace. She realizes that she must have left it there and runs out into the street and all the way back to her friend's house only to have the friend point out that the necklace was around her neck the whole time. The question he now asks is: was it necessary that the lady make the effort of going round to her friend in order to find the necklace?

"Clearly she already had the necklace but, equally clearly, she did not know that she had it. And this is the key point of the metaphor. We already are free but we do not know it. The effort of sAdhana and j~nAna yoga is to acquire the knowledge that will remove the notion that we are bound.

"Enlightenment is of the mind; the Self-knowledge that destroys the Self-ignorance takes place in the mind. There is no frustration at all when Advaita is taught correctly. On the contrary, it is a joyful process in which aspects that caused confusion are replaced by clarity. It is also the person that seeks enlightenment and the person that finds it, even though the 'finding' also includes the realization that there never was a 'person' in reality".

The point about your pen and PC: Yes, these are Brahman. Everything is Brahman. The problem is that you are caught up with the name and form. Everything has what might be thought of as five 'properties', according to the dRRigdRRishya viveka (a short scripture attributed to Shankara). These are asti ('is-ness' or existence), bhAti ('shining-ness' or cognizability), priya ('dearness'), nAma (name) and rUpa (form). The first three belong to Brahman (more usually described as sat-chit-Ananda), while the last two belong to the world. You miss those 'attributes' that would point you to satyam, the real, and get caught up with those aspects that enmesh you in the mithyA world.

So thanks for the question – a very worthwhile one, because I am sure there are many in your position. Hope it has helped.

Q.311 Clearing the mind

Q: I come across a lot about clearing the mind ... but if there is no person, no one that can have a will of his/her own, surely a desire or will to clear the mind is nonsense? The mind cannot be tamed because there is not a person to whom it belongs, someone with their own free will? Is that at all right? Surely a clear mind would only arise because it is the will of Brahman?

A: It's only nonsense once you know that you are not a person!

Also, you have to be very clear when you are talking about Brahman. Strictly speaking, the term 'Brahman' refers to the non-dual reality and, if you are using it in this sense, it is not meaningful to speak of 'the will of Brahman' – Brahman does not have any will; there are no 'parts' to Brahman and there is nothing other than Brahman.

If you are talking about the person (appearance) within the world (appearance), then you have to refer to Ishvara as the 'creator' and the dispenser of body-minds in accordance with accumulated karma from past lives.

You have to be clear in your own mind about this distinction because, for example, the Brahma Sutras uses the word 'Brahman' in both of these ways – Brahman and Ishvara – and expects you to know which one is being referred to in any given instance!

Q.341 Positive thinking

Q: There are moments when I think I am the one that is creating my world with my specific positive thoughts – is that true?

Or is it the consciousness bringing me those positive thoughts or negative thoughts? I know that I don't have to ask for anything because in that way there is an infinite possibility of something fresh and new and totally different.

How do I pray? In silence or meditation?

A: The reality of the world is the same as the reality of yourself. It is as a result of believing in the separate existence of the world and assigning names to perceived separate forms that you effectively create 'your' world. The choices that you make here are governed by your particular nature, which is governed in turn by your past actions.

Consciousness, which is what you really are, is unlimited. There is no need to look for anything 'fresh and different'. Such an idea results from believing yourself to be limited.

Silence and meditation (and prayer) will help prepare the mind but only Self-knowledge will solve your (perceived) problems.

Q.383 Alzheimer's

Q: Does an enlightened one stay enlightened when he gets Alzheimer's disease? You seem to be saying that enlightenment is knowledge, self knowledge. Can one lose that knowledge again?

A: This is the sort of question that first requires very careful definition of terms. What do you mean by 'enlightened'? Who is the 'one' you are asking about? Who gets Alzheimer's? Who loses the knowledge?

It is the individual person (jIva) who has a mind and it is this mind that may gain Self-knowledge. But the body, mind, intellect and world are all mithyA. Who-you-really-are is the Atman, which is equal to Brahman, which is non-dual, perfect and complete. Brahman has no mind to acquire dementia. So, the answer to your question is that the jIva's mind may get Alzheimer's and the person may effectively lose the knowledge. But this cannot affect who-you-really-are. Consciousness is the only satyam. And Consciousness does not get Alzheimer's.

Have you read my 'chidAbhAsa' and 'manonAsha' articles? See Q.405 ('States of Consciousness' section) and Q.235 (this section) for references. These should help clarify the situation.

Q.391 Dissociation

Q: Does the psychological concept of dissociation have any role in Advaita? In other words, the subjective experience of being detached, depersonalized, or wholly uninvolved in any given situation – is this the same as what Advaita might call 'awareness' or 'just happening?' If not, how are they actually different?

A: Who-we-really-are is not the mind; we are the Consciousness in which the mind arises. However, it is the mind of the person that realizes this in what is termed 'enlightenment' or (better) Self-knowledge. A mind that is not balanced and controlled/disciplined is most unlikely ever to be able to attain this Self-knowledge; it will be more interested in avoiding fear, satisfying desires etc. A mind that is unbalanced/disturbed etc. is even less likely to be capable of assimilating the teaching of Advaita. As far as I understand the term 'dissociation', it refers to just such a mind – one in which the functions of the mind are out of balance, with some parts functioning normally and some not at all. So, no, it is not the same.

For a discussion on the distinction between 'consciousness' and 'awareness', see Q.156 earlier in this section.

Q.400 Consciousness and the person

Q: A few questions or clarifications please…

1. As you've said to me before, to focus on this world and everything within it, is really the wrong focus, because it's mithyA. And what we really are, is that in which all of it occurs?

A: You are not the body-mind; you are Consciousness. There is only Consciousness in reality; the 'rest' (i.e. this world and everything within it) is just appearance and mistaken interpretation.

2. Am I correct in saying that Vedanta is truly a specific system or process to know who you really are as well as understanding the functioning of everything?

A: Advaita is a teaching methodology to bring you to the realization of who-you-really-are.

3. So the elements or energy is not who we are, since they

are dependent on Consciousness. As Nisargadatta said, *"without Consciousness nothing is"*.

A: Elements, energy etc. are name and form of Consciousness. The words 'dependent on' Consciousness could be misleading, maybe implying that elements are separate entities. If you understand the meaning of mithyA, no problem – elements and energy are mithyA. 'Who-you-really-are' is Consciousness.

4. To gain Self-knowledge however, there must be a body with a nervous system. So the body does matter in relation to Self-knowledge? But, Consciousness doesn't care whether it's manifested or not?

A: In reality, there is only Consciousness. From the perspective of the person, there is a body-mind. The realization that there is only Consciousness has to take place in the mind of the person in order for the person to realize that 'All there is is Consciousness'. So yes, Advaita says that you specifically need a *human* body and mind in order to gain Self-knowledge, and therefore freedom from saMsAra (rebirth).

5. Words cause confusion, so what is the difference between Consciousness and Awareness from your understanding?

A: You can define words how you like. As long as you do this, there need not be any confusion (as long as you are then self-consistent as you develop your philosophy and end up with the same conclusion as Advaita!). The way I use these terms is that Consciousness (capital 'C') is the reality (better called 'Brahman' to avoid confusion); and 'awareness' (capital or not) and 'consciousness' (small 'c') refer to the person's perceiving/conceiving ability.

6. The mind is discussed a lot, and many say that to have 'no mind' is the key to peace and freedom. Is the mind a part of the brain or something entirely different?

A: The 'person' requires a mind in order to function in the world. This applies whether the person has Self-knowledge or not. The mind as defined by Advaita is a subtle organ, which survives death, whereas the brain returns to dust, like all organic matter. Obviously the mind depends upon signals from the senses, which science now knows are processed in the brain. And loss of limbs and other organs does not seem to affect one's ability to think and act. So it makes sense to think of its being located in the brain. But this is really not important.

7. Upon gaining Self-knowledge, does the mind continue or fade away if you will, leaving the brain to function in its normal and natural way without the mind blocking it?

A: The 'person' requires a mind in order to function in the world. This applies whether the person has Self-knowledge or not. It is likely (though not necessary) that the mind of someone with Self-knowledge will be less prone to disturbance by desire/fear etc.

Q.415 Having the same thoughts

Q: If thoughts arise from Consciousness, and Consciousness is the Absolute, *and* we are all connected to the Absolute, why do we not all have the same thought simultaneously?

A: This is one of those many questions which confuse reality and appearance. The absolute reality is that there is *only* Consciousness and, from that perspective you cannot say any more. At the level of empirical reality, there is clear duality – world, objects, separate people etc. At this level, separate people have distinct thoughts, which are private.

You cannot mix these two levels except to acknowledge that the empirical level is only an appearance (even though we believe it is real most of the time). As a crude metaphor, you might suppose that you take a lump of gold and make a ring and a bangle from it. If you drop the ring in some chemical and it is tarnished, you might ask why, since the ring and bangle are the same gold, doesn't the bangle become tarnished as well. But this metaphor has its limitations!

You might enjoy reading the discussion (http://www.advaita.org.uk/discourses/teachers/mindreading_benjamin.htm), where

Benjamin asked a similar question: Why can't I read your thoughts?

Ego

Q.12 Why am I not all-powerful?

Q: If I am the Source, why do I not have the powers of the Source? Why can I not create worlds for example?

If what I will is the Source's willing, why is it not instantly fulfilled?

How do you experientially move from living in your ego to being the Source?

A: Sounds like delusions of grandeur!

This is another one of those questions where you have to clarify from which level you are speaking. From the standpoint of absolute reality, there is only the 'Source' as you call it. Therefore you could say that, being the Source, you *do* have the power of the Source – what is happening now is exactly what you (the Source) want to happen! The problem is that you (the ego) are seeing 'everything' through a 'cloud of ignorance'. In reality, nothing is happening at all; it is just your mistaken view that thinks there is. (Moreover, the 'Source' has no desires, since it is limitless, and does not act, so that it does not 'want' anything.)

But, of course, you are asking this from the standpoint of the appearance, in which, because of ignorance, you think that you are a separate person with your own particular desires which, naturally enough, you want to fulfill. Unfortunately, this is not possible – see the section on free will. All that you, the apparent person, can do is be thrown backwards and forwards at the mercy of the various forces acting upon you.

So what you (the ego) will is not what the Source is willing. What you 'will' depends upon which thoughts arise and which seem the more attractive. Whether an action follows or not is again not a question of 'will' but simply of cause and effect within the brain-body mechanism. Basically, you cannot 'will'.

Finally, 'you' do not move from living in the ego to being the Source. 'You' do not exist as a separate entity. The idea that you do is a mistake – mixing up real and unreal. When this is truly realized, it will also be realized that you are already the Source and always have been.

Q.20 Can I have any effect on reality?

Q: Does our 'sense of self' have the egoic power to manipulate the content of reality or is what 'I' seem to experience just random?

A: There seems to be a number of misunderstandings here.

I assume that you appreciate that in reality there is only the non-dual Self. So what we are talking about here is simply the illusory appearance. But even at the level of the phenomenal there is no such thing as 'egoic power' because there is no such thing as ego. (I assume that your 'sense of self' is another phrase for ego.) The ego is really just a bunch of ideas with which we identify. (Or, if you prefer, the process of identifying with body-mind-ideas is what we call the 'ego'.)

Furthermore, no one does anything. Even ignoring the fact that there is no one to begin with, the seeming appearance is just a cause-effect nexus with one thing following on from another in a totally automatic way. So what happens is not random but entirely deterministic. (Note that I am not saying '*pre*-determined' – see the section on 'Free Will' for a more specific discussion.) However, one of those determining causes is our own mental makeup, itself the result of all of our upbringing, education, genetic makeup etc. Therefore it is inevitable that the way that we see 'things' will be determined by the nature of our mind. Someone sees a particular event or situation as exciting, another as frightening, yet another as mundane.

Thus, our experience is certainly dependent upon our ego (as defined above) but there is no manipulation. All that is happening is that all perceptions are filtered through our preconceived thoughts, habits etc. in a manner quite beyond any control.

Finally, all of this only affects the appearance, of course – reality is forever changeless, perfect and complete.

Q.25 Is the 'calling' of a spiritual teacher obeying ego?

Q: I am a spiritual teacher and have considered teaching to be a 'calling'. In this calling is also heard the call of the ego, most definitely. One wants to help, as you have so ably, but it is clear that wanting to help, perhaps especially that desire, is problematic.

Even in the call of the quiet, there is the still small ego. Even 'doing nothing at all' is suspect. In this passing evening, given the implicit impurity of altruistic prompting, there seems nothing but to follow the Invisible wherever It may lead, in spite of the potential emptiness of even This. Perhaps teaching and learning, humbled always in the obscure awareness of Reality, is the form of the infinite for now. Perfectly imperfect.

A: I feel that there is free will issue here as well. What 'comes up' for the person is whatever has been conditioned – genes, education, upbringing etc. There is no choice here. The action that is taken is then, similarly, the result of the (automatic) mental discussion and discrimination – again no free will. After the event, there is the tendency (again automatic) for the thought to arise: 'I decided this', 'I did that'. This thought is effectively the 'ego'.

So, these thoughts will continue to arise for the 'realized man' since they have nothing to do with who-we-really-are. To this extent, the 'realized man' still has ego-thoughts but, now, there is no identification with them. The crucial difference is that it is now known that all this is simply a part of the appearance. The rope-snake metaphor is useful here. Once it is known that the snake is really a rope, it is no longer possible to be deceived.

Accordingly, if one's natural role is that of a teacher, the related thoughts and actions will continue as before, including the thoughts 'I want to teach', 'I enjoy teaching others' and so on. No problem. Once the ego has been seen through, it will no longer be possible to be deceived by those thoughts into believing that anyone is doing or enjoying anything. There is nothing 'empty' or 'imperfect' – reality is always perfect and complete.

Desire and Fear

Q.43 How can one instill a desire for the Self?

A: My book 'How to Meet Yourself' is all about this topic. All desires are effectively for the Self; a wish to 'return to' who-we-really-are. Of course, we already are That but unfortunately do not know it. And so we mistakenly go after objects and experiences to try to find that ultimate happiness, continually looking outside when it is really already there inside, as it were.

Even the desire to harm or destroy something or someone arises because the person or thing is seen as a threat or limiting agent. Removal of the limitation allows the desire (or fear – which is a 'negative' desire) to fall away and, at least temporarily, allows the natural happiness to shine through.

You will never get rid of desire – it is a function of the mind and our particular makeup (prArabdha saMskAra). The important thing is to recognize its intrinsic nature and not be taken in by it. Once this is completely understood, you can accede to a particular desire or not, depending on reasonable considerations rather than the demands of an ego.

The overriding desire to discover who-you-really-are and the nature of reality – to 'gain' mokSha or 'liberation' from saMsAra, the eternal round of birth and death – is called mumukShutva. This is the only desire worth having but you cannot *choose* to have it. Rather it is something you grow into. In the course of the usual pursuits of life, you are repeatedly disappointed by finding that the results of your endeavors do not bring the happiness and fulfillment that you had anticipated. You grow disillusioned with this way of life and begin to look for what might be termed 'spiritual' pursuits and explanations. This outlook, once begun seriously, becomes a passion. It is colloquially referred to as 'putting your head into the lion's mouth' – once there, you are obliged to follow it through to the end!

Q.352 Sexual desire and happiness

Q: I have read the book 'How to Meet Yourself'. I think that I understand about desire; that it is a searching for a return to our natural state of happiness. I understand that we are already that, but when around women or just bored I start moving toward pornography to get relief from the desire. How exactly can I just access this happiness? Do I not take the desire seriously and not look at women, or do I need a more practical way to cope and avoid that route?

A: I have just re-read the section on 'Sex'. (I wrote this quite a long time ago!) I pointed out that the sexual element of desire and enjoyment is really an aspect of Darwinian evolution – an urge associated with intense enjoyment so that we are encouraged to propagate the species.

This is all part of the 'working of the world' and has nothing to do with 'who-we-really-are'. It is all mithyA, irrespective of how real and pressing it might seem. Dwelling on it in any way will only take you away or keep you away from ever finding out the truth of the matter. And, let's face it, you cannot prevent your body and mind from functioning in the way that nature has intended! Stop worrying about it! Turn your attention to the only thing that really matters, namely getting rid of Self-ignorance by trying to discover the nature of the world and your Self.

Of course, unless you retire from the world by becoming a monk or recluse (which wouldn't really solve your problem anyway), you still have to function in the world. Participate to the extent that you need to – work and social life – and endeavor to function normally within it, whilst retaining a 'witness' attitude towards it so that you never lose sight of the real aim. If you can turn your efforts towards spiritual seeking, ideally with the guidance of a qualified teacher, then your desires will settle down into a more proportionately useful balance.

As you say, 'happiness' is your true nature but you don't find your true nature by seeking to satisfy desires and thereby becoming happy. It is the other way round; you discover your true nature and then realize that you are happy (regardless of personal situation)!

Happiness

Q.48 Should we be happy, whatever we are doing?

Q: I've just finished reading your new book (How To Meet Yourself ... and find true happiness) and it's turned my life upside down!

I want to offer my congratulations on such a superb piece of work as I can't disagree with any of your arguments. However, Dennis, it's left me realizing how much I've been identifying myself with my mind for most of my life. And I'm now 49 years old. [I suspect the majority of the population is doing the same.]

I've also read so many books explaining why it's important to have 'a purpose for existing'; otherwise we'll drift aimlessly through life. They then explain how to go about finding our 'purpose in life'. I'm therefore beginning to realize this advice is wrong, because you say on the last page of your book that 'ambitions and purpose are irrelevant'.

Your book has brought up one major question: I can't deny that when I do certain things, for example, a favorite hobby, it makes me feel 'happier' than an action such as ironing. Is this because I'm letting my mind dictate to me what I find happy? And if I am Happiness (consciousness) should I be equally happy no matter what I'm doing?

Do you, Dennis, still find, with all your knowledge on this subject, that writing books is something that fulfills you more than, say, completing a tax return?

Do we find certain actions more fulfilling than others because of the conditioning in our childhood? If I have understood the conclusions of your work, should I be aiming to be equally happy no matter what I'm doing?

A: The reason that 'purposes' are never going to lead to fulfillment is that they are based upon a false premise, namely that you are a separate person. 'The Book of One' explains a lot more if you are interested in pursuing it and 'Back to the Truth' deals with the subject in all its amazing detail. And it is all totally logical and unarguable.

As regards your main question, what you 'like' is dictated by your nature and upbringing – genetic, family, education etc. All that is happening is that, when you are doing what you like, you are without any desires and desires are the source of unhappiness. No desires = satisfaction with the way things are = happiness. So, if you are doing something that you don't want to do, there will be a desire to be doing something else. Consequently, you won't be happy. My own 'upbringing' has resulted in an endless fascination for Advaita so yes, I am happy writing about it and definitely do it in preference to filling out tax returns.

There is no point in aiming to be equally happy whatever you are doing. There is no real choice in the matter. You will be influenced by all of the factors with which you come into contact. Hopefully, you will encounter influences that push you in a direction which leads you to understanding. If you do go on to read 'Book of One', it is possible that this understanding will grow and that eventually you will realize the truth about yourself and the world. Once that happens, the problems that arise no longer trigger the same degree of concern, since you now know that they do not *really* matter.

The whole point of How to Meet Yourself' was precisely to appeal to those people concerned about meaning and purpose and point them in the direction of a philosophy (i.e. Advaita) that resolves all of these issues for ever. But it is not an instantaneous process because we have a lifetime of conditioning in wrong thinking and it all has to be laboriously unraveled before the mind gains sufficient clarity to be able to see the truth.

Q.463 Improving one's life

Q: Can you recommend any book that talks about how traditional vedAnta can improve one's life, and give deep peace as a result of j~nAna phalam [the 'fruit' or benefit of gaining Self-knowledge]?

A: I doubt that such a thing exists. You've really got this the wrong way round. vairAgya – being dispassionate about one's life, good or bad – is one of the pre-requisites for enlightenment. And the phalam or 'fruit' of Self-knowledge is a spin-off rather than the prime objective. Enlightenment brings freedom from saMsAra; our aim is to get off the treadmill altogether rather than to get cushioned seats! [For a clarification of the distinction between j~nAna and jIvanmukti, see the sections on 'Enlightenment' and 'Enlightened Man'.]

Suffering

Q.24 Is suffering 'necessary'?

Q: Pure Land Buddhism teaches, 'The lotus blooms in fire' and, 'Bits of dung are transformed into gold'. These aphorisms point to the apparent paradox of the relative, the conditioned, the illusion of separation, and that which is beyond the beyond, all here and now, in and out of time and space.

Advaitins seem to agree with the more realized and radical of Zen masters that 'nirvANa is saMsAra' (and vice versa) , with the Buddha who would call these descriptive terms mere words having no basis in Reality, and with Nagarjuna that 'Is' is not and 'Not' is, but then 'Not' is also not and 'Is' is.

Thus comprehended, is suffering, at any level, in any sense of word or action, real or unreal, ultimate or illusory, necessary? Is there any point, pointless or provisional, to preservation of illusory life, the alleviation of illusion? Try? Teach? Care?

No problem. Or Is There? Thanks.

A: Your question is posed in a very intellectual way. Whilst the mind is the tool that we use to try to highlight the source of ignorance, and thereby undermine it, it is also in a very real sense the cause of all of our problems. So it is a constant balancing act. Another problem is that my knowledge of Buddhism (in any variant) is virtually zero.

So, bearing this in mind, the first point I would make is that traditional Advaita initially differentiates between appearance (vyavahAra) and reality (paramArtha), because we start off with the belief that the world and the separate self are real. The first task is therefore to undermine that belief and show us that we are not the body, mind etc. Only after the final stage of dis-identification has been undergone can this differentiation be taken back and can it be admitted (and realized to be true) that the world is in fact not other than who-we-really-are. This I understand to be what you mean by 'nirvANa is saMsAra'.

You then ask whether suffering is necessary or whether there is any point to the alleviation of suffering. The phrasing implies that the full consequences of the above have not been taken on board. To whom or for what could anything be 'necessary'? For whom could anything have a 'point'? Suffering is an intrinsic part of vyavahAra so will (appear to) continue for all of those jIva-s still mired in mAyA. Anything that appears to be done to alleviate this would itself still be a part of the dream and would inevitably only be temporary anyway. The only way out of it is through the realization that it is only an appearance – name and form imposed upon the non-dual reality, which is always perfect and complete and totally unaffected by the seeming change, whether it be deemed (by the jIva) to be good or evil.

Ultimately, nothing in the appearance matters because it is only an appearance. Whilst still (apparently) trapped in the appearance, it matters very much and the way out is through removal of the ignorance. This can only be achieved through knowledge, which can arrive from scriptures or from a guru or preferably both. But nothing can be done (because there is no one to do it) so we rely on the operation of cause and effect. For example, reading this, someone might be caused to read more, track down a teacher etc. The teacher, similarly, teaches because teaching is part of the nature of that body-mind in the (apparent) creation.

Q.32-3 Suffering of an enlightened person

Q: In your review of the book 'A Natural Awakening' (by P. T. Mistlberger) you wrote that: *"Many students of Advaita think that to become enlightened is to attain a permanent state of peace and happiness"*. Is this not so? According to everything I've read it is.

Maybe you were saying that a person with an ego thinks that the ego will become enlightened, etc. Then I would agree. But if you're referring to Self-Realization, then I think I'd have to disagree; enlightenment is a permanent state of peace and happiness, etc.

A: When I say 'I want to be happy or have a peaceful life', I am talking about the (non-existent) person, am I not? There will still be times for the 'enlightened person' when there is physical pain in the body or emotional distress in the mind. The difference now is that it is known that 'who-you-really-are' is not the body or mind and is therefore unaffected by any of these things – satyam, j~nAnam anantam brahma.

Incidentally, it *is* the ego (or, at least, the mind) that becomes enlightened! The Self is always free and unlimited – there is *only* the Self in reality. [See the section on 'Enlightenment' for further elucidation.]

Q: Thanks for responding. I think I understand your view now, but am not sure if I agree with it. On the one hand, there was physical pain for both Osho and Sri Nisargadatta. Later in his life, I think Osho made the statement that *"This body has become a nightmare"*. I can accept that there may be physical pain as long as the body lasts, but I'm not so sure about emotional distress. There has to be an ego for there to be emotional distress.

As regards suffering in general Sri Ramana tells us that, when individuality is lost, suffering will be non-existent. I would categorize both physical pain and especially emotional distress as suffering. Some quotes from discussions with Sri Ramana:

Sri Ramana:

"If one scrutinizes one's own Self, which is bliss, there will be no misery at all in one's life. One suffers because of the idea that the body, which is never oneself, is 'I'; suffering is all due to this delusion".

"When you remain as the Self, as in sleep, the world and its sufferings will not affect you. Therefore look within. See the Self! Then there will be an end of the world and its miseries".

To me these statements and others seem to state very clearly that one who has realized the Self cannot experience suffering, as there is no individual to experience it. So the problem I have with your statement that an enlightened 'person' suffers are thus:

Statements like those of Sri Ramana declare that an enlightened one cannot suffer.

Even if your statement is correct, the residue of human problems would be nothing compared to the peace of the Self experienced at the same time.

Even if your statement is correct, and even if there was acute suffering, the life of the body will be over in a flash, along with all of the suffering. Then one will be abiding as the Self forever in perfect unalloyed bliss.

If you are saying that a person, the small 'I', won't have permanent peace and happiness, then that's true. However, the statement is confusing then because it implies that permanent peace and happiness, etc. aren't attributes of the Self, which they are. And, even if the small 'I' doesn't have peace etc., what does it matter, because the universal 'I', our true nature (which is infinitely greater than the ego) does have peace?

You said that 'who-you-really-are' is unaffected by these things (suffering). Why make the statement at all then that an Advaita student thinks that there is no suffering upon enlightenment, when you admit that it's true by saying that they don't affect your true nature?

A: This is a language problem again – as are many of the confusions in this teaching. I have never used the word 'suffering' with respect to 'enlightened persons' and would agree that this is something from which they do not suffer!

However, I do maintain that their bodies and minds are still subject to physical/emotional pain. Ramana is, I believe, reported as having been moved to tears by external events or the reports of others. (I don't recall details but can probably locate them if you like.) The key difference is that there is no *identification* in the case of the realized man. The pain or emotion is felt but let go with no subsequent attachment, whereas the ordinary 'person' will dwell upon it, recollect it etc. It is not the case that there has to be an ego for there to be emotional distress. Emotion is to the mind as pain is to the body and the realized man still has both body and mind, though he knows that he is neither.

The other frequent point of confusion relates to the word 'happiness'. As used by the 'person', it is invariably in the sense of 'I want to be happy', as opposed to being miserable. In fact, in the phenomenal realm, happiness and misery are the two poles of the emotional state. The word traditionally used in relation to the non-dual Self is Ananda, which is usually translated as 'bliss'. This would seem to be paradoxical in that it implies that, if the realized person is experiencing bliss, he/she cannot simultaneously be feeling misery. The paradox is resolved, however, by understanding it as 'limitless'. This is the word actually used in the phrase '*satyam, j~nAnam anantam brahma*' (from the Taittiriya Upanishad) which I quoted above. According to Shankara, this is 'effectively' a definition of the Self. The point is that the Self is always truth-knowledge without limit, regardless of whether happiness or misery happens to be temporarily dominant in the mind.

In conclusion, therefore, I only use the word 'suffer' when there is identification with the emotions or with physical pain.

Consequently, since there is no identification in the case of the realized person, there can be no suffering. There may still be happiness and misery but it is known that 'I' am not them and they pass much more quickly, leaving no residue.

Q: I can allow the possibility that a realized man may have physical or emotional pain but be dis-identified with it. You say that pain will not be dwelt upon, or brought up again by a sage. However, in the original statement we were discussing you say that an Advaitic student thinks that there will be no worries and fears, implying that there are.

'Worrying' is thinking about problems of the past and projecting them onto the future, which doesn't fit with your statement that a sage won't dwell upon or recollect pain. As to fear, Sri Ramana tells us that one quality of the guru is *"unshakable courage at all times, in all places and circumstances"*. You say that Sri Ramana was known to show emotion based on external events or reports (please provide a credible source for this). I find this hard to believe, considering He knew the world to be an illusion and was always telling others so. Also this is contradictory to a response by Sri Ramana to a question:

Seeker: When we suffer grief and complain and appeal to you by letter or mentally by prayer, are you not moved to feel what a pity it is that your child suffers like this?

Bhagavan: If one felt like that one would not be a j~nAnI.

In your second paragraph you wrote *"The paradox is resolved, however, by understanding it as 'limitless.'"* Are you referring here to the Self, Bliss, or both. I did a search for satyam j~nAnam anantam brahma, and found one translation as Truth, Knowledge, and Infinity. Is this the same as sat-chit-Ananda, different, or at odds with it?

Also, I'm still wondering why you made a point of saying that many students of Advaita think that pain, etc. are not part of the enlightened 'state' when it doesn't seem like a big deal even if they are, as the Self isn't affected by it and these problems will end with the death of the body. My apologies if it seems like I'm debating just for the sake of debate; I'm just trying to clear confusion and gain a greater understanding.

A: We are still arguing about the meaning of words here and how you choose to use them. The point is that, in the body-mind, cause-effect actions take place just the same for the 'realized' as for the 'unrealized'. The difference is that, in the case of the 'realized', there is no identification and thus no claim that 'I am happy' or 'I am miserable'.

I have chosen (arbitrarily, perhaps) to define 'suffering' as being an identification so that this means the realized man cannot suffer. I have chosen, again arbitrarily, to define 'misery' as being an automatic activity of mind so that this means everyone is subject to it, realized or not.

Since you have been confused or even misled by this use of the words, I am willing to concede that perhaps it would be better to make 'misery' an identification word, too. I have no problem with this. With regard to the words 'worry' and 'fear', these were used without sufficient thought. I do agree with what you say – both are 'projecting' present emotions into the future and imagining the outcome. It is unlikely that one who knows that 'everything is Brahman' would do this. (I use the word 'unlikely' deliberately. I would still say that it is possible to know the truth and yet sometimes behave as though one didn't. This is determined by the extent to which one's mind was 'prepared' prior to enlightenment. See sections on 'Preparation/Practice' and 'Enlightened Man'.)

Nevertheless, the main argument still stands. Many seekers do labor under the misapprehension that enlightenment is all about 'me' attaining eternal happiness, never being sad henceforth etc. and of course this is not true. Also many teachers do cater for this type of seeker, teaching psychology rather than Advaita and judging success by the extent to which the seekers feel better. As you rightly say, the physical and mental pain is not a 'big deal' afterwards anyway but there isn't going to be an 'afterwards' for seekers who still have this attitude.

Regarding a quote of Ramana illustrating emotional or physical pain, I am sure there are several but quotations on any topic are not easy to locate because of the lack of indexes in most books. Here is one that I did manage to find:

"Bhagavan related how Echamma, after she lost her own daughter, brought up her brother's daughter, this Chellammal, and added, 'Chellammal used often to go to me as a school girl. Afterwards too, she always thought of me. In every letter of hers, she would refer to me both in the beginning and the end. She died soon after she gave birth to Ramanan, the boy who is now in Bombay. They brought the boy here, (it was soon after we came here and we had only a small thatched room in which the tomb was located and I was also staying). On seeing the babe, I could not help thinking of its mother and I wept for her.' (Bhagavan was moved even now after several years when recounting the event to me)". (From Day By Day with Bhagavan, 2002 p. 315)

When I said "The paradox is resolved, however, by understanding it as 'limitless.'", I was referring to the Sanskrit word 'Ananda'. The word 'anantam' means 'without limit'. The term sat-chit-Ananda is the one most often encountered in 'descriptions' of Brahman and 'Ananda' does mean 'happiness'. This direct translation leads to confusion, however, as we have discussed, so I was pointing you instead to the 'definition' in the Taittiriya Upanishad, which is also favored by Shankara. This does not have the same propensity for confusion.

Q.94 Can some people not be sufficiently detached?

Q: I am coming to believe that some people's 'innate nature', for lack of a more precise term, simply precludes them from ever truly achieving the detachment so essential to Advaita. (And I think this applies to me!) While they may totally understand Advaita intellectually, it can never be realized in a 'total' sense due to this inability to achieve the necessary detachment. Is this true?

A: 'No' is the short answer. Suppose that I ask you to close your eyes and then hold an object in front of your face. When I ask you to open your eyes, you will see the object and (assuming it is a familiar one) you will have no choice but to recognize it. It is similar with Self-knowledge. You already are Brahman. It is just that this obvious truth is covered over by ignorance. If I present you with the salient pieces of Self-knowledge that counter those mistaken views, you have no choice but to recognize them as true.

Of course it is also the case that you must be able (which also implies 'willing') to pay attention and listen to all of the relevant arguments. And, in order to do that, you must have a degree of mind and sense control etc. An aspect of that *is* dispassion/ detachment (vairAgya). And you must *want* to! (These pre-requisites are discussed in the section on 'Preparation'.)

People's nature may predispose them to be particularly interested in this or that in the world and this may make them unwilling to look into Advaita. One of the key requirements is mumukShutva – the desire for enlightenment – and if someone does not have this, they are most unlikely to expose themselves to the teaching. This may have the same effect as your theory but the essence is quite different.

Q: On the one hand, I know that what Advaita says is true but, on the other I still suffer emotional upheavals of fear and anger at the destruction and suffering that I see all over the world, and frequently feel helplessness and despair. Although I am still aware of the truth, it seems at such times to be reduced to the level of simply concepts or beliefs. It seems that Truth has no Power. I still *know* I am Brahman, the world is in me, and that all of the destruction and extinctions and global warming etc. are 'the dream of appearance' only, but I cannot waken from it.

It seems that some people are simply not suited to Advaita. Maybe it will take many life times before I have a full realization. Despite all my longing for and understanding of Truth, I seem to be just as mired in the nightmare in those bad periods, as if I had never heard or read about the Truth.

A: I do understand what you are saying and can sympathize.

I think the main point to note is that enlightenment does not bring the appearance to an end. Nor does it necessarily signify an end to personal unhappiness or even despair. If the mind was insufficiently prepared prior to enlightenment, then you will not automatically gain peace of mind – this will only come gradually as a result of a deepening understanding. And, of course, the body-mind will continue until its natural death, along with any pleasures and pains that accompany this. Knowing the truth, as you do, all that you need to do when the despair comes is remember that these apparent lapses will happen from time to time but that they always pass.

As regards being affected by suffering, the Buddhist story of the woman who has just lost her child is a telling one. She is told by the Buddha that if she finds a house in the village which has not suffered the loss of a loved one, then he will bring the child back to life. She goes about the village, knocking on all the doors but of course is unable to find anywhere unaffected. Eventually, she realizes that suffering is intrinsic to life as long as we seek happiness outside of ourselves.

Enlightenment includes the knowledge that you are not in the world; the world is an appearance within you, along with all its excitement and suffering. Who-you-really-are is totally unaffected by it, as in the cinema screen metaphor. Again, as with the cinema, there is the danger of becoming so involved with the story and the skilful acting that we take it as real and end up frightened or tearful ourselves.

The key practice in traditional Advaita is shravaNa, manana and nididhyAsana. Once you have heard and understood all of the teaching, meditation on those truths will eventually bring the sought-for peace of mind.

Q.98 'Giving up on the relative'

Q: I wrote to you over a year ago about seeing something new in my life. You stated that *"Advaita is for those who have seen and done it all and have found there is nothing that works"* (paraphrased) but I didn't listen and pursued it anyway. There was much misery witnessed daily and I identified with all of the misery and ideas about who I am. I started to question everything via the books of an Advaita teacher. I read everything from his basic books to his advanced books but too quickly. I even started studying Maharaj consciousness and the Absolute.

I suffer from alcoholism, PTSD, depression etc. – I feel like I have gone really crazy and can't get out of it. The teacher advised that I should not yet attempt to 'abide as the Absolute' but should get all the above issues resolved first, and that is happening. My question is: what should I do about 'giving up on everything that is in the relative'? How do I get out of this hole which some state as being sane and others think is insane?

A: Did you read 'How to Meet Yourself' as I suggested? This is the book that looks at the traditional views of meaning, purpose and happiness and provides a gentle introduction to Advaita.

The point is that life is all about misery and happiness (not always in equal proportions!) and nothing you can do will alter that. But who-you-really-are is not the body-mind that is living this life. In fact, this life, this world and universe, time and space are all no more than names and forms of the non-dual reality that you already are. As long as you believe yourself to be the very limited body-mind, you will continue effectively to be bound by all of these things about which you complain.

You cannot really decide to 'give up on the relative'. What happens is that, as understanding of the truth grows, these things naturally assume less importance. It is like the child growing up and losing interest in toys. It may be that some discipline will help steady the mind and make it easier to assimilate this knowledge. (Certainly, it would not be possible to appreciate it if, for example, you were drunk all the time!) Ultimately, the only solution is Self-knowledge.

Practices may prepare the mind for this but what is eventually needed is a reliable source of this knowledge and for that you really need a teacher who has it and is able to convey it. If you firmly believe that you have found such a teacher then you will be able to listen to what he says and follow his guidance. (Presumably I will have heard of him if he has written books. The fact that you are writing to me to ask about it implies that you are unsure whether to have faith in his teaching.)

The bottom line is that you are not in a hole, neither sane nor insane. All of these are just mistaken ideas because you do not yet know who-you-really-are.

Q.133 An alcoholic looking for happiness

Q: I'm going to be 50 years old very soon and have done everything and can't find a true, lasting solution. I feel that the more I've done and the more I've read, the more I get confused. I feel so much guilt in my life about so many things, so many problems with fear and depression. I just can't seem to be able to be consistent and happy. I'm an alcoholic and have been sober for nearly three years now, and still find myself unable to feel happiness. Is there a little hope that maybe I might be able to live in this world without it affecting me, regardless of the insanity and contradictions?

So I come to you asking for a possible way of just being happy, regardless of all the problems in the world and all the problems of my physical, mental and spiritual life. Can you suggest something? I'm in therapy; I'm in and out of Alcoholics Anonymous and have worked the 12 steps strenuously, still not getting what they promised me. And if I wasn't feeling okay, all these alcoholics would tell me that I'm not putting my trust in God. It seems that all of these alcoholics eventually come together to worship this punishing God, that I don't even want to know. For so long I believed that I should suffer because these so called 'spiritual beings' were more connected than I was, so that they knew better than me. Help, please!

A: If you are looking for personal happiness or an end to personal unhappiness, then Advaita is not the answer. Advaita is about the realization that there is no person, that who-you-really-are is already limitless, full and complete. One comes to Advaita when it has been accepted that lasting happiness is never going to be found in people or things (including alcohol!). How can anything that is transient and ever-changing bring lasting happiness?

If your nature is not amenable to belief in an external god that can be trusted and worshipped (as is my own), then it is pointless associating with any teaching that insists that this is necessary. My suggestion would be that you accept once and for all that this world and this life will never provide true happiness for anyone (not just you). This does not mean that you reject the world but that you determine to look elsewhere, namely within rather than outside for any 'truth'. If you can genuinely do this and resolve totally to pursue the truth without reservation, then you have a purpose that can overcome any obstacle. All that you then need to do is commit to some clear path to help you pursue that end.

Q.145 Do the enlightened suffer pain?

Q: I am not clear on the teaching of Neo-Advaitins, which seems to be echoed in some more traditional schools of thought, that 'there is no one'. No individual is actually real. The more traditional paths teach that, but do stress practice and a progressive path to realizing what one already is. This is not so easy as thinking 'There is no me', 'I am That'.

But the traditional paths (and I have read your book 'Back to the Truth') do seem to state that one's experience of being an individual, separate self is the result of ignorance. And once this ignorance is dispelled, one's suffering ends because it is seen that 'there is no one who is suffering'.

Pure ignorance does not seem to be something that could cause sensations of body and mind. Especially it seems that intense sensation could not be caused by simply harboring erroneous ideas. Take pain, for example. How could the intense, excruciating agony of being burned by fire be 'caused' by simply holding erroneous views that you are an individual self? Would not even a fully realized person experience excruciating pain, if burned by fire?

A: I have to say that your concern is one that used to worry me, too. I think that the way to look at it is firstly to differentiate between pain and suffering and secondly to ask what is meant when we refer to 'I'.

As far as the unenlightened are concerned, 'I' is the body-mind. This means that, when there is a pain, I firmly believe that 'I' have the pain and start worrying: how serious is it? How long will it last? Will it get worse, and so on? Instead of simply acknowledging that it is a symptom of some malfunction in the body and doing whatever is necessary to get it fixed, we magnify it into something much more than it really is and give it a disproportionate amount of attention. In other words, we 'suffer' in addition to having the pain.

I always remember an occasion when I was in a cross-country race in my early teens. I had run quite well and, in the last couple of hundred yards even sprinted to overtake another runner. It was not until sometime after I had finished the race that I noticed the back of my sock covered in blood from a burst blister, which only then began to be very painful. In other words, it was only when I gave it my attention that it became a problem.

So, to answer your question, of course the enlightened still have pains, possibly very severe ones such as Nisargadatta with his throat cancer. But knowing completely and irrevocably that they are not the body, they know that 'I' do not have the pain and that makes a world of difference. There is no concomitant suffering.

This is the theory anyway. My knowledge of history is atrocious but I am sure there are instances in all religions of people being tortured and/or killed because of their beliefs, yet not recanting and dying (to be sainted or whatever in later years). I don't think anyone claims that they did not feel the pain, just that their beliefs were able to sustain them. In the case of true enlightenment, it is no longer simply 'belief' but knowledge. Since the perception of pain is in the mind, it is genuinely the case that the enlightened can say that the pain is simply another mithyA form of that non-dual reality that I am.

The idea of non-duality will not help in the slightest. Moreover, for the unenlightened person in a torture situation, there will be heightened attention to the identification of 'I am the body' and this will make the feelings of pain even worse and there will be no possibility of remembering the beliefs of non-duality. But the enlightened person does not have mere ideas or even beliefs. Such a person has certain, direct knowledge of the fact that 'I am not the body', 'I cannot be touched by anything', 'everything is appearance only, name and form of my Self' etc. The pain is still observed, naturally, but is known not to be happening to 'me' but to the body-mind.

The bottom-line is that non-duality will not help an awful lot as far as experiencing the pain is concerned (although the relative lack of concern about it by the enlightened person may well ameliorate it) but then so what? You could just as well have said that 'despite non-duality, I will still die.' This is also untrue. Who-you-really-are was never born so cannot die. But the body will still grow old and die. Non-duality cannot stop any of those things happening that are part of the appearance of duality. The show must go on!

Q.173 How does one cope with anger?

Q: I seem to be full of anger and hate (at times). I am frustrated and do not want to be. Sometimes I am afraid that this may even lead to physical confrontations. It seems to disappear for several months and then, the next thing I know, I am swept away it seems and arguing with people over nonsense, screaming and honking my horn in traffic. I think: 'how did I get here again?' Most times

I am very well liked and helpful. Any help would be extremely appreciated?

A: I am sure what you say will be recognized by many, though some may not be honest enough to admit it. It really comes back to the, now quite numerous, questions that touch on the subject of j~nAna and j~nAna phalam – enlightenment and the 'fruits of enlightenment' such as peace of mind, fearlessness and, in your case, tranquility, not being angered or frustrated by events in the seeming world.

According to traditional Advaita, your nature (in the sense of personality) is determined by past karma. This functions as cause and effect so situations will occur and you will tend to act according to that karma. There are really only two practices that you can follow to ameliorate these effects. The first is karma yoga and the second is meditation and they do go together. You will experience a still and clear mind more frequently and for longer periods if you practice meditation regularly. And, with a still mind, it is much more likely that you will be alert in the present moment so that you can you can respond to events appropriately, as they arise, rather than reacting to them in an habitual manner.

The thing about meditation is that you really need a mentor for the first six months at least who can comment on your experiences and provide reassurance/explanation etc. so, although the essential practice can be explained very easily, it is not recommended that you simply pick up a book and follow written instructions. If you practice assiduously, you will benefit but it *does* require commitment – we are talking about two half-hour sessions per day religiously for years. This actually turns out not to be a problem once you get into it but it certainly seems so at the outset!

Q.377 Ability of Advaita to relieve suffering

Q: I am a Theravada Buddhist considering changing my views and practice to Advaita Vedanta. I still have many reservations, and would appreciate your thoughts:

It seems to me that Advaita Vedanta has the wrong question and goal. The teaching aims at Self-knowledge, which does not necessarily equate to the ending of suffering (which, as a Buddhist, is top on my list! – a very personal agenda indeed). If happiness is the aim of Advaita Vedanta, and not Knowledge, then shouldn't we be asking: "What is suffering/happiness? What is its cause? What is its cessation? What causes its cessation?" instead of "Who am I?".

Does the Knowledge of the Self eradicate the arising of suffering? Doesn't the arising of suffering indicate that the conviction/knowledge of the Self is not yet firmly established in the mind of the seeker? And what I mean by suffering is any mental affliction, pain, or anguish arising.

I read very conflicting statements, sometimes by the same people in the same book, about this. To me, Self-knowledge just sounds like a belief, but if there continues to be suffering, then it just sounds like a bit of a cop-out to say, "Yea, there is suffering, but it's not me, I am desireless". If that statement were true, what would cause suffering to arise in the first-place?

On the other hand, so much in the Advaita Vedanta tradition and the Vedas and Upanishads makes so much sense, is so beautiful, intricate, and rigorous, that I just keep thinking to myself: "There has to be a reason the rishis chose to focus on Self-knowledge, because they (and countless yogis and seekers following them) were ultimately seeking liberation".

A: As you obviously know, the 'bottom line' of Advaita is that there is only Brahman or Consciousness if you prefer. And who-you-really-are is therefore That. It is the person (who can be regarded as '*reflected* Consciousness') who realizes this. Once it is realized, it does not mean an end of pain and empirical unhappiness. But it is now known that these things do not happen *to* you; rather they happen *in* you, as part of the endless play within apparent creation. You now know that *you* are not affected by them, whatever happens. 'Suffering' occurs because you believe it is happening to you; that who-you-really-are is somehow being diminished by the events. And this, of course, is not true. If interpreted correctly, it is possible to say that suffering *does* end.

Similarly, desires do not end on enlightenment. These result from the particular nature of the person. Prior to enlightenment, the belief is that my happiness is dependent upon those desires being satisfied. After enlightenment, it is known that I am already perfect and complete and that the outcome of any desire has only limited, temporal, empirical value – and this does not really matter at all because all this is mithyA.

Ignorance

Q.249 Ignorance and existence

Q: Two questions:

1. Who is ignorant? It would be begging the question to claim that the ignorance is illusion, or the experiencer of that ignorance doesn't exist, for then one could ask who, or what, is experiencing an illusionary ignorance, and in what sense can there be an experience of illusion without an experiencer? If it is the 'one Self' that assumes the illusion, then it posits a dualism within that Self; a 'part' that is aware and a 'part' that is not yet aware that it is aware, or some other clumsy statement. With this approach, we've introduced both a dualism of being and of time.

2. It seems to me that there is a dualism at the basis of the distinction that Brahman, the One, is 'real', and the other stuff around isn't, or doesn't exist. It would seem to me that the distinction 'exists, or not', or 'real or not', is misleading here. The table is real; it exists, as does the ego. A table may be a world of pulsating energy with more space than 'material', if looked at from a different perspective, but that doesn't make its existence as a table less valid. It may be other than what we perceive it to be, but it exists, just as a whirlpool exists even though the water is not so much spinning around as flowing through. It may not

exist as an independent structure; it perhaps exists as a temporary construction, a form of a more basic 'energy' that stands out temporarily from its surroundings by an act of interpretation and some other process of distinction – but it still exists.

I understand that 'emptiness' does not mean not real or non-existent, but empty of the illusion of independence, just as Brahman isn't real if it is seen as an independent reified being distinct from non-Brahman stuff. Please correct me where you feel I have gone awry in this thinking.

These two questions are, of course, quite connected. I am just beginning to read your books, and besides a response from you, I would appreciate if you can refer me to writings of yours or others that deal with this topic of the subject of the illusion.

A: Your questions are really going right to the heart of the teaching of Advaita and if I tried to answer them fully (as indeed they deserve), I would end up writing another book. They are certainly answered fairly comprehensively in the second edition of 'Book of One'. I don't think they were satisfactorily covered in the first edition, unfortunately – probably because I didn't really understand the teaching completely myself at that time. If you have 'Back to the Truth', I think that may also clear up the issue – but you won't read that overnight! (Also, 'Back to the Truth' is made up of lots of material from many other teachers and writers, so there is a lack of consistency of style etc. The second edition of 'Book of One' is a more mature presentation of my own understanding so I would recommend that in the first instance.)

The two topics that you really need to understand first are the two-level teaching of Advaita – paramArtha and vyavahAra – and the concept of mithyA. There are lots of essays and definitions of terms at the website which address these, as well as many of the other questions in this book.

Very briefly, the person does exist at the empirical level (vyavahAra). And it is the mind of the person that is ignorant. At this level, the ignorance is just as real as the person, and the experience of duality is equally real. From the standpoint of absolute reality (paramArtha), where of course 'we' can't stand, there is no person, no ignorance and no duality. If one attempts to explain this in a few sentences, it is very likely to sound clumsy and unconvincing. If it is explained gradually, by a qualified teacher who understands and can interpret the scriptures, the hearer is left with no doubt at all that this is how it is. (But if you have no prior understanding of Advaita at all, this could take quite a long time!)

Regarding the question of the 'reality' or 'existence' of the table, I suggest that you read the story I wrote (http://www.Advaita.org.uk/discourses/definitions/Advaita.htm). When you say that the table 'exists', there is no doubt that there is something that has existence. That 'something' is Brahman. Brahman is the essential reality of all apparently separately existing things. There is only Brahman. The 'table' is simply name and form of that.

For the reader of this book, other sections such as those on 'Nature of Self' and 'Reality' will provide more detailed answers to these questions. In particular, look in the index for references to 'mithyA'. (Unfortunately the questioner at the time did not have the benefit of these references!)

States of consciousness

[In this section, as well as other parts of the book, please differentiate 'Consciousness', with a capital 'C' from 'consciousness'; and 'Self', with a capital 'S', from 'self'. The words with capital letters refer to Brahman/Atman and with lower case to the individual person. The scientist or materialist does not believe in Brahman, so he will never talk about Consciousness with a capital 'C'! (Accordingly, at the beginning of sentences, the reader will have to exercise discrimination or viveka!) For example, humans exhibit consciousness only by virtue of Consciousness.]

Most people will say that there are three states of consciousness: waking, dream and deep-sleep. Occasionally, you will find someone who argues for other states such as hypnotized, anaesthetized, comatose or just plain dead. I have written an article 'States of Consciousness – 2, 3, 4 and 1/2?' (http://www.Advaita-vision.org/states-of-consciousness-2-3-4-and-1-2/), to entertain such people! It does not really matter how many you decide on, the underlying reality of all of them is the same, called turIya in Advaita. (The word 'turIya' is used when speaking about states of consciousness. It is the reality 'behind' all states. It is, of course, the same as Consciousness or Brahman. The various words used for the non-dual reality relate to the context and must not be thought to be indicating that the reality is *not* non-dual!)

Q.90 samAdhi

Q: What is the difference between samAdhi and the deep-sleep state?

A: Both samAdhi and suShupti are states of consciousness – they have a beginning and an end in time – and they are both characterized by absence of duality (note that I am talking about nirvikalpa samAdhi her, not savikalpa). This being the case, one could say that it does not make any sense to differentiate between them – non-dual is non-dual! (Swami Dayananda did make a joking differentiation when he said that samAdhi was sitting up, while deep-sleep was lying down!)

One might be tempted to say that there *must* be a difference – in deep-sleep, one is aware of nothing while, in samAdhi, one is aware of one's own awareness/existence. But, as has been pointed out, in order to know that one was 'aware of nothing' in deep-sleep, one must have been aware that one was aware of nothing! So the two 'states' are not dissimilar.

More importantly, however, both are also characterized by a return to the normal waking state in which there is still ignorance of the non-dual reality. Both are experiences only, with a beginning and an end in time.

samAdhi does not actually have any relevance in traditional Advaita – the word does not even occur in any of the major

Upanishads. It is a practice in the Yoga philosophy, although it has been taken up as significant by many more recent proponents (especially in the Ramakrishna tradition). The word does not even occur as such in the major Upanishads. You might want to read Michael Comans' essay (http://ccbs.ntu.edu.tw/FULLTEXT/JR-PHIL/comans.htm).

According to traditional Advaita, our problem is one of Self-ignorance and this can only be remedied by Self-knowledge. No experience can bring this about.

Q.232 Consciousness, Brahman and samAdhi

Q: I am finding it difficult logically to counter the claim by modern psychologists that consciousness/awareness arises from the body. The basic issue for me is that the usual Advaita arguments on the subject don't consider the value of third party observation. For example, regarding the argument that, since the body 'disappears' in deep-sleep, you can't be your body, one could easily say that it didn't really disappear, since a third party could see you the whole time and wake you up at any moment. It was merely that your body has a process by which, during deep-sleep, thoughts dreams, and sensory perception as we usually understand them were shut down. Carrying the idea further one could say that the body is actually a constant between waking, dreaming, and deep-sleep, as evidenced by the fact that a third party can verify its presence throughout the day.

It is not that I totally disagree that 'I' am consciousness; it is that I'm not seeing a compelling case for why this 'I' is not dependent on the body (i.e. brain) or does not arise from it. The implication is that, if the body were to die, my consciousness/awareness would also cease. Have you read anything (from Advaitin authors) that directly counters the assertion I've outlined above?

A: This is a very deep question and not one that can be answered satisfactorily in a few sentences. I am not aware of any books that specifically address your question. The one I know of which covers all of the topics in this general area is D. B. Gangolli's 'The Magic Jewel of Intuition' but your chances of obtaining a copy are virtually zero. I had great difficulty a few years back – there were only 1000 copies published in 1986. But it is in any case not very easy to read because the author did not have a very great command of the English language and some of the sentence constructions are terribly convoluted. Reading it caused me to write to him to ask a question that was not too dissimilar from your own. Unfortunately, he has died so I never received an answer! [Note that, since this answer, the book has now been made available electronically. The PDF file may be downloaded (http://www.adhyatmaprakasha.org/Volumes/PDF/english/032/index.pdf).]

I have since written a book which is a presentation of the Mandukya Upanishad and Gaudapada's commentary on that. This deals with states of consciousness and proves, in a totally reasonable way, that who-I-really-am is the non-dual turIya and that the waker, dreamer and deep-sleeper are simply that same turIya 'confused' by ignorance and error. So this may well clear up your concerns ('A-U-M: Awakening to Reality').

It should help you to think of the problem in terms of subject and object. The reason that science can never provide any ultimate answer is that, by definition, it is always a subject trying to find out about an object. Whatever I investigate is always an object, with 'I' as the subject. I cannot make 'I' the object because that would necessitate another 'I' to do the investigation.

Your problem of 'third party' is, to some extent, an illusory one. If 'I' am conducting the investigation and trying to understand the nature of the objective universe, that universe has to include everything – all other persons and even 'my own' body and mind. I must certainly take into account the observations of 'others' and, indeed, this is how all teaching takes place, including Advaita. But, when it comes down to it, the only reality of which I can be absolutely certain is 'I am'.

Another very helpful way to approach the subject is from

the concept of mithyA (http://www.Advaita.org.uk/discourses/definitions/Advaita.htm). This effectively explains the concept (and it appears as the explanation of 'mithyA' in 'Advaita Made Easy'). Once you appreciate that the entire world is mithyA, and that it is appearing to you, the observer, who are the only reality, you are almost there.

The point about deep-sleep is that, in it, you are ignorant of the nature of reality but you do not, as a result of this, erroneously project a separate universe (as happens in waking and dream). Nevertheless, you are still present as consciousness. When you wake up, you are able to say that, 'during the deep-sleep, I was not aware of anything'. How could you say this if there was no conscious entity to know this? Some people have a problem with this explanation (I know that I did!). But consider: if I ask you 'did you know anything?', you will answer 'No'. If I now ask you: 'How do you know that you did not know anything?', you can say 'I know' with absolute certainty.

As regards dying, of course you can always argue that anything that anyone says about this is being said by someone who has not died! Whilst you still believe it to be a possibility that the world has a reality separate from you, the turIya consciousness, then the argument about the world being absent during deep-sleep will not be of any help. Once you understand that this consciousness is the only reality, however, then you will know that nothing actually happens upon the death of the body. It is a mere rearrangement of molecules; new names and forms for the same 'stuff', which remains as the non-dual Brahman, totally unaffected by any of the apparent changes. So you can take the view that 'death' can, at worst, be no different from a prolonged deep-sleep. At best, of course, it can be like deep-sleep minus the ignorance, if you have realized the truth prior to death!

Q: How much intellectual capacity is required for enlightenment? Based on my reading of 'traditional' sources I believe the answer is that one must actually be fairly bright to have a shot at samAdhi.

Several pieces of evidence come to mind:

Knowledge is required to remove ignorance: Advaita concepts can be complex and therefore gaining this knowledge would require a fair amount of intellectual capability.

The Gita implies that those with sattva tend to be bright, while those filled with tamas are dull.

Many of those who are well respected in the tradition seem fairly bright. Clear examples include Swami Dayananda, Swami Rama Tirtha, A. Parthasarathy, Shankaracharya, etc. Even those without formal education such as Ramakrishna Paramahamsa possessed sharp critical thinking abilities.

The reason I ask is because I have not read any text that calls out this need for intellectual capacity in any explicit way. In addition, it also implies that not everyone has the ability to reach samAdhi in this lifetime even if they devote themselves as needed to sAdhana. What do you think?

A: The first point about your question is that samAdhi has nothing to do with enlightenment. samAdhi is an experience, with a beginning and an end in time, however blissful. Enlightenment is about Self-knowledge. But, no, it is not intellectual. It is true that a tAmasika mind will not even think about enlightenment, let alone have the control and discrimination to be able to seek it. So, for most people, some degree of mental preparation is needed. But we already are Brahman, so when it comes down to it, there is no need to do any thinking to see this. It is rather an intuitive leap that is made when a teacher gives us the right pointers.

Here is what Swami Dayananda says about it:

"Seeing yourself is something like seeing me. When you see me, it is not inferential, it is not intellectual – it is direct perception. Similarly, you exist – you are there to be seen – and the existing 'you' has its own experiences. The teacher analyzes these experiences, your experiences. He does not talk about some strange personal experience. When you see what is being taught and discover it to be true, there is nothing intellectual or perceptual. It is self-recognition, born out of the teaching. It is direct

knowledge. It is direct, just like the direct knowledge you have when you open your eyes and see me. It is a conditioning to think that knowledge of the Self is intellectual. We should knock off that conditioning. There is no intellectual knowledge about Atma". [Dialogues with Swami Dayananda, Sri Gangadhareswar Trust, 1988. No ISBN.]

If you read the explanation of bhAga tyAga lakShaNa in Q.345, you will see what I mean.

Q.144 On communication with the dead

Q: I understand that this world is simply an illusion, played out by our minds. In the end, once one has become fully aware of Self, then the mind can cease to exist and the Self is One with Reality (much like the ocean-wave metaphor). I have read on your site and others that when it comes down to it, nothing really matters. However, I have researched quite a bit on phenomena such as Near-Death experiences, Out-of-Body experiences, medium-ship, etc. Dr. Sam Parnia ('What Happens When We Die?: A Groundbreaking Study into the Nature of Life and Death') suggests that in a NDE, we actually are seeing the afterlife. So, to this end, the Self is actually still thinking, observing, realizing, even during clinical death (brain and heart death). How can the teachings of Advaita explain such a phenomenon? There have been numerous studies conducted over the years which imply a complete transcendence of spirit/After-Life; e.g. dreams of deceased loved ones, offering information not presently known to the experiencer.

I have personally had a dream of my deceased Father, but it was not like a 'normal' dream. I hugged him, after brief conversation, but it was the most joyous experience I have ever known. I woke up with a feeling I had never experienced before – it was real. I was so excited I called my family, to inform them of this great experience. One could say this was my mind, coping with a great loss. However, why has my mind not had such dreams in the past? There are many reports of similar dreams, but the dreamer explains their loved one carried a very unique, provable message;

one that could not possibly have been known to either the deceased (because they're dead) or the dreamer (because they didn't know the information).

It is the understanding of teachers such as Dr. R Craig Hogan, Dr. Peter Fenwick, etc., that our Mind (which is Spirit) is simply having a physical experience in a virtual reality world, played out by our Brain-Mind system. The importance of NOW is stressed, because this life, this physical body, is simply education for our soul. As we live, we learn. As we learn, our Soul develops and matures. In the afterlife, there are infinite planes of growth, of which we 'ladder' through and progress.

So, as I am learning of the teachings of Non-Duality, you can see where I come to a crossroads. It is difficult for me to understand that the ultimate goal is not to experience our earthly lives, but to let go and know Self. Isn't the purpose of our earthly existence to further develop Self? And is Self not simply our consciousness without the physical body? If so, it would make sense to me that Self actually carries on after death, in a very similar state. However, ego would no longer be a part of it, being attached to our physical realm. So then Self would be our Mind, without ego, which would be comprised only of happiness, peace, brotherhood, and the like.

A: First of all, I'm not sure what you mean by 'illusion' when you say that: "this world is simply an illusion". The world has the status of 'relative reality' – it is real for the jIva or one who believes himself to be a person. It is called vyavahAra, as distinct from the illusory status of dream, called pratibhAsa, or the absolute non-dual reality of paramArtha. An even better word to use to describe it is 'mithyA' – that which is neither totally real nor totally unreal. All these terms are explained in detail at the website and in other questions in this book. Certainly, when the mind realizes the true nature of the Self, the mind does not disappear. (Nor does the Self become one with reality – it already is 'one with reality' since That is all that there ever was, is or will be.) [Incidentally, while editing the original question from quite a few years ago,

I checked out the references. I also noted an interview with Dr. Parnia (https://skeptiko.com/sam-parnia-claims-near-death-experience-probably-an-illusion/) in which he confirms that near-death experiences (NDEs) are probably an illusion.]

Near-death-experiences have no relevance whatsoever to Advaita and studying them will not help you to realize the truth in the slightest. Who-you-really-are was never born and will never die so that 'near-death' has no meaning. Secondly, there is no value in seeking experiences of any kind. You already have the experience of being your true Self; you already have the experience of Advaita or non-duality – in deep-sleep. No further experience will bring you to the realization of your true nature. The reason you do not appreciate this is that you have Self-ignorance and the only remedy for this is Self-knowledge. Knowledge of anything in the vyAvahArika realm (or the prAtibhAsika!) will not bring about Self-knowledge.

Having said that, if you really want to pursue the topic, I strongly suggest that you read a more sober view such as that by Susan Blackmore. The book: 'Beyond the Body: an investigation of out-of-the-body experiences', Academy Chicago Publishers, 1992, ISBN:0897333446, presents an extremely reasonable, researched, objective view of the whole topic and reaches conclusions which provide satisfactory explanations without any of the New Age mysticism. All remains firmly in the realm of vyavahAra and nothing conflicts in the slightest with the tenets of Advaita.

Even if the 'after-death' experiences, heaven, hell or whatever you like were empirically 'real', this reality would still be relative and would not cause any problems for Advaita. The Upanishads themselves speak of such 'realms' of existence, gods and demons etc. Used as teaching strategies, these may be perfectly valid if they bring about clarification in the minds of the seeker.

One other point of misunderstanding – you say: "the Self is actually still thinking, observing, realizing, even during clinical death (brain and heart death)". The Self never does any of these things, even when the body is alive. It is the mind that thinks etc.; the Self does nothing. It is because of the Self that the mind is able to think but this is a crucial distinction.

You also ask: "Isn't the purpose of our earthly existence to further develop Self? And is Self not simply our consciousness without the physical body?"

Here, you are mixing up 'self' (body-mind-ego) and 'Self' (Consciousness/Brahman). The Self is already whole, perfect and complete. It is non-dual. How could it be 'developed' or 'improved upon'? The self with a small 's' is mithyA. Within the empirical world, you the person can make your body fitter or study new subjects at college, thereby 'improving' your self.

In fact, Self is everything – there is nothing that is not Self because Self is all there is. So the physical body, too, is Consciousness. And not 'our consciousness' – the sense of ownership only results from identification with this particular mind and body.

Finally, all dreams are nothing but the mind of the dreamer. Irrespective of the seeming reality, vivid, larger than life, 'things which I could not possibly have known' or whatever: it is all a creation of the mind.

Hope this all provides an answer to your questions (even if they are not the ones you wanted!).

Q.148 Why do people have near-death experiences?

Q: If we don't exist, why do people have near death experiences of heaven/hell, and some have life reviews?

Is it your positive view that there is no judgment or punishment when we die?

A: Whatever a person's experience might be, this has nothing to do with reality. You can choose whatever 'explanations' you like to rationalize the world appearance – creation, gods, heaven, hell etc. – but the reality is that no one is ever born, no one dies, there is no creation. It is all an appearance whose essence is the non-dual reality. Yes there is a cause-effect relationship within the relative reality of the world and judgment and punishment fall within this. It is all effectively real while you believe it to be real. What you must do to realize its lack of absolute reality is to gain Self-knowledge.

Q: So, if we don't exist, then that means that I won't see any of my deceased relatives or even my deceased dog? But will my consciousness still be aware?

A: You do exist! (You are existence.) We do not exist *as persons*. Bodies and minds are mithyA. Who-you-really-are is the same non-dual reality as who-your-relatives-really-are, is the same as who-your-deceased-dog really is. There are not two in reality. As regards consciousness, you as a person are aware because of the non-dual reality, Brahman. You are aware of 'things' as separate entities because of Self-ignorance. When you have Self-knowledge, you still perceive 'things' through your senses and mind but now know that they are not separate. It is not really meaningful to ask 'what will it be like to simply be Brahman without a body and mind' because this is now beyond the realm of words or thought.

Q.254 Yet more on near-death experiences

Q: I've studied Advaita for years but I can't understand why the philosophy takes the stance it does on life after death. Everything else makes sense except for the fact that it says that Consciousness needs a body to exist. If all you know for sure is that you are, and that you exist as awareness, how then can you infer from that that you don't continue to be aware after the death of the body or that you don't leak into some higher dimension or more subtle plane where you continue to exist as an individual?

I have seen the other questions that you have answered concerning life after death experiences, but the reference to a book by Susan Blackmore, written in 1993, as your evidence that Consciousness as an individual doesn't survive death, seems kind of weak to me, especially with all the recent cases of people being monitored and verifiably having no chemical or electrical activity in their brain and still having incredible tales of a life after death not dissimilar from all the others.

I've really liked Advaita for a while but this discrepancy has been bothering me and it seems no one has any real explanation for it. Perhaps I will have to start a new branch of Advaita allowing for the possibility of Consciousness surviving the death of the body, seeing as how traditional and Neo-Advaitins don't have the balls to admit that enlightenment in this life doesn't mean you've figured everything out!

Ramana Maharshi or Nisargadatta Maharaj might have already been re-born into new physical bodies and could currently be having to re-enlighten themselves all over again. Or perhaps they were surprised at the time of 'death' when they didn't merge into Brahman and instead found themselves in a higher, more subtle plane where they encountered beings with a spiritual knowledge more advanced than their own.

A: Consciousness does not 'need a body to exist'. From the standpoint of absolute reality (i.e. Consciousness), there is *only* Consciousness. Bodies are simply manifestations (names and forms) of that same Consciousness. There are no 'individuals'. Who-you-really-are does not exist as an individual *now,* let alone in the past (or future). The purpose of referring to the Susan Blackmore views is to provide what might seem like an adequate argument for one who firmly believes that he is an individual and who finds science a persuasive approach.

There is no question of 'merging into Brahman' on death, since you are already Brahman. Also, you should not rely on reported experiences. After all, you do not accept reports of dreams as true. Why should you accept reports of experiences when the brain was nearly dead? Advaita does not merely "allow for the possibility of Consciousness surviving the death of the body", it insists that Consciousness is prior to the birth of the body. The body arises in Consciousness, not the other way round. Ramana Maharshi and Nisargadatta were physical forms whose minds realized the truth of all this. But they were never born in the first place – where is the question of their reincarnation?

Q: I truly appreciate your responding to my enquiry. I understand the Advaita doctrine and tenets thereof so when I say things like Consciousness surviving the body, I've been convinced that it does. And when I refer to them as 'him' or 'his', I'm speaking of that individual as impersonal Consciousness. But my quarrel isn't the nature of the 'I', it's the manner in which it's reported to exist after death.

Now if Ramana Maharshi showed up in his last life as he did, being raised from a baby, being fed concepts, creating an ego, and finally having to realize his way out of the whole thing, what's to say that even though he or Consciousness had realized itself, it didn't blink out for a period of time, and then re-implant itself directly into another physical body and have to re-do the whole thing over again?

There is verifiable evidence of people during brain surgeries being closely monitored and having no electrical or chemical activity in the brain and still regaining consciousness and telling tales of 'being' there all along, from popping out of their bodies and witnessing what the surgeons were doing and talking about it, to being led by other beings into heavenly realms where they were privy to knowledge and understanding that wasn't accessible in our world. I don't know if you've ever researched NDEs [Near Death Experiences] or the detail and the accounts and circumstances of the stories but it seems a bit hasty to pass them all off as mere dreams, especially given the fact that there are a few that can be scientifically verified as not being able to be produced by a dying brain.

I recently came across a reported NDE that seemed to support Advaita where a man talked about having an NDE and was allowed to approach 'God', which to him was perceived as a bright, radiant, intelligent light, and on his approach he was told that the closer he came to this oneness with God, the more psychologically painful, so to speak, it would become. As he approached 'God', he became aware that if he wanted to merge into this light completely, he was going to have to shed all forms of individuality and self-identification. At a certain point, his 'ego' objected, refusing to let go of a few remaining dearly-held self-identifications.

I'm not trying to argue or debate and I do appreciate your taking the time to listen, but it just doesn't make sense to me that all these NDEs are reduced to dreams and make-believe just because they are ephemeral. The only way that I can work it out is that if one is enlightened before one 'dies', then one merges automatically and has no more experiences. Maybe the NDEs are reserved for the people who still believe themselves to be individuals.

The Hindu outlook on life after death just seems to be a little cold, and it seems to me that seeing as how most traditional Advaita came from India and Hindu people, that coldness has leaked into the Advaitin concept of life after death. I can't for the life of me reconcile how realizing the true nature of what you are gives you an all-pervasive, iron-clad knowledge of what will become of you and what other experiences you may have in the eternal now. This is obviously all just sprouting from my over-active ego and exaggerated fear of death but I thank you for taking the time to read and hear me out.

A: No worries. I do understand that this is a tricky topic and sympathize with your attempts to come to terms with it. It is actually a problem that I have worried about myself in the past so I can appreciate your frustration.

I think that the NDE aspect is a red herring. Let us accept that there is such a thing. Even so, it is only another 'state of consciousness'; like waking, dream, deep-sleep, hypnosis, hypnagogic imagery, etc. All of these states are valid only in the context of the state and lose that validity once you move to another one. Thus, the dream world is valid for the dreamer and the waking world has no relevance. Once the waking state is re-established, you (the waker) now know that the dream world was only a manufactured image of your mind. From the standpoint of absolute reality, only Consciousness is real. Consciousness is not a state; it is the background and substance of all states.

When you are in the dream, you the dreamer – the subject of your dream experience – is the 'real you'. Although, in waking life you might be married with children, in your dream you might be a rich bachelor running after nubile young women. As far as the dreamer is concerned, you are the bachelor – the married waker does not exist.

The situation regarding the waker is somewhat different in that the waking world seems to be independent of 'your' state of consciousness, i.e. the world that was there when you, the waker, transferred to the dream, seems to be still there when you 'return' to the waking state. This is because the dream is a product of your personal mind, whereas the waking world is a product of the 'universal mind'. But don't get hung up on this because who-you-really-are is Consciousness and it is the same Consciousness which manifests as personal or universal mind anyway.

Hinduism also accepts the existence of a heaven, with gods and demons, etc. If you are very, very good but do not become enlightened, you might go to heaven or even become a god yourself. But you have to come back eventually as a man in order to gain enlightenment. So NDE is not a problem for Hinduism. But all of these possible states, worlds, gods, etc., are all ultimately irrelevant from the absolute perspective of Advaita, since all are only manifestations of Consciousness; name and form of the same non-dual reality.

Similarly, the traditional teaching is that, although the gross body dies, the subtle body of mind and vAsanA-s continues after death, if that person did not become enlightened, and is then reborn into another body. But again, this is only Consciousness manifesting in different forms. There aren't really any separate individuals ever.

So, yes, you could say that Consciousness was in the form

of Ramana Maharshi, say. And then the mind of Ramana gained enlightenment, thus ensuring that 'Ramana' would not be reincarnated. And then you might want to argue that this Consciousness that was Ramana does in fact come back as Fred, even though Ramana had gained enlightenment. And then you will ask: what was the point of striving for the enlightenment in the first place?

The problem with this view is that you are confusing levels of reality. At the level of appearance, there was Ramana, Ramana gained enlightenment, Ramana died (and supposedly his subtle as well as gross body died too), and Fred is then born who has to begin a spiritual path to attain enlightenment. Now, even if Fred claims to have memories of having been Ramana (contradicting the teaching of traditional Advaita), this would still not be a problem from the perspective of absolute reality. From that perspective, there has only ever been Consciousness throughout all of this. Forms are born and forms die. If you think of the wave-ocean metaphor, waves die and new waves are born that may or may not contain water from earlier waves; but all is always water only.

The dream analogy takes you all the way. You, the dream bachelor, effectively die when the dream comes to an end. Who-you-really-are was the waker-mind, manifesting the entire dream world, including the bachelor you. In the next night's dream, you might be a beggar, starving on the streets of Mumbai. Has the bachelor been reincarnated as a beggar? You could say this – in the dream, the beggar might have memories of his previous life. And he might ask: what was the point of having all the money that he had then – after all he didn't even spend most of it – if he is now to be reborn as a penniless beggar. But the point is that both bachelor and beggar are manifestations of the waker's mind only and have no existence of their own.

Similarly, you the seeker might go on to attain enlightenment in this waking life and your body-mind die a jIvanmukta. And then, sometime later, someone might be born who is seriously not enlightened but who claims to have memories of a previous life in which he was 'you'. So what? In reality, both are only manifestations of the one eternal, limitless, complete Brahman and have no separate existence of their own.

You see, enlightenment only has relevance to your personal mind in this lifetime. Whatever happens to the person, who-you-really-are remains untouched.

Q.245 The enlightened dream?

Q: When one 'becomes' self realized/enlightened, is the person's dream state affected? For example, is there any change to the types of dreams one has?

A: No. The enlightened person still dreams and is (usually) unaware in the dream that the dream-world is unreal. You could view it all as the playing out of prArabdha karma. The person still functions in life as before and to all external appearances is mostly unchanged (although someone who knew the person well before might notice differences). The difference is in one's outlook. It is now known for certain that the world is mithyA; that the reality is the non-dual Brahman and 'I am That'. Both waking world and dream world continue to be experienced as before.

Q.262 Consciousness and the brain

In the following discussion, there is considerable scope for confusion. Throughout this book, the word 'Consciousness' (with a capital 'C') has been used as synonymous with Brahman, the non-dual reality spoken of by Advaita. Usually, this does not cause any problem. In questions such as this, however, it may easily do so. The topic of discussion is the 'consciousness' (with a lower-case 'c') exhibited by animals and in particular by humans in the waking state. In this latter case, the word is synonymous with 'awareness'. Advaita uses the specific term 'chidAbhAsa', which means Consciousness 'reflected' in the mind of the jIva. There is only one Consciousness, since it is non-dual; there are very many 'consciousnesses' or chidAbhAsa-s because there are many jIva-s, even though they are all mithyA!

In order to try to obviate this confusion, I am putting the word 'Brahman' 'awareness' or 'chidAbhAsa' in brackets after occurrences which appear uncertain. In the case of the questioner's usage, my bracketed insertions reflect my own understanding and not necessarily that of the questioner!

Q: You said in your article 'Science and the nature of absolute reality' (http://www.Advaita-vision.org/science-and-the-nature-of-absolute-reality-part-1/):

"The idea that consciousness [awareness] is an epiphenomenon of matter is not, it may surprise the reader, an invention of modern science. This same view was held by the chArvAka-s (a materialist philosophy) in the time of Shankara (around 8th century AD) and Shankara rejects their position in his commentary on the Brahmasutra (III.iii.54). He says that consciousness [awareness] must be distinct from the body since it does not exist in a dead body, whereas all of the other attributes persist (for a time, at least!). Furthermore, we can perceive other attributes, such as form and color of the body but we cannot see consciousness [chidAbhAsa]. Nor can we see its non-existence (e.g. it might transfer to another body at death). So, if it does not consist of material elements, what else is there (since materialists deny that there is anything else)?"

I think these are all bad arguments, because they assume that consciousness [awareness] is a low-level feature of matter. If you assume that consciousness [awareness] is analogous to digestion, for example, then these arguments do not go through. Digestion is non-controversially an epiphenomenon of certain biological organisms. However, digestion does not exist in a dead body, and it cannot be directly perceived. We can observe the intake of food, the initial breakdown of the food by bile, the removal of essential nutrients in the small intestine, and the excretion of waste. However, digestion itself cannot be directly observed, and it could be argued that consciousness is perfectly parallel. We can observe the behavioral manifestations of being conscious, of gaining consciousness, and of losing consciousness. We can also observe correlations between states and structures of the brain and the content, presence, and absence of consciousness.

Of course, the Advaitin will object that only relative consciousness [awareness] is gained or lost in these cases, that there is a principle of Consciousness [Brahman] that underlies the relative states of being awake, dreaming, and deep-sleep. However, this assumes the very point at issue, viz. whether consciousness is an epiphenomenon of the brain or it is something outside of space/time. I'm not sure I see anywhere in the Advaita tradition an independent argument for the claim that Consciousness [Brahman] is a basic, metaphysical feature.

You go on to say: "Finally, Shankara points out that matter is an object of perception. If consciousness [awareness] is only matter, then we have the contradictory state of affairs that consciousness is 'acting on itself'. This, he says, cannot happen. For fire, though possessing heat, does not burn itself, nor does an actor (or acrobat), trained though he be, ride on his own shoulder. And it cannot be that consciousness which is an attribute of the elements and their derivatives, (and hence is one with them), will perceive those elements, etc. Hence just as the existence of this perception of the elements and their derivatives is admitted, so also must its separateness from them be admitted".

I don't follow this argument. The claim that consciousness is 'only matter' is stronger than the claim that consciousness is an epiphenomenon of matter, I think. The first claim implies that consciousness can be identified with physical structures of the brain, for example, whereas the latter claim only entails causal relations between consciousness and the brain. If consciousness is the product of matter, why can't it act on matter? Digestion, again, is clearly the product of matter, and it acts on matter.

And you say: "Moreover, though perception takes place when light and other accessories are present, but not when they are absent, it does not follow that from this that perception is an attribute of the light, etc. That being the case, it does not follow that consciousness [awareness] should be an attribute of the body just because it occurs where the body is present and does not occur where the body is absent".

The example of perception and light shows, I think, that light is a necessary condition for perception. Perception is not an 'attribute' of light, because light is not a sufficient condition for perception – a suitable perceptual apparatus like that of the human visual system is required. Again, I think the analogy with digestion is instructive. Digestion requires a complex (though relatively easily satisfied on Earth) set of conditions, but it is still, for all that, an epiphenomenon of the body.

Finally, you say: "One other point with respect to science's idea that consciousness [awareness] arises in the brain is that this would explain nothing. Conversely, Advaita's explanation that everything arises in Consciousness [Brahman] explains everything".

I don't see this at all. The claim that all there is is Consciousness [Brahman] has to confront two enormous explanatory challenges: the coherence/persistence of our perceptions and the cosmology of science. As for the first challenge, nobody will deny that there is an extraordinary coordination between various perceptions, between those of different agents, between those of the same agent at different times, and between different perceptions of the same agent at the same time. Mary can tell me about a new statue in the park, and I can go there and appreciate it for myself. I can return to my bedroom each night, and see that that the bed, the nightstand, the floor lamp, and the dresser have the same appearance and configuration as they did on previous nights. I see, hear, and pet the barking dog, and these various perceptions are resolved into a single, coherent experience of the dog. How are these familiar occurrences possible if there is not a world of independent, existing things, a world that has some sort of inter-subjective reality that is more substantial than fleeting forms of awareness?

As I see it, Advaitins try to defuse this sort of objection by permitting only an appeal to 'direct experience'. It's true that external objects are not part of my 'direct experience'. As far as my own experience goes, there are only perceptions, feelings, and thoughts. But can't one reasonably infer the existence of external objects from one's own direct experience and the reports of others? Doesn't the behavior of even Self-realized Advaitins indicate that this inference has been made? It seems to me that someone who really took seriously the notion that her sensations do not correspond to a substratum of independent, existing things would regard the world as a series of disconnected flashes of images, feelings, and smells.

Another problem with the restriction of evidence to 'direct experience' is that it seems to be tantamount to solipsism. I have no 'direct experience' of the awareness of others, and, thus, shouldn't I also discount my own belief and the claims of others that they are aware?

As for the second challenge, it seems to me that the Advaita position is not easily reconciled with a naturalistic cosmology. If all there is is Consciousness, then how are we to make sense of the claims of science that there was a Big Bang, that stars and planets coalesced out of the remnants of the Big Bang, that life on Earth evolved from single-celled creatures, etc. If these events happened, they happened when no one was around to observe them. Hence, if they occurred, they occurred outside of awareness. Of course, they are now, in some sense, part of consciousness [awareness], because we and many others are discussing them. However, if the Advaita position is right, these events did not become existent until theories about them were created. Again, this is extremely counterintuitive, and I think both of the challenges I've outlined explain why, at least as it stands, the Advaita position is explanatorily inadequate.

A: I don't think your attempt to draw a parallel between digestion and consciousness [awareness] succeeds. I would argue that digestion is a 'process'. You acknowledge that you can observe the various stages of this process. Surely digestion is nothing more than the stages of which it consists? Consciousness [Brahman] on the other hand is something absolute, without which nothing else is. You are confusing Consciousness with awareness when you say that we 'gain' and 'lose' Consciousness. It is the brain activity and sense organs that cease to function in the normal way under anesthesia for example. To say that we are not conscious is not at all the same thing as saying that Consciousness is absent.

I'm not sure what you mean when you say that you can't find 'in the Advaita tradition an independent argument for the claim that Consciousness is a basic, metaphysical feature'. The entire scriptural purport is to show that 'all there is is Brahman'; 'Brahman is real, the world is mithyA and the jIva is not other than Brahman; 'thou art That'; 'Consciousness is Brahman', etc.

And the continuation of your parallel with digestion does not stack up (for me) either. Digestion is a series of cause-effect relationships at the material level. When you mix starch with saliva, the enzymes chemically convert the starch to sugar – the first stage of the digestion process. This is simply cause and effect. To claim that Consciousness [Brahman] was like this would mean that the effect became the cause which would be counter to the second law of thermodynamics.

I don't see that digestion is an epiphenomenon of the body either. It is simply the chemical process whereby some sort of solvent acts upon a substrate to extract something more subtle that was previously in combination with the substrate. (Clumsily put but I think you should get the point!) Consciousness [Brahman] doesn't do anything but it is nevertheless that without which nothing gets done. It is certainly not a process or the result of anything.

Regarding the existence of separate objects, no one denies that this is our empirical experience but that does not mean it is really the case. The example of dreams amply illustrates this. The dream world is perfectly real for the dreamer and only realized to be illusory upon waking. And knowing the truth about Brahman does not affect the experience of the world – we still experience the sun rise despite knowing that it does no such thing.

Where does your understanding that we have to rely only on 'direct experience' come from? Advaita relies primarily on shAstrIya pramANa – testimonial evidence from the scriptures. Ideally this is backed up and explained by the guru – shabda pramANa. This is then subjected to reason. Only then may we realize for ourselves that what they say is true. There is no solipsism. There is 'only the Self', not 'only me' – a big difference!

Your point about cosmology does not hold water. Irrespective of the arguments that the idea of creation makes no sense, there is no problem with the idea of evolution. Since there is only Consciousness [Brahman], this could all happen without the need for any 'intelligent' life form present to observe it.

Q: I agree with you that the analogy between digestion and consciousness [awareness] is misguided. (Incidentally, this is the philosopher John Searle's analogy.) Digestion clearly does have coordinates in the space-time continuum, and, on the other hand, it is difficult on reflection to assign temporal and spatial boundaries to consciousness [awareness]. However, I'm not convinced that to say that someone is 'unconscious' is not to say that Consciousness [Brahman] is absent. In fact, one way of framing the Advaita position, I think, is to say that it regards 'unconsciousness' as the consciousness of absence rather than the absence of Consciousness. I think the crux of that matter is whether Consciousness can be assigned temporal/spatial boundaries. If it cannot, then it is limitless; it makes no sense to speak of its appearance and disappearance, and it must be the absolute reality.

A: Sounds like a good summary of the position to me! And is this not our experience? When we 'come to' after being under anesthesia, do we not 'know' that we have been 'unconscious'? It is not an inference, made only after we look at the clock and see that time has passed. As T. S. Eliot says in the Four Quartets: 'Or when, under ether, the mind is conscious but conscious of nothing…'

Q: You said: "I'm not sure what you mean when you say that you can't find 'in the Advaita tradition an independent argument for the claim that Consciousness is a basic, metaphysical feature'. The entire scriptural purport is to show that 'all there is is Brahman'; 'Brahman is real, the world is mithyA and the jIva is not other than Brahman'; 'thou art That'; 'Consciousness is Brahman', etc.".

Well, the Advaita literature is, of course, full of these 'assertions'. As I see it, there are two pillars of argumentation in the Advaita tradition: dRRigdRRishya viveka and avasthA traya. I don't see that either of these lines of reasoning establishes that Consciousness [Brahman] is the ultimate reality.

The first shows that Consciousness is not a 'thing', but then gravity, solidity, etc., are not things either (though they are features of the world and not the ultimate reality). The second line of reasoning shows that our self is not the body or the mind, but it does, I think, leave open the question of what the self is. In particular, it does not immediately follow that the self is Consciousness. Couldn't the self be some sort of potential of the body, i.e. I am an expression of the body (or a part/subsystem of the body) functioning in a certain way just as, for example, a song is an expression of a track on the CD and the stereo functioning a certain way?

A: You will not find any 'proof' that Consciousness [Brahman] is the ultimate reality in the scriptures because none is possible. You will only find assertions and pointers. 'Proofs' relate only to the phenomenal world. Enlightenment is the realization in the mind that Consciousness is the non-dual reality. It comes as the final recognition when the ignorance that causes us to see duality everywhere finally falls away.

Q: You said: "I don't see that digestion is an epiphenomenon of the body either. It is simply the chemical process whereby some sort of solvent acts upon a substrate to extract something more subtle that was previously in combination with the substrate. (Clumsily put but I think you should get the point!) Consciousness doesn't do anything but it is nevertheless that without which nothing gets done. It is certainly not a process or the result of anything".

I agree that it is difficult to regard consciousness [awareness] as a process, both because it seems irreducible and because it is difficult to situate it within space/time. I don't agree, however, that it doesn't do anything. In fact, it seems absolutely essential to cognitive relations like knowing, understanding, intention, etc., in a way that it is not essential to running, speaking, dancing, etc. On the face of it, at least, consciousness seems to be part of the causal nexus for cognitive relations (I can't understand something without being conscious of what's understood), but we can imagine unconscious zombies running, speaking, dancing, etc.

A: You are using 'consciousness' [awareness] here in the sense of 'intelligence'. But this is not the sense in Advaita. Rather, intelligence is Consciousness [Brahman] reflected in the mind. All 'action' relates to prakRRiti – the mithyA world of people and objects, not to Consciousness itself.

Q: I understand your point that ultimately there is no creation, according to Advaita. However, I'm still unclear about how we can make sense of evolution or any other part of scientific cosmology at the relative level of existence if all there is is Consciousness [Brahman]. As I understand it, to exist at the relative level on the Advaita view is to be an object of relative consciousness [chidAbhAsa]. However, there were no animals for the first 3.2 billion years of evolution, and, thus, there was, for all we know, no relative consciousness [chidAbhAsa] during this time frame. What can it possibly mean to say that this phase of evolution occurred if there was no awareness of it and Consciousness [Brahman] is all there is?

A: Again, you are confusing the non-dual Brahman (which is synonymous with 'Consciousness' as I have been using it, with a capital 'C') with the consciousness (small 'c') 'exhibited' by a person. The latter is better called chidAbhAsa, which literally means 'false appearance or reflection (AbhAsa) of Consciousness (chit)'. Evolution is simply our attempt to rationalize what we now see, or infer, with respect to the changing form of Consciousness (capital 'C') at the level of appearance. There are, no doubt, theories and mathematical descriptions of the changing form of waves in the ocean but, in the final analysis, it is all only water. Also, 'existence' relates to Consciousness itself, not to the object. When we say that the chair exists, what is actually the case is that Brahman exists in the form of the chair. The chair itself is mithyA.

Hope all of this answers your questions... although I have a sneaking suspicion that it won't!

Q.313 Under anesthesia

Q: I recently had an experience that leaves me baffled. I have read your books, the sections on deep-sleep consciousness, and it does not seem to match. The incident occurred when I was given anesthesia for hip replacement surgery. I went from eyes open in the operating room to eyes open in the recovery room without any sensation in between at all. The experience was seamless and continuous from one consciousness to another. Time was absolutely absent. There was no reflection possible on the three-hour interlude. There was no interlude. There was no feeling of having slept well or otherwise.

This experience has left me with a problem. This was the nonexistence of any kind of consciousness; even in retrospect, it seems neither the small self or the real self existed at all. Please comment.

A: The 'Consciousness' (= Brahman) of Advaita should not be equated with the 'consciousness' of 'being conscious, or aware'. The former is non-dual, the latter is dual; being conscious entails a subject and an object of which he or she is aware.

The states of consciousness refer to the person and require a mind (and a body). One should always bear in mind the concept of chidAbhAsa; that idea of 'reflected Consciousness'. The sense of separate identity is the result of the non-dual Consciousness being reflected in the mind. Hence I see what I see, you see what you see and I do not know what you are thinking. If your mind is shut down, whether by anesthetic or by death, it ceases to reflect Consciousness for the duration. But of course that does not mean that Consciousness is not there. If you hold a mirror in such a way as to reflect the sun's rays into a darkened room, you will be able to see the objects in that room. If you then cover up the mirror with your hand, you will no longer see those objects – but of course the sun is quite unaffected.

My article (http://www.Advaita-vision.org/chidabhasa/) gives a much extended explanation of this. I also discuss how many states of consciousness there are in my blog (http://www.Advaita-vision.org/states-of-consciousness-2-3-4-and-1-2/).

Q.371 Deep-sleep state

Q: In Advaita, we use the recall of a 'good deep-sleep' as a very important argument for proving continued presence of awareness… the question is, how does this recall happen? We have a process in Advaita by which 'the presence of a pot is known'. How is deep-sleep known? Or – How is the fact that one slept well, recalled?

A: Consciousness is always present, throughout all so-called 'states of consciousness', including deep-sleep, anesthesia, etc. It is the 'turIya' of the Mandukya Upanishad. When we say that we 'slept well', what we mean is that our sleep was not disturbed by periods of wakefulness or dreams. In fact, we could say that we were 'aware of nothing'. And this is not an inference, based upon some memory; rather it is certain knowledge. If I ask whether you are sure that you were aware of nothing during your anesthetized operation, you will insist that you are sure. And the only way we could have such certainty is that Consciousness was present, even though awareness was not. Awareness requires mind (to reflect Consciousness); Consciousness requires nothing.

Consciousness reflects in the mind to animate the body and

senses but these are resolved in the deep-sleep state; there is only Consciousness, knowing nothing – it is the bliss of ignorance. Since there is no subject-object differentiation, the deep-sleep state is 'without division' – nirvikalpa.

If you are looking for a vyAvahArika explanation of the mechanism, I suggest you are doomed to failure! An explanation for 'knowing a pot' is possible (though all is mithyA) because pot and 'knower' are both in the gross realm of the waker. But when you ask 'How do I know that I slept well?' you ask a meaningless question. You are trying to ask how the waker ego knows that the deep-sleeper ego did not know anything. But waker-ego, dreamer-ego and deep-sleeper-ego are distinct states which can never interact. Waker and dreamer can 'pass messages' via the mind, but the mind is unavailable in deep-sleep. (And so, to be pedantic, there is no 'deep-sleeper ego', since ego is an aspect of mind.)

Of course, who-I-really-am is none of these but the Consciousness that pervades them all. I am present throughout but I do not 'know' in any objective sense; I simply know.

Q.388 Fear of deep-sleep

Q: From the age of around seven (I am now 51), I have had a morbid terror of sleep, equating it with 'unconsciousness or non-consciousness' or death, which leads to death anxiety. How can this be our natural state? Is that all there is – a kind of acceptance of annihilation of this ego-mind... forever?

A: In deep-sleep, you do not experience anything. But this is because there is nothing to experience, not because 'you' have disappeared. You see neither external world (because the senses are inactive) nor internal thoughts (because the mind is inactive). But the Self that is the witnessing Consciousness in deep meditation is still present in deep-sleep. It never 'sleeps' (or dies) because it is the only thing that really exists. It is who-you-really-are.

Q.405 Persistent Vegetative State

Q: Recently, a relation suffered cardiac failure and was declared as 'dead' by one of the doctors in the local hospital. 30 minutes later, a doctor at a bigger hospital used a defibrillator to restart his heart. Unfortunately, for this span of 30 minutes, his brain was not receiving oxygen and, consequently, 50% of it was damaged leaving him in a 'Persistent Vegetative State'. He has been in this condition for the past 2 years.

Currently I am studying various Upanishads along with Advaita Vedanta philosophy and I would seek your help on the following questions:

1. According to Advaita Vedanta and Upanishads, the soul departs on the death of a person. So in my relative's case, does that mean that the 'soul' had departed and came back again or did it never leave?

2. Does Vedanta recognize a person in a 'persistent vegetative state' as 'alive'? How would Vedanta describe this state in terms of the usual 4 states (waking, dream, dreamless sleep and turIya)?

3. Does the soul leaves the body because the heart stops functioning or does the heart cease functioning because the soul has departed from the body?

A: Sorry to hear about your relative's situation. It is understandably distressing.

Advaita is a progressive teaching. In other words, the scriptures or a teacher will provide one explanation for a new seeker and a different one for an advanced student. Ultimately, as you must realize, there are 'not two things'. Therefore, the final understanding must be that there are no persons, no world, no mind etc.; there is only Brahman and 'you' are That.

The most useful way of answering your question depends upon an understanding of the concept of chidAbhAsa, the 'reflection' of Consciousness in the mind. The principal article has already been referenced (http://www.Advaita-vision.org/chidabhasa/). There is also an extended (quite technical!) discussion on the subject between myself and Peter Bonnici (http://www.Advaita-vision.org/discussion-on-chidabhasa/).

The point is that the jIva (which you are calling 'soul') does not really exist; it is only a 'reflection' of Consciousness as it were. It is possible to provide explanations for how the subtle body 'separates' from the gross body at death and eventually transmigrates to a new body. There is a blog on this topic – 'Between Lives' (http://www.Advaita-vision.org/between-lives/) followed by 'The Fires of Reincarnation' (http://www.Advaita-vision.org/the-fires-of-reincarnation/). [The process that the jIva has to go through in between lifetimes is described in the Chandogya Upanishad V.3 – V.10 and the Brihadaranyaka Upanishad VI.2 and is referred to as the 'five (mystic or sacred) fires' (pa~nchAgni).] But these explanations again are only for those not yet prepared to accept the reality. (To be fair, the reality is probably more acceptable to the modern mind than those mystical 'explanations'!)

So, to answer your questions:

1. The interim teaching would probably say that the subtle and causal bodies have left the gross body. There is therefore no longer any reflection of Consciousness to 'animate' the brain. (I say 'probably' because, of course, this state was presumably unknown to the ancients as there were no life-support facilities to maintain vital functions!)

2. Again, I speak from my own understanding here – I very much doubt that anything is said about such a condition in the scriptures. You could probably say that the body is alive in the same way that a plant is alive. Just as the plant needs sunlight, water, carbon dioxide and a few minerals to remain alive, so the body in PVS needs the life-support functions of a hospital to remain alive. As far as a 'state of Consciousness' is concerned, this does not apply, since there is no Consciousness being reflected by a mind. Consciousness is still present in the sense that there is *only* Consciousness, so all is still turIya, if you like.

3. The subtle body depends upon the brain for its operation in the context of the jIva. When the heart stops, blood is no longer supplied to the brain, which begins to cease functioning. You

could say that when this reaches a critical level, the mind (subtle body) leaves the gross body.

The reality of the situation is that there is only ever Consciousness or Brahman. All apparent things/bodies are only name and form of this Consciousness. Nothing is ever born or dies. Realizing/ remembering this is the simplest way to accept the appearance, be it something desirable or something one wishes were otherwise.

Q.419 E.S.P.

Q: I can hold an object that I know nothing about in my hands and start meditating. Within about 10 minutes I receive images related to the object, such as where it has been, who previously owned it, sometimes where it came from. At times I have visual images of walking through the original building or house where it previously belonged. I would like to know what this is called; is it dangerous; should I persevere and try to expand this experience? Is it valuable or beneficial to practice it?

A: It's called 'psychometry'. [Wikipedia: *Psychometry (from Greek: ψυχή, psukhē, 'spirit, soul' and μέτρον, metron, 'measure'), also known as token-object reading, or psychoscopy, is a form of extrasensory perception characterized by the claimed ability to make relevant associations from an object of unknown history by making physical contact with that object.*]

It has nothing to do with Advaita, which is about gaining Self-knowledge – the knowledge that there is ONLY Consciousness. Pursuing this 'ability' will not help; indeed it will almost certainly take you away from Self-knowledge, down a blind alley, if you like. True (and worthwhile) meditation is about cultivating a still, quiet mind and the self-discipline to control that.

Q.426 Flow

Q: In response to my question "Can one ever know that reality is non-dual?" Ramesam wrote: "Yes, when you are in the 'zone', (the flow of Mihály Csíkszentmihályi)".

I'm a big fan of flow, know it quite well, teach it in fact to my students. I'd like to know what your take is on flow, specifically: Do you agree with Ramesam, that being in flow is knowing that reality is non-dual?

Is being in flow a desirable 'state' according to Advaita Vedanta? In other words: if, as often happens, I spend most of the day in flow, is this a 'good thing' for my Advaitin development?

The reason I ask is because I've often wondered about the difference between pure awareness and flow. Flow is very goal oriented; pure awareness is not. Also, when in flow, you are deeply aware of that which you need to be aware of to keep flowing (holding a conversation, skiing a narrow downhill trail, etc.), but you are typically *not* aware of your awareness. In fact, if you become aware of your awareness, you'll probably lose the flow, get tripped up in the conversation, fall down on the trail, etc. It's as if you were completely lost in the activity.

So, is flow a less desirable state than pure awareness? Or some other state that Advaita recommends?

A: I came across Csíkszentmihályi when I was writing 'How to Meet Yourself' and of course the feeling of 'flow' is recognizable. And it is a great feeling, obviously invaluable for sports and other activities. It represents single-mindedness, concentration etc. – the control of the mind and senses – dama, shama etc. And it is in this sense that it has some relevance for Advaita – mental preparation to make one 'ready' for taking on board Self-knowledge.

But that is as far as it goes. It has nothing to do with actually knowing that reality is non-dual. In fact, I would suggest that the vast majority of people who know about 'flow' have no interest (and have probably never heard of) non-duality. They are interested in its value in furthering their materialistic ends (by this, I don't mean obtaining objects but improving their sporting achievements or whatever). If one also has spiritual 'ambitions', then pursuing flow could even be counter-productive. It is said that mokSha has to become your sole, overriding aim in life to the exclusion of everything else if you are to gain Self-knowledge in this lifetime.

So your assessment is correct, except that you do not really become 'aware of awareness'. The non-directed stillness of the mind in deep meditation is the nearest you come to such a thing. nirvikalpa samAdhi has nothing as its object whereas, as you say, flow is invariably goal-oriented.

Q.437 Lucid wakefulness

Q: Many Eastern traditions refer to what we think of as the waking state as a (subtle) dream, meaning that things are not real in the sense that we think they are real. An elephant in a dream is 'dream-real', not 'waking-state-real'. Similarly, an elephant in the waking state is not real in the sense we think it is either. It is a story, an interpretation, a creation of the mind.

Lucid wakefulness enables us to see this: that the waking-state elephant is just as un-real as the dream elephant. I see this as a third state of consciousness: not the default wakeful state, not the dream state, but the lucid wakeful state.

A: This highlights one of the principal problems of teaching Advaita – use of language. Unless each key word is carefully defined and understood by the listener as was intended by the speaker, the 'teaching' will not work. Confusion and/or misunderstanding will result.

You know that there are three states – waking, dreaming and deep-sleep – and a non-dual reality, turIya. Any attempt to introduce further states can only confuse and will certainly not tally with traditional Advaita. Also, although waking and dream are both mithyA, waking is vyavahAra while dream is pratibhAsa – not the same! Try walking in front of a (waking) stampeding elephant if you don't believe me!

Q: But ... In order to see that dream objects are mithyA, you need to be looking from one level higher: the waking state. Similarly, in order to see that waking objects are mithyA, you need likewise to be looking from one level higher. This is what I'm calling lucid wakefulness.

How would it be described in traditional Advaita, this 'ability' to see that waking objects are mithyA? And totally, not just intellectually.

A: It's called 'Self-knowledge' or (in modern parlance) 'enlightenment'. But it is still the waking state.

Q.466 Awareness in deep-sleep

Q: In your article on chidAbhAsa (http://www.advaita-vision.org/chidabhasa/) you quote from the Brihadaranyaka Upanishad:

"The Brihadaranyaka Upanishad (IV.iii.23) states: 'That it does not see in that state [i.e. deep-sleep] is because, though seeing then, it does not see; for the vision of the witness cannot be lost, because it is imperishable. But there is not that second thing separate from it which it can see.'[1] *I.e. the reason that we are not aware of anything in deep-sleep is simply that there is nothing to be aware of".*

But the organism remains aware of many things during deep-sleep. Otherwise, it wouldn't wake at a suspicious sound, or detect coldness from an open window, etc. How do you explain this?

A: As the essay explains, when we say 'I am aware of X', what this means is that Consciousness, reflected in the mind, is aware of the percepts or concepts that 'appear' in the mind. Percepts come via the senses and concepts via manas. In deep-sleep, the mind is inactive. This means that there are neither percepts nor concepts. Nor is there any chidAbhAsa, because there is no mind to reflect Consciousness. But Consciousness itself is ever present, since there is only Consciousness in reality.

Also, as is explained elsewhere, the world appearance of forms is also present to other jIva-s. The interim explanation for this is that the world is created by Brahma and 'governed' by Ishvara according to His laws. The body and mind are part of this 'creation' and operate according to those laws. Whilst the body is alive, its bodily functions continue to operate. Blood is pumped, lungs breathe and so on. You might say (according to a modern scientific viewpoint) that the 'lower' aspect of the brain that controls all of these. The senses, too, must continue to function at some level, in order to maintain the body in an operational state. If the temperature falls such that the body is no longer comfortable, one might say that it is necessary to stimulate the 'higher' brain out of its resting mode. Similarly a loud noise, or someone calling our name, is a stimulus recognized by the brain at some subliminal level, which triggers an 'awakening' response.

All of this may be regarded as being part of the mechanical brain operation, and does not require what we would call conscious awareness to be present. It is simply an automatic 'nudge' by the brain to move us from the deep-sleep or dream state into the waking state.

One could reason that the 'mind' (and hence chidAbhAsa) is associated with the 'higher' brain. If this is considered helpful, then fine. Obviously the scriptures do not address such things because science had not investigated the workings of the brain at that time. You will find many differences between the scriptural 'explanations' of experiential phenomena in the world and modern scientific explanations – science has come a long way in the past 2000 years! But none of this matters, since all of it is mithyA.

Q.469 Consciousness versus consciousness

Q: Consciousness (capital C) is Brahman is ineffable; consciousness (lowercase c) is the state of being aware (of something).

These are fundamentally different 'things' ... they really have nothing to do with each other. They might as well be called x and Y instead of x and X.

What am I missing here? What justifies consciousness and Consciousness being portrayed (linguistically, in any case) as the same thing except for the capitalization?

How is consciousness similar to Consciousness?

Or is it as simple as: **What we call consciousness is <whatever**

happens to arise mentally when> Consciousness reflects off the mind? In other words: There is no consciousness per se, there is only reflected Consciousness in ALL its forms?

The feel of consciousness ... qualia, presence, what it is like to be a particular mind-body at a particular moment.

How is this *feel* similar to Consciousness? If they are utterly dissimilar, why use the same root word with different spellings?

A: Interesting questions, although I think maybe you are making more of this than is really there.

Firstly, Consciousness and consciousness have to be the same in reality, since there is *only* Consciousness. How can you say they have nothing to do with each other? In the light analogy I used [If you look at the analogy of light, the light reflected off a mirror is still light, still photons of electromagnetic radiation, even though the mirror itself is not the originator of those photons] the reflected photons are the *same* photons, not newly originated imitations. We call the reflected Consciousness 'consciousness' but it is still only ever Consciousness. The reason that we want to differentiate is to explain aspects such as why Consciousness manifests differently in different minds. You could say that a clear, disciplined mind 'reflects' Consciousness much more 'brightly' than a dull, identified mind, in a similar way to a clean mirror reflecting light much more brightly than a dirty one.

You say to begin with that "consciousness (lowercase c) is the state of being aware (of something)". But it is Consciousness that enables us to be aware of anything. When Consciousness enlivens the mind, we just happen to call it 'being conscious'. Your statement "There is no consciousness per se, there is only reflected Consciousness in ALL its forms?" is one way of putting it.

The 'feel' of being conscious is one aspect of the mind's response to the reflection of Consciousness. There is no 'feel' under anesthesia, for example, because there is no reflection taking place since the mind is inactive.

Q: Yes, ultimately (paramArtha) there is ONE (Brahman). But consciousness (small c) does not exist at this paramArtha level. Similarly Consciousness cannot be said to exist at the vyavahAra level. (Per Shankara: Consciousness neither exists nor does not exist.) So at what level are these two things 'the same?'

A: You always have to remember that vyavahAra is mithyA. In reality, there are no levels; in reality there is only Consciousness (Brahman). This is why I was saying that effectively, small 'c' or big 'C', there is only one. But of course, you can use whatever 'explanations' you like if it helps lead you to this understanding.

Q: I would have thought that Advaita would say Consciousness keeps reflecting off the mind during deep sleep or anesthesia, but there are no objects for it to reflect onto, hence the lack of feeling. To use sunlight as a metaphor, the photons keep reflecting off the mirror even when the mirror is 'inert', but there are no objects in range for the photons to reflect off of (a chair or a table, for example) to form a reflection of any object in the mirror.

A: Metaphors are slippery things! In order to see a reflection in a mirror, you (the observer) have to be separate from the mirror so you move into a new scenario. Consciousness is certainly still present in deep-sleep. Otherwise we would not know (on waking) that we did not know anything (whilst asleep). I wonder if it would make things easier if you replaced all iterations of 'consciousness' with 'awareness'? In deep sleep, we are not *aware* of anything but Consciousness (as if) 'witnesses' this fact. (It doesn't really, because Brahman-consciousness is akartA.)

Meaning

Q.353 Witness to the boredom

Q: I have a problem with the boredom of everyday life. Nothing seems to satisfy me. I find it so difficult to be just here in the moment and be content with that. You say: go through life and work etc., but as a witness to it all.

Am I living in the moment as I should? Should I give all my

attention to each action, so that the ego is absent or should I just be the witness of everything, every action on a moment to moment basis?

Maybe if I understand how to live in the moment better and had some clarification, that would help me stay present and focused on just living. My mind lives in the future.

A: The instruction to be in the moment (do what needs to be done without allowing personal desire into the equation; witness the activity and do not dwell upon the outcome, etc.) is an aspect of karma yoga and its purpose is to train the mind to be your slave rather than your master. (This is necessary if one is to begin the process of gaining Self-knowledge – j~nAna yoga.) But, in itself, it is not going to do any more than that. If you have come to the realization that the usual pursuits of life are ultimately not going to give you anything (other than transient pleasure or pain), then what you are really looking for is Self-knowledge, colloquially (and misleadingly) referred to as 'enlightenment' or 'self-realization'.

In order to gain this, there is no alternative but to study. Ideally (as has been said so many times in these answers) with a qualified traditional teacher, but otherwise reading, discussing, asking questions of those more advanced on the same 'path'.

I said in one of my early books that disappointment is the result of unreasonable expectation. I could have said this about boredom also. But what I meant then was that you act anticipating a specific outcome and, when that does not materialize, you feel let down. But, when it comes to boredom, it is much more than that. It is due to a lack of participation: thinking that you simply need to sit there and fascinating experiences will come and find you. It doesn't work like that. You have to go out and look for it! Take up photography for example! Whether macro – examining flowers or insects close up; landscape – the wonder of mountains, lakes and forests; or street/urban – the endlessly interesting behavior of fellow humans and their artifacts. Or reading; or writing. Or endeavoring to discover the nature of yourself, 'life, the universe and everything', by studying Advaita. Every moment is potentially interesting and fulfilling if you are alert to it – in the moment!

The bottom line, however, is that the only thing that can ever give you lasting satisfaction it the certain knowledge that you do not have to do anything at all because you are already perfect, complete and without limitation of any kind.

Q.407 Why not commit suicide?

Q: Since the world as perceived by our senses is mithyA, and we are Brahman, any suffering or pleasures that we derive during the waking or dream state are mere illusions. As this realization dawns, I am forced to conclude that living or dying (both concepts being associated with the waking state) are meaningless.

Rather than meditating etc., and deciding to live life as it is with the knowledge that it is mithyA, why shouldn't someone just end his existence in this state? He is Brahman anyway and it doesn't matter if he lives or dies in an illusory world born out of his senses.

Rest assured, this is more of a rhetorical question, to understand if any of the proponents of Vedanta have addressed this.

The very act of my writing to you is in itself irrelevant in the broader context.

A: This is the sort of question that Ramana or Nisargadatta would answer with the question 'Who is asking?'

The point is that the world and its vicissitudes are real *for the jIva* – hence the teachings about karma and rebirth. If the jIva ends his/her life before gaining Self-knowledge, there will be rebirth according to the accumulated karma. Also the pleasures and sufferings during waking and dreaming are not illusions; they are mithyA – a world of difference! Whilst your mind and body are still alive, pleasure and pain continue. They do not affect who-you-really-are but, if you don't yet know this, they will still be believed to be real and accorded corresponding importance.

It is only from the vantage point of absolute reality that you can say that living and dying are meaningless. The unenlightened never question the reality of the world. They commit suicide because some aspect of their lives is considered to be real and unbearable. The enlightened do not kill themselves even though they know that their life as a jIva is not real. Every aspect is known to be mithyA. They know that no harm can come to who-they-really-are and, more to the point, they *know* that their true self cannot be killed!

The State of the World

Most people would not even question the reality of the world. The solidity and separate existence of objects and other people is apparently self-evident. Yet many religions and philosophies have done precisely this and we have theories such as Berkeley's idealism, solipsism, and nihilism. Advaita is a non-dual teaching methodology. Its philosophy is simple – there are not two things. According to Advaita, there is only Brahman or, as a concession to the more modern, scientific outlook, there is only Consciousness.

This means that the world cannot exist as something separate from Consciousness. Note that this is not to say that the world is unreal. Rather, the reality of the world, the existence of everything, is 'borrowed' from Brahman. (By 'world', the entire universe is meant.) This, in turn, means that there has never been any 'creation', whether by a 'god' or as the result of a 'Big Bang'.

Usually, in both waking and dream states, we are ignorant about the truth and misperceive what is there. In deep-sleep there is no misperception so that we directly experience the non-dual Self. But there is still ignorance there and, as soon as we wake up the same old snake is projected onto the rope. There is only the Self, so that, inevitably, we must always be experiencing that. The problem is that we do not know it – the only solution is to gain Self-knowledge.

In fact, it is worse than this. Shankara says in his commentary on the Gaudapada kArikA-s that the world is unreal (mithyA) *because* we experience it. If you can experience something, you know by that fact that it must be unreal.

Needless to say, such ideas are bound to lead to some astonishment and it is no surprise that many questions arise.

Appearance

Q.2 Do thoughts create our reality?

Q: Do thoughts create our reality? I have played with this for years and watched how 'my' thoughts created my so-called reality. Can you explain?

A: You use the adjective 'so-called' reality, regarding your thoughts, so you obviously appreciate that the 'true' reality is not something that is at all relevant to your thoughts. It was, is and always will be the only, non-dual reality before your body-mind-personality was born and after it has died.

So who-you-really-are (the non-dual Self, Brahman, Absolute or whatever you prefer) is totally unaffected by any of that. At the level of appearances however, i.e. you the person, the world and others, this Self is presumably identified with a body and mind and the mistake is made that 'I *am* this body'.

Whilst this error continues to be made, there will be the belief that you are limited by the body-mind. To this extent, your apparent world will appear to be your reality. If there are thoughts of fear, you will say 'I am afraid' and your world will become very small. If you are in love, all will seem well and the world very large and full of happiness.

So yes, you are right, in the normal state of man and woman our thoughts *effectively* create our reality. But this normal state is one of error, mixing up real and unreal.

It is very much tied up with the way that our mind separates out forms in the world and gives names to them, thus creating a seeming duality where there is really none. See Q.73 in the section on 'Mind and Thinking' for more on this.

Q.21 Can our attitude to life change without free will?

Q: How is it that if everything simply happens, if there is no mind and, accepting that in reality there is no person as such, that a person's attitude to life can radically change their perspective of, appreciation of, and attitude towards that life?

A: It is just a cause and effect relationship. Those thoughts that are particularly attractive (i.e. with which there is identification) exert correspondingly more influence on everything else. It automatically follows that some things will be appreciated (and appear to be chosen) and others will not. Positive feedback reinforces particular ideas; negative feedback loosens their hold.

Not sure why you say "if there is no mind", incidentally. At the level of empirical reality (experiential world), there are people and each person has a mind – they would find it very difficult to function in the world if this were not so! It is only when we are speaking as if from the level of absolute reality that we can say that there is no world, no persons, no minds.

See the section on 'Free Will' for lots more Q&As on this subject.

Q.22 I thought that there was no thinker or doer

Q: I cannot disagree with your answer (to Q.21) as this is how it appears to be. But it seems to fly in the face of Advaitic teaching which says that there is no individual and therefore no-one to have thoughts; there is no doer; everything simply happens. How come something that doesn't exist influences something else which doesn't exist either? Quite apart from that, it does appear that it is not just that which we find attractive that is drawn to us but that also that which we fear. This seems to imply an individual volitional mind – and Advaita denies that. Dr Amit Goswami, who is a non-dual physicist, posits that the brain [individual mind?] perceives a potential and the mind [universal mind?] collapses the wave function into particle form and manifestation. Advaita would also contend that cause and effect only appears to be the case. No?

A: You are confusing reality and appearance. If you ask about thoughts and influence, I assume you want an 'appearance' answer. At the level of the phenomenal, everything proceeds according to cause and effect (or the laws of Ishvara if you prefer!). Also, there appears to be free will (although I have argued – and believe it to be the case – that the evidence is that there is no free will even at the level of appearance). Again, at the level of appearance, there are clearly individuals (jIva-s) and they are affected by all of the influences (including their own apparent volition) according to cause-effect laws.

It is only *in reality* that there are no individuals, laws, influences etc.

As I have noted before, you can blind most people with quantum physics since so few understand it. Science is intrinsically objective and there are no objects in reality. (See the section on 'Science' for more on this.)

Q.23a Do those who have awakened live in reality?

Q: Are you saying that those who are awakened live in Reality, not 'down here'? You see, I cannot get past the idea that 'awakening to Reality' is nothing more than viewing this world from the perspective of That rather than from a perceived individual viewpoint; i.e. free from prejudice, conditioned response and misconceptions (without concepts of how things should be). After all, both the apparent individual and the enlightened can only function through the perceptions taken in by the senses, should they wish to continue existing. Again, after all 'This is It'.

A: 'Awakening' doesn't change the appearance. Contrary to what some seem to claim, the world does not effectively disappear. Everything is seen as before; the difference is that it is now known not to be separate. All the 'people' are still there, living out their apparent lives, still acting as though there were free will, including the body-mind in which 'awakening' has occurred. So yes, what you say is true – the world is now viewed *"from the perspective of That rather than from a perceived individual viewpoint"*. However, the body-mind is not necessarily free from prejudice. Conditioned responses will still take place, all according to the same laws as before. But it is now known that it is not 'me' who is doing any of this. As you say, functioning takes place through the body-mind by virtue of the Consciousness that enlivens it.

Q: Thanks for that; really clear. Hence, there is no need to worry about our little inconsistencies or what may be conceived of as imperfections. They are not a barrier to awakening and neither do I own them, they are a part of the play.

A: Everything is perfect!

Q.30 Is it true that nothing matters?

Q: I am working my way through your book ('Book of One' 1st edition) and last week got to a section where you talk about us not having the sonar senses of bats or the ability to see in ultraviolet etc. You then talk about sensory perception being a conversion of electromagnetic stimuli. The more I thought about that – that in fact the whole of bodily experience is just electromagnetic impulses, indeed that thought is really just the same – the more I began to lose touch with what the body/mind set up is. In fact, it began to seem to me that it is little more than a very complex piece of electronic circuitry and when I realized that, I had the impression of my whole identity dissolving – very unsettling but also strangely reassuring. If I don't exist, and neither does anyone else, then nothing matters.

I wanted to ask you first whether I have understood what you said and secondly, how do we know that the notion of anything above and beyond this complex circuitry, i.e. the Self, isn't just another construct of mind?

A: All of the stuff in the book about bats etc. was background to explaining how western philosophers had effectively reached similar conclusions to those of Advaita. It wasn't really intended as any sort of prakriyA (teaching method). But you are right. Atmananda Krishna Menon uses this (Direct Path) approach to bring one to the realization that all of this (matter, thoughts, feelings etc.) simply arises in Consciousness and is just witnessed. Since 'I' am observing it, I cannot be it. You can download the 'Notes on Spiritual Discourses of Sri Atmananda' (http://www.advaita.org.uk/discourses/downloads/notes_pdf.zip). This is a tremendous book and it is very well indexed so you can easily look up what he has to say on particular topics.

My book 'How to Meet Yourself (and find true happiness)' is aimed at someone who knows absolutely nothing about Advaita; who simply wants to find some sort of meaning and purpose to their life. This uses all of the latest findings from sociology and psychology to analyze what we mean by happiness and then shifts into a gentle deconstruction of our self-image along the lines you are indicating. And it concludes that the only pursuit that is really worthwhile is discovering the truth that we are already 'perfect and complete'.

My book 'Back to the Truth: 5000 years of Advaita' addresses your more difficult second question. One obvious way of thinking about it is to consider the three states of Consciousness. You enter the deep-sleep state every night and, in it, there is no mind present. Do you worry that who-you-really-are will disappear when you go to sleep or do you actually look forward to it and feel great resentment if you are kept from it? Of course, 'you' are still present in deep-sleep, despite the absence of mind. To come back to the witness concept, 'you' can see the mind and thoughts so cannot be either of those. But, yes, you are ultimately right – the 'witness' concept of Self has to go eventually too. In the final analysis, all of this is just appearance, and the true non-dual reality transcends appearance.

Q.40 How can elements be both real and unreal?

Q: In Sri Nisargadatta Maharaj's discourses the five elements and the three gunas appear to be permanent and immutable but these are the characteristics of the Absolute, the only Reality. At the same time the elements and gunas are part of the manifested reality, i.e., the world which is not 'real'. So how can they be both real and unreal?

A: Can you quote the reference that states that the elements and/ or guNa are real in any sense? This must be a misunderstanding. The really real is unmanifest and undifferentiated. The world, elements, guNa or whatever are mithyA only, name and form dependent upon the reality. Please rephrase or ask additional questions if this is not clear.

Q: This is actually my question. Are they? My reasoning (quite possibly faulty) goes as follows:

1. The Real is permanent and unchanging.
2. The gunas and elements are – apparently – permanent and unchanging, since it is they that always govern the manifest reality.
3. Therefore, the gunas and elements are real.

I do have a nagging feeling that this conclusion is based on an error but I can't put my finger on it. We could also say that this question is unimportant, or 'who wants to know?', etc. However, I wonder if receiving an answer on the same epistemological level is possible. Alternatively, I would like to know where I am taking the false step in my argument. Perhaps the criteria of immutability and permanency are not sufficient to make 'something' real?

A: Right, now I see where you are coming from! Good reasoning, faulty premise.

The point about all traditional Advaita teaching is that it is aimed at taking us from where we think we are now (separate, limited etc.) to the recognition of our identity with Brahman. And everyone cannot be at the same level of understanding. Accordingly, Advaita has carefully gauged prakriyA-s which the teacher will use as appropriate for a particular student. (A prakriyA is a set procedure, story or metaphorical explanation which the student will understand from his or her own experience and which will give insight into what is being discussed.)

Ultimately, all prakriyA-s are false. Once the related ignorance has been dispelled, the knowledge that brought it about is discarded, too. All knowledge is equally mithyA. So, the story about five elements and three guNa-s is a useful fiction, devised to help the sAdhaka along the way towards understanding. The only reality is Brahman and this cannot be divided into elements or anything else. If it could be divided, it would not be non-dual, as you have already appreciated.

Incidentally, you use the term 'manifest reality'. This is not strictly accurate and could be misleading. The world is not other than Brahman so, in that sense, is real. But it is only a particular form of Brahman, in the same way that the ring is a form of gold. The correct appellation is that the world is mithyA – dependent for its reality on Brahman. Only Brahman is ultimately real – satyam. The ring is always gold but the gold may or may not be the ring.

Q.52 Is truth relative?

Q: Is Truth always one or is it the case, for example, that reincarnation actually happens if we believe in it or are still in some way caught up in mAyA? Is Truth relative?

A: Advaita is a gauged philosophy. A skilled teacher will answer the questions at the student's level of, or readiness for, understanding. For some students, the concept of reincarnation is one that 'strikes a chord' and provides satisfactory answers 'for the time being'. There comes a time, if the student continues to study, assimilate and validate the teaching, when these explanations no longer satisfy and a different approach is needed. All study, question and answer, experience, student and teacher and the world of objects are at the 'empirical' level of reality. 'Truth', in the absolute sense, is always only One – there is only the non-dual Brahman.

At the level of empirical reality, there is simply the ever-changing names and forms that we, in our ignorance, take for the truth. But that, too, is actually only the non-dual Brahman. The material form that is referred to as person X will certainly eventually 'die' and decay and change into more basic forms. The more subtle forms that make up the saMskAra-s of X may continue according to the law of karma and reappear sometime later 'attached' to a new physical body. This might be regarded as the 'reincarnation' of X. But the Truth is still the same.

Q: As I am a scientist, it is inevitable that 'Why?' questions are going to crop up in the mind. After all, the objective universe is ruled by a cause and effect chain. When Vivekananda was asked why Brahman projected the 'illusion', the magic of mAyA, the pair of opposites, the universe, he always replied that while we are still caught within mAyA, the question cannot be answered for as yet we are not ready. The intellect which answers questions is also bound in mAyA. And once we have 'become', then the question, the questioner, and the answer, will no longer exist for us.

I still have a couple of questions: Why is there the empirical reality in the first place? And why are there these subtle forms? They must come into existence at some stage, since the law of karma operates in time. Of course there is also the question of who made the law of karma. How did it come about and who defined the rules?

I have read Vivekananda, Ramana Maharshi and listened to Swami Chinmayananda's lectures on the Gita. Could you recommend one or two books? On saMskAra and reincarnation, there must have been a point in time in this transmigration process when they were sattvic and then got contaminated with rajasic and tamasic tendencies. Also there was a time when this planet was just a ball of fire i.e. no humans and therefore no subtle bodies. Then humans appeared and the population has now expanded to nearly 5 billion. Are these subtle bodies being manufactured on-line so to speak and if so why? Also, prior to the birth of the planet, the sun came into existence from the dust left behind by a supernova. Now since there were no humans to observe this, can we say this never happened?

A: In truth there has never been any creation – this is the ultimate teaching of Advaita – ajAtivAda. There appears to be a manifest universe because of adhyAsa – our mistakenly superimposing a separate reality on the forms; mixing up real and unreal as with the rope-snake metaphor. So, in truth, there is no empirical reality, only the non-dual paramArtha.

The 'law of karma' is part of vyavahAra, too; an attempt by the deluded mind to make sense of what it thinks it sees. According to it, saMskAra-s accumulate as a result of action, in the cause-effect manner that you mention. They must have their effect in due course, even if this requires another 'life'. It is not ultimately meaningful to ask questions about who made the law etc. If your mind is of the nature to be satisfied with being told that 'Ishvara' made the law, then fine. I suspect from your comment about being a scientist that your mind is not. (Neither was mine, since I too had a scientific education.)

If you want a detailed explanation that will satisfy the most critical scientific mind, you will have to study something like Gaudapada's kArikA on the mANDUkya upaniShad. This is the 'advanced' Advaita text, if you like, for those who have moved up through the earlier material. Having read virtually all of the available translations of this and studied it for a number of years, I eventually wrote my own commentary to explain it to Westerners. This was published in 2015 – 'A-U-M: Awakening to Reality'.

Books that I would particularly recommend are:

'Methods of Knowledge According to Advaita Vedanta' by Swami Satprakashananda.

Practically anything by Swami Dayananda – you can get a 'Collection of Talks and Essays' from 'Arsha Vidya Bookstore' (http://www.arshavidya.org/Bookstore.html).

For a clear and rationally acceptable explanation of karma, 'Karma and Reincarnation' by Swami Muni Narayana Prasad is very good.

Your questions about the provenance of subtle bodies etc. are not worth pursuing. Any questions about the nature of the empirical realm are equivalent to asking whether the snake in the rope-snake metaphor is poisonous. Once you realize that it is a rope, the question no longer has any meaning. Hope these answers provide a degree of satisfaction for the scientific mind!

Q.60 How can the Self be actionless?

Q: How can the statement that the Self is the still, silent observer who does not act, be reconciled with the action that is taking place in the universe, which is a manifestation of the Self?

A: This is essentially a paramArtha-vyavahAra question (most of the seemingly difficult ones turn out to be). A good way into this is to consider the dream state. There usually seems to be lots of action in dreams – whole cities with transport and people all going about their apparent business. But what is seen when you wake up? That nothing was 'really' happening at all; it was all an imagined scenario taking place in the mind. The 'actions' were only movement of 'mind-stuff', to which we had temporarily assigned name and form.

The same applies to the 'real' world, which isn't real at all. In reality, there is only ever Brahman, unchanging, eternal etc. The apparent world with its objects and people and action is our mistaken interpretation as a result of adhyAsa. In fact, it is only the movement of names and forms of mithyA objects whose essential nature is the same non-dual Brahman.

Q.64 Appearance of the world

Q: From the point of view of a seeker, I have difficulty accepting that *"the movement of names and forms of mithyA objects"* is as insubstantial as movements in a dream. Surely the world and its movements (from the heavenly bodies to the minutest thought) have a degree of reality, albeit a dependent one. Even though everything is Brahman, they are still movements, so my question still stands. To accept the Advaita position would be to deny reason, experience and science.

A: Of course the world has seeming reality from the vyAvahArika standpoint – but then the dream world has seeming reality from the standpoint of the dreamer. It is only when you wake up that you can 'look back', as it were, and realize that the dream was all in your mind.

Advaita's view certainly denies experience and science – both these are subject-object 'activities' in the dualistic world. Advaita is not contrary to reason, however. Indeed, it is one of the precepts of Advaita that you must employ reason to verify what you are told or read. From the pAramArthika standpoint, there cannot be any action because there is no 'actor/thing-to-be-acted-on'; there is no 'cause-effect'; there is no time or space; there is no duality.

But you must also be careful not to think that the world and objects are 'unreal'. You have to be quite sure that you understand the difference between 'unreal' and 'mithyA'. What you can say (and think) is that the world is not real *in itself.* It derives its reality (existence) from Brahman. It is like the pot made out of clay and the lump of clay from which it was made. The pot is not real in itself. Take the clay away and the pot ceases to exist.

Q.116 Does mAyA have a context?

Q: My question is simply: Does mAyA have a context, and if so what is it?

It seems to me that unless mAyA has a context there is a piece of the puzzle missing. It must be a truth that we are all born in an enlightened state but such is the attachment power of mAyA that we are under the spell of the illusion before we are able to rationalize and exert any apparent control over the function of the mind. However I have the proof with my own children that if you are sensitive to the fact that we fundamentally feel our way into this world and help them to come to terms with the crude communication of words, it manifests in them staying more in touch with their true selves.

If mAyA doesn't have a context, then everything we do or say in this world is an irrelevance. Also, how do you reconcile the changing behavior of 'enlightened' individuals with an irrelevant mAyA?

Maybe I am confusing a Neo versus traditional Advaita principle but it also seems to me that there cannot be any fundamentally meaningful difference between Neo and traditional Advaita.

I look forward to hearing an answer to my simple question. I'm 224 pages into 'Back to the Truth' – an impressive tome. I think I am somewhere along the path without knowing precisely where. I'm intrigued, though ultimately not bothered, by the seeming lack of retro-engagement possibility of the enlightened state.

A: Enlightenment is not a state; it equates to Self-knowledge and is effectively a permanent disposition of the mind, once attained. It is one of those modern myths that we are born enlightened. According to traditional Advaita, we are 'born' (at the relative level of the world) because of past karma and because we are *not* yet enlightened. (Of course, at the absolute level, no one is ever born because there are no individuals and no creation; there is only the non-dual reality.)

Given that we do seem to be in a world of separate people and objects, mAyA is the 'force' that is postulated to provide an interim explanation of what is going on. It goes along with Ishvara, who wields the force, and all of the jIva-s, who are subject to it. But it is only an interim explanation. As our understanding grows, traditional Advaita provides successively more subtle explanations and withdraws the previous, course explanations. In reality, mAyA is just as false as every 'thing' else. So, the simple answer is that the context of mAyA is vyavahAra; in paramArtha, there is no such thing.

When enlightenment occurs, all of this is known as unarguably true. Nevertheless, just as the sun still appears to rise and set, even though we know that it is the earth rotating around the sun, so the world, with its objects and people continues to appear just as before. The enlightened man knows that everything is just name and form of Brahman but he continues to play his role for the remainder of his life. Indeed, the role is played better, knowing that who-he-really-is is totally unaffected by the seeming appearance.

For the unrealized, whose 'context' remains as vyavahAra, everything is relevant – vyavahAra *is* the effective reality. There is the possibility of seeking, finding a path and a teacher, gaining Self-knowledge and becoming enlightened. For the realized, all of this is mithyA – an appearance of Brahman and simply a game to be enjoyed, with no winners or losers. This is mAyA.

The problem with Neo-Advaita is that it denies the existence/relevance of vyavahAra and tries to 'impose' the absolute reality upon ignorant and enlightened equally. This is not helpful!

Not sure what you mean by 'lack of retro-engagement possibility'. It seems you are implying that, for the realized man, the world disappears somehow. This is another one of those myths. As noted above, everything continues as before; it is just now known to be mithyA. Having been previously confused himself, the realized man has compassion for those seeming others who are still confused and he is perfectly willing to help them. The extent to which he is able to do so depends upon his teaching skills and knowledge of appropriate methods etc.

Q.176 After all are enlightened, might lIlA start again?

Q: After all the jIva-s realize their true self and return to the Source/Brahman, will it be a real possibility that Brahman will create another lIlA or 'divine game' and so Brahman will start manifesting as form again and we will once again be under mAyA and start seeing everything as separate again?

A: This question is again confusing the two levels. From the standpoint of the apparent world, Hinduism has its creation theories etc. just as Christianity does. The story is that Brahma (*not* Brahman but the particular god who is currently playing the role of creator) creates the world according to the fruits that had accumulated on termination of the previous creation. He also (re-) creates all of the jIva-s. Some of these will be reincarnating; some new ones will have progressed from lower life forms; gods will now be being reborn as jIva-s to try to reach enlightenment. This new creation passes through four stages (yuga-s) of decreasing purity and increasing anarchy until that creation reaches an end and is 'folded up'. There is then nothing for a while (pralaya) until the whole sequence begins again. This has always been going on and always will.

As I have said before, from the standpoint of absolute reality, there is no creation; there are no jIva-s or gods; there is only Brahman who does nothing and wants for nothing because it is already perfect and complete.

Q: You say that the yuga-s will keep going on and on forever but what if all the jIva-s achieve enlightenment in the future, even if this takes a long time? Then the new creation and yuga-s will stop, surely?

Also have you realized yourself? Will I be able to realize myself for sure in this lifetime by focusing on the feeling 'I am'? I have read that David Godman, who dedicated his whole life to Ramana's teachings and practiced Self-enquiry, has still not realized his self. Ramana is said to have realized the self at a very young age. Does this all depend upon how good one's karma is?

A: Since there is really no creation in the first place from the standpoint of absolute reality, it is not meaningful to ask questions such as this. It is like the waker asking if the accident victim in his dream recovered or not.

Regarding my own 'enlightenment', as I have told everyone else who asks this question, it depends what you mean by the term. It is like asking me whether I believe in god. You define exactly what you mean and I will give you an answer according to that definition.

As far as your spiritual search is concerned at the level of empirical reality, simply repeating 'I am' or meditating upon this will not bring enlightenment. If you think of enlightenment as 'Self-knowledge', you will appreciate that you need to learn things about the nature of yourself and the world in order to remove the

Self-ignorance that presently exists. Whether or not you attain enlightenment in this life might be thought of as karma-dependent to the extent that your choice to pursue Self-knowledge and your ability to do so are the 'effect' of past influences.

Q.182 adhyAsa

Q: In the description of mistaken superimposition (adhyAsa), it is said that we superimpose the 'is-ness' of the rope onto the snake. How is this possible, when the snake is unreal and never existed in the first place? Also, the 'is-ness' of objects is not an attribute, it's their very essence, and therefore not superimposable.

A: I agree that it is a strange way of putting it and you could certainly argue that pedantically it cannot be so. However, the actual situation regarding the rope-snake is that the snake does not exist while the rope does exist. Yet we say with certainty 'there is a snake'. What it seems that we have done is to take the 'is-ness' of the rope and superimpose it upon the illusory snake, thereby giving it seeming existence.

A more rational way of speaking about this is to say that we have projected the mental image of a snake onto the rope but (pedantically speaking) this is superimposing the illusory snake onto the real rope and the 'is-ness' still belongs to the rope (which it does anyway of course). But, since we believe that the snake exists, we must also believe that the snake has 'is-ness', even though this is ultimately discovered to have been illusory. To this extent, we must have 'borrowed' the is-ness from the rope.

It's really only playing with words in order to understand what is happening and it is probably best simply to say that we are mixing up real and unreal.

There is an excellent 5-part series of articles on adhyAsa, as described by Shankara in his introduction to the brahmasUtra bhAShya. It was written by AchArya Sadananda of Chinmaya Foundation and edited by myself (http://www.advaita-vision.org/adhyasa-part-1/). As evidenced by the fact that Shankara chose to preface his commentary in this way, the concept of adhyAsa is one of the most important in the entire methodology of Advaita. Accordingly, all serious seekers should insure that they understand it!

Q.189 Aren't 'truth', 'justice', 'faith' etc. real?

Q: According to the principles of Advaita, there is no difference between jIvAtman and paramAtman. If so, why should an Atma ever be encapsulated in a body (of ignorance)? Also, why is such an encapsulated Atma not capable of performing actions that 'paramAtman' is capable of?

When everything in this material world that you can perceive is unreal, how can it be that everything in the 'higher world' is real? Even in this unreal world, there should exist something real to guide the 'worthy' ones. Of these 'real' things, there should be 'Truth', 'Justice', 'Faith' etc. When one is exposed to what is perceived as 'Injustice', is it unfair to expect the perception of 'Justice'?

A: The absolute truth is that the Atma has never been 'encapsulated in a body'; there are no jIva-s; there is no world; nothing has ever been 'created'. There is only Brahman. Also, paramAtman performs no actions at all.

The world, the people in it, their actions, concepts such as truth, justice, faith etc. are not 'unreal' but neither are they 'real' in themselves. All is mithyA – name and form of Brahman only. What guides you to this truth is the shAstra, and ideally this should be unfolded by a skilled, self-realized guru.

Q: What do you mean by saying "The world, the people in it, their actions, concepts such as truth, justice, faith etc. are not unreal but neither are they real in themselves"? Please correct me if I am wrong: what is not 'unreal' is the same as 'real' (double negation = positive). Also, please explain what you mean by saying "neither are they real in themselves". (Specifically the stress seems to be on" in themselves".)

A: The sort of example that is used to illustrate the 'neither real nor unreal' problem is that of gold and ring. The ring clearly exists since you can see it on your finger. Therefore it is not unreal. However, it is not a thing-in-itself; ring is not a substance. I could say to you that I will take the gold and let you have the ring! The fact of the matter is that the ring is only a particular form of gold, which we have chosen to honor with a name of its own to recognize its shape and function. The reality is only ever gold. Similarly, the world and the jIva are not things-in-themselves. They are only forms of Brahman to which we have chosen to give names to recognize their roles and appearance.

Q.272 How does a plant grow without an observer?

Q: If I leave a plant in my backyard and there is no one to look at it for three weeks, then how we can explain an inch of growth after I return?

A: This is one of those 'confusion of levels' problems. From the point of view of absolute reality, there is only Brahman – no plant and no observer. At the level of empirical reality, there is a separate plant and a separate observer and they are born, grow and die quite independently (although if you leave it for three weeks without watering, you might just bear some moral responsibility for its death!).

Since there is actually only the non-dual Brahman, even at the 'empirical' level', it follows that all attempts to explain things must be wrong in the final analysis. Explanations are interim only, to provide some satisfaction for the inquisitive mind. The interim explanation that is usually employed by traditional Advaita is that objects have an independent existence because they are created by Ishvara. So the plant continues to grow, even though there might not be any observers. (Or, if you follow Berkeley, Ishvara is watching!)

Another way of looking at it is that the plant and its soil substrate are simply name and form of Brahman. Food from the soil Brahman is simply moving into the plant Brahman, which therefore grows. It is all simply changing name and form of Brahman.

Yet another 'explanation' is given in the Chandogya Upanishad. This describes the process that the jIva has to go through in between lifetimes and is referred to as the 'five (mystic or sacred) fires'. Effectively this indicates that the jIva 'travels' via vegetation. So you could regard your plant as a jIva in its own right! If you want to read lots more about this bizarre version, read my 3-part essay beginning (http://www.advaita-vision.org/between-lives/). (But, despite its scriptural origin, I would not put too much credence in it!)

Q.301 Why do we see duality?

Q: From the pAramArthika standpoint, everything is Brahman, and nothing exists other than Brahman. Thus, the world that we observe should be names and forms of Brahman, which must be 'real' (since it is indeed Brahman). Given this understanding, the following question arises: Why do we observe ever changing and diverse forms of the non-dual Brahman?

If the apparent world is nothing other than Brahman, which is homogeneous and non-changing, why do we not recognize the world as such? Is this the result of adhyAsa? At the vyAvahArika level, I cannot believe we always perceive the rope as a snake. Without accounting for this seeming contradiction, Advaita suffers from logical inconsistency, even if it rejects any creation theories. Or is this question already subject to category errors? Or is it simply that we cannot explain this, using language that presupposes the duality? Does the world of pAramArthika truth deny any attempts to make verbal explanations? I would greatly appreciate it if you could provide some comments on this question.

A: This is really a formulation of the unanswerable question which has been asked before in many forms, such as 'Why is there something rather than nothing?' (By the Western philosopher, Schelling) or 'Why, if Brahman is already perfect and complete, does he create the universe?' or even 'Which comes first, the jIva or ignorance?'

The yoga vAsiShTha (II.xxi.35) sums up Advaita's view: '*This universe of plurality is verily an illusion. The reality is the undifferentiated Absolute and I am That. The proof of this is the Upanishads, the great Teachers who have realized the truth of the Upanishadic doctrine, and one's own personal experience,*' (translation A. J. Alston in, A Shankara Source Book, Volume 1).

We fail to see this because of ignorance, which as you say gives rise to adhyAsa. In truth, there is no ignorance; you only think there is (hence the question about it). But, if you believe you are affected by ignorance, you must be 'seeing' ignorance as an object – which means that it does not belong to you, the subject. The Self only appears to be deluded and subsequently liberated. [This is paraphrasing Alston's summary of Shankara's views.]

And, as regards the ontological status of ignorance, see Q.261, where I quoted from Shankara's Brihadaranyaka Upanishad bhAShya (I.iv.10).

Q: Thanks very much for your always insightful comments. Although I still need some time to fully understand your comments, it seems that the formulation of the unanswerable question is caused by my jAgrat state. Is it correct to say that paramArtha ways of understanding reality are only made possible by the person in the turIya state?

If this is correct, we can only imperfectly describe the pAramArthika satya using language since, by definition, we are in the jAgrat or svapna states in this case. Using a metaphor, we do not really understand how to swim by reading the text, only once we actually get into the water and practice swimming (but then, the serious problem is that we are not sure how we can get into the turIya state).

Besides these concerns, my tentative understanding on the seeming contradiction between our perception and Brahman is as follows. Since we can only observe the Absolute through the lens of time-space-causality, as Vivekananda described, we can recognize only a limited set of the Infinity. In this respect, I assume nirguNa is a set of infinite attributes. Then, observed diversity is owing to this imperfect recognition of the infinity as oneness, while the change is attributed to our changing recognition of a finite subset of the infinite attributes, owing to the mAyA of time, although the Absolute itself does not move. Thus, apparent diversity and change are caused not by unchanging Brahman as oneness, but by our limited cognitive power, which could be defined as avidyA. Is this understanding valid? Or does it still suffer from some serious logical inconsistencies? I greatly appreciate your comments.

A: You can never understand Brahman intellectually – Brahman cannot be 'known'; you are Brahman.

There is no such thing as 'pAramArthika ways of understanding reality'; paramArtha is itself a concept (in vyavahAra). There are only vyAvahArika ways of understanding anything. Advaita presents concepts, metaphors, etc., which only point to the reality. It says things about Brahman which enable you to discard previous false ideas but, eventually, you have to drop the new ideas as well. All ideas about Brahman must fail to capture the true essence because you cannot predicate anything whatsoever about Brahman.

turIya is not a state; it is effectively a synonym for Brahman, which you already are. All states are mithyA. nirguNa is not a 'set of infinite attributes'; it is an absence of attributes of any kind – 'nir' guNa means 'beyond' the guNa; having nothing to do with them. The observed diversity is because of adhyAsa; mistakenly superimposing false notions upon the non-dual reality.

Q.318 Gunas and history

Q:

1. If the triple gunas are the matrix of the 'reality', aren't they immutable and therefore truly real?

2. What is the ontological status of the course of human history?

Is it objective, or just a sort of shared mass illusion that somehow gets transferred from generation to generation?

A: The guNa-s only have reality in sAMkhya philosophy, where they are the substantial parts of prakRRiti or pradhAna (primordial matter). In Advaita, they are the *attributes* of prakRRiti, which itself is only mithyA.

Regarding history, this too is mithyA. Everything is mithyA. Only Brahman is satyam. If you think of one of your dreams, it clearly had a history for its duration, i.e. a beginning and an end and a succession of events in between, even if these did not seem to have logical succession (when viewed from the vantage point of the waking state). What we call the 'real world', which we perceive in our waking state, does seem to have logical succession and also a content that is agreed amongst different observers. But it can be regarded as Ishvara's dream if you like and it lasts a very long time from our standpoint (4,320,000,000 years, I believe, according to Hinduism). At the end of the creation, the universe returns to unmanifest form, along with all the jIva-s and Ishvara. But, in between creation (sRRiShTi) and dissolution (pralaya), history is maintained and appears to be to be objective from the standpoint of the jIva.

Q.338 Not the 'doer'

Q: It seems like a contradiction to me to say that we are the observer and not the doer and, at the same time, suggest that we can do something such as 'paying attention'. I encounter this apparent contradiction often when I read about Advaita. If there is no doer, why are there suggestions as to how to remove ignorance, for example? Who would remove the ignorance if there is no doer?

– Is it that in the dualistic world it appears as if there is a doer and therefore we act 'as if', even though we might know that there is no doer?

– If we realize that there is no doer but we act 'as if', is it like playing our part in a game?

– If the ignorance is removed, who apperceives the truth?

A: You are quite right. The fact of the matter has to be that, if we are being 'true' to the non-dual nature of reality, we could never say anything at all. Who could say what to whom when there is no differentiation?

In practice, what we try to do is point to that reality from the dualistic world of transactions. This is where we start from – we are ignorant of the truth. This ignorance is very much in the dualistic mind of the dualistic individual. And the only way to 'apperceive' the truth is via the 'explanations' of scriptures and teachers. This, in turn, necessitates saying things which cannot be literally true but which have to be taken as intermediate truths, if you like, in order to progress in understanding until able to make the final leap of realization.

You just have to get into the habit of appreciating from which viewpoint you are speaking (thinking). From the standpoint of the empirical world, we cannot help but act. We are constantly breathing, circulating blood etc.; we have to eat and drink to maintain the body, and move about in order to achieve these. And I (the individual jIva) think and speak, trying to get the mind to understand and dissolve its ignorance. All of this is actually happening from the vyAvahArika viewpoint. And, most of the time, it is definitely not a game!

But in reality, there is only Brahman – non-dual consciousness if you like. There are no individuals doing anything at all; no actions and no objects upon which to act.

So what is happening here is that we are, for all practical purposes, living in a dualistic universe but trying to understand and appreciate the non-dual reality in our minds. If you want the crude analogy, we seem to be individual waves in a huge and constantly threatening ocean. But in reality there is only ever water.

Q.372 Superimposition and memory

Q: What is the relationship between memory and superimposition (adhyAsa)? In the metaphor of rope and snake, we say that we fail to see the snake clearly, because of inadequate light – there is partial knowledge and partial ignorance. When we superimpose a snake on the rope, we are drawing on fear and memory. We must have seen a snake (or image of one in a film or book) before in order to be able to mistake the rope for one. Similarly, we mistake Brahman for the body and the world etc.

But what about a baby or someone who has no memory as a result of brain damage? Is there still superimposition in this case?

A: The mechanism of perceptual error is one of the key issues for Indian Epistemology. The example most frequently encountered is that of seeing silver in the nacre of a shell. Mistaking a rope for a snake is similar – both are examples of seeing an object as something totally different. The other type of perceptual error is mistaking an attribute – an example of this is seeing the transparent crystal as red because of the proximity of a red cloth. But essentially there is an illusory appearance upon a real substratum in all cases.

Since knowledge of objects is based purely on the attributes that the senses manage to gather during observation, doubts and errors can arise. Depending upon which philosophy you take, there are at least 7 different theories which try to explain what is happening in detail.

The two schools of (pUrva) mImAMsA claim that the 'silver' misperception arises from memory (although they argue about the mechanism). But in essence, as far as I can make out, what they claim is that there is a failure to discriminate between the object and the memory (of the wrong object). They claim that all knowledge is valid so that any error is caused by 'non-apprehension' rather than misapprehension.

The nyAya philosopher thinks that we actually perceive the wrong object. Because of insufficient light, defective vision or whatever, we fail to see the actual object and instead somehow see the remembered object instead. The wrong object must actually be seen because, they say, it would not be meaningful to say that we saw an absolutely non-existent thing.

sAMkhya philosophers claim that the error arises because we see the shell as both real and unreal – real as the present object and unreal as remembered silver – and fail to apprehend the distinction.

The vishiShTadvaitins believe that there really is silver in the shell and that a defect in the vision of the one who 'misperceives' causes them to see the particles of silver instead.

The mAdhyamika Buddhist believes that everything is unreal so all that is happening here is that we are seeing an unreal thing superimposed upon another unreal thing, as a result of our particular vAsanA-s.

The vij~nAna vAda Buddhist thinks that all appearances are manifestations of (momentary) Consciousness so that silver is just as good (bad) as shell as far as the perception goes.

And so we come to the Advaitin's view of things. Suitable arguments are offered against all of the above theories. What Shankara says is that, in the case of an erroneous conclusion from the perception (e.g. seeing silver instead of nacre), we are 'mixing up' real (there is an object) and unreal (it is silver). Partial knowledge gives us the former and partial ignorance the latter. The partial knowledge comes from the real object. The partial ignorance comes from a memory, which has no real object as its substratum; instead the remembered object is superimposed upon the present, real object.

The perceived object (silver) is not real, because when we go closer, pick it up etc., it is found to be nacre – the silver is sublated. But it is not unreal either, because we perceive it. (Hence the Advaitin theory is called anirvachanIya khyAti – apprehension of the indefinable.) Nevertheless, Advaita rejects those theories which talk about confusing the real shell with remembered silver because we actually see the silver here and now, in front of us, not as some image in memory. If there were not an actual (mis) perception of silver, the mistake would not be made.

So we actually see silver. When we bend down to pick it up, we realize our mistake. The silver perception is sublated and we now know that it is nacre. The silver was not unreal – because we experienced it; but it was not real either, because the subsequent examination found it to be nacre. It was mithyA (in the context of the nacre).

The nyAya philosopher argues with the Advaitin, trying to claim that the silver which is seen is the real silver previously seen, taken from memory and superimposed on the nacre. As noted above, the Advaitin rejects this, saying that we actually perceive silveriness *now*, in the object. Because 'silveriness' is the predominant attribute of silver, we thus conclude that the object is silver. It is thus a real and present attribute that we see, not a previously seen total object.

And this, I think, is the key to answering the question. We see an attribute and correlate it with any memories we might have of things which possess that attribute. Silveriness is thus highly likely to make us conclude that it is silver, if we do not know better. In the case of the rope, in a situation (country) where we might have reason to fear snakes, poor illumination of a coiled-up rope may well make us suspect a snake – if we know what a snake is. Even if we haven't actually seen one (in a zoo, for example) we have probably seen them on TV or in a book. However, a baby or toddler may well not have seen one and I suggest that, in this case, he or she will *not* think it is a snake. They are unlikely to be fearful of the thing – maybe they will suspect it is a discarded umbilical cord...

If you want to read lots more about perception and error, read AchArya Sadananda's series on 'Knowledge', edited by myself (http://www.advaita.org.uk/discourses/knowledge/intro1.htm).

Q.448 Are animals real?

Q: I am struggling to understand where reality ends and mithyA begins.

I understand that everything in my experience is Consciousness. But I cannot reconcile this with seeing 'things' in the 'world'. I appreciate that, if I am Brahman, meaning that my little jIva consciousness is actually Brahman, then it is my consciousness that is generating this entire perception of nature and mammals. In other words, the only thing going on with the 'jIva seeing world and objects' is Consciousness.

But what is going on for the animals and objects? Are they really there or not? Are they appearing just through my human mind via Brahman/Consciousness? Are there no objects in reality? When I see a leopard, all that is real is Consciousness seeing Consciousness? Then how are the leopards appearing with so much complexity and purpose?

I realize that time and space are appearing in Consciousness; I realize that leopards are appearing in Consciousness. But what are they? Do you have any way to answer this that doesn't rely on the Advaita Vedanta language since that language isn't getting through to me? In other words, dependent reality, Ishvara, mAyA, mithy**A:** none of these words seem to be pointing me in the right direction.

A: Here is a story reported as told by Swami Dayananda:

"There was a King in whose court there were a number of preceptors from various philosophies, including one from Advaita. The King was very close to the Advaitin and the other philosophers were looking for the first opportunity to prove the Advaitin wrong. One day, when the King and his retinue were walking in a forest, suddenly there appeared a wild elephant. *The Advaitin was the first one to take off and run for cover. Later, when all of them assembled in the King's court, preceptors of other philosophies wasted no time in grasping the opportunity to point out to the King, that though the Advaitin taught everything was mithyA, he was the first one to run on seeing the wild elephant – and they asked*

'Why would the Advaitin run on seeing the wild mithyA elephant?' The Advaitin answered them calmly 'yes I did run – but who said my running was satyam – it was also mithyA'".

Your viewing animals and objects etc. is all within the realm of the empirical – the world of experience. And, within that context, the animals are real. It is like talking about dreams. The world of the dream, with all its characters and places and objects is real for the dreamer. It is only when you wake up that the waker can say that the dream was 'not real'. For the waker, the dream is mithyA, being dependent upon the waker's mind for its existence.

For the jIva, the separate entity in the empirical world, the animals are real. The jIva is real. But the consciousness of the jIva is a reflected Consciousness only. This reflected Consciousness nevertheless has the power to animate the body-mind of the jIva and to impose name and form upon the Consciousness 'out there', making it appear to the mind that there are separate entities, when there is really (from the 'perspective' of absolute reality) only non-dual Consciousness.

Within the context of the waker-world, the animals are separate entities with their own reflected Consciousness. You might imagine that there are countless mirrors in existence, each reflecting the sunlight. Vegetable life-forms are very poor reflectors, animals are much better and humans are the best. Humans reflect the Consciousness so well that the mind is self-aware and can even become enlightened!

Q: So are you saying that the animals exist only in the reflected consciousness of the jIva's mind? Meaning that when the jIva's mind dies or the reflection wakes up to its reality, the animals will not (really) exist? Or will the animals still exist in the minds of all the other reflections?

Who is dreaming this dream of the universe with animals? Because I don't think it's Brahman ...

A: "So are you saying that the animals exist only in the reflected consciousness of the jIva's mind?"

– No. That would be solipsism. In the waking world, the animals exist in the reflected consciousness of everyone's mind (including those of other animals).

"Or will the animals still exist in the minds of all the other reflections?"

– Yes!

"Who is dreaming this dream of the universe with animals?"

– Within the context of the waking world, the only answer is 'Ishvara', I'm afraid. But remember that it is your mind that, through ignorance, is imposing name and form upon the formless Consciousness. From the vantage point of absolute reality, there is no waking world ...

Q: I have been reading Swami Dayananda's teaching where he shows a flower and then starts to take it apart to find out which bit is the actual flower. And I suddenly had an insight. Oh, what they are saying is: when you think about an object, it is obviously appearing in your consciousness but when you perceive an (external) object, it's actually the exact same process! An image appears in your consciousness – you are never experiencing an object that does not appear in your consciousness because perception is simply the prompting of imagery in the mind, same as any thought! There is never direct contact with any external object, ever, even your own body.

This is correct, right? I mean even scientifically correct? This opens up a floodgate of insight. I am only this consciousness, everything is in it and *is* it, and so am I – the end!

A: What you are saying here is effectively Kant's distinction between phenomenal and noumenal. Our senses are so limited that we can never perceive the ding an sich – the thing in itself. Our senses pass on a small amount of the total available data from objects to our mind and we are aware of that mind-presented thing, not the actual object.

But this is not quite what Advaita is saying. Kant is acknowledging that there are actual objects, just that we can never really apprehend them. Advaita is saying that there are *no* actual objects, that our minds effectively fabricate them by separating them out from the rest of what is 'out there' and giving them names.

The deconstruction of the flower is showing that the name 'flower' only applies to a particular form for which we have an idea in mind. If you take the thing to bits, there is no actual object which we can say is the flower. Have you read my 'story' based around this? (http://www.advaita.org.uk/discourses/definitions/advaita.htm.)

Your last sentence is, of course, correct!

Q: I see what you mean about Advaita versus Kant. What I'm seeing is that the entire world is not actually out there as a bunch of stuff. All of it is being produced, so to speak, in and via consciousness. The names and forms are obviously an error, but that isn't where I've been stuck.

I've been stuck because I have believed that what my senses tell me about the world is a direct result of the objects in the world being real. In other words, I see a rock because a rock is there. And when I see it, I think I see an exact replica because I believe that the mind is a perfect mirror of reality, at least to scale.

But now I'm seeing none of this is correct. When I see a rock, all that is happening is that an image is being generated in the mind which is 'made of' Consciousness. The rock is in Consciousness; the image is in Consciousness; and the name and form are in Consciousness. And Consciousness is one continuous whole with no parts or limits – there is no inside/outside Consciousness.

A: Sounds great! If you genuinely believe that, no problem at all! It's only a way of looking at it, of course, from the vantage point of the jIva in a world where everything is Consciousness. But you cannot get any 'closer' to reality than that via the spoken or conceptualized.

World

Q.37 Does the world exist without a perceiver?

Q: A few quick questions relating to the reality of the world.

A: Quick question?! Books have been written about this topic! Advaita has several theories, gauged for the level of understanding of the questioner. All these are addressed in my book 'Back to the Truth'.

Q: Does the reality of the world depend on a perceiver?

A: The world is not 'real'; it is mithyA. It has not been 'created'; it has 'dependent' reality, being simply name and form of the non-dual reality. What it depends upon is Brahman, not the perceiver which is part of that mithyA world.

Q: Does the world or universe exist independently?

A: I could say that, having answered the first question, all the rest are irrelevant and effectively meaningless. There is only Brahman. Seeing something other than Brahman is the mistake of adhyAsa – mixing up real and unreal. The mind sees forms and assigns names based on its particular nature, saMskAra-s etc. Accordingly, what it thinks it sees and what it *calls* what it thinks it sees will be dependent upon that nature. Thus, in that sense at least, the mind does create its own world (heaven or hell).

Q: Are there as many worlds as there are perceivers?

A: As above. Most questions of this sort depend upon the level at which you are speaking (paramArtha or vyavahAra) and confusion arises when the question is at one level and the answer is at the other. In reality, there is no world and no perceiver – obviously, if you are talking Advaita, since there are 'not two things'. At the level of appearance, you can apply whatever theory you like. Ultimately, it will have to be discarded. The approach to use is called svataH prAmANya vAda, which means not needing to validate knowledge acquired from one pramANa by another.

The theory that you are referencing is called dRRiShTisRRiShTivAda, where the perceiver combines what he (thinks he) sees with memory etc. and superimposes this upon reality, thus effectively bringing a 'world' into existence. This theory supersedes the more common-sense sRRiShTidRRiShTivAda, which says that the world has been created and then we see it. The theory that sublates both of these is ajAtivAda – there has never been any creation.

Q: When I look at an object with another person, for instance say the Statue of Liberty, is there just one that we both perceive or are there as many Statues of Liberty as there are sentient beings perceiving it?

A: As above – use whichever theory you like, really! I hope you can see that this is not being flippant. Wherever you think you are, use that theory which satisfies the mind for the time being. But the mind likes to play – and this is not always very helpful! Ultimately, there is no statue of liberty and no perceiver. There is only Brahman.

Q: Independent of a perceiver, what actually exists besides undifferentiated, infinite, eternal Consciousness?

A: Nothing – and what is this 'perceiver' that it is independent of? The differentiation only comes about in the manifestation as a result of a mind imposing name and form. (And this 'mind' is itself only name and form ...)

Read the book. There are many other sources explaining all of this in addition to my own inadequate attempts!

Q.59 Communicating with others (about Advaita)

Q: One of the questions that I ask myself is this: How do I live in the world of duality, in which everyone is asking my opinion on a whole range of topics? If I answer according to the teaching of Advaita, they don't like the answers they get and think I'm mad! I know there are really no answers or questions but I can't seem to communicate this in a way that can be understood ... and what's the point anyway?

A: You cannot escape the world of seeming duality, even if/when you gain enlightenment. There will always be 'seeming' others asking questions and being happy (or not) with the answers they receive. While you actually believe that the word is real, you are obliged to ask questions yourself if you are less than 100% happy with things (as is inevitable!) It is only through asking questions and receiving good answers that you can come to the realization that the world is mithyA and you are actually Brahman. When you have come to this realization, it no longer matters that there are still these questions from the seeming others. You then know that the 'others' are not separate and, if they are seriously interested in understanding the nature of the world and themselves, you may even be able to help them!

That is the point!

Q.93 Concerns for the environment

Q: Recently I've been having long, complex, endless conversations with a dear friend who is tremendously obsessed with, and depressed by, the environmental crisis: global warming, species extinction, the end of the oil supply, the coming water shortage – the whole situation.

She is a very intelligent, extremely compassionate woman, and her painful awareness, which never lets up, of all the suffering she sees going on has totally destroyed the 'faith in Life' she once had. She is in deep despair. I have no idea what to say to her as I have no 'answers' myself.

My question: In the Advaitic view, how does one deal with the, albeit apparent, suffering and terrible effects of this worldwide 'Environmental Crisis'? The (seeming) fact that we, as a species, are destroying the very planet we inhabit? Other species, our victims, go extinct daily, there is human suffering, especially of the very poorest people, on an unprecedented scale, and not only are no solutions of any merit put forth, there is, indeed, very little acknowledgment of what is happening.

I am going to assume that you will say one must cultivate detachment, as that does, indeed, seem to be the only 'real' answer;

and I accept that. But for those like myself, and my friend, who have not 'awakened', or truly realized Absolute Truth, and are people who feel all this as personal suffering and, worse, feel helpless to do anything, detachment is an attribute profoundly aspired to, yet seemingly inaccessible.

Here I am going to 'go out on a limb' and put forth a sort of theory of my own; I am coming to believe that some people's 'innate nature', for lack of a more precise term, simply precludes them from ever truly achieving the detachment so essential to Advaita. While they may totally understand Advaita intellectually, it can never be realized in a 'total' sense due to this inability to achieve the necessary detachment. I also think, or suspect, that many people are in this category with me.

A: For the person who is involved with the world, convinced of their separateness and mortality, there will always be suffering. Someone who is particularly attached to ideas of worldly problems will be able to see them everywhere – the world is a big place and there are many people. And obviously there is little or nothing that one can do about the majority of those problems, so that despair is not an unexpected outcome.

If you are asking what one should do as an 'individual' about all of this, I can only refer you to the metaphor of the reservoir, which I used in 'Book of One':

"Sri Parthasarathy speaks of four levels of helping others. At the lowest level, one can give money to a charity. This is impersonal and, once the money is handed over, is probably instantly forgotten. The next level is to give some personal possession. For example you might hand over your coat to a beggar in the street. Again, this is a brief transaction and carries little in the way of personal effort. The third level is to give oneself in the sense of personally assisting in a positive way. One might, for example, give up several hours a week to help with a local charity. Here there is actual involvement, interacting with others, directly giving of oneself. The highest level, however, is to seek enlightenment. This is total renunciation of one's ego, giving everything 'in service' to the truth

and ultimately benefiting all.

"He uses the metaphor of the water supply to help explain this. When we want a drink of water, most of us think that we just need to go and turn on the tap. It doesn't occur to us that this is not actually the source of the water at all. Ultimately, all of this water comes from a distant lake or reservoir up in the mountains. When new towns are constructed, men must travel to the reservoir and tap into its resources, bringing the water down to the houses so that we may benefit. The lake itself does nothing. It simply sits there and collects the rainwater from the heavens. When people discover that they need it, they have to come and connect into it. The realized man, he says, is like the reservoir. He sits there (in his cave), holding the knowledge of life, the universe and everything, and people who wish to learn go to him to discover the truth. He does nothing, yet makes available the most valuable knowledge there is – to those who seek it".

Also, of course, the dream metaphor is always a good answer to most questions of this sort. Suppose you have a dream in which you find someone injured, say, and you are just about to call for an ambulance when you wake up. Having woken up, your concern for the injured person disappears completely because you now know that the entire incident was illusory. Similarly, the enlightened mind knows that the world, with its separate persons, global warming etc. is mithyA only. All is Brahman and nothing needs to be done (or can be done because Brahman does nothing). [Note that this is not to say that the realized man ignores those who are suffering around him. On the contrary, action will take place in response to the need, without any attachment, according to the nature of his body-mind.]

There is a nice quote by David Carse: *"Taking the dream to be real is not what causes suffering; it is the suffering".*

I have actually answered questions about suffering before. See 'Q.24 Is suffering necessary', for example.

The solution is not to cultivate detachment as you suggest. If you still believe that there is suffering and you are ignoring it, this could only be construed as callous. The real solution is knowledge – to realize that there is no one who is suffering, that there is no world existing as a separate entity to be destroyed or unique species to become extinct etc. These are only the constantly changing forms of the non-dual reality, to which we in our ignorance give separate names and thereby conjure up problems where there are none.

Ramana Maharshi said: *"The world is alright as it is; it is we that are to blame, because of our own mistaken way of thinking"*. Ultimately, you have to realize that the world is in me; I am not in the world.

As regards how you should act towards your friend, simply stating ideas such as those above is unlikely to help. Knowledge of Advaita has to be presented in a gradual way, ideally by a qualified, realized teacher. Bottom-line conclusions will simply be ridiculed by most intelligent people. All you can do is be sympathetic and supportive and perhaps hint that a philosophy exists which can bring us to the realization that things are nowhere near so bad as they might appear; in fact, quite the contrary!

Q.135 Are there other people?

Q: I understand that we are all the same being. But are other people out there having their own subjective experiences like me? Or are they simply projections?

A: From the standpoint of absolute reality, there are not two.

While this truth is still covered over by ignorance, there seems to be a separate world containing separate people, although all of this is simply name and form of that absolute reality. Advaita provides an 'interim' explanation, for those as yet unable to appreciate the absolute truth. This is that the world is created and that the illusion of separateness is due to a power called mAyA, which is wielded by Ishvara, the Lord of all.

From this relative standpoint, the world and people are a reality. It is not projected by you, the individual – that idea is called solipsism. And, of course, we 'each' have our own separate experiences (*you* are communicating with *me*).

The best metaphor to think of, if you find this concept difficult, is the one of wave and ocean. At the 'relative level', the wave is a part of the ocean (the individual is a part of Ishvara) but from the standpoint of 'absolute reality', both wave and ocean are always nothing but water (individual and Ishvara are both actually Brahman).

In fact, the solipsistic interpretation of the world – I, the jIva, project the appearance of other people – was held by a few Advaitic philosophers post Shankara. The Sanskrit term is 'eka jIva vAda', meaning 'the belief that there is only one jIva'. And arguments still rage today between people who would each claim to be representing the 'correct' vision of Advaita. Some of these discussions may be read at my website – see, for example, (http://www.advaita-vision.org/shruti-support-for-eka-jiva-vada/) and see Q.393 for links to other articles on the subject.

Q.163 Are dreamed people real?

Q: (continuing on from Q.135) What about the dream state? Are the people that we see in dreams real, as in the waking state (from the relative standpoint) or they are solipsistic (i.e. do I create them)?

A: From the standpoint of the dreamer, the people that you meet in the dream are real. From the standpoint of the waker, it is all a creation of the mind. But you can't call this solipsism since the dreamer ego is not real either (from the standpoint of the waker).

This is why dreams are such a good pointer for the seeker looking for the truth! You know that, while you were in the dream, everything seemed so real yet, on awakening, you find that none of it was real. So it is with the waking state, too. Just as the dream was a creation of your individual mind, the world is a creation of the macrocosmic mind (Ishvara). Both are mithyA.

Q: So, to rephrase what you said: From the standpoint of the waker, the people that you meet are real. From the standpoint of the macrocosmic mind (Ishvara), it is all a creation. But you can't call this solipsism since the waker ego is not real either (from the standpoint of Ishvara). Is that right?

A: No, that is not quite right. Certainly, from the standpoint of the waker (empirical reality), other people are real and creation is real (and we say that Ishvara is the creator). From the standpoint of absolute reality (turIya, paramArtha, Brahman), you the waker are not real, the world is not real, Ishvara is not real. Ultimately, only Brahman is real (sat). Everything else is mithyA.

Q.207 On the 'changelessness' of Brahman.

Q: My question concerns the ring of gold analogy for the changelessness of Brahman.

I understand from the analogy that the ring is mithyA and the gold is Brahman. The implication being that 'change' as we perceive it is only at the apparent level while the substance (Brahman) remains unchanged. Is it then correct to say that Brahman does indeed change but only in form? I believe the answer is 'no', since the Upanishads clearly state that Brahman is changeless. That said the fact remains that, although I don't perceive an object's substance/essence (i.e. Brahman), my senses do gather information that results in thoughts leading to the experience of change in the world of objects. But if Brahman doesn't change even at the level of 'form' then I don't know how to rationalize changeless Brahman with the experience of a changing world. Can you point me in the right direction on this one?

A: This is one of those 'mixing levels' questions. The changeless Brahman refers to paramArtha; the changing world refers to vyavahAra. Brahman is never amenable to objectification in any way, is attribute-less and without name or form. The world is intrinsically dualistic; ever changing and *only* name and form. So Brahman doesn't change. The apparently changing appearance of duality is the result of adhyAsa. In the end it is part of the adhyAropa-apavAda teaching of Advaita. First read Chapter 6 of the Chandogya Upanishad with Shankara's commentary to learn all about vAchArambhaNa and then read the Mandukya Upanishad with Gaudapada's kArikA-s and Shankara's commentary to learn about ajAti vAda.

The following is not associated with a specific question

In the rope-snake metaphor, when one realizes the rope, the snake *does* disappear – it does not remain as a mirage. This is contrast to another example – that of a clear crystal appearing to be colored because of an adjacent colored object refracted in it. One may realize this to be the case but, nevertheless, the crystal *still* appears to be colored.

As regards realizing the mithyAtva of the world, this has to be done within that mithyA context because that is where we find ourselves. It is the mind (which is mithyA) which realizes that the world is mithyA. And it does this with the help of scriptures and teacher, which are also mithyA.

Q.218 How can I be the creator if the world is an illusion?

Q: How can 'I' be said to create the world when, having attained self-realization, I then see that the world is an illusion?

A: This is one of those questions in which there is confusion of levels. From the standpoint of the unenlightened person, there is a real world. This is analogous to the dream world being real for the dreamer – it is only discovered to have been illusory after he wakes up. (Note that it is the content of the dream, not the fact that there was a dream that is illusory.)

The analogy is not quite true, however. When the person becomes enlightened, he does indeed realize that the world is not real but the world does not thereby disappear (as did the dream on awakening). The enlightened person still sees the world and continues to act in it as though it were real for the remainder of the life of the body-mind. However, the enlightened person knows that this is appearance only; that all is simply name and form of the non-dual Brahman. Advaita explains this by saying that, although the person creates the dream world himself, it is Ishvara who creates the waking world. Whereas the dream world exists only for that dreamer, the waking world exists for all persons. This is the distinction between the microcosmic and the macrocosmic, as explained in the Upanishads, particularly the Mandukya.

All of that, then, relates to the level of transactional reality. From the perspective of absolute reality, of course, there never has been a world; no person has ever been born; no God has ever created anything. Some teachers, particularly Neo-Advaitin ones attempt to make only such statements and attempt to deny the experiential world of duality. Traditional Advaita, however, utilizes the former explanations as stepping stones to an appreciation of the absolute truth.

Q.237 Relative status of jIva, world, Ishvara and Brahman

Q: I have been listening to Swami Dayananda's lectures and also I have been reading about Advaita. Please go through the following and see if my understanding is correct.

The only truth is consciousness. 'I am conscious' is the fundamental fact and everything else (including my mind, body, this world that includes Swami Dayananda and even God) are secondary and so do not have independent existence. This implies that if I am not conscious of something, that something does not exist. Upon the death of my body, I am not conscious of my body, mind and this world, which means that they cease to exist. This seems logical to me until I come up with this example: if I walk into an unknown place with my eyes closed, and I am not conscious of the presence of a wall, will I bump into it or not? Logic says that I will. Can you please help me reconcile this paradox?

Let us ignore the above problem for the moment. I understand that there is only one knower in this world and that is 'I'. Everybody else is an apparent knower and everybody else and everything else (including my body and mind) just go by a script that was written by me (in so many lives before), unconsciously due to the incorrect thinking on my part that I am my body/mind/intellect. The actions that I did (with my erroneous ideas) form the seed for this entire universe. Everything in this universe exists just for my own sake. Some good things I did are the cause for Swami Dayananda's (and even Lord Krishna's) existence and their teaching and the only intended recipient of that teaching is 'I'. Once I come out of the habitual thinking that I am separate from the rest of this world and realize that this entire universe is just a manifestation of my karmas and I am just 'I am', the game is over and there is no necessity for this world (or any world). This world will continue only so long as my body/mind remains alive.

The conclusion is that, once I realize my true nature, I will not suffer since I know that nothing in this world (including the sufferings of other people) is really real. And, I will not have any necessity to teach anyone since no one is real.

A: I'm afraid you have some very confused ideas here. If you continue reading Swami Dayananda and listening to his talks (or those of Swami Paramarthananda, which I can recommend even more highly as far as listening is concerned) you will undoubtedly clarify them.

The areas of confusion relate to Brahman versus jIva versus Ishvara, and the status of the world with reference to karma. The net result is that your ideas sound more like solipsism than Advaita.

It is probably best if you do not use the word consciousness, which you seem to be confusing with 'being conscious of' (i.e. aware of) something. Call who-you-really-are Atman or Brahman – the non-dual reality. There is only That from the standpoint of absolute reality. But there is an apparently dualistic world, with other people and this appearance continues after you are enlightened and after the death of your body. It is only an appearance even now; in reality, it is only name and form of Brahman but the ignorant mind mistakes it to be something separate.

When you wake up from your nighttime dream, your dream world disappears because it was all in your mind. But when you 'awaken' to the reality (i.e. become enlightened), the world does not disappear because it is not inside your mind. The world is not your projection. According to traditional Advaita, the world is the projection of Ishvara, using the power of mAyA. From the standpoint of absolute reality, Ishvara too is Brahman alone. In reality, there is no creation, no separate jIva-s and so on. But while the appearance lasts, the interim explanations are needed.

Your own body, mind and environment are the result of your past karma. The present world is the result of humanity's combined karma. So your 'not being aware of something' does not make it cease to exist – Ishvara is still aware of it, as are all of the other jIva-s.

And you cannot talk about there being only one knower in the world (you). This is again confusing levels of reality. If you speak of there being only One, you are speaking as if from the standpoint of absolute reality (paramArtha). On the other hand, if you speak about there being a world, you are talking from the relative or empirical standpoint (vyavahAra). You cannot talk about both at the same time because this would be meaningless.

Who-you-really-are can never suffer, whether you are enlightened or not. Equally, the body and mind may suffer irrespective of your enlightenment. Enlightenment is permanently to realize that you are not the body and mind, even though these will continue until their death.

Q: I read your response, thought about it and I write the following. Please see if my understanding has become better.

I understand that 'I am conscious' (not of anything, but just the fact that I am conscious) is more fundamental than the fact that I am conscious of something.

I understand that the world will continue as it is even after I am enlightened but with full understanding on my part that the world is just nAma-rUpa.

The appearance of the world even after my enlightenment is due to the continuation of my body and mind which are due to my prArabdha karma still being active (and so my body may still suffer). But I still don't understand how you can say that the world will continue after my death. Even in my deep-sleep, when I am supposedly still 'alive', there is no world.

The continuity of this world after I come out of my deep-sleep is due to my memories, which still existed in some form during my deep-sleep, due to the force of my prArabdha karma.

And so I still tend to think that when I am not conscious of the world, the world does not exist. (I do admit that this idea that the world will cease to exist upon my death gives me a certain peace of mind, for there is no family I leave behind to suffer.)

I do understand that the world is not a projection of my mind since I group my body, mind and the world in the same order of reality. The world is not my projection; myself and the world are all projections. All 'idam-s' are projections (that includes my body, mind, thoughts and the world). If I say that these are Ishvara's projections, then if Ishvara is 'not I', the subject, he also becomes an idam and so becomes another projection. So Ishvara should be the same as the 'I', the subject. What is mAyA, then? Can I say that mAyA is nothing but the ignorance in the mind of myself?

A: I think you are still missing the point about Consciousness, with a capital 'C'. This is often used as a synonym for Brahman, the non-dual reality. It does not mean 'conscious' as in self-aware. Everything is 'Consciousness', including a stone, which is clearly not 'conscious'.

Presumably you have had friends or relatives that you knew and who have since died? And the world did not end when they died. Why should it end when you die? From the standpoint of empirical reality, the world is real, people are real and separate and the world carries on when one of them dies. From the standpoint of absolute reality, the world is mithyA, as is your body and mind.

This reality is forever unaffected because there is no world and no people. This differentiation has to be very clearly understood.

You cannot deny that your experience is very much that the world does continue when you are asleep. It is still there, the next day when you awake; your body is refreshed but now hungry; the ground is wet from the night's rain etc. From the standpoint of the waker, the reality of the waking world is undeniable, just as from the dreamer's standpoint, the dream world is real. You can say, if you like, that 'your' waking and dream worlds are in potential or unmanifest form when you are in deep-sleep. But, as I explained before, while your dream world is entirely within your own mind, the waking world has apparent external reality and this is in common for all wakers so you have to postulate Ishvara as the creator of this. It does not work to say that it is a projection of your mind unless you say that you are the only 'real' person in this waking world. This view, as I pointed out before, is solipsism.

Again, from the absolute standpoint, you can indeed say that you are Ishvara but, while you still believe you are a separate body-mind in a separate world, you are clearly not. Ishvara is said to be sarvaj~na – all-knowing. He does not have any ignorance but uses the power of mAyA to create the world according to humanity's karma. But again we are at the level of the waking world, which is mithyA.

Q.357 Existence of Objects

Q: I bought and read two of your eBooks and liked them so much that I then looked at your blog and came across your article (http://www.advaita-vision.org/advaita-is-not-idealism/).

You say that objects really exist; Advaita is not idealism, it is realism. I don`t understand this. In your book you use the 'dream' and 'cinema' metaphors. You even said in your book 'Back to the Truth':

"He goes on to explain that our normal states of consciousness – waking, dream and deep-sleep – are at the level of appearance.

Reality is the non-dual background to these states. Just as our dreams seem real to the dreamer, so this world-appearance seem real to the waker. But, on waking, it is realized that those dreams are nothing but an illusion generated by the mind.

Similarly only on awakening to god-consciousness will you appreciate and realize the staggering truth that there exists nothing other than Brahman everywhere. Until that supreme state is reached, the universe will appear real. Living in your present state of ignorance you will have to accept the world that you experience. But at the same time try to contemplate and realize the truth proclaimed by Self-realized souls that Brahman alone exists".

So you changed your mind after writing the book and now you say that the world-appearance is real, Advaita is realism and there is no illusion at all?

I`m confused, can you explain?

A: Good question! If you've read my 'Jungle' book, you will know that I criticize Satsang and Neo teaching because of their 'out of context' and 'lack of continuity' nature. It's interesting to think that I could be accused of the same problem!

Actually, though, the quotation to which you refer is from Swami Parthasarathy and not myself. 'Back to the Truth' is intended to be a compendium of related material from lots of teachers and writers and their styles, and content, do not always tally. That may be fine, as long as you have a good understanding or as long as you are actually following just the one source. I do refer to 'Back to the Truth' as being intended for mature seekers and not 'beginners'.

The key point here is that, in the article, I refer to idealism in the sense of Berkeley – i.e. the notion that objects are only constructs of the mind and have no independent existence. According to Advaita, this is not the case. If I go out of the room, the table in the room really does continue to exist as a (seemingly) separate entity.

But if we now switch to (as if) talking of paramArtha instead of vyavahAra, then of course there are no separately existing objects (or subjects). Every seeming thing is mithyA and is only name and form of the satyam Brahman. So in this context, only Brahman is real and we could certainly say that the table, the room, and the person (whether inside or outside the room) are all only appearances. But they are not illusions; they all have Brahman as their real substrate. From the perspective of our minds, they each have a form and we give them unique names which, in turn, impart a spurious separate existence.

Hope this is clear and not further confusing the issue! I certainly haven't changed my mind. But hopefully I may have become a little better at explaining what I mean!

Q.439 Universe is Consciousness

Q: Is the following summary correct? The universe is pure Consciousness (non-dual) – one big mass of it that manifests (at least, in the illusory sense) as separate forms, objects or organisms. The reason(s) it does this are ultimately unknowable, but speculations include out of playfulness, to know itself, or due to boredom.

A: There is only Consciousness so, yes, you can regard the universe as Consciousness also. But don't think of it as a 'mass', since that would imply a 'lump' of it existing in something else, and there is nothing else.

An interim teaching is that Brahman 'manifests', and the 'reasons' for this are sometimes given as lIlA etc. But Brahman does not do anything, need anything, know anything etc. That would be duality, wouldn't it? Strictly speaking, if you are considering this, those qualities have to be applied to Ishvara – saguNa Brahman; not Brahman – nirguNa. At the level of the empirical world, you have to allow the existence of Ishvara. How you think of this is up to you. If you are happy with the concept of a God, that is fine. If not, think of it as the nexus of laws that governs how the universe operates. In reality (absolute), Ishvara as well as universe and jIva are only Consciousness/Brahman. In reality, there has never been any creation.

Q: I think that one of the problems I'm having is the whole 'The Tao that can be spoken is not the eternal Tao' dilemma (i.e. we're trying to discuss something in words that can't really be conceived of using a language system that is steeped in dualism). But I'm not sure there's an actual solution to that; although I definitely appreciate your efforts at linguistic clarity.

Anyway, if we want to use the term 'Ishvara' when discussing the height of empirical/created (vs. absolute/Brahman) reality, that's cool. I'm just trying to get a provisional understanding/cosmology in my head. So we have Brahman above/containing/*is* all. Then a hypothetical hierarchy from there would be Ishvara, underneath which is (depending on your belief system) ... what? The heavenly host, other gods, archetypal beings, spirits? Then extraterrestrials, then man, then animals, plants, inanimate objects? (I'm thinking in terms of evolution here).

And Ishvara, this *"nexus of laws that govern how the universe operates"*, would hypothetically include both physical/scientific laws as well as laws governing magic, the supernatural, etc.?

A: It is definitely the case that you cannot really describe or define Brahman. If you say or think something about it, you know that cannot be true because you are limiting it in some way – if it is A, then it is not B etc. To some degree you can actually say that it is the use of language itself that causes the problem (see the vAchArambhaNa sutras from the Chandogya Upanishad – referenced elsewhere). All you can do is to 'point' and use metaphors until the mind makes an intuitive leap to understanding.

As regards understanding the 'hierarchy' of gods or whatever, there is not really any point in this. The Hindus have very many gods (and demons), the idea being that whatever they might be doing they can be aware of the higher meaning behind the mundane, if you like. But since all that is mithyA, it is not really going to help.

Again, your hierarchy does take account of plants and animals. Each is a jIva and progresses 'up' to man, man being the only stage that can gain mokSha. Bad karma in this life will result in a retrogressive step in the next! But I really regard all this stuff as mythology, useful for a low level of seeker but one assumes that it would not be of any value for the 'sophisticated' (i.e. 'educated') Western mind!

Ishvara is responsible for ensuring the lawful operation of the universe, whatever aspects you might be interested in.

I think you should be aiming to understand/acknowledge the mithyAtva of the world rather than looking for any sort of meaning in the 'illusion'.

Creation

Q.373 Which creation theory is correct?

Q: The scriptures talk about several theories to explain creation, as well talking about things like 'lIlA'. Which explanation is correct?

A: Advaita uses the technique called adhyAropa-apavAda. This means that a 'more acceptable' explanation is given in the beginning but then taken back later, and a more sophisticated explanation given, as your understanding grows. Ultimately, *all* explanations are rescinded.

All of the theories used to 'explain' why there is a separate creation or what happens when we die are mistaken. They are mistakes consequent upon the fundamental ignorance in thinking that there is separation to begin with. Since there has never been any creation, there is no need to look for an explanation for it. Since we have never been born in the first place, there is no need to try to explain reincarnation.

Yes, these aspects are dealt with by the scriptures but their value in explaining life, death, heaven and rebirth etc. is analogous to the dreamer trying to explain why the elephant in his dream has just turned into a chair. prAtibhAsika is real from the standpoint of the dream and vyAvahArika from the waking standpoint. When the dreamer wakes up, there is no longer any meaning in trying to explain the elephant transformation. (And it is not relevant to bring Freud in here, because he was trying to explain the dream from the *waking*, not the *dreaming* standpoint. And it was not the waker who was having the dream!) These explanations are of value only to the interim seeker who needs explanations for things that will later be realized to be unreal.

There cannot be any lIlA because Brahman has no desires, does not act and does not enjoy. Advaita takes you all the way; don't allow yourself to be diverted by the distractions along the way. Don't try to discover whether or not the rope-snake is poisonous!

Q.103 On the relationship between Brahman and mAyA

Q: In my understanding, mAyA is the appearance of appearances. It cannot be separated from Brahman. Brahman is real and mAyA isn't – even though it seems to appear in Brahman. Does this accord with shruti or am I missing something?

In 'Back to the Truth' (page 272), Dr. K. Sadananda is quoted as saying *"He (Brahman) cannot have avidyA (ignorance), since if he has it, he cannot be Brahman"*. Is not vidyA (knowledge) as well as avidyA part of the world of appearances, which is and is not Brahman?

Similar, on page 361 Prof. V. Krishnamurthy says: "The base of activity of mAyA cannot be Brahman because the latter is absolute luminosity and there is no place in it for ignorance or darkness". Why not? All is Brahman, so how can mAyA, ignorance or darkness be excluded?

Is there a difference between dRRiShTi sRRiShTi vAda (the theory that it is our perception that effectively 'creates' the world) and vivarta vAda (the theory that the world is an apparent 'manifestation' of Brahman; an illusory appearance as a result of ignorance). If yes, what is it? Would you agree that dRRiShTi sRRiShTi vAda is what modern neurological research points to?

A: I think the key consideration regarding your questions is the distinction between paramArtha and vyavahAra (it usually is!).

In reality, there is only Brahman and that is already saying too much. From the relative viewpoint, where all question and answer take place obviously, everything is mithyA. This is really only to say that whatever you can conceive or perceive is not ultimately real in itself; it is only name and form of the non-dual (pAramArthika) reality. What happens in the teaching of Advaita is that interim 'explanations' are put forward to provide an understanding that is a little closer to the truth (or at least less false) than the supposed understanding that was there previously. (This is the technique of adhyAropa-apavAda that is explained above.) And there is no exception to this because we can never say anything about reality that is really true. Accordingly, the concepts of Ishvara wielding the power of mAyA to create the appearance of the world etc. are no more than interim explanations to satisfy the seeker at a particular point in his or her 'path'. The reality is that there has never been any creation. There are no separate jIva-s and no mAyA to delude them. There is only Brahman, as you have noted.

That it 'seems' as though there is a world and that we are separate and so on is attributed to mAyA until we are better able to appreciate the truth. It is like telling a child that babies are brought by the storks (perhaps!). If they are unable to appreciate the unexpurgated details, it at least shuts them up for the time being! Advaita also tells us that we are 'not the body, mind etc.' (neti, neti) but, since all is Brahman, they are ultimately Brahman too.

Explanations have to be provided at the present level of understanding.

Your next question also seems to be confusing vyavahAra and paramArtha. The point is that duality is never real. There is only seeming duality within vyavahAra as a result of the beginningless, inexplicable ignorance. Because of this, the apparent, separate jIva superimposes false attributes upon the non-dual reality. Yes, there are paradoxes throughout this teaching but this is because of the same problem described above. So there appears to be knowledge and ignorance, light and darkness. Pedantically, I would have to agree with your objection to Profvk's statement. You cannot really talk about Brahman being 'absolute luminosity'. This is why we have to postulate Ishvara as the one who controls mAyA and not Brahman. It is a dualistic solution to an apparent problem which may satisfy until we are better able to appreciate that it is really not a solution at all (because there is no problem).

The subject of creation theories is a bit like the waker trying to decide whether person A or person B was correct in some discussion that took place in his dream last night. The ultimate truth is that there has never been any creation. In any case, questions about the relationship between a perceiver and creation make no sense. Ask yourself whether the perceiver is part of the world or not and see where that leads you!

dRRiShTi-sRRiShTi-vAda is not part of Advaita anyway, really. Shankara said that an object had to exist in order for it to be perceived. vivarta vAda goes along with Ishvara and mAyA and provides the temporary explanation that the creation is effectively an illusion created by Ishvara, which is not the same as being created by the jIva. It is true that the jIva is really Brahman and Ishvara is really Brahman but this does not equate Ishvara with the jIva. It is like saying that the wave and the ocean are both water but a wave is clearly not the ocean. Incidentally, you might find it helpful to read Vidyasankar Sundaresan's essay on creation theories (http://www.advaita.org.uk/discourses/teachers/theories_vidyasankar.htm).

Q.297 Cause of creation

Q: I would like to ask a question regarding the relation between karaNa-sharIra (causal body) and Brahman. You mentioned the analogy of pot and clay. The pot corresponds to the world, and the clay to the causal body. The causal body in this case is also a material cause, which can be called mAyA. But the clay as the material cause cannot generate the pot by itself. To create the pot from the clay, what is required is a pot-maker as an intelligent cause, which is called Brahman. So this world is created by Brahman, using the karaNa-sharIra as the material cause.

Now, my question arises: how is the clay created? Is this created by Brahman? If this is correct, then, logical difficulty arises, since in the karaNa-sharIra, time and space as materials do not exist, as the form of the pot does not exist in the clay before the pot is created. Since no time exists in the causal body, we cannot say Brahman creates the causal body, because this statement presupposes that Brahman exists before the causal body. But since no time exists in this stage, this is obviously wrong. Maybe, the causal body and Brahman exist all the time, and we cannot say when both are created. Is this the correct interpretation? If yes, then, it seems the Advaita story fails since the causal body as the material cause exists just like Brahman.

One way to get around this, I think, is that although we must admit the causal body is not created by Brahman, the former depends on the latter as mithyA. But then, I cannot get a clearer picture of how the causal body depends on Brahman. Without Brahman, the causal body cannot exist. Why? The clay cannot exist without the pot-maker? It seems the clay can live without the pot-maker. Then, we must abandon Advaita, and instead, adopt dvaita vedAnta.

A: You will always get into trouble if you attempt to speak of the world and Brahman at the same time. Strictly speaking, if you want to talk about Brahman, you cannot talk about anything else, because there is only Brahman in reality. (Of course, being really pedantic, you cannot talk about Brahman at all, because words relate to such things as attributes, relationships, actions, etc., none of which apply to Brahman.)

And you almost always run into problems if you attempt to push metaphors too far, which is what you are doing here with the clay-pot metaphor. Metaphors serve the purpose of giving insight. Once the intended insight has been gained, it is best to drop the metaphor.

In answer to your question, then: first of all, when speaking about creation, world, etc., you have to talk about Ishvara, not Brahman. Ishvara is Brahman + the power of mAyA. The causal body is not the material but rather the instructions. In relation to a jIva, this is where the saMskAra are stored from past actions, which will dictate the future body and lifestyle on reincarnation. The 'material' could be regarded as prakRRiti or mAyA but is perhaps best thought of as Ishvara Himself – like the web spun by a spider. The spider is both efficient and material cause for the web – it creates the silk out of its own substance. Ishvara is the efficient and material cause for the universe. So Ishvara (Brahman) does not create the material for creation; He *is* the material.

There are logical problems associated with any 'explanation' for creation. But Advaita does not have any of these because the ultimate teaching of Advaita is that there is no creation at all. There is only Brahman in apparent manifestation of name and form. The 'causal body', too, is also only Brahman; there is no question of there being 'two things' ever. 'Causal body' does not exist as a separate thing.

You might also find the distinction between macrocosm and microcosm helpful; or samaShTi and vyaShTi – the 'whole' and the 'individual'. In pralaya, when the universe goes into its 'Big Crunch' prior to a new 'Big Bang', the entire set of individual 'causal bodies' is held in causal form (vaishvAnara) so as to maintain the continuity of individual karma-s.

But it is best not to get too hung up about all of this, since these are interim explanations only. If you do not find them helpful, then it is best just to ignore them. They all have to be dropped eventually anyway.

Q: Thanks very much for your insightful answers. I agree with most of your replies, but it at the same time causes one final question:

You are quite correct to say, 'Ishvara is the material,' and Brahman is both the efficient and material cause. But according to my understanding, Brahman is pure Consciousness, which is defined as the cause of all knowledge, and it never acts and changes. How does Consciousness transform itself into the material and the universe?

In one metaphor, Brahman is the light of a movie projector and mAyA is the movie film. Light itself does not change at all, but with the changing movie film, the light projects the movie vision onto the screen. The movie film corresponds to prakRRiti, which is nothing but 'guNa', and I believe (maybe wrongly) the guNa must be different from pure Consciousness. In order to 'project' the universe out of Brahman, the guNa or some reflector is required. According to your reply, it seems this reflector is also Brahman, pure Consciousness. This statement is hard to understand and very confusing to me.

Or is it correct to say that the material is nothing but vibrating energy, and pure Consciousness is also in the form of energy or vibration, and no distinction exists between the two. Or another possibility is that the law of karma plays the role of the moving film, which realizes the whole universe out of Brahman or Ishvara. Probably, I am asking the same question in a slightly different manner.

A: I didn't say that 'Brahman is both the efficient and material cause'; I said that Ishvara was. You are quite right when you say that Brahman never acts or changes – Gaudapada says that it is kArya kAraNa vilakShaNa – it has nothing to do with either cause or effect. As I said: you cannot really talk about Brahman at all.

Again you are trying to press metaphors into service beyond their field of applicability. It also seems that you might be confusing Advaita and sAMkhya teaching. It is sAMkhya philosophy that differentiates puruSha and prakRRiti and says that prakRRiti is 'made up of' the three guNa-s, with differing proportions for each person, thing, etc. In Advaita, the guNa-s are attributive descriptions only; all matter is only name and form of Brahman. In reality, the universe is not 'projected out of Brahman' – there is no creation at all. Creation 'stories' are interim teaching so that your understanding may grow gradually, rather than giving you a 'final' explanation that is totally unpalatable.

Incidentally, in his 'ghaTa bhAShya' or 'clay pot commentary' in the first chapter of the Brihadaranyaka Upanishad (1.2.1), Shankara argues that the effect (pot) *has* to be contained in the cause (clay) prior to creation. The naiyAyika philosophers say that, if the pot was there before, then it would not need to be created. But Shankara says that it *was* there – in *unmanifest* form.

Note that this topic is later discussed by Gaudapada, with Shankara's commentary, in his kArikA on the Mandukya Upanishad. The conclusion is that the pot is simply another form of the clay – that nothing is actually created at all. Similarly, the world is just another 'form' of Brahman and has not been created. (Read my book 'A-U-M: Awakening to Reality' to find out all about this.)

Q.374b Creation according to Ramesh Balsekar

Q: I recently bought a book called 'Final Truth' by Ramesh Balsekar. I read the book and now see it as one of the most 'deep' and 'philosophical' books on Advaita.

I saw an idea in the book and it resonated with me so much. In my opinion, it even explains (on some level) why there is mAyA or why the appearance exists or why there seems to be a 'creation' in the first place. The idea is this: The formless Consciousness can be experienced only through the multitude of sentient bodies with names and forms, just as light can be seen only through refracting agents. It is thus not that the multitude of names and forms exist independently of Consciousness but that Consciousness can express itself only through these forms.

So the other way of saying this is that God or Brahman or Consciousness experiences himself through us. We and the universe are God looking into himself.

Brihadaranyaka Upanishad 2.5.19 has this verse

"He transformed Himself in accordance with each form; that form of His was for the sake of making Him known. The Lord on account of Maya (notions superimposed by ignorance) is perceived as manifold, for to Him are yoked ten organs, nay, hundreds of them. He is the organs; He is ten and thousands – many and infinite. That Brahman is without prior or posterior, without interior or exterior. This self, the perceiver of everything, is Brahman. This is the teaching".

What do you think? Does traditional Advaita accept that idea or not.

A: As it seems with most questions I get these days, this one also revolves around the reality-appearance, paramArtha-vyavahAra question.

Regarding the 'purpose' for the seeming creation, this does not hold water. There can be no meaningful attribution of purpose at all. Purpose implies some sort of deficiency in Brahman, which is a contradiction. Experience of any sort is a limitation, so cannot be applied to Brahman. It is best just to think of everything as name and form, including the ignorance and the experience; the experienced and the experiencer. But, as an imaginative way of thinking about it, God looking into himself is fine, as long as you don't take it literally.

Q.431 Emergence vs. Consciousness

Q: In Advaita one learns to 'unravel' objects: table as wood, wood as cells, cells as molecules, molecules as atoms, atoms as subatomic particles, etc. (neti neti!) all the way down. What Advaita says 'lies at the bottom' is Brahman, the oneness from which all apparent objects of form manifest.

What seems just as (if not more) intuitively plausible to me is that what lies at the bottom is a few primal emergent 'rules'. Perhaps even just one rule: attraction/repulsion. Electrons are attracted to protons and repelled by other electrons giving way to atoms, atoms are attracted to other atoms giving way to molecules, and so on, all the way up to the forms we know and love.

In this view of reality, there is no top-level, overarching 'organizational' principle: Consciousness. There is instead a vast web of 'stuff' that arises from a few simple, low-level, emergent rules. As with all emergent systems, the application of these rules, once sufficiently complex, creates a system that seems to have an overarching top-level intelligence/intentionality/organizational principle, but in reality doesn't.

So, who wins? Emergence or Consciousness? Or is it a non-zero-sum game: Are emergence and Consciousness not mutually exclusive?

A: If you have read my articles about science and its views, you will know that I do not regard it very highly when it comes to consciousness and reality!

The 'unraveling' is an explanation of the concept of mithyA and provides an intuitively reasonable explanation as to why all 'things' are just name and form of Brahman. If you try to turn this around you are then tacitly assuming that the empirical reality has some absolute reality, which it doesn't (unless you are just accepting that 'everything is Brahman'). Or are you just attempting to use science to 'explain' Ishvara? Because Advaita would call your 'fundamental laws' or 'primary emergent rules' Ishvara. Ishvara is both the intelligent and material cause for the (apparent) creation. In reality, of course, there has never been any creation. Both the ocean (universe) and the wave (individual) are always only water.

Q.441 Creation and morality

Q: I've heard/read from multiple sources that the universe/non-dual everything-there-is/whatever you want to call it is 'love'. How do we know that, and why couldn't it be hateful/evil/neutral/any other way?

A: This is the sort of statement made by 'new-agey' teachers. Nowhere in the scriptures (to my knowledge) is such an expression used. There is *only* Brahman/Consciousness. The 'universe' is mithyA, which means it is not real in itself; it is just name and form of Brahman. Brahman is said to be unlimited (anantam) existence (sat) Consciousness (chit) but these are only for the sake of definition/pointers. See also Q.100 and 120.

Q: In answer to Q.120, you said: "Indeed, according to traditional Advaita, part of your preparation for enlightenment involves acting unselfishly, not harming others, living a moral life etc. All the opposites do exist at this level and, if you act knowing your action to be wrong, you will incur the lawful penalty (karma)".

I'm having trouble understanding why one should act 'morally' or 'good'; i.e. why does karma exist at this level? Why is it set up this way?

A: The 'bottom line' of Advaita is that there has never been any 'creation'; no jIva has ever been born etc. – there is only Brahman. Obviously it does not seem like this; there is the appearance of duality and we initially believe this to be real. Accordingly, traditional Advaita has a progression of teaching to accommodate this appearance. For those who still believe in duality, the teaching is aimed at the preparation of the mind to accept the more advanced teaching. This includes a world, a creator and laws applicable to the operation of the world and the action of the jIva. And the operation of cause and effect is one of these laws. If you act purposefully, you will reap the fruit of that action; if not in this life, then in the next.

Summary

The proposition that the effect is already pre-existent in the cause is the belief of Sankhya philosophers. It is called satkArya vAda or pariNAma vAda. (pariNAma means transformation or modification.)

As mentioned above, the nyAya-s (and vaisheShika-s) put forward the opposite claim, called asat kArya vAda, namely that the effect is not pre-existent (asat) in the cause. They say that the statue only comes into existence as a result of the action of the sculptor. They say that, if the effect is already there, then what does it mean to produce it? It is like saying that the stone and the statue are at one and the same time both different and identical.

The sAMkhya-s object that this amounts to claiming that something is coming out of nothing, which is clearly nonsensical. So effectively the nyAya-s & sAMkhya-s cancel each other out and both theories are rejected.

The various theories of creation are dealt with extensively in the first part of Chapter 4 of gauDapAda's kArikA-s on the mANDUkya Upanishad. As far as Advaita is concerned, you will find various, seemingly contradictory explanations for creation in the scriptures. Essentially, however, like many other topics, it follows the process of adhyAropa-apavAda.

The initial explanations involve actual creation but this clearly has to be rejected for various reasons (Brahman is non-dual, having no desires, not acting or enjoying etc.). vivarta vAda is the 'intermediate' theory, which says that we superimpose the world upon Brahman as a result of ignorance. This goes along with the concept of mAyA. In the end, all of these theories have to be dropped. There cannot be any creation at all; there is only ever Brahman. This is ajAti vAda. Every seeming thing is simply name and form of Brahman.

The use of the word 'manifestation' is specifically to imply that there is no actual 'creation' involved. It only appears to us that there is multiplicity ...

From the sAMkhya perspective, the 'creation' of the clay pot is satkArya vAda; from Advaita, it is vivarta vAda. But remember that the clay-pot is a metaphor for creation. We can say (indeed the Chandogya Upanishad does say) that everything in the universe is just a name of a form of Brahman. The act of 'naming' as if gives the thing a separate existence. The reason I am being pedantic (and possibly repetitive!) is that one would not want to get into an argument as to who it is that brings the pot form into manifestation from the clay (jIva or Ishvara or Brahman)!

The bottom line is that there is no difference between cause and effect. Shankara uses the example of a rolled up piece of cloth and the unrolled version. We may be ignorant of certain attributes of the cloth while it is unrolled (e.g. its length), but it still the same cloth when those attributes are revealed (manifest). The various theories are only ever of any value as steps along the way to understanding. They all have to be discarded eventually. Nothing ever changes in reality because there is only Brahman.

[There is an extensive discussion of creation in 'Back to the Truth' but the refutation aspects are addressed in 'A-U-M: Awakening to Reality', which is specifically on the Mandukya and kArikA-s.]

Good and evil

Q.85 svadharma and Hitler

Q: I would like to ask a question relating to dharma, after reading your book ('The Book of One'). When you say that a person should act according to his own svadharma or essence, I was wondering what if one's essence is that of a Hitler or Saddam, or if a person is inclined towards violence, a rapist etc. If your prArabdha karma determines these negative attitudes, is this what you would follow even if it is faulty?

A: dharma in this context refers to the unwritten moral laws governing behavior in the sense that 'this is what you should do if you are working towards enlightenment'. svadharma means one's own particular obligations or duty. The idea is that one should behave in a certain way in order to 'cancel out' the accumulated saMskAra resulting from past actions. If one continues to behave badly, it will simply accumulate more pApa (demerit). One has to endeavor to act morally (but inevitably constrained by one's own particular nature) in order to cancel out the accumulated fruits of one's own past actions.

The idea of karma is that you are presented with situations in life in accordance with past actions. Your vAsanA-s (prior conditioning; latent tendencies) will certainly incline you to act in the same way that you always have (i.e. badly in the case of a Hitler or Saddam Hussein!). In the new situation, there is the opportunity to act in response to the needs of the moment and not out of habit. Thus, following svadharma is the opposite of acting in accord with one's vAsanA-s in this case.

Q.100 Is there evil in Brahman?

Q: According to Advaita, the Brahma is the absolute reality and nothing besides him. He is infinite, he is in all and all is in him. So, Is evil also present in Brahma?

A: The name given by Advaita to the absolute reality is 'Brahman', and Brahman is not a god. Brahman being the unmanifest absolute reality, 'knows' no duality (hence 'Advaita' – not two). There is nothing other than Brahman. ('Brahma' is the name of the 'creator god' in Hindu mythology.)

The apparent, empirical, dualistic universe is mithyA only, having no reality of its own, being simply name and form of Brahman. Therefore, from the standpoint of the world, you could say that Brahman 'contains' all apparent dualities, including good and evil. But these terms only have any meaning from the viewpoint of a jIva; one who believes the world to be real and himself to be a separate entity. Good and evil are relative terms; how could they have any meaning from an absolute non-dual standpoint? (They do, of course, have their understood relative meanings from the standpoint of the world.)

Q.120 Problem of good and evil

Q: I've been studying non-duality for some years now, and Advaita for the past two. I've read your books 'How To Meet Yourself' and 'The Book of One'. I'm on my second reading of the latter. I asked this similar question of other authors on the subject and have not really received a clear answer. Could you please help?

My question concerns good and evil, right and wrong. As I understand it, from the Advaita point of view, these opposites don't exist. Is there no way to determine what is right and wrong?

Is anything that happens ok? Is Mother Theresa no better than Hitler? I know these questions have probably been asked many times. I understand that there is no 'I' to whom these things should be of concern, but still, they are a concern, at least for now.

Does nothing really matter? If a man driving down the street sees an injured child on the side of the road, does it make no difference morally whether he helps or runs over that child? How can I look at moral issues like these and say that it doesn't matter?

I read somewhere once that above the human level of right and wrong is absolute right; above the human level of good and evil is 'absolute good', but we just cannot see it because of the illusion. Does Advaita see it like this?

A: Your difficulty, as with most questions in Advaita, is caused by failing to differentiate the point of view. The purpose of philosophies such as Advaita is to point you towards an appreciation of the essential non-dual nature of reality. However – and you must never lose sight of this – the world always continues to appear, along with separate objects and people. Post enlightenment (when you have gained Self-knowledge), you will know that this appearance is only name and form of the essentially unchanging, limitless One, just as bangles and necklaces are name and form of the same gold. Even so, the appearance will continue.

So, you need to decide at what level you are asking your questions. From the absolute standpoint, all is Brahman. Nothing can ever be affected by anything else because there are not two things. But from the relative standpoint, there are people, subject to happiness/unhappiness, pleasure/pain and so on. Suffering *is* 'not knowing' that there is only Brahman! Until you are enlightened, you are very much in the world. That is your reality and you are forced to live by its rules. Indeed, according to traditional Advaita, part of your preparation for enlightenment involves acting unselfishly, not harming others, living a moral life etc. All the opposites do exist at this level and, if you act knowing your action to be wrong, you will incur the lawful penalty (karma).

The term that best helps you to understand this is 'mithyA'. It does not get much of a mention in 'Book of One' first edition unfortunately ('Back to the Truth' goes into all of these aspects in much greater detail and it is fully explained in the second edition of 'Book of One') but have a look at (http://www.advaita.org.uk/discourses/definitions/mithyA.htm). The name and form is always there. Prior to enlightenment, we think that is the reality; afterwards, we know that the substratum or essence is Brahman. Ideas of 'right and wrong' are equally mithyA. In reality they *must* be meaningless ('right' for whom?). But at the relative level, they always apply.

Q.134 Good, evil and enlightenment

Q: I have come to understand that Advaita makes sense but obviously don't know all the implications.

Here is my understanding:

Good or bad does not exist: all that exists is karma and its fruit.

If a particular path is pursued it leads to mokSha [for the unrealized].

For the realized this definition has no meaning, for even 'bad' is as neutral as 'good'.

For those who are still unrealized, if they perform tasks without attachment, the words 'good' and 'bad' lose their significance.

Does this understanding make sense?

A: Good and bad *do* exist at the relative level of world and people. While you still believe yourself to be a person, acting in the world, you are obliged to follow the moral code of society and you should never act so as to injure another. By acting intentionally for good or bad you incur karma. All this is saying is that effect will follow cause in the usually accepted manner (although we may not always see the connections).

Doing good in the world will incur good karma (puNya); doing bad will incur bad karma (pApa). Neither leads to mokSha.

Realization of the truth (that we are already free) only comes when the ignorance (that tells us that we are not free) is removed. Thus, what is needed for mokSha is Self-knowledge.

The realized man does not lose his senses, his mind or his memory. Though he now knows that the essence of the world is non-dual, he still *sees* the duality. He sees the forms, remembers the names and that the 'other' jIva-s are still ignorant. He still remembers the meaning of good and bad from that relative viewpoint, even though he now knows that the Self is totally unaffected by either and, indeed, encompasses both.

Q.416 More on evil

Q: If everything is the manifestation of consciousness, is there any explanation for so much pain, suffering, illness, disease, starvation, depression etc.?

I have read and understood that Consciousness manifests itself in everything and through human beings in order to experience the life (or dream) it created.

If this is so then one comes to the conclusion that sadism and masochism are experiences Consciousness also wants to feel, bearing in mind the atrocities that humans are committing nowadays.

A: In addition to the points that have been made above, here are a couple of ideas that may help.

If, by 'Consciousness', you mean the non-dual reality (which I assume you do – so do I) then you have to concede that from that point of view there can be no 'experiences' and no value judgments. If you accept the conclusion of Advaita – 'all there is is Consciousness', then Consciousness is all there is! It is a bit like using steel to make scalpels and also to make daggers. From the standpoint of the steel, both are steel only. It is only the person who says one is good and the other bad. And the person, too, is only Consciousness.

Another way of looking at it is by comparing it to dream.

Presumably you have dreams in which 'bad' things happen? Why do you do this? Why not always dream about good things? But, when you wake up, does it really matter? Was the bad thing *really* bad? When you realize the truth, you also know that the waking world is ultimately no more real than the dream world. Both are turIya, only.

Finally, you should note that Consciousness does not do anything, does not desire anything. Nor does it experience anything, either for itself or 'through' the supposedly created entities. The 'bottom line' of Advaita is that nothing has ever been created.

What we can do

What can we do to become enlightened and realize the truth of non-duality? Well, since our problem is that we are presently ignorant of this fact, the only thing we can do is to seek and gain knowledge of it. This bears repetition: it is the ONLY thing will enable us to realize that we are already infinite, perfect and complete… because we already are – we just do not know it.

This extremely simple fact has an equally obvious corollary: there is nothing that we can *do* to become enlightened. (And there is nothing anyone else can do – there is no 'transmission' of enlightenment for example, despite what some unscrupulous people might claim to the contrary.) Bhakti (devotion) or samAdhi (deep meditation) cannot bring enlightenment. Enlightenment is the 'event' in the mind when the truth is realized. (There is more about this in the section on 'Enlightenment'.)

Simply telling someone that reality is non-dual and they are infinite Consciousness, however, is most unlikely to achieve anything (other than make them doubt your sanity). Preparation of the seeker's mind is needed and (probably) lots of preliminary teaching leading up to the final revelation.

Many seekers unfortunately believe wrongly that experiences are the aim; that somehow we can attain to a state wherein we experience permanent bliss and the feeling of oneness with everything. This is not what it is about at all. We each remain associated with these bodies until their death and consequently are aware of their ups and downs, pains and pleasures. What we are seeking is the knowledge that this is all mithyA; that the reality is non-dual and we are That. This knowledge is only assuredly gained through proper teaching, which ideally means finding a qualified guru and committing to studying with them for as long as it takes.

Q.462 Lost enthusiasm

Q: I am not enlightened. I seek to become so. But why bother? The cause of my lack of enlightenment is the illusion set up by ego. When 'I' die, my ego dies – once it's dead it can't cause an illusion. The only thing that's left is consciousness. So surely we all become 'enlightened', or wake up, at the point of death. All I need to do to become awake is to die! Yes, no?

A: Afraid not! For those not enlightened, all actions have their effect and, if you don't reap the rewards/punishments in this life, you are reborn to live through them in future lives. According to Advaita (from the point of view of relative, empirical reality), you have already lived through countless lives and this will continue indefinitely until you become enlightened. It's called saMsAra. Only the gross body effectively dies for the unenlightened; the subtle and causal bodies continue until reborn in another body. (For a description of the 'three bodies' of a jIva, see http://www.advaita.org.uk/discourses/venugopal/venugopal23.html.)

Q: Ah well, worth a try. I guess it does matter what we do then?

I don't know if this makes sense Dennis but I find it amazing how many times I can read something from a book and it doesn't seem to have real meaning but hear the same thing when actually directed to me and it works.

I have found myself in a very dark place in recent years. Having spent my life working along my 'spiritual' path I found that I didn't (don't) seem to have moved from the starting point all those years ago when I read Paul Brunton's, 'Search in Secret India' and first came across Sri Ramana. I ended up following a Zen path for many years but, despite many retreats and even a little time in a Zen monastery, nothing seems to have changed in me. Eventually I found a darkness was creeping in and I could no longer sit, nor concentrate on anything to do with Buddhism, or Advaita – it just didn't ring true anymore. Around 5 years ago I stopped my daily sitting and effectively gave up.

Occasionally I'd read something you'd written and it so

resonated that I almost felt the spark again – but it rapidly died and I couldn't rekindle the flame (sorry for the metaphors). I guess that now I've retired I've no excuse for not being able to commit the time – I just hope that eventually this phase will pass and I will reconnect to these wonderful teachings.

A: I think the problem with most written (and maybe lots of the hands-on variety) 'teaching' is that it sounds good, positive and even inspirational but, when analyzed in the cold light of reason, it doesn't really add up. So, while you are in the right frame of mind, it seems you are making some kind of progress but then, when your mood inevitably sinks, you realize that nothing has actually changed.

I suggest (as I do to most people these days, it seems) that you buy and read Swami Dayananda's 'Gita Home Study Course'. It's now available in 9 hardback volumes, although I think you can still purchase the 4-volume ring binder version. It is also available at the time of writing in a number of downloadable electronic formats (https://archive.org/details/BhagavadGitaHomeStudyCourse_SwamiDayananda). I don't think anyone can do better than to read and study this slowly (unless they have direct access to one of his disciples). Probably most aspects of Advaita are covered and nothing contradicts reason. Teachers like Ramana and Nisargadatta were no doubt brilliant, if you could live with them for a few years and ask questions etc. but one hits too many irresolvable problems trying just to read transcripts of their talks.

Seeking

Q.38 Depression and anti-depressants

Q: Do you know of any teacher who addresses the problem of so-called 'Major Depression' and especially Antidepressants, from the non-duality viewpoint?

A: Most teachers do not specifically address the problem of depression. This is understandable since all suffering stems from mistaken identification with the body and mind and the belief that happiness can be found externally, in the future, in objects, people or events. If the general issues are attacked, the more specific ones are automatically covered too. Furthermore, if depression is regarded as a malfunction of the brain and is treated by chemicals that affect its operation, it is all at the level of the body and therefore not of much interest to Advaita.

Having said that, depression is of course a very real problem affecting many to a greater or lesser degree and it is not easy to practice sAdhana of any sort whilst the mind is flooded by depressing thoughts. Practically speaking, therefore, the best thing to do is to treat the symptoms using conventional methods and, as soon as it passes, return to the teaching. Once the ignorance that prevents realization of our true nature is removed, no form of physical or mental dysfunction can cause true suffering again.

Q: It's not about the 'cause' of the depression, but more about the effects of Antidepressants on the illusory self.

A: The effects of antidepressants on the illusory self are illusory, as is true with LSD and other drugs. They affect the mind but Who-we-really-are is not the mind. Neither are we any state of consciousness but the background against which they arise. And so on.

Perhaps what you are really asking is whether antidepressants would affect the ability of the 'person' to become enlightened? The answer to this is almost certainly 'yes'. Enlightenment is effectively of the mind, when the ignorance that obscures the truth is finally removed and the mind 'takes on the form of the undivided'. The ability of the mind to do this is likely to be severely hampered if depressed or under the influence of antidepressants. This is part of the reason why practice and mind preparation are necessary.

So perhaps the answer to your question is that you should treat the depression medically first and *then* attack the ignorance using the methods of Advaita.

Q: Isn't the depression itself caused by ignorance?

A: I wouldn't say it was ignorance that causes depression. My experience would say that it is rather an entrenched identification with a particular situation and failing to see a way out. But this has nothing to do with Advaita.

Also, the depression would not necessarily go away on gaining Self-knowledge. But, as noted above, if you could gain Self-knowledge whilst suffering from depression, then it presumably could not have been too bad! In this situation, you would clearly still have pratibandha-s (the mental obstacles to the final peace) but, after those have been resolved (by nididhyAsana), the depression should disappear too.

Q.132 Anti-depressants and spiritual progress

Q: I've been taking antidepressant medications for some time. As a pharmacist who dispenses countless prescriptions for these drugs, my observation is that they may have some value in severe clinical depression, although their mode of action is unknown and their efficacy and safety cannot withstand rigorous scientific scrutiny.

When I was going through a difficult period some years ago, I became somewhat depressed and, as is generally the case, an MD prescribed Effexor, a popular AD drug. It was not particularly helpful, if at all, but I continued its use based on the doctor's recommendation.

I'm still taking antidepressants, although my doctor thinks at this point they're probably irrelevant to any existing emotional problems I have, which are few. However, withdrawal from these meds can be extremely difficult, even when tapered slowly and, although I consider my progress and development unrelated to ADs, I'm nevertheless frightened to discontinue them.

I read your viewpoint on this issue in the Q&A section of your website, and found it very discouraging. I've progressed well and learned much about Oneness, with your work as one of my prime sources! Knowing, of course, that neither of us is a physician, can you definitively say that these drugs will preclude the development of spiritual progress?

I only ask because, as I've stated, I've put a lot of time and effort into studying non-dualism, and I'd hate to think I've been operating at half-power and am limited in my progress by virtue of taking these meds. I love this area of study, and any encouragement at this point would be very welcome.

A: I stand by what was written in principle but I am no expert on the effects on the brain of modern anti-depressant drugs. It may well be that they do not affect one's ability to reason or discriminate. Perhaps they only dull any negative emotional reaction to external events. If this is this case, then perhaps their possible role in the mind's ability to realize the truth is minimal or even non-existent. Certainly, if the result of stopping the medication were depression or any other activity decreasing clarity of the mind, then to stop them would be worse than continuing… at least in the short term.

What I would recommend (what I would do in your situation) is that you see your doctor and explain the problem – namely that you want to come off the ADs but are concerned about the withdrawal symptoms. Maybe it is possible to counter these by short-term treatment with other drugs that do not have any withdrawal problems of their own?

Whatever the case, the bottom line is that you are not the brain! It is an instrument for your use in this apparent embodiment. Any instrument functions optimally when it is well looked after, polished, lubricated etc., as appropriate. But you do have to work with whatever instrument happens to be available. Some can run a marathon with the body that they happen to have, others cannot. Running marathons is not an essential part of life. It is clear from your writing that you are perfectly able to think logically and put ideas into order etc. You certainly do not have to be a professor of philosophy in order to become enlightened!

So, I would definitely pursue the giving-up of ADs, since it does sound as though you no longer actually need them. But I would also stop worrying that taking them (or not taking them) is impeding your progress. The whole topic is a side issue that is taking away your attention from the true path. Your real progress will be determined by the extent/degree to which you seek to answer questions relating to Self-knowledge and assimilate what you learn.

Q.175 What if one blasphemes against Brahman?

Q: In the Bible, Jesus said that one who blasphemes the Holy Spirit is guilty of eternal sin. As we all know, even Hindu sages agree that Jesus was a fully enlightened person. Therefore, can it also be said that one who blasphemes Brahman is guilty of the eternal sin that Jesus was talking about and therefore never able to attain salvation?

A: I think you are missing the point of Advaita here. The absolute truth is that there are no 'people', whether Hindus or Christians, Krishna or Christ. There is no universe, nor any god that created it. The concepts that you speak of are only relevant at the level of the apparent world.

At the level of the apparent world, Brahman is not a god anyway; Brahman is the word used to refer to the non-dual reality. So you *are* Brahman. It would not make any sense to speak of blaspheming against Brahman.

At the level of the apparent world, the principle responsible for 'rewards' or 'punishment', through the process of karma, is called Ishvara. But this is rather viewed as the wielder of the laws of the universe etc. and is not regarded by Hindus as a 'personal' God. At the level of personal gods (of which there are many in Hinduism), I suppose it might be meaningful to talk about blasphemy. But this is now way outside the philosophy of Advaita and I don't know anything about it.

Q.256 Self-realization – why bother?

Q: What I can't seem to understand is why the sages such as Nisargadatta or Ramana Maharshi devoted so much time to helping others to realize their true Self. From what I read, Ramana spent quite a bit of 'time' with his mother to see that she gained enlightenment before her body died. Why bother if, when she dies, everything that was 'her' dies and Consciousness continues? So my question is: why should one bother to 'seek' realization in this body? Why not just eat, drink and be merry and look forward to death to end any miseries we may suffer.

A: The answer is entirely grounded in Advaita's teaching of 'levels' of reality. You really have to take your stance in paramArtha or vyavahAra when you discuss this topic. You simply cannot mix the two or you end up with irreconcilable problems.

As far as paramArtha is concerned, there is only Brahman – end of subject. There is only ever Brahman; no world, no Nisargadatta, no you, no seeking, no finding. Even that is saying too much because language itself is dualistic.

As far as vyavahAra is concerned, the world is real, Nisargadatta and 'you' are real. What you do will result in saMskAra, which will likely not be exhausted by the end of 'your' life. Then, karma will dictate that your subtle body will have to undergo further rebirth in order to deal with the accumulated saMskAra. This is simply the law of cause and effect, which operates infallibly within the universe. You know that perceptible things that you do have their effect – you press the light switch and the light comes on. Motives and their results in terms of puNya or papa are obviously subtle and you might want to argue about them, but the principle is the same.

Within vyavahAra, so the teaching goes, if you become a seeker and eventually realize the truth, you will cease to accumulate any new saMskAra and, when the existing prArabdha saMskAra is exhausted, you will die and you (the subtle body) will no longer be reincarnated.

Realized teachers know all this so they also know that teaching anyone is, *in reality*, unnecessary since every (seeming) individual is already Brahman. But they also know that the seekers' minds, being clouded by ignorance, do not appreciate this so that they consequently suffer. Since the teacher was also once in this position, he or she has compassion and willingly teaches, answers questions, etc., so that maybe whoever listens will also realize the truth in that lifetime.

Still within vyavahAra, despite the fact that an individual is not really an individual but unlimited Brahman, ignorance imposes a life of intermittent suffering. And failure to realize will incur further such lives in the future. Eating, drinking and merrying is short-lived anyway. Happiness is invariably followed by suffering (and vice versa) in this human life. Once you are aware of the teaching and have some faith in it, you 'have your head in the lion's mouth' and are obliged to follow it through to its conclusion.

Q.288 Need for a 'path'

Q: I would like to refer to the notion that enlightenment requires a 'path' that leads to it. There are going to be some who do see themselves on a path heading towards an endpoint or goal. Then there are going to be others who may have been on a path for a while until they realize that they are already what they are searching for, and that they always were. Furthermore, there might be some who never knew of any path or anything called enlightenment, who one day find that they are 'no longer in Kansas anymore'.

The point is that I do not know what good it makes claiming that one way is better than another. I would rather people make up their own minds, instead of being influenced by experts in a particular field.

A: All that you say may be true to some degree. The bottom line, however, is that enlightenment = Self-knowledge and Self-knowledge is prevented by ignorance. So the *only* way to attain enlightenment is to remove the ignorance. This is a mental activity and a still, perceptive mind, able to exercise discrimination etc. is the one most likely to succeed. An approach is needed which cultivates this condition of mind and simultaneously provides knowledge appropriate to removing the ignorance. Traditional Advaita is such an approach. Some other 'paths' do not provide either.

Q: What does one need to do to attain realization? How does one go beyond the limitations of this world of vyavahAra?

A: You have to remove the ignorance that obscures the truth that you are already unlimited. This is effectively a two-stage process, though these usually proceed in parallel. Firstly, mental preparation (there are various Q&As on sAdhana chatuShTaya sampatti); and secondly, studying under a qualified guru (there are lots of other questions on this, too).

Q.305 Spiritual Progress

Q: What are some indicators of progress on the spiritual journey? Is witnessing consciousness an indicator of progress?

A: Most people actually don't go along with the idea of 'gradual' progress. The enlightenment 'event' if you like (akhaNDAkAra vRRitti) is rather a catastrophic reorientation of the mind (in the mathematical sense of course, rather than the emotive!).

The progress indicators are rather in terms of mental preparation, as in sAdhana chatuShTaya sampatti. We notice that we are less prone to emotional disturbance, avoid emotional reactions, see issues more clearly and make right decisions without selfish motive and so on. And maybe we have increasingly frequent glimpses of the unity and increasing conviction of the truth of the teaching. If, by 'witnessing consciousness' you mean seeing what is going on around you with a dispassionate eye, yes – that, too.

Q.322 Seeking – do I have to give up pleasures?

Q: I can see I need to live more austerely, and I am prepared to sacrifice much to bring about a more lucid and disciplined spiritual practice, but if I am honest, sacrificing those pleasures will have their cost and I will miss them. I would give up nearly anything to find a way forward, but I have heard that unless giving up pleasures is seen as so necessary it isn't actually a sacrifice, it won't produce any progress, making it pointless. I am confused. Living austerely definitely means sacrifice, and I could do it, but what's the point in doing it if it won't work? I hope I have been clear. If you could tell me what you think, I would be most grateful.

A: You do not have to give up pleasures. And living austerely will not bring about enlightenment. Here are a several points to clarify this:

1. Doing (anything), i.e. karma or action will never bring about enlightenment; only Self-knowledge can do this, since only knowledge is opposed to ignorance.

2. Regarding attitude to pleasure and so on, you have to want mokSha more than anything else and, this being the case, it will be perfectly natural always to put that desire before all others. But you can still enjoy a good meal etc.! You only really need to give something up if its pursuit is interfering with your pursuit of knowledge. And, if you have the right attitude, then giving up will not be any problem; indeed there would probably be no interference in the first place.

3. The purpose of disciplined spiritual practice is only to prepare the mind so that it is in a fit state for taking on board the knowledge. If it is not fit, the j~nAnam will not have its effect. Once this has been achieved, you need to drop the karma yoga.

Q.355 Faith in a Path

Q: How do we get the conviction to go on a spiritual quest? Unlike science, there are no indicators to give feedback if this is even the right path. We need to have blind faith in the general idea itself before we venture into it. Can we only do this through negation of the other paths, where apparent validations are possible by material feedback?

A devil's advocate argument could be to dismiss everything associated with the Vedas as nonsense, since nothing can be proved. Another way to look at this is to acknowledge that the ancient sages have come up with practices such as yoga and meditation, which sort of proves their intellect and extrapolates on their ability to see things farther than an average person can, and therefore we should have faith in their judgments.

A: Most seekers seem to go down a few cul-de-sacs to begin with. This is not a problem as Advaita sees it. If you keep trying, it proves that you have the genuine desire – mumukShutva. It does not matter how many lifetimes you take (according to the scriptures!), no matter which religions or philosophies you try, you must inevitably come to Advaita, since that it the truth.

You have to put your trust in something or someone in the first instance – someone who says 'this is the way; it works'. Common sense tells you to point this trust in the direction of someone or something that you have reason to believe is sincere rather than something or someone which has already been shown to be false on at least one occasion. The 'proof' that you are looking for is not in the form of a geometric theorem. It begins with unlikely-sounding statements in the scriptures. You then investigate these, with the help of someone who has been down this path before and is familiar with all of the signs and can guide you through the fog and avoid the cliff edge. Ultimately, you see the destination for yourself with total clarity and there is no doubt in your mind that this is it. Faith is not blind; it is trusting in your guide dog!

Faith only means putting provisional trust in someone that you feel justifies that provisional trust, until such time as you realize the truth yourself. You never have to 'leap' anywhere!

Q.356 Signs Along the Way

Q: I'm firmly convinced that nothing outside myself can give lasting fulfillment, I have acquired quite a facility for playing the piano and am still improving that skill, and when I do make an improvement it's usually after a long period of practice until the next breakthrough, ad infinitum. I'm in a fulfilling relationship with my girlfriend and I have a great job at a pharmacy. I'm in good health as well, but beneath it all is this sense that it will eventually change, and I ask myself 'is this it?'.

All my needs are met but I still feel incomplete. I have good karma and predominantly sattvic tendencies, so how will I know I'm making progress on my path? Are there certain objective milestones that I will definitely notice and see that I'm closer to realizing who I am? You said the mind needs to be receptive and mostly controlled but I just wish there were more specific instructions.

A: As I repeat many times to questioners, enlightenment is the same as Self-knowledge. It 'occurs' in the mind when you become certain of the truth of the pronouncements of the scriptures. This is not merely an intellectual conviction; there are no doubts remaining. So progress can be seen on those (hopefully numerous) occasions when you hear or read something and are aware of a flash of recognition in the mind – Ah! That's how it is! Also, when you read or hear other things, you will experience doubts, and questions will arise that require an answer. Progress can be seen when such occasions reduce in number and eventually cease (even though you continue to study).

Note that what I am saying here must be differentiated from the perceived worldly benefits (equanimity in the face of adversity, no longer fearing death etc.). These fall under the heading of jIvanmukti and there are questions on that in the section on 'Enlightened Man'.

Q.384 Dark night of the soul

Q: Please help me. I had a temporary glimpse of reality around 15 months ago by following the '8 fold path'. I tried to penetrate the question of suffering and learned that everything wants to come into equilibrium (a known chemistry fact) due to which my thought trains stopped and I got an instant realization of something called reality. After that, I experienced I am a silent witness and not mind, body, ego, etc.

This faded away after some time and now I am in mental anguish and turmoil. I don't know what is happening in my mind but it is disturbed or in what people call the 'dark night of soul'. Every joy is lost now; I get angry easily and have feelings of despair from something. Maybe it is because I didn't discipline my mind with ethics before starting this practice for enlightenment. Please save me now. Whatever is going on in my head, save me from it. I don't know how to complete surrender unto reality and may be this is due to the hold of ego. Please help!

A: The teaching tradition of Advaita is all about Self-knowledge. You listen to the teaching from a qualified teacher (ideally) or read about it and discuss it (less good). You ask questions about it to resolve your doubts. Eventually, you realize that what is being said is true and that is that. In theory!

The problem is that you need a clear, self-controlled mind and some trust in the teacher, the ability to discriminate and so on. These 'skills' are not really a part of Advaita – they are mostly lifted from Patanjali's Yoga system. If you have no mental discipline along these lines, you are never going to be able to assimilate the teaching. You need at least a medium level of attainment. With that you can take on board the knowledge and then continue your practices until you reap all the other benefits (peace of mind, security and so on).

From what you say, I would advise that you forget about Self-knowledge for a while and concentrate on acquiring the mental skills. Meditation is invaluable. And, if you have no religious-type outlook (praying to a god and so on), then the practices of karma yoga are the other main route – doing what is in front of you because it needs doing, ignoring desires and not expecting any results. And so on!

I do not know anything about Buddhist methods so cannot really comment. I would forget about 'dark nights'. The main thing to remember, even if you don't yet believe it, is that the world is not absolutely real. Your body, mind and everything else have empirical reality only, depending ultimately on Consciousness, which is the only reality. And you are That.

Q: How does it happen that one can know 'in the mind' that one is free, and yet continue to fall back into the conundrum of no longer feeling this freedom? Moments of complete freedom, knowing that it's not my business to 'do' life, not even to attempt to not 'do' life… and yet slowly fall back into the habit?

A: There are quite a few questions on this topic. Try the section on 'Suffering' for starters! What you are differentiating between is the j~nAnI (who is enlightened) and the jIvanmukta (who is established in peace/stillness etc. all the time). The obstacles are called pratibandha-s (obstacle, hindrance, impediment, opposition, resistance). And they are there because there was insufficient mental preparation (discipline, control etc.) prior to enlightenment. So the mind is still prone to fall into old habits. If nothing is done, it is possible to 'fall back' to some degree. The solution is to continue to do nididhyAsana in the form of reading, studying, teaching or whatever; continually reminding oneself of the teaching and the truth of its conclusions.

Q: One of the ways to liberation some Neo Advaita teachers recommend is to focus on the question "Who am I?" Accordingly, from an examination of this, it is not hard to perceive that the 'I' is simply a concept, and to ignore it as such.

However, it would seem that the roots to this 'I' may go deeper, and may in part be based on past negative experiences, which are much harder to dismiss as mere concepts, even though they happened 'in time' (also a concept).

Would you have any advice regarding the 'I' and past negative experiences, and how to resolve these within the Advaita teachings?

A: Experiences, whether positive or negative, can never lead one to an understanding of the nature of the Self. They are necessarily dualistic – experiencer-experience-experienced – and reality is non-dual. This understanding has to come from another source. The real value of negative, past experiences is in leading one to the realization that happiness is never going to be found in worldly things. Eventually, the desire to search for the truth becomes the overriding one and, with a bit of luck (grace) one finally comes to the teaching of Advaita.

Preparation and Practice

It is necessary to bring the mind under sufficient control first so that it is still and clear and able to exercise dispassion and discrimination so as simply to listen to the teacher and then ask questions later to clarify. Any emotion just gets in the way.

'Practice' is a requirement for preparing the mind to be able to take on board the knowledge (through shravaNa-manana). Once the mind is ready, practice serves no further use. Our problem (saMsAra) is the result of Self-ignorance and the only remedy for this is Self-knowledge. Practice is not opposed to ignorance and therefore cannot help. Shankara is quite clear about this. He refutes the idea that both are needed (samuchchaya vAda) in the first chapter of upadesha sAhasrI and the early part of his aitareya upaniShad bhAShya.

Q.6 Is watching thoughts/feelings of any value?

Q: Is the watching of thoughts and feelings of any value to a seeker?

A: Contrary to what some modern teachers might tell you, preparation and practice *are* needed by the seeker. This is not for the result ('you' are already the Self) but in order to prepare the mind so that it may be receptive to the knowledge which will remove the ignorance that obscures the truth. Remove this apparent ignorance from the apparent individual and the mind is able to re-cognize the Self, non-dual Consciousness, which is then realized (in the absence of the ignorance) always to have been who I really am.

Watching our thoughts etc. is valuable to the extent that it allows us to appreciate that we are not the thoughts or feelings. If we can see them, we cannot be them. But it is the knowledge that can then be gained through listening to a qualified teacher that can bring about 'enlightenment', not the practice per se.

Q.55 Stopping the mind

Q: The whole 'problem' with Advaita seems to be that *it* – i.e. Realization, Enlightenment, non-dual awareness – must be so simple that 'we' just have a hard time getting down to that simplicity. 'I' intuit that it *must* be utterly simple, the simplest thing of all and yet I constantly seem to 'work toward it', make effort for it, usher it in as if it were apart, something separate.

Well, I don't know what else to do other than continue questioning 'Who am I?'; 'For whom are these images and concepts?' Questions like those – and really question, not just pay lip service to it. I do find that those questions, asked with intensity, do momentarily shut off thinking. And I wonder if that's what it is really about, inquiring so intensely that thought stops for a moment and then the moments become longer with the questioning, longer and longer until at some point the mind of duality just stops.

A: You are right; it is simple. Unfortunately, all of our lives, everyone and everything around us – parents, teachers, friends, newspapers, TV, etc. – have been pointing us in the wrong direction and it is difficult to think outside of the conditioning. Even some of the modern western 'teachings' on non-duality may inadvertently be doing this. Neo-Advaita in particular is constantly trying to apostrophize this 'I' as *you* are doing in your question. This 'I' is just a story, they say; there is no seeker, no path, nothing to do; everything is already perfect as it is. This view is most unhelpful.

The essential feeling of 'I' that you have, without adding on any 'thought' of anything at all: this 'I' is Brahman. You are That, regardless and always. Nothing that you do can bring this about since it is already the case. Trying 'harder', 'inquiring more intensely' will probably only give you a headache. There is no need to stop the mind. The mind is the problem only in the sense that it has wrong ideas and you have identified with these. Get rid of the wrong ideas and you will see that there is no further problem. The mind must be used (with logic, reason, discrimination etc.) in order to do this so 'stopping the mind' would be counter-productive!

Q: That feeling of 'I' seems to get lost in the midst of activity. I just came from my step father's funeral. I was greeting people, etc., all the things we do at funerals. The 'I' didn't' seem to be in the midst of those activities. I was 'doing' stuff, talking etc.; responding to the circumstance; thinking about other people; what to do next; thinking about what was said; paying attention etc. It seems as if 'I', the awareness of it, isn't present in most daily activities. I'm not aware of it then.

The above paragraph is essentially what I can't seem to reconcile. I forget that I'm the witness and get involved in 'doings'.

A: Yes, I understand. But clearly you cannot be aware of 'I' in an objective sense. Even the witness concept is just another stepping stone. In the ocean metaphor, all of the doing is only movement of waves on the surface. You think that you are one of the waves interacting with another wave but there is never anything other than water in essence. Everything else is just form. It is the nature of the mind to get involved and carried away. You may discipline it but never really change it. As long as the knowledge is there, don't worry about it!

But, if you still have doubts, then it is those that need to be addressed. Ideally, you would find a qualified (i.e. traditional!) teacher and affiliate yourself for as long as necessary to answer your remaining questions. Failing that, read recommended books and ask questions on the Internet of those who have progressed further down the notional path.

Q.118 Reading ('Back to the Truth') and practice

Q: I enjoyed your 'Book of One' and began to see some things in there that were new to me in a sense. At the end of the book, you mentioned the 'Direct Path', though this does not seem to be something that I would be interested in following at present, maybe later. I will be moving on and purchasing 'Back to the

Truth' soon. Is there any particular way to look at this book or is it something that should just be incorporated into my practice; just a book to enjoy? The three paths of yoga, that you have mentioned in 'Book of One' are where I am at and am very pleased with them, along with the meditation practice twice a day. Although, sitting for a half hour is a really difficult thing to do!

A: Glad you enjoyed 'Book of One'. It ended with Direct Path really because that was 'where I was at' at the time. (This was the first edition; the second edition goes on to talk about Neo-Advaita.) As it transpired, although I found Sri Atmananda's 'Notes on Spiritual Discourses' to be very good, I eventually settled with the traditional approach epitomized by Swami Dayananda and his disciples as probably being the best for most seekers.

'Back to the Truth' was intended to cover all of the essential topics in Advaita in some depth and uses extracts from other teachers/writers/scriptures so as to give the reader a very wide exposure to lots of different sources. They can then pick and choose those which resonate. You can just dip in anywhere but I did try to organize it all in a logical way so that front to back reading is probably optimal. I hope that the book does actually convey some real knowledge so that it will 'move the reader along the path'.

It does deal with practices but it must always be remembered that practice is for mind preparation and does not in itself bring about enlightenment. shravaNa, manana and nididhyAsana are the true 'practice', acting directly to bring about Self-knowledge (which equals enlightenment).

Regarding the 'three yogas', read the relevant sections – the situation is not quite as you appear to think.

Meditation is certainly valuable in helping to still the mind and giving a measure of mind control. Indeed, it is possibly the best practice, so stick with it! It does become easier. When I was a student with the School of Economic Science in the UK, we were supposed to get up immediately we awoke and meditate for half an hour. If it happened to be 3am so be it! The optimum times are supposed to be sunrise and sunset, when sattva is at its natural peak. Anyway I kept it up for quite a number of years (10+?) and the benefit was clear. Ideally, you should have a mentor to whom you can talk about your experience – someone who has a number of years more experience of meditation than yourself. For example, it is very easy to get the idea that 'there must be no thoughts', when in fact thoughts are inevitable – you just have to learn to see them and let them go, not allowing the mind to run with them.

Q.196 On shravaNa, manana and nididhyAsana

Q: Can you advise how one can 'make real' the teaching or information that we read or hear? Even if one does not actually attain enlightenment, can one at least gain relative ease in one's life? I am thinking of the practice of shravaNa, manana and nididhyAsana. It seems that people are often so involved with the first (shravaNa) that they never get around to the second two. They want more and more information until their heads almost explode, but they don't know how to go beyond the information presented via teacher, or book.

These people may not actually be seeking enlightenment, but rather, freedom from a lot of 'issues', such as depression, addiction, attachments, etc. With correct teaching, might they begin to find some peace in their lives? Is it possible that shravaNa, manana and nididhyAsana can function in a specifically therapeutic setting? And am I correct in assuming that that is why most therapy does not work; i.e. because they focus too much on shravaNa, but lack manana and nididhyAsana? How does one truly awaken to the information presented, so that it becomes Knowledge? How does one go about truly learning?

A: I would not call shravaNa, manana and nididhyAsana (SMN) 'practices'. These are for the gaining of Self-knowledge or enlightenment. Listening to a teacher is essentially a 'passive' action. The 'practices' of karma yoga are needed to cultivate a mind that is able to listen without constant mental commentary. SMN do not in themselves have anything to do with 'finding peace in one's life'. Solving the problems of desire, fear, attachments, anger, blame etc. are a 'side-effect' if you like of the karma yoga.

These practices are collected together under the heading of sAdhana chatuShTaya sampatti and they are described in such documents as tattva bodha (or see pages 216 – 224 of my book 'Back to the Truth'). Following karma yoga practices or the rAja yoga techniques of Patanjali covers all of these. And they really need to be undertaken with the guidance of a teacher, who can set exercises, monitor progress etc. If you join an appropriate organization, these will be covered in parallel with the SMN.

It is a slow, methodical process to break down the bad habits that we have acquired from birth and you cannot expect to see many immediate results. Mental disciplines, viveka [discrimination], vairAgya [dispassion] etc. gradually develop over the years rather than weeks so that, hopefully, they mature as understanding grows from the teaching itself. Then, when enlightenment dawns, jIvanmukti may quickly follow.

Advaita uses the terms shravaNa, manana and nididhyAsana to describe the 'process' of learning, understanding and total conviction that one goes through on the 'path' to enlightenment. shravaNa is the initial phase of reading, listening to the teacher unfold the scriptures and so on. manana is the stage of asking questions and clearing doubts. But the final stage is the one of consolidation, until the mind is no longer disturbed by the day-to-day problems, thoughts, desires etc. that naturally take one away from this knowledge.

nididhyAsana can take various forms – reading, listening, discussing or teaching on all aspects of the subject. It's really a gradual wearing-away of the old habitual thought patterns, allowing them to be naturally replaced by a 'correct' outlook on the world, until everything is seen always as Brahman only.

I guess the only way of speeding up this process would be to endeavor to exercise discretion and not 'indulge' in activities which you now know to be associated with a dualistic outlook. You might think that, if manana has been completed successfully, such inclinations would no longer arise anyway. But habits acquired through a long life are difficult to dispel. Reactions such as impatience and intolerance, for example are likely to happen automatically if you are not extremely vigilant. But don't worry too much about it!

Q.204 My understanding is only intellectual

Q: I understand what you have said about Consciousness and how I am that. Sadly my understanding is only intellectual. I have no experience of that Consciousness (or to put differently, I am not yet aware that I am that very Consciousness). This is where I am stuck. I wish to do something to experience that Consciousness but it is said that I cannot do anything – it will happen when it happens.

A: I think that, like most people, you underrate 'intellectual understanding'. This is really the first stage of the Advaitic 'method', called shravaNa – hearing the message and understanding it. This must simply be followed up by manana – which is the process of removing doubts. To do this, you read more, discuss aspects, ask questions and generally go over the teaching learnt in Part 1 until you are thoroughly familiar and happy with it. The third stage, nididhyAsana, is the 'living with/in that knowledge' which has the effect of the gradual eroding of all of the bad habits we have acquired with respect to dealing with the world, seeing separation, having desires for objects etc. What you should not expect is that there has to be some clear moment of revelation, before which you were confused, and after which all is crystal clear. And, in particular, you should be very clear that there is no enlightenment 'experience'. As I have said before many times, enlightenment equates to Self-knowledge. This arises when all Self-ignorance has been removed. There is nothing new to 'experience' – you already are the Self and always have been.

Q.211 Can one reconcile spiritual seeking and career?

Q: I'm having problems reconciling my daily life and career with the wish to pursue a spiritual path (which is the most important aspect of my life). I believe that the world is an illusion but how does this help when I have to earn money to live? I hold a senior position in an IT company and there is considerable pressure to work all hours, seek promotion and so on but none of this really interests me. Accordingly I am finding motivation very difficult. I have also had the feeling for a long time that I would really find satisfaction working with the disadvantaged but am worried that, if I gave up my current job to do this, I might regret it later.

How should one reconcile the self-interest of a job in modern society with the desire to gain Self-knowledge? What does Advaita (and in particular the Bhagavad Gita) have to say about it? Is there always a 'right action'? Is it the case that each person has a 'calling' or is this just another ego-based desire?

A: This is a very real problem as opposed to the many theoretical or academic questions which are often posed. And you are right to say that it is a 'Gita problem'.

It is not the sort of problem to analyze and go over and over in your mind – this will only obscure the issues. It is rather the sort of question that you put on hold for a while and then later pose in silence, following meditation for example. In fact, if you relate to the phrase, it is something that is answered by the heart rather than the mind.

The way that you describe it, it does sound as though serving the disadvantaged might be your 'destiny'. The phrase 'svadharma in the Gita refers to that which you ought to pursue as required to fulfill your own particular destiny (neutralize your saMskAra). Earning lots of money, gaining status etc. can never be svadharma – these are the false aims instilled by modern society. I tend to think of 'career' in the sense of a car 'careering' downhill, out of control! But, as you and the Gita point out, you do have to act. Knowing that the world is mithyA is no excuse for failing to get up in the morning!

But, of course, you are nervous at the idea of giving up your job and going into the unknown; this is certainly understandable. I think that the most important thing you should do is to try to find a qualified teacher. Sign up with one of Swami Dayananda's disciples and attend classes regularly without fail. There is no question but that gaining Self-knowledge is the single most important thing that you can do. As long as you are doing this and know that you are on a clear path to achieving this, the other issues can assume lesser importance. This need not conflict with your existing job as long as your priorities are clear and the job does not demand too much of your time. You may know (or, if not, will be interested to learn) that Swami Parthasarathy, who has been giving Gita talks around the world for many years, also gives talks to high-powered executives about action, efficiency etc. There is certainly no reason why any job cannot be approached with the mindset of a Gita student and a seeker of truth.

Q.224 Watching the thoughts

Q: When I try to watch my thoughts, all I feel is a form of resistance in my stomach and head – sometimes quite painful – but it is really hard to see my thoughts. It's almost as if my mind has gone blank, even though I am trying to see them. Is there a reason for this?

A: This is a very common problem, especially noted by people trying to get into a regular meditation routine. Watching your thoughts is not really an active task at all and trying to make it into one will give rise to the sort of symptoms you mention (and will not give any benefits either!). The reason why you find it difficult to 'see' your thoughts is because you get carried away by whatever you happen to be doing. The key is attention. Simply attend to whatever is happening in a passive way, almost as though you are sitting outside of your body and mind and simply watching what is going on as an observer. Our habitual tendency is to jump in and get involved because the belief is 'I am doing this'. In fact, there is just 'doing' or 'thinking' going on and who-you-really-are is not doing anything at all. But you will not see that this is really how it is unless you can cultivate the detached witness attitude. Again, this is something that a good teacher will address and get you to practice as part of the teaching.

Q.260 Different approaches and practices

Q: I wonder if you are familiar with subliminal technology (https://www.innertalk.com/). I ask because I am a seeker (or in the process of becoming one) and am using 'subliminal spiritual awareness' CDs. It uses barely audible messages like, for example, 'I am unconditional love', 'I am Consciousness', 'I am awakened', 'the kingdom of God is within me', etc. to target the subconscious mind in order to accept these messages without the conscious mind censoring them.

I was wondering if it will hinder my progress spiritually. I find the subliminal CDs my only hope to help my sisters who have serious OCDs [obsessive compulsive disorders] and they seem to respond well to them. I am taking lessons at Chinmaya and I heard that you endorse this approach.

A: There are no shortcuts to enlightenment, I am afraid. You have to follow the due process of mental preparation (karma yoga) and then the key practices of shravaNa and manana (j~nAna yoga). Subliminal messages, hypnosis, autosuggestion, etc. may well be very helpful for psychological conditions but they can never provide Self-knowledge. This requires scriptures and, ideally a qualified teacher, accompanied by attention, listening, discrimination, reasoning and so on. And it will take however long it takes. I don't suppose recorded messages will do any harm but they won't help either – so why bother? (I have certainly never recommended them.) If you are attending Chinmaya regularly, with a good teacher, you will get there eventually!

Q: Thank you very much for your answer. Do you suppose that if I study your books – The Book of One and Back to the Truth: 5000 Years of Advaita – I can get there? I have trouble understanding the Indian accent and Sanskrit and it took me a very long time to be able to accept that praying to a statue of Krishna or Ganesha is OK (I still feel awkward because I used to be a Christian, and was told that praying to idols is evil and against God).

A: After many years of reading, discussion and study, my considered view is that only traditional Advaita has the variety of techniques and teachings available to enable any suitably qualified seeker to become enlightened. Neo-Advaita may 'tip the balance' for someone already well versed in the subject. Direct Path may offer a suitable route for a certain type of mind (very intellectual!) but again, I feel that adequate preparation is needed first. Since you are already blessed by having access to a traditional path, I would really advocate sticking to it and not looking elsewhere.

A teacher is really needed – there is no one to ask questions of when you are reading a book. It would not do any harm to read books which are in keeping with the traditional approach, whilst still attending Chinmaya, but there is a danger of encountering conflicting ideas if you read outside the tradition and this will only bring about confusion. The second edition of Book of One is now entirely in keeping with traditional teaching (the first edition was not).

Praying to statues is not an essential part of Advaita. But I wouldn't get hung up about it. The statue represents an aspect of the Self (which you are); it is largely a means for focusing the mind and for taking the ego out of the equation. For those to whom it appeals, it can be very helpful indeed. But if it really does not appeal to you, can you not drop this aspect entirely? If it is bringing about resentment or rebellion in you, this is obviously the opposite of the desired effect so is not helpful!

Q: I will definitely continue Chinmaya, knowing that I am blessed to have it 40 minutes away from my home. I guess it's natural to get hung up with idols, since present-day Christian ideas were instilled in my mind, and it's time to get rid of them to arrive at the ultimate goal. Lord Krishna said it's easier for one to reach Him through form and yet it's difficult to go to Him through the formless.

I was initiated into kuNDalinI by the Parajonthi Mahan group, which brings up the energy from the first chakra to the eyebrow chakra. I tried to surrender to the Lord but sometimes the pulsation at the eyebrow starts on its own! I asked two swamis from the Chinmaya Mission: one said Consciousness should not be limited to that one spot, while the other said even this kuNDalinI could lead me to Brahman.

I don't know what to do. I know if I meditate on the ajna chakra, I feel blissful with a peaceful mind and it sometimes happens on its own when I am at a swami's talk and concentrating on their discourses. Of course, if I can observe the kuNDalinI, it can't be the unmanifest unconditioned Brahman since I, as Brahman, cannot observe my Self as the subject but only as a projected object.

What's your view? The other reason why I still sometimes do kuNDalinI is it relieves my asthma and I see radiance and peace (a halo effect).

A: I'm afraid that the only thing I know about kuNDalinI is that it has nothing to do with Advaita! Enlightenment is about removing the ignorance in the mind that prevents Self-knowledge. You are already the Self, which is not other than the non-dual Brahman. You are not the body, nor the mind, nor its habits or inclinations. You really should not get hung up about those things. Giving attention to them means that you are not giving attention to shravaNa and manana. Sense control, mind control, stillness of mind, etc., are all important practices as preparation.

Q.274 Practical requirements for studying Advaita

Q: I registered to take the Chinmaya Foundation Introductory Advaita Course about a year ago. But after working through the first chapter (several times), I ended up feeling so stifled by what was being asked of me as a student (to study only at certain times, to build an altar with a picture of a great spiritual teacher, to significantly change my everyday living habits, etc.) that I gave up. The teachings delighted me; the trappings did not.

My questions are:

Can one study Advaita without making the kind of life changes that the Chinmaya course asked of me? In other words, can Advaita study accommodate itself to one's life rather than the other way around?

Does one need a teacher to study Advaita effectively?

If yes, can it suffice to have an online teacher with whom I can exchange emails?

If not, where/how do I create a personal study program?

A: It is not necessary to change one's lifestyle. Certainly, worshipping at altars is not something that would appeal to Westerners and, whilst it can certainly be very beneficial to the right sort of mind, it would only be counter-productive to the 'wrong' sort. Apart from attending regular classes with a qualified teacher (if possible) or regular study on your own (if not), the only really beneficial but time-consuming practice that I would recommend is meditation. Half an hour morning and evening is very helpful for the mind – and the practices that you need are all geared to instilling mind and sense control, enhancing your ability to give attention, discriminate, etc. [See the later sub-section on 'Meditation' for much more on this topic.]

Having a teacher is extremely helpful. Some would say that it is essential but I would have to disagree with that since I have not had one for the past 20 years – and the ones I had before that did not really understand Advaita! But, if you don't have a teacher, you are likely to pursue wrong paths, pick up incorrect understanding, etc. Coping with this involves lots more time. I was only able to do this, I think, because I was without a job and decided to write books on the subject. This meant I had to read lots, ask questions on Egroups and was able to devote most of every day, including weekends (and still do)!

I don't know of any teachers (that I could recommend) who

teach via email, although it is certainly possible that many of those who take formal classes will also respond to occasional, individual questions via email. And I haven't come across any websites or books that deal with 'personal study programs'. If you know what you need, it comes down to personal discipline I guess. And if you don't know what you need, read lots of recommended books.

Q: Do you feel that not having had a (good) teacher did any permanent 'damage' to your Advaitin development? I'm thinking of some self-taught guitar players who learned the technically 'wrong' left-hand position and, 20 years down the road, feel that their playing suffers from this early bad habit.

A: Interesting idea – and I'm aware of the guitar problem; I did exactly that! (Though can no longer play because of arthritic fingers.) But enlightenment is binary and irreversible. The process of acquiring Self-knowledge is gradual. But, once the 'penny drops', it drops to the same place however you got there.

The best teacher to read, bar none (to my knowledge) is Swami Dayananda. Probably anything by him is worth reading and likely to prove helpful. Go to Arsha Vidya bookstore and order some!

Q: He's written so many books! Might you be able to recommend, say, three that would be appropriate for a (relative) beginner like me?

A: Three books:

1. Self-Knowledge

2. Dialogues with Swami Dayananda (both these are short books but excellent)

3. Talks and Essays of Swami Dayananda (these are large books and there are two volumes)

Best of all, and recommended probably several times amongst these questions and answers, is his 'Bhagavad Gita Home Study Course'. The Bhagavad Gita is said to embody the entire teaching of Advaita – a summary of the Upanishads if you like. And Swami D's course covers everything at an easy pace with great authority, yet entertaining as well. (See details in answer to Q.462.)

Also, my books 'Advaita Made Easy' (to start with) together with the second edition of 'Book of One' cover all of the key concepts in Advaita in what I consider to be an easily readable format.

Q.315 Does practice make any difference?

Q: I have read your books (and appreciate them) and many books and tapes from many teachers on Advaita and Neo-Advaita. There have been glimpses and experiences here in the last 15 years, resulting in much lightness in this life. The real freedom came when it was realized there was no more need to 'decide' who to listen to or follow and 'I' have followed them all. I have one question which seems to separate your views from Tony Parsons yet he, you and the others all state that 'the bottom line is nothing matters' and whether or not an apparent person gains self knowledge makes not the slightest difference to reality-oneness.

The question is this:

If the truth is that, ultimately, only oneness is always present, what difference does it make whether 'I' as a separate individual meditates or doesn't, prepares myself for awakening or doesn't etc.? If I want to rob a store, why shouldn't I? Whatever apparently happens is going to apparently happen anyway with no 'doing' by 'me'.

A: What you say about nothing making any difference to 'reality-oneness' is, of course, true. The gold does not care whether it is in the form of a ring or a necklace in the sense that it is always only gold. But what happens in this 'apparent' world makes all the difference to the 'apparent' person! At a purely practical level, if you rob a store (and are caught), you will be punished by society. If you go through life believing that you are the body-mind, you will be dependent upon the satisfaction of trivial desires for your transient happiness.

You can't choose what thoughts occur to you; these are dependent upon your particular nature and will arise regardless of your degree of spiritual attainment. But traditional Advaita says that you do have the choice as to whether to act upon the thoughts. Whether you do or not is itself dependent upon how well developed your discrimination is; and this, in turn, is dependent upon mental preparation, such as learning to control the senses. Even if, like me, you do not believe that we have free will, it is still the case that the performing of those practices which produce sAdhana chatuShTaya sampatti will increase the likelihood that you will not give in to inappropriate desires. And you can regard this entirely as cause and effect.

The enlightened person, knowing that he or she is actually Brahman, cannot act unlawfully in any case. Everyone naturally knows the difference between right and wrong and it is impossible to do harm to another, knowing that that other is one's own self. Again, you can regard this as cause and effect if you like.

Q.316 Repetition of practices

Q: I can see that whatever is seen cannot possibly be me, the seer. The perceiver cannot be perceived because it is perceiving. That seems really obvious and clear.

Whatever practices, meditations I've ever done always end up at the same place: I come back to I/me, the perceiver. Whatever experiences of bliss, ecstasy, I've had always end up going away: I come back to 'I', the perceiver. I've gotten to the point where I don't care whether some bliss state occurs because I know it won't last, and, ha, it took many years of going through the same thing over and over again. I'd have that bliss state, or whatever we might want to call it, try to hold on to it, be disappointed when it went away and then 'work' to get it back again! Seems absurd now ...

I understand that I can't be what I perceive, whether outwardly, in the world, or inwardly; I am the 'I' perceiving all this. I don't know whether I should continue as I'm doing, keep coming back to the understanding that I, the perceiver, can't be perceived or is there something else I should do, the 'next rung on the ladder' so to speak. Is it sufficient to understand that I'm not thoughts, etc.; that nothing seen can be the seer? Is it sufficient to stay with that and let that deepen, maybe, or is there some practice or attitude beyond 'the perceiver cannot be perceived'?

A: The practice that is needed is investigation into the nature of the Self – Atma vichAra, j~nAna yoga, shravaNa, manana and nididhyAsana. And it has to be repeated until such time as the understanding finally 'clicks'. If you think of a difficult subject in the 'worldly' realm – say quantum physics – you know that you cannot simply get a book out of the library, read it once and all will be understood. How much more difficult, then, is something like Advaita, which addresses the very nature of reality and consciousness?

You know that Shankara's 'statement' of the truth of Advaita is: brahma satyam, jaganmithyA, jIvo brahmaiva nAparaH. The first element of this –that Brahman is the only reality – is not something that is immediately obvious; you cannot see Brahman, and even understanding what the statement means is not easy. The second element – that the world is not itself real, depending for its reality on that very Brahman which we have not yet realized – totally contradicts our everyday experience. We perceive the world through all our senses from the moment we awake and most of the time it is not to our liking! But the third element – that I am Brahman – is the most difficult of all to swallow.

Accordingly, it should come as no surprise that we should ideally go through all of the Upanishads, Gita, Brahma Sutra and prakaraNa grantha-s with a qualified teacher, continually asking questions where we don't follow; reading, reading, discussing, discussing – for a l-o-n-g time before it finally sinks in.

Be patient! There are no 'rungs of a ladder' to realize the Self – you are already Brahman – but there are effective rungs in mentally reaching this understanding.

Q.359 Some potential practices

Q: As a long-time Krishnamurti fan, I often 'practice' awareness (mindfulness): when a thought arises, I watch it live out its life and disappear; when I sip coffee, I am aware of the feel of it, the taste, the fact that I am sipping coffee, etc.

1. Is it okay for me to continue doing this while I am studying Advaita Vedanta? (OK in the sense of not undermining the Advaita learning process.)

2. Does Advaita hold that is valuable/beneficial to practice this kind of nonjudgmental awareness? Is there a similar practice in Advaita?

A: According to (traditional) Advaita, you are supposed to have gained sAdhana chatuShTaya before you embark upon the formal path of self-enquiry (shravaNa-manana-nididhyAsana). This includes shamAdi shakti sampatti, the six fold 'accomplishments'. And the first of these are shama and dama, tranquil mind and sense control. This is obviously a similar sort of idea to mindfulness. So any practice which helps bring the mind under control, so that it is not thinking about something else while supposedly giving attention to Advaita, is fine. But very definitely the idea is to become disciplined first, so that you can direct the whole of your attention. If you try to do it at the same time, you will end up doing neither well!

Q: Yesterday on my daily walk, which I usually treat as a laboratory for consciousness experimentation, I said to myself "Stop trying to make 'spiritual' things happen, just sit back and enjoy the ride, trusting that Consciousness is at the helm. In other words: Get out of your own way!"

The result was, more than anything else, a sense of deep relief: not struggling to achieve anything, not feeling I had to be deeply aware or transcendent or anything at all. Just... walking, looking around, having thoughts that came and went – being; trusting in Consciousness to steer the ship.

From this description, does it sound to you like this is a

useful/helpful attitude for me to nurture? I'm wary of latching onto something because it feels good, but that is, in reality, a misstep.

A: It's a useful sort of attitude to have up to a point. But this is the state of mind that Neo-Advaitins claim is 'it'. And it isn't.

Enlightenment is not an experience or an attitude or a state of mind. It is knowing without the shadow of a doubt that your essential nature is Consciousness, which is all there is, and that everything is That. And your mind must not accept anything less, no matter how pleasant or how much of a relief. We are used to going after anything which we think will give us happiness, not realizing that happiness is our own nature and that any external pursuit is bound to fail sooner or later. This includes the pursuit of a certain feeling, emotional or mental state.

As long as you appreciate this, enjoy the peace that comes with accepting whatever happens… and press on with the enquiry!

Q: Regarding the teaching of Nisargadatta Maharaj: central to Maharaj's teaching is the sense of 'I Am', which he instructs us to hold on to (as do some other teachers – even Ramana posits the 'I Thought'). I was sure that I understood the meaning of that somehow enigmatic notion, which became the center of my practice. I understood it as some sense of being, not 'I' (a sense of a subject) and not 'I am this' (grasping onto yourself as any observable object, such as the 'I thought', 'I image', body, mind and so on). But I am not sure that this is correct. Could you shed some light on that?

A: This is precisely the problem with relying upon written material rather than a live teacher. Translated and transcribed material is even worse – it relies upon the understanding of the translator (who may not even have been present at the original discussion, so that the context may be missing).

Practice of anything can never bring you to enlightenment. Practice is 'doing' and this is not opposed to ignorance. Since the problem is one of ignorance, only knowledge can cancel this out.

You are already Brahman or Consciousness (or Awareness if you are following Nisargadatta's terminology) so you do not need to do anything to 'become' That.

I have written elsewhere about some aspects of Ramana's teaching (see the 'Advice on Teachers' section). I would say that the 'Who Am I?' instruction is an exhortation to conduct Self-Inquiry. It is certainly not telling seekers to go away and repeat the question endlessly like a mantra! Similarly, I would say that Nisargadatta's telling people to 'abide in the I am' was effectively telling them: "discover who-you-really-are and then do not forget it, irrespective of what actions are going on in the empirical world". The point is that 'who-you-really-are' does not say 'I am' or 'do' anything. All sayings and doings are by the body-mind in the context of the world. And body-minds and world are all mithyA – merely names and forms of you, Consciousness. Once you have realized this, you can then carry on an outwardly normal life but knowing (in your mind/intellect) that who-you-really-are is not the body-mind and is not doing anything. Nothing can ever affect you – you are eternally unlimited and free – but now you know this to be so. That is enlightenment.

Q.364 Dispassion

Q: I think I understand dispassion and its importance, I've read that even 'loathing for worldly objects' is required. But I do have some passions or so it feels like it. For instance, I enjoy fabric and sewing a lot. Is this just Brahman? At times it feels like an addiction. Is there relative condemnation of whatever passion one may have?

A: I believe it was Greg Goode who once said that you have to want to realize the truth so much that you are prepared to die for it. This may be a bit extreme but it is probably true to say that, whilst you have lots of other desires or one particularly strong one, unrelated to truth-seeking, then you will never get Self-knowledge. viveka and vairAgya are important but mumukShutva – the over-riding desire to discover the truth is also very important! You have to get things into perspective – viveka – and become dispassionate – vairAgya – to the extent that you recognize those traits and activities that help you on your path towards Self-knowledge and those that do not.

If you have a desire that takes your mind away from its seeking, this is clearly counter-productive. But simple likes and dislikes are not usually a problem, unless being deprived of a like makes you angry, for example! I would not have thought that sewing would be a problem – that may well improve your concentration and attention abilities.

Q.367 shraddhA (faith) – Is it necessary?

Q: I come from an atheistic upbringing, and in addition I have studied a good chunk of modern Western philosophy and science. Such a position has become my 'default mode'. A day came a couple of years ago when I found myself in a deep existential crisis (one that is most certainly still ongoing), and so I looked for a spiritual path that could reconcile what I knew of philosophy/science with spirituality. Advaita seemed to be the one that not only fit the bill the best, but also resonated with me the most.

But on this path, I find myself constantly slipping into the habits of thought that I am used to. I try to cling to the pieces that don't fit neatly into the materialist story, but I'm very much aware that I'm hanging on to them because I'm worried, not because I have a strong belief in their truth. If there is a teaching that goes against the grain of most scientific thought, even slightly, I tell myself I must discard it – "otherwise you're just fooling yourself", I say.

I notice this thought process, and it's disturbing to me. I want to be open to what Advaita has to offer, but it's incredibly tough – I worry often that a spiritual path of any kind is not possible for someone like me. I have a good deal of mumukShutva, but no shraddhA. Can someone without shraddhA somehow gain it? How necessary is it? And how can I break through my old habits of thinking, and gain that faith that there's something more than just this body?

A: The situation is not as bad as you think. My background is entirely scientific. (I have a Chemistry degree and nearly 30 years working with computers.) My book 'A-U-M: Awakening to Reality' is about Gaudapada's teaching. He was one of the earliest Advaitins and said that you should not believe anything you read in the scriptures unless it is backed up by reason. Faith does not mean 'having to believe in something that you really have grave doubts about'; it is just being prepared to set aside judgment for a while until such time as you can ratify what is being said for yourself.

The sort of situation to which I compare it is hearing a friend describe something to you. Although you have not (yet) experienced the thing for yourself, you feel that you can accept what is said as true because you know and trust the friend. Maybe at some future date you will verify it for yourself. This is another very strong reason why you should seek out, and affiliate yourself with a qualified, traditional teacher. Over time, you will come to regard the teacher in this way and accept what you are told in good faith until you discover its truth for yourself.

Of course you have to be prepared to suspend your presently entrenched belief in the reality of the world etc. But this is not really any different from accepting the often incredible claims of science. The frontiers of scientific knowledge are usually at odds with the prevalent understanding of common people. And increasing numbers of scientists are not so ready to reject the claims of Advaita!

Q.376 Is preparation necessary?

Q: As I consider devoting myself to the path of Advaita Vedanta, I find that I keep coming up against a few constant, nagging protests:

First, it seems that the tradition and methodology (although I also assume that there is quite a lot of variety in how Vedanta is taught and realized) are overly academic and scholastic, at least as I view it from the information that I've gleaned during my research. The unfolding of the teaching of Vedanta seems to leave the student engaging in a lot of analysis, rather than a deep exploration of how they genuinely experience the world. This lacks transformative power because it remains something objective.

Second, according to some of the sources that I've gleaned, it seems to place Vedanta on an extremely high pedestal, as something engaged in only following years of other preparatory practices. But modern practice appears to demonstrate that such preparation, while helpful, is not necessary. I cite websites like 'Liberation Unleashed' (http://www.liberationunleashed.com/) and Scott Kiloby's excellent work which show that directly exploring and inquiring into the truth of statements like, "All there is is pure awareness", etc., can still be highly transformative outside of the context of a more robust regime of spiritual purification and development.

My fear is that, if I follow the traditional route, I will end up entangled in these preparatory practices. I'll just be getting the appetizer for years before getting the meal, in other words, but, in my opinion, why wait?

Is this perception true (given that there will be a lot of diversity)? Do most AchArya-s make their disciples engage in such practices for prolonged periods of time before discussing Vedanta?

I have heard you and many other teachers in the traditional Advaita lineage say things like, "Unless you have a very pure mind…" or "Unless you are highly developed…" etc., the practice of Vedanta will be fruitless. But, if you read the logs, for example, of the website 'Liberation Unleashed', you will find some very impure people – depressed, addicted, desperate, you know, the usual seeker lot!, who come out transformed after only a few days of directly looking into their experience.

I appreciate your thoughts on this and your generosity in helping so many confused seekers.

A: A qualified (sampradAya) teacher is never academic. But it is certainly true that a lot of the books around *are* overly academic. If you look at the books in the library pages – http://www.advaita.org.uk/library/library.html – probably 60% of them are written by university types as theses or critiques, with far too much Sanskrit content and lots of refutations and affirmations rather than elaboration and clarification. So you do have to be very careful when purchasing a book on Advaita that sounds as though it ought to be good!

Good teaching does not encourage analysis; it elicits recognition.

The correct (i.e. the one that works) approach to Advaita is the traditional one – shravaNa, manana and nididhyAsana. There is no question about this. But not everyone is immediately able to assimilate the teaching. A degree of sAdhana chatuShTaya sampatti is necessary. Again, this is a proven fact. Someone with no qualifications will simply not 'get' it. But it does not require 'years of preparation' before you can embark upon listening to/reading Advaita. You can still gain Self-knowledge. The only thing is that you will not immediately gain the full benefit (jIvanmukti).

On its own, exploring and inquiring is extremely unlikely to bring about enlightenment. You will not discover that everything is Brahman by looking! And simply hearing the words, without the methodology, is not very useful.

Q.404 Practicing Advaita

Q: I need some practical guidance on practicing Advaita in daily life. Please advise me of the best course of action.

A: You cannot 'practice' Advaita. Advaita is a teaching/philosophy. Its aim is to bring you to the total understanding that reality is non-dual; that all-there-is is Brahman or Consciousness, and that who-you-really-are is that Brahman. Only the body-mind can 'practice' or 'live a life' and you are not that. The body-mind and the world are mithyA, which means that they are not real in themselves; their real substratum is Brahman.

Q: Many thanks for the response. I still have a question though.

I understand that Advaita is a philosophy. But what does one do with a philosophy? Try to understand? Try to live it? What is my next course of action? I know that action should be ruled out. But what is the next step for me? What do I do or where do I go from here.

A: Advaita is a teaching methodology. It provides a step by step 'education' for the seeker to bring him or her Self-knowledge. Ideally, this teaching is given by a qualified teacher. This is someone who already has Self-knowledge and also has the skills to teach it to someone else. Since the original teaching derives from the scriptures, a deep understanding of those and a knowledge of Sanskrit is also deemed by many to be a necessary qualification for a teacher.

Accordingly, the next step would ideally be to find such a teacher and study with them for as long as necessary – usually at least a few years. Failing that, you have to read widely (but only those books that do not confuse!) and ask lots of questions (of someone who can answer them!).

Q.417 Value of practices

Q: Knowing that you have extensive knowledge regarding various pathways to enlightenment, I would like to ask your views, if you have any, on the combining of Holotropic Breathwork with perhaps Vedanta.

I have done some Breathwork in the past, and have had some energetic and some emotional experiences, for which I had no knowledge base to anchor my experiences to (to borrow the explanations I have heard from Vedanta).

Now that I am aware of the conceptual explanations (at a basic level) for reality (e.g. James Swartz's videos, Rupert's videos, Pure Light of Knowing meditations, etc.), I wonder if the 'jarring' of my energy/emotional bodies might trigger the internalizing of the knowledge that is perched in the mind, ready to 'colonize' my Awareness/Intellect/Mind(?) and create an awakening experience that will stick if I continue my sAdhana-s.

A: The bad news is that I have never heard of 'Holotropic Breathwork'; the good news is that this does not matter as far as answering the question is concerned.

'Enlightenment' means Self-knowledge. And knowledge is the *only* thing that can bring enlightenment. Actions of whatever kind will never do so, because action is not opposed to ignorance. Also, any 'awakening experience' is incidental to the gaining of Self-knowledge and not necessarily indicative of it. You can have the most amazing experience (as a result of drugs for example) but remain totally ignorant of your true nature.

Unless you can think of some mental 'purification' that may result from this 'breathwork', I would ignore it to be quite honest. Meditation is good because it does aid in control of the mind, improves mental discipline, increases stillness etc. All these are pre-requisites of a mind ready to assimilate the teaching so will be of use to most spiritual seekers.

Look into Shankara's sAdhana chatuShTaya sampatti. Then ask yourself about any potential 'practice': "Will it help bring about any of these elements?" If the answer is clearly 'yes', then by all means take it up. Otherwise, direct your efforts to something more fruitful!

Q.451 Nothing to be done?

Q: After reading and listening to non-duality teachers I got to know that there is nothing that can be done; there is nothing to attain and nothing to achieve. Whatever 'is', simply *is*.

So what should we do actually? After knowing this truth how should we live our life? Earlier I wanted to do sAdhana to attain self-realization and enlightenment. Now I have understood that it is the ego which is asking that.

Now in my life I have a feeling that, whatever activity I undertake, it's just about keeping my mind and body engaged. Be it any activity – reading a book, doing meditation, working at the office – I feel that there is a separation between 'I' and the 'mind'. When an activity or any kind of work starts, then the Mind and body are involved in it but I am separate from all of them. When the activity finishes, I again have my body and mind available to be engaged in another activity.

A: You seem not to be differentiating between absolute and empirical reality (paramArtha and vyavahAra). From the absolute viewpoint, there is only Brahman so that doing, enjoying, knowing etc. have no meaning – there is no one, no thing. But from the empirical perspective – from your personal viewpoint – there is a world and people. And there are j~nAnI-s and aj~nAnI-s (people who know the truth and those who do not). If you do not know the truth, you will suffer in life, so what can (and should!) be done is to find out the truth: that who-you-really-are is Brahman. Of course it is the ego that wants to do this but this desire is the one desire that is not only permissible, it should be encouraged!

Once your mind truly and irrevocably knows the truth (this is the meaning of being 'enlightened'), you can then do whatever happens to be your svadharma or 'calling'. This may just be carrying on doing your everyday job, living a family life, or whatever. But you may need to continue nididhyAsana in the form of study, reading, teaching, discussing Advaita so that the Self-knowledge is consolidated and you benefit from peace and happiness etc. for the remainder of the jIva's life.

Yogas

It is often thought (I once did) that there are numbers of discrete 'paths' to enlightenment. As far as Advaita is concerned, the relevant ones are usually referred to as karma yoga (the yoga of action), bhakti yoga (the yoga of devotion) and j~nAna yoga (the yoga of knowledge). This was the way in which I described the situation in the first edition of 'The Book of One' – and it is not correct!

In fact, there is only one way, as I have stated in the answers to a number of questions in different sections of this book. The seeker's problem is Self-ignorance, and the *only* remedy for this is to gain Self-knowledge. Accordingly, there is only one 'path' to enlightenment and that is j~nAna yoga. However, I have also stated the need to gain certain mental 'qualifications', namely discrimination, dispassion, discipline and the desire for liberation – the 'four Ds' as Swami Paramarthananda calls them. These are referred to in the Bhagavad Gita under the effective umbrella of karma yoga. Accordingly, karma yoga *is* relevant and necessary but as a preparatory tool, not as a means on its own.

Bhakti yoga is not referenced anywhere in the scriptures as a stand-alone method for gaining enlightenment. The term used (by Shankara, for example) for 'devotion' is upAsana but this is usually used to mean 'meditation' as a practice, in which case it is more correctly referred to as dhyAna yoga! As far as the idea of bhakti is concerned, rather than referring to a single-minded worship of a god, this means a general attitude of mind – not doing things for personal gain and surrendering the 'fruit of action' for example. Accordingly, the spirit of this is required at all times.

The fourth yoga that seekers often speak of is raja yoga. In fact, this is a branch of Yoga (with a capital 'Y', meaning the actual Yoga philosophy, one of the six branches of Hinduism). It is also called aShTA~Nga yoga in Patanjali's system of Yoga. Shankara actually utilizes some aspects of this in his recommended preparatory practices for karma yoga. But, again, it is not on its own a method for reaching enlightenment. (Yoga, after all, is a dualistic philosophy!)

Swami Paramarthananda provides an excellent breakdown of the nature and function of relevant 'yogas' in the introduction to his series of talks (240 hours' worth!) on the Bhagavad Gita. He says that the aim of every human is essentially the same: to gain security, peace and happiness. Initially, we think these will be found outside in the world. Eventually we realize that they are our own nature... so that our task is to reconnect with them. In order to do so, these yogas are prescribed.

The purpose of karma yoga is to remove impurities (mala) in the mind. (Guidance is contained in the part of the Vedas called the karma kANDa.)

The purpose of upAsana yoga is to remove the extravert disturbances (vikShepa) from the mind. (Guidance is in that part of the Vedas called the AraNyaka-s.)

The purpose of j~nAna yoga is to remove AvaraNa – the covering of ignorance – from the mind. (Guidance is in that part of the Vedas called the j~nAna kANDa or Upanishads.)

karma yoga

Q.101 Some questions about karma yoga

Q: According to karma yoga, We have to *"Work incessantly. Our duty is to work but not to expect the fruits thereof and you should not be attached to the work"*. But, how do we know what actions to do (good) and what to skip (evil)? For example, if you encounter a criminal who has a dangerous weapon and puts your life in danger, should you kill him (action) or allow him to kill you (inaction)? This is the extreme example.

And also if we go on doing actions (karma), which is an endless cycle, when will we attain liberation, which is renunciation of actions?

A: Karma yoga is about acting without any personal desire for a particular outcome at the moment of action, as well as non-attachment to the results. You act simply in response to the needs of the moment as perceived in the moment. Problems arise when you start to think about it before acting, trying to decide what you 'ought' to do, what is likely to produce the optimum outcome and so on. Actions to 'do good' generate saMskAra just as much as those that 'do evil' – the former results in puNya (merit, leading to happiness), the latter in pApa (sin, leading to misery). Acting in response to the need generates no saMskAra. The decision as to what to do in such a situation is made by buddhi (the intellect) as opposed to manas (the discursive mind) and it is not possible to generalize. The 'correct' action will depend upon the situation.

In the case of the criminal attack on your body, defense mechanisms are genetically built into the brain so it is extremely doubtful that such considerations would ever enter into it! It is conceivable that a j~nAna niShThA (a fully realized person) might naturally respond by allowing his body to be killed but this is somewhat hypothetical. (Also, even a fully realized person still has inbuilt personal behavior mechanisms.) As pointed out in the Gita by Krishna to Arjuna, *"Whoever thinks that Atman, or the Self does the killing or can be killed misunderstands. That (Self) doesn't kill, nor is it ever killed. It is not born and it does not die. Unborn, eternal and ancient, the Self is not killed when the body is killed"* (II 19-20, Swami Satchidananda translation).

Regarding your last question, liberation has nothing to do with action or inaction. It is attained when Self-knowledge is gained.

Q.217 Is karma yoga needed to understand the teaching?

Q: Is it necessary to follow an ethical lifestyle, practice karma yoga etc. before one is able to appreciate the higher teaching of Advaita? James Swartz says that a 'qualified' student is one who is 'mature'.

A: It is certainly the case that one cannot 'take on board' the teaching of Advaita if the mind has not been sufficiently prepared. This preparation is what Shankara referred to as sAdhana chatuShTaya sampatti, and you can find more about it in many of the sections in this book – it is so fundamental. He said that an immature student could never gain enlightenment without a degree of attainment of sAdhana chatuShTaya sampatti.

Someone with a medium degree of attainment could become enlightened but would not immediately gain the 'fruits' of enlightenment (peace, fearlessness etc.); someone who was fully qualified could easily gain enlightenment and would then immediately gain the fruits (j~nAna phala or jIvanmukti). So, yes, you are right in what you say. If you find a good, traditional teacher, you will find that he/she addresses both aspects and you will gain 'maturity' along with Self-knowledge. This is probably more acceptable to the western mind than trying to acquire a mature mind before beginning to study the scriptures!

Q.264a japa and karma yoga

Q: I was reading your 'The Book of One', and found it to be interesting and thought provoking. I saw Byron Katie on one of the lineage links at your website. I was wondering if her four-question process of questioning any limited thought is useful in applying viveka in practical terms, for example, concerning the belief that people should be 'nice':

1. Is it true/do I know if it is absolutely true?
2. What do I feel or think about with this thought?
3. What would I be without this thought?
4. Turn the belief around: people should not be nice if they don't want to be, etc.

I am trying to use the intellect to tackle life problems but find it hard to relate to scripture. I keep having to remind myself, for example, to eat for the Lord but instead end up strengthening doership. One swami said to do nAma japa when doing everyday activities, in order to strengthen focus, but it can be very distracting.

A: Byron Katie is only mentioned once on the site in connection with the book 'The Awakening West' by Lynn Marie Lumiere. As far as I know, she has little to do with Advaita but I haven't read any of her work so I can't really comment on her teaching.

Viveka (discrimination) is not something that can be taught like mathematics – there is no logical formula that can be applied to insure that you make good decisions. Viveka is something that is developed as a result of cultivating such qualities as dispassion, unselfishness, stillness of mind, and so on. As the mind develops such qualities, it is also naturally able to exercise viveka more effectively.

I do not see that the practice of japa (mentally repeating a mantra for meditation), whilst giving attention to a task, can be particularly helpful. I would say that simply letting the attention rest on the place where the work is taking place and not giving any attention to thoughts in the mind is the optimum way of performing karma yoga.

Q: Thanks for explaining karma yoga. If I can get to the point of focusing on the task or my duty without the ego coming in to exert doership, I guess I am on the right track. Does this mean anything can be done in the spirit of karma yoga? How do I discern if I am really doing something for the Lord or my own selfish needs? If I merely observe the act of doing things, can I temporarily remove the idea of doership? (If I can observe 'myself doing' something, I cannot be the doer doing it!) Or should I be so focused with the task that I lose myself in it, but which can strengthen the desire to do the task again?

A: 'Doing' anything, including japa, will never lead to enlightenment. (I use the word 'enlightenment' rather than 'liberation' because you are already 'free'.) Only Self-knowledge will remove Self-ignorance. So if you do not have access to a qualified teacher, reading (including listening to or watching recordings), reflection and discussion are the next best.

Karma yoga is doing something because it needs to be done, not for yourself or another person. Dedicating your action to the Lord can be an aspect of this. If you are giving your complete attention to the task, you will not have any space for anything else. But this is not at all the same as getting lost in an action, such as playing a computer game, for example, where you are identified with the character in the game. This is better regarded as 'identification' and is not useful!

bhakti yoga

Q.314 Being a bhakta

Q: I take no great pleasure in what the Buddhists call 'samsaric' existence, and, over a long number of years, by intellectual hard work, have extricated myself from sectarian Christianity. However, I have come to realize that my progress has been not so much spiritual as intellectual. In practice, I find that I seem to be incapable of devotion, or any emotional attitude to any avatar or guru. For me, bhakti seems to be impossible even though I really try to avoid obvious 'sins', and try to be altruistic in my outlook. It seems as if I am damned to be merely a seeking, learning intellect, with very little emotion in what I do, except in times of crisis. For instance, in desperation at what I see as my condition, I have prayed to Ramana Maharshi, asking him to open my heart, and to allow me to feel more emotion/devotion than I do. Sometimes, on such occasions I have shed tears, but they pass, and soon, I am back to my usual practical self, doing the usual, practical things, and taking an 'intelligent interest' in things.

Years ago, I used to attend a Buddhist meditation group under a very able teacher who, it was obvious, had seen through the ego and was beyond it. After a number of years' attendance, this teacher made it clear to me (I must say, very skillfully, by implication and not directly) that I was not a suitable attendee. This was even though there had been many of what I would call transcendental experiences, and insights (all, I think, thanks to the darshan of this teacher) that have now been lost. For many years, since leaving the group, I have been a loner, living a very quiet and studious life, mainly. I try to do all the good for others that I can, by being helpful to others, and as generous as I can afford to be (I think) with money. Yet, I feel as if I am damned, having lost my chance to practice with a realized teacher. And all because (it seems) I was not able to forswear sex within marriage at that time of life. Even now, in old age, when such an obstacle cannot exist, there is still the problem of a lack of a capacity for devotion — only a capacity for intellectual understanding.

What can be done? I am afraid of being re-born in unpropitious states because of my condition.

A: My own situation was similar to yours in that I never had any inclination towards bhakti (as I understood it). But I believe that you are being much too hard on yourself. And (if your situation is like mine was) you have an incorrect understanding of the meaning of bhakti in the context of spiritual seeking.

The bottom line has to be that enlightenment or self-realization means Self-knowledge; and it is an 'event' in the mind, a rewiring if you like when realization of the truth of non-duality dawns. Prior to this, a qualified teacher 'enables' this and it would certainly be natural to feel devotion towards such a one but neither is absolutely necessary; it is your attitude to the teaching itself that is important. Presumably you read and are drawn to the teaching of Advaita. This very feeling that the scriptures embody the truth about the nature of reality, and the respect and heartfelt gratitude you would naturally have for those who have written about it since, can be regarded as an attitude of bhakti.

Not sure where your comment about sex within marriage comes from. This is natural and desirable, and an accepted part of the gRRihastha Ashrama (householder role) in traditional Hindu society. It is only given up when you give up the marriage and go off into the forest to prepare for complete renunciation (and I don't think this sort of thing happens much these days!).

So I would suggest carrying on as you are already doing. It seems to me that your real obstacle is the idea that you have an obstacle!

Q.63 bhakti and j~nAna

Q: Could you say something about practice with reference to bhakti and j~nAna in bringing about enlightenment?

A: Practice is about mind preparation. So, to the extent that the mind is not fully prepared, practice is at least useful and possibly essential. Ultimately, however, the root problem is Self-ignorance and the only remedy for that is Self-knowledge. Knowledge is objective (in the sense of being dualistic), so it is not in itself 'real' (in the Advaitin sense of the word). But then who-you-really-are does not need enlightenment!

So-called 'enlightenment' is when the Self-ignorance in the mind is replaced by Self-knowledge. So the effective procedure for becoming enlightened is to acquire Self-knowledge. This is the only method. Listening to a qualified teacher 'explaining' a scriptural text is the best way. Then ask questions to clear any doubts and reflect upon what you have learned. In the absence of access to a traditional teacher, read recommended books.

It really does not matter very much if you 'cover the same ground' several times. Different teachers will have different perspectives and you will usually learn something new. Despite all of the books I have read, covering effectively the same material probably dozens of times, I still learn new things from new sources. The problem with this approach as a 'path' is that some writers will themselves not have understood correctly. If you go to the original material (effectively Upanishads etc.), these are not readily understood – especially if you do not know any Sanskrit! So, ideally, you do need assistance from someone who already understands.

Bhakti is not an alternative path, because it does not provide Self-knowledge. Indeed, 'bhakti' is not really a practice in Advaita at all. The term used in the scriptures is upAsana, and this relates to devotional practice (worship, meditation) on a deity or symbolic object. Its value is in preparing the mind for j~nAna.

j~nAna yoga

Q.108 On being in the present and j~nAna yoga

Q: How would I go about approaching the material in the 'Book of One' in order best to understand it? My 'practice' recently has been therapy/psychodrama, AA once in a while and, around it all, just trying to be more in the present. The problem is that I keep falling asleep and then get caught in some persona or another; but I try to realize this and get back to just staying present. I spend as much time as I can just seeing the background of it all.

A: I think you should treat the book just as an enjoyable (hopefully!) but thought-provoking way of passing the time. It is not a manual for realizing the truth so there is no particular way of going about reading it. If, having read it, you are convinced that Advaita provides a means of understanding the truth, then perhaps you should go about finding a genuine teacher, who can address your own specific problems. Note that you are unlikely to discover the truth on your own. That there is only a non-dual reality and that 'you are That' are not intuitively obvious! If you are still not convinced, you can read 'Back to the Truth', which looks at everything in more detail through the words of many other teachers and writers.

Enlightenment is only secondarily about peace of mind and reconciliation with life. It is primarily about Self-knowledge. It is not about being in the present per se, nor about avoiding bad experiences. But it is true that identification with the roles that you play will occur less and less as your understanding grows.

It is relatively easy to gain information from books but much less easy to gain Self-knowledge. It is, however, true that you need a receptive mind in order to be able to assimilate the truth of Advaita. So the therapy etc. may well have been useful in this respect. If your desire to find out the truth about yourself is sufficiently intense, you will not have any problem.

Q: In the book, you mention j~nAna and TM. I know how to practice TM twice a day but j~nAna – I haven't got a clue what to do with that or where to even begin. Can you suggest a starting point for j~nAna?

A: You are already doing it! The 'person' 'follows the path' of j~nAna yoga, the yoga of knowledge, by learning all about the nature of self and the world. This is not in the sense of acquiring information but in the sense of seeing for oneself what is actually the case. It is done ideally with the help of a teacher. The next best thing is to read good books and discuss them/ask questions from others 'further along the path'. When you have realized the truth of the teaching for yourself, the mind is said to have gained Self-knowledge and the person is said to be 'enlightened' or to have become a j~nAnI.

Meditation

Meditation (dhyAna) is an integral part of the process of seeking the truth but cannot, on its own, give mokSha. It is a preparatory practice whose principal purpose is the acquisition of mental discipline.

In order to be able to meditate, one should have a degree of mental equanimity. Obviously, if the mind is anxious, angry, imagining, fearful or in any other way not at rest, it is not going to be able to rest attention on an object of meditation. The other main prerequisite is vairAgya. Effectively, this means that one has relegated all other concerns in life to a lower priority – the most important thing is to gain mokSha. This is mumukShutva. So, as Swami Paramarthananda puts it, vairAgya is the maturity of being clear about the priorities in life.

Then one finds a suitable location – relatively (but not too) comfortable, and quiet with a reasonable guarantee that one will not be distracted. Ideally, find an upright chair which puts no strain on any part of the body but also does not encourage falling asleep. If the object of meditation is a mantra, close the eyes and allow any other sensory input to just be – given them no attention – and simply attend to the repeating mantra in the mind. Just as you would not chase after every vehicle passing by in the road outside, allow any arising thoughts to pass by also, without following them.

Focusing the mind on the object of meditation is dhAraNA; keeping it focused for the duration is dhyAna; becoming absorbed in the process is samAdhi. When the absorption occurs, the meditation becomes effortless and, in the case of mantra meditation (japa), the mantra may cease to repeat altogether, leaving total stillness (although stillness is not the purpose of the exercise).

Q.15 Enlightenment

Q: Can meditation bring about enlightenment?

A: Meditation is a valuable rest for the mind, providing some welcome freedom from thoughts. But the point to bear in mind is that the root cause of all of our problems is ignorance and the only thing that can remove that is knowledge. Experiencing a still mind is still an experience! Even an ascetic who goes into a cave to meditate for days at a time will come out and be no more enlightened than when he went in – just thinner!

Meditation is of value when the mind is very active. If thoughts, objections, problems, ideas etc. are continually being thrown up, the mind is not going to be receptive to knowledge – a still mind is needed. But nothing can take 'you' (the ego) anywhere, whether to enlightenment or to hell, because 'you' do not exist.

Who-you-really-are is already free, perfect and complete. The problem is simply that there are thoughts that there is a separate entity that exists and is not free. These thoughts (ignorance) have to be shown to be mistaken. This involves the mind, paradoxically. New knowledge is input, from scriptures or a teacher, and reason shows the previous notions to be false. Obviously this process cannot happen in the absence of mind. Hence, meditation could never itself bring about recognition of Self; it can only help prepare the mind to be more receptive to the knowledge. In fact, meditation (dhyAna) is not even part of the traditional preparation of Shankara's Advaita (sAdhana chatuShTaya sampatti). It is the seventh of the eight steps of aShTA~Nga yoga, which is an aspect of Yoga philosophy.

Q.36 Meditation – 'One without a second'?

Q: If meditation is to be 'One without a second' is it therefore much broader than 'dhyAna' (is this what 'formal' meditation is called)?

Is it therefore an integral part of Advaita (how does 'one' prepare' for that which already is?) and synonymous with Life/Essence/Source/Religion/Background?

This may be connected to a Tony Parsons' sentence from 21.12.2005 in a conversation posted on his web-site, *"... the reality is that everybody in the world is meditating"*.

Perhaps the only point of any practice is to see through it to the pregnant void of no one to practice, nothing to practice until the next seed sound vibrates up from the deep?

A: The fundamental point about seeking, practice etc. is that, as you say, we are 'already That' – we just don't know it. Enlightenment is something that happens when the realization is triggered in the mind that 'I am Brahman', I am not a separate, limited person but the undivided, changeless reality.

But this is not to say that things cannot happen to make this realization more probable. If we continue resolutely along a path of selfish, desire-fulfilling, worldly pleasure, it is most unlikely. If, on the other, hand, practices such as Shankara's chatuShTaya sampatti are carried out, scriptures are read and reflected on, qualified teachers are consulted etc., then the state of the mind is likely to be more conducive to this mental modification occurring. (This mental occurrence is called akhaNDAkAra vRRitti incidentally.)

Meditation is a practice which stills the mind and thereby helps quell disturbing thoughts and emotions, making it potentially more receptive to any thought, event etc. which might trigger akhaNDAkAra vRRitti. That is all it is. It is not 'One without a second' – we are always that anyway and meditation does not usually bring about realization of this. After the meditation, we soon return to the usual mental turmoil. I can't imagine what Tony meant by his statement!

Q.302 Guidance on Meditation

Q: You stress the importance of meditating, and I have been meditating for a number of years. I somehow feel that while I meditate on a regular basis, it is all a little unstructured. Which way of meditating would you suggest for the best results in regard to Advaita?

A: What do you currently do?

Q: I lie down, counting my breath from one to ten when exhaling. When I have done that for some ten minutes, I stop and let go, i.e. 'connecting to' Brahman/Big Mind/Supreme Being. This is based on 'Big Mind Meditation' by Genpo Roshi. It was from here I went on to find Advaita, and it appears to me to be quite similar. I think it works rather well, but I feel that it is somehow not very organized, and sometimes I mix it with other methods.

I started to read 'I Am That' (Nisargadatta) and tried to meditate on 'I Am', and it seemed to work as well. I have a feeling that perhaps I should avoid mixing different methods, but on the other hand I don't know if it matters. Often, I also use meditation tapes with theta sounds as well.

A: You can read the principles behind meditation, and its purpose, in 'The Book of One'. From my own experience, I do not believe that a duration of less than 30 minutes can be effective. Also, twice per day seems necessary for a prolonged period (years) before the benefits start to be realized. And I do feel that, in order to insure that your practice is correct, and to address any problems that you are having, you should have regular counseling from someone who is very experienced in your method. I also agree that you should find an 'approved' method and stick to it. Ideally, you would receive guidance from the teacher by whom you are being instructed in Advaita. If you do not have a teacher, you could do worse than TM (Transcendental Meditation) and I think you would probably be able to find an approved instructor in any major city in the world. Failing this, find a book on the subject of mantra-based meditation and use 'OM' as the mantra. Tapes of so-called 'guided meditation' are not really meditation at all.

Q: Did you do TM yourself, and is there any difference between it and japa?

A: The meditation I did was effectively identical to TM (initiated via an offshoot of Maharishi Mahesh Yogi, called 'The School of Meditation' in London). And it is a japa meditation.

It is not only for stilling the mind though (shama), but also as part of karma yoga preparation, i.e. rigorously regular practice, two half-hours per day (ideally with the first being when you wake up, irrespective of how early it might be!). I kept it up for quite a number of years (though the 'when you wake up' for not quite so long). I also taught it for a couple of years and, by then, I was able regularly to reach total stillness of mind during the meditation. The combination of the practice and the discipline are very powerful as preparatory techniques, i.e. to make you 'qualified' (in the sense of sAdhana chatuShTaya sampatti) to do Atma vichAra under a qualified teacher.

Q.330 Depression

Q: For years now I've been severely depressed and it doesn't seem to be changing. What led me to Advaita, I think, was the intense desire to know what I guess I can only meaningfully refer to as God.

I read a lot about how we are not our bodies and how if we can be aware of something, then that 'something' cannot be us. I understand all this. There is a formless awareness that appears to be prior to everything, prior to my body, my mind and the suffering of depression. I can see that.

One book I've read, not specifically about depression, advises that we remain with that awareness, as that awareness that is prior to both body and mind. However, I find this difficult. The body and mind come out of the Self and thus must be the Self. Beyond this, the reasoning and experience of it gets quite subtle, but I'll give it my best shot. Yes, there is an awareness that is before the mind and body, something that you might call the Ultimate subject, but It is only apparent because of the body and mind – without the body and mind, the Self wouldn't know itself.

When a person first starts to study Advaita, they are constantly told that they are not their body and mind, but I believe that this is only to get them to see that the body and mind is temporary and thus to 'disconnect' from it. However, I'm struggling a bit because, the way I see it, the body and mind is the Self, since they come out of the Self although, it would seem, they are an apparently transient expression.

So when it appears that teachers are trying to get you to abide in this awareness, I get confused, because I don't see how you can abide anywhere but the body and mind, for without them, this awareness would not know of itself. The only thing I can see that one could do, is simply keep in mind that 'this is not me' and nothing else, although Buddhists would say to abandon even that. So it therefore seems that there probably is no difference between a so-called 'enlightened' person and an 'unenlightened' person, other than that the former knows a particular something, if you see what I mean.

Is my understanding askew? Or is it really possible to abide in this awareness?

A: Sorry to hear about the depression. Have you taken or are you taking prescription medicines? These only relate to the body/mind after all so there is no 'stigma' in any sense. Certainly a pre-occupied mind will not be so amenable to taking on board the truths revealed by Advaita – this is the reason for sAdhana chatuShTaya sampatti.

What you say is all effectively true; your understanding is correct. It is, of course, even more amazing than that – it is not simply that your mind and body are the Self; the whole universe is only a manifestation of your Self; you are everything. The teaching initially tells you to 'disconnect' to remove the mental identification and the final truth comes as a later revelation.

But knowing this truth intellectually does not necessarily bring about the peace and bliss that you might have thought came with it. If you read the material, and other questions, on the site relating to jIvanmukti, you will see what I mean. What I would prescribe for you actually, is serious and dedicated meditation. You need to meditate twice per day, for 30 minutes at a time. And it will be some months before you get into the swing of this. But eventually, you will start to experience true peace and stillness during these periods and this will ultimately carry you through the rest of the day. People without any spiritual understanding attest to this but, with your understanding in the background, everything should start to come together. But, when you are actually feeling depressed, be very wary. Meditation may well help but it *could* make you feel worse (studies are ambivalent). If you find that it does not help, don't persist – consult a doctor!

Regarding type of meditation, I am only familiar with mantra-based, similar to that disseminated by TM, but others presumably work as well. Ideally, you would learn with some suitable organization so that your progress might be monitored and any concerns be quickly resolved. As I say, the entire exercise requires real commitment –but it does work. If you have access to proper, traditional meditation, such as that guided by an Arsha Vidya organization or by the Advaita Meditation Center, then definitely go for that.

Q: I am on medication, yes, and have been for about seven years. It may be true that my mind, in its current state, may not be able to take on board the truths of Advaita, but I won't give up – ever.

To be honest, I'm not sure that I want peace and bliss so much, as these are surely transient as well? All I want is to 'know' 'God', for want of better terms. I want to touch the highest peak, the heart of God, not just for the sake of it or for rewards or bliss, but because it is where I should be, it is the only place that matters. I will gladly give up friends, family, fortune and even life for that one thing. I am depressed, yes, and one might suggest that I say such things because of the depression, but, truthfully, that feeling I just expressed is just as strong in me when I am happy and not worrying about life; i.e. when I am not feeling depressed.

I was worried about meditation because it would seem that there is the meditator and the thing meditated on, implying duality; do you see what I mean? But I suppose its purpose is to make away with an intellectual understanding of things and encourage an intuitive understanding of things?

A: Your feelings are those of a true mumukShu! And you are perfectly right – you feel that that is 'where you should be' because that is precisely what you are – you are 'God'!

Meditation only begins as duality. The mantra (or whatever is objectively meditated upon) disappears in the latter stages of meditation and you are left with simple, silent awareness – a tremendously powerful and healing state. It is certainly not 'intellectual' in any sense.

Q.457 Using meditation to 'find the self'

Q: Undaunted by my belief that meditation to find the self (soul) is difficult, I would like to try, but there are no teachers in my area. Therefore, in the first instance, I would really appreciate your advice regarding a book to follow for this type of meditation that is suitable for a beginner.

A: The purpose of meditation is to help gain control of the mind and senses so that you can cultivate dispassion and discrimination and still the mind when listening to the teacher.

Meditation cannot enable you to 'find the self'. You are already the Self – you just have not realized this. What has to happen is for the mind to receive knowledge about the Self, clear any misunderstandings, resolve any doubts etc. Ideally, you need a qualified teacher for this – someone who knows the truth and is able to convey the relevant steps (via story, metaphor etc.) to help someone else come to the same understanding.

As an introduction to Advaita, there are three books I would recommend:

1. 'Introduction to Vedanta' by K. Sadananda – see http://www.

advaita-vision.org/vedanta-introduction-sadananda/;

2. 'Book of One' (2nd edition) by myself – http://www.advaita.org.uk/discourses/thebook/thebook.htm;

3. 'VEDĀNTA the solution to our fundamental problem' by D. Venugopal (This is serialized at the website (http://www.advaita-vision.org/vedanta-the-solution-part-1/).

samAdhi

Q.266 samAdhi

Q: I read one of the books that you had previously recommended: 'Methods of Knowledge according to Advaita Vedanta' by Swami Satprakashananda. Could I ask you a couple of questions?

The book makes a distinction between the Vedantic nirvikalpa samAdhi and the yogic asamprAj~nata samAdhi (p. 301). From what I could understand, both paths recommend discriminating the Self from the not-Self. In vedAnta, towards the end of the jIva's sAdhana, the jIva must focus exclusively on the Self to realize that the infinite Brahman is the Self, the sole reality. For the yogi on the other hand, *"the liberated soul is omnipresent spirit/Consciousness pure and simple but not the sole reality; and there are countless souls"*. And, according to the book, the yogi's mind is detached from the Self in liberation while in vedAnta the mind is fused with the Self, but both minds are modeless (p. 302). Is there a difference between the realization of the yogi and the Vedantic sage? It sounds like there is, according to the book, but in non-duality, there can't be, can there?

Also, the book only talks about nirvikalpa samAdhi, not at all about sahaja. Ramana Maharshi and Jean Klein both said sahaja samAdhi is liberation. Jean Klein said in a book that there's still duality, however subtle, in nirvikalpa. Could you comment on these points?

A: This question is crossing boundaries to other disciplines – I'm afraid I have no in-depth knowledge of yoga, sAMkhya, etc.

According to Advaita, all 'samAdhi-s' are states only – they have a beginning and an end in time. The mind is an aspect of the subtle body, i.e. 'Who-we-really-are' is not the mind. This, of course, is speaking within vyavahAra. From the pAramArthika standpoint, since there is *only* Brahman, there is nothing that is *not* Brahman.

Discrimination of Self from not-Self is one of the techniques used to bring us around to Self-knowledge. But, whilst the jIva can 'focus on' the not-Self, it is not possible to 'focus on' the Self. The scriptures point you in the right direction but, ultimately, you realize that you *are* the Self. This is direct and immediate knowledge, not in the sense of perceiving or knowing objectively.

Since yoga (and sAMkhya) are dualistic, their so-called enlightenment, if this word is understood in the same way as 'the mind gaining Self-knowledge', cannot be the same as Vedantic enlightenment, can it? Because the 'Self-knowledge' they end up with is incorrect. Reality is non-dual, but they mistakenly believe that it is dualistic. Consequently, according to our understanding, they are not really enlightened at all.

Q.370 nirvikalpa samAdhi

Q: Should a person necessarily have experienced nirvikalpa-samAdhi in order to know that he has a mind which is prepared for j~nAna?

A: No. Of course, a good degree of mind and sense control is required (as part of sAdhana chatuShTaya sampatti) before the mind is capable of taking on board the teaching of Advaita. But nirvikalpa samAdhi is a practice of Yoga or Neo-Vedanta and leads nowhere. Meditation is perhaps necessary – it is certainly an invaluable practice for the mind – and NS may well come as a result of this. But it is important not to be diverted or seduced by the experience; only Self-knowledge matters in the final analysis.

Here is a quote from 'A-U-M: Awakening to Reality': *"Swami Paramarthananda jokes that it is called 'nirvikalpa samAdhi' if you are in a sitting position and 'sleep' if you are lying down! And, if you think about it, they do have to be the same – you cannot have two types of non-duality! The bottom line here is that enlightenment cannot be an experience. We are already the non-dual Self; we just don't know it. Accordingly, enlightenment has to be simply Self-knowledge".*

pramANa-s

Q.427 pramANa and reason

Q: Regarding the relationship between scripture, logic, and experience in the context of Vedanta being a pramANa: It seems like the 'rule' is that for scripture to be considered valid it must be both supportable by reason and non-negatable by reason. But what exactly does that mean?

A: Basically, according to Advaita, *the* pramANa is scripture (shruti). In practice, this should be unfolded by a qualified teacher, who you trust not to mislead you. You make the conscious decision to take what is said 'on trust' until such time as you realize its truth for yourself. Shankara said that you should not accept any scripture that is contrary to reason. But 'unreasonable' scriptural statements usually turn out to be gauNa, which effectively means 'figurative', and are explained (reasonably!) somewhere close by in the text in which they occur.

Experience

Q.78 Experience versus faith

Q: I have read most of your books, in fact I am re-reading 'How to meet yourself'. I have also read most of the direct path authors. Everything resonates deeply but this apparent me finds it difficult to accept without some definitive 'peak experience', which all these authors seem to have had where once glimpsed acceptance is not questioned.

All I can say for sure is that the very possibility that 'it' is all there is makes me feel lighter and at peace, so why do I find myself wanting this genuine article stamped on it, and does it really matter as long as it feels right? The common theme here is that 'it' cannot be understood by the mind ... which only leaves an apparent leap of – let's say for want of a better word – 'faith' in 'it'.

A: It is not the case that some sort of experience has to happen. After all, experiences have a beginning and an end in time whereas the reality is beyond time. The process whereby Self-knowledge removes Self-ignorance is most likely to be gradual. This means that there will, in all probability, be a number of 'mini-experiences' if you like, each of which represents a leap in understanding in a particular area. The final removal of Self-ignorance by the so-called akhaNDAkAra vRRitti will also represent a quantum leap but there is no law that states that this will be experienced as a blinding flash of light. It is natural for the ego to want some 'seal of authenticity' but ignore it. The ego naturally loses its dominion with the gain of knowledge.

It is certainly the case that 'it' cannot be understood objectively by the mind but this is not a problem. Who-you-really-are *is* That, so there doesn't need to be any ability to pin it down by description. The faith really only applies to having a degree of trust in the sources of that Self-knowledge, be it written or (ideally) spoken by a true teacher. Good teaching is always reasonable and able to be validated for oneself. If a good and totally trustworthy friend describes something to you which is outside of your own experience, it does not occur to you to doubt them. This is the only sort of faith that is needed.

Q.151 Religious experiences

Q: I've had a powerful religious experience and wonder if it is enlightenment.

A: The thing to remember in relation to experiences such as these is that enlightenment is the same thing as Self-knowledge. Self-knowledge is not an experience; all experiences have a beginning and an end in time. I have had several discussions in the past with various people on the subject of near death experiences (NDE) – see section on 'States of consciousness'. People who have had these or read about them set great store by them and genuinely believe that they have some sort of transcendental meaning. But if you read the books of Susan Blackmore you will discover that there are perfectly reasonable scientific explanations for these, down to the finest detail. All is explicable without any need to resort to gods, life after death etc.

Similarly, one is often told, when embarking on a formal, prolonged practice of meditation, that strange sounds, lights, visions etc. have nothing to do with it. If and when these are experienced, put it down to sensory deprivation, heightened imagination, dream or hallucination. They never have anything to do with reality or enlightenment. The true benefit of meditation is in the silence. True silence, without thought or perception, is also without duality. It is the (reflected) Consciousness alone illuminating nothing.

None of this is intended to negate the value of any experience you might have had. If such a thing is causal in instigating a spiritual search, it has been of value. But, in reality, there is no god, no ego etc. – there is only the Self.

Don't worry about the idea of progress. If you are understanding and learning from whatever source, then that is enough. You are already free; you just don't yet know it!

Q: Wouldn't Swami Paramarthananda say that 'Consciousness alone illuminating nothing' is the same as deep-sleep? Then why bother meditating?

A: No. Both deep-sleep and deep meditation can be called nirvikalpa – without division. There is no subject-object division. However, there is a crucial difference: in deep-sleep, the mind is inactive and unavailable, whereas in meditation it is fully alert but silent and perfectly controlled.

Q.230 Non-dualism & experience – definitions

Q: In your review of Rupert Spira's book (http://www.advaita.org.uk/discourses/teachers/transparency_waite.htm), you make the following comment: *"Any experience must involve an experiencer and an experienced thing (otherwise, how can there be an experience?). I.e. it is firmly rooted in a dualistic world".*

This statement is at odds with the non-dualism of many other traditions: there is a non-dualism of subject and object that does not necessitate the monism of systems like Advaita. The non-dualism of Buddhism is such a case – it's the realization that the duality of an agent/doer in relation to the object/world is an illusion. In other words, the world is not given twice – it is of 'one taste'.

In relation to Direct Path teachings, I would suggest re-reading the chapter 'Your Experience' from Greg Goode's excellent book, 'Standing as Awareness'. The last four paragraphs express clearly this insight that *all* experience is already non-dual – without a subject/object split.

Another book that I would very much recommend to you is 'Non-duality: A Study in Comparative Philosophy' by David Loy, where he discusses the various meanings of non-duality.

A: In the review, I pointed out that I was looking at what had been written from a traditional viewpoint – this means the accepted distinction between paramArtha and vyavahAra. Thus, an experience has a beginning and an end in time as well as having a subject and an object. So yes, it is firmly rooted in the dualistic world. Of course, from the pAramArthika standpoint, there is only the non-dual reality; there has never been any creation; there are no subjects and objects. But then neither is there such a thing as experience.

The problem of any teaching is to reconcile the experience of duality with the reality of non-duality. I am well aware that Direct Path attempts to argue the non-dual even in the apparently dualistic experiences of life. And, where it succeeds, I have no argument. I wrote the foreword for Greg's book (although I understand he omitted it in later issues at the request of his publisher) so had no argument with that presentation. I have also endorsed Atmananda's work. (I also have two copies of David Loy's book, but I confess to having abandoned it because most was not relevant to my studies and I found it very difficult to read.)

Finally (if I didn't already say this in the review, I know I say it quite a few times in this book), since our problem is one of Self-ignorance, only Self-knowledge can remedy the situation. We already experience the Self in deep-sleep but we still wake up to the same old dualistic world.

I have no significant knowledge of any other non-dual teaching so all I can do is speak from the standpoint of traditional Advaita.

In the second edition of 'Book of One', I have added the following 'proof' from Shankara that there can be no such thing as an 'experiencer'. It seems appropriate to record this here:

"*(The following argument is made by* Shankara *in his* brahma sutra bhAShya *I.ii.12, though I am indebted to Swami Paramarthananda for the explanation in his recorded talks.) From the standpoint of the world, there are two things: Atman, or Consciousness, and everything else (anAtman). The process of doing something (or enjoying or knowing something) necessitates that some sort of change take place. We move from a state of 'not knowing' to one of 'knowing' for example. It follows, therefore, that whoever or whatever 'does', 'knows' or 'enjoys' has to be subject to modification. 'Change' in Sanskrit is called* vikAra *(transformation, modification, change of form or nature). Something that undergoes change is called savikAra – 'with change'; something that cannot undergo any change is called nirvikAra – 'without change'.*

"When we discuss the nature of the Self in chapter 17, we will see that it is eternal, unlimited and ever the same – it is nirvikAra. It is only the limited, finite, apparently separate things of the world that are born, grow, decay and die, i.e. undergo change – they are savikAra.

"If you think about it you will appreciate that, in order to do, enjoy, experience, know etc., I also have to be conscious and intelligent – chetana in Sanskrit. So it follows that there are two conditions for the doer,

enjoyer etc.: firstly, it has to be conscious; and secondly, it has to be able to change – it has to be chetana-savikAra. But, to go back to the beginning of this discussion, there are only two things: Atman, which is chetana-nirvikAra, and anAtman, which is achetana-savikAra (inanimate things have no consciousness of their own). Consequently, there can be no such thing as a knower, enjoyer, experiencer, thinker".

Q.309a When is an experience true?

Q: I'm trying to understand how one can know whether an experience is valid or not e.g. if one saw an apparition of Christ, is one to interpret it as real/unreal, true/untrue etc. and how would you know one way or the other? Questions about truth and validity are always crossing my mind.

However, earlier today, I remembered how clear things become when you don't ask people questions, when you don't talk excessively about life, when you don't actively seek truth, when you stop asking questions and just let things 'be', when you just stay silent, still, focused and almost renounce life. However, it's hard to maintain that way of being when life seems to force you to ask questions and engage in it. I can see why some people retreat to a life in the mountains or a forest.

I was wondering whether, as someone with knowledge of Advaita, you would comment on this.

A: Experiences are 'valid' within their own terms of reference. Thus, the dream is valid for the dreamer (e.g. only dream food will satisfy the dream hunger). Similarly, our waking experience is valid for the waker. But, ultimately, neither is 'real', in the Advaitin sense of the word, since they are dependent upon something else for their existence. So an apparition of Christ would be real for the state in which you were (dream, hallucination or – much less likely – waking experience) but it wouldn't, indeed couldn't, be absolutely real. Only Brahman, the non-dual reality, is really real.

[The definition of 'real' as 'independent' refers to the term mithyA, which is exhaustively covered by other questions. If you haven't (yet) encountered this term before, think of the ring and gold metaphor. Advaita says that the ring is not itself 'real'; it *depends* for its reality upon the gold from which it was formed. It is the gold that is real, not the ring. The ring is simply name and form of the gold.]

And of course an experience which is seemingly inexplicable can have a perfectly reasonable explanation. For example, in 'How to Meet Yourself', I described a room that I had encountered at London's Science Museum. What one saw, looking through a window into the room, was that a person entering a doorway at the other side started off with a small body which increased in size as it advanced into the room. When you looked from the other side, you realized that the shape of the room was distorted, with a floor that sloped up to the window. It had all been a misinterpretation by a mind that expected the room to be 'normal'.

Q.433 Seeking 'non-dual experiences'

Q: For the better part of four decades, I was on the hunt for spiritual experiences that would 'expand my consciousness'. I now realize and understand that only Self-Knowledge can provide lasting peace, and any experience is something that comes and goes in time and therefore can never be a permanent condition. However, I still find it very difficult to drop the search for a 'Big Bang' event, after which I can safely say: "Ok, now I am enlightened for sure".

What is confusing about this is that there are so many teachers who seem to have a pretty clear grasp of non-dual teaching and still speak in terms of what happened during their awakening or enlightenment event. Francis Lucille, for example, talks about his experience in Eternity Now. (*"For a few moments, the pure I-thought seemed to vacillate, just as the flame of an oil lamp running out of fuel, then vanished. At that precise moment, the immortal background of Presence revealed itself in all its splendor".*) Franklin Merrell-Wolff provides an amazingly clear description of the 'Recognition' events that happened to him after studying Shankara. Ken Wilber talks of having been consciously aware for 11 straight days, even through deep-sleep, etc. Clearly, Ramana Maharshi and Nisargadatta Maharaj both went through Big Bang type spiritual awakenings, and of course, there are numerous other similar reports by various sages and gurus.

Recently, I came across a work by Michael Langford, titled, 'The Most Rapid and Direct Means to Eternal Bliss', in which he recommends a specific meditation technique. After 27 years of various Yoga and spiritual practices which proved fruitless, he discovered the method of 'awareness watching awareness', and promptly woke up and obtained the result he was after. The method basically consists in sitting quietly for a couple of hours a day, with awareness watching awareness, as the most direct means of finding the I-sense and abiding within it. He says that over time, there is an opening and deepening of bliss that takes place, etc. We also have the talk by Maharaj of *"sitting with the I AM"* for three years, and *"then I realized"*.

I guess my question is twofold: are any of these methods of self-inquiry via sitting in meditation worth pursuing, or am I still fooling myself in looking for the Big Bang? And if so, how do I drop this lust for a major transformative event?

A: The impossibility of a non-dual 'experience' and the distinction between knowledge and experience in Advaita have already been discussed above. But it is such a common misunderstanding that it bears repetition:

It is not the case that one gains 'intellectual understanding' and then has to go on and gain anubhava – the 'experience' of something that will provide the actual 'enlightenment'. If you understand and fully accept the tenets of Advaita – if you have heard the teaching (shravaNa) and had all of your doubts removed through asking question, further reading etc. (manana) – then that is it. It may take longer to 'internalize' all of that (nididhyAsana) and for it to become the background to your entire outlook on life, but there is nothing more to be done.

What more could there be to do? You are Brahman because you always have been Brahman. It was just that you did not appreciate it. You were 'experiencing it' all of the time without realizing it. Once the ignorance has been removed, you know it. Where could there be a question of experiencing something else? There is nothing else!

In my experience, meditation is useful. But its value is in conditioning the mind, since it is in the mind where enlightenment takes place. But unless the knowledge is there, stimulated by the appropriate input, nothing will happen. In other words, meditation cannot be a means to enlightenment on its own. If the truth has already been heard and considered then maybe the stillness of mind brought about by meditation will allow the 'event' to occur. But the meditation is only providing more conducive conditions. In the case of Michael Langford, assuming he is enlightened, this may just have had something to do with the assimilated knowledge over the previous 27 years!

My own experience and belief is that there need not be any 'event'. It may simply be realized one day that there are no more questions and no more doubt. Further reading, discussion, etc. may help consolidate this and help answer others' questions but it does not 'add' to the truth, which is already known. In what, in any case, could a 'transformation' consist? Who would be transforming into what?

Q.442 Witnessing and the Self

Q: Seeing-feeling that 'I' am not this body (aggregate of cells) and not this external world (job, house, possessions) is much easier for me than seeing that I am not this mind (thoughts, memories, personal history, feelings). The body seems like a suit of clothes, and the external world like a bunch of random stuff. But the mind seems real. At a deep level, I identify with it, feel I am it.

It's hard to see mental 'arisings', particularly those that have strong emotional resonance, as impersonal objects. It feels like my internal, mental life is the 'real' me.

A: If you are the mind, what happens to you in the deep-sleep state?

Q: I've been on the direct path for a few months, limiting the scope of 'what I know' to what I directly experience. Speaking from that point of view, I have no clue what happens to 'me' in deep-sleep. I don't even know there is such a state as deep-sleep, because I have no memory of having experienced it.

A: Presumably there is elapsed time between waking/dream periods. Since you have no experience or knowledge of it, do you think the Self ceases to exist during that period?

Q: No. But I can't prove it from first-hand experience. I can't prove that the Self exists or doesn't exist from first-hand experience, even from my waking state. Perhaps I might have an experiential 'realization' that Self is eternal and all-that-is (= Brahman), and I might feel that I know this afterwards. But I haven't had an experience that has left me utterly sure (knowing, rather than speculating) of this, so I can't say.

Barring first-hand experience, presumably I have to rely on logical inference and trust/faith in the word of the Vedantic sages?

A: Who is this 'I' that you keep talking about?

Q: 'I' is what feels like the subject of all that is experienced (sensory perceptions, thoughts, emotions, feelings, etc.) and done (actions).

A: 'Feels like' to whom?

Q: Again, more 'what' than 'whom'. Awareness/consciousness does the low-level 'pure' feeling and then the mind jumps in and 'storifies it' (walking > I'm walking > I'm taking a walk > I love taking walks, etc.).

A: I'm sure you know what I am saying. No matter what is thought, felt, done, said, etc. there is always an 'ultimate' subject who does not take part but 'witnesses' what is happening (or can do if the ego does not get in on the act and claim responsibility). This 'witness' is the nearest you get to the 'Self'/Brahman/

Consciousness, which is 'who' you really are. It witnesses all of the intellectual ratiocination indulged in by manas and witnesses the blankness of the deep-sleep state.

Q: Yes, I understand. Witnessing (for me at least) divides the world (subtly) into witness/witnessed. When I relax or surrender, this division disappears and all that remains is 'things as they are' (or something like that). So it's no longer subject/object, witness/witnessed, self/world. It's just 'what is'. That's why my answers to your questions "Who is this I? Feels like to whom?" are not really answers. I'm sure you know what I mean, yes?

A: "When I relax, surrender…" is an event in time. This 'just is' has a beginning and an end in time. Happenings in time are all experiences and do not really help you to understand who you are. But you must appreciate that, if you can 'see' something (body, thoughts, feelings, world) then 'you' who are doing the seeing must be separate from what is seen. You cannot appreciate this ultimate subject by 'seeing' it. It is always the 'seer' and never the 'seen'.

You (the ego/mind) are never going to 'experience' the Self/Brahman because that is who-you-really-are. It would be like the mirror that is reflecting the sun wanting to know what it was like to *be* the sun. (But would it make any sense at all for the mirror to question the existence of the sun?) What the ego/mind should be aiming to do is to gain and make-firm this knowledge. Never forget that, in the context of this metaphor, who-you-really-are is the sun, not the mirror! It is the sun that is Consciousness; the mirror is inert.

Initially, you are right, you do have to trust that the teacher is being truthful and that what is said by the scriptures is correct. But this is only provisional.

Understanding grows with repetition and differing views of the same concepts. A new metaphor may suddenly make a concept crystal clear. Eventually, all comes together and no questions remain unanswered.

Q.450 Witness – mind or Brahman?

Q: Talks that I have been listening to use the terms 'witness', 'eternal witness' and other synonyms. Is pure consciousness or Brahman this 'Ultimate Witness'? If so, obviously, it can't witness unless there's a manifesting medium to do so, correct? But 'to witness' implies duality. Also, it is often said that Brahman is transcendent or beyond the body-mind, and something other than the mithyA universe. So that means, again, that it can witness everything.

How do you reconcile the fact that knowledge is in the mind with Brahman being the witness beyond and apart from it? And how does this fit in with non-duality – there can't be two things?

A: The effective explanation is 'adhyAropa-apavAda'. The reality is that there is only non-dual Brahman or Consciousness. You begin with the conviction that the world is real, you are your body etc. Advaita gradually disabuses you of such notions by use of prakriyA-s (teaching 'ploys') such as analysis of the states of consciousness, cause and effect, real and unreal, seer and seen. Each of these takes you a little further in understanding. But, once the particular example has served its purpose, it is discarded. Analogy and metaphor can only take one so far; they are means to an end. Metaphors to illustrate this are leaving the boat behind once you have crossed the river, and letting go of the pole in pole vaulting before you go over the bar.

So, your understanding begins with falsity, ignorance, body, objects and progresses to an appreciation of pAramArthika reality, the opposite extreme of the ignorance – Self-knowledge spectrum. In between you have ideas such as Ishvara and mAyA, karma and reincarnation. Even further towards the 'reality' end of the spectrum, you have the concept of witness-consciousness. It's just a process of successive sublation of the ideas until you reach the final understanding that there is *only* Consciousness.

If you are talking about Brahman as the non-dual reality, then there cannot be anything else for it to witness or know. It is satyam, not mithyA, and there cannot be any 'manifesting media' or 'mithyA manifestation' that is not Brahman.

Only the mithyA mind can 'know' things objectively. The best that you could say about Brahman in this regard is that it *is* 'Knowledge'. (But again that is a mithyA concept in the mind!)

Q.142 On the notion of a 'witness'

Q: The notion of the witness as found in some Advaita writing is troubling me. It seems like a distinction that steps back from self in a 'process' to find Consciousness, Reality, Self, et al. This sometimes strikes me as inserting a 'layer' in the apprehension of Self. When there is some understanding, intuitive or intellectual, of 'witness', the moment is simply consciousness.

This 'witnessing' seems like 'doing' to me.

A: What you say is essentially correct. It is part of the process of getting the mind to see that we are not those things that we have always taken ourselves to be. (It is yet another example of the adhyAropa-apavAda method of Advaita.) It is relatively easy for us to accept that we are not the body. It is less easy for us to see that we are not the mind, since this is where all of the rationalization takes place. Accordingly, the natural step is to say that 'that which can see the thoughts and recognize that it is not those' is 'something which is a step removed from the mind'. Since this 'entity' is *seeing* the mind, 'witness' seems an appropriate term.

But, when you examine this idea more closely, you see that a 'witness', 'seeing' thoughts and the mental process, would still be a part of duality and so this cannot be the final answer. The witness ultimately has to go, along with everything else. In the end, 'all there is' is Brahman or Consciousness.

Probably Sri Atmananda Krishna Menon is best for examining all of this in detail. You will find lots of references in the 'Notes', which you can download from the web site (http://www.advaita.org.uk/reading/free_sages.htm#atmananda_notes).

Q.464 The 'witness'

Q: What exactly is the 'witness'?

A: The 'one' who is totally identified with something inside or outside of the mind is the ahaMkAra or ego – the one that 99.99+% of people believe they really are. It is an aspect of the mind.

The 'one' who can see this happening and remain detached from it is what is usually referred to as the 'witness'. But the recognition of the witness is also effectively done by the (same) witness. There is not more than one witness per jIva. The witness is still the chidAbhAsa jIva but now operating in stillness and with knowledge. Similarly, the acknowledgement that who-you-really-are (and have always been) is the Atman is still done by the chidAbhAsa. Consciousness can only (appear to) 'do' anything through a mind or jIva. This is why there is the distinction between jIvAtman and paramAtman. The jIvAtman is the one who seeks and becomes enlightened, realizing that in reality there is only paramAtman.

All this stuff is really playing with words now, and you have to do lots of background reading/listening over many years to be able to play with them confidently. And maybe others might put things slightly differently.

Q.445 Experience and Brahman

Q: What exactly, *in reality* (Brahman is the only reality) is experience?

I know that there is a relative level where there are jIva-s and objects and minds and Ishvara, but if we talk about the absolute reality – Brahman – then I believe that there is no experience possible.

Brahman is the only reality and Brahman does not have experiences of any kind – yes?

So if I realize myself as Brahman, then I have to see all my experience as mithyA, yes?

So, if you are agreeing to the above, and if I am following correct logic: why do so many teachers of non-duality and even of Advaita Vedanta say that experience is the only means through which we can explore reality?

As jIva-s in the relative realm, the only thing we have to navigate reality is our experience. So again: what is an experience? Is there no reality to an experience?

Many teachers who are famous and well-respected point to the 'Presence of God' as a palpable experience of peace, fullness, truth, love which comprises the reality of all our experiences. They say 'Presence' is Brahman in manifest form and is eternal.

Is experience comprised of Brahman-as-Presence?

A: You are essentially correct in your analysis here.

The best quote to remember for this sort of question (what is real?) is that of Shankara, often used to summarize the teaching of Advaita: "brahma satyam, jaganmithyA, jIvo brahmaiva nAparaH" – Brahman is the reality; the world is mithyA; the jIva is not other than Brahman. So, if you are trying to speak of the ultimate reality, you are obliged to say that there is only Brahman. Consequently, Brahman does not act or enjoy; there is nothing else. And, crucially, there is no 'experience'.

You have to be very careful with the words you use when talking about this. You go on to say "then I have to see all my experience as mithyA". Certainly, you have to realize that this is so. But you (the jIva) will continue to see the world as separate. You cannot 'see' Brahman, or 'see' the world as Brahman or Consciousness.

It is certainly true that some teachers claim that 'experience' plays some part in enlightenment. For example, they might say that, having understood the teaching intellectually, you then have to go on to 'directly experience' this. This is nonsense. It may be a misunderstanding or possibly a conflation of Advaita philosophy with that of yoga. (The Neo-Vedantins – Vivekananda and followers do this.) Yoga is a dualistic philosophy and it claims that nirvikalpa samAdhi has to take place in order to realize the truth. Only the particular teacher could explain the reasons behind their statements (perhaps!).

How could one 'explore' reality, if it is non-dual? Who would be exploring what? We cannot 'navigate' reality. Or rather we must be navigating reality all of the time because that is all there is! It is just that most do not realize the mithyAtva of this.

To return to Shankara's statement, although the world is mithyA, the substantial aspect of this world is Brahman. The world is name and form of Brahman, mistakenly seen by the jIva as separate. So, at its heart if you like, the 'experience' is 'real' in the sense that everything is Brahman. It is just that there is no duality in any of it. You cannot even say that Brahman is 'experiencing itself', since there is *only* Brahman. But putting it like that may help, and some teachers do.

Attempts to 'explain' any of this by bringing 'god' into the equation do not really help. The best way of looking at Ishvara to my mind is as the 'laws of nature' which govern how everything (apparently) takes place in the world. References to peace, stillness, harmony etc. are of no help in understanding reality except in so far as a still and peaceful mind is necessary in order successfully to conduct shravaNa.

Q: If there is no experiential basis for self-realization then are you saying it is an intellectual theory that one has to sort of decide on and commit to? Like the sub-atomic field of potentiality in quantum physics maybe? In other words, "this makes good sense so I'll commit to this?"

What other than an experience of the 'truth of Brahman' would make an individual mind feel convinced enough to gain Self-knowledge that the Self is Brahman and Brahman is All?

The truth is true and knows the truth because it is the truth? Isn't that truth experiential for the jIva?

A: It is not a theory. But it is a fact that it is the mind that has Self-ignorance so that it must also be the mind that eliminates this when it gains Self-knowledge. The best way to appreciate this that I have come across is the idea of bhAga-tyAga-lakShaNa or jahadajahad-lakShaNa. Read the explanation of this in Q.345 and see if it helps. And knowledge is not experience.

Q: The whole problem we humans are having, as opposed to the problems of animals, plants etc., is that we human jIva-s are suffering because we feel that we are in a dualistic, hostile world with little to no freedom from problems.

So then the reason we are in this predicament is ignorance – yes? The solution comes in the form of knowledge that we are Brahman, the non-dual reality of All.

What I don't get it is: what is this non-dual 'Brahman reality' knowledge going to do for the jIva? The jIva will still see duality; it will still have the experience of living in duality, which is nothing but pain.

How does the 'knowledge' solve the problems of the experienced mithyA-world-jIva situation? What does the jIva get in terms of better experiences after gaining the knowledge of Brahman?

To me it seems like your husband or wife dies suddenly; the agony mows you down; you think all this is only apparently happening in non-dual consciousness, which I and my husband both are and always were and will be – but it doesn't do anything to help the agony!

A: The dream state is a useful one to think of in reference to this question. Have you ever had a lucid dream? Dreams can be wonderful or terrifying experiences but they are manifestations of our own mind and, if this is recognized in the dream itself, then we can modify events according to our inclination and simply enjoy it all.

The waking world is said (in the interim teaching) to be a manifestation of the cosmic mind. Hence, the individual is unable to modify events in the same way as in dream. Nevertheless, knowing that none of it is real inevitably ameliorates any suffering. For example, the child may initially be terrified of visiting the dentist, worrying about imagined pain and discomfort. Once it is discovered that the situation is nowhere near so bad as was thought, future visits can be made without that initial level of anxiety. (This may not be such a good example but I'm sure you get the idea.)

I'm not suggesting that Self-knowledge makes one unfeeling in a situation such as you describe. The initial response is likely to be no different from that of an ignorant jIva. But knowing the truth that all of the appearance is mithyA makes 'recovery' much more rapid!

I suggest that you read the answers to questions 24, 32-33 for more insight into this.

The point is that 'experience' is not just what is happening outside, it is also very much dependent upon how I interpret this. Knowing that everything is Consciousness and that who-I-am cannot be affected by anything makes all the difference.

Free Will

Introduction

Before even beginning this sub-section, I need to make it clear what I mean when I use the words 'choice' and 'free will'.

If a person is to act, when there are several ways in which that action might take place, then a 'choice' has to be made by that person. This 'choice' is unlikely to be random. But the question is whether the choice is freely made or whether it is driven in a (theoretically) entirely predictable way, according to that person's prior conditioning (i.e. genetic makeup and upbringing). If a sophisticated computer, with full knowledge of that person's character, were able to predict how the person would act with 100% accuracy, then there is no 'free will' involved.

You might argue that, of course you are influenced by external factors and personal disposition when you make your 'choice' but still maintain that such a choice is 'freely' made. I would say that these factors are deterministic.

The philosophical positions regarding the existence of free

will vary considerably. At the free will end of the spectrum is the extreme 'Libertarianism' of philosophers such as St. Augustine and Sartre. This says that, as long as we are physically able to do something, have the opportunity to do it and are not constrained from doing it by some outside force, then we may freely choose to do it (or not) without anything, inside or out, 'making' us act one way or the other.

Universal determinism is the general belief that everything that happens does so necessarily as a result of the causes that precede it.

Theistic determinism (or *Predestination*) claims that these causes are the will of a God or gods. Some variants of this allow that we ourselves may have some free will within the overall constraints. This is effectively the general view of Advaita at the vyAvahArika level, i.e. our actions are largely determined by our karma but there is a limited scope for free will within this. (Karma is 'effectively' the same as control by a god in the sense of being a 'ghostly power'.)

Fatalism is not quite the same thing. This maintains that some events (such as the time, place and nature of our death) are totally predetermined –nothing that we do can prevent these from happening – but for the rest of the time, the status quo is maintained (e.g. karma + limited free will).

Naturalistic Determination is the belief that every event is the natural outcome of prior causes such as genetic and environmental factors (and that no god is involved). *'Soft' Determinism* allows that some of these causes are our own desires, thoughts and feelings at the time of action (this is my own view). *'Hard' Determinism* denies that these are relevant. This is the view of people like B. F. Skinner.

Soft determinism is also called 'Compatibilism' meaning that belief in both free will and determinism is not necessarily logically inconsistent (both libertarianism and hard determinism are therefore '*Incompatibilist*' beliefs). The crucial, practical aspect here is that compatibilism makes moral responsibility meaningful, whereas it is not meaningful for incompatibilism.

The 'bottom line' as far as I am concerned is that the absolute reality of the situation is that there is no one to have free will so that the entire discussion is academic. We know that it is the case that Advaita utilizes teaching methods that are appropriate to the level of understanding of the student. 'Explanations' are given and later withdrawn as the understanding grows. Ultimately, all explanations must be withdrawn, since Brahman is beyond any description or understanding. The Mandukya kArikA explains that there has never been any creation and yet descriptions of the creation are given in many of the other Upanishads. This need not be a problem as long as the other Upanishads are taught first!

It seems perfectly reasonable that karma should be taught to the early seeker, so that he starts to act rightly and without claiming the result of the action. [Advaita refers to the 'fruit' of action – karmaphala]. And it is reasonable that free will is allowed so that the seeker can 'choose' to seek the truth. It does seem that other teachings are potentially dangerous, however. For example, see Q.9 below and Q.114 in the section on 'Advice on Teachers/ Scriptures', regarding the teaching of Ramesh Balsekar.

I feel that ideas such as that our death is totally predetermined may also be used in a negative sense. It seems necessarily to follow that everything leading up to that event (i.e. one's entire life) must also be predetermined (in a hard sense). This being the case, what would be the point in pursuing any path to the truth? This will either happen or it won't, according to whether it is en route to the appointment with death.

Q.9 What is your view on free will?

Q: What is your view on 'free will' and the position of Ramesh Balsekar saying that we are mere puppets on a string (the body-mind mechanism)?

A: The teaching of Advaita regarding the existence of free will (or any other topic for that matter) really depends upon the current level of understanding of the student. For one who believes that he or she is a separate person, Advaita teaches that it is possible to exert self-effort in order to discipline the mind, acquire Self-knowledge etc., and ultimately attain liberation. As you know, the 'bottom line' of Advaita is that everything is Brahman and you are that. There *are* no persons who could choose to do anything. The world-appearance is simply the ever-changing form of the never-changing reality. So clearly, in the end, the concept of free will is meaningless. Apparent individuals are just following a chain of cause and effect at the level of appearance.

Even ignoring the teaching of Advaita, it is possible to see that within appearance you do not actually exercise free will. The experiments of Libet and the theory of Daniel Wegner suggest that the feeling of having chosen to do something only occurs after the action has been set in motion anyway. Thoughts arise and actions happen and that is the most that can be said. Unless you can choose to originate a thought, you are logically forced to acknowledge all of this.

Note that there is an article explaining my belief in the non-existence of free will, and lack of a need to believe in it, in the face of a contrary statement from Swami Dayananda, at http://www.advaita.org.uk/discourses/past_messages/freewill_waite.htm.

Q.137 How do you rationalize your lack of belief in free will?

Q: I understood you were a traditional Advaitin. How do you rationalize your lack of belief in free will with this?

A: No problem. All of the teaching of Advaita is provisional, appropriate to the level of understanding. The ultimate truth of traditional Advaita is the same as that of the Neo-Advaitins – no creation, no persons to have free will, no god(s), no time. It's just that, for me, the concept of free will has never been helpful (or, alternatively, the concept of no free will has never been an obstacle).

Q.13 Does the acceptance of Advaita lead to a life of passivity?

Q: From your explanation I understand that you are saying that 'will', as the origin of something, doesn't exist. Why things happen is because of the law of cause and effect.

Isn't the natural conclusion of this a life of passivity – a total acceptance of things as they are – with no wish to develop or progress? Perhaps even reverting to living in the jungle?

A: At the level of appearance, yes, there is only causality to account for actions. But this does not lead to passivity. Darwinian selection naturally inculcates competition, 'development' and 'progress'. And there is no escaping the fact that we *feel* as though we have free will. All of this stuff will carry on regardless but there is no need to feel negative about it. It really is all quite amazing, isn't it? It is all arising within you, for your enjoyment, as it were!

Q.16 'Angering' God

Q: If everything is Brahman, and nothing is non-Brahman, then nothing can be 'counter-Brahman' or 'anti-Brahman'. In other words, in contrast to dualistic Christian philosophies, wherein people can 'anger' God, in Advaita, assuming the basic premise is correct, it is impossible to do anything that Brahman does not want, because there is nothing other than Brahman.

Is this correct?

A: Sort of – but you are anthropomorphizing Brahman, which is not a valid thing to do. Brahman cannot be compared to a human (or a god). Things appear to happen in the phenomenal world but they are all only the ever-changing form of the non-dual Brahman – nothing really changes at all. And Brahman does not 'want' anything – it is already perfect and complete (and there is nothing other than Brahman that it could want).

Q.17 Then we cannot do anything 'wrong'?

Q: (Continuing from Q.16) If so, then the logical extension of this idea is that there is no way we can do anything 'wrong', and that absolutely everything we humans do on this planet is 'right' (and is in fact pre-determined). If there is only one thing – Brahman – and we are all manifestations of Brahman, and Brahman is omnipotent, then Brahman (us and everything) knows exactly what will happen, because Brahman is beyond time, space, and causation, because these things are part of mAyA anyway.

A: There are two issues here. Firstly, 'right' and 'wrong' are purely human concepts, usually relating to a particular society. And they are obviously dualistic so could never have anything to do with Brahman. These ideas of omnipotent and omniscient do not relate to Brahman but to Ishvara. Just as the idea of an individual (jIva) corresponds to Atman (jIva = Atman + avidyA, where avidyA is ignorance), so the idea of Ishvara corresponds to Brahman (Ishvara = Brahman + mAyA).

Within the context of the world-appearance, everything proceeds in a cause-effect manner. This is deterministic, yes, but in accordance with our past actions. The 'soft' approach allows us 'self-effort' to influence our future karma; the hard-line recognizes that this self-effort, too, is conditioned. But, again, the idea that Brahman 'knows what will happen' is not a valid way of looking at the situation.

All of your dreams are generated within your mind and proceed according to some cause-effect principle but this does not mean that you (whether from the vantage point of the dreamer – the 'I' in the dream – or the waker) know what is going to happen next. (N.B. This excludes the special case of the lucid dreamer.) At the level of the empirical reality, Advaita says that the world is created and jIva-s are reborn in such a way as to enable them to work through their accumulated karma. All of this proceeds by cause and effect within the constraints of Ishvara's laws. The jIva has a degree of free will in each situation encountered. The current in the river may be strong but you have a rudder to help you to steer!

But the best way of looking at the situation (from my own point of view) is to say that the jIva lives a deterministic existence but you are not the jIva. Atman is always totally free. You are That.

Q: In other words, because Brahman is beyond time, and there is *only* Brahman, and Brahman cannot do anything that angers itself, or that runs counter to its own desires, and because Brahman brought mAyA into existence, then there's NO FREE WILL, ever, only the illusion of free will that jIva-s (incarnated souls) feel is actually real.

A: This is anthropomorphizing again. Brahman does not have desires and does not act. In reality there is no creation. In ignorance, there appears to be individuals, the illusion of free will and determinism. You are never going to be able to make unambiguous or ultimately meaningful statements about Brahman because all language and thought are necessarily limited and dualistic. We say that Brahman (= Atman) is free, perfect, complete, unlimited etc. These adjectives are not intended to be 'attributes' (since Brahman is attribute-less) but indicators of an infinite, absolute reality. We cannot really say *anything* about Brahman, but we have to say something to convey this to the seeker.

Q.18 Is everything 'scripted' by Brahman?

Q: (Continuing from Q.17) As you say in your book, knowing these things, we can just watch the play unfold. This also implies that even our attempts to prove our supposed but illusory 'free will' to ourselves or others is scripted and known by Brahman before we know we'll do it. Furthermore, this implies that every good thing, every bad thing, every mediocre thing 'I' have ever 'done' was pre-destined to happen. If I become a Nihilist and say 'why do anything?/nothing matters', then that's scripted, too.

A: This idea of a script is just another metaphor. It is useful in that it helps us to understand that people cannot act other than the way in which they in fact do. It is unhelpful in that it implies that a god has 'decided' in advance what is going to happen. Also, you must be careful about attributing anything to Brahman. Brahman does not 'know everything in advance'; there is nothing other than Brahman to be 'known'.

Q: While I understand these concepts and am beginning to see the truth of them (reading John Wheeler, Vivekananda, and Ramana, also), I still don't know *how* or *why* Brahman can exist. Human life may be a play of lIlA to amuse Brahman, but that doesn't explain how Brahman came into being. I recognize that Brahman is said to be eternal, beyond time, homogeneous, etc., but I can't conceptualize these things with my puny brain, and my ego rebels against these thoughts, quickly hitting a resistance point beyond which it can't go.

A: Brahman did not 'come into being'. Brahman is the non-dual reality, 'beyond' time and space. There is (has been and always will be) only Brahman. Concepts such as lIlA are provided only to help people towards that final truth. The mind can never comprehend Brahman. You need not, because you *are* Brahman!

Q: There seem to be two main schools of thought on the subject of self-realization: one says that all jIva-s are reincarnated until they self-realize, that this is the end-goal, and the other that it doesn't matter either way whether or not we self-realize, that Brahman really doesn't care what happens in that regard.

A: It's not that there are different schools of thought so much as that Advaita aims to teach at the level of understanding of the seeker. Initially, reincarnation is taught so that one might believe that one will get there eventually. Once all of the theory has been understood and intellectually accepted, however, it can be appreciated that there is nowhere to get and no one to make the journey. And you are anthropomorphizing Brahman again – there is only Brahman; 'caring' is not something that is relevant in absolute reality.

Q.65 Subsidiary choices in the 'decision process'

Q: You have said that we cannot will our thoughts. I fully accept this with regard to what might be called 'primary thoughts' but do we have some influence over subsidiary thoughts? For example a thought arises, unbidden, that I will go to town. Do I not then will thoughts such as whether I go by bus or car and what the advantages of each might be?

A: The traditional view is that the jIva has limited free will: to choose to do, not do or do differently – within the constraints of his or her mental make-up (vAsanA-s). But it is perfectly possible to believe (as I do) that there is no free will whatsoever. In the example you state, the logical process of 'deciding' is all quite deterministic, based upon your past experience and knowledge of advantages, disadvantages, frequency and cost of buses etc. In theory, a computer programmed with all of your knowledge on the matter (and your reasoning processes) would come to the same answer. And if you decide to choose the opposite answer just for the hell of it, that would be because that response was also part of your nature – so you can't win!

Q.79 Do we choose whether to become enlightened?

Q: As you and many others have pointed out we don't really have any volition, just apparent choice, so you can guess what question is arising, which is, does this apparent me really have any choice whether or not acceptance of what *is* happens or not?

A: I think the belief in free will (or not) really depends upon the nature of your own mind. I personally have never really had any problem with the concept of no free will but of course many do. Certainly the traditional view is that we should consider that we *do* have free will until such time as we know differently.

As to the question of enlightenment, I don't believe we have any choice there either. Imagine that I ask you to close your eyes and then I hold an object in front of your face. I then tell you to open your eyes but not see the object I am holding. Maybe if I hypnotized you, you really would believe that you couldn't see it but, in the normal scheme of things, you would simply see it. You would not be able to choose not to do so – the perception would be immediate and direct. Similarly, if the mind is suitably prepared and you are normally intelligent (!) and the relevant Self-knowledge is unfolded to you by a qualified teacher, enlightenment will necessarily follow eventually. When the last of the Self-ignorance is removed, there is no choice involved.

Q.171 Problems with the notion of 'choice' and 'doing'

Q: I still have problems with the notion of 'choice' and 'doing'. If choice is an illusion and action takes place regardless, why do I need to worry about it? For example, I want to drink less (alcohol) since I know that it affects my mental energy the next day. I would prefer to have a clear mind so that it will work more efficiently. It seems that I can make plans to do all this and it seems to work but who then is doing this? Do I only 'play' at being the chooser, knowing that in reality I am not doing anything and this will all happen (or not) regardless? Do you, for example, make an effort to write your books? I often feel that, unless I make an effort, I would just eat, play and enjoy the moment.

A: One of the metaphors I often use is the sun rising and setting. Even though we know that it doesn't really, it still seems to do. Similarly, even though we know that there is no person choosing and making effort, it still seems like that. You really have no choice but to continue seeming to choose! It will happen anyway. Something will always happen to force the issue; why bother about it? I often feel lethargic but eventually the pressure of things that 'need' to be done 'forces' me out of the chair and things start happening again. Just let it be and enjoy!

Of course the mind plays its part in all of this. Knowing that life will improve without the alcohol is a significant factor in the equation of all the forces playing their part. As this is born out in practice, the force becomes stronger and the result is in accord with all of this. No real choice in the matter.

Q.178 Is there choice at the moment of awakening?

Q: When I wake up in the morning, is there a moment of 'choice' when I can decide either to continue to behave in the same way that I have always done (leading to misery) or instead to break that habitual cycle and act in such a way as to lead to happiness?

A: I would have to say that there is no choice – everything functions automatically in a cause-effect manner at the level of appearance. But intrinsic to that cause-effect nexus are the outcomes of prior experience. Thus, for example, it may have been seen that certain habits have repeatedly led to misery and you may have read that certain practices such as being in the present, acting dispassionately etc. can break such habits. Thus, there may come a point where the balance tips and you act in a non-habitual way. This may lead to a satisfactory outcome, thus reinforcing the tendency to act in this new way and building a new habit. Thus, changes can come about despite the fact that there is never any conscious choice in the matter.

Q.200 Freedom to dedicate bhAvana (attitude)

Q: You said in a previous email that free will is an illusion. Shantananda Saraswati, Shankaracharya in Feb. 1974, responds to a question about bhAvana [the 'attitude or outlook' that one forms in the mind]: *"The laws of the universe bind man in every aspect of his existence except in one aspect. The individual is free in bhAvana. An individual can dedicate any bhAvana to anyone. He can deliberately create a bhAvana within himself and work accordingly. Even in miserable conditions, people become happy, or in happy conditions become miserable, because they choose it like that"*.

Doesn't this suggest free will?

A: If you read the rest of this section, as well as my essay on the topic (5 parts beginning http://www.advaita-vision.org/free will/), you will see that I make it clear that absence of free will is only admitted as part of the final teaching of Advaita. During the earlier stages of the teaching, limited free will is certainly acknowledged, within the restrictions of the law of karma. Otherwise the practical teaching (puruShArtha) would make no sense.

As regards Shri Shantananda Saraswati, he has certainly left a legacy of some excellent quotations. However, there is in his teaching often a very confusing admixture of material from philosophies other than Advaita, including sAMkhya, sphoTa and yoga so I would never recommend him to anyone not very familiar with the correct Advaita teaching.

Q.248 Ambition and changing our destiny

Q: When we say we do not have free will and everything is happening spontaneously, then one naturally assumes that all is governed by the universe or the Self. It is also said that whatever happens is fixed according to the will of God. So what is the point of having ambitions or trying to do anything at all?

A: According to Advaita, you, as a person in the world, do have a limited degree of free will – as it is put in the scriptures 'to do, not to do or to do differently'. The extent to which you are able to exercise this free will is restricted by your particular nature, upbringing, etc. There are many factors affecting any given situation and most of them are outside of your control. Things do not happen 'spontaneously'; they happen according to the laws of creation (or the will of God if you prefer). But you, the jIva, are an aspect of this creation and also play a part in the happening. Your 'free will' is also an input to the cause-effect nexus.

From the point of view of absolute reality, of course, there is no free will. There is none because there are no persons to have any. There is only the non-dual reality. And who-you-really-are is That.

So, when it comes down to asking 'what I want', it makes no sense to have as your ambition 'to become rich' or anything similar. In reality, such things have no more meaning than does your dream after you have woken up. The only meaningful aim is to attain enlightenment so that you realize the truth of the matter whilst still in this body and world.

Q: What you say above becomes our reality only when realization happens. So, when it does happen, does it not mean our will becomes God's will; and so now can we at this stage know what my will would be for me? (Not from an ego point of view but from the Self's point of view.) The reason why I ask this question is because I heard Ramesh Balsekar saying that after Self realization, certain tendencies of the body-mind organism would remain as they are, as per their destiny and the will of God; but when we, as awareness, become aware of ourselves, can it not affect the body and mind's destiny as well, because the choice maker is source itself? For example, when we come across the law of karma and the law of attraction, it appears that we can bring in changes for our body-mind destiny, though the silent witness we are will be unaffected?

A: There is a confusion of levels of reality here.

From the absolute perspective, the Self does not act and there is nothing other than the Self – nothing else to say.

From the standpoint of the world, everything happens in a cause-effect manner, according to universal law or 'the laws of Ishvara (Brahman + mAyA)' if you prefer. Your free will is also subject to the same laws, which means that you find it extremely difficult to act outside the scope of your own nature. The state of the mind inevitably affects the outcome, as you know. For example, your actions will differ according to whether you are feeling depressed or elated. And in particular, new knowledge affects the way that you (choose to) behave. For example, the new knowledge that what you thought was a snake is in fact a rope changes your outlook considerably. It stands to reason, then, that Self-realization will affect your outlook radically.

But, enlightened or not, what we are speaking of here is the behavior of the person. Whether or not the person is enlightened, he is still a person, with all that this entails. Although I may now know that the world is mithyA, I still see the world and still have to interact with these people, even though I now know them to be none other than myself. And the tendency will still be for the body-mind to act in similar ways to before.

I don't know what you mean by asking 'can we know what my will would be for me'. The Self has always been the Self. This person has always been, in reality, the Self – he just did not know it prior to realization. After realization, there is still a person. The difference is that the mind now knows that the person is mithyA and 'I am Brahman'. But this knowledge is still in the mind and, at the empirical level, actions and choosing continue as before.

To say that 'we as awareness become aware of ourselves' is not to make a really valid statement; or it is at least misleading. This is where the mixing-up of levels comes in and seems to be causing your own confusion. From the pAramArthika standpoint, Brahman does not do anything, including 'becoming aware'. The best you can say here is that Brahman *is* awareness. But even that is saying too much. And at the vyAvahArika level, it is effectively the *reflection* of Consciousness in the mind that 'becomes aware'.

Q.287 Choice

Q: When you say that we do not have a choice in what we do, do you mean that the ego does not have the choice and that it is Consciousness that makes the choice at that particular moment in our spirit's evolution?

A: Choice (or not) only relates to the person – Consciousness does not do anything. Who-we-really-are is Consciousness – now and always. There is no 'evolution of spirit', only diminishing degrees of ignorance in the mind.

Q: Thank you for that. Tell me, once you realize the Truth, how do you go on in the world and pretend, in order not to make anyone uncomfortable, and yet still live by your Truth? Is leaving the world a solution to not exposing your mind to the distractions and the pretentions of life? Or should you just be where you are and be aware of Consciousness and still continue to pretend?

A: You don't have to do anything. The world-appearance

continues and your body-mind and its apparent involvement in the world continue also. The difference is that you know it is only an appearance and who-you-really-are is totally unaffected by any of it. There is neither any need to pretend nor any need to disturb the ignorance of others (blissful or otherwise) unless they should ask questions, believing that you have some answers. You simply know that everything is Brahman and you are That.

Q.365 Free Will and mumukShutva

Q: In response to what you said in your answers to Q.12 and Q.22:

If there's only causality to account for actions, there should be no space for free will. And if there is just a 'feeling that we have' of a free will, then there is no free will. To put it in other words, if there is no free will, how can I actually gain mumukShutva (if desire also is a kind of a free will)? For intense 'Longing for Liberation' to happen, I should be blessed with Free Will.

A: In the world, we react to stimuli according to our pre-existing nature and intellect. In response to the offer of a cream cake, for example, we will want to eat it if we like cakes and are not too full. We probably won't be interested if we have a history of being sick after eating them. Simplistically, mumukShutva is itself the effect of a long history of a 'failure to be satisfied' by those things that we are led to believe will make us happy. We consequently give up on material things, status etc. and turn towards the spiritual. There is no need to posit free will.

You must always bear in mind that such explanations are interim only and apply to the world-appearance. All concepts have to be dropped eventually, Just as we are effectively dropping free will here, so causality has to be dropped later, too.

Q.413 Yet more on free will

Q: http://www.advaita.org.uk/discourses/past_messages/freewill_waite.htm is about your convincing argument that there is no free will. The Q (for which I have no free will!) is whether the lack of

free will is an obstacle in pursuit of Self-realization? It would seem that one has no 'choice' in the pursuit for it will follow the law of cause and effect.

A: Lack of free will is not an obstacle, because it is not relevant.

Whether or not one has the overriding desire to discover the truth/gain enlightenment (mumukShutva) depends upon one's upbringing, education, experience in life etc. In other words, those are the causal factors which determine our outlook on life and our judgment as to what things are important.

If one has true mumukShutva, then one overcomes apparent obstacles to pursue the truth (perform regular meditation, seek out a genuine teacher etc.). If one doesn't have this, then the question does not really arise, or one gives up at the first difficulty or when some material pleasure comes along and so on.

So the entire process is a matter of cause-effect. The lack of free will is not itself an obstacle; free will just does not come into it at all. (And could not, since it doesn't exist!)

Q: I am still not clear. What you say means that a person will not 'seek' unless it is not supported by the cause-effect principle. But my understanding of free will is that, if one has it, he/she can break this cause-effect pattern and seek self-realization. That is to say, free will could be an aid to seeking. Conversely, in the absence of free will, one is deprived of this aid thereby making 'to seek' that much more difficult.

This view is seemingly in conformity with the Advaita teaching, as can be seen from your 'Advaita Made Easy': "Our actions are therefore mostly triggered by pre-determined prArabdha but we have some free will. Since we cannot know which will be effective in any instance, we have to assume free will and endeavor to insure that we act in accord with dharma".

On the other hand, the debate of free will is a non-starter if it assumed that the free will is also an outcome of cause-effect, notwithstanding the ego having an illusion that it has free will. I refer to your query *"Can anyone explain please why 'choice of action*

based on rational thought' is not itself just a chain of cause and effect?"

A: It is true that traditional Advaita teaching says (in the early stages) that we have free will. Obviously there can be none ultimately, since there are no jIva-s to have free will (since there is no creation). It is simply that (personally) I see no point in admitting free will even in the early stages. We will follow sAdhana chatuShTaya sampatti if our prior circumstances dictate that such a course seems favorable. And this seems to be as good a 'definition' of free will as any: 'Choice' occurs when our mind deems that a particular action is more favorable than alternatives. But this 'choice' is simply the mind balancing the possibilities according to prior disposition, assessment of likely outcome, desires etc. and determining which has the highest 'score' – all quite automatic, despite appearances to the contrary. And this is no 'choice' at all.

At least, this is how I see the situation. You may feel that this is precisely a description of 'choice' – that one examines and weighs the various factors and makes a decision accordingly. You may believe that, for there to be no free will, we would have to be *prevented* from doing this. I would argue that, in a real sense, we *are* prevented from seeing the situation from any other point of view than our own. We *are* constrained to act in the way that we do in fact act. Our brain computes the 'best' outcome, based upon its existing data and learned manner of operation, in a precisely analogous manner to an electronic computer. And this is not 'free'.

Knowledge

Q.42 What is knowledge?

Q: What is knowledge? How does knowledge affect ignorance? What understands knowledge?

A: The short answer:

Ontologically knowledge, like everything else, is mithyA, having no existence apart from Brahman. Epistemologically, at the level of vyavahAra, knowledge is that which removes ignorance,

even if in the end it turns out itself to be mithyA. Both ignorance and knowledge belong to the mind.

The much longer answer:

In Advaita, knowledge is said to be valid when it is not contradicted. The sort of example that is used is that of rope and snake. Knowing the object to be a snake is invalid knowledge, since it is contradicted later when we discover it to be a rope. Knowing it to be a rope, however, is not contradicted. This is only a temporary situation, though, which is why we have svataH prAmANya vAda, the theory of the 'self validity of knowledge', i.e. not needing to validate knowledge acquired from one pramANa by another. This is because, if we examine the rope closely, it is found to consist of woven strands of fiber, perhaps hemp. Therefore, the rope is actually only a form of hemp and not an object in its own right at all. But this applies to the hemp, too. If we continue to analyze, we end up with molecules, then atoms, then sub-atomic particles and eventually just energy. The forms are imposed by the mind; the reality is always and only Brahman.

This is less obvious with things like perceptions and thoughts, but they too are just movements of organized energy. Everything without exception is ultimately just a name and form of Brahman. Thus it is that, what we thought we knew (to be true) turns out not to be. Our so-called knowledge turns out to be ignorance and it is sublated by a new knowledge. The only knowledge that cannot be sublated is the ultimate non-dual truth so that Knowledge (with a capital 'K') could be said to be a 'description' of Brahman, in that it is 'what is left' when no new, sublating knowledge is possible. Some teachers speak of 'Knowledge' as a synonym for the Self. This is using the word in a metaphysical sense rather than an empirical one. At the level of the mind, knowledge comes and goes and may be valid or invalid but transcending this in a sense is 'absolute knowledge', which equates with Consciousness itself and has neither beginning nor end.

Krishna Menon also points out that 'knowing' is clearly different from 'doing', 'perceiving', 'feeling' and 'thinking', being

always present and not coming and going like the others. Thus, he says, it is 'of the nature of the Self'. Similarly, he says it is the 'I-principle' that is the knower.

Pedantically (and Vedantically!) the mind itself cannot know anything since it only comes about itself as a result of Consciousness acting through the insentient matter of the brain. The knowledge of some object 'arises' when the mind is impacted on by the object. But what is actually happening is that Consciousness, as the object, is manifesting to itself through the mind, which is itself also operating only by virtue of Consciousness. Thus, a good definition of knowledge is that it is the manifestation of Consciousness (to itself) through the mind.

It is possible to follow all of this and acknowledge its validity but I prefer to keep things as simple as possible on subjects such as this, which can become exceedingly complex. Modern teachers talk about our being 'knowingness' and many other artificial words. All language operates in and describes duality so it seems to me that this sort of thing can only confuse and mislead. Perception, thoughts, mind and knowledge itself are all meaningful only in vyavahAra. To my mind, knowledge too is mithyA as much as are the knower and the known. In the end, I prefer the view expressed by the Tripura Rahasya: *"The greatest of all delusions is the conviction that knowledge is not a delusion"*.

If you are not satisfied with the above answer, please ask something more specific. As stated, it is a bit too general and it really would be possible to write a book on the subject, though I'm not sure I would want to attempt it! (For example – see Methods of Knowledge according to Advaita Vedanta, Swami Satprakashananda, Advaita Ashrama, 1965. ISBN 81-7505-065-9. I can heartily recommend this as both erudite and readable, if that is not a contradiction!) Or read the series about knowledge (analysis of the vedAnta paribhAShA (http://www.advaita.org.uk/discourses/knowledge/intro1.htm) by Dr. Sadananda, edited by me.

Q.91 Knowledge, science and enlightenment

Q: I have been studying the teachings of Ramana Maharshi interspersed by writings by some 'modern' teachers of self enquiry. I won't go into the differences or confusion that creates in my understanding. Ultimately, I tend to stick with the 'real deal': Bhagavan's teachings. However even his teachings in the form of dialogues seem contradictory at times. Similarly, the Buddha's teachings seem contradictory at times as well. Nevertheless, having been blessed with a tendency to think analytically and logically the essence of Bhagavan's teachings and that of the Sakyamuni Buddha seem to come through if one persists and tries to understand the essence of what they are trying to say.

1. So my first question is: What is it that the Buddha or Ramana Maharshi experienced as 'knowledge' that is different from the type of knowledge that is revealed through scientific investigation?

Despite all the scientific knowledge that I hold in my intellect that points to the oneness of all beings, I still feel a sense of separation and I am sure many other scientists feel the same way. Yes, I feel a sense of bond when I watch chimpanzees or elephants at the wild animal park, or I can 'feel' what someone else might be going through (joy or distress) under specific circumstances. But the sense of 'Oneness' that enlightened/'Awakened' people and teachers talk about isn't there.

So the knowledge that erases ignorance apparently is still present at the intellect-mind level. What needs to happen for someone to experience the Oneness?

2. There are instances both in the teachings of Ramana Maharshi and the Buddha that, when someone heard a certain teaching, suddenly they became enlightened. However when we hear the same teachings or discourse such sudden awakening isn't occurring. Were people in those days more 'ripe' for an Awakening experience? Or is it similar to the experience when suddenly a student understands a difficult problem posed to a group and the light bulb goes on?

3. In some of the discourses, Ramana Maharshi explains that what we know as our mind (the 'daily grind' mind) is in fact nothing other than an emanation of the Self itself. Why does the Self create such a farce? And why does the Self hide behind the illusory everyday mind?

4. I am convinced that the ego is nothing more than thoughts that arise and fall and when teachers personify ego by using terms such as the 'ego doesn't want to die' and so on, they are making it more solid than it is. What are your thoughts on this?

A: First of all, the 'real deal' as regards the teaching of Advaita is the traditional kind. This has been tried and tested for over a thousand years and has proven methods appropriate for all types of seeker. A good teacher who is familiar with these methods, knows the scriptures and is enlightened, will be able to gauge the needs of a seeker and use the best method, story, metaphor etc. to remove relevant areas of ignorance. The problem with reading a book, even one with dialogs from someone as good as Ramana, is that the answers he gives are the ones that were relevant to the questioner. They will not necessarily be appropriate for you and may even mislead. Anything that can be spoken or thought necessarily falls short of the truth since it is in the realm of dualistic vyavahAra. Hence the confusion.

This is probably worse for someone with a scientific background since they will tend to analyze everything very carefully and pick holes in what is said.

One of the key areas that continue to elude science is the nature of consciousness. Scientists continue to try to explain how the brain can manifest consciousness. The idea that everything might be an appearance *in* consciousness is one which seems to be alien to them. This consciousness is the ultimate subject, the essence of all the appearances, which are themselves only name and form of that non-dual consciousness. This is the knowledge that enlightenment entails and it can never be revealed through scientific investigation because the subject cannot investigate the subject – science is necessarily dualistic.

Experience of any kind, including that of 'oneness' is not 'it'. Experiences have a beginning and an end in time and time is intrinsic to vyavahAra (along with space and causality). Enlightenment is nothing other than Self-knowledge, when all of the Self-ignorance has been removed. The body-mind will continue to operate and the world will still appear but all of these are now known to be mithyA only. Feelings of oneness or duality may also occur and will also be known to be mithyA. You are right – enlightenment is in the mind – where else would it be? There is a further distinction, namely between j~nAna and j~nAna niShTha. Basically, the enlightened mind will not necessarily feel the benefits of enlightenment (peace, love etc.) immediately, if there was insufficient mental preparation beforehand. There are other Q&A's covering this aspect.

On the question of hearing something and becoming enlightened, yes, that may happen to a particular person but not to another. The point is that there will usually be many 'blind spots' in the understanding of a particular mind. As the teaching is heard, knowledge 'vRRitti-s' are acquired (mental modifications) and there will be 'mini' realizations in response to particular revelations. In the final revelation, the akhaNDAkAra vRRitti, the mind 'takes on the form' of the 'undivided' reality. The light bulb metaphor is a good one for the knowledge vRRitti-s. The removal of ignorance may be gradual but enlightenment is binary. This subject is dealt with in detail in my book 'Enlightenment: The Path Through The Jungle'.

The questions as to why the world appears, why there is ignorance etc. are not 'valid' questions in Advaita. From the vantage point of reality, there is no creation, there are no minds, there is no ignorance. The confusion is only in the mind of the person, which concepts (confusion, mind, person) only have validity in relative reality. Yes, it is all paradoxical from the mind's point of view but all is resolved in Self-knowledge.

On the subject of ego, whilst you believe yourself to be a

separate entity, a doer and enjoyer, the concept of ego has validity. And a teacher has to begin from where you believe yourself to be. All of what a teacher tells you has provisional validity only and is *all* rescinded in the final analysis – this is the technique of traditional Advaita.

Q.92 Ignorance and enlightenment

Q: (Continued from Q.91, following above answer) I agree that enlightenment is not an experience that has an end. However, people do talk about 'before their enlightenment'. Although teachers say that there is no enlightenment and nothing to attain (since there is no self and nobody there), people definitely talk about the 'transformation' that happens.

Yes, it may be progressive, or spontaneous as in the case of Ramana Maharshi. We have reason to believe that these people's 'experience' certainly marks their transformation. It is something that brings about a revelation that most of us seekers strive for.

Again, to say there is no ignorance amounts to saying what the Neo-Advaitin teachers say: "nothing to do; nowhere to go". Surely, the sages did not tell us that. So what actually do you mean when you say, "all is resolved in self knowledge?" What self knowledge need arise to wipe out non-existent ignorance?

Many teachers clearly talk about ignorance being the source of all our suffering and enlightenment amounts to removal of that ignorance. All the sAdhana-s are geared towards removal of ignorance. Even with a few years of practice one begins to see where our ignorance stems from – from our attachments to the illusion of our 'self' and how such attachments cause suffering and continue to keep us bound in the cycle of saMsAra.

I still would like to ask the question as to why the Self (the big Self) creates the egoic self and at what point it decides to seek itself. It seems like an elaborate game. What's the point of it all? Why did consciousness in the human form begin to build this 'egoic mind' that has brought about this strong identification with our bodies resulting in a sense of separateness?

A: It seems that your missing the point I was making is caused by failing to recognize clearly the distinction between paramArtha and vyavahAra (and this is the principal problem of the Neo-Advaitins, too!) and also not understanding exactly what enlightenment is (a common problem).

'There is no ignorance', 'no person', 'you are already enlightened' etc. are typical Neo-Advaitin statements and they are true only when referring to absolute reality (which you cannot do anyway, pedantically speaking). In reality, there is only the non-dual Brahman – end of discussion.

At the relative, empirical level of you and I discussing this in an apparent world of separate things, there is definitely ignorance and there are definitely people, nearly all of whom are not enlightened. Enlightenment is an event in time, in the mind of a person, when the Self-ignorance about all of this is replaced by Self-knowledge. And, yes, when this occurs it is quite possible that it will be accompanied by an overwhelming feeling of revelation (though not necessarily so).

In order to become enlightened, this Self-knowledge must be acquired and the best (some would argue only) way is from a qualified traditional teacher. Part of the process also entails the acquisition of certain conducive qualities of mind – discrimination, dispassion, self-control etc. – this is the 'practice' element that is often referred to. In itself, practice cannot bring about enlightenment. The problem is ignorance, the only solution is knowledge.

This Self-knowledge is irrevocable and unarguable. It is known that the world is only name and form etc. and that all is one. It is not an experience. Indeed the experience continues as before, seeing everything as separate, but it is like still seeing the sun rise in the morning yet knowing that it is the earth that orbits the sun.

I'm not sure what it was that I said which implied I was claiming you do not have to do anything. It is true that you do not have to do anything to *be* the non-dual Self but if you want to *know* this, you have to acquire the knowledge. And the two-hour satsang of a Neo-Advaitin (or any other) teacher will not provide this knowledge. It runs counter to a lifetime of programming by society, parents, friends and teachers. Accordingly, it takes prolonged effort over a long period (the scriptures refer to lifetimes of effort but let's not go into that!).

I'm afraid you are not going to get an answer as to why the 'big Self creates the egoic self'. As I said, from the vantage point of that 'big Self', there has never been any creation – how could there be when reality is non-dual?

Q.126 Is there only knowledge?

Q: Do you think that it is true to say that only knowledge exists and that there is nothing beyond knowledge?

A: How do you define knowledge? In reality, only Brahman exists. From the standpoint of the apparent world, a person must gain Self-knowledge in order to realize that.

Q: When I say knowledge, I mean all the notions, names, concepts, ideas, theories which arise as a result of culture, science, religion and philosophy. Even the basic concept of 'I am' is just knowledge which you learn as a child.

My question is: Does that mean that beyond what you learn (knowledge) there is nothing? Or, if theoretically someone were able to erase all that knowledge, what would be left?

A: All the stuff arising from culture, science etc. is what you should rather call 'information'. There is no end to it – the more that you find out, the more there is to find out. 'I am' is not information. It is absolute and irrevocable. You do not need anyone to tell you this. At the website, there is a series of essays on the subject of knowledge. These are (my edited version of) Dr. K. Sadananda's posts to the Advaitin Egroup on his understanding of the vedAnta paribhAShA of dharmarAja adhvarIndra. This is the definitive book on Advaita epistemology (theory of knowledge). I suggest you read these. The first of the series can be found at http://www.advaita.org.uk/discourses/knowledge/intro1.htm.

Q.140 On shabda pramANa and knowing the Self

Q: On reading several of the essays by Dr. Sadananda, it struck me that there should be no means of knowledge required to know the Self, since it is not an object. But I guess a means of knowledge is required to drop that veil and purify the mind as they say. At some point, maybe one doesn't require the guide and that 'knowledge' is recognized.

But, his essay on 'Vedanta as Pramana' had me confused. He says:

"...For the spiritual knowledge that we are seeking, perceptual and inferential knowledge are both useless. At the best they are secondary or supportive but do not give direct knowledge because the subject 'I' cannot be objectified. If it can be objectified then it is no longer a subject. Hence the only means of knowledge to know about the self is shabda pramANa (words of dependable reporters), which in this case is veda pramANa or shAstra pramANa. ... Therefore what is pramANa has to be clear – it is the means of knowledge and Vedanta provides that means of knowledge about the Absolute..."

Can you clarify: what exactly is shabda pramANa required for? Why is it necessary to know who I am when there is no distance between the two? If it is required to clean up the mind, then why can't other methods be useful to clean up the mind? Why is the Vedanta the only means to do so?

This leads me to a second question. Does that mean that Bhakti Yoga and other forms of Yoga are *not* alternate paths to the state of j~nAna but preparatory stages?

And what about other paths such as Buddhism, Zen, Tao etc.? Are these considered to be in keeping with Vedanta or not? Are they valid means to recognize the true Self?

A: I do not need anyone or anything to tell me that I exist. But

I do not initially (think that) I know anything about Brahman. Brahman is not and cannot be an object of knowledge or experience. Therefore, I am never going to discover Brahman by looking for it. The scriptures provide pointers and metaphors etc. to explain to us what Brahman is and then they reveal A. that 'I am Brahman' and B. that 'everything is Brahman'. There is no other source for this knowledge.

The fact that Advaita tells us that I *am* Brahman often makes it difficult to appreciate that I cannot 'know' or 'experience' Brahman. But you can appreciate that a torch can illuminate all objects in a room except for itself (unless there is a mirror present!). Most of the time we are aware of other objects or concepts – even in dream our mind manufactures what we think of as an external world. All of these apparent 'others' are also Brahman but we do not realize this; thinking instead that they are separate entities. Only in deep-sleep do both the external world and the internal thoughts fall away and there is only Consciousness. Unfortunately, I am ignorant of it.

It is because of this ignorance (in all states of consciousness) that Self-knowledge is the only solution. Worship (bhakti), right action (karma), meditation etc. cannot themselves bring about Self-realization. You should also be careful not to confuse relative and absolute – it is the mind that is seeking to understand all of this at the relative level, despite the fact that I am (already) Brahman.

I assume that Zen, Taoism etc., also have valid methods but I'm afraid I am no expert in other traditions.

Q.219 All-knowing on enlightenment?

Q: As an individual, I am ignorant about most things but God is said to be all-knowing. When I become enlightened, I become 'one with God'. Why then do I not simultaneously become all-knowing too, able to predict the future, win the lottery etc.?

A: The problem with your conception of ignorance and knowledge is two-fold really. Firstly, enlightenment is about the dawning of Self-knowledge and the elimination of Self-ignorance.

This is the realization of the nature of the Self and reality (Everything is Brahman, Thou art That etc.). As you probably know, Shankara is said to have summed this up as 'Brahman is the ultimate reality; the world is mithyA; the jIva is not other than Brahman'. The key to your problem is in the second of these – the world, together with its knowledge of 'things', and the dualistic 'knower' of those things, is mithyA. It is not really real, deriving its semblance of reality from Brahman. It is name and form of that Brahman only. There are not really any separate things, including a knower knowing facts about other things. This is the one aspect.

The other aspect is not dissimilar from the question of what happens to the mind of an enlightened 'person' when they become Self-realized. The answer hinges on the distinction between the microcosm and macrocosm at the level of transactional reality. The point here is that 'knowing' things at the level of the person involves that person's mind. And that person's mind will only know of 'things' with which it has come into contact, whether that be familiarity with a physical location or understanding of quantum mechanics. If you haven't spent many years learning Chinese, you are not going to be able to understand or communicate with a Chinese speaker, whether or not you are enlightened! And you are certainly not going to be able to see into the future – the human mind does not have an organ for this function!

The idea of 'knowing everything' is not a concept that applies to a person; it is a concept that applies to Ishvara – the Lord who effectively creates this world and allocates all of the jIva-s their particular roles in life according to their accumulated karma. Of course, Ishvara too is mithyA from an absolute standpoint but this is how the concept is used in the teaching of Advaita.

The oft-quoted metaphor is that of seeing the sun rise and set. Even after learning that this is really an illusion caused by the rotation of the earth, one still sees this happening. So it is with the rest of Ishvara's projected illusion. The enlightened man can no more read minds or predict the future than he could before. So no winning lotteries by other than pure luck, I'm afraid! (The good news is that, once enlightened, winning the lottery will carry no interest for you.)

Q.261 Is Advaita necessary?

Q: Is there really such a thing as ignorance? Most answer in the affirmative – do they not? But, to hold that Consciousness is either ignorant or awakened is a dualistic viewpoint. Is it not?

I have had years of arduous study, and prescribed meditative practices, and I have to ask whether this study, absorption, and assimilation of all the Christian dogma, Theosophical speculation, and Hindu religious tradition were, in the end, necessary to effect an awakening? Does one need all of the this in order to perceive the Self; to grasp the mystery of One?

If Consciousness is One, and if 'All that Is' is Consciousness arising, where then is room for differing opinion or argument? What difference does it make if Traditional Advaita, Neo-Advaita, Pseudo-Advaita, Traditional Path, or Direct Path are spoken for or against? Is it important? It just Is What It Is. Do you not agree? Is there, in truth, a purpose and meaning for Advaita?

A: Reality is non-dual in spite of the appearance of duality, like the sunrise metaphor. To the ignorant, this appearance is the reality. Self-knowledge removes the ignorance, not the appearance.

As to the ontological status of ignorance itself, Shankara says: *"We agree that the Absolute is not the author of Ignorance and that it is not deluded by it either. Even so, there is nothing other than the Absolute which is the author of Ignorance, and no other conscious being apart from the Absolute that is deluded by it"* (From Brihadaranyaka Upanishad bhAShya (I.iv.10).

Basically, everything is Brahman, including so-called ignorance! This is one of the inevitable paradoxes that you run into when trying to talk about the indescribable. The objector in the Brihadaranyaka Upanishad bhAShya goes on to say that, *"In that case the scriptural instruction is useless"*. Shankara replies: *"Quite so, let it be, when the truth has been known"*. And he points out that we can actually see for ourselves that the knowledge imparted by the scriptures removes ignorance; so that to deny it would be contradicting your own experience.

So, is all this teaching necessary? See Q.307 in the section on 'Mind and Thinking' for a story told by Swami Paramarthananda which illustrates this very well.

Q.268 'Knowing' an object

Q: I have been reading the mANDUkya upaniShad translated by Swami Chinmayananda, and on p. 249, he talks about how, when one knows an object (a flower for example), the object cannot exist for me apart from my knowledge, and that this great truth has been dealt with in other scripture. Which scripture is he talking about and which translation? Do you know other books that talk about this clearly?

A: The scripture that discusses the means by which we find out about the world is vedAnta paribhAShA by dharmarAja adhvarIndra. This is available in a translation by Swami Madhavananda from Advaita Ashrama. But I wouldn't really recommend this original version – it is virtually unreadable. If you are really interested in this topic, I suggest you start reading Sadananda's 'Knowledge' series at the website (http://www.advaita.org.uk/discourses/knowledge/intro1.htm) which is an attempt to make this work comprehensible. I have edited it and tried to make it as reader-friendly as possible but I confess to still finding it hard going at times. And, although there are some 65 parts, it is still nowhere near complete. I suggest you read a few pages and see how you get on.

To address your answer from a metaphysical, rather than an epistemological point of view:

In reality, there is only Consciousness (Brahman). At the empirical level, our mind effectively separates out this non-dual 'substance' into 'forms' and gives these 'names'. In this way, one effectively 'creates' the dualistic world. The scripture that specifically talks about this is the Chandogya Upanishad. The relevant section is Chapter 6 – the vAchArambhaNa sutras – and it would be Shankara's commentary on these that would be most relevant. (You might also need a more modern commentator's commentary on Shankara to understand clearly!)

Q.312 How can we know Advaita is right?

Q: How can I know that Advaita is correct and not just another interpretation, another 'way' of seeing the world? Everyone has their own ideas about the world; even science is found to carry the weight of uncertainty that it tries to overcome. All the different knowledge in the world just doesn't fit together. There are contradictions and complexities that never get solved. Everything is so complex. Does Advaita offer any solution?

A: 'Knowing' that Advaita is right is what is called 'enlightenment'! Until that time, you have to keep an open mind. Place provisional trust in someone whom you have reason to suspect does know (i.e. find a qualified teacher). Listen to what they say over a prolonged period of time – years rather than months – subjecting this to your own reason and experience. Eventually, with application, diligence, faith, determination etc., you can realize the truth for yourself. [The literal meaning of the word 'realize' is 'to make real'. The dictionary gives the definition "become fully aware of (something) as a fact; understand clearly". You cannot 'know' Brahman, as has been pointed out many times, but you can know that you *are* Brahman and that there is *only* Brahman. This is 'Self-realization'.]

Worldly knowledge is infinite – the more you discover, the more there is to be discovered. Advaita is not about that knowledge; Advaita is about knowledge of Self, which you already are. In fact, a better way of looking at it is to say that it is about removing the ignorance that covers over the knowledge that we already have. It is about knowing That through which all else is known.

Q.362 Knowledge, belief and experience

Q: What does it take to become God-realized? Is it simply to accept that I am Brahman, or to really believe I am Brahman, or to really, really believe I am Brahman, etc.? I understand that to have knowledge of something does not automatically transform me. I believe that in order to really know something one has to assimilate and implement the teaching. I know I am already That, but then, how can I insure the attainment of mokSha in order to stop the illusion of saMsAra?

A: Many seekers think that the essence of enlightenment is 'experience'; that they need to actually experience something for themselves before they can be regarded as enlightened. In line with this, they denigrate the notion that a teacher can convey whatever it is that the seeker needs by simply talking to them, answering questions and so on. Even worse, they feel, is the idea that enlightenment can be gained by reading a book!

Maybe the term 'Self-inquiry' is largely to blame for this misconception. Seekers attached to this idea think that subjecting their own experiences (perceptions, ideas, theories etc.) to close examination is somehow the key.

Whatever is the case, such seekers are seriously confused and need to distinguish carefully between 'experience', 'belief' and 'knowledge'. I would like to give an example from my own experience, which (for me) provided a very clear distinction between these three.

The experience occurred about 30 years ago. You will have to bear with me as it takes a little while to explain.

I used to attend philosophy seminars at a school called SES, which held its talks in rented buildings scattered about the UK. This particular building was a large private house on a circular avenue. To reach it, the final stages of the journey were as follows:

1. I drove for a few hundred yards along a major road.
2. I turned left into a short side road that led to the avenue.
3. I turned left again to enter the circle, drove around it clockwise

about one-third of the way, and stopped at the house where the talks were being held.

After the seminar, I retraced my route:

1. Anti-clockwise around the circle.
2. Right into the side road.
3. Right again back into the major road.

Now, this is what happened:

Experience stage

One evening however, when I left SES for home, I decided to take a different route and continued clockwise (instead of anti-clockwise) around the circle. I reached the side road from the opposite direction, turned left into it, then right as usual into the major road. But then I suddenly encountered traffic lights which had not been there before! I soon recognized where I was and took corrective action but was completely mystified as to what had happened.

Belief stage

I puzzled over this for several days, wondering if I'd had some sort of mental blackout or been so involved in thinking about the lecture that I hadn't been paying attention and had gone the wrong way. But I didn't really believe that; I believed that there had to be a simpler explanation.

Knowledge stage

And then, at some point, the explanation suddenly came to me: I knew beyond any doubt what must have happened, even though I hadn't looked at a map or spoken with anyone about it. There had to have been a *second* side road exiting the circle leading to a *second* major road at right angles to the one I usually took! And so it was of course.

The key point here is that when the answer finally came to me, it came as utter certainty, not as some working hypothesis or plausible explanation. I *knew* it was true.

This is the certainty of knowledge rather than belief. All of the information has to be there in the mind. In this example, the data concerning starting point, end point and location of the school were all there; I just hadn't seen the connection. The realization comes of itself when your mind is ready. You simply know that there is no other answer, even if you cannot look at a map to check your conclusion. If you have the belief (of the reality of non-duality) already, you have presumably had sufficient shravaNa (hearing the truth from a qualified teacher or scripture). You simply need to give yourself more manana (questioning the truth to dispel doubts) and nididhyAsana (repeatedly 'dwelling upon' the truth in various ways).

Knowledge, according to Western philosophy, occurs when you believe something and that belief is both justified (by experience and reason) and true. In order to become Self-realized or enlightened, you have to subject the ideas of Advaita to doubt and questioning and repetition and consideration etc. until such time as your beliefs become knowledge.

Q.387 Value of Self-knowledge

Q: At the end of the day, what does knowledge of Self give us? It does not help to answer the burning question of why the appearance/dream/mAyA that we are experiencing as humans or animals exists. Also, it appears that even if one attains knowledge of Self in one life, he/she can actually become a cockroach in the next due to karmic effect, i.e. we are not really liberated from the birth-death cycle. The only benefit I do see in a life in which one attains knowledge of Self is that one might lead a life devoid of misery in the mind as we sail through good and bad times, even though we may experience physical pain.

A: Self-knowledge removes Self-ignorance and it is the latter which makes us think we are limited, unhappy, doomed to old age and death. With Self-knowledge we realize that we are not human, living in an inhospitable world; we are Brahman. The world appears as separate because of our ignorance. On gaining Self-knowledge, we realize that its substance is nothing but Brahman.

From the perspective of the ignorant person, there is rebirth (possibly as a cockroach) and we are subject to karma. With Self-knowledge, we realize that there is no person, no birth or rebirth, no death, no creation.

The idea that knowledge is pointless is actually the main argument of the pUrvamImAMsika philosopher. They believe that only the karmakANDa portion of the Vedas is relevant – rituals that we have to perform in order to gain benefits. They say that the Upanishads etc. are only supporting material to be meditated on. In the Brahmasutra, I.1.4, Vyasa effectively refutes all those philosophers who deny that Brahman is the principal topic of the Vedas. He says, (expanding the abbreviated sutra 'tattu samanvayAt'): "But that (Brahman is to be known only from the Scriptures and not independently by any other means is established), because it is the main purpose (of all Vedantic texts)". [Translation by Swami Sivananda]

In his commentary on this sutra, Shankara agrees that knowledge in itself is often useless – we need actually to *do* something in order to gain some benefit – but there is one situation in which *only* knowledge bears fruit. That is when the problem is one of ignorance. The classic example is the rope mistaken for a snake. As soon as we find out that it is a rope, all our fears etc. disappear. And our essential problem in life is that we believe we are a limited person. The knowledge that is to be gained from Advaita is that we are Brahman – and that reveals that we have no real problems at all.

Q.396 Atman cannot be known

Q: Swami Paramarthananda makes the following comments in his talks on upadesha sAhasrI:

"Atma, though a knower of everything, is not a known object, because, if Atma were to be a known object it will need another Atma to know, leading to what is known as infinite regress (anavastha doSha). Atma cannot be known by itself, because, to be known by itself, it has to become both the subject and the object, which is not possible as one and the same entity cannot function as subject and object simultaneously.

"We cannot also say that one part of Atma can be known by another part, as Atma is by definition part-less. Thus, Atma is ever the knower but not known by others or by itself.

"As Atma is self-evident, its existence needs no proof. That 'I am conscious' is evident to me. The very search for proof is possible because of my being conscious. Thus, Atma is revealed as self-evident Witness-Consciousness which illumines everything and which cannot be objectified by anything. This Atma is my real nature. All the known attributes belong to the known objects and cannot belong to the knower, Atma (Consciousness)".

Atma cannot know Atma (Atma cannot be known), but Atma is said to be self-evident (I know I am conscious). So does it mean that the self-evident Atma is due to the chidAbhAsa?

I know my face only because I can see my face in the mirror and recognize it. But my face can exist without the mirror and its reflection. Like the Tenth Man Story, he couldn't know himself unless the guru told him.

Mind, which is acting like the mirror is only mithyA; its substratum is Brahman/Pure Consciousness only. So the self-evident quality is also mithyA. When the body and mind are destroyed, there will be no chidAbhAsa; after that nothing can be said or known or thought or described. A videha mukta will never say: "I am self evident; I am Pure Consciousness; I exist".

Although, ultimately, there is no videha mukti or liberation either because, since beginningless time, there is only Brahman; body and mind are like golden ring and golden bangle.

Is my analysis correct?

A: There is always a problem when trying to talk about absolute reality, because the reality is the non-dual Brahman. *All* discussions, explanations, rationalizations etc. take place in vyavahAra, which is dualistic and mithyA. chidAbhAsa is a metaphor, and a very useful one; it can 'explain' aspects which are otherwise difficult to rationalize. But *all* those explanations etc. have to be dropped in the end. This is why the key methodology of Advaita is pointed out as being adhyAropa-apavAda.

Most of what you say looks ok but the answer to the question "So does it mean, the self-evident Atma is due to the chidAbhAsa?" is No. You can say 'Atma is self-evident', as in 'I know I exist'. In reality, there is no such thing as chidAbhAsa because there is no world and no jIva. At the level of the empirical world, you can say: "that the Atma is self-evident is realized by the intellect of the jIva. chidAbhAsa provides a sort-of-explanation for how this operates if one assumes a real world and jIva".

Q.465 Removing the Ignorance

Q: If all we can do is to remove the ignorance that prevents us from seeing the truth, who is removing it? If there is something that can be done, it implies that there is someone who can do it. Who is that someone if we do not really exist?

A: This is just confusion between paramArtha and vyavahAra, between satyam and mithyA.

At the level of the world, there is a person; there is ignorance and there is the possibility of removing it so that the person can understand this teaching and realize that, in truth, there *is* no person, ignorance or realization, since there is, in truth, no creation at all.

No one 'removes' the ignorance exactly. The words of the guru act as a pramANa and bring about a direct realization of the truth in the mind of the seeker. Again, at the transactional level, there is someone speaking and someone listening, and words passing between them, but in reality no one is doing anything, since there are no individuals. All there is is Brahman or Consciousness if you prefer. 'Everything else' is just name and form of that Consciousness.

Q: Does this mean that the realization occurs in the mind?

A: Yes indeed. 'Enlightenment' occurs when the mind realizes the truth of the non-dual nature of reality. Note that this is not an 'intellectual understanding', though, but the sudden, certain knowledge as in bhAga tyAga lakShaNa (see Q.345).

Q.460 Talking about the Absolute

Q: Given the fact that it is impossible to speak 'from an Absolute standpoint' or even to speak accurately/directly about the Absolute (since it is attribute-less), should we (teachers and students) limit our inquiry and discussions to the relative/transactional/vyavahAra world? Isn't all talk of the absolute conjecture? And what place does conjecture have in a 'science of reality?'

A: Let me ask a counter-question. If we limit our discussion to the transactional world, how are we going to realize the nature of reality? The methodology of traditional Advaita is to look at what we presently (in our Self-ignorance) consider to be desirable, worthy, and apparently 'real', and question whether this really is the case. The usual candidates are examined and found to be wanting – objects, body, mind, ideas, status ... The aim, as I put it in 'Book of One', is that of Sherlock Holmes: when all has been investigated and rejected, whatever remains, however improbable, must be the truth. The Brihadaranyaka Upanishad calls this the 'neti, neti' method.

So, in a sense, you are right. We do limit ourselves to the relative world. But there has to be some talk of/around/about reality. Firstly, there is the need to inspire mumukShutva and keep us moving towards an understanding. This is the cultivation of shreyas rather than preyas; what is good and beneficial, rather than merely pleasing and enjoyable. And we need to be pointed towards the Consciousness that we really are and away from the entire mithyA prapa~ncha (world). It may be impossible to speak about the Absolute, and it is impossible to know it in an objective sense, but it is not impossible to 'realize' it, since we *are* it.

It is true that we cannot 'investigate' reality objectively, since it is non-dual. Similarly, there can be no attributes, no cause-effect characteristics and so on. The 'realization of the truth' is an intuitive leap. I attempted to give a personal example of this in Q.362. What happens colloquially is that you move from a position of merely believing that something is true, based upon hearsay, to knowing that it is true, based upon a personal realization.

Q:

1. You say *"It may be impossible to speak about the Absolute but it is not impossible to know it, since we are it"*. Please define 'to know' in this context. To know as in I know the answer to this question? Or I know how this works, what it's made of? Or I know the feeling of looking at this sunset (qualia)? Or I know this old friend of mind I now see on the street etc.?

2. I'm a huge fan of the via negativa 'neti neti' approach. And of Sherlock Holmes and his famous "... whatever remains, however improbable, must be the truth". But in my experience, 'neti neti' can be applied endlessly, to every apparent thing: physical objects, mental objects, no matter how subtle and apparently real these might be. To draw on the Sherlock Holmes quote: What if one finds that nothing remains after thorough neti-neti'ing, that it's all mithyA?

A:

1. 'To know' is in the sense that 'I know that I exist'. It is also in the sense that 'I know, but until I gain Self-knowledge, I do not know that I know!' I always refer to the example of bhAga tyAga lakShaNa in this scenario (see Q.345).

2. Fine! But it is not 'nothing' that remains, is it? There is still *you*, the observer, finding that there is nothing else ... The observer can never be negated.

Q: I actually have trouble knowing that 'I exist'. Maybe I'm over-thinking it, but here's how it works, perhaps you can help me figure out what's going on? When I ask myself "Do I exist?", my brain short circuits at both 'I' and 'exist'. At 'I' because the questions arise: Who or what is this 'I'? Where is it? Is it real or a phantasm? And at 'exist' because existence, like any other word/idea, is a man-made concept, and I know the danger of mistaking concepts for the real thing. The only thing I can say that I know for sure is the qualia-feeling-experience of whatever is being felt/experienced (in this moment). And I wouldn't say 'I' know this ... rather: It is known.

A: 'I' is the one who is asking the questions 'Who or what is this I?' etc. It is Consciousness reflected in the mind. Existence is having 'being' for a period of time. You, the jIva, have 'being' for the period between birth and death. Advaita says that Consciousness has eternal 'being'. And, according to Advaita's definition of 'real', this means that only the 'being' of Consciousness is 'real'. It is no coincidence that the Sanskrit word for this – sat – means both 'existence' and 'reality' (as well as 'being')!

The Teaching of Advaita

Advaita is a 'teaching methodology' rather than a philosophy. (It is certainly not a 'religion', except in the literal sense of the word – 'leading one back' to the truth.) Traditionally, it is taught from teacher (guru) to disciple, who then becomes the teacher for the next generation. It begins with the Vedas (hence Advaita 'Vedanta') and ends when the seeker gains Self-knowledge ('enlightenment'). There are numbers of key concepts and procedural teaching techniques (prakriyA-s) which are also part of the tradition, because they have been proven to be efficacious in transmitting fundamental principles of the teaching. To some degree, it is inevitable that all sections of this book will deal in part with these aspects. But some specific concepts and 'strategies' are covered in this section.

General points

Q.119 & Q.224 Some general questions

(Note: the questions here were prompted by the free E-Book containing excerpts from 'Enlightenment: The Path Through The Jungle':

http://www.advaita.org.uk/discourses/downloads/extractsv6.pdf)

Q: What is the Truth? I think Wittgenstein would not speak a single word on this, nor would Buddha or Lao Tse. 'Definitions' such as yours are always given from a relative point of view. How do you define the word 'rich'? If I say I am rich because I have £1 in excess, then I am rich. If I say I am not rich because I can't afford a second boat, then I am poor. Not to speak about the definition of enlightenment!

A: What is truth? I assume you are referring to the non-dual reality, called 'Brahman' in traditional Advaita? In which case, the answer is easy – Brahman has no attributes and, since we can only describe attributes and not the 'thing-in-itself', the question is essentially unanswerable. This is why Wittgenstein would not say anything.

As you go on to say, all 'definitions' are relative. This is necessarily the case since every 'thing' takes place at this level – both our ignorance and our enlightenment.

Q: Is methodology a must? Do I love my children because of a methodology? Do the Eskimos, the aboriginals etc. follow any methodology?

A: Teaching is a progressive and a skilled pursuit. You cannot teach quantum mechanics to someone who doesn't first have a thorough grounding in math and physics. So, equally, with spiritual teaching. You can tell someone outright that 'you are That' but without lots of 'grounding' preparation, they are unlikely to make much of it. The 'grounding preparation' in a systematic manner is what I mean by 'methodology' and, yes, I believe it is required.

Such things as loving your children are 'programmed in' – they do not have to be taught. Not sure what you are getting at with Eskimos. I'm sure their parents teach and demonstrate no end of things. The 'methodology' may not be written down but I guess an alien might observe, take notes, and write a book if so inclined.

Q: Sri Siddharameshwar teaches to focus on 'I am' whereas Sri Ramana teaches to ask the question 'Who am I?' Do you call this also a methodology, a progressive and skilled pursuit?

A: Ramana's 'Who am I?' teaching is a technique, not a methodology. A methodology incorporates many techniques so that a skilled teacher may select whichever one is appropriate at a given time for a particular student and those techniques/metaphors etc. are graded to suit any seeker from beginner to advanced. Ramana's one-off technique is given by many modern satsang teachers to anyone, regardless of their present level of understanding. (Note that I am not criticizing Ramana or suggesting that the technique is not valuable.)

Q: Referring to the example of the programmed love for our children, I believe the 'path' from ignorance to enlightenment is also somehow programmed in the lIlA of Brahman. Why should there be any difference regarding the experience of the non-dual reality? Since the 'path' from ignorance to enlightenment has also been programmed this 'path' should forcibly lead to enlightenment (the experience of the non-dual reality)!

A: From where do you get the idea that one's spiritual path is 'programmed'? If you do nothing, nothing will happen. Effort has to be made in a direction which is contrary to our habitual behavior.

Q: My point about the Eskimos is that maybe there is no Eskimo-shruti, which would be a quite unfair handicap for those guys.

A: There was no English shruti either until relatively recently. If there was the interest, I'm sure someone would translate and publish relevant texts.

Q: Do I need to study Arts to enjoy a beautiful painting or the science of wine to enjoy a bottle of wine? A dog can be happy without any teaching method because he is here and now! People are first of all looking for happiness, not for the truth says Ramana, says the Buddha.

A: Art and wine may be appreciated. I'm sure they are better appreciated when the subtleties are explained by someone more knowledgeable. But I don't know what point you are making. Dogs may be happy but can they be enlightened? I agree that most people are looking for happiness. But the vast majority are looking for it outside, in 'things' (objects, people, status and so on). Even if they do find it, this sort of happiness does not last. The only true happiness is to be found as one's real nature. Looking for, and finding this, requires teaching from someone who already knows this truth.

Q: The point about wine and art is that according to my experience they can be fully appreciated without studying with a teacher. Using a manual while I am drinking a glass of Champagne would not improve the experience. I would even say that it could hamper the fullness of the experience and appreciation. Again, why should this be different for the experience of the non-dual reality?

A: I disagree about the wine tasting. Someone knowledgeable can draw your attention to those aspects (tastes, smells, color, and transparency) which could easily elude the inexperienced. Even more so with art. But I don't think this is really a good analogy because in both of these cases, there are actual attributes to be observed. In the case of Brahman, there are no attributes. Since we already are Brahman, you could ask why there should be any need to observe anything anyway, let alone require a teacher. The point is that, although we are That, we do not *know* it.

Q: What is the difference in reading a book from Shankara and reading a book from a modern satsang teacher? Is it because the scriptures are so old that they can claim the final authority?

A: The difference between reading a book by Shankara and one by a modern satsang teacher is that you will probably understand the latter. (Yes, I did say 'latter'!) But neither is likely to bring enlightenment on its own. A qualified teacher can, in time, provide all of the pointers needed to bring about Self-knowledge. You can find one in India (almost certainly, though apparently it is becoming more difficult!). Disciples of Swami Dayananda teach in the USA and India and there are Chinmaya Missions scattered around the world. There are undoubtedly other sources but they do not always advertise!

The shruti are ancient, yes; passed down by word of mouth through enlightened men for a long time before being written down. Their authority lies in the fact that the knowledge of what they essentially say (that 'all there is, is Brahman' and 'you are That') cannot be obtained in any other way (apart from direct realization). The ways in which they explicate these truths have been used successfully for thousands of years by traditional teachers.

Q: Are more advaitins enlightened than Neo-Advaitins? Are you enlightened?

A: Every sensible person who writes about non-duality is very wary of stating whether or not they themselves are enlightened because the understanding of what is meant by this term varies so widely. You tell me what you understand by it and I will tell you whether I am enlightened according to that definition.

Q: The nature of things is evolution. The science of the mind is evolving, so why not the science of the heart? Is real knowledge coming from the mind or from the heart? Knowledge from the mind is indirect knowledge. Knowledge from the heart is direct knowledge. Silence is the non-dual way of the heart and reason is the dual way of the mind.

A: "The nature of things is evolution", you say. No it isn't, I say – the essential nature of things is Brahman. Evolution is simply changing forms at the level of appearance. I don't know what you mean by 'science of the heart' or 'knowledge from the heart'. Knowledge takes place in the mind. The heart is a physical organ for pumping blood. There is an extensive section in the 'Jungle' book talking about direct and indirect knowledge etc.

Q: Concerning the science of the mind, I mean that this science is suited for the study of the 'outer world' whilst the science of the heart is suited for the 'preparation' towards 'enlightenment'. By 'heart' I am just referring to 'intuition' which takes you 'beyond' the limited knowledge of the brain and which is needed to experience non-dual reality. What is your experience?

A: 'Heart' as used in Advaita is really synonymous with mind. [See Q.61] The heart has nothing to do with any of this. Traditional teaching is always reasonable – although it may sometimes be counter-intuitive. As regards 'experiencing non-duality', it has already been pointed out that we *cannot* experience non-duality. But, having acknowledged that, one could say that, since there is *only* non-duality, we '*always* 'experience' it! The point is that every 'thing' is always non-dual, but we do not know it – it is Self-knowledge that is needed. Alternatively, one could ask: how *can* you experience non-duality? In non-duality, there is no experiencer and experienced, since this is duality.

Q.334 Different teachings

Q: How do you explain two enlightened people (in the Advaitic sense) that have different teachings? For instance, I think someone like Greg Goode and Swami Dayananda would disagree on many things despite both arguably being enlightened. For example let's take Greg's essay on idealism (http://www.advaita.org.uk/discourses/teachers/idealism_greg.htm).

I don't think Swami Dayananda-ji will agree with the core position that an object doesn't exist unless perceived. In fact I have asked Swami Tadatmananda this question (in the form of 'does a rock exist before someone sees it?') and he answered in the traditional sense saying that it does. From your point of view does this still fall under the umbrella of differences in teaching style? I also believe we could get a debate between the two on the topic of Ishvara and free will.

A: All teachings are mithyA and ultimately have to be discarded (pole vault metaphor), traditional and Direct Path Advaita included. If a teaching removes Self-ignorance, it brings enlightenment, by definition. paramArtha is not amenable to objectification, so even the enlightened have to use mithyA words to teach others. So I don't think Swami D and Greg would disagree about the nature of reality, just on the most appropriate way of teaching it. In particular, they might differ on their descriptions of empirical 'appearance-reality'. Traditional Advaita teachers are quite happy to accept vishiShTAdvaita (and even dvaita) as interim positions of understanding en route, as it were, to Advaita.

Whether someone takes an interim idealist stance or a realist one does not really matter very much as long as they reach the final understanding that there is only Brahman. Certainly, I would agree with you that traditional Advaita uses a realist position for vyavahAra. So, yes, they will differ from Greg in the way that that they teach this. But this need not pose any problem unless a seeker who doesn't appreciate all this attempts to mix the two teachings.

The world is real from a vyAvahArika standpoint so the pole and the veda-s, the bar and mokSha, are all real too. You cross the real bar using a real pole; you use real veda-s as a real pramANa to gain real mokSha. All of the same order of reality. From the pAramArthika standpoint *all* are mithyA. veda-s are a pramANa in just the same way as pratyakSha is a pramANa in vyavahAra. *No* pramANa-s are relevant from a pAramArthika standpoint.

I don't believe any Advaitin will complain about claiming that the veda-s are also mithyA. I believe that the 'unauthoredness' is a red herring as far as this discussion is concerned. Their utility as pramANa would be the same even if their authorship were attributable to past sages. [See Q.242 for a discussion of the concept of apauruSheya – the notion that the Vedas were 'unauthored' and, instead, passed down by Ishvara when the world was created.]

Q.434 Modern debates about Advaita principles

Q: As I work through the Brahma Sutras, and having read Alston's 'Shankara on Rival Views', I have a nagging concern that all of the refutation of alternate theories is too self-contained. What I mean is that much of it seems like a straw-man setup, where Shankara defines his opponent's views for them and then shreds those views. The objections are being written by the same author that is refuting those objections. I would like to find texts that carry the debate outside of the closed circle, so to speak. Say, for example, a Buddhist took exception to those refutations and wrote a compelling argument against them, and then a traditional Swami responded in kind. Are you aware of any more modern works along these lines? In particular, I would like to see Shankara's logic analyzed by a scholar and compared to our modern updated view of logical argumentation, etc.

A: Are you sufficiently certain of the Advaita stance on all issues that you would want to look at critical appraisals? I haven't come across any easy work that deals with these. If you are studying Brahmasutra now, there is a version which is fairly readable and actually occasionally funny (in a superior, knowing sort of way), which looks at the other commentaries and interpretations. It's called 'The Brahmasutra and their Principal Commentaries: A Critical Exposition' by B. N. K. Sharma. It's in 3 volumes and almost certainly very expensive in the west. You can probably get it cheaper from India, though.

Another book which I haven't looked at is 'A Critique of Vedanta' by L. V. Rajagopal. It looks at the three Vedantic schools and applies Whitehead's approach to philosophy to critically analyze them (so says the book cover!). It looks like a very serious read to me!

The other book which might interest you is Sri Swami Satchidanandendra's (SSS) book 'The Method of the Vedanta: A Critical Account of the Advaita Tradition'. It looks at pre and post Shankara authors and endeavors to establish Shankara's views as the correct ones. But it is a huge book of nearly 1000 pages and really not terribly readable. It is, however, translated by A. J. Alston so is at least understandable with some effort. But I can't honestly actually recommend any of these. It's up to you if you want to give any a try. From what you say, maybe the Rajagopal would serve your needs.

Q.452 Why is non-duality teaching 'cold'?

Q: I am wondering why none of the teachings on Advaita/non-duality address the seeker with compassion or answer the question directly in a manner that would embrace the seeker.

I have read several questions regarding thoughts and the creation of observed reality. Understanding that the person asking is still seeking, why would the near hostility of the answer that there is "no person to think, no concrete reality to experience, etc.". possibly be acceptable from the standpoint of pure awareness.

Wouldn't it be aware that this is not just 'not an answer', but a steering away from the question, and in terms of attaining a nondual experience not helpful? I would think awareness should know to first answer the question and then provide the next level view.

This is by far not the only site/teaching/vision of non-duality where this semi-hostility and often circular logic is present. I frequently see angry articles that just say "LOOK, it's all right there, just LOOK", as if that is helpful for someone who is seeking to understand. It's not. It's off-putting.

By far the worst answer I frequently come across is: "but who is asking?" That answer, while I have yet to see it here, is reprehensible. It is not an answer intended to help; it is intended to put people off and convey a sense of superiority. It shows less than no compassion and is ostracizing.

Why does it seem that the modern teaching of non-duality is hostile, cold and harsh with an almost elitist and upper crust air that defies an idea of an ever present awareness? What am I not seeing? Is there no teacher that can lead without being dismissive?

A: The problem with emailed Q and A is that they are one-off; not part of a continuous, probably years-long teaching. Ideally, a seeker finds a teacher whom they can trust and are prepared to listen to for as long as it takes. Then that teacher begins from the seeker's present level of understanding and takes the teaching one step at a time. The specific teaching methodology of Advaita is called adhyAropa-apavAda, which means that one explanation is given to begin with. Later, as understanding grows, that explanation is taken back and another, slightly more 'advanced' explanation is given. And so on. Obviously this is not possible when someone asks a single question, gets an answer and then goes away, probably never to ask anything again.

Accordingly, when someone emails a one-off question, there is a potential dilemma. Does one give an 'interim' answer, aimed at where one thinks that particular seeker presently stands, knowing that it is actually not like that? Or does one give the 'bottom-line' answer, even though the seeker may not be 'ready' for it?

What I try to do is to state the truth of the matter, while at the same time pointing out that to do this is going against the intention of traditional Advaita teaching. And the 'bottom-line' answers are inevitably going to seem 'impersonal' because the truth is that there are no persons. The answers are going to seem abrupt because it is not possible to give long, complete explanations to everyone. (I usually recommend that they read one of my books. And the one I recommend depends upon what I judge to be the level of their present understanding.) Because answers are inevitably short, I also take great pains to insure that I use language which is clear and unambiguous. I always re-read my answers, often several times, and make changes as necessary to insure this objective is met. Accordingly, it may sometimes appear 'cold'. But I certainly never say anything like "LOOK, it's all right there, just LOOK"!

I can certainly sympathize with your general attitude. My book 'Enlightenment: the Path through the Jungle' specifically addresses the very many problems with most of the modern-day, Western teachers. I do not even accept that they have precisely the same problem that I am talking about here – namely the need to answer one-off questions out of context – because this problem is one of their own making! If, instead of travelling the world holding two-hour satsangs in different cities, they remained in one place and held regular meetings to the same audience for years at a time, this problem would not arise. If you were to attend the classes of a qualified, traditional teacher, you would soon find that there is no suggestion of a "hostile, cold and harsh with an almost elitist and upper crust air that defies an idea of an ever present awareness".

I hope you feel that this has answered your concerns. And thank you for raising it – it is a topic which merits clear explanation!

General concepts

The key tenet of Advaita is that there is only Brahman or Atman (or, if you prefer, Consciousness). There is nothing else – reality is non-dual. [Note that Brahman, Atman, Consciousness, Absolute are synonymous in this context. Atman is used when referring to an apparent 'person'; the others tend to be used when speaking of the 'impersonal' reality.]

All explanations for how there seems to be a separate world are, like the world itself, mithyA. There is only Brahman. The explanations are only intended to be interim, in order to satisfy the intellect until such time as you realize the truth. They are like the pole in pole vaulting; this pole must be discarded before you can 'pass over' the bar of ignorance. This includes the explanations of Shankara, as he would be the first to admit.

For example, it would certainly be possible to put forward alternative theories for creation etc. But, to be frank, why bother? The various explanations provided in the shruti have worked for innumerable people for several thousand years. You can read about and hear them presented in slightly different ways in many books and from many teachers until they finally work their magic and the Self-ignorance is dispelled. But then you throw them away just like all ideas about the truth. It is simply not possible to speak about the ultimate truth. Attempting to devise some alternative approach to do the same thing would seem somewhat ambitious and entirely a waste of time.

Q.130 Does Advaita endorse man's dominion?

Q: In your story about Advaita (http://www.advaita.org.uk/discourses/definitions/advaita.htm), you use the example of taking a rose to pieces to illustrate the meaning of mithyA. So that you know how your readers are affected emotionally by what you write, when the master ripped apart the rose, you lost me. I saw this as an unnecessary act of violence, killing a living creature to make a point. For me it harkened back to western science and the Judeo-Christian ethic: human dominion over all. This in turn made me suspicious of Advaita — does it 'endorse' this sense of dominion? Does it extend to animals? Again, this is not a criticism of the story, which is good, rather an insight into how some readers might react to the rose vivisection.

A: Point taken, though a cut rose in a vase already has a somewhat limited life expectancy!

But, as the Gita points out, the Self does not kill, nor is it killed; is not born and does not die. Death of a 'living creature' is only rearrangement of form, with the essence forever unchangeable. There is no question of human 'dominion' in Advaita – the essence of every seeming thing, rock or human, is the same non-dual reality. The point is made in the traditional teaching, however, that man alone is capable of realizing the truth of this. To that extent alone you might regard man as 'superior'. Even the gods have to be reborn in human form before they can obtain enlightenment!

Q.220 Are the vAsanA-s in the causal or subtle body?

Q: Are the vAsanA-s stored in the causal body (kAraNa sharIra) or subtle body (sUkShma sharIra)? In 'Back to the Truth' you state the former but I have heard that the kAraNa sharIra is a state of ignorance and that the vAsanA-s are stored in the subtle body.

In the subtle body camp I got a response from one of Swami Dayananda's senior students saying that the causal body is pure ignorance with no attributes and that vAsanA-s "definitely belong to the subtle body". In addition, from my own quick review of some of Shankara's basic works I can find no passage that says the causal body is anything but 'avidyA' and find no mention of the term 'vAsanA-s' anywhere.

In the causal body camp I have James Schwartz and multiple pieces of Chinmayananda literature. In fact I have seen them equate vAsanA-s to avidyA by pointing out that avidyA and vAsanA-s are both caused by the guNa-s.

A: Both answers could be regarded as 'correct'. If you are talking about how we behave in the waking or dream worlds, then the vAsanA-s 'belong' to the subtle body. But both gross and subtle resolve into the causal state in deep-sleep, so these 'belong' to the causal body. Obviously in this state, we know nothing (the mind is resolved), so it is often 'equated' to ignorance. A better way of putting it is that deep-sleep is characterized by ignorance but there is no erroneous mistaking of the real for something else. Waking and dream states are characterized by both ignorance and error. (Who-we-really-are, of course, is characterized by neither.)

I think one has to concede that, since the mind is resolved in deep-sleep, the vAsanA-s have to be stored in the causal state. There is no avoiding this conclusion – they must be *somewhere* in deep-sleep (and between lives of course!). Hope this resolves the confusion.

Remember, though, that these are only concepts to help to move the teaching forward. Eventually, they have to be dropped before you can reach the final understanding.

All this is explained by Gaudapada and Shankara and covered in my book 'A-U-M: Awakening to Reality'.

Q.236b Organs of the mind and mokSha

Q: What is the relationship between antaHkaraNa (ahaMkAra, chitta, buddhi, manas) and the physical brain? Modern neuroscience and psychology have conclusively proven there is certainly some sort of link between the physical and subtle entities – clearly different electrical brain activities correspond to different functions such as perception, memory, emotion, etc.

A: Both antaHkaraNa and brain are mithyA so there is no future in pursuing such questions. It is like asking about the relationship between entities in the dream that you had last night. From the vantage point of absolute reality, both are simply name and form of Brahman so that there is no question of 'relationship' – you can only have a relationship between two things.

At the empirical level (which I appreciate is the level at which you are asking the question), it really doesn't matter. By all means, take the latest scientific explanation to be the most reasonable and accurate way of representing the situation. Any 'explanation' you may derive from the traditional Advaita scriptures will only be the best that their 'science' was able to describe.

Q: The fact that ingested food and drugs DO have an effect on the antaHkaraNa – e.g. you can take LSD or ecstasy and experience 'blissful' states associated with the subtle realms perceived/enjoyed/known by the antaHkaraNa – this suggests that the antaHkaraNa is *not* a subtle instrument as I think vedAnta would claim, but that it is gross, owing to the fact that physical matter can be affected by it? What is Vedanta's view?

A: Advaita would not argue that the mind depends upon the brain for its functioning. The sense organs initially send their signals via nerves to the brain. (Let us not get into any discussion of mind-body duality or how the 'mind' receives the nerve-transmitted signals. Advaita certainly cannot help here!) In the empirical realm, the traditional teaching of Advaita claims that the mind 'travels' to a new body upon death of the brain so there is no question but that the view of Advaita is that the mind is subtle.

The point is that all of the teaching at this 'interim' level was intended to satisfy the minds of the seeker for the time being. Scriptures of 2000 years ago were suited to the mind with a 'scientific' understanding of 2000 years ago. If you read answers to questions in other sections, you will see that I point out that such teachings as reincarnation and even free will have to be recognized ultimately as false. This does not contravene the traditional teaching of Advaita. But, whereas the refutation of such ideas used to be delayed until an advanced stage of the teaching, I now feel that it has to be admitted much earlier for the benefit of the more 'knowledgeable', more 'sophisticated' seeker. (I put those words in inverted commas because of course, in many ways, the modern seeker may be *less* knowledgeable and sophisticated!)

Q.265 Rituals

Q: If all is He, then who is it performing religion? Is there any necessity to perform rules and regulations as described in Holy Scripture? As I am He, how can I worship me? It is worthless or a kind of cheating. Please clarify.

A: If you know that you are Brahman (i.e. are enlightened), then obviously none of this is necessary or relevant. Worship, etc., are interim means for preparing the mind to be able to truly realize this fact.

Q: Almost all religion says at the beginning there was nothing but He. To express Himself, He has created the world of forms, still remaining formless/unseen behind the form. So everything is He, as the clay remains as clay in the pot of different shape, size and color. My question is: if He is He, then what is the necessity for performing prayers, uttering mantras, sacrificing animals at His feet, etc.? My opinion is that religion is for those who possess mind (duality); in no-mind (non-duality), there is no need for performing rules and regulations of religion. Whether I am right or wrong, please clarify.

A: From the perspective of absolute reality, there is indeed only Brahman. At the level of appearance, there is the jIva, the world and Ishvara. The seeker can use worship of a god to help to prepare the mind for Self-knowledge. But even the enlightened can continue to worship, recognizing the distinction but still appreciating the beauty of the apparent creation and knowing that 'I am Ishvara'. Read someone like Swami Dayananda to gain more understanding about this.

One should certainly bear in mind, however, that rituals cannot bring about Self-knowledge, contrary to the beliefs of those who claim that it is the karma kANDa portion of the Vedas that is important and that the Upanishads are of little value. But Shankara acknowledges their value for preparation of the mind. And the j~nAnI does still have, and need, a mind for interactions in the world until death of the body! No one 'lives' in non-duality!

Q.350 Heaven and hell

Q: In Advaita, it is said that heaven and hell are mithyA. They are just ideas for bhakti-natured people. But Advaita says the world is mithyA too. So even though heaven and the hell are mithyA, we are still going to go there – they are as real as this world. Is that the correct interpretation?

A: Apart from the comment about 'bhakti-natured people', what you say is correct. There are many loka-s in scriptural Advaita, not just the world, heaven and hell. But all are mithyA. This does not mean they are unreal. It means that, whilst you still believe in duality, you are effectively bound by all the seeming dualistic aspects. Your subtle-causal bodies are doomed to rebirth (saMsAra), in accordance with the principle of karma, until you realize that you are not those bodies. This may include periods in heaven or hell as well as periods as plant or animal. So goes the empirical cycle of birth and death.

Of course, who-you-really-are is none of these and none of them 'really' exists (as something separate). Everything is name and form of Brahman. And you are That.

Q.398 Use of metaphors

Q: There are two concepts – superimposition and manifestation – in Advaita to describe the 'relationship' between Brahman and the empirical world. Superimposition means that the world is superimposed on Brahman. Manifestation means that the world is a manifestation of Brahman. My doubt is as to how a manifestation can be superimposition also? My gut feeling is that there is a subtle link between the two concepts which I am unable to 'see' because of the proverbial 'ignorance'.

A: They are each a metaphor to give the mind some insight into the nature of reality. The reality is non-dual so that all metaphors and all 'explanations' are ultimately untrue. The world and the jIva are mithyA. Brahman has no relationships. Use the metaphors and explanations of the scriptures and teachers to help guide the mind to realization of the truth but don't ever take them as more than what they are. And do not worry if one 'explanation' disagrees with (or even contradicts) another. They all have to be dropped in the end!

The idea of 'manifestation' is one which suits the person who starts off with the idea of a god who created the world. It introduces an interim concept which moves away from the notion of a 'creation' and towards the reality of there not being a world at all.

The concept of 'superimposition' is a crucial one for seeing how it might be that our preconceptions are preventing us from realizing that our mind's Self-ignorance may be the cause of all our (seeming) problems. It is so important that Shankara addresses it (adhyAsa) in the introduction to his commentary on one of the most important scriptural texts – the Brahmasutra.

dharma

Q.127 On the desire for making money

Q: I work as a freelance musician so that most of my money comes from TV and radio advertisements but sometimes it seems that contracts never arrive when I need the money. And then my girlfriend gets somewhat stressed! (I try to explain to her the Advaita point of view on this but...)

Do I just have to stay in and wait for contracts etc., or should I 'do' something else to makes some money? (But how can I when there are no doers?) It seems a bit hard to change to have no desires, since society is so geared up to desiring and satisfying those desires. So, while it seems like a good challenge for me to let go all desires for gain, at the same time I am afraid I might lose everything and become homeless! Something inside me says that, if I have the guts to live the 'real life', then pain cannot exist, since the big snake that I see is really just a rope!

A: At the relative level of the world, and you cannot avoid acting even though, as the Gita tells us, it is not the self that acts but the guNa-s. Traditional Advaita advocates that you pursue your 'natural inclinations' (svadharma) but without any attachment to the outcome. Unfortunately, most people do not live in India, where such an attitude is (or perhaps it would be more true to say 'was') both permitted and laudable. There, one could give up one's job, home, family and possessions without worrying that one might starve.

It is really a case of exercising discrimination and reason and of adapting one's style of living to one's circumstances without feeling hard done by or resentful and without wishing that things were better. I once had a highly paid job in computing but was made redundant. I could have tried for other jobs, whether minor management or shop-related or whatever. Instead, I decided to write books on Advaita and accept a vastly reduced standard of living. And I have never regretted this decision (although my wife, like your girlfriend, used to complain bitterly about it!).

One should aim to sublimate the materialistic desires. Eventually, the only really important one should be mumukShutva – the desire to realize the truth; to gain Self-knowledge.

Q.208 On selfishness and svadharma

Q: Quoting from Swami Dayananda's introduction to his Bhagavad Gita commentary:

"... one who desires a particular end, any artha or kAma, does so for his or her own sake.

"Suppose you say, 'No, Swamiji, it is not for my sake; it is for the sake of my son.' This only means that your 'me' has become a little extended, but it always reduces to 'me.' Your 'me' can extend to the community in which you live, to your religion and to your nation also. It is your ego – an extended ego – and the more extensions, the healthier the ego. Still, the end is always for your sake alone.

"If you pray for your mother, father, children, humanity and all living beings, you do so because you can only be happy if others are happy. How can you be happy if everyone else is unhappy? When you know that whatever you do is for your own sake, everything becomes meaningful".

Questions:

1. What does he mean by "your own sake"? Is he referring to Atman? It seems as if he is referring to ego.

2. Does this imply that true altruism/selflessness doesn't really exist? From my personal experience, everything I do is for me, even 'selfless' thoughts & actions. All the sAdhana I do is for my happiness, not yours. (Although, incidentally, shruti would say that your happiness is my happiness which is why I must strive for selfless action – but selflessness is not my actual motivation as I do it for my own happiness. I guess this is the same for all of us?)

3. In this light, the whole notion of selflessness as advocated in Vedanta seems to be fairly superficial since those who do act 'selflessly' do so for their 'own' mokSha, or their 'own' spiritual progression (where 'own' = ego). I thought that, according to Vedanta, selfishness is not a desirable quality. But is not the desire for mokSha (which is a key pre-requisite for mokSha) intrinsically selfish? Isn't *everything* we do for 'our own sake' as Dayananda says?

I suspect I may have totally misunderstood Swami Dayananda's point here. I would really appreciate your clarification.

A: While you believe that you are a separate individual, everything you do is ultimately for that imagined individual. You are right – every action is selfish, even the so-called self-less ones. However, part of the preparation for the mind (sAdhana chatuShTaya sampatti) involves such things as vairAgya (dispassion) and control of the senses etc. Also, karma yoga (which is also a valid preliminary for j~nAna yoga for those who are not yet ready) involves action for its own sake, i.e. endeavoring to transcend both selfish and selfless action. Once you actually attain self-realization, you understand that there are no others. And, once this knowledge becomes established, the concepts of both selfish and selfless lose their meaning.

So, concepts such as altruism are meaningful in vyavahAra for those seekers who are practicing karma yoga. And, since every concept and action only has meaning in vyavahAra, this is fine. The entire karma kANDa (the first part of the Vedas) is concerned with such things but it is all in the nature of preparation for those who are not yet ready to take on board the final truth of Advaita. It is more than superficial in an absolute sense – it is totally meaningless! But, from the point of view of a beginning seeker, it is very important indeed because the world and our interactions within it constitute reality for them.

Q: The notion of karma yoga transcending both selfish and selfless action is entirely new to me (I thought it was all about selfless service). This is an interesting point, which raised a few more questions:

1. If selfless action is ultimately selfish (for the ego), why should I be engaging in so called 'selfless activities' (which are actually just me being selfish, but with a slightly extended ego as Swami Dayananda puts it)? This would surely just serve to reinforce my identity with my own selfish ego (which is contrary to the truth of Advaita).

2. Karma Yoga enables us to transcend selfish & 'selfless' action. So does this imply that so called selfless action may be contrary to karma Yoga? This seems to be what Swami Dayananda also suggests in one of his books 'The teaching Tradition of Advaita'. For example, say I have started voluntary work in an attempt to increase the amount of so called 'selfless service' I am performing. Does this have no value (in terms of my spiritual progress) at all?

3. According to Swami Dayananda, the key factor in defining the practice of karma yoga, is the performance of dharma (whether I happen to like my dharma or not). So, if it is my dharma to perform relatively selfish acts for the sake of my own survival & happiness, then is this OK according to shruti?

It seems to all boil down to this notion of dharma. I have never really understood what exactly my 'svadharma' is. In 'The Book of One', you say *"we all know what our duties are"*, without much further explanation. It always seems to be a rather gray area. I really don't know what my 'duties' are. For example, a big dilemma I can never fully resolve is whether I must follow the house-holder life style, or that of a saMnyAsin (I'm 23 yrs old). I know there are certain qualifications for both. However, I feel kind of stuck in the middle. I'm certainly not qualified for the life of a saMnyAsin at present. However, I feel I may have a realistic potential to develop those qualities fairly quickly if I were in the company of a guru. But then everyone always seems to advise the safe route of a householder. I can appreciate this but I don't know if that is my dharma. I figured out the only way I will know is if I go to India & spend some time with some mahatma's. Any advice?

4. If I don't know my svadharma, is the practice of karma yoga impossible? (I guess it is.)

A: When I used the word 'selfless', I actually meant 'unselfish' – apologies for the confusion! The idea behind karma yoga is that neither doing something with the intention of benefiting yourself, nor doing something with the intention of benefiting someone else is beneficial – both incur karma phalam, which furthers saMsAra. The aim is to do action purely in response to the need without any thought of 'benefit' for anyone – simply because that is the appropriate response to that situation. You might call this type of action 'selfless' – because there is no 'self' or ego involved in the motivation. If so, then selfless action is good and is the aim of karma yoga. Hope this is now clear.

But karma yoga cannot bring about enlightenment. No action can, since enlightenment is purely the result of Self-knowledge, i.e. eliminating Self-ignorance. Karma yoga functions as a preparation for the mind, instilling self-discipline etc.

The concept of dharma is a difficult one unless you are brought up with the idea, which I wasn't! But, in general in this context, it relates to behaving in accordance with the laws of society and accepted standards of morality. svadharma is simply that which applies to ourselves in our particular job and social environment. We know what our job responsibilities and family responsibilities are and know that we ought to follow these. But, again, this is part of the preparation for the mind so that it is ready and able to take on board the teaching of Advaita when it is presented by a qualified teacher.

I shouldn't get too hung-up on the nature of your 'lifestyle'. The four Ashrama-s are related to Hindu culture rather than a necessary path to be followed by the spiritual aspirant. If your aim is enlightenment (as I assume it must be), this can be gained at any stage of life. It is Self-knowledge only. It can be pursued whilst following an everyday job if you are prepared to make that commitment, study, try to find a teacher, forego the more usual pleasures of life etc.

Q.323 Advaita for mothers

Q: My question is: as a mother, is it ever possible to not be very attached to my child, and be a mother only (following dharma and avoiding the clutches of moha for my child)? How do I do that? I would greatly appreciate if anything here can help me because I truly am looking for it, and struggling with the issue for a long time.

A: I think you are misunderstanding and misusing the word moha here. This means 'delusion' and is one of the 'impurities' to which the mind is prone. This 'dirt' or mala is said to tarnish the mind and prevent us from seeing clearly. Making up this dirt are such sentiments as raga, dveSha, kAma, krodha, lobha, moha, mada, matsarya. (These are, respectively: attachment, aversion, desire, anger, greed, delusion, pride and jealousy.)

Swami Dayananda, in his 'Gita Home Study Course', equates moha to having what he calls 'false values', inculcated by society. And there are no end of these in modern Western society, propagated by television and films, such as thinking one has to go and drink alcohol whenever something goes wrong.

Clearly, looking after and looking out for one's child, until it is old enough to do these things for itself, is not a delusion or false value. On the contrary, it is the duty of a mother in the same way that it was Arjuna's duty as a kShatriya to fight the battle. The strong emotional feeling that is associated with this duty is simply Ishvara's way of ensuring that even those who might not be aware of dharma, nevertheless still (usually) end up doing the right thing.

Q.454 How should one live one's life?

Q: One of the problems I encounter with Advaita is that, even though it makes sense and resonates with me, it does not help from the point of view of providing guidelines on how to live my life. If we consider Buddhism, for example, we find a clear path on how to live one's live that goes in accordance with the deeper philosophical explanations of what reality is, etc.

This is the part in which I find myself discouraged and not knowing how to move forward. What could you tell me about this? What would you recommend that I read?

A: All of the guidance given by Advaita regarding 'how to live' is directed at preparing the mind so that it is optimally able to gain Self-knowledge. Once this has happened, you know that in reality there is no world, there are no persons. 'Life' is just the apparent movement of forms of Brahman. An enlightened person will simply continue to operate according to prArabdha karma until death of that body-mind. Of course, cause and effect still operates at the empirical level. So, now knowing the truth and probably feeling sympathy for other apparent (and ignorant) jIva-s, there will be a tendency to behave more considerately towards them! If you look at someone like Swami Dayananda, you will see that he was not only a brilliant teacher but also very active in charitable works etc. But the bottom line is that it is not really meaningful to talk about 'how should a realized man behave'. The Bhagavad Gita has a chapter on how a realized man does behave, but that is more to do with recognizing such a person.

Possibly the best text I have come across regarding the 'life path' of a seeker is jIva yAtra by Swami Jnanananda Bharati of Sringeri. Swami Paramarthananda gave a 15-hour talk on this at a residential course some time ago. You can download these (http://hinduonline.co/AudioLibrary/Discources/LectureonJivaYatraParamarthananda.html) and they are very good, but there is a lot of Sanskrit in them (he breaks down each verse for the Sanskrit students). This is not a problem really, since you can just ignore those aspects if you do not understand them. You can also download a transcription of the talks (http://arshaavinash.in/index.php/download/jiva-yatra-swami-paramarthananda/).

karma

Q.216 'Right action' and helping others

Q: I understand the basic concept of 'action without attachment to the fruits of the labor or action'; to just do something simply because it is the right thing to do, but without any desire for a specific outcome, either for yourself, or for another, etc. – removing 'ego' from the action.

I was curious as to doing a 'right action,' but wanting the outcome of that action to benefit that being; to relieve their suffering, make them well, heal them, calm them, etc. As long as it is a 'right action' and you do not want it for 'yourself,' why is that wrong? For instance, I have a dog, or a child. I love and care for this dog, or child. I am responsible for their well-being and welfare. The dog gets hit by a car and breaks his leg, or the child gets very ill. I must nurse and treat them. I have to take them to the doctor, change bandages, give medicines, feed them by hand, sit by the bed, soothe them. I only want for them to get better – for them, not for myself. I want them to get better so that they can live their own healthy life.

Can you want 'something good' for someone else and not for yourself? Or would you say the ego would never allow this; that even if you thought you wanted it for the other person or animal, you really wanted them to get better for yourself... because you love them, and you wanted them to live so they'd be around for example; and love is an 'attachment.'

How did Mother Teresa and many others like her apply this concept to their works? How does compassion and love fit in? What about ministering to the mortal body, nursing care, veterinary care, feeding the hungry, etc.?

A: The various types of action relate to the theory of karma, which in turn is supposed to 'drive' the person's life and determine future rebirth etc. There are three classes of motivation influencing any action: a selfish motivation is deemed to be 'bad' and incurs demerit or sin (pApa); an unselfish motivation is deemed to be 'good' and incurs merit (puNya); an action which is purely in response to the need of the moment, with neither selfish nor unselfish motivation is 'right' and incurs no karma at all. If you have accumulated mostly pApa by the time of the body's death, your next life will be 'lower', i.e. an animal, insect, tree or stone (in descending order!) If you have gained puNya, you will have a better life. Lots of puNya may even take you to heaven (svarga) for a while, although you will eventually have to come back as a human, since the ultimate aim it to achieve enlightenment and then not come back at all.

So goes the theory. And its value as a guide to living one's life is obvious. From the standpoint of absolute reality, of course, there is no world to begin with and, since you were never born, the question of rebirth has no relevance.

The way to reconcile this with one's everyday life is essentially: initially one follows guidance such as that above and aims to gain such virtues as viveka, vairAgya and the shamAdi shakti sampatti as described in the scriptures (and 'The Book of One'). The purpose of this is to prepare the mind to be able to understand and 'take on board' the Self-knowledge-teaching of the guru. At some point, enlightenment will occur and the truth is then realized for oneself. Thereafter, one will naturally come to act in accordance with this knowledge. (Initially, the habits of a lifetime may mean that apparently selfish acts still take place but these will diminish as further nididhyAsana is done.)

Note that there is never any question of 'striving to eliminate the ego'. You cannot do this (who would do it?) and there is, in any case, no need to do it. Whilst the body-mind remains, there will always be an ego. What you are aiming for is simply Self-knowledge.

Advaita is that branch of Indian philosophy which accepts the authority of the shruti (Upanishads) and interprets them in a non-dualistic way. 'Orthodox' or 'strict' are not appropriate adjectives. There are other branches which accept shruti but interpret them dualistically or partially so. And there are some that do not accept shruti at all. (Vedanta simply refers to the end portion (anta) of the veda-s, i.e. the Upanishads or j~nAna kANDa.)

Q.320 saMskAra-s, svadharma and karma

Q: I read about the above topics in your book and struggled with them, not only because there are a number of things to remember, but also because how exactly they function is complex.

I thought about what you said regarding svadharma – how not going with it, using the example of Arjuna in the Bhagavad Gita, is bad for one's karma. And I wondered about Hitler.

You might say that it was Hitler's svadharma to do as he did. Had he become an ordinary politician, for example, would that then have given rise to bad karma for him, (in the same way as going against his duty would have caused Arjuna bad karma, when Krishna told him: 'slay thy foes')? But then that seems unfair to him (Hitler), since surely his 'bad actions' (genocide, etc.) as a result of following his svadharma brought him bad karma anyway. So Hitler would seem to lose out either way! Then one might say that what Hitler did was not really his svadharma. I would personally agree with that, since a 'person' cannot act 'outside of Brahman', i.e. everything we do, feel, think is Brahman. This would mean that even Hitler's 'evils' were also Brahman?

The only way I can see out of the complexities of karma and related ideas, is to realize that karma, and such, only apply to a person, not to the Self. So it is a person that has karma and not Self. When there is belief that there is a person, then there will be karma?

However, if that is right, I do struggle with it, since I've concluded already that since body-mind, world etc., come out of Self, then they too must be Self. And so when there is a body-mind, it surely follows that there must be karma? So karma is inevitable? Or does simple knowledge of the Self defeat all this?

A: I can see you have got yourself into some mental knots here but it is a confusing topic.

karma is really simply about cause and effect. If something happens, it must have its consequential effect. The classic example used in the scriptures is that of the arrow leaving the bow (or to bring it up to date, the bullet leaving the gun). Once the arrow is on its way, it cannot be stopped. Similarly, any action of a person must have its consequence for that person. If you do bad things, you will reap the pApa or retribution eventually; good things will bring puNya or merit. If these do not come in this life, they will come in the next, since the consequences are at the subtle level of causal, rather than the gross bodily level.

So, yes, you can say that Hitler was born into a life in which he was presented with the 'opportunities' (to become powerful and commit evil acts etc.) resulting from karma from previous lives. And certainly, the path of least resistance is always to act out of habit, without thought, in accordance with one's existing nature. But this is not to be confused with dharma. dharma has to do with what is right and lawful, in accordance with moral precepts. So svadharma has to do with the way in which one ought to act oneself in order to be in accordance with truth and justice etc. Clearly, Hitler did not act in accord with any universal principles of right and good; at least none with which the rest of the world is familiar! So one has to presume that he was deliberately or unknowingly ignoring his svadharma and following instead the egomaniacal demands of his nature and compounding his 'bad karma' instead of clearing it.

Doing the 'right' thing (according to dharma) is always good, i.e. results in puNya, whether one's own nature is good or bad. The point about Arjuna is that the people against whom he was fighting were 'bad' (they had done unjust things to himself and his family in the past) so they had to be punished. And it was Arjuna's duty, being a warrior, to exact that punishment. And doing the wrong thing is always bad. So you can say that, had Arjuna not gone into battle and killed his enemies, he would have been doing the 'wrong' thing.

The real difficulty comes if you try to reconcile the theory for more than one person at a time. In the case of Hitler, it seems that you can only say that Hitler's actions were in accordance with his karma if you simultaneously accept that it was the destiny of all of those Jews to die in concentration camps. And this seems to stretch the bounds of reason.

You are correct in your assumption that karma only applies to the person. Once I realize that I am not a person (i.e. gain Self-knowledge) then there is no more AgAmin saMskAra generated (because there is no longer anyone acting). And that saMskAra stored up from past lives but not yet maturing is also destroyed. Only the prArabdha saMskAra continues, because this is the 'arrow already released from the bow'.

The entire theory of karma and reincarnation is, as I think Eliot Deutsch described it, 'a useful fiction'. It serves the same purpose as theories of creation, namely to provide an interim explanation of the empirical reality until such time as we come to realize that it is all mithyA. The book to read, if you are really interested in all this, is 'Karma and Reincarnation' by Swami Muni Narayana Prasad, D. K. Printworld (P) Ltd., 1994, ISBN 81-246-0022-8.

Q.390 karma and judgment

Q: On the subject of karma please could you explain who or what decides on the destination of the 'soul' to a higher or lower life form. It would seem to be a judgmental decision based on our behavior so presumably cannot be 'Self' which is unaffected and affects nothing?

A: You have to distinguish between paramArtha and vyavahAra. The absolute reality is that there is only Brahman – non-dual Consciousness. There is no world separate from Consciousness, no people separate from Consciousness. The world and people are mithyA. So, in reality karma has to be mithyA also; there is no birth, no death, no reincarnation, no one who acts and no one to be reborn as a cockroach.

Explanations at the level of vyavahAra are interim explanations for the benefit of someone who does not yet appreciate the above. At this level, there seems to be cause and effect and all the apparent scientific laws that operate in the world. Ishvara is the name given to the 'entity' of 'Brahman + mAyA' who lays down these laws. But the laws are not operated by Him on an individual basis; they are simply the 'rules' that are necessarily followed by everything in creation (such as gravity, Newton's Laws etc.). There is no 'judgment' involved at all.

Q.420 Honoring the truth

Q: I have heard a teacher say that, if you have listened to Vedanta/ Upanishads teaching, you have heard the truth; if you do not honor this by continuing to deepen the listening, there are the following consequences: you will not hear the truth for thousands of lifetimes, and have to be reborn starting again from plants, insects and so on. Can you shine some light on this please?

A: What you have heard is nonsense. The most important

requirement for pursuing Advaita is what is called mumukShutva, which means the 'burning desire' to discover the truth. Once you have that, you are going to continue seeking anyway. The other requirements are things such as a still mind, ability to concentrate and discriminate, ability to control the mind and senses so that your attention is not easily distracted, being prepared to put provisional trust in what is said by the teacher.

The theory of karma says that your actions will have lawful consequences in this life or the next. But this is interim teaching, anyway. The 'bottom line' is that who-you-really-are was never born in the first place and is already perfect, complete and free. You just don't realize this; hence the requirement for finding and listening to a qualified teacher.

Death and reincarnation

Q.19 Are jIva-s reincarnated until they realize?

Q: There seem to be two main schools of thought on the subject of self-realization: one says that all jIva-s are reincarnated until they self-realize, that this is the end-goal, and the other that it doesn't matter either way whether or not we self-realize, that Brahman really doesn't care what happens in that regard.

A: It's not that there are different schools of thought so much as that Advaita aims to teach at the level of understanding of the seeker. Initially, reincarnation is taught so that seekers might believe that they will get there eventually. Once all of the theory has been understood and intellectually accepted, however, it can be appreciated that there is nowhere to get and no one to make the journey.

Also, you must be careful about anthropomorphizing Brahman. Brahman does not act or enjoy (it is akartA, abhoktA). If you are talking about nirguNa Brahman, you cannot simultaneously speak about anything else because there is *only* Brahman. If you want to talk about interacting with the world, you must speak of saguNa Brahman – Ishvara.

Q.66 Do 'spirits' exist?

Q: How does the message of Advaita deal with the possibility of spirits? My own wife claims to see the dead, and some modern, so-called mediums seem to be very convincing. If there is no self and we are just life, 'being', is there some accounting for the possibility that the energies we identify as our selves exist somewhere else after the individual mind dies?

A: The bottom line is that there is the reality (paramArtha) and there is the appearance (vyavahAra). The reality is that there is only the non-dual Absolute (or whatever you want to call it) and that is the (beginning and) end of the matter. The appearance – people and the world etc. – has the effective status that a dream has when viewed by the waker. Within it, what is seen is always mistaken because, in reality, there is no duality of subject and object.

Traditional Advaita does speak of gods, spirits and demons, heavens and hells etc. and such teaching may be useful for some seekers at some time in their apparent lives. But all of these forms are ultimately mithyA – their reality is Brahman. Who-we-really-are was never born and will never die so there is no question of spirits, mediums, heaven and hell etc. having any absolute existence. Conversely, if you believe the individual person to be real, then you may claim the gods and demons also to be real!

As regards survival of the 'soul' after death, traditional Advaita claims that the subtle and causal bodies transmigrate. The gross body returns to dust, or is usually cremated (they used to be left out for the vultures). The jIva is then reborn in a body suitable for working out the accumulated saMskAra. But, during the interim period between lives, the jIva is not available for communication as far as I am aware. (It is not a topic that is usually addressed in traditional Advaita.)

Q.138 Body, memory and reincarnation

Q: I am having difficulty with something that Nisargadatta Maharaj is quoted as saying: "Once you know that the body alone dies and not the continuity of memory and the sense of 'I am' reflected in it, you are afraid no longer".

Surely, when the body dies, there can be no memory as there is no instrument to cognize with. The brain holds the memory which is made up of 'mind stuff', and when that dies surely there can be no persistence of memory? Maybe the quote is a translation mistake?

A: Nisargadatta was part of a formal sampradAya, which meant that he was essentially teaching traditional Advaita (although he became somewhat extreme, especially toward the end of his life!). According to traditional Advaita, the mind is *not* part of the gross body but an effectively separable 'subtle' body. This does not die when the physical body dies but transmigrates. Actions in this life generate merit and demerit according to the motives of those actions. Every 'cause' must eventually have its 'effect'. These stored 'causal' elements *do* survive death and are reborn in a new body in order that the effects may ensue in due course. But the personal memory is not an aspect of this and does not reincarnate. As you note, the memory dies with the brain.

Accordingly, Nisargadatta must have been referring to the continuity of the jIva, with the saMskAra held in the subtle body. A skilled teacher will answer the questions at the student's level of, or readiness for, understanding. For some students, the concept of reincarnation is one that 'strike a chord' and provides satisfactory answers 'for the time being'. There comes a time, if the student continues to study, assimilate and validate the teaching, when these explanations no longer satisfy and a different approach is needed. All study, question and answer, experience, student and teacher and the world of objects are at the 'empirical' level of reality. 'Truth', in the absolute sense, is always only One – there is only the non-dual Brahman.

Q.169 Are only unenlightened jIva-s reincarnated?

Q: My understanding is that only the unenlightened jIva is reincarnated but not the realized man – is this correct?

A: There are some questions that touch on this already: 19, 23a, 50 and 52. Also, question 168, although I was actually answering a slightly different question, will throw some light on this.

Basically, reincarnation is a teaching which is given to fit in with the apparent causality in the world. It is also in accord with Vedic/Hindu teachings about how one should behave in the world (morality/dharma). It is logically necessary for the theory of karma, which states that we must reap the fruits of our actions. Even so, they relate to the jIva – the apparently separate individual living in the world. It is the subtle aspects (vAsanA-s) that are said to transfer from one body-mind to another and, as you say, this ceases once there is enlightenment in the present incarnation.

Q.241 karma and reincarnation

Q: Researching into sharIra trayam [the causal, subtle and gross bodies], I realized there is some mix up in my mind, especially concerning what happens with the sharIra-s [bodies] after physical death, the nature of kAraNa sharIra [the causal body] as such and concerning pralayam [the 'big crunch' when the universe is terminated for a while].

First, allow me to outline my understanding so far:

- for the jIva as well as jIvanmukta, sthUla sharIra [gross body] dies with physical death;
- for the jIva, sUkShma sharIra [subtle body] survives death and then travels to 'find' another physical body;
- for the jIvanmukta, sUkShma sharIra dies with physical death;
- for the jIvanmukta, karaNa sharIra dies with liberation.

If this so far is correct:

1. From Swami Paramarthananda-ji, I have learned that karaNa sharIra dies with liberation. I understand this to mean that, as the

jIvanmukta has stopped taking mAyA for real, karaNa sharIra 'dissolves'. Is this understanding correct?

2. karaNa sharIra being mAyA seems to be entirely collective. But, as it is part of sharIra trayam, I would think that it must also have an individual aspect. If this is so, in what way is it 'attached' to the individual jIva? Is it attached entirely through belief in its reality? Or is there another concept regarding this question?

3. As far as I understand, only sUkShma sharIra travels after physical death. karaNa sharIra does not travel. It is the 'pool' into which sthUla and sUkShma sharIra merge in physical death and (for the jIva) out of which they emerge again. Is this understanding correct?

4. In pralayam, do all the sUkShma sharIra-s of the jIva-s merge into karaNa sharIra? Does karaNa sharIra being mAyA survive pralayam in dormant form?

A: If you try to reason out the fine detail of this, you are bound to become unstuck (i.e. fail completely). In the alAta shAnti prakaraNa (4th chapter of the mANDUkya kArikA-s), Gaudapada systematically refutes the theory of karma on the grounds that, however you try to relate karma and sharIra-s, you are bound to run into logical inconsistencies and fallacies. You are eventually forced to accept that there has never been any creation of world or jIva (ajAtivAda).

You should just stick with the simple idea that the attitude to our actions brings inevitable consequences that, in turn, affect our future behavior. This interim belief persuades us to cultivate 'right' action, which then helps to discipline the mind, direct attention, increase discrimination etc., all of which help prepare for receiving the Self-knowledge that can bring about realization.

In the final analysis, all of this mental argument is tantamount to discussing whether or not the snake is poisonous, what the antidote might be, how far it is to the nearest hospital etc., when all the time what we have in front of us is actually a rope. Obviously I appreciate that the theory of karma exists for those who are still in thrall to the world-delusion, which is why I suggested that simply accepting the basic ideas is sufficient, without trying to pin everything down to the finest detail. This will never be possible.

I can recommend the following book as particularly valuable on this subject (in fact I am not aware of any other that specifically addresses it): Karma and Reincarnation, Swami Muni Narayana Prasad (DK Print World, 1999) [ISBN-10: 8124600228, ISBN-13: 978-8124600221].

It is very readable!

Q.263 Death

Q: When a person overcomes ignorance and realizes there is only One, I think this is understood by the feelings/senses. What happens when this person dies? Can he still feel/sense that only One exists and nothing else. If so, how is it possible? Is this because in order to feel/sense, an individual self should exist? Let me exemplify – do the Buddha, Sri Krishna, Bhagavan Sri Ramana Maharshi still feel Oneness?

A: You have to differentiate between empirical and absolute reality. At the level of the world, a person is born and dies. Traditionally, if the person does not become enlightened, he accumulates karma according to his actions and the net result determines what form and position he will take in a next life. If he does become enlightened, no further karma accumulates and, when the present karma is exhausted, he dies and is not born again.

However, from the standpoint of absolute reality, there is no person. No one is born and no one dies. There is only Brahman, forever unchanging, perfect and complete.

Feelings, perceptions, thoughts, all require a body-mind. When the body dies, the brain dies too. You, as the Consciousness in which the forms arise, remain unchanged. The Buddha, Ramana Maharshi, etc., as persons, died when their bodies died. Their teaching remains. Consciousness was never affected by their birth or their death or their enlightenment.

Q: Everything we understand/conceive we do by our mind/ intellect. What is the value of understanding/feeling the Oneness if death engulfs, and that after death, there is no one to understand/ feel Oneness. Even in deep-sleep, we do not know/feel who we are. So I conclude, only He understands/feels Himself because He alone is living/being. All writings are, ultimately, bogus/nonsense.

A: Nothing is born; nothing dies in reality. The body is formed from the food we eat and eventually becomes food for worms. It was, is and will be only matter – but even that is Brahman. There is only Brahman. The world is Brahman. Consciousness is Brahman. You are Brahman.

Believing that you are the body and that you will die gives little consolation. Knowing that what is said above is the truth, on the other hand, takes the 'sting' out of death.

Q.293 prArabdha karma and reincarnation

Q: What happens once I realize Brahman and let's say I complete my prArabdha karma? Isn't it all just static and boring once I realize that there is nothing at all?

A: Upon exhausting the prArabdha karma, following enlightenment, the body falls away and there is no rebirth.

What do you mean by 'realizing that there is nothing at all'? The truth is that you are everything – unlimited, complete, lacking nothing. How exactly can this be 'static and boring'?

Q: Thanks very much for your kind words and I appreciate your reply. But my question is can there be interaction between jIvAtman and Brahman?

A: At the level of the apparent world, you can worship gods, etc. In reality, there is only Brahman so where is the question of interaction?

Q: Can you please explain multiple birth and incarnations in the material world (vyavahAra)?

It appears that millions of souls interact with each other and all those souls see the same effect of mAyA (universe and its principles) and each of those souls preserves their memory and carries over their karma through multiple generations.

The interesting fact is that, in order to preserve the memories, jIvAtman has to live eternally, even in the world of vyavahAra, so that the same jIva continues to bear the fruit of his karma; otherwise, don't you think there would be cross connection between different jIvAtman-s when they are reborn, because in reality, all the jIvAtman-s share the same memory source?

A: No one can explain why there should be the appearance of multiplicity. In reality, there are no jIva-s or world but equally there is no denying that this is how it appears.

Although saMskAra is carried over to future births in accordance with past karma, memories are not – do you have memories of past lives? From the vantage point of the jIva, there is reincarnation until mokSha. But Brahman was never born and will never die so where is the question of reincarnation?

Q: Well, I may not have memories of my past life but there are instances where people do carry memories of their past lives (for instance Ramana). Please let me know if what I say below is right:

Let's say in vyavahAra:

1. jIva 1 in body of Person A performed some actions and then Person A died. Owing to his prArabdha karma, jIva 1 is reborn as Person B and so it continues until jIva 1 realizes that he is the ultimate Brahman;

2. jIva 2 in body of Person C performed some actions and then Person C died. Owing to his prArabdha karma, jIva 2 is reborn as Person D and so it continues until jIva 2 realizes that he is the ultimate Brahman.

A: As far as I know, there is no *scientifically proven* case of anyone ever remembering a past life. Those instances that have been written about in the West tend to have anecdotal evidence only and are consequently open to deliberate or unintentional deception. (And this deception has been proved in some cases.) I understand that some traditions may have different views on this.

What you say in 1 and 2 is correct.

In a sense, you could go with whatever explanation you like for the vyAvahArika appearance. In the final analysis, all such explanations are mithyA, whether they are scriptural ones or your own invented ones.

Q: As far as I know, there are many theories.

Dvaita philosophy says that soul and Brahman are different and soul can never completely merge into Brahman but can go as close as possible, so that the relation between God and disciple is maintained. Another Western philosophy says that God divided himself into many souls in order to experience himself (so in other words, the main purpose of the soul is to experience itself by allowing God to experience himself as a whole).

All these theories seem to be true. Which one to believe?

A: It depends what has influenced your mental development in the past. If you read the questions on free-will, you will see that I conclude that there is no real choice involved.

Q: I am really thankful to you for replying to my questions but I still have doubts:

1. You say you have realized the real Brahman, so how come it is possible that you don't know anything about other religions (you have stated this in some of your answers)?

2. You say you have realized the real Brahman; do you know your past and future in the world appearance?

3. Can you do miracles?

A: I don't believe I have ever explicitly stated anything about my own 'Self-realization'. What I have said is: "tell me what you understand by the term and I will give you an answer". But, in any case, enlightenment is about Self-knowledge; this has nothing to do with worldly information. Becoming enlightened does not mean that one can subsequently speak Chinese, know what someone else is thinking, predict the future, etc. Nor has it anything to do with miracles of any sort. If such things are at all possible, they are associated with yoga siddhi-s, which again have nothing to do with enlightenment or with Advaita.

Q.308 Nothing dies

Q: I've been thinking about death for a long while and last night something came to me that I wanted to share with you. It's not so much a question, though. Rather, I'm just wondering whether my thinking is 'on the right lines'.

Ok, imagine a dead body lying in a coffin. Let's say that this person lying there is called John Doe. Many people would believe that now John Doe is dead, something would have left the body, that this 'John Doe' identity is no longer there. My thinking from what I've learned about Vedanta so far, is that this 'John Doe' was probably never there as was perceived in the first place.

When a child is born, it can (usually) speak, look, hear, smell, taste, touch and interact with its world around it. This functionality of the body is what we give an identity. We say that these abilities, these functions that the body has, are what constitute the 'self' and so one would have labeled that 'self' as John Doe. And when the brain ceases to function as it had done in life (i.e. the person dies), all the abilities that the body once had stop and so those characteristics that we had labeled as being integral to John Doe's self would also stop (the ability to speak etc.). So we believe that something has gone, something has left, that the John Doe that was once a part of the body is no longer a part of the body.

My understanding is that John Doe as a 'self' never really existed anyway, so nothing is lost when a body dies. All that happens is that a few functions of the body mechanism cease to work; that is all. The 'self' is what gave the body the power to exist in the first place – Brahman. So the self is still there, in the coffin, only now it has moved around a bit. I am no different from the body I am looking at in the coffin, because my true self is not X, it is Brahman and since the body in the coffin is also Brahman, we are exactly the same – non-duality.

What I've tried to explain here hasn't come out exactly as

I understand it. I'm finding it a little difficult to put into words. What I'm basically trying to say is that the true self is not confined to mechanical abilities like talking, looking and thinking; the true self is that power that allows such functions to come about. In death, these abilities do cease, but since the body is still there, so is the self, in a sense anyway. In truth, the 'self' is also a part of the coffin, the pillow in the coffin and everything around it. Nothing is really lost. As the analogy goes, it's like putting salt back into the sea. When a body dies, the self merges with the rest of existence that is Brahman ... but this brings me on to my next concern: the localization of consciousness.

If everything I am is Brahman and everything around me is Brahman, why do I not experience existence from other perspectives? When I walk on the pavement, why am I the one walking on the pavement and not the pavement on which one is walking? Why does my consciousness seem localized to the body? Or is this just an illusion?

A: Very well thought-out questions! Essentially you are right but there is still a slight misalignment of understanding.

Firstly, there is only Brahman in reality – ever and always. So the perception of a separate entity, John Doe, is an error; a superimposition brought about as a result of ignorance. The John Doe form emerges from the womb of his mother, takes in food and grows, takes in ideas and forms opinions and so on. And eventually the body develops diseases, grows old and ceases to move, returning to the earth from which it came. Consciousness animates the form whilst 'alive' and – this is the answer to your second question – it is reflected in the mind of John Doe, thus appearing to give independent existence to that form. But, like the image in a mirror, it does not really have any independent existence at all; there is only really the original source – in this case, Consciousness itself.

So you might imagine a pool of water on the ground. The sun is reflected in it and you might be misled into thinking that the pool has its own source of light. But, eventually (ignoring the possibility of rain for the purpose of this metaphor!), the pool dries up and the light disappears. But the sun is completely unaffected throughout. The brain ceasing to function is the equivalent of the pool drying up. Similarly (an answering your last point), there could be many separate puddles of water on the ground after heavy rain. Each appears to be separate and has its own reflection of the sun but each one is reflecting the same, single, real sun.

And, you are right, everything is Brahman – including the coffin. Everything is Brahman (and Brahman does not move – it is already everywhere). But there is only the appearance of life and consciousness in a form that is capable of reflecting it. Plants have limited capability; humans have correspondingly much more. Similarly, there is no 'merging' with Brahman on death (or enlightenment); it is like the rise and fall of waves on the ocean. Nothing really changes; it is all always only water.

Q.335 Reincarnation

Q: As you know, all spiritual traditions in Tibet, many in India and even the early Christians took reincarnation for granted.

In Advaita however the idea is blatantly refused. Balsekar says that, since there is no ego and the idea of an individual person is an illusion, what or who is there to be reincarnated?

Does this mean that the other traditions are wrong or is it a question of understanding, meaning that the people who argue differently do so from a different level of understanding/ consciousness?

A: It is a question of the level of understanding. Advaita certainly *does* teach reincarnation. The theory of karma is fundamental. Cause and effect operate at the level of empirical reality, as you know from your own experience. It is only from the level of absolute reality that there is no reincarnation, because there is no world, no individual etc.

The entire teaching of Advaita proceeds via adhyAropa-apavAda. The concept has been discussed earlier. Explanations are provided to suit the present level of understanding of the seeker. An example is with respect to creation itself. To begin with, there are elaborate explanations of how the elements proceed from God. Later it is admitted that creation is actually a product of mAyA, like the illusion in a magic show. Only ultimately is it explained that there is in fact no creation at all. This is why Advaita is such a powerful teaching system. It caters for the whole spectrum of seekers, taking you from total immersion in the wrong beliefs that you are the body in an objective world to the ultimate realization that there is only Brahman, and you are That.

It is the subtle body, sUkShma sharIra, which is said to be reincarnated. So the accumulated saMskAra from past actions is carried over to 'bear fruit' in future births as per the theory of karma, satisfying the principle of cause and effect. But this is from the empirical, worldly viewpoint. From the absolute point of view, all this is mithyA only.

Q.344 Death of the small I

Q: While I'm drawn to the apparent peace that sages such as Ramana Maharshi seemed to enjoy, I feel I'm failing to grasp something.

Advaita seems, sometimes, to be totally nihilistic and bleak (although I accept that this would not constitute an argument against its veracity).

It's all very well to say that the 'self' can't die but this seems (from my perhaps benighted viewpoint) to be playing with semantics.

If, with 'my' death, comes only oblivion such as in deepest sleep/ anesthesia, where is the comfort or meaning in this knowledge? The end of my small 'I' would seem to be, in effect, the end of everything since, without my consciousness to perceive it, how can anything be said to exist?

Does one take comfort from the fact that other apparent 'I's continue to experience within the one reality? It may be that my existence is only apparent and that, whether it is followed by oblivion is irrelevant – but it doesn't feel like that from where I'm sitting!

A: Whilst you remain Self-ignorant, you will continue on the 'wheel' of saMsAra, with the consequent ups and downs determined by the fruit of past actions. This is the 'bleak' picture for those who do not make the effort to pursue enlightenment. Death is then a long 'sleep' until rebirth in a new body, which will not necessarily be one that you would choose!

But your question seems to be implying that you think that the death of a j~nAnI would be no different; that striving to become enlightened is a worthless pursuit because you only end up dying anyway. You are correct in identifying all the small 'I's as 'apparent' but wrong in denigrating the real Self.

The reality is that there is only Consciousness, always. All of the rest is simply name and form – mithyA. Nothing can die because nothing was ever born from the perspective of absolute reality.

From the perspective of this empirical world (which has the status of a dream, looked at from the point of view of absolute reality), of course you seem to exist. But this 'small I' is simply a reflection of Consciousness in the mind associated with 'your' body. This body-mind and its experiences are not ultimately real.

In verses I.12 – 15 of the kArikA-s, Gaudapada compares the states of consciousness with our true status – turIya. He explains that the waking and dream states are conditioned by both ignorance and error – we are unaware of our real nature and we mistakenly think that we are separate body-minds living in an alien world of separate objects. In the deep-sleep state, we do not make this mistake because the mind is inactive – all is resolved into its unmanifest, causal state. But there is also total ignorance – the 'cause' is still there, waiting to give rise to the 'effect' of misapprehension as soon as we move back into waking or dream. turIya, however, has neither cause nor effect, neither ignorance nor error. turIya is the 'I am', bereft of attribution (because all attributes are erroneous). Death of the 'small I', as you put it, occurs in both deep-sleep and death, but is only temporary for the aj~nAnI. With the death of the j~nAnI, it is permanent.

Q.375 Conditions affecting next life

Q: I agree that Reincarnation, the next life, isn't real. But it's as real as this life... and, for most of us, this life seems pretty real, even if we know better.

And, as we all know, very, very few people are going to achieve Enlightenment (liberation, realization, mokSha) in this lifetime.

For the above two reasons, I suggest that reincarnation is a reasonable thing to be concerned about.

It's been said that one's next incarnation depends greatly on one's thoughts and state in their last moments of this life. I hope that isn't true, because we aren't always in the best of condition when we die, are we? A person, at death, might be delirious or heavily sedated at a hospital. What then? How does that affect that person's next life?

Has there been discussion, from theory, regarding how this life – and, in particular, a person's condition in the last moments of this life – affect that person's next life?

A: Your position on this topic seems a bit ambivalent! You claim to accept that 'the next life is not real' yet say that 'it is as real as this one'. Does this mean that both are real or both unreal? Whatever you decide, you are never going to have any conclusive proof that there is another life after this; it is this life about which you should be concerned!

Related to this, you think that enlightenment is a rare event. What evidence do you have for this? Many think that, on the contrary, it is not so rare at all; just that many who achieve it do not make a fuss about it!

For both these reasons, then, I would argue that reincarnation is *not* a topic about which you should be particularly concerned. To reinforce this, and hopefully convince you that reincarnation is more of a teaching device than a reality, I suggest you read 'Karma and Reincarnation', by Swami Muni Narayana Prasad.

I, too, have read somewhere that one's thoughts at death influence or even determine the next life. This cannot be literally true based upon the (rest of the) teaching of Advaita. The next birth is determined by the accumulated but unfructified karma from previous lives. Random thoughts at death could only be a whisper compared to these. I suggest that the purpose of any such statement could only be to impress upon the listener's mind the need to change ones attitude and outlook, as well as any actual actions. It is, after all, the motive behind actions which affects saMskAra rather than the action itself.

This sort of teaching counts as karma yoga and its purpose is to purify the mind so that it is in a better state to hear and assimilate the teaching of Self-knowledge – j~nAna yoga. It is *that* which is important!

Q.379 Practice, enlightenment and reincarnation

Q: My understanding is that the purpose of spiritual practice is to purify the intellect so that it 'reflects' Consciousness without distortion. This enables the mind to recognize the delusion caused by ahaMkAra. This would mean that 'enlightenment' is a function of the mind. Is this correct?

If this is so, it would seem to mean that any 'benefits' gained from enlightenment would only apply to this body-mind, in this life. Is this so?

Scriptures indicate that one may have to undergo many lives before gaining mokSha, and suggest that fruits of previous lives accumulate to enable this. But, if enlightenment is an event in this mind, how can previous lives be of any benefit? Is there something in the mind that is 'carried over' into future births?

A: First of all, you should be clear that the whole of this question relates to vyavahAra, to the seeming 'person' who has an apparent life in what seems to be a separate world. All of this is appearance only – it is mithyA, which means that it has no reality of its own, depending upon Brahman for its existence. (A metaphor that is often used is that streams, rivers and oceans seem to have a separate existence but have no reality of their own, depending upon water for their existence.)

Within this mithyA existence of ours, the person carries out various 'spiritual practices' in order to purify the mind so that it is able to take on board this teaching. The practices do not in themselves 'enable the mind to recognize the delusion'. In order for it to do this, it has to be told (by a teacher or book). Then it has to reflect on what it has learned and usually ask questions of the teacher in order to clear up confusions and doubt. Subsequently, usually after further time to assimilate, the realization of the truth of the teaching takes place in that mind. This 'event' in the mind is often called 'enlightenment'.

'Benefits', in the form of peace of mind, lack of disturbance from desires and fears etc., accrue from the mental practices rather than from the 'enlightenment'. But of course you are correct: these 'benefits' only apply to this body-mind in this life. However, according to the traditional teaching, both 'past' and 'future' karma are destroyed upon enlightenment and 'present' karma runs out with this life. Since extant karma is the determining factor for future lives, the realized person is not reborn, because there is nothing remaining to bear fruit.

Karma that has still to come to fruition can be 'good', in a spiritual sense. Someone may have been practicing karma yoga and pursuing the teaching of Advaita and the benefits of this will be carried over to a future life, thus reducing the effort required next time, so to speak. (This explanation has been given to rationalize how Ramana was able to gain Self-knowledge without needing to follow the usual path.)

The mechanism that 'explains' how this can happen involves the storing of karma. The subtle body (which incorporates the mind) resolves into the causal body at death and it is this that eventually dictates the nature of the future life and situation. There are complex processes involved in this. See my blog on this topic if you are interested (http://www.advaita-vision.org/between-lives/ and http://www.advaita-vision.org/the-fires-of-reincarnation/) but suffice to say that it is for 'mythological' interest only!

Q.422 loka-s – 'planes' of existence

Q: I've just started reading about Advaita and Hinduism and wondered about the concept of loka-s. Are these physical or mental places or do they not really exist at all? What do Advaitins believe now, after 2000+ years of advancement of scientific knowledge?

A: Advaita is a 'gauged' teaching – read about the methodology of adhyAropa-apavAda in other answers. The teaching of loka-s etc. is an 'early' one, and was aimed at Hindus who were used to worshipping gods, believing firmly in reincarnation and so on.

If you are interested in reading about it from an academic point of view, the Chandogya Upanishad (around 6.2.9 onwards) tells you all about what happens 'between lives' – pa~nchAgni vidyA. Or read the articles referenced in the answer to Q.379 above. But what matters is the understanding that supersedes this: the world and the jIva are mithyA; there is no birth, creation or reincarnation in reality; no gods or loka-s. There is only Brahman and you are (already) That.

Q: I guess the main issue when I first posed this question to you was that if karma, reincarnation etc. are all illusion, due to our ignorance of who-we-really-are, what purpose do they serve? I mean once we realize we are not the jIva, then karma and reincarnation are irrelevant or better yet don't exist (and never have because we were always Brahman). So they seem to serve no purpose since, although they seem to exist on that level, they are not true.

A: The world seems to be real until you know that it isn't. This includes all of the 'laws' that go along with this from gravity to cause-effect relationship. And who-you-currently-think-you-are will continue to be subject to all those laws, one of which is the law of karma. You are obliged to be aware of, and abide by the laws as long as you believe you are a separate entity in an alien world.

Q: So how does reincarnation fit into this? I mean it isn't really a 'law' is it? So who I think I am reincarnates into a next life based on my karma? But if it's not actually me that's reincarnating (since I am Brahman), then what is it that reincarnates on the empirical level?

A: The subtle-causal body – essentially mind (though not memories) – is what reincarnates. Since you presently identify with your mind-ego, you naturally believe that who-you-really-are reincarnates. In fact, you were never born in the first place. karma is a 'law' just as much as Newton's laws of motion, as far as the Upanishads are concerned.

Q: Obviously we have been born in the past so as to have taken this present birth. A soul polluted by worldly contaminants such as love for family, money etc. is said to be the cause. For the self-realized soul there is no attachment and no birth. My question is how is that a pure soul (before it could have taken its first birth) was still forced to take birth? This would mean that some factor forced the pure souls to take birth for the first time. Does this not contradict self-realization per se which is going back to the purity of soul and ending the chain of births and deaths?

A: All 'living things' have an associated jIva according to traditional Advaita. The nature of the next birth for a human is determined by past karma. Non-human organisms do not gather new karma but could still have karma from earlier human lives – you can go round and round, up and down in saMsAra until such time as you gain enlightenment. Only then are you not reborn. But, as you will appreciate there are countless plants, insects and animals still to come to a human birth, as well as gods and heavenly beings that did not attain enlightenment, to come back down to earth as humans.

But all this is vyAvahArika explanation only – for those who want it and can feel satisfied by it. From an absolute point of view, where is the question of a 'rebirth' when there has never even been a first birth at all? Don't confuse the two levels!

Ishvara

saguNa means 'with attributes'; nirguNa means without attributes. These words go along with vyavahAra and paramArtha respectively. Ishvara or saguNa Brahman is a concept that may be useful to some seekers and relates to 'explanations' within the empirical world, such as cause and effect, karma and reincarnation and so on. From the perspective of absolute reality, none of these things are real. Only Brahman is nitya (eternal). When talking about creation and dissolution etc., Ishvara effectively has to be eternal in order to 'oversee' these throughout eternity. But the bottom line is that anything and everything in the transactional reality has to be mithyA – simply name and form of Brahman.

Q.82 What does 'one with God' mean?

Q: What do you make of the notion that qualitatively we are one with God, but quantitatively we cannot be God? For example, qualitatively, if God is the ocean, then we are waves on that ocean. We are capsules of the spirit soul of God. Quantitatively, however, we cannot be one with God, because God is not susceptible to sin and temptation, like us. Do you think that Advaitins forget the quantitative relationship/disparity we have with God?

A: There is much confusion over the wave-ocean metaphor. The best way to understand it is that the wave is a part of the ocean but both are one and the same water. Similarly, at the level of vyavahAra, the jIva is a part of Ishvara but, in reality both are one and the same Brahman. The notion of god only has relevance at the empirical level. (Advaita is one of the philosophies within Hinduism, and Hindus have many gods.) In reality, there is only non-dual Brahman.

Q: You mentioned that the notion of God only has relevance at the empirical level. Do you mean that our notion of God, then, is dualistic, because our own concept of God does not have its own identity? For example, we cannot know and appreciate 'good' without knowing 'evil'. Does this same dualism apply to the notion of God? Is this how you would come to the conclusion that the only reality is non-dual Brahman?

A: I'm not sure what you are saying here regarding qualitative/quantitative. The point is that, in reality, there is *only* Brahman; it is not that 'we' are one with god. At the empirical level, there is effective duality so that there are jIva-s and there is Ishvara. Yes, these are concepts and are only relevant in vyavahAra. All concepts are necessarily dualistic since there is a subject-object relationship. And, of course, god is also a concept.

That fact that reality is non-dual (whatever you want to call it – Brahman, Absolute, Consciousness etc.) – is something that is passed down from guru to seeker. The oldest recorded 'telling' of this is in the Vedantic scriptures. These effectively tell of the sages who first passed on the teaching. But this is not to say that the seeker accepts it entirely on faith (as do religions that accept the existence of god because this is recorded in a trusted scriptural text). The fact is something that is eventually realized by seekers for themselves.

Q.309b Grace

Q: One is liberated through grace, is that correct?

A: If you take up meditation, you will find after you have been practicing for some time (maybe years), you find that you are able quickly to reach a state of stillness and clarity, in which everything simply rises and fades away without causing any distraction. But, when you return to your normal waking state, any ignorance about your true nature that you had before will still be there. This is because experience (of any kind) cannot bring about the knowledge that there is only Brahman and you are That. The only way to arrive at this understanding is through listening to a qualified teacher explaining the scriptures and subsequently asking questions in order to remove your doubts.

Grace is the word used to rationalize the seemingly random element in all of this. It is through 'grace' that we start to think about all of this in the first place, that we find a suitable teacher and that we finally obtain Self-knowledge. According to traditional Advaita, what we 'get' now is the result of the fructifying karma from actions performed in the past (and not necessarily in this lifetime). For those who believe in a god and routinely worship and/or perform rituals for/to a god, the 'grace' (anugraha) is understood to have been 'awarded' by the god in recognition of the devotional acts. And a seeker may offer prayers to the god for grace to be given relating to the search for truth.

It remains a fact, however, that Self-knowledge can only come as a result of j~nAna yoga (shravaNa, manana), not through prayer, devotion, ritual etc.

Q.346 Brahman, Ishvara and mAyA

Q: I am not clear about the relationship between Brahman, Maya and Ishvara. Maya is said to be inherent in Brahman. Like Brahman, it is ever existent. Ishvara is said to be a product of Brahman and Maya. However, while the universe is governed by Maya, Maya does not govern Ishvara. Ishvara governs Maya although he is a product of Maya. This is confusing.

Secondly, did Shankara deviate from the teachings of Upanishads? The invocatory verse in IshopaniShad – OM pUrNamadaH pUrNamidaM pUrNAt pUrNamudachyate [This is Perfect, That is Perfect, Perfection proceeds from Perfection; you take Perfection from Perfection and what remains is Perfection] – seems to indicate that this world is born out of that Brahman. Shankara does not seem to agree with this view. According to him, the imperfect limited world cannot emerge from unlimited, perfect Brahman and the world is only an illusion created by Maya. What is the correct position?

A: The absolute answer is simple (and the same as the absolute answer to every other question): there is only Brahman; end of story. When you ask questions about the nature of empirical reality, it is like the dreamer asking questions about his or her dream, whilst in the middle of the dream. An answer can be provided which may be deemed to be satisfactory (or not) but, from the vantage point of the higher reality, it has to be effectively illusory, i.e. mithyA. So yes, a frequently given explanation for the world-appearance is that Ishvara manifests it using the power of mAyA. (Ishvara is not a 'product' of mAyA!) But you cannot say that mAyA is 'inherent' in Brahman. That would be two things and Brahman is by definition non-dual.

In order satisfactorily to explain the world as a separate entity, you really need an intelligent and a material cause. Ishvara is posited as these causes and mAyA is the supposed 'magical power' that He uses in order to do this. But such explanations are really for the non-seeker. The true seeker has to go beyond this and realize that there has never actually been any 'creation'; that what is erroneously perceived as separate is only ever name and form of Brahman, the only real, non-dual substrate.

You should also bear in mind that Shankara uses the term 'Brahman' for both the nirguNa (Brahman) and saguNa (Ishvara) aspects. If you read his bhAShya on the brahmasUtra-s, you need to understand this and be able to differentiate; otherwise, you will get confused! But it does emphasize the point that they are really one and the same. It is just helpful to speak of Ishvara when we are talking about the world and the jIva because then we can remember that all these aspects are mithyA.

If you want to understand the relationship:

Ishvara = Brahman + mAyA

jIva = Brahman + avidyA

Since Brahman is non-dual, you also have to recognize that all the other parameters have to be mithyA.

Q.436 Ishvara and the existence of fossils

Q: Dinosaur fossils point to a world history that greatly exceeds the history of human beings. I realize that from the Absolute perspective, there is no creation, no world, and therefore no fossils. However, I also realize that Advaita is not equivalent to solipsism. When 'I' die, the relative world will still continue in 'my' absence. What is puzzling is why there should be any such consistency. When I go to sleep tonight, I do not expect to pick up the dream from where I left off last night. Yet on waking, I definitely expect to be in the same room I went to bed in, with the same clothes hanging in the closet, etc. In short, there is a direct continuity that occurs in jAgrat that does not apply to svapna. Doesn't this very continuity (e.g. fossils having existed for millions of years before 'I' was born) point to a definite need for a Creator, aka Ishvara or saguNa Brahman? Otherwise, I don't see how the continuity would make any sense. 'I' as the jIva cannot have had anything to do with it!

A: Ishvara is just as real as the world. Ishvara is the order that we see, the laws that govern it and so on. All this is empirically real, not absolutely real; it is mithyA. You and I and Ishvara and the world and jAgrat and svapna and suShupti are all mithyA. So yes, if you are talking about fossils and dinosaurs, Ishvara is needed as the creator of the world and of the laws of evolution etc. that enable such things to be a part of our history. Ishvara maintains the waking dream so that I have some clothes to put on when I wake up.

mAyA

Q.141 Question about mAyA and its origin

Q: I am confused about the concept of mAyA and its origin. If Brahman has no attributes and does not act, then what is the origin of mAyA? Is it something that is outside of Brahman? That would negate the whole non-duality idea. I have heard people say mAyA should be understood like waves in a ocean, but then that would require either action by the ocean or an external influence like wind. The explanation that I am under the influence of mAyA and that it is impossible to understand its origin seems inadequate.

A: Have a look at the essays on the subject of Appearance and Reality – these are listed on http://www.advaita.org.uk/discourses/teachers/discourses_by_topic.htm. Quite a few of them deal with mAyA.

You must understand that all explanations about the world appearance are ultimately themselves mithyA because the world itself is mithyA. It is analogous to the dream. Within the dream, you might invent all sorts of explanations for what is happening but, when you wake up, all are superfluous since everything was your mind alone. You are not going to find answers, as such, to question such as: 'why does the universe appear to exist?', 'why is there ignorance of the fact that we are already That?' etc.

There is the reality (satyam) that is Brahman. And there is the appearance (mithyA) which is just name and form of Brahman. There is nothing else. Concepts such as mAyA and Ishvara are there to help us along the way to understanding this.

Q.284 Brahman and mAyA

Q: In Advaitic philosophy, Brahman is everything. How does mAyA have a separate existence? How does Brahman come under the influence of mAyA? Why does Brahman get influenced by mAyA? jIva-s are the result of Brahman's being influenced by mAyA. Are they real or illusionary? Do they represent a deterioration in the original condition of Brahman? The goal of jIva-s is liberation. Does this mean that Brahman under mAyA's influence is to seek Brahman outside mAyA's influence? The number of jIva-s is infinite. What does it mean if a few of them attain liberation?

A: Briefly, your question is confusing paramArtha and vyavahAra – real and apparent. From the vantage point of absolute reality, there is only Brahman. But we seem to see a world of multiplicity and, in order to explain this appearance, we postulate a magical force called mAyA, which we say is wielded by Ishvara in order to create the world. But the world, Ishvara and mAyA are all mithyA – they have no reality of their own, being essentially Brahman only. So, to answer your questions, mAyA does not have a separate existence; Brahman does not come under the influence of mAyA. jIva-s are similarly mithyA (neither real nor illusory); in essence they are Brahman only. Their goal is liberation only because they do not know that they are already free. The aim of Advaita is to remove the ignorance that obscures this knowledge (and the ignorance and knowledge are also mithyA).

The 'formulae' relating to this, incidentally are as follows:

Ishvara = Brahman + mAyA

jIva = Brahman + avidyA.

This 'explains' relationships at the level of the world. In reality (paramArtha), Ishvara, jIva, mAyA and avidyA are all mithyA. Brahman is the only reality.

On the question of why everyone does not become enlightened when one jIva does, see Question 168.

Q.358 mAyA and avidyA

Q: If Atman is perfect, how can it ever be deluded by mAyA? What is the source of avidyA? If there is only Brahman, how and why does avidyA exist?

A: Read the 'Several warnings' section at the beginning of the book!

Atman is never deluded by mAyA. Atma is satyam or real; mAyA is mithyA – it does not really exist as something separate from Brahman; it is only a provisional explanation to account for the appearance. avidyA is a provisional explanation to account for our failure to appreciate the non-dual reality of Brahman. It is also mithyA in the final analysis.

Q.421 Creation and mAyA

Q: I understand that Brahman is Eternal, Changeless Being; it's the mAyA aspect that is puzzling. Why create an illusion and then ignore it through dispassion, observation, witnessing, spiritual practice, etc.? The very thing you (Brahman) made for your play, of a world/dream you now must awaken from? I have often pondered that Brahman did not make/create the world but the mind/Self did through a type of mis-creation or false identification. Does this make any sense?

A: The 'final' message of Advaita is that there is *only* Brahman (i.e. really, *really* 'non-dual'). Ideas such as mAyA are part of the interim teaching to help lead the mind to that final realization. Eventually, they have to be dropped. Brahman did not create anything – there is no world as a separately existing entity – it is all only Brahman.

So yes, you are correct; the apparent separation is effectively generated by the mind as a 'false identification'. In a sense, it is the separation into 'forms', and the 'naming' of these that 'creates' the seeming duality. (But don't overlook the fact that the mind that does this is also a supposed part of this creation and therefore also just name and form!)

Read the adhyAsa series that I posted (http://www.advaita-vision.org/adhyasa-part-1/) or better still read my book 'A-U-M: Awakening to Reality', which is all about this 'final message'.

Brahman

Q.14 Origin of Brahman

Q: How did 'Being' come into being? In other words, how did Brahman, i.e. us and everything, come into being? How can something arise from nothing? And isn't nothing a form of something, anyway? I guess I'm wondering *how* the uncaused first cause (Brahman) could come into being. I just can't conceptualize it. If Brahman is concealing this truth from us (i.e. from itself), then why?

A: I think this is the one they call the 'devil's question'! 'Why is there something rather than nothing?' There isn't ever going to be an answer that is understandable by the mind. How could the infinite ever be comprehended by the insignificant, finite mind of man which after all is only a transient form within that infinitude?

Having said that, Advaita teaches that Brahman is existence 'without limit' (anantam). (This is often translated as 'eternal', but you cannot even say that, since Brahman is outside of time.) In other words, it did not come into being; it has always been all there is and ever will be. There never was 'nothing' but, equally, you cannot call Brahman 'something' for that would imply that there could be some other thing (or nothing) and this is not the case (hence 'Advaita' – 'not two'). So, no, Brahman did not come into being and, more to the point, as I said to begin with, 'you' cannot conceptualize any of this.

As for concealing the truth from itself, this is traditionally the sort of explanation given for creation, namely that, not knowing itself, man was created in order that there could be objective knowing through the mind. Of course, this is just an idea that might appear to some to provide the explanation that is ultimately not achievable. There is no creation, as discussed in the Creation section, earlier in the book.

Q.153 Brahman indescribable yet sat-chit-Ananda?

Q: Absolute Reality is said to be free of or beyond all qualities and yet it is also said that Its nature is sat-chit-Ananda. Since Vedanta is a logical and reasonable path, please help me understand this apparent contradiction.

A: It is certainly true that absolute reality (Brahman or turIya) cannot be 'described'. Language is dualistic so that this must be so. However, this is not the same as saying that we cannot 'point' in the right direction. Words such as sat (existence), chit (consciousness) and anantam (limitlessness) are called lakShaNa-s. [The word sachchidAnanda – sat-chit-Ananda – is often used to 'describe Brahman but the word Ananda is better understood as anantam. Translating it as 'bliss' gives it the sense of a relative degree of happiness, which it isn't.]

The word lakShaNa is often translated as 'pointer'. The dictionary translates it variously as 'accurate description, definition, illustration' and 'characteristic, attribute, quality' but 'indicating, expressing indirectly' is the best translation. It is a 'definition' in the sense of 'revealing' the object, rather than restricting it in any way. Since there is only Brahman, words such as these do not function to differentiate (c.f. the 'red' apple as opposed to the 'green' one).

We cannot 'know' Brahman in the way that we know a fact, as something objectively defined. We 'know' it by virtue of 'being' it. But, to begin with, we are ignorant of our true nature so that words are needed to 'show us the way'. But straight descriptions are not available. Even obvious concepts such as 'sweetness' cannot be described – they are known by direct experience. But if I give you some sugar and ask you to taste it, there is no longer any need to describe it; I can simply say that the quality of that taste is called 'sweetness'.

Brahman is not an experience in this sense but we can still use words, whose meanings we understand, to point to that which is not itself an experience. Thus, for example, we know the difference between 'real' and 'unreal' from everyday experience – the chair on which I am sitting is real and the face that I see in the pattern on the carpet is unreal. 'sat' also means 'real, existing, true'. If Brahman is the only reality, then it clearly must be real and existent, even though we do not know it in any objective sense.

The 'right' words can trigger direct understanding because we are already Brahman. The classic example that I often tell people about is called bhAga tyAga lakShaNa and it is so expressive that it is worth reading again, even if you are already familiar with it (see Q.345).

Obviously lots more could be said here. Answering this one

question fully could constitute an entire course on Advaita! But I think you should get the general idea.

Q.337 The changing world

Q: Since Brahman is non-dual, attributeless, changeless, and eternal, and since Brahman is everything, it must follow that everything is also non-dual, attributeless, changeless, and eternal. So how can it be that we experience duality, attributes, change, and impermanence in the world? How can the changeless manifest change, even if this change is in appearance only (mithyA)? How can there be anything but the 'perfect' unchanging oneness if everything *is* this oneness?

A: If you look at Mandukya Upanishad mantra 7 – possibly the most famous mantra in all of Advaita (and justifiably so) – Brahman is 'described' as achintyam, avyapadeshyam and agrAhyam. The first word means it cannot be thought about; it is beyond the mind or inconceivable. The second means indefinable, not an object of experience. The third means not graspable, beyond understanding or comprehension – it cannot be 'caught' by any of the organs of action.

In fact, here is something I wrote in Nov 11 – I can't recall in what context or whether it was published anywhere:

Absolute Reality (Brahman or turIya) cannot be 'described'. In order for something new to be 'describable' at all, it has to satisfy one or more of five conditions:

- *It can be available for direct perception via at least one of the senses. Then we can give it a name and refer to it.*
- *It may be a species of something with which we are already familiar.*
- *It can have describable properties, such as color.*
- *It can provide a describable function.*
- *It can have some describable relationship with something that we know.*

Since Brahman doesn't have any of these aspects, we cannot talk directly about it. However, that is not to say that we cannot speak of it indirectly. And this is how the scriptures operate.

Some ways in which they manage to achieve this are:

- *Speaking of Brahman as the 'witness' is analogous to saying that the sky is blue – it is an 'apparent' attribute.*
- *Speaking of Brahman as 'Consciousness' (in relation to the body). This is acting as a 'pointer' from something that we know to something that we cannot describe. The classical example is describing a house as 'the one on which a crow is (temporarily!) sitting. It is an 'incidental' attribute.*
- *Speaking of what Brahman is not. The example often used is identifying a man by his baldness – the fact that he has no hair. Thus, Brahman is described as adRRiShTam – (it is) unseen (by any of the senses); avyavahAryam – nothing to do with 'worldly' things; agrAhyam – beyond understanding; alakShaNam – without any characteristics; achintyam – inconceivable; avyapadeshyam – indefinable. (And this is just in one mantra of the Mandukya Upanishad.)*
- *Speaking about something else and about Brahman only by implication. This is what is often referred to as 'neti, net', 'not this, not this'. When we have finished negating, whatever is left must be Brahman by implication. The example that Swami Dayananda's disciples use is speaking of the elder son as being very intelligent (and thus implying that the younger is relatively stupid!).*

So you are fighting a certain-to-be-lost battle if you are trying to 'pin down' Brahman in some way! What is truth, reality or Brahman? Brahman has no attributes and, since we can only describe attributes and not the 'thing-in-itself', the question is essentially unanswerable.

The aim of Advaita is not to tell us what Brahman is but to remove all our false notions, Hence the 'purpose' of neti, neti.

When all attempts to define Brahman have been rejected, as Karl Potter puts it: *"pure consciousness will remain unqualified by adjuncts, and that state of understanding will constitute liberation"*.

And Shankara says, in the BSB II.1.14, that the means of knowledge can only operate in the realm of ignorance so they must inevitably fail to tell us about reality. When you wake up, the dream monsters disappear.

Q.351 Attributes of Brahman

Q: Advaita says that 'sarvam khalvidam brahma – all this (including all objects, which have form) is Brahman'. Therefore, how can we say that Brahman is without any attributes at all (including form)? Surely Brahman must be both with and without form? Isn't this what neti, neti means (not this, not that)?

A: Here is a passage from 'A-U-M: Awakening to Reality':

"... in order to be 'real', a thing must not be subject to change. If A changes into B, it effectively becomes what it was not to begin with; it ceases to be A. How, therefore, can A be said to have been 'real' if it entails non-existence?

Accordingly, only Brahman, Atman or Consciousness is truly 'real'. Anything else – world, cup of coffee, tiger, you and me – is not, in itself, real at all; it is only a particular name and form of Brahman, much as we know that the ring is only name and form of gold.

"There is no word in English to describe this peculiar state of affairs. The Sanskrit term is mithyA. The universe and everything in it, from the grossest brick to the most subtle imagining, is mithyA. These things are not unreal but neither are they real-in-themselves; they have 'dependent reality', depending for their ultimate existence on Brahman.

"That which is 'true' or 'real' is called sat in Sanskrit; 'truth' or 'reality' is satyam. 'False' or 'unreal' is asat (putting the letter 'a' in front of a Sanskrit word usually gives it the opposite meaning). The word mithyA, then, means neither real nor unreal, neither sat nor asat. This is an effective definition of mithyA – neither real nor unreal (sat-asat-vilakShaNa – the word vilakShaNa means 'differing from; not possible to

define exactly')".

The world, then, is sat-asat-vilakShaNa – neither real nor unreal. It is unreal in itself, dependent upon the reality of its substrate (Brahman) for its existence. Name and form are 'imposed' by the mind (which is also mithyA). Brahman itself is without form or any other attribute. Any attribute would limit it, since it would exclude the opposite attribute.

Regarding neti, neti:

At the beginning of the related section of the Brihadaranyaka (2.3.1), it is stated that *"Brahman has only two forms – gross and subtle, mortal and immortal, limited and unlimited, perceptible and imperceptible"*. Simplistically, therefore, when the Upanishad repeatedly utters the pronouncement 'neti, neti' in later mantras, the first 'neti' negates the gross aspects of the universe, i.e. tangible, material aspects (mUrta prapa~ncha), such as the physical body. The second 'neti' negates subtle aspects (amUrta prapa~ncha), such as the mind and intellect. Whatever we can experience, see or think cannot be who-we-really-are, since there is always a subject witnessing these things. I am the consciousness-witness which remains when there is nothing to experience.

The teaching of Advaita is adhyAropa-apavAda. Everything has to be 'given up' eventually, including the concepts of Brahman and mithyA and Advaita and…

(General comments from Q.378, which is not included):

Brahman is attribute-less. You cannot apply logic here. Brahman is outside of time, space, causality (or rather these are mithyA concepts appearing in Brahman). One of the definitions of mithyA is being dependent upon something else for its existence. Everything is dependent on Brahman; Brahman depends on nothing. Also, Brahman cannot be experienced. But it is not non-existent because I, the witnessing Consciousness who cannot experience it *am* Brahman and it is not possible to deny my own existence. Brahman is also changeless, and without limit of any kind. There isn't anything that ever could be that is not Brahman.

[But always remember, from the point made above, that Brahman too is a concept and ultimately has to be given up – absolute reality is ineffable!]

'Consciousness' is used as an English 'equivalent' to Brahman. But it is not the simple consciousness of the person that we say is lost under anesthetic. Consciousness (with a capital) is always there, no matter what the state of body and mind. And it is not the same as the 'awareness' to which we refer when someone is cognizant of some object being present. (Unfortunately, Nisargadatta uses these terms the other way round, just to confuse you!)

(And from Q.385, which is not included – note that these questions are not included because they mainly do not add anything to what has been said elsewhere):

In reality there is only Brahman… ever.

Brahman does not 'do' anything, has no desires etc. So it is not role playing or enjoying the world at 'our' expense, or any other thing that you can imagine, because there is nothing other than Brahman, not even a 'dream'.

But, from our perspective, there does seem to be a world etc. All explanations and reasons are at this level. And everything at this level is not real in itself, it is all just name and form of Brahman; the rope mistaken for a snake. Trying to decide whether or not this snake is poisonous is really a waste of time! What matters is realizing that it is a rope.

In reality, there is no such thing as enlightenment, because there is no one to enlighten. Everything is already Brahman, always was and always will be.

Q.428 A dialog on getting to know Brahman

Q: I'm struggling (a lot) with 'believing in' Brahman.

I realize the problems inherent in this struggle: 1. It's probably futile in my early stage of Advaita studies; 2. Brahman is beyond mind, so any attempt to truly apprehend it is doomed to failure. And yet I persist.

I can walk with Advaita Vedanta through all the 'neti-ing' – I/ Truth am not this, not this – but when Advaita makes the leap to *is* This, I shake my head and turn away. Brahman seems like an abstraction born of fear/uncertainty, like other similar abstractions such as Heaven, The Ground, The Truth, etc. (I am not saying I know that Brahman *is* an abstraction born of fear, rather that it seems to me that it could be.)

So I keep looking for analogies, things I can do or believe in that might be similar enough to Brahman that I could relax into it a bit.

Today I thought: Perhaps Brahman is (quasi-)synonymous with Nature? Nature – 'everything that is' – is all-encompassing in a way that suggests Brahman to me. Science's take on Nature is conceptual, but the essence of Nature is, I think, not conceptual.

So: 'Everything that is' + non-conceptual – this sounds Brahman-esque to me. Yes? No?

A: In a sense, it seems as though you are saying that you want to be enlightened before you are enlightened. You will accept Brahman for what it is when you gain Self-knowledge. Until then, it is best not to try to leap ahead. Advaita is a stepwise process: hearing a bit, asking questions until you understand, and then letting it sink in. Intellectualizing in this fashion is trying to bypass the process.

So, to provide a not very satisfactory answer to your question: you can think that 'everything is Brahman' if you like, but not 'Brahman is everything'. (It is a bit like saying that the ring is gold, but gold is not the ring.) A better way of thinking about it is that 'everything is mithyA', where 'mithyA' means name and form of Brahman. Also, Brahman is not 'non-conceptual'; rather it is itself a concept, pointing to the non-dual reality. It is the name that we give to that which is that reality, which cannot be conceived.

Q: Could be. Though how I feel it is: wanting to know what I'm getting into before I commit. To take a crass example, I might find the initial stages of Scientology very compelling. But if I found out what the path of Scientology had in store for me, the foundation upon which it was built so to speak, I'd no doubt run away screaming!

Advaita says: You will *know*, once you have gone through the program. But I can be manipulated enough to be convinced (for a while) of most anything, provided it is presented in a compelling way. And Advaita is compelling.

A: You have to commit at some point and stop dabbling! In Advaita, 'faith' is being prepared to put your trust in someone/thing that you perceive as being trustworthy, until such time as you realize the truth for yourself. As I said, you want to know it's true before you discover it to be so for yourself. Not possible!

Q: Intellectualizing in this fashion is, for better or worse, a key part of my process.

A: Not too serious a problem. Always been partial to a bit of intellectualizing myself!

Q: As I'm sure you know, saying that 'Brahman is a concept' is confusing, since I've been reading over and over in your books, James Swartz's books, online, etc., that the only thing that *is* real and not a concept is Brahman.

But I'm guessing you mean that the word 'Brahman', and any thought or image of Brahman (no matter how subtle/sophisticated), is a concept. Yes?

A: Correct. Unfortunately, we can only think/talk about Brahman from a vyAvahArika perspective and Brahman is the next level up. Imagine the characters in a dream talking about a 'waker' who is really 'dreaming' them all.

Q: So the thing I'm reading about, the thing I understand Advaita to be founded upon is only an illusion? In fact, I will not know what Advaita is founded upon until I spend more time studying it. Is that about right?

A: You need to be very careful with the word 'illusion'. Rather use the word 'mithyA'. Brahman, although it is concept from the empirical standpoint is nevertheless the only reality. You know that you exist, quite irrespective of a body growing old or a mind trying to understand Advaita. You *are* Brahman.

Q: I hope you're not getting too frustrated with me? For whatever reason, getting it right is terribly important to me, and I will not leave any stone (that I'm aware of) unturned.

A: Not at all. You are asking very intelligent questions and I recognize where you are! I was there up until some years back.

Q: As part of my daily practice, I've been 'Neti neti'-ing a bunch. Yesterday on my walk I realized that everything I sensed, perceived, thought was mithyA. How cool is that?!

Neti-ing comes easy/natural for me. Being aware of Self (= Brahman) does not. But with a little finagling/effort, I sometimes (feel like I) can get there; apprehend 'what is' as a non-dual oneness. The problem is that I don't know if I'm fooling myself, talking myself into seeing what I'm not really seeing. I'm good at that, as are we all, right?

So my question is:

Is it of value, at my current level of understanding, for me to try to apprehend the world as Self/Brahman? (Gently, not violently, more like: to encourage the apprehension to arise on its own.) Could this be a good practice, a way to switch my focus from mithyA to satyam? Or is it best to stick with Neti-ing? Or not to try to do anything at all?

A: That's good, yes. 'Glimpsing' how things really are is always reassuring. But you are still talking about practice and seemingly trying to equate it to knowledge. 'Trying' (to see everything as Brahman or whatever) is 'doing'. 'Doing' is not opposed to ignorance so can never bring about enlightenment.

You can never 'see' or 'apprehend' non-duality anyway. Even the j~nAnI still sees duality in the world; the difference is that he/she knows that it is just name and form of Brahman.

So, no, you shouldn't try to increase the frequency of these glimpses. They are not really important anyway. What you are after is the certainty that, irrespective of what you see or feel, there is only Brahman. That will happen only when the ignorance is swept away by knowledge.

Q.430 Brahman = changeless, eternal?

Q: I'm aware that I'm on (very) shaky ground when I talk/think about Brahman. But there's something that's been bugging me for a long time now about the 'definitions' of Brahman I've read.

Brahman is always described as changeless and eternal.

Let's start with 'changeless'. When I think about a changeless 'force' (for want of a better non-object word), I envision something static and dead, without animus, without vitality. But I can't reconcile this idea with Brahman, the 'mother of all existence and vitality'. How could utter stillness give rise to such a vibrant universe?

On to 'eternal'. Why does Brahman have to be eternal? Why couldn't it have arisen with the Source Event (Big Bang, etc.) and evolved into its 'current' fullness? Likewise, why couldn't it end with the collapse of the universe back to a zero-dimensional point?

So changeless and eternal elude/confuse me. But I suspect that's because I'm trying to image-ine them, which is an oxymoron: conceptualizing the non-conceptual.

This wording works *much* better for me:

Brahman is not of change, and not of time ... both of which are human concepts.

Is this translation accurate? Does changeless not mean unchanging (which is built on the concept of change), rather: beyond change? Does eternal not mean never-ending (which is built on the concept of time), rather: beyond time? Instead of thinking changeless and eternal, can I more accurately think: the concepts of change and time do not apply to Brahman?

A: You are essentially correct. Brahman is 'beyond' time and space in the sense that every thing/concept exists 'within' Brahman and is ultimately mithyA. Thus Brahman is changeless because change requires time – a 'state' at one moment in time and a different state at some later time. 'Eternal' is not really a good word because it presupposes existence in time; it means 'lasting forever', i.e. for all time. Time and space come into existence with creation, as you suggest with the big bang; and cease to exist with the end of the universe (pralaya). The scriptures say that the entire duration of creation is but a day in the life of Brahma, And then there is another ... and another ...

You should not think of 'changeless' as dead or static. Think of the axle at the center of a wheel. Everything moves around it while it remains still. As T. S. Eliot says (Four Quartets, Burnt Norton):

"At the still point of the turning world. Neither flesh nor fleshless;
Neither from nor towards; at the still point, there the dance is,
But neither arrest nor movement. And do not call it fixity,
Where past and future are gathered. Neither movement from nor towards,
Neither ascent nor decline. Except for the point, the still point,
There would be no dance, and there is only the dance".

Q.432 'Definition' of Brahman

Q: So Brahman is, 'by definition', that which is beyond mind, conceptualization, understanding etc.?

If one takes this seriously, not just metaphorically/allegorically, how can one validly say anything at all about Brahman? For example, Brahman is: unchanging, timeless, attribute-less.

If it's unknowable, how can we know these attribute-less attributes about it? We are told that Brahman is real, we are Brahman. But if we can't know/fathom Brahman, how can we know it is real or that we are it? Does it ultimately all come down to believing the conclusions/insights of the scriptures?

A: Brahman is not anything 'by definition', because we cannot define it.

It is true that you cannot, strictly speaking, say anything at all about it. All of these statements from the scriptures are simply pointers. You know what those words mean so that your mind can gain some insight. Ultimately, the accumulation of insights enables the mind to make that catastrophic (in mathematical terms) 'rearrangement' that we call enlightenment. The problem is simply that all concepts and objects are 'known' so cannot be Atman-Brahman. Atman is the 'knower' and there would have to be another knower to know it. Since there is only Brahman in reality, there cannot be anything else to know it.

But Atman is not something that is not known. Indeed it is known more intimately than any concept-object because we *are* the Atman. And the Atman is neither an object nor a concept. Here is what Sureshvara says (naiShkarmya siddhi III.47-48):

"Because the Self is of the form of constant awareness, it requires no second means of knowledge to reveal it; because it is without sound or other attributes it is beyond the sphere of doubt. The Self cannot be known through the empirical means of knowledge such as perception, etc., which are but phlegm coughed up by the thirst for life. Indeed, it is not a possible object of empirical cognition, since it is the innermost Self and since it exists for its own sake".

Another reason is that all forms of perception are directed outwards, so that we could never 'perceive' the Self. And, since inference is itself based upon perception, we cannot infer the Self either.

So, yes, you are effectively right that, when it comes down to topics such as this, the scriptures are the final, indeed the only, authority. But it is not exactly 'faith' as this word is normally understood. The scriptures do not ask us to believe in anything that is unbelievable. That we are the Atman is effectively self-evident. What the scriptures tell us is that this Atman is Brahman.

[Note that I have posted a series of four articles, entitled 'What is Brahman?' that discusses this whole subject and explains the two ways in which we can talk about Brahman – svarUpa and taTastha lakShaNa-s, intrinsic and incidental definitions (http://www.advaita-vision.org/what-is-brahman-part-1/).]

Q.467 Existence of Brahman

Q: Western philosophers disagree about whether 'existence' is or is not a property/predicate. What does Advaita say?

If existence is seen as a property/predicate, 'Brahman exists' would (at the paramArtha level) be un-true ... another assertion about Brahman that is ultimately meaningless.

If existence is not seen as a property, 'Brahman exists' would mean that Brahman is not non-dual, because existing only makes sense if there is a non-existing, and that is two.

A: You are falling into the vyavahAra-paramArtha trap. You are trying to say something about that which 'cannot be spoken of'. If you say anything at all about Brahman, you are effectively saying that Brahman is dualistic. And of course it isn't. That is why, ultimately, you cannot say anything at all. What Advaita does is to use pointers, (as if) attributes, negative statements… and so on, in order to bring the mind closer to understanding. In the end, they are all 'taken away' again, having served their purpose. This is the meaning of adhyAropa-apavAda.

Atmananda says: *"Any question which has the slightest reference to the Absolute cannot be answered in the relative and the question does not arise in the Absolute".*

Here is what Shankara has to say on the matter (commentary on Gita 13.12):

"Only an entity which is an object of sense-knowledge can become an object of affirmative predication of the form 'it is' or an object of negative predication of the form 'it is not'. Reason also proves that Brahman cannot be expressed by words denoting existence (sat) or non-existence (asat). All words used by speakers for the purpose of conveying meanings and listened to by the hearers do convey their meanings through the categories of class (jAti), action (kriyA), attribute (guna), and relation (sambandha), and not otherwise, for no instance to the contrary is seen. Now when we say 'cow' or 'horse' we do so through the category of class; when we say 'cooks' or 'reads', we do so through the category of action; when 'white', 'black' etc., through the category of attribute; when 'rich',

'having cows' etc., through that of relation. But Brahman has no class and hence cannot be expressed by words like 'existent' etc.; nor has it attributes... It stands to reason to hold that, not being an 'object' and being the Atman, it cannot be expressed by any word whatsoever".

Q: Great quotes, both. It's as if I asked Atmananda and Shankara the questions directly!

I've ended up at the following point many, many times. It seems to be my final hurdle with fully accepting the teachings of Advaita. And I honestly don't know if it's just another mind trap-game that I shouldn't pay much heed, or if it's an indicator that Advaita might not be the most fruitful path for me:

If Brahman has no attributes, cannot be expressed by any words/images/ideas (even that it exists), cannot be seen or found or understood by the human mind ... how can it be established that Brahman is real(ity) and not a figment of group-mind imagination, an invention devised by ancient philosophers to lend the chaos and suffering of life a sense of order and salvation? In other words, and to be (respectfully) blunt: How can it be established that Brahman is not wishful thinking, a kind of God/protector delusion as is seen in so many religions? The two answers to this that I know are: 1. The word of enlightened sages. 2. One's own conviction after going through the learning process. But sages are human and humans can be self-deluded and wrong (singly or collectively), and the human brain-mind can convince itself of pretty much anything given enough time and motivation (such as freedom from suffering).

A: Your position sounds like that of the (would-be) 'Christian' or whatever asking 'How can I know that God exists?'. You know that you would eventually hit the same problem if you followed any other so-called path. After all, all paths must lead there (or somewhere similar) eventually. What you are really talking about is being on the cusp of enlightenment. And the (only) solution is to keep repeating the shravaNa-manana cycle until the penny drops. You are not going to get proof in the repeatable scientific manner, are you? Because you are attempting to cross the uncrossable boundary between empirical and absolute.

Q: I just ran into something I find very interesting, because it's a kind of bridge between my two favorite teachings: Advaita's Atman is Brahman, and Buddhist emptiness (shUnyatA).

(Note that I'm conflating vyavahAra and paramArtha here; consider it 'poetic license' for bridge-building.)

I was thinking up to now that since Brahman has no attributes, one could say that Brahman does not exist (assuming 'existent' is an attribute). But now I see that 'non-existent' is also an attribute. So it would be more correct to say: Brahman neither exists nor does not exist. And this is just a step away from emptiness's glorious tetra lemma: 'Brahman neither exists, nor does not exist, nor both, nor neither'.

A: As I have said, I don't really know anything about other teachings. I also said that Shankara rejects Buddhism in both his Brahmasutra and Gaudapada kArikA commentaries. Read 'A-U-M', where I deal with this to some degree. None of what you said seems convincing. Advaita, too, says that you cannot say anything about Brahman *as an object*. But your arguments say nothing about Brahman *as the subject*. You can deny things as much as you like but you can never deny the consciousness behind the act of denying.

Q.449 Definition of Consciousness

Q: Do you have the perfect definition of Consciousness as per Advaita Vedanta?

A: Traditional Advaita prefers to use 'Brahman' as referring to the absolute reality, although the aitareya upaniShad says 'praj~nAnaM brahma', which is translated as 'Consciousness is Brahman'. Probably the most famous 'definition' (as far as that is possible) is the one in the Taittiriya Upanishad (2.1.1): satyam j~nAnam anantam brahma – Brahman is real/truth/existence – knowledge/consciousness – limitless.

And in 3.1.2, the same Upanishad says that one should strive to know that from which all these beings are born, that in which they live and exist, and that to which they return – that is Brahman.

Brahman is the sRRiShTi sthiti laya kAraNa – the cause of the creation, maintenance and destruction of everything.

And so on! There are lots of 'pointers' but no definition as such, as explained in the answers above.

Q: Maybe I'm asking about consciousness with a lower case 'c' – I just want to know how you would define *that* word.

A: Nothing special here. The Sanskrit word is 'chit'. Swami Dayananda's definition is 'limitless self-effulgent awareness; the self-revealing'. The book 'A-U-M' tells you all about the 'states of consciousness' and that their 'substratum' is turIya. See the article I wrote about 'states' of consciousness (http://www.advaita-vision.org/states-of-consciousness-2-3-4-and-1-2/).

satyam and mithyA

Read my essay on mithyA (http://www.advaita-vision.org/origin-and-meaning-of-the-word-mithya/) for more, general information on this topic.

Q.3 Purpose, satyam and mithyA

Q: I understand that everything is a concept, that all that is really here is Consciousness. And yet, isn't the mind also Consciousness? Isn't the whole idea to witness the concepts, know that if they are coming from Consciousness that there is some truth to them as well, and yet it is not the whole truth? Therefore I am not attached to the concepts – for example I play a lot with Vedic astrology and have yaj~na-s (large pUjA-s) performed for me (incredible experiences with both, and I know that I am just playing, having fun, opening more to the awakening) – and I know that these practices are not the 'whole truth'. Does this make sense? Perhaps you have more to add to this?

A: The only sensible purpose for the presumed person must be to discover who they are, to realize the truth, to understand the nature of reality.

Practically all of the words in the above sentence should really be put into quotation marks, in recognition of the fact that they are concepts and, as such, do not correspond with the way things actually are. The fact of the matter is that we cannot 'under'-stand reality; we can only stand 'as' reality. It is only the mind or ego that seeks, that wants to reach somewhere and get something. And the mind and ego are nothing more than concepts themselves so the whole idea is a non-starter.

Yes, the fact of the matter is that all 'things', including concepts, are nothing but Consciousness but until this is directly realized, we are in the position of the man seeing the rope but thinking it is a snake.

The Sanskrit word for 'truth' is satyam and this is also the word for reality. The only reality is Brahman. Everything else in the world, including concepts, is mithyA. There is no English equivalent for this word.

The metaphor that is often used to explain it is that of clay and pot. The clay exists before the pot is made. Whilst the pot is in use to hold something, it is still clay. And after the pot has been broken, the clay is still there. Advaita defines 'real' as being that which exists in all three periods of time (past, present and future), so that it is only actually the clay that is real by this definition. Yet whilst the clay is in the form of the pot, it would not be true to say that the pot does not exist. Clearly it has some reality but it cannot be described as real according to the definition. But neither is it false, since we can use it to carry water about, while the clay can almost certainly not. Its reality is entirely dependent upon the clay and, moreover, it is always clay and nothing but clay whether it is in the form of the pot or not. The pot has a 'dependent reality' and is said to be mithyA.

Similarly, the world did not exist a few billion years ago and will be swallowed up by the sun in few more. The reality upon which it depends is Brahman. Brahman exists before during and after the world. The world, whilst it exists is nothing but Brahman. Brahman is the only reality; the world is mithyA. And the same with concepts, emotions etc.

Ultimately, of course, everything is satyam because that is all there is. It is the mind that mistakes separate things as real. In fact, everything you experience is mithyA. But the essential, unqualified feeling of existence about which you can never have any doubt, is Atman, the reality. This is what I am referring to as 'I am'. This 'I am' does not disappear in deep-sleep – it is the world that disappears. Also, the idea of lIlA – that Brahman manifests as the world to enjoy/know itself is part of the interim teaching. The final truth is that there has never been any 'manifestation'.

Q.51 Why can't I feel your sensations?

Q: Awareness seems only to include the sensations that *this* mind/body seems to have, not those that *that* mind/body seems to have. Your pain doesn't hurt me, or even seem to. If there is only one awareness, and I am that, it would seem to follow that there are no sensations that any other mind/body seems to have (none are present in *this* awareness; therefore none are present in awareness; therefore none exist, even in the realm of illusion).

However, I don't understand you to be saying that other apparent people are any different from 'me', or that this particular mind/body is somehow a focal point for the one Self. I hope you see my confusion. I imagine the answer is something to do with the concepts of this and that being dualistic in nature, but in a sense that is my point: awareness seems to be differentiated and to exist in separate pockets, but this would contradict the idea that it is 'the real', and that reality is non-dual. Perhaps I have not grasped what is meant by non-dual yet. I would certainly be grateful for any clarification you can offer.

A: This sort of question is indicative of too much thinking! The mind can tie itself into all sorts of knots trying to sort it out.

A metaphor that might help is that of the sun reflecting from different media. Suppose that there are some different objects on the ground – a clean mirror, a dirty puddle of water, a white ball, a matt black card. You can see all of the objects but you cannot see the reflected sun equally well in each of them. The mirror shows a clear bright image, the puddle an imperfect one; the ball reflects bright light but no sun image and the black card just looks black. Each object reflects the light in a manner related to its own particular nature. What you see is the end result – the reflection alone. By looking at the object, you do not see the original sun. Similarly, the mind of a person reflects Consciousness according to its own particular nature. A criminal, with many conflicting desires and motivations, lack of inhibitions or concerns for others, will behave quite differently from a spiritual person who thinks and acts selflessly with a quiet mind. You see the individual behavior, which is a manifestation of the 'reflection' of Consciousness in the mind, but you do not see the 'original' Consciousness. Similarly, the manner in which you 'see' depends upon your particular nature. Both physical aspects (eyes and brain) and subtle aspects (mental acuity, concentration etc.) will affect what is seen.

The reality is non-dual but the appearance in the world is that of duality. Knowing the truth does not change the appearance or functionality. A clay pot is nothing other than clay but a lump of clay will not carry any water! Read the other questions and answers in this section and on Appearance and Reality for more explanations on all of this.

You should also avoid confusion of levels of reality – the source of most of the confusion in Advaita. It is safest to refer to the non-dual reality as Brahman. Awareness of pain or objects requires a body and sense organs and these only 'exist' at the empirical level of reality. Actually they are all mithyA, names and forms of Brahman. If you are speaking 'at the level of' Brahman, there are no other bodies. *Nor is there a body-mind of your own*. There is nothing to sense (as something separate from yourself) because there is nothing separate.

An even simpler way of looking at it is this: at the level of absolute reality there is only Brahman; at the level of empirical reality, there appears to be many separate things, all of them perceived as 'other', but again there is actually only Brahman. This truth is obscured by ignorance. Brahman is satyam; all appearances are mithyA.

Q.411 Action and knowledge

Q: Brief scenario: While walking I notice the floor is wet. I decide to walk carefully because I fear I might slip and fall otherwise.

I could think that the entire situation takes place within Consciousness; all of it is in fact Consciousness alone. This would mean that the fear of slipping and falling, and the decision made to walk carefully (or even the decision not to walk carefully) are also Consciousness. Am I correct here or do I depart from Consciousness each time I make a decision and execute it etc., as in that scenario?

A: Floors, walking, slipping, deciding etc. are all mithyA – they are not real in themselves. Their substratum – Consciousness – is the only reality. But neither are they unreal. From your standpoint in the world, they are real. So walk with care!

Swami Dayananda often referred to the story of the sage running from a rogue elephant. Here is how Krishnan Sugavanam (one of the other bloggers at Advaita Vision) told it:

"I remember a story which once Pujya Swami Dayananda Saraswati narrated. There was a King in whose court there were a number of preceptors from various philosophies, including one from Advaita. The King was very close to the Advaitin and the other philosophers were looking for the first opportunity to prove the Advaitin wrong. One day, when the King and his retinue were walking in a forest, suddenly there appeared a wild elephant. The Advaitin was the first one to take off and run for cover.

Later, when all of them assembled in the King's court, preceptors of other philosophies wasted no time in grasping the opportunity to point out to the King, that though the Advaitin taught everything was mithyA, he was the first one to run on seeing the wild elephant – and they asked 'Why would the Advaitin run on seeing the wild mithyA elephant?' The Advaitin responded calmly: 'yes I did run – but who said my running was satyam – it was also mithyA'. :-)"

Q: Just to clarify (because my focus is on the decision made and the execution of that decision): my decision to walk carefully on the wet floor and the Advaitin's decision to run from the wild elephant are the same – the decisions made were just mithyA?

A: Decisions take place in the mind, and the mind is mithyA. Everything that is part of the dualistic world is necessarily mithyA. The only reality is Brahman-Consciousness-Atman-Absolute (whatever you want to call it) (although, to be pedantic, the 'calling' of it is also mithyA).

Q:

1. Does that mean that each time I make a decision in my daily life, I am departing from Consciousness and reinforcing my dualistic mind, which in turn will keep me in saMsAra?

2. How does an Advaitin go through the dying process, death itself and after death state?

3. How does one who lives and works in the world ('householder') insure that he is totally thought-free? (Otherwise, if he cannot be totally thought-free, he will not realize his Self fully etc.?)

A: Have you read any of my books? The latest 'A-U-M: Awakening to Reality' may be the one to read, though 'Book of One (2nd edition)' is more general.

You seem to be under the illusion that something is either mithyA or Consciousness. There is only Consciousness, ever, whether you are a seeker or a j~nAnI. You cannot 'depart from' Consciousness.

There are descriptions in the scriptures about the process of death and rebirth. But the 'bottom line' is that who-you-really-are

(Consciousness) will never die because you were never born.

Thoughts are part of living in the world. Having Self-knowledge does not mean that you no longer think!

Q: I failed to state clearly my problem so far. From 'The 40 Verses on Reality' by Bhagavan Sri Ramana, which I read long ago, my conclusion was that if I perceived the truth that 'I am a body' is mithyA only, then all thoughts including decisions and choices will also be perceived as mithyA only .

I started having problems when I re-read again the 11th and 13th paragraphs of 'Who Am I?' by Bhagavan Sri Ramana in which all thoughts (including decisions and choices) must be annihilated immediately and consistently (11th paragraph), and in which in which no thoughts are allowed to arise (13th paragraph). I thought those two paragraphs meant that no thoughts should *ever* exist or arise.

Looking back, comparing both '40 Verses On Reality' and 'Who Am I?' together, I think what Bhagavan meant was simply to view all thoughts that arise (including decision making and choices) as simply mithyA and nothing more.

A: Self-knowledge *is* enlightenment. You don't realize the truth 'intellectually' and then have to go away and *do* something. Action is not opposed to ignorance, so no amount of 'doing' can ever bring about enlightenment.

Much as I respect Ramana, books such as 'Who Am I?' and '40 verses' etc. are not really very helpful. (The 'Talks' are better in a general sense, because they cover lots of useful independent aspects.) The idea that you have to somehow 'destroy' thoughts (manonAsha) is positively unhelpful, because the literal understanding is wrong. Read my article (http://www.advaita-vision.org/manonasha-not-the-literal-death-of-the-mind/) to (hopefully!) appreciate this.

Q: So everything that we see/experience is mithyA; nothing really matters ultimately. It is like when one wakes up from a dream – whatever was happening in the dream is just done and gone and meaningless. So having a very firm knowledge is the whole key or else one can easily get caught up and identified with this appearance again – and suffer the consequences.

A: Nothing matters from the vantage point of absolute reality because nothing is changing; all is already and always Consciousness only. But from the vantage point of the world, things clearly do matter. The truly important aim is to move from the position of believing the world is real to knowing that it is mithyA (whilst still acting as if the world were real). You must never forget that, within the context of the world, one does suffer the consequences of one's action.

Q: Having read the article by Peter Bonnici (http://www.advaita-vision.org/can-you-accept-that-the-world-is-mithya-12/), I clearly understand that objects depend on Consciousness for their existence.

However, I don't understand why there can't be Consciousness *plus* matter, which thus produces the 'real' world/universe that the waker sees.

A: The philosophy that claims there are two principles – matter and spirit (prakRRiti and puruSha) – is sAMkhya and this is refuted by Shankara in the brahmasUtra. Can I ask if you have you read 'A-U-M'? It covers all of this material in depth. Peter's article addressed just a few verses of Gaudapada.

One point is that you should not think that Advaita claims that there is no matter in an empirical sense. At the level of practical experience, duality is a given. What Advaita says is that, if you listen to the explanations of the scriptures and use reason to analyze this, you are led inescapably to conclude that there cannot have been any creation. Consequently, since Consciousness/Existence is also unarguable, there cannot be anything else. This is a very abbreviated summary obviously.

Therefore, it is not just that objects *depend* upon Consciousness for their existence; they actually have to *be* Consciousness.

Q.461 mithyA and vyavahAra

Q: What is the difference between mithyA and vyavahAra?

A: vyavahAra refers to the empirical waking world of objects and people etc. It is what most people would call 'reality'. But, of course, it isn't real from the dreamer's point of view – to the dreamer, it is the dream that is 'reality'. When we wake up, we know that the dream could not have been real – we were lying on the bed for the entire time and the lakes and mountains would not fit in the bedroom. The dream world is called pratibhAsa – it only appeared to exist whilst we dreamt. There is only one 'absolute reality', and that is called paramArtha. The absolute reality is Consciousness or Brahman. These can be thought of as the three 'categories' or 'levels' of reality. Something that is 'impossible', such as the 'son of a barren woman' is called tuchCha – completely unreal, empty, and utterly non-existent.

Neither the waking nor the dream worlds can be called 'unreal', since we actually perceive them – there must be something there, even if it is only an image in the mind. So, if these worlds are neither real nor unreal, what are they? The answer is 'mithyA'. Their reality is 'borrowed', as it were, from Brahman. All of the vyAvahArika and prAtibhAsika levels are mithyA – they are name and form of Brahman. The pAramArthika level is real or satyam.

You cannot talk meaningfully about Advaita without accepting the traditional stance of absolute and empirical levels of reality. The empirical level, though ultimately mithyA, is the one that we irrevocably occupy until the death of the body, whether we are 'enlightened' or not. It is here where the ignorance takes place and here where the clarification has to be made. If you appear in the middle of my nightmare and say "don't worry, you are actually lying on your bed and none of these monsters are real", it is not going to help because it is the 'dream self' that is frightened and the dream self is definitely not lying on a bed!

Teaching Devices

Q.50 If lIlA is true, why is there enlightenment?

Q: If the whole point of lIlA is for the Self to be playing games of illusion with itself and pretending to be separate beings, why is it that in some of these games there is the seeing through of the illusion? What would be the point of the Self revealing the illusion to itself, because surely once the illusion is revealed, the game is up and there is no point in the continuation of the game?

That's the main question, but I also have a side question. I've been reading the essays on your website written by Dr. K. Sadananda, and somewhere he writes about how the progress made towards enlightenment in this lifetime is not lost in the next lifetime. This looks to me like an allusion to the Buddhist doctrine of reincarnation, but if there is no separate individual entity, how can there be continuation between subsequent lifetimes of such non-existent entity? To say that a person for whom enlightenment happens very quickly upon hearing about Advaita must have made great spiritual progress in previous lifetimes in order for this sudden enlightenment to have happened is, surely, creating causal links in the mind only? Isn't reincarnation an unprovable theory? Perhaps useful as a paradigm or a metaphor maybe, I'm not sure. It could be a bad metaphor though, as it could induce fear and anxiety about making spiritual progress in this lifetime to avoid hardship in future lifetimes.

A: Good questions!

The main thing to be borne in mind about lIlA is that it is just a placebo device to satisfy the questioning of the enquiring mind until such questions no longer arise. (See other sections for details about adhyAropa-apavAda.) It is simply not possible to make any statement about the nature of reality, much less to assign motivation to a supposed creator. So, yes, at a certain point in a seeker's progression, it can be useful to talk about 'playing games etc.' – this may stop the seeker from asking lots of unanswerable

and unhelpful questions. But, beyond a certain point, these ideas cease to be helpful or meaningful.

The particular adhyAropa that is helpful at any given time really depends upon the particular seeker's nature. For some, i.e. those who subsequently ask questions such as the one you have asked(!), the lIlA concept is not particularly useful. Accordingly, my suggestion would be to apply apavAda now and move on to some more useful prakriyA!

The more fundamental aspect of your question – why some 'people' become enlightened and some don't – is much easier to answer once you have dropped the idea of a Self wanting to 'play games'. It is simply the case that in some minds, knowledge arises/arrives, which nullifies the ignorance that is covering over the truth. If you want to pursue the metaphor of game, however, you could say that there would not be much point in a game if there were not sometimes winners!

The same argument applies to reincarnation (which belief is prevalent in Hinduism as well as Buddhism). At the level of the empirical world (vyavahAra), where we believe ourselves to be bodies and minds, if bodies are considered to be real, then birth and death are also real and the process is cyclical. In order to explain the principle of karma, with cause and effect through action, it is necessary to postulate that minds accumulate saMskAra as the 'fruit' of those actions. For the whole process to work, it is then necessary to suppose that the mind, with its accumulated saMskAra, survives death and the 'soul' is reborn. As with lIlA, all of this is retracted once there is greater understanding but, for many, it serves a necessary and very useful function in preparing the mind. As you can imagine, it inculcates a very positive and unselfish outlook on life if you believe that bad actions may bring about rebirth as a cockroach!

Q.104 On reading a single text as a practice

Q: Advaita seems to require a lot of reading. As a student who

aims at enlightenment, I wonder if it is sufficient to study one text intensely and repetitively instead of studying many different texts.

I also wonder if it is sufficient simply to consider the three propositions (Brahman alone is real; The world is mAyA; jIva is Brahman) over and over again.

I find myself frequently doing this following exercise. I consider the mistaken equation 'I am this thing or that thing'. And then I consider that this I, this pure subject, this pure awareness, cannot possibly be 'this thing or that thing'. I wonder if this method is sufficient for enlightenment.

A: Studying a single text is not really a good idea. The problem is that, if you misunderstand something, that misunderstanding is simply going to be reinforced by repeated reading. If, on the other hand, you read a different presentation of the same topic, you may see the contradiction and then rectify your view.

A good example is in your suggestion of reflecting on 'Brahman alone is real; the world is mAyA; jIva is Brahman'. This is a crucial misunderstanding of the statement, which should be that the world is mithyA; mAyA is the supposed power that brings about the world appearance.

This also illustrates that reading is not actually a very reliable source of knowledge. Ideally you need a qualified teacher who can discuss a topic with you and insure that you have the correct understanding.

Finally, doing exercises of any kind is not likely to bring about enlightenment. We are already Brahman, we just do not realize this – i.e. there is Self-ignorance in the mind. What is needed to eliminate this is Self-knowledge. The main source of such knowledge is the scriptures, which really need to be explained by a teacher.

Q.128 Neti, neti – not this, not this

Q: As Self-ignorance is replaced by Self-knowledge, there arises an understanding of the utter purposelessness and lack of meaning

in our apparent 'lives'. Yet sensations, thoughts and emotions continue to arise – aches and pains in our aging bodies; doubts over future choices, concerns over finances, etc. – universal human experiences. What then arises is a sense of hollow emptiness, that nothing really matters, and that there seems no point in making any effort.

If 'waking up in the dream' results in such bleak despair, it would appear preferable to go back to sleep and continue with the dream of having a life and a future to control. Being lost in a relative reality is more comfortable than having awareness of an absolute reality that sweeps away all sense of direction and purpose.

However once the illusion is seen through (the rope is seen, not the snake) it seems as if there's no going back. It is seen that any effort to change or achieve happiness is a movement away from 'what is', and that 'just this' is absolutely appropriate and perfect. But where is the 'bliss' of pure Being? Is there such a thing as the 'dark night of the soul'?

A: *"That which is only living can only die"*, as T. S. Eliot says. Is a flower not beautiful? Is not the whole process of bud to flower to dropping petals a marvelous process? Could you have one aspect of that process without the others?

All of that is part of the movement of the apparently separate in the seeming creation. In reality, each supposed object is only name and form of the unchanging, unlimited, non-dual Brahman. Where is there a problem?

The teaching of Advaita is a two-stage process effectively. The 'neti neti' is to distance us from those things with which we initially identify – principally body and mind. In the end, however, they have to be brought back again since there is nothing that we are not. How could there be when there is only Brahman?

* * *

A recent question I had before yours is relevant:

Q: I keep getting stuck on something. I have been studying the various writings of the Upanishads and find them very beautiful. My question is: If all is the Self, and all that we see, taste, touch, hear, smell, feel, witness is a manifestation 'out of' Self (it comes out of Self, so it *is* the Self) then why is it to be negated as not this, not this? All is Self, but then: 'not this thought, or not this feeling, or object, or not this or that', etc.?

A: This is just a teaching technique in Advaita (neti, neti). The idea is that you start off being identified with something – e.g. you really believe that you are your body. You have to be disillusioned of this before you can move on. Once you have moved nearer to an appreciation of how things really are, this is also admitted to be a wrong notion. Since there is only the non-dual reality, the body must also be this. It is sort of complementary to the adhyAropa-apavAda technique – see earlier Q&As. In that technique, we initially attribute something to Brahman and then later take it away. Here, we are initially taking it away and then later giving it back. You might also have come across the Buddhist saying that 'mountains are initially seen as mountains, then later they are seen as not mountains but finally they are seen as mountains again.' This is the same idea because, although we eventually realize that we are not the body, nevertheless, the body is still seen as a separate entity. In the final stage, however, it is known that despite seeing the form, the essence is nevertheless Brahman.

* * *

It sounds as though you are temporarily stuck at the second stage. Happiness and misery are the two inevitable polarities of relative existence. The despair that you feel is identification with the negative aspects of the polarity. Both are emotions that arise in the mind of the person. See them as that but identify with neither. You are that in which everything arises: person, emotions and all of

those seeming objects and events that gave rise to those emotions. You cannot achieve lasting happiness as a person... but who-you-really-are is already unlimited and free.

Q.223 The observer and the observed

Q: I have read J. Krishnamurti over and over again and I always thought that he was telling us that the observer is the observed and that there is no difference. Have I misunderstood him? I read in the 'Introduction to Vedanta' at your site that the subject is different from the object. This teaching on Vedanta seems to give me more space. However, I am still confused. Also, 'A Course in Miracles' teaches that we are all one and everything is one. Is the subject really different from the observer or are these different teachings or have I misunderstood?

A: First of all, the 'Introduction to Vedanta' series is by Dr K. Sadananda – I only edited it. Also, I have only read a little J. Krishnamurti so cannot really answer any detailed questions on his teaching. (If you have any, I can pass them on to Sadananda, who began his studies with JK.)

Having said that, the bottom-line of all non-dual teachings is that there are not 'two things', 'we are all one' etc. The difference lies in the way that the teaching brings about this understanding in the mind of the seeker. You will appreciate that, on the one hand, there is the claim that 'everything is one' and on the other there is the experience that 'I am here and the world is there'. There is a clear disjoint between what we experience and what the teaching is saying. This has to be resolved by the mind before any 'realization' or 'enlightenment' can occur.

The way that Advaita brings about this understanding is by beginning with our current, dualistic experience. 'I', the subject, am clearly 'here', while 'you' the object, are 'over there'. Obviously, I cannot be you. Similarly, I am not this computer in front of me. I am not even this body, since I can lose bits of it and continue to exist without them. Neither am I the mind. Thoughts come and

go but I remain. And so on. The teaching takes us forward from that basis and only later starts to 'take back' some of what has been said earlier, in the light of our growing knowledge. It is a bit like beginning with Newtonian mechanics and later introducing relativity.

There is no point in trying to feel 'I am everything' to begin with, because all your prior knowledge, your peers, the media etc. will insist otherwise. Such a strategy will only result in frustration. Find a good, traditional Advaita teacher if you want to take things slowly, using proven techniques.

The answer to your basic question (for the record!) is that you, the 'ultimate' observer, are Brahman or Consciousness. The observed is seemingly separate in the empirical realm but is actually only name and form of that same Consciousness. But this is the 'final' understanding. Usually, a seeker has to approach this via several interim positions.

Q.410 Teaching the blind

Q: How do you teach Advaita to a blind person? I am talking about a person who has been blind since birth, who has no vision of external reality/unreality. The adhyAsa bhAShya talks about superimposing the subject and the objects. But both subject and object are not perceived by a person who has been blind since birth. All that he/she would be aware of is taste, smell, sound, sensations. How would you proceed with such a candidate? The theory of negating the superimposed almost fails for such a person, for he/she cannot 'see' or 'perceive' what is superimposed!

I am not saying the avasthA traya is not a good way to start here, the avasthA traya prakriyA holds good for even a blind person. That is, your dream is just like your waking state. But the problem is, there is no perception in either dreams, waking or deep-sleep for such a person. Here's a video that confirms that people who are blind since birth don't see anything in their dreams (https://www.youtube.com/watch?v=XpUW9pm9wxs).

A: Self-realization is about knowledge, not experience. Self-knowledge is gained by listening to a qualified teacher unfolding the scriptures and asking questions to resolve doubts. Sight is clearly an important sense, especially to someone who has grown up with that sense! Sight is obviously not at all an important sense to someone who has been blind from birth!

The scriptures use many metaphors and stories, and a fair number of these relate to the sense of sight. But they are adaptable to other senses and adhyAsa relates to 'perception', not specifically to sight. One can imagine hearing something, not altogether clearly – maybe one was attending to something else at the time and therefore not 'tuned in'. One can imagine that in such a situation, one might erroneously conclude that it was X when it was really Y. Upon investigation – approaching the source of the sound and listening carefully – the truth of the matter would be realized. This is perfectly analogous to the rope-snake example and would carry the same meaning. Obviously you would need to think of something appropriately dramatic – say a squeaking door that sounded like a vicious animal.

I agree that the avasthA traya prakriyA might not be quite so useful to someone who did not experience visual dreams. Congenitally blind people do have dreams involving other senses though, so I don't think they would have any difficulty translating to their own experience.

Q.423 Logical proof

Q: Is there a logical proof that all souls are multiple personalities of the same self, and of what therefore to do?

A: 'No' is the simple answer. If there were, scientists would not still be looking for the origin of consciousness in the brain! It is rather that there exists a body of knowledge from those who have realized that this is how it is. 'Teachers' draw on this, together with their own experience, to explain things to seekers until such time as they realize the truth for themselves. To one who has been

through this process, there is no problem in understanding that this is perfectly acceptable. To one who has not, however, it seems quite unacceptable and not really any different from the 'faith' of religions.

Incidentally, the phrasing of your question indicates that you do not appreciate the 'bottom line' message of Advaita. There are no individual 'souls' or 'personalities' and nothing to 'do' in reality. There is only the Self – and you are That (already). You just do not realize this. I.e. all that needs to happen is to remove the ignorance that is preventing you from seeing what is already the case.

Q.459 The unbridgeable gap

Q: I have a few doubts regarding Advaita. I was fascinated by this philosophy when I started perusing different philosophies but, on reflection, I found it to be untenable or a logical travesty at best.

I suspect that ajAtivAda is the ultimate tenet of Advaita – creation never happened, ontologically speaking. And yet, inexplicably, this vyAvahArika world with its jIva-s exists. And, to end his purported suffering, the jIva has to realize this ontological oneness or sole existence of unqualified Brahman.

Now, to be a little antagonistic, according to the frame of reference of the jIva, his realization will not have any effect on the pAramArthika Brahman because jIva, world and liberation are all only vyAvahArika truth. As ajAtivAda explicitly states, jIva, world, liberation and bondage do not exist.

I suspect that Advaita is also not a realization (mental state) of the jIva as Brahman cannot be an object of knowledge or experience so, at the apparent instant of realization (apparent because of ajAtivAda) nothing really happens from the point of the jIva also. Even for the jIvanmukta, his mind and body exist, yet neither his body nor mind can get liberation because it would turn Brahman into a subject.

What can a jIva know other than the conceptual and hardened knowledge about Advaita and the pAramArthika reality? It can neither be direct experience nor realization as it would fall in the domain of experience. Even nirvikalpa samAdhi is an experience. And Advaita maintains that, for anything that can be an object or is experienced, beginning or ending in time doesn't have an absolute reality.

I think there is an unbridgeable gap between absolute and relative reality. Even if you strive for liberation, that process itself has no meaning in the absolute sense (and by the way, the jIva cannot make Brahman an objective thought in the mind). As has been pointed out, from the absolute viewpoint it is as if there is an unchanging screen and, from the relative point of view, nothing ever enables the jIva to experience that reality.

Even gurus like Ramana say that 'destroying the questioner' is also just another thought in the mind. I mean to say that, from the point of view of the world, nothing would ever make the jIva realize Brahman, as he cannot escape his cognitive closure and, from the point of view of absolute reality, he is already Brahman.

Even if one's life is extremely dissolute, it won't be a problem, since you are eternally Brahman. From the pAramArthika viewpoint, you (the jIva) do not exist at all and you can do absolutely nothing as regards realizing, experiencing, or knowing Brahman as that would reduce Brahman to an object. So there's no real difference between being a highly revered saint or the most corrupt, mass murderer.

As two unbridgeable realities will never bridge, it renders the entire Advaitic tradition moot and futile. It's like solipsism: even if it's true, you can never escape from it. Similarly, even if Brahman exists, your life (whether good, horrendous or saintly) has no relevance.

I think this tradition was invented to escape from the poor living conditions of the world – they made elaborate jugglery to convince themselves that world is unreal. Even if pAramArthika reality is true, it does not benefit the jIva in any way as he cannot close that gap. And from that absolute viewpoint, the jIva does not even exist.

I now sincerely believe that this whole Advaita is just a mental speculation like solipsism and that its unfalsifiable concepts have no bearing for anyone in this world. I believe that investigations into AI and neural correlates of consciousness may eventually show that it is all parallel, time lag processing in the extremely complex brain.

To summarize my question succinctly: in the Advaita tradition, does an unbridgeable gap exist that no teaching can reconcile?

A: You say: "I suspect that ajAtivAda is the ultimate tenet of Advaita – creation never happened, ontologically speaking. And yet, inexplicably, this vyAvahArika world with its jIva-s exists".

This really sums it all up. The 'bottom line' of Advaita is that there is no world (separate from Consciousness) and that no jIva has ever been born (i.e. all apparent jIva-s are also nothing but Consciousness). And Advaita does not offer any explanation of why there appears to be a world. It is anirvachanIya – inexplicable.

When a jIva attains enlightenment, nothing really happens. The jIva was already free because there was no jIva separate from Consciousness. All that happens is that the mind-intellect of the jIva now knows that he or she was and is already free and is nothing other than Consciousness. It is not true that "nothing happens from the point of view of the jIva" – this is to confuse paramArtha and vyavahAra. Lots of things happen all the time in vyavahAra, as I'm sure you know! But, to repeat, nothing gets liberated in reality (as you say) because there is only Brahman, which is already unlimited.

The other point of misunderstanding is that knowledge and experience are not regarded as synonymous in Advaita. 'Loss of Self-ignorance' is not an experience. Experiences have to have a beginning and an end in time. Thus, nirvikalpa samAdhi is an experience, as you rightly point out – it has both a beginning and an end. But loss of ignorance has only a beginning. Once Self-knowledge has dawned, it is permanent.

This distinction between vyavahAra and paramArtha is crucial in Advaita. At the empirical level, behavior is important. It does make considerable difference whether you behave well or badly, as I am sure you will admit. This is why traditional Advaita devotes so much of its teaching to topics such as dharma and karma. It is not meaningful to say that, from a pAramArthika viewpoint, a jIva could 'live a dissolute life' because, from that viewpoint, there are no jIva-s! You can only speak of jIva-s and their behavior at the vyAvahArika level.

There is no need to look for a 'bridge' between the two levels. In reality, there is only one level, so the idea of a bridge is meaningless. It is 'no benefit to the jIva' because he/she does not exist as a separate entity. There is only Brahman.

I doubt very much that you will be convinced by any of this. But it is also the case that you cannot convincingly argue otherwise! Impasse.

Q: You said that, from the jIva's point of view, the only thing that changes on gaining Self-knowledge is that he gets a new understanding of the world and of himself. To be as precise as possible: in the body-mind-consciousness of that person, on the relative plane, his mind-intellect will have a new understanding that only the Absolute is non-sublatable. He will still experience the world like the rest of us.

In response to Q.383 (Alzheimer's), I think you responded from the Absolute level. But what will happen to that person's mind in the relative plane? Imagine a person, after years of austerity and shravaNa, manana and so on, became a jIvanmukta (i.e. his mind developed an understanding) and then slowly the Alzheimer's eats away that achievement.

A: Enlightenment means gaining Self-knowledge. It relates to the jIva and is an event in the mind. It does not confer immunity to disease, as was exemplified by Ramana and Nisargadatta. Alzheimer's is a disease of the brain, which is a part of the gross body of the jIva. Bodies grow old, cease to function correctly and die. If a brain suffers a stroke, those functions that were governed by the affected part of the brain, be they speech, movement or whatever, become disabled or inoperative. If that part of the brain responsible for reasoning or retrieval of memory is lost, the related functions are lost.

So, yes, if a j~nAnI succumbs to brain disease, the functions of the body-mind will inevitably be affected but this does not matter to Atman. If your dream-self was involved in a serious accident last night and ended up in intensive care, is your waking self concerned? You are not your waking self either. Consciousness does not get Alzheimer's.

Language and Sanskrit

Q.34 Pronunciation of anusvAra

Q: Why is the capital 'M' that you put in words like ahaMkAra and saMsAra not pronounced as an 'm'?

A: I am not actually a Sanskrit expert and don't even know any declensions or conjugations. The 'a' and 'M' together, in words like saMsAra is called an 'anusvAra' and this combination is rather regarded as a vowel than a consonant. All consonants sound with 'a' by default (unless something else is specified) and the anusvAra is represented by putting a dot over the 'm' in saMsAra when it is written in Romanized form: saṁsāra. Now the sound of the anusvAra is determined by the succeeding consonant and takes the sound of the nasalized consonant that is in the same group as that succeeding consonant. 's', which is the succeeding consonant in saMsAra, is a semi-vowel and is in the 'dantya' or 'dental' group of letters and the nasal consonant at the end of that group is 'n'. Therefore it is pronounced as 'n' instead of 'm'.

The philosophy of sAMkhya yoga has an anusvAra which sounds using the ~N nasal (sounded at the back of the throat) because the consonant 'kh' is in the kaNThya or guttural group whose nasal is ~N. The only time that the anusvAra will actually take the 'm' sound is when the following consonant is in the oShThya or labial group of letters. An example would be saMbodhana, which refers to the vocative case ending of nouns, since 'b' is oShThya.

Q.107 How do you pronounce 'Advaita'?

Q: How do you pronounce 'Advaita'? Is it 'ad-vay-ta' or 'ad-vye-ta'? I've heard both used.

A: The (pedantically) correct way to pronounce it is actually 'a – dwye – ta' ('dwye' sounding like 'why?' without the 'h') and, if you live in the UK, you are likely to hear it this way. (SES teach this.) If you live in the US, you are more likely to hear 'a – dvie (as in pie) – ta', since the American Sanskrit Institute teaches that. If you abide by the logical structure of the language, the SES way is the correct one, since the semi-vowel 'v' is formed by combining the two vowels 'u' and 'a'. And, if you say 'oo' and 'a' quickly one after the other, you get a 'wa' sound and not a 'va' one.

Useful question – I am sure lots of others fail to pronounce it correctly, even though they pursue the philosophy! Incidentally, although I live in the UK, and learnt the 'w' way of pronouncing it, I now use the 'v' version, since the majority of seekers seem to live in the USA. But you still have to spell it when you speak to others, since so few people have ever heard the word!

Q.113 The 'power' of Sanskrit

Q: I have enjoyed reading your books and I am intrigued by the questions raised in my mind by the extracts of your 'Jungle' book. I get the sense that you feel that the ubiquitous 'Neo-Advaitins' are leading modern would-be j~nAnI-s down the primrose path. Is it really true that Sanskrit syllables have special innate vibratory power, not possessed by most other languages? Or could it be possible that the books 'Nothing Being Everything' or 'Emptiness Dancing' could be the Astavakra Gita of 1000 years hence?

I am trying to familiarize myself with the Advaitic teachings of the Vedas and the treatises of Shankara but the talks of the modern (so-called sages) are very seductive. What to do?

A: The situation is rather (as I see it) that there are many seekers out there who genuinely want to discover the truth but are finding only frustration or worse as a result of visiting various satsang teachers or reading their books. I certainly would not presume to claim that the Neo-Advaitins are merely cynically taking advantage of this.

Sanskrit is by no means a *sine qua non* of good teaching. Its value is simply in that all of the historical classic works in traditional Advaita were written in this language. Many of the words are still used simply because there is no equivalent term in English, and a good teacher wants to avoid the danger of a student understanding a word in the way he has always misunderstood it rather than in the way that will point towards the truth.

My belief is that many of the modern works can alert one to the possibility of a non-dual reality but, if you want systematically to undermine all of the erroneous beliefs built up since birth and introduce a certain knowledge that 'all-there-is is Brahman' and 'I am That', then the best option is a prolonged course of traditional teaching by a qualified traditional teacher.

Q.174 Do I need to learn Sanskrit?

Q: It is somewhat discouraging to entertain the possibility that the way is blocked until the proper meanings of many Sanskrit words are assimilated.

Somehow Nisargadatta was able to get away with teachings like "Stay open and quiet; that is all. What you seek is so near you that there is no place for a way", and "Stop making use of your mind and see what happens. Do this one thing thoroughly. That is all". This type of idea provides more hope of success for a linguaphobe.

I have no idea whether my current mental preparedness is enough to allow traditional Indian words to do their job, or whether more familiar English words might be enough. From where I stand, I can see I'm not qualified to judge what might work; only that one road looks easier than the other. Maybe both eventually reach the same vista, and maybe not, but at a fork in the road, the path with fewer boulders tends to beckon.

A: I can understand your concerns about Sanskrit terms. I rebelled against it for years before finally giving in (to learning basic Sanskrit) – and then found that I enjoyed it.

The essence of what teachers such as Nisargadatta and Ramana said (together with all of those modern teachers who claim to be following in their footsteps) is of course true. You are seeking your Self and you already are that. Ironic really! But the problem is all of the mistaken ideas that point us in the wrong direction. Simply stating that you do not need to do anything to be who you already are does not help. The mistaken notions have to be analyzed and seen to be false. Only when all of the Self-ignorance has been eliminated can the truth be clearly seen.

There are well established and proven techniques for guiding seekers through this process but it requires knowledge and skill. And, unfortunately, a little Sanskrit seems unavoidable because it is not always easy to express an idea in English when the concept is alien and no suitable English word exists. Obviously we can provide a nearest-equivalent word but then there is the real danger of misunderstanding.

As an example, much confusion arises when people attempt to discuss such topics as 'the soul' or the 'unreality' of the world. This could be obviated by introducing and defining the key terms of 'jIva' and 'mithyA'.

The word that Advaita uses to describe the world is 'mithyA'. This is sometimes translated wrongly as unreal or illusory. It is better translated as 'neither real nor unreal'. Best of all, though, it is not translated at all, since there is no equivalent word in the English language. Its meaning is that it has 'dependent existence'; the essence of the thing is real but it has a name and form which are changing and non-eternal (thus effectively not real). Therefore, a sufficient definition of 'reality' is that it must be *unchanging* or *eternal*. The Sanskrit word which is normally used to define 'real' is trikAlAtIta, which means 'that which transcends past, present and future'.

So, to say that the world is not real is not correct. The essence of the world *is* real; it is the *form* that is unreal – the world is mithyA.

Also, to say that the 'self' or 'soul' of any sentient being is also unreal in that it is subject to change and contingent on innumerable factors is also potentially very misleading. The essence of each 'person' is called 'Atman' in Sanskrit and this Atman is the same as Brahman (there are not two things). When the Atman is identified with body and mind as a result of ignorance, that 'embodied Atman', as it were, is called a 'jIva'. This is what is often poorly translated as 'soul'. Part of the early teaching of Advaita is that, when the body dies, mind leaves along with the jIva and is reincarnated in a new body.

It is not correct to think of the jIva as unreal. What is effectively happening is that the Atman, which is real, appears to be limited as a result of ignorance. In Sanskrit, the jIva is said to be the Atman together with the upAdhi (limiting adjunct) of avidyA (ignorance). The metaphor that is often used to explain this is that of the space 'in' a jar. We think that an empty 1-liter jar 'contains' 1 liter worth of space. But it is rather that the unlimited, unbounded space happens to contain a jar at that location. You can say that there is 1 liter of air inside it, but not 1 liter of space. If the jar is moved to one side or broken, the space is totally unaffected.

Q.446 satyam, j~nAnam anantam brahma

Q: Does the phrase satyam j~nAnam anantam brahma mean 'truth-knowledge limitless' or 'Existence-consciousness limitless'? (The latter is the definition given by Swami Dayananda in one of the summer camp tapes.)

A: Strictly speaking, sat means 'real, existence or being'; sattA means 'being or existence'; satya means 'truth or being'. If you look up 'existence', you will probably find asti or astitvam. If you look up 'sat' in Monier-Williams, one of the meanings is 'that which really is, entity or existence, essence, the true being or really existent'. If you look up 'sattva', you get 'being, existence, entity, reality, true essence'.

So the answer is that both are used in either context and there is no clear meaning associated with either (and I have come across both being used in both meanings). I am fairly sure that Swami D has used both to mean 'existence' and both to mean 'truth'. Sanskrit is a very versatile language.

In mitigation, the words 'existent' and 'true' could be considered to be synonyms in Advaita...

The suggestion that j~nAnam is translated as 'consciousness' is a little more difficult. It is, indeed, one possible correct translation – but it is in the sense of 'I know' equating to 'I am conscious of'. If it was used in this way by Swami D, it would seem to me to be perhaps a 'slip of the tongue', momentarily confusing 'satyam j~nAnam anantam' as the 'definition' of Brahman with 'sat chit Ananda' as the other common definition. chit, of course, does mean 'Consciousness' in this context.

Q: I am a student of James Swartz. I wanted to find a good reference book for learning the terminology of Vedanta in Sanskrit. James recommended I contact you to ask which one of your books would the most helpful. If you have time to point me in the right direction it would be much appreciated. Thank you.

A: That's an easy one! The best book by far (of which I am aware) is John Grimes' book. See first entry at (http://www.advaita.org.uk/library/i_indian.html).

From another unpublished question:

Q: I always thought that the use of Sanskrit terms was a little spiritually pretentious (mainly because I'm lazy and had to do Latin at school!) I can now see the need for it in spiritual investigations. So where would I start with this to catch up?

A: I wouldn't really recommend learning the language seriously (pity we didn't learn it at school instead of Latin, though!). You pick up the main terms just by reading and joining email discussion groups. There is a dictionary at the website – see 'Dictionary' under the 'Sanskrit' menu (http://www.advaita.org.uk/sanskrit/sanskrit.htm). But some Sanskrit terms are essential because there are no English equivalents – mithyA is an obvious and key example. There are detailed entries on some of these terms – see 'Terms and Definitions' under the Sanskrit menu. Or read my book 'Sanskrit for Seekers' (http://www.advaita.org.uk/extracts/sankrit.html) if you want to understand a bit more (and even how to read the Devanagari text) without learning the language as such. [Note that the Glossary provides a list of all Sanskrit terms used in this book.]

Guru

Q.277 Need for a guru

Q: Sri Atmananda proposes that simply reading the writings of the guru is ineffectual in evoking the experience of the truth as written. He says that only the spoken word of the guru can be correctly understood and experienced. To what extent would you say that a seeker has to have a physically-present guru in order to gain Self-knowledge?

A: The physical presence of the guru may be valuable in focusing the mind, making one more alert and attentive etc. From the guru's side, he or she will be able to pick up on the unspoken element of your questions – body language, hesitation and so on. The spoken word of the guru may be extremely valuable in being able to clarify your understanding, explain difficult concepts and so on, which you might not be able to take in from merely written material.

The extent to which written material can succeed depends on many factors – knowledge of the author, with respect to both the subject itself and the language for expressing it; writing skill; understanding of the precise nature of the question etc.; and it depends upon the prior knowledge and understanding of the questioner, language skills and do on. Asking and answering questions via email is difficult enough, when there is opportunity to clarify misunderstanding, rephrase the question and/or answer, but in the case of a written book there is only one chance to get it right.

So my view is that a guru is extremely valuable but not absolutely essential, providing that you approach the subject in the right way, read extensively and critically, and have access to a source for clarification if necessary (e.g. Advaitin group). Logically, it seems that this must be so. The truth is not directly communicable because words themselves can only speak of the dual. Words point to that truth, whether read or heard and, once rightly understood, the truth is directly apprehended because we are That.

Q.282 Qualified guru

Q: I have just found out about Advaita and have recently finished 'How to Meet Yourself' and will start reading 'The Book of One' very soon. I understand that you stress the importance of a guru. My question is can you could recommend one in Sweden, preferably in Stockholm?

A: I'm afraid not. I get quite a few requests like yours and it is surprising and disappointing how few countries are served by a traditional teacher or organization. What I tell people is that, whilst a qualified guru is extremely valuable, I do not believe one is absolutely essential. If you have the commitment and time, and are prepared to read widely without accepting anything as the truth immediately, and if you ask questions of more knowledgeable seekers (such as via the Advaitin Egroup for example), then you can still acquire Self-knowledge eventually. Asking questions when you don't understand or in order to gain clarity is very important. And obviously you cannot do this if you only read books.

Q.349 Guru's grace

Q: Do you have any comments on the concept of 'guru's grace' or 'shaktipat guru' – the idea that some teachers are able to 'induce' experience in seekers or 'transmit' knowledge or 'spiritual power'? Numerous reports of this sort of thing abound in the literature, and I myself have experienced something along these lines many years ago from a 'mystical teacher' I followed for several years in 1978-1980. I wonder what is actually going on in this sort of incident. Is it just 100% psychology at work, pure self-deception? Such 'transmission' experiences can often be the seed or catalyst which spurs further effort on the path. There are so many examples of an aspirant 'feeling something' in the presence of a teacher or guru that it seems inappropriate to just dismiss such claims outright.

A: There is no way that a guru can 'transmit' knowledge, other than by expressing his understanding verbally. I think what is really meant here is that, if a guru is actually in the presence of the seeker, the former may be able to pick up on non-verbal clues so as to intuit whether the seeker has understood and rephrase answers as required. But enlightenment has to take place in the mind of the seeker when understanding occurs. There is no scope for mysticism here.

It is because of this element that most (all?) traditional teachers recommend physical presence. Swami Paramarthananda, for example, does not actually condone people listening to his recorded talks unless this is as nididhyAsana after attending the talks in person. My own view is that, providing your level of understanding is already quite high, this *is* ok and actually works almost as well as attending personally. The possible proviso here is that you have access to someone who can answer any problematic questions that might arise.

My feelings regarding induced experiences is that it is caused by being 'inspired' by the guru's obvious wisdom, peace, 'aliveness' and so on. These aspects can be picked up by someone who is paying attention without the need to resort to mystical powers.

Swami Dayananda has said that grace comes as a result of the seeker's karma, and not as a 'free gift'. Basically, you 'earn' karma as a result of past effort.

Advice on teachers/scriptures

General comments and questions

My emphasis in this book (and at my websites) is on traditional Advaita. I am not familiar with other non-dual traditions so these are definitely excluded. The 'bottom-line' of all non-dual teaching has to be the same but, within Advaita, only traditional teaching provides a consistent, reasonable, systematic approach. I advise against satsang-based teaching because it cannot do that (my book 'Enlightenment: The Path Through The Jungle' gives very many reasons for this stance). Also, given that it is necessary to talk about the subject indirectly, choice and definition of words is so important if confusion is to be avoided.

I don't even recommend Ramana and Nisargadatta. They do not teach from a sampradAya background; practically all their material is 'satsang' question-and-answer format and is even translated by others (who may or may not have fully understood what was being said).

The websites (http://www.advaita-vision.org/ and http://www.advaita.org.uk/) have developed into somewhere for people to come when they are confused by the sources they have encountered and are looking for a clear explanation and resolution of their problem so that they can then continue on whatever path they are pursuing. That is the purpose of this book also. The 'clear explanations' that they get are from the vantage point of traditional Advaita since that is the only teaching methodology I am aware of that takes one all the way, from total Self-ignorance to total Self-knowledge. And it does so in a way which never contradicts reason or experience.

Of course, there must be other paths that achieve this but they will have their own peculiar definition of terms etc. which will not agree with those of traditional Advaita. (There are also some Sanskrit terms which are used because there is no unique corresponding concept/word in English. The English words often used in translation also have other meanings – hence the confusion.)

Q.380 Finding a teacher

Q: I've been reading books about the perennial philosophy recently and they often state that to develop spiritually you need to be attached to an exoteric tradition or you probably won't detect any errors, and will be essentially wasting your time or worse. I'm not attached to any tradition, never have been, and can honestly say that the only one I'd be interested in would be Hinduism.

Hinduism strongly suggests that you need a teacher, but my question is, how are you supposed to get a teacher when there are so many experts out there taking advantage of our ignorance, and money.

A: A true teacher will never take advantage of your ignorance and will only take money to support basic needs (travel, hotel, food etc., as relevant). If someone is charging lots of money for large gatherings, be sure that their teaching merits this!

That is one point. The other is that you could spend a lifetime doing the rounds of the various traditions and not feeling comfortable with any. There may be a single truth behind them all but the finer details of the process, and even the final positions, differ. You cannot even refer to 'Hinduism' as a single approach. Vedanta, which is probably what you mean, has three branches with quite different teaching. Advaita uses scriptural-based arguments, logical reasoning and experience to refute other Indian philosophies.

Ideally, the optimum way forward would be to read widely in all the traditions and then decide on one to pursue in depth. Only then, look for a teacher – and do that by asking those who have already been following that path for some years to make recommendations based upon their knowledge. The problem with this is that you do not know which books to read to begin with. I, for example, have read very many books on Advaita and I am now able to say that a large percentage contains erroneous or at least misleading statements. Either that or they are so academic as to be unreadable! All this makes things very difficult for the new seeker!

I can't really help any further, I'm afraid. My knowledge is really only in Advaita. I know that this 'works' but why should you believe me? And that is the third point. Eventually, you have to resort to 'faith' to some degree, where this means putting trust in someone whom you believe to be trustworthy.

Q.26 Who most embodies the principles of Advaita?

Q: Would you say that there is one person who embodies these principles in the world today? I have met some UK teachers (Nathan Gill and Tony Parsons) and am not sure about their depth of understanding, although they are great guys to spend time with. Will you be holding any seminars? If you are please let me know.

A: There are many teachers out there and it is really a question of who most resonates with your own particular nature. To my mind, the best living teacher is Swami Dayananda – crystal clear explanations of the most difficult topic and a humorous style. (Note: Swami Dayananda died in 2015. I would say that one of his disciples, Swami Paramarthananda, now qualifies for that role.) Of the modern writers, I must say that I was most impressed by David Carse's 'Perfect Brilliant Stillness'. He does not teach but what he says comes across in such a way as to leave one in no doubt of his authenticity. He also has some very original metaphors. His book is long, though, and takes a while to 'get going'. I guess I would probably have to recommend Sailor Bob as one of the best modern satsang teachers.

I do not intend ever to hold satsangs. I would have been prepared to hold something like a year-long course on Advaita, one lesson per week, but this does not seem very likely. Unfortunately, I do not live within easy access of London, which is probably the only location where this might be viable. The aim of any such course, though, would be to teach Advaita as a philosophy rather than in any sense help 'people' attain 'enlightenment'! If such a thing is ever planned, it will be advertised on the website.

Q.31 Laying-on of hands

Q: I went to a satsang a few weeks ago. At the end of the last session, someone came forward to ask to be accepted as a disciple (at least I think that was what was going on). The teacher put his hands on the man's head and there was a moment of quiet. I wondered if you could explain what the implication of this ritual is.

A: Regarding your description of the satsang, I do not actually know the teacher or his writing. I have heard that he does have a strong presence but you should be careful not to be taken in by this. The way in which anyone 'presents' themselves is part of the nature of the body-mind organism. This is obvious in the case of a deep, commanding voice for example, which is clearly dictated by the construction of the larynx etc. But things such as self-confidence, persuasive power, oratory ability etc. are all learned or conceivably inherited characteristics and have nothing at all to do with non-duality. I cannot imagine what he was doing with respect to the 'laying on of hands' but this could never achieve anything other than simple physical reassurance or comfort. If someone makes a habit of this one would have to assume it was an affectation to encourage guru worship – hardly something which could be interpreted as authentic. All of our 'suffering' (or whatever you want to call it) is the result of ignorance and ignorance can only be removed by knowledge. Knowledge cannot be transferred by touch unfortunately! [Note that the name of the teacher has been excluded for two reasons. Firstly, this is a general principle. Secondly, it is a reported incident by a questioner; I did not witness the incident myself.]

Q.69 (part 2) Recommended reading

Q: Can you recommend some reading? What about Patanjali and

Christian scriptures?

A: Patanjali is useful preparation but the final beliefs of Yoga philosophy are dualistic. Christian scripture (and almost certainly others) is most unlikely to help. It has been distorted and censored too much by others with self-interest. The Upanishads are best by far but often too cryptic to appreciate without guidance. Of all the material I have read, the easiest to read and embodying the most wisdom has been that by Swami Dayananda. Read practically anything by him (see Arsha Vidya Gurukulam for books to buy and Arsha Vidya Satsangs and Yoga Malika for free downloads). I did not find his spoken material quite so good – he speaks so slowly, I sometimes forgot what he was talking about by the time he reached the end of the sentence!

I am currently listening to the lectures by Swami Paramarthananda on the Gaudapada kArikA-s and this is the most informative of anything I have ever found. But there is lots of Sanskrit and the Mandukya Upanishad is the most difficult by far. There are loads of other mp3 files of his talks though and, on the strength of those I have heard (e.g. Mandukya Upanishad, Brahmasutra, Dakshinamurti Stotras) I would recommend any of them. You can download most of them (http://hinduonline.co/AudioGallery.html).

I would recommend the Mundaka as the first Upanishad to study. There is an excellent two-volume text on this by Swami Dayananda. The best introductions to Advaita are probably those prakaraNa grantha-s attributed to Shankara, such as vivekachUDAmaNi, Atma bodha and vAkya vRRitti. Hope these are useful.

Q.77 'A little investigation is all it takes' (Charlie Hayes)

Q: I just have to comment on Charlie Hayes' essay: I *really* have a problem with *anyone*, (and I 'know' Charlie – we've talked and emailed in the past) who writes: *"Correcting the error is simple, A* *little investigation is all it takes"*. These are the kinds of statements that have made my life *hell* for so many years because, if this is true, then there is something seriously flawed with 'me'. I have been 'investigating' this error for about 20+ years now, and no matter how much I *know* the Truth, the error still runs my life 99.9% of the time. Maybe some people are just not 'meant for' Advaita. Very discouraged!

A: The fault is not with you but with the Neo-(non)teaching. And you are not alone! Many (most? all?) seekers whose exposure to Advaita has only been via the modern Western satsang and Neo-style of teaching are similarly frustrated and confused. My book 'Enlightenment: the Path through the Jungle' is all about this and will hopefully clarify the situation once and for all.

All of our lives, upbringing, education, experience are dualistic in nature. This teaching is contrary to all of that. It is scarcely surprising that it takes time (the scriptures talk of lifetimes, of course, but it is not really that bad!). Self-knowledge is needed to remove the Self-ignorance and that has to be taught by someone who not only has the Self-knowledge but is able to utilize proven methods to convey it to others. The vast majority of Western teachers do not have this capability and the satsang medium is unable to provide the environment in any case.

(Note that Charlie's essays were removed from the website at his request, because of the sort of ideas I am expressing here.)

Q.111 Guidance on teachers

Q: I am a bit confused that you have written a book about the shortcomings of the Neo-Advaitins and yet list quite a few of their books in your Recommended section, including those of Sailor Bob, Francis Lucille, Nirmala, John Wheeler, etc.

Perhaps I have missed something, but this appears to me to be a contradiction.

Do you recommend living teachers in your book 'Enlightenment'? It's a very confusing spiritual scene out there today. There are hundreds of teachers, including Buddhist, Tibetan Buddhist, Sufi, Nondual, etc. and it would be impossible to check out even a small number of them.

As they say, *"When the student is ready, the teacher appears"*. Perhaps I should stop looking for a teacher as it has been a very frustrating and disappointing process.

A: The teachers you mention are not Neo-Advaitins (by my definition). Francis Lucille is Direct Path, which is very different. The others you mention are what I call 'satsang' teachers. Sailor Bob and John Wheeler actually belong to the Navnath sampradAya through Nisargadatta Maharaj, although they do not teach according to any traditional method now. Nevertheless, I do also recommend books by teachers such as Leo Hartong and David Carse, who *are* Neo-Advaitins. The reason for this is that I acknowledge the value of all these books as pointers to non-duality. If reading a book such as one of these alerts the reader to the possibility of a non-dual reality and sets them off on a path towards discovering the truth, then they have served their purpose. I also prefer to let readers make their own decisions about which 'path' to follow. I will certainly indicate the dangers and suggest what I believe to be the better routes but, in the end, it is for each seeker to decide for him or herself.

The 'Jungle' book does not specifically recommend any teacher. What is does do is suggest that no satsang based 'path' is likely to lead to realization at all. Only a traditionally based, prolonged course of teaching, given by a realized person who is a good teacher and is fully conversant with the proven techniques of the past thousand years is likely to provide that. In the west, the only sources I am aware of which can do this are Swami Dayananda and his disciples, the Chinmaya Mission and The Philosophy Foundation. (Note that I only have any knowledge of Advaita teachers. I do not know anything about other traditions.)

I'm afraid I don't believe in the teacher 'appearing' when the student is ready. It is rather that the continued probing by the seeker eventually finds the connection. But I do agree that the search can be very frustrating.

Q.121 Can one 'get it' overnight?

Q: I have been listening to the various talks on yogamalika.org. These are very powerful. I enjoy them as well, but it is very difficult to follow all the ideas of the tattva bodha. I have four questions:

1. Is this something that one can expect to 'get' overnight or is this something that is manifested over one's lifetime?

2. Can following the principles given by the talks at Yoga Malika be important as far as enlightenment or gaining knowledge or removing ignorance is concerned?

3. Can listening to speakers on Vedanta in all forms be a substitute (for the time being) for the voice of a teacher, until I find one?

4. Am I even doing all of this seeking in the 'right' way from what you may know of what I have written so far?

A: You really cannot expect to understand everything and gain full Self-knowledge instantly. The scriptures say that it takes many lifetimes! But even optimistically, you can expect to continue learning for many years. I don't know which 'principles' you are referring to at Yoga Malika. When you are learning with a traditional teacher, 'mind preparation' and 'gaining of Self-knowledge' tend to go hand in hand but it is the pointers to truth that bring about enlightenment, not the practices. When you do not actually have a teacher, any reading/listening/discussion is likely to help. Doing this, you will undoubtedly pick up ideas that are not useful but, providing you keep an open mind and always use reason to question everything you read/hear, you should eventually get to the truth – it will just take much longer. From what you have said, it does sound as though you have the right attitude. You probably no longer have any choice about pursuing this (head in tiger's mouth and all that) so just be patient!

Q.136 Are teachers X and Y Neo-Advaitins?

Q: Although Krishnamurti famously said that truth is a pathless land, I do look forward to your book 'Enlightenment: the path through the jungle'. In the meantime, before I get my hands on your new book and my feet on the said path, may I ask you if you consider teachers X and Y to be Neo-Advaitins or would you place them in some other category? [Names removed to protect the innocent!]

A: I think the simplest way of answering your question is to say that there is only one traditional path in Advaita and that is the one that follows the proven methods of the past thousand-plus years, ideally presented by a teacher who is both enlightened and a part of that tradition. And those whom I call Neo-Advaitins are the ones who deny that there is a seeker, a path and a world of duality that is seemingly real; and who claim that practice is pointless because there is no doer and nothing to do ... and so on.

In between, if you like, there are those teachers who 'teach' by answering questions at satsangs and on residential courses. What they teach varies tremendously. A few may be familiar with Advaita scriptures and make some use of them; many may loosely 'follow' Ramana or Nisargadatta; more and more seem to be adopting the Neo-Advaitin 'message' (possibly because it is easiest to pick up and pass on?); and a lot adopt various new-age stances or address the psychological well-being of the 'seeker'.

What I attempt to demonstrate in the book is that only the traditional approach is likely to be effective in bringing about enlightenment.

Q.195 On the need for a teacher

Q: I feel that I am lacking a sense of direction or needing some 'light to be shed on my darkness'! I feel that I am not 'at peace'. The truth is I often get fooled into believing I am this character who is stressed out and has lots of problems. I know that I am not, but I still get sucked into buying the 'Theater of the lie'. I love the idea of 'As if living' but can truly say that I haven't really experienced it. That is to say this manifestation, driven by programming and conditioning, believes itself to be the 'real deal' and believes its own thoughts to be truth.

A: Basically, there is no quick solution to the sort of problem you describe. Some may give you a glib answer implying that you do not really need to do anything at all. This is not the case (try it and see!). The only way to realize that there are not really any problems at all is to gain Self-knowledge. And the only proven way to do this is to go to a good, qualified teacher who can systematically remove your Self-ignorance. This requires complete commitment for an indefinite period. It has to be the only thing that really matters. If you tell me where you are, I may be able to recommend a school or teacher.

Q: The closest teacher that I know of is X. I have attended one of his meetings but a 65 hour workweek, a wife and two kids won't always allow me to go. I understand what you are saying: that this takes commitment and there is no response that you can give me in an e-mail that will bring about the required Self-knowledge. I was helped much by Y. who is the one who recommended your books to me. I see that he was able to deconstruct every concept, idea and belief system I had, exposing the conditioning and programming for what it was. Other teachers like X were able to show me the real me that never changes, always is and so forth. I guess the point of the e-mail was to say that because I am often attached to a false sense of self, there is pain. I think I was looking for a quick fix to the problem but as you guessed that didn't happen.

A: I'm afraid a 65-hour working week is not conducive to spiritual seeking! As you probably know, those seekers who are really serious in India give up family, work and possessions to devote full time effort. It does sound as though you need to take a proper traditionally-based course from first principles as it were. The most widely available organization is that founded by Swami Chinmayananda. The Central Chinmaya Mission Trust (http://www.chinmayamission.com/index.php) lists missions and ashrams throughout the world and Chinmaya Mission West (http://www.chinmaya.org/) lists centers in North America. You do have to attend on a regular basis in order to really benefit.

It is said that, when a seeker is ready, a teacher will appear. I prefer to think of it as prioritizing of time. When it matters *enough*, you will find the time! Lest this seems harsh, you can always remember (even if you do not really believe it) that none of 'this' is really real and 'who-you-really-are' is already perfect, complete and unlimited.

Q.198 Traditional teaching and 'methods'

Q: Why did you write 'Enlightenment: the path through the jungle'?

You seem to be saying that Advaita is best taught by 'tradition', and you name some teachers but without any strong endorsement. You like Swami Dayananda who pretty clearly thought little of the Maharshi*. (The latter is given credit in your book for 'enlightened' but not 'traditional'.) You don't think satsang is a good place to actualize enlightenment, but give Sailor Bob some credit for being helpful. You seem to qualify so many of your statements, especially finding a 'real' teacher. You clearly 'bad-mouth' satsang (I have never attended, but I have read those who seem to use this delivery method as a core of their presentation of the Truth).

Your emphasis on 'tradition' puzzles me when you return over and over again to the assertion that only traditional teachers teach with a method. Again, from my world of appearance, how can method take on such importance? Wouldn't the reality/actuality of 'Consciousness is all there is' be more important even if it came without a 'how-to' manual? If you are simply intending to contrast the need for method as opposed to some whose method dwells only on the absolute, then you have a point.

Is it safe to conclude, since Poonja (apparently) favored 'transmission' over instruction and scripture, that he lacks legitimacy?

[* Note that, as far as I am aware, there is no evidence for this. According to one of his students, "Swamiji has a very high regard for Ramana. He even visited Ramana's ashram during his own spiritual search trying to find someone there who could help him, though Ramana himself had already died by that time". He has also written a book: 'Talks on Upadesa Saram. (Essence of the Teaching) of Ramana Maharshi'.]

A: Why did I write it? I explain this in the Introduction.

Many teachers and writers have useful things to say and I particularly recommend, for example, Leo Hartong and David Carse, who are both Neo-Advaitins. The point is that enlightenment is Self-knowledge and the seeker begins from the position of not knowing who he/she really is. If a teacher simply says 'You are That (non-dual reality)', it is unlikely to be of any help at all because it is counter-intuitive and against everyday experience. What is needed is gradual, reasoned explanations and pointers that bring about successive sublations of prior understanding, until such time as the realization occurs of itself. Some satsang teachers do utilize proven techniques but, as the book points out, an occasional 2-hour meeting, on random topics is never going to provide a gauged education for all attendees. Traditional teachers would never attempt to do this. Seekers have to commit for however long it takes. Qualified traditional teachers have many techniques at their disposal and can bring them out at the right time as part of a steady progression.

What you are objecting to with respect to 'strong endorsement' (or disapproval) may simply be that I specifically set out not to single out any teachers. I wanted to emphasize principles rather than people so as not to antagonize anyone.

Papaji did not belong to any sampradAya so could not be regarded as 'traditional' (this also applies to Ramana of course, but there will always be occasional ones who prove to be brilliant teachers simply because of their deep understanding and ability to transmit this to others, irrespective of any 'formal' qualification).

Q.215 Payment for teaching

Q: I understand that, as long as we hold on to the idea that I exist as an individual entity, I will continue to act as if I have to do something in order to get something or somewhere. David Carse, in his book 'Perfect Brilliant Stillness', says that one should not charge money for anything spiritual. The bible says that God *"clothes even the birds and the flowers, how much more will God take care of his own"*. Even some of the satsang teachers, e.g. Stephen Wingate, Sailor Bob, don't concern themselves with donations or charging.

They have seemingly realized that, since nothing matters and all is just happening, everything is being taken care of by the 'One'. There is no need to 'do', or 'have', but to just *be*! And allow 'It' to take care of our needs. That, in my understanding, does not mean to 'not act', but to leave the results to God. It is not in your control.

Can any so-called enlightened person charge for anything? None of the sages such as Ramana Maharshi, Nisargadatta, Atmananda Krishna Menon ever charged, at least to my knowledge.

A: Traditionally, teachers never asked for money but then most such teachers were probably saMnyAsin-s and either lived in an Ashram or traveled around accepting only food and minimal clothing from others. I don't think this style of living would work very well in the West!

If you have read my book 'Enlightenment: the Path through the Jungle', you will know that I do not condone satsang teaching, since there are many reasons why it cannot satisfy the needs of the seeker. But clearly such teachers need to pay for their accommodation and travel expenses etc. so would obviously need to charge *something* unless they were independently rich. And Ashrams that provide accommodation and food for visitors today (at least in the West) have to pay for that somehow. So I think the point is that it must be reasonable to charge something. What is not reasonable is for a successful teacher to become rich on the proceeds! The other point is that teaching should never be refused to someone who asks but is unable to pay.

You should also bear in mind that an enlightened person is still a person, i.e. their 'personality', likes and dislikes, skills and propensities do not suddenly disappear. Over time, a j~nAnI is likely to become a jIvanmukta and will 'acquire' the serenity, love etc. of the stereotype sage but, initially at least, it is likely that someone who is both enlightened and has teaching skills will still exhibit 'human' traits!

Q.244 Teachers

Q: I have been getting advice from a certain teacher (not as a guru-disciple), who said one should be careful about choosing a teacher because there are so many false teachers these days and that one should Google for scandals around the teacher and check blogs that talk about him/her.

If you were a seeker and found some very negative comments about a potential teacher, would you ask him/her about it if you wanted to study under him/her? Are there really no codes of behavior that a teacher should be held to? Besides Swami Dayananda, who else do you hold in high regard?

A: The problem is that you will often find bad reports about someone if you go looking for them! It is certainly true that there are teachers around who take advantage of seekers, usually in order to make money but sometimes in other ways too. And it is difficult to know what to believe. If you ask someone's opinion, all that you will get is an opinion, coming with no guarantee of truth. This includes opinions given by teachers!

If the opinion is given by someone that you know and trust and that person says that they have justification for their view, then it is reasonable to accept that opinion. If you find many negative opinions expressed on the Internet (say), then you are justified in being suspicious. Certainly you could ask the teacher in question to give their side of the story if you were considering long-term commitment.

But, regardless of all of this, any teacher is valuable to the extent that you learn something useful from them. You should know that someone may be a good teacher and be self-realized and still act in a way that you feel 'unbecoming'. This is possible when the person still needs further nididhyAsana in order to gain the 'fruits of their knowledge'.

From my own experience, I could recommend any teacher who studied for a long period with Swami Dayananda. Alternatively, it seems that the Chinmayananda organization is reliable. The only other organization that I am aware of and can recommend is the Advaita Meditation Center (http://www.advaitameditation.org/) in Massachusetts, US.

Ramana Maharshi

Q.53 On the teaching of Ramana Maharshi

Q: Regarding Ramana Maharishi's recommended practice of asking, 'Who Am I?':

When asked 'what is tapas?', he always replied "seek the source of 'I' and the mind will sink into That; seek the source of thoughts, and the mind will sink into That – that is tapas".

Now there is some confusion regarding the 'I' here. As I understand from David Godman's book ('Be As You Are: The Teaching of Ramana Maharshi'), 'I' was a reference to the ego. Some however are of the opinion it is the 'I' of the 'Self'. I wonder what you make of it. Also, I would appreciate your comments on Ramana's teachings, especially the Self Inquiry method, in the light of the Vedantic teachings.

A: The Self is already the Self and doesn't do, or need to do, anything. It is the identified self that thinks it is limited and has to seek liberation. Seeking takes place until such time as the ignorance is dissolved by knowledge.

The problem with asking oneself the question 'Who am I?' is that, if one only has oneself to provide an answer, it is unlikely to lead anywhere. The fact that reality is non-dual is, for most people, deeply counter-intuitive. Everything that the senses and the mind tell us goes against this. To take us from the apparently self-evident to the wildly implausible usually requires many years of gauged instruction from a qualified teacher.

As regards the 'Who am I?' practice, I have written about this in many places. If you are serious about utilizing the teaching of Advaita to gain Self-knowledge, then the only reliable route is via traditional teaching. (Practice of any kind can never bring about enlightenment, since it is not opposed to ignorance.) If you cannot access a genuine teacher, then reading recommended material, listening to mp3 talks from teachers such as Swami Paramarthananda, then asking questions from trusted sources is the way. Ramana was a brilliant teacher – no question – but the material you access now is from transcribed talks, where he was answering questions from specific seekers (whose level of understanding and particular problems would have been quite different from your own). Papaji had his moments, but was also (unwittingly or not) the initiator of the whole 'satsang' movement, with its emphasis (intentional or not) on making easy money for the leaders and doing little to aid the understanding of the seeker.

Ramana was a brilliant teacher and had a particular knack of being able to gauge his words for the particular level of understanding of his questioner. Accordingly, it is very dangerous to take his words out of context. You should always read his complete answers to complete questions, ideally within the context of the larger discussion in which the question took place. Even then, there is a danger of jumping to the wrong conclusion. Essentially, though, Ramana was a traditional teacher, but not part of a sampradAya and not always therefore using the proven techniques for unfolding the scriptures.

Q.71 Self-inquiry

Q: I am following the teaching of Shri Ramana Maharshi on Self-inquiry but I have one doubt: when I ask the question 'Who am I?', I get the answer 'body + mind + intellect'. Why can't we consider ourselves to be this composite which is ever-changing but keep our identity at that moment as 'I'?

A: You could consider that you have answered this question yourself. 'Who-you-really-are' does not change. Whenever you consider the body-mind-intellect, what you see is always different from when you last looked; yet 'you' who are looking is always the same. Therefore, you cannot be these things. Another, even simpler way, is to say that since 'you' are the subject seeing the body, mind or intellect as an object, therefore you cannot be them.

However, that is the traditional way of analyzing the situation. Ramana does not advocate this. He says you should not analyze. When the answer 'body + mind + intellect' arises, you should ask 'to whom does this answer arise?' and carry on enquiring.

Q.331 Beyond stillness

Q : I am a 'solo practitioner' following the guidance of Ramana Maharshi, as I understand it. My enquiries move between an apophatic and cataphatic flavor.

When I do this, I am moved to an absolute stillness. Upon 'coming back', there is a sensation of still not passing the barrier of stillness. I am not sure how to continue. Should I continue to practice just like this? Until I have destroyed differentiation? Should this be a lesson on what the 'real' really is?

[Note: Here are the meanings of those terms from my Oxford dictionary:

apophatic/ap'fatk – adjective Theology (of knowledge of God) obtained through negating concepts that might be applied to him. The opposite of cataphatic.

cataphatic/kat'fatk – adjective Theology (of knowledge of God) obtained through defining God with positive statements. The opposite of apophatic.]

A: Here is what I said in response to a similar question several years ago:

"I'm not actually the best person to ask about Ramana's Self-enquiry; A. because I have never really practiced it and B. because I can't say that I really believe in its efficacy. You may ask how I can make the latter claim when I admit to the former! But, as I repeatedly tell people, since our problem is one of Self-ignorance, the only remedy is Self-knowledge to eliminate that ignorance. 'Doing' anything or 'experiencing' anything is not really going to achieve anything (other than maybe highlight the ignorance so that one is prompted to try to obtain the knowledge). So, to my mind, the value of repeatedly asking 'Who am I?' is to bring about the realization that I am not any of those things that I might have thought myself to be – body, mind, intellect etc. Basically, if I can observe it, I cannot be it, since I am the observer. This might lead one to the conclusion that 'I am the witness'. But the point here is that this witnessing is only possible through the body-mind equipment. Furthermore, the very concept of 'witness' is meaningless if there is no witnessed object – i.e. we are still in duality. So, in reality (paramArtha), there can be no witness.

"So, it is this understanding that has to be garnered and not more, specialized experiences of witnessing or inquiring. All of this is fully and completely explained in the scriptures, but ideally needs a qualified teacher to unfold it in terms which are immediately recognized by the seeker".

I read in one of the Mountain Path journals [produced quarterly by Sri Ramanasramam, Tiruvannamalai) an article effectively stating that shravaNa, manana and nididhyAsana are of value 'only as a preliminary step' whereas the Self-inquiry as described by Ramana is the 'direct path'. This is contradicted by several thousand years of tradition. Traditional teaching works by negating the false understanding that we have about ourselves and the world and then pointing to the truth of Brahman.

The facts that reality is non-dual, that everything is Brahman, that 'I am That' are not realizations that are likely to be made by simply being still or asking 'Who am I?' This knowledge is only contained in the scriptures and has to be conveyed by a suitably qualified teacher in order that it should be believable, reasonable and ultimately eliminate our Self-ignorance. Also, the end point of seeking is not 'extinction of the mind' as this same article suggested.

I would certainly never suggest either that Self-inquiry is valueless or that Ramana Maharshi was not a brilliant teacher but it does seem to be an unfortunate fact that some of the things he said have been taken out of context and are lauded by some modern teachers as efficacious in their own right, bypassing the methods proven by many generations of teachers.

Q.76 Michael Langford on Ramana Maharshi

Q: I have long been interested in the diverse schools of mysticism. I have a rudimentary knowledge of Vedanta, having taken several Indian philosophy classes in university.

A few days ago, I chanced upon Michael Langford's 'The Imposter', which was inspired by Ramana Maharshi. I was very impressed by the clarity of its exposition. The author says he is enlightened. Later, I read some more documents on the main site, specifically, 'Sahaja – What is Liberation according to Sri Ramana Maharshi?' The ideas therein horrify me.

According to Michael Langford and his interpretation of Ramana's teachings, after sahaja samAdhi, the mind is dead. The sage does not perceive particulars (names and forms) but resides in reality. Objective knowledge (perception of particulars) is no longer possible. Reality is defined as non-dual awareness.

That the appearance of the sage continues after his enlightenment is merely the body-delusion of unenlightened people. Basically, Ramana had no awareness of anything in this world after his enlightenment, because he was perpetually in sahaja samAdhi. It is other people's delusion which created the appearance of Ramana, after he ceased to be aware.

All phenomena are unreal. Nothing ever happened. All paths other than self-inquiry lead nowhere.

Normally, given my background in Indian philosophy, I would

assume that the author has fallen into extreme views, e.g. asserting ultimate reality while denying conventional reality. Previously, I assumed that, after enlightenment, objective knowledge persists. For instance, if I'm crossing the road, I become aware of cars, etc. Basically, the mind-body nexus persists, and my ego with it. In fact, I have read in some Yogic exegesis that without the ego, aham, perception and activity are impossible. And that the aham, rather than dying after enlightenment, actually functions better, because it is no longer entangled by desires.

Now the author asserts that after enlightenment, the ego dies, and that perception and activity are no longer possible, and that one resides perpetually in non-dual awareness. Now if this were pure speculation, then I wouldn't pay much attention to this, since it contradicts everything I've been told. The problem is that the author claims that he is personally enlightened, and that he testifies to this, etc. And he has quotations from Ramana to back his assertions:

"In sahaja, however, the mind has resolved itself into the Self and has been lost. Differences and obstructions mentioned above do not therefore exist here. The activities of such a being are like the feeding of a somnolent boy, perceptible to the onlooker (but not to the subject). The driver sleeping on his moving cart is not aware of the motion of the cart, because his mind is sunk in darkness. Similarly the sahaja jnani (liberated sage) remains unaware of his bodily activities because his mind is dead, having been resolved in the ecstasy of Awareness (Self)".

And he (Langford) goes on to say:

"From the above talk by Sri Ramana we can see that the liberated sage is not aware of objects, the world, the body, the universe, activity, walking, talking, etc. However, the onlooker who is still under the illusion of the ego imagines a sage with a body walking, talking, etc.".

After reading the above quotations, I was very shocked. I wanted to burn all of my spiritual books. Now I'm simply confused. What if he is right and everyone else is wrong?

This problem is too difficult for me. If it is within your power, please give me some definitive explanation and clear up my confusion. I seek the truth sincerely.

The document containing the views of the author on sahaja samAdhi (https://albigen.com/uarelove/sahaja.htm).

Main site (http://www.albigen.com/uarelove/).

'The Imposter' (https://albigen.com/uarelove/most_rapid/contents.htm).

A: I have read some of Michael Langford's material in the past and he certainly appears to be confused regarding some key concepts. Your existing understanding is much more nearly correct.

Regarding the principal point of concern, the mind is *not* destroyed upon enlightenment. Enlightenment is, after all, an event in the mind! On the contrary, the mind increases in strength and peacefulness following enlightenment. As you say, 'it is no longer entangled by desires' (to the same degree). The realized person clearly continues to function in the world and this would not be possible without a mind! The confusion possibly arises by misunderstanding the terms:

nirvikalpa samAdhi is the state in which the person is no longer aware of the outside world – but it is a state and the mind returns to normality after a time.

sahaja sthiti is not a state and simply means that one never forgets that 'I am the Self' and 'this Self is all there is'. Nevertheless, the world appearance continues and the body-mind continues its role in the world. It is just that it is known irrevocably that the world appearance is mithyA. It is like still seeing the sun rise and set but knowing perfectly well that the earth goes around the sun.

(It is ok to say that the ego dies – this is just the process of identification of Self with some supposed other thing in creation. So this mistake no longer occurs post-enlightenment.)

It is true that all phenomena are unreal from the absolute

standpoint but transactional reality is from the empirical, vyAvahArika standpoint. This mixing up of absolute and empirical is the cause of most confusion in Advaita. Similarly, there is only Brahman in reality – no differentiation at all. But at the relative level, there are separate people going about their business in an apparent world. The realized person has no problem accepting this seeming duality, knowing that the reality is non-dual.

Regarding paths, there are many of these. Pragmatically, those paths which have been proven over thousands of years must be the most reliable to tread. Traditional Advaita has withstood this test of time. Ramana's Self enquiry (and I regard Ramana very highly indeed) has only been around a relatively short time.

As regards the quotations, it is very dangerous to take these out of context. Ramana, as with other teachers, gauged his replies according to the perceived needs and understanding of the questioner. Traditional Advaita teaches many things that are later withdrawn, after the understanding of the student has grown. (An obvious example is creation itself.) A critical observer might ask: If Ramana no longer perceived a world, how could he have made these statements?

Q.408 Ramana's Atma vichAra

Q: I would like to ask a question about the practice of Sri Ramana's teachings and in particular the way of carrying out the self-enquiry 'Who am I?'

According to what I've seen so far regarding instructions, when a thought arises one enquires 'to whom has this thought arisen'. If the answer to that is 'to me', the enquiry continues with 'Who am I?'

At this stage, the mind becomes silent. Are we supposed to remain in this silence until another thought arises or should we continue enquiring 'Who am I?' every few seconds or so?

Would you be kind enough to clarify this.

A: If you are committed to following those ideas that are frequently claimed as representing the essential teaching/method of Ramana, then I am not the best person of whom to ask these questions.

Ramana was not a traditional teacher; he was not trained in the methodology of any sampradAya. There is no doubt of his status as a j~nAnI and transcriptions of his talks show brilliant insights into many aspects. But I have to say that the 'enquiry' as you describe it is most unlikely to lead to Self-knowledge. I prefer to think that such practice can only lead eventually to the realization that one needs a teacher to provide the guidance via the proven succession of shravaNa, manana and nididhyAsana. It is primarily an intellectual process – the mind is both the problem and the solution. You have to hear the truth, expounded in a convincing manner; ask questions to clear doubts; then repeat in whatever manner is available. Silence will not tell you anything.

Q.179 Yet more on 'Who am I?'

Q: I've just been enjoying your book 'Enlightenment: the Path through the Jungle'. You say that enlightenment is an 'event in the mind' but isn't the seeing-through of the illusion heart-based rather than intellectual? And surely practice is what brings this about? Ramana Maharshi advocates asking 'Who am I?' to achieve this.

A: Yes, you are right that practice is necessary. I don't think I said anywhere that it isn't. What I said is that practice in itself cannot lead to enlightenment. Since enlightenment is an event in the mind, the mind has to be in a suitable state for the event to occur. It won't, for example, occur in the mind of someone whose mind is full of worry, desire, fear or whatever. The purpose of practice is to learn how to control the mind, give attention, exercise discrimination etc. Without some preparation (practice), there is no chance of gaining Self-knowledge. The other aspect is that, although with some practice, it is possible to gain Self-knowledge, if the practice has been insufficient, there will be no 'fruit of knowledge' (jIvanmukti). In other words, although the person may become enlightened, there will be none of the 'good stuff' associated with this – peace of mind, fearlessness etc.

The knowledge that 'I am Brahman' is not something that can be gained from any experience or any of the usual sources of knowledge (perception, inference etc.). The pointers to this fact come from the scriptures. When 'unfolded' by a competent teacher, it is possible for there to be direct apprehension of this truth (since we already are That).

The second point is regarding your 'heart' concerns. This is a red-herring. The reason that many teachers have become hung-up on the 'heart' being the centre for the 'self' (or however you want to put this) is that, at the time that the Upanishads etc. were being written, it was believed that the mind was located in the heart. The fact is that enlightenment takes place in the mind (which is where the 'light' of Consciousness is 'reflected'). Self-knowledge then replaces Self-ignorance and that is all there is to it. (!) [See Q.61 for definitive reference.]

If you accept the bottom line of Advaita, namely that the reality is that there is only Brahman, then it follows that we are already That. Nothing we can do will liberate us because we are already free. So what is the problem then? We don't know this fact. We know that we exist and we know that we are conscious but we don't know that we are unlimited. Ramana advocates Atma vichAra – investigation into the Self. An element of this is asking 'Who am I?' but simply repeating this like a mantra is not going to achieve anything. What is lacking is Self-knowledge and some external teaching is required to provide this. Of all the means of knowledge available to us, the only one that can provide this knowledge is shabda pramANa – scriptural knowledge, ideally imparted by a teacher. Yes, it is the ideas in the mind that bind us but the mind is also where the Self-knowledge takes place that brings enlightenment.

Q: But Ramana says that Enlightenment (Self-Realization) is the dissolution or destruction of the 'I'-thought in the heart. Don't you agree?

A: It is not like that. The 'I' thought is the reflection of Consciousness in the mind. This continues after enlightenment and, indeed, until the death of the body-mind. What enlightenment brings is the knowledge of this. Before, one thinks 'I am this body-mind'; after one knows 'I am Brahman; this body-mind is simply name and form of that same Brahman'.

Q: Have you ever actually attempted a sustained Ramana-like Self-Enquiry practice?

A: Not as such, no. But then, as noted above, this practice is an aspect of Atma vichAra. I think that its main attraction for many seekers is the idea that doing this on its own circumvents the need for following a traditional path and this notion is mistaken.

Q: Isn't the argument which says that direct experience is not necessary, or cannot bring about Self-Knowledge, really a 'clever' trick or ploy engaged in to avoid exposing the lie which our identity is usually based on – i.e. a 'personal' self?

A: No. If you accept that the Self is non-dual, it is a contradiction in terms to talk about 'experiencing the Self'? Who would experience what?

Self-enquiry means investigation into Self, not investigation 'by yourself'. (An obvious point perhaps but one which may often be assumed to be otherwise.) As Swami Chinmayananda pointed out, asking ourselves 'Who am I?' is only going to return the answer 'the same old fool'.

The seeker begins with the mistaken belief that he is a jIva (independent soul with a body-mind-intellect). And he really believes this so that investigation is going to be from this standpoint. Compare the rope-snake metaphor. We mistakenly believe that the thing ahead of us is a snake. If we begin our investigation from this standpoint, we are going to be looking into types of snake, occurrence, characteristics, precautions, poison remedies etc. and none of these are going to lead us to rope-realization.

According to traditional Advaita, the only pramANa (means of knowledge) for Self-knowledge is shabda pramANa, which means scriptures and guru. They are needed to point us in the right direction – away from the snake and towards the rope.

Nisargadatta Maharaj

Q.212 Consciousness 'coming out of' Awareness

Q: I was going through some of Nisargadatta Maharaj's sayings In 'Seeds Of Consciousness' He said: "There is the true Awareness, from which comes consciousness, which is your feeling 'I am'. Be one with your consciousness and that is all that you can do, the Ultimate must come to you. You can only watch what happens – there is nothing you can do to get it".

My question is: what is the point in his referring to consciousness 'coming out of' True Awareness? Is Awareness another term for the Absolute? I have not heard many teachers doing that, except in Dzogchen where Awareness is our True State prior to anything else. Is that what Maharaj was referring to?

A: Nisargadatta uses the terms in the opposite way to most teachers. Most teachers tend to equate Brahman with Consciousness (with a capital 'C'). When we are still identified with this body-mind, we nevertheless claim to be conscious, both of ourselves and of other people and things. To avoid confusing this 'personal consciousness' with the absolute Consciousness, we might call it 'awareness'. Nisargadatta simply interchanges these terms for some reason. So, yes, Nisargadatta's usage of 'Awareness' is another name for the Absolute.

You have to remember that this is a transactional distinction. From the standpoint of absolute reality, there cannot be two things.

Q.342 Teachings of Nisargadatta and Ramana

Q: Is there a difference in the teachings of Ramana Maharshi and Nisargadatta Maharaj?

A: This is too general a question, really. The short answer is that the bottom-line message of any teacher of Advaita must be the same, obviously. But the methodology depends upon the teacher lineage. Nisargadatta did have a lineage, although he developed his own style somewhat! And Ramana did not have a lineage at all. The absence of a lineage means that what is said is not supported by generations of proven efficacy and is subject to differing interpretations etc. This is why the recommendation is always to try to find a qualified, traditional teacher.

Q: I do realize that my question was too general and could not be dealt with in a short answer. What I had in my mind was with regard to their approaches to meditation/self enquiry or the 'path' recommended by them. In self enquiry Ramana stated that while enquiring into 'who am I?', the 'I' that is enquired into is the individual or the ego and not the Self. According to him, focusing on the ego or 'I' would make one realize that it is a phantom and thus lead one to the Self. Nisargadatta, on the other hand, seems to suggest that one should focus directly on 'I am', which is the same as the Self. In this sense, I thought there was some difference in their teaching.

I also read somewhere that Nisargadatta's later teachings were more advanced than his earlier teaching. I do not know whether this is correct and if so, in what respect his later teachings were different from his earlier ones.

I also have a problem with Ramesh Balsekar. I had met him in Mumbai, have read his books and I find that, like Rajneesh (Osho), he is a brilliant writer but his personal life is not quite exemplary. Should one ignore their poor standards of morality and read their writings for the very clear exposition of Advaita, just as one goes to a cancer specialist for his expertise and is not concerned about his personal life, or should one ignore them altogether?

I fully agree that one should go to a qualified traditional teacher, but the problem is of finding one and (even more difficult) knowing whether he or she is genuine. Ideally, the teacher should be one who is Self realized, but unfortunately, a truly realized teacher will not declare that he is realized. It seems that finding a genuine teacher is a minefield and I have decided to continue my sAdhana by following the teachings of Ramana and Nisargadatta and hope that, when I am ready, a teacher will appear and take me further.

Incidentally, Nisargadatta said that a personal guru is not essential – books can be taken as one's teacher. Further, although Ramana did not have any lineage or sampradAya, as Nisargadatta had, I find his teachings are fully consistent with traditional Advaita as formulated by Shankara in his prasthAna traya commentaries; are extremely precise and clear and are not open to varying interpretations.

A: The teachings of both, as far as we have access to them, are inevitably episodic since all we have are recorded talks as opposed to a systematic explanation of an Upanishad for example. Furthermore, the talks are usually translated – not necessarily by someone who could be guaranteed to have understood them. So the extent to which a seeker can understand them as they were intended depends upon how thoroughly they have studied all of the other writings and transcriptions. It is all very hit and miss.

The latter transcriptions of Nisargadatta read almost like the writing of some Neo-Advaitins, speaking as they do as if from the standpoint of absolute reality.

Based on what I have read (not much), Ramesh initially sounds good but later seems repetitive, almost to the point of obsession about the absence of free will. The best of Osho is very good indeed but again lacks a systematic approach, a problem exacerbated by the fact that he looks at so many different traditions.

As far as I know, scarcely any of those current teachers who claim to be disciples of Nisargadatta or Ramana can actually be regarded as genuinely and consistently good teachers. I suggest that this observation must be significant.

You should not worry too much about behavior. There is no

necessary relationship between this and either the ability to teach or enlightenment.

I'm afraid I have never had much faith in the notion that a good teacher must inevitably come to a sincere seeker! But you are right that a good teacher is hard to find. I always recommend trying to find a nearby disciple of Swami Dayananda or a Chinmaya Mission. Failing that, read good traditional stuff – systematic! – rather than random books of talks which may or may not say something useful to you at that time. The best I know of is Swami Dayananda's Gita Home Study Course. This is expensive but will provide wonderful material which will take you months to cover. See Q.462 for details.

Regarding your claim that Ramana is not open to differing interpretation, I beg to differ. I wrote an article some time ago which neither Mountain Path nor the Ramana Maharshi UK Newsletter would publish because it disagrees with, for example, the interpretation of Michael James. See (http://www.advaita-vision.org/manonasha-not-the-literal-death-of-the-mind/).

Q.444 Prior to Consciousness

Q:

1. Is there or could there be an Absolute Nothingness that everything, including Awareness, comes from or out of? Part of this question is the possibility that Awareness or Consciousness is only in this world and for this experience.

2. Without a brain and nervous system, or a manifesting medium, Awareness doesn't even know it is. Therefore, it is still temporary, or a state? And, as Nisargadatta says, what we are is *prior* to this.

A:

1. The confusion of 'awareness' versus 'consciousness' a la Nisargadatta has been addressed in other questions. 'Awareness' in traditional (my) terminology is a characteristic of the mind of a jIva. A sharp, controlled mind has more awareness than a dull,

undisciplined one. But 'awareness' is not a 'substance' in its own right, so it cannot 'come out of' anything. And 'absolute nothingness' is just that – and nothing can come out of it by definition. (Or, perhaps more accurately, *only* nothingness can come out of it!) The concept of 'absolute nothingness being the reality' is shunya vAda, which is a Buddhist idea refuted by Shankara in his brahmasUtra and mANDUkya upaniShad commentaries.

'Consciousness' (as defined by Advaita) is all there is in reality. In the world, Consciousness appears as the world and jIva-s to a Self-ignorant person. To a jIva who has gained Self-knowledge, Consciousness still appears as the world and jIva-s but he/she now knows that it is really only Consciousness.

2. I would have to rephrase this as 'Without a brain and nervous system, a jIva would not be aware.' Then I agree with the statement. As you have phrased it, it has no meaning. We are only 'aware' when awake or dreaming. Deep-sleep is a state in which we are not aware.

I would stop reading Nisargadatta and stop worrying about aspects there that you have not understood. I gave up with his last books because they had stopped making any sense! The traditional teaching of Advaita is all perfectly reasonable. Never be prepared to abandon common sense when reading any spiritual literature!

Ramesh Balsekar

Q.114 Was Ramesh enlightened? (Part 1)

Q: I've just read 'Confusion no more' by Ramesh Balsekar and got pretty confused by lots of statements like the following:

"I believe that each of us is a separate entity, but none of us has the real power to do anything. I am an ego, you are an ego, but the difference is, Ronald's ego thinks he is the doer of his actions, but my ego is totally convinced that no one is the doer, neither me nor you ..." (p. 252).

"Therefore, what can we do? Very simple. I accept that basically all there is, is the 'I' and so long as the 'me' is there I live my life thinking and doing whatever I think I should be doing at any moment and leave the 'I' to itself. Forget the 'I'. Live my life with the one understanding that whatever happens is what the source does. I am not the doer" (p. 265).

Balsekar 'admits' very directly (and pretty boldly!) that to him Advaita is just a belief, or a philosophy, making life a little easier (for the ego) by removing sin and guilt from the equation (by removing the personal responsibility for one's actions). Is that really what Advaita is all about? Has Balsekar totally misunderstood, or is he just more 'honest' than most teachers?

A: [NOTE: Ramesh died in Sept. 2009] This is an excellent question and voices concerns that I think will have been felt by many. Ramesh was generally recognized as one of the greatest living sages – after all, he was a direct disciple of Nisargadatta – but it has to be said that it is statements such as the ones you quote that are likely to give Advaita a bad name! The sense that is carried by them, to those who may not be as 'enlightened' as Ramesh, is just as you say; namely that we can 'do what we want' as long as we believe that it is not really 'me' who is doing these things.

This is not what Advaita says. The point is that, once we reach the stage where we truly know that there is no separate self (i.e. once we have complete Self-knowledge or are 'enlightened'), we also know that there are no 'others' either. We know that there is only the Self. Accordingly, we have total compassion/empathy for so-called others. We also no longer have any vested interest in the outcome of any action. Nothing can ever make any difference to the unlimited fullness that we now know ourselves to be. We may still have desires (these are the result of so-called prArabdha saMskAra) and we may even act in such a way as to fulfill them (providing that this does not impact adversely on others) but it matters not whether the result is in accord with that desire or not. The 'wants' that the enlightened have cannot be compared to those of the unenlightened.

Secondly, the doctrine of 'no free will' is not one that is generally acknowledged by traditional Advaita. On the contrary, it is said that, although the scope for our actions is limited by past karma, we do have scope for modifying our behavior. The metaphor of a boat on a river is often used. The current of the river acts on the boat regardless, but we may use the oars or a motor to try to counteract that current. Often the current is far too strong and our limited free will counts for naught but it is still there. It is only when we (try to) speak of the absolute reality that it has to be said that there is no such thing as free will because there is no one to have it.

This idea that there is no one to act, no free will and therefore no responsibility is one of the most dangerous ideas to have been taken up by Neo-Advaitin teachers. It runs completely contrary to traditional Advaita by failing to recognize that, at the level of the world (apparent though it may be), people exist as separate individuals who act and interact. It is intrinsic to the whole process of seeking on a path and eventually becoming enlightened. This process cannot be bypassed by attempting to deny it before the mind is ready. As you say, these false ideas effectively license the ego to do whatever it wants. This is, of course, completely contrary to what Advaita is really about.

Q.374a Ramesh Balsekar scandal

Q: I recently bought a book called 'Final Truth' by Ramesh Balsekar. I read the book and now see it as one of the most 'deep' and 'philosophical' books on Advaita. But then I read Balsekar had some sex scandals and preached 'do whatever you want; you are not responsible' philosophy and I'm shocked.

A: Who-you-really-are does not act, so cannot be 'responsible' in the sense that you mean here. The person, on the other hand, does act and *is* responsible, and gets puNya-papa as a result of those actions. It is especially the responsibility of the realized person to act in accordance with dharma – the awareness of right and wrong – since he is setting an example to others. However it is also possible that, because of insufficient prior mental preparation, an enlightened person is still attached to desires and fears. Even knowing that he is perfect and unlimited, he could still act in accordance with these feelings, which are called pratibandha-s (obstacles or impediments). These will go in time, with further nididhyAsana.

It has to be assumed that this was the position regarding Ramesh, as far as the 'scandals' are concerned. However, if it was the case that he was actually preaching "do whatever you want you are not responsible", as you say, then this is not a clear presentation of the truth of the situation and should be condemned.

Osho

See Q.264b in the section on 'Enlightened Man'.

Other Teachers

Q.172 Could you give me your opinion of Gangaji?

Q: I would be grateful if you could give me your opinion of Gangaji.

As I said in my previous emails, I am very new to the study of Advaita. I have been on the spiritual path for about 40 years on and off, and after visiting a healer in 1972 had glimpses of something inside that was very pleasant and lasted for several months. I was changed immediately but I didn't know how it came about ... I just discovered God I suppose and didn't study much scripture before or after. This happened several times again years later (long story!) and it faded away each time.

The fact is I have become very fond of Gangaji over the past few months. She seems compassionate and very dedicated and very knowledgeable of human behavior. I retired sick nearly ten years ago; I don't know how much time this body has left and don't wish to waste it on listening to anything that is not worthwhile.

As you have much more experience than me, are you able to

say whether I am on the right track with Gangaji? She claims to be in lineage from Ramana Maharshi through Papaji. I have studied him as well and find him very good too, although hard to follow sometimes, most likely due to his English.

I have practiced basic self enquiry and experienced a calm mind for extended periods, but it fades away again as soon as I have a problem. Today, for example, I had printer problems for hours and felt really fed up afterwards!

A: I'm afraid that I do not have much knowledge of Gangaji, never having met her or read any of her books. I know that many believe her to be an 'authentic' teacher but her lineage is not particularly auspicious since, according to David Godman, Papaji did not really recognize any of those that visited him as worthy and merely sent them off to act as 'evangelists' to get people to come to Lucknow (the city in India where Papaji held his satsangs).

The value of a spiritual experience is in reinforcing the resolve or pointing you in the right direction. Our problem is not lack of experience (we experience non-duality every night in deep-sleep) but lack of knowledge. Practice is a precursor rather than an end in itself, in that it is easier to listen and understand with a still mind than one that is in turmoil.

I do appreciate your concern regarding not wasting time. If it is any consolation, time is as much an illusion as the body – both are real from the empirical standpoint but have no absolute reality. As regards recommending a course of action, I presume that your involvement with Gangaji is mainly through listening to CDs and reading books rather than one to one personal interaction. (Otherwise, I don't imagine that you would be asking my advice.) If that is the case, then I would definitely recommend that you listen to Swami Paramarthananda and read Swami Dayananda. (Specifically this way round, not the other, since Swami P is easy to listen to and Swami D difficult.)

Many short essays and transcribed material from Swami Dayananda may be downloaded (http://www.avgsatsang.org/

hhpsds.html) and his books may be purchased (http://books.arshavidya.org/). Many of Swami Paramarthanda's talks may be downloaded (http://hinduonline.co/AudioGallery.html under 'Discourses – General Topics' and 'Discourses – Vedantic Topics (Advanced)').

Since you are new to Advaita, I would recommend that you particularly look for books/talks on Atma Bodha, Tattwa Bodha, Vivekachudamani, Kena Upanishad, Mundaka Upanishad from these sources as a starter. I can almost guarantee that you will find these rewarding, whereas I obviously cannot speak for the Gangaji material. With Swami P, you will also be getting a consistent and complete picture of Advaita – and therefore knowledge about who-you-really-are.

I shouldn't worry about the fading away of the calm mind. There is Self-knowledge (j~nAnam or enlightenment) and there is peace-of-mind, fearlessness etc. (j~nAna phalam) and the two do not automatically go together unless you were fully qualified (having followed sAdhana chatuShTaya sampatti) prior to gaining the Self-knowledge or you have fully 'assimilated' the knowledge post enlightenment (nididhyAsana).

Q.201 On the Ramakrishna order

Q: I noticed that you rarely cite any work from the swamis of the Ramakrishna Order (apart from a few quotes from Vivekananda). Is there any particular reason for this or is that just that your own interests lead you to focus on other authors (Chinmayananda, Dayananda, Parthasarathy, etc.)?

A: The reason that I do not often quote from the Ramakrishna tradition is that, following Vivekananda, their teaching began to diverge from that of traditional Advaita, embodying teachings from the dualistic Yoga tradition and blurring the original clear messages. This has been so significant that their teaching is actually given a name in India – Neo-Vedanta (not to be confused with Neo-Advaita!). This is not to say that many of the books written by monks of the Ramakrishna order are not to be recommended – some of them are excellent – but one does need to be careful if still unsure of the 'correct' teaching.

Q.202 Paths to enlightenment

Q: I have several questions:

Q1: Ignorance blocks knowledge. The removal of ignorance allows knowledge. To remove ignorance, we must study Advaita philosophy. Is this correct?

A: 'Enlightenment' equals Self-knowledge, which results from removal of Self-ignorance. I know that Advaita 'works' in this regard. I presume that other traditions also work but have no direct knowledge of these.

Q2: I would like to start studying Advaita philosophy, but much of it seems irrelevant – e.g. the minutiae of philosophical argumentation and cultural conceptions. Are there just a few concepts I can study over and over, rather than having to study the vast, unending ocean of Advaita literature?

A: For any given person, it is no doubt the case that some aspects of Advaita will be superfluous. The problem is in knowing which ones! You are almost certainly not the best judge of this – the aspects that you consider unnecessary might be precisely the ones that help remove the blocks. This is one of the reasons that a teacher is considered to be virtually essential. If this is not really an option in your present circumstances, the best you can probably do is to read a variety of good books by various acknowledged experts. And discuss aspects that you do not understand in a good discussion group. I have suggested books by Swami Dayananda – I know of none better.

Q3: I have recently bought 'The Nature of Man According to the Vedanta' by John Levy. It is fairly short. If I just read that over and over, would that be enough to remove ignorance?

A: I haven't read the John Levy book but I can say that Direct Path teachings are not for everyone, whereas straight traditional teaching does cater for all. It is most unlikely that a single book such as this would answer all your questions and persuade you of the reality of non-duality.

Q4: What are your views of Adyashanti? He seems to have the peace of mind which characterizes j~nAna-phalam. But he doesn't recommend any specific practice. How about Eckhart Tolle? Both seem to have different understandings of enlightenment from you. They seem to believe that if you remain 'in presence' long enough and frequently enough, eventually the presence will take over.

A: I have not read any books by Adyashanti or heard any of his talks. Some of the material that I have read on the Internet is very good indeed – but his teaching is not pure Advaita. In fact, I understand he began in the Zen tradition. If you were being taught one to one for a prolonged period, then maybe he would be a good choice but, as I have written at length, satsang (occasional, short, group question and answer) is hopeless as a teaching method. The same applies to Eckhart Tolle – his books (as far as I have read) are excellent for providing useful practical approaches but I feel that they are short on theory (and not in accord with traditional Advaita). 'Remaining in presence' is an experience in time; it has a beginning and an end and has nothing to do with enlightenment.

Summary

Q: Many thanks for a great web page. I've been through all of the Q&A section, and it really cleared up a lot of things for me.

I really like Swami Dayananda's way of teaching. His explanations are really excellent. I've been watching some old videos on YouTube with him (at a time when he didn't talk so slowly!) and I've read his 'Introduction to Vedanta'. Now I want to read more written by him. I've visited the bookstore (http://books.arshavidya.org/) and there's quite a collection of books, which makes me a bit confused as to where to begin. So, I want to ask you if you could please write me a list of a recommended order in which one should read his books. They are not that expensive, so I might buy a bunch of them straight away.

A: Regarding Swami Dayananda's books, I have not read all of them but all that I have read have been readable and useful to some degree. It really depends on the level or topic that interests you. If you want short talks on a wide variety of subjects, the two-volume 'Talks and Essays of Swami Dayananda' is excellent. You buy these separately, rather than as a set incidentally. Each is quite thick. I can highly recommend 'Self-Knowledge' and 'Dialogues with Swami Dayananda' – both short and 'introductory' in nature. 'The Value of Values' and 'Teaching Tradition of Advaita Vedanta' are both classics. If you don't mind a fair bit of Sanskrit (but English equivalents are usually given when a word is introduced), then the two-volume 'Mundaka Upanishad' and 'Vivekachudamani: Talks on 108 Selected Verses' are both excellent. If you want really advanced, try the Taittiriya Upanishad, which is published in a ring binder – but I haven't yet read this myself. But the highest recommendation has to go the Gita Home Study Course (which I have still not completed myself). See Q.462 for details.

The Goal

Enlightenment

Here is what I consider to be the definitive statement of what is meant by 'Enlightenment'. It is by Shankara, in his commentary on the Brihadaranyaka Upanishad (I.iv.7) as translated by A. J. Alston in Volume 1 of the 6-volume 'A Shankara Source Book' – a truly excellent source reference:

"Attainment of the Self is nothing other than knowledge of the Self. Attainment is not here, as it is in other contexts, attainment of something that one does not already possess, because there is here no difference between the attainer and that which he wishes to attain. If the Self wished to attain the not-self, then the Self would be the attainer and the not-self the object of his attainment. And the object of its attainment would be something not already possessed, something which required action for its attainment or even production. It would have to be attained by some act brought about by the requisite instruments of action. Such an object of attainment, not yet possessed, would necessarily be impermanent. It would proceed from action, which in turn proceeds from desire, itself born of wrong knowledge. Its 'attainment' would be like the 'attainment' of a son in a dream.

"But this Self is the opposite. As it is one's own Self, it never becomes separated from itself through the typical forms of activity such as production. Being eternally attained by nature, the only impediment to its possession is ignorance. One may be perceiving a piece of nacre and yet not perceive it on account of its appearing through error as a piece of silver. Here, the only barrier to the possession of the nacre is wrong knowledge, and right knowledge is the only means for its attainment, because right knowledge has the quality of cancelling wrong knowledge, the obstacle to the attainment of the nacre. The same is the case with the Self. In non-attainment of the Self, the sole barrier is ignorance. Therefore attainment of the Self can never be anything other than removal of ignorance regarding it through right knowledge".

Q.369 mokSha

Q: What is meant by mokSha as a puruShArtha?

A : Someone who has come to the realization that he/she is never going to find happiness through worldly pursuits of any kind – be it objects, other people, status or whatever – may eventually realize that what is really wanted is freedom from the presumed bondage to all of those things. 'Gaining' mokSha is acquiring the certain knowledge that one is already free of those things, since they are all mithyA and who-one-really-is is the unlimited, perfect, ever-complete, non-dual reality.

Q.412 Definition of 'Enlightenment'

Q: In your writings you use quite often the word 'enlightenment'. In 'Back to the truth: 5000 years of Advaita' you give the following definition:

"Enlightenment is a sudden recognition that non-duality is, has always been, and will always be the reality of our experience"

and further you explain:

"[...] it refers to the transition from the position of believing oneself to be a person – body, mind etc. as described earlier – to the position of knowing, that there is only the non-dual Self [...]".

This is probably a pretty good definition; however the words 'recognition' and 'knowledge' here can be easily misunderstood. 'Knowledge', in the view of most people, including most of the spiritual aspirants, is a kind of intellectual knowledge or insight. As a result these people hearing the Advaitic non-dual doctrine usually just add to their ideas a new one: 'I am non-dual Self, I am Brahman', thinking that this is the required knowledge (or recognition) they have missed so far and that this is the enlightenment.

Moreover, the term 'enlightenment' is used by many religious/spiritual traditions/movements and is differently defined/interpreted by them. In fact, there is a wide range of interpretations/definitions. Further, many claim that there are 'stages' of Enlightenment, saying that that there can be a deep or shallow enlightenment, full or partial.

Advaita defines 'knowledge' or 'true knowledge' differently and according to Advaita such an intellectual knowledge or mental recognition of non-dual truth is not the true knowledge at all. So, such an 'enlightenment' has relatively little value in Advaita spiritual system, being seen just as an intellectual understanding of the non-dual truth. From this point there is still a long way to the authentic realization of the truth, called 'true knowledge'.

Taking all that into account I am rather against using the term 'enlightenment' in the context of authentic Advaita teaching. In my view it doesn't bring much clarity, confusing many. Why not use original Advaitin terms, which are meaningful, concrete, almost free of misconceptions and leave little room for interpretations?

Would you please explain if the term 'enlightenment' has any origin in traditional Advaitic texts? Which ones? Please give the exact examples. What is the original Sanskrit word which is translated into English as 'enlightenment'?

A: I do use the word 'enlightenment' quite a lot, because this is the word that many modern seekers associate with their 'objective' in pursuing Advaita. But I also agree that it is a much misused word and I devote a whole chapter to this misuse in my 'Jungle' book.

I would not define the word in quite the way that I did in 'Back to the Truth'. That book is quite old now and my comments would probably change quite a bit if I were to produce a second edition. (I may indeed do that when I have completed this one!) Very simply, I equate 'enlightenment' with 'Self-knowledge' and not in any way with 'experience'.

The stance of claiming that one gains 'merely intellectual knowledge' and then has to 'do' or 'experience' something else to 'convert' this into 'real' understanding is a mistaken one. One can certainly have 'provisional understanding' of something and need to submit this to further examination – this is the purpose of shravaNa and manana respectively. But firm Self-knowledge is 'it' – there is nothing else to do.

You can define knowledge as 'justified, true belief' if you like. I attempted to illustrate this with a personal example – see Q.362 – but I don't know how successful this was!

It has always been the way of the teaching of Advaita to start with the current level of understanding of the seeker and move forward from there (adhyAropa-apavAda) so I do not see a problem with using English words, providing they are correctly defined. But I also agree that it is often necessary to use Sanskrit terms, because there is no corresponding word in English ('mithyA' is a good example). sAkShAtkAra is probably the closest Sanskrit word for enlightenment used in Advaita texts, but it is not often encountered. mokSha is what is spoken of – liberation. And of course we are already free. We were never bound – we only thought we were.

The Varaha Upanishad states (2.41): "*A man is said to attain parokSha (indirect) wisdom when he knows (theoretically) that there is Brahman; but he is said to attain sAkShAtkAra (direct cognition) when he knows (or realizes) that he is himself Brahman*". I am not aware of any other scriptural reference for this word.

I sympathize with your views – and, if you have read practically any of my books, you will know that I use the same arguments to justify my own use of Sanskrit terms. The problem is that many Western seekers are tentatively investigating traditional teaching with a background of only Satsang teaching (or, worse, Neo-Advaita or some other system altogether). They tend to have an actual antipathy to Sanskrit and would be likely to turn off completely if one insisted on using correct terms and actively refusing to recognize the terms that they are used to.

Q: I am not sure that I understood your explanation of how the belief 'becomes' the true knowledge. You said "this is the purpose of shravaNa and manana respectively. But firm Self-knowledge is 'it' – there is nothing else to do".

I think nididhyAsana is missing here, it cannot be disregarded on any account, it is essential. nididhyAsana in its last aspect is the practice of abidance in the Self. Self-abidance is a practice of being, not doing, so it is correct in a sense to say that there is nothing to do. However, before one becomes mature enough to undertake the Advaitic practice of mere being (Self-abidance) a lot of effort is required in order to make the mind still (which is necessary for Self-abidance) and this is a kind of 'doing'. shravaNa and manana also require some conscious effort and have an element of 'doing', otherwise how are we going to perform them?

In other words, using Advaita's metaphor, if we want to see the real rope instead of the false picture of the snake superimposed on it, we must withdraw our attention from all other objects, direct it to the snake and investigate it in order to find out the truth (i.e. source) of the snake. Then, in due course, the false snake disappears and only real rope is left – this is the true knowledge.

Do you know how – if not through the efforts of the practice taught by Advaita's sages – can we withdraw our attention from the thoughts, direct it to the 'snake' and keep it there?

A: Several questions deal with the topic of j~nAna versus jIvanmukti – look up 'pratibandha' in the index, or search for the term at Advaita Vision – and I follow the position taken by Swami Dayananda in maintaining that the function of nididhyAsana is to 'make up for' deficiencies in sAdhana chatuShTaya sampatti so as to benefit the 'person' and give j~nAna phalam. Self-knowledge results from shravaNa and manana. By all means read more, study, continue attending talks by a qualified teacher if you are lucky enough to live near one, etc. This will avoid the danger of any recurrence of doubt, and further cement the understanding. But there is nothing else to be done as far as mokSha is concerned. The only question is whether or not you enjoy the 'fruits' (peace of mind, security etc.) for the remainder of the life of the body-mind.

Q.129 How does one move towards enlightenment?

Q: How does one move towards enlightenment in Advaita? Does it offer the equivalent of a eightfold path to awakening or is it more like Krishnamurti – any attempt to get 'enlightened' leads you further into delusion?

A: In Advaita, 'enlightenment' is synonymous with Self-knowledge. The acquiring of this at the practical level is a process of hearing the teaching from a qualified teacher, clarifying understanding through questioning, discussion, repeated hearing etc. and absorbing that knowledge. Simple, really! Also, it is logical and reasonable, unlike many other so-called paths.

Q.150 I'm not sure that my goal is enlightenment

Q: About seven years ago, I embarked upon a spiritual quest through the Christian path, a quest to attain liberation and live from my authentic nature, whatever that might be. I became involved with a group of spiritual Christians who were very open to mystical things. We met on a regular basis to discuss scripture, pray, meditate etc. and there appeared to be a lot of spiritual activity, but in the end I became very disillusioned. We all considered ourselves to be quite spiritual but I had the sense that this was all an egotistic illusion and ultimately not Real.

On the other side of this realization was a certain amount of freedom. For the first time in my life I was happy, and I had a desire to be in a relationship with others for the pure joy of the relationship. Now I find myself in an Advaita group. The whole focus is on the teachings and the goal of enlightenment. I am reading your books, learning a new language and engaging with others. There is an Advaita teacher who is a beautiful expression of the Self, and yet for some reason I'm not sure my goal *is* enlightenment, I know that's not what's driving my involvement. My interest seems to be in opening up to another perspective, another language in order to gain understanding of others and the oneness of it all. Does this make any sense? This is obviously not an intellectual question.

A: Yes, I understand your views. I used to belong to the SES organization in the UK and attended for many years. Although, ostensibly teaching Advaita, this was much more of a group who were sharing their common practices, environment and cultural values, if you like. It seemed to me that they were using the supposed aim merely as the trigger that had brought them together and the purpose was now forgotten. The group itself had become the raison d'être.

In my experience, the true pursuit of enlightenment is generally confined to those who are deeply dissatisfied with their lives and the supposed values of society. Those who actually enjoy life or who seek to find satisfaction through dualistic means (ambition, money, objects, finding a partner etc.) are not suited to the enlightenment search and are unlikely to have the determination to follow a serious path. To put it brutally, if you are enjoying the dream, why bother waking up?

The problem is of course that life, being dualistic, will always have its ups and downs. If things are going well, they are likely to get worse (and vice versa of course!). There is no problem with this. You are the non-dual Self whether you seek to discover this or not (and whether you like it or not). If knowing that your true nature is unlimited, that 'you' cannot die etc. is important, then you will (eventually) become a seeker. Whatever happens is ok from the absolute perspective, so if you are happy from the relative perspective don't worry about it!

If you are more interested in psychological aspects, learning an attitude to life that will optimize your outlook (feeling at one with everything etc.), then why not try some of the western satsang teachers for whom this is often more important than genuine self-realization?

Q.11 Enlightenment of the person

Q: Is enlightenment personal?

A: Yes or no, depending on your point of view! The question arises as a result of the concept that there are individual persons, some of whom are not currently enlightened but may become so at a future time. This is from the empirical (vyAvahArika) perspective. So, from that point of view, the answer is 'yes'.

The mind of the unenlightened person superimposes duality upon the non-dual Brahman and sees the world, other people and self as all separate. If this mind is disciplined and seeks out a qualified teacher, it is able to gain knowledge that will dispel that ignorance and permit realization of the truth that there is only Brahman or Consciousness. That entails the realization that there was no separate person in the first place.

In reality, there is only Brahman and it is obviously not meaningful to speak of Brahman becoming enlightened – Brahman is unlimited Consciousness. In reality, there are no persons, egos or individuals – no one who could become enlightened. So it is not altogether meaningful to speak of the person having become enlightened (but then, if anyone has become enlightened, it has to be the person)!

The Brihadaranyaka Upanishad (IV.4.19) states that *"It is only through the mind that the truth can be realized"*. And when so-called realization occurs, the world continues to appear exactly as it did before. The crucial difference is in the mind – the mistaken concept of a 'world' and 'separation' has now disappeared.

Hence the expression 'Nothing ever happened' or the Zen term: 'the gateless gate'.

David Carse's book 'Perfect Brilliant Stillness' addresses precisely this question (his material is specifically not copyrighted, in case anyone should wonder):

There is a sense in which there is no 'awakening,' no enlightenment, because there is no 'one' to awaken. Who would this be? Who is awakened?

'Me,' david? Of course not: david is a dream character, an idea, a fiction; not the dreamer, and therefore obviously cannot awaken. There is no 'david' to do anything, including awaken.

Or is it 'Who I Really Am' that has 'awakened;' Presence, Awareness, All That Is?

But of course Awareness has never been asleep, has no need to awaken to anything; Awareness is always already All There Is.

Clearly then, there is no one to awaken. 'Awakening' is only an analogy, a concept, a pointer. The seeker community tends to take it literally, but like most analogies it only takes you so far.

What has happened is more like this: in the dream, in the case of the dream character 'david,' All That Is stops pretending that 'It' is asleep. What has always been awake lets the misunderstanding that there is someone to be asleep and someone to awaken, fall away.

That is all. And the dream continues, as before. The misunderstanding has fallen away, but the misunderstanding was not real anyway, so what has happened? Nothing. The character 'david' now knows he is only a dream, not 'real;' knows it is all a dream. But even this dream character's 'knowing' is part of the dream, part of the unfolding of the script of the dream for that dream character, and nothing has happened. The dream character goes on being the dream character.

But, if this is couched in language which seems too 'Neo-Advaitin', the simple answer is this: it is the person who has Self-ignorance so it is the person who must gain Self-knowledge. This takes place in the mind. When this ignorance has been replaced by knowledge, the person can be said to be enlightened.

Q.39 My 'awakening'

Q: Would you please tell us about your own Awakening?

A: The short answer is 'no'. Why do you ask and what difference could it make to anything?

The longer answer is that I used, in my early twenties, to feel generally dissatisfied with life and believe that everyone else (at least those who appeared to be happy) was deluding themselves in believing that anything in this life had any real meaning. I began an investigation that was to last for several decades, during which time I learnt about Advaita and felt that I was following a path that would one day lead to enlightenment. I used to imagine that I might one day meet a guru who would pass on the crucial knowledge that would make the breakthrough. All this was self-delusion, still believing that there was a separate 'I' that could somehow become an eternal Self.

There was no obvious, final piece of knowledge, no event, no special guru. I carried on reading and discussing these matters, latterly with many contacts on the Internet. Then, though my interest continues (as evidenced by the fact that I am still writing on the subject), the personal element imperceptibly diminished until, sometime in the noughties, I realized that I was no longer 'seeking'. The understanding of the truth was just simply there, not just as an intellectual conviction but as something unarguable, requiring no external validation.

Life goes on; the nature of this body-mind has not changed and will continue to operate as though the world is dualistic but it matters not. There is not the shadow of a doubt that 'I' am not the body or mind, simply 'I am'. There is no free will, no creation etc. All of the key tenets of Advaita are simply self-evident.

Q.45 Is it possible to 'transmit' enlightenment?

Q: Do you have any views about organization X, which advertises courses in which the leaders claim the power to transmit enlightenment? They last several weeks and cost thousands of dollars.

A: I have not heard of the organization that you mention. However, I can tell you categorically that it is *not* possible to 'transmit' enlightenment. As you no doubt appreciate, we already are That (the Self, Consciousness, Brahman or whatever). The reason that we do not realize this is that it is obscured in the mind by ignorance. The only way that ignorance can be removed is through knowledge and that is transmitted in the usual manner – by a qualified teacher via word of mouth over a prolonged period. Furthermore, a genuinely qualified teacher will never ask for money in that way.

Q.46 Who is it who awakens?

Q: Since the person can't awaken (since awakening is the seeing through of the person), and, since oneness, consciousness, being is the ground of everything, *it* is already always awake. So, what exactly is it that awakens?

A: As you say, who-you-really-are is already the Self. The Self is the only reality so it makes no sense to speak of this Self 'becoming enlightened'.

Although *in reality* there is no person, it is at this empirical level of reality (vyavahAra) where there appears to be a separate person. The reason for this mistaken view of things is ignorance at the level of the mind. Specifically, the nature of this ignorance is mixing up the real and unreal – this is called adhyAsa. (Remember we are still talking about the empirical level, where there seem to be such things as minds.)

The only thing that can remove this ignorance is knowledge, which has to take place in this mind, since that is where the ignorance is. Accordingly, like it or not (and despite what other teachers may say – especially Neo-Advaitin ones), enlightenment takes place in the mind. It is the mind or person that 'awakens'.

Of course, once this awakening has taken place, it is realized that the seeming person, mind and knowledge were all part of the mistaken view and that before, during and after, there was only the Self and no actual person to become enlightened.

You can see some definitions of adhyAsa (http://www.advaita.org.uk/discourses/definitions/adhyAsa.htm) and you may find the essay on 'Self-knowledge and the Mind' will help understand this topic (http://www.advaita.org.uk/discourses/durga/knowingself_durga.htm).

Q: So, since the Self presents as the ignorant/separate person in the first place (so to speak), it also presents as the separate person seeing through this illusion of separation. In this seeing through of the unreal the person is no more.

In a way, it still seems inaccurate to say that the person awakens – since at the point (I understand it is not an event in time) of awakening, there is no person. I suppose it's similar to saying that someone is dead. To say John is dead is not true since death is the absence of John (John of course does not experience his own death). Is it a convenience to say that the person awakens (as in the above example about death)?

Sorry to be picky here – I suspect it's got something to do with the mixing up of levels.

A: No problems with being 'picky' – I can see you really want to get to the bottom of this and that is good. But it is very difficult to put clearly into words.

There is only ever the Self in reality. So the apparent persons and world that we perceive in our ignorance are already only and always the Self. The person in ignorance and the person seeing through the ignorance are equally only the Self. I think this is what you are saying in the first part.

You then say: *"In this seeing through of the unreal the person is no more"*. In reality, there never was a person to begin with. There only appeared to be whilst there was ignorance. So, 'in the seeing through', there is not actually any change in reality. But the mistaken view that there was a person has now been dissolved.

The apparent confusion of levels occurs when we try to speak of a person being enlightened. There are only (thought to be) persons in vyavahAra. Enlightenment means seeing through vyavahAra and knowing that there are no persons in reality. Thus, enlightenment does not really have any meaning at all for the enlightened 'person'; it only has meaning for the 'person' who is not yet 'enlightened'.

But you are not entirely correct when you say that "it still seems inaccurate to say that the person awakens". It is certainly reasonable to quibble over saying 'the bottle is broken' for example since, as soon as the breaking occurs, there is no longer a bottle. But, when the person is enlightened, that person does not cease to exist. If that happened, there would be no enlightened teachers! After enlightenment, the mind that has been enlightened continues to exist until its associated body dies. Even the ego continues, albeit perhaps in an 'attenuated' form. It is simply that this mind now realizes the truth about the non-dual nature of reality. And it is likely that it will no longer be swayed by desires/fears etc. The extent to which that is the case, however, is dependent upon the mental preparation that was carried out prior to enlightenment.

Q.152 Who is it who awakens (another questioner)?

Q: Is it valid to ask 'who awakens?' How this question is answered reveals the major underlying difference between traditional Advaita and so called Neo Advaita. Traditionalists say that it is the person that awakens, becomes enlightened. Most 'Neo Advaitins' would say that Oneness is already the case, therefore enlightenment has no significance.

Each perspective recognizes difficulties in the other:

1. The person becomes enlightened.

It appears of course that a body/mind is necessary for recognition to occur, but at the 'point' of recognition it is known beyond doubt that the body/mind is just an appearance in what I am. It cannot be correct therefore to say that the body/mind has become realized. Realization is not an attribute of the body/mind.

2. Oneness is already the case.

Yes, Oneness is already the case but unless that is 'known' beyond doubt, insight (enlightenment) has not 'occurred'. The 'Neo Advaitin' might respond that absence of recognition is Oneness appearing as 'not recognizing'. But this understanding itself assumes recognition (and thereby confirms its necessity).

How is this resolved?

Perspective 1 works from the stance (so to speak) of 'prior' to the 'realization event' within the appearance of separation. Here it seems wholly correct to say that it is the body/mind that becomes realized since this is all we have to work with via the gradual unfolding of knowledge.

Perspective 2 works only and always from the 'outlook' of realization. From here, the body/mind, 'prior-ness', *and* the realization itself are known to be appearances in what I am – and what I am, could never be lacking.

Conclusion:

Both perspectives are consistent with their respective context of either 1. teacher or 2. reporter.

1. The teacher starts with how we appear and guides us to the recognition of what we really are.

2. The reporter starts and ends with the description of what we already are (that which is always already the case).

The validity of the perspective and the lucidity of its statements etc. is dependent on recognizing the context of the communication, guide or report.

P.S. The mode/means of communication of reporter and teacher are probably as distinct as painter and film maker – yet both point to the same reality (only one employs a method of unfoldment).

A: Yes, I agree with all you say.

In order to avoid confusion, I prefer to use the term 'liberated' or 'free' to refer to what we already are, whether or not this is realized. This then allows a definition of 'enlightenment' as 'the realization that we are already free'.

I think that the sunrise metaphor explains why what the Neo-Advaita teacher says cannot really work. Suppose that there is one scientist, who understands the output of Newton, Kepler, Copernicus etc. and actually knows that the earth rotates and goes round the sun. But suppose that all of the people to whom he is talking have the 'scientific' understanding of the Middle Ages. Their direct experience is that the sun rises, moves across the sky and then sets. How can you tell them the truth such that they immediately realize the reality? It simply would not work. You would need to explain some basic principles, show them models, let them look through a telescope and so on before they started to appreciate what it was you were actually saying.

Recognizing that the Neo-Advaita teacher is a 'reporter' does not give them special credibility when there are also reporters around who claim that they communicate directly with dead people or aliens etc. What is said has to be reasonable and not conflict with other sources of valid knowledge.

I have always acknowledged that what the (genuine) Neo-Advaita teachers say is the truth, just that simply stating this has no utility for most seekers (i.e. the unprepared ones).

Q.69 (part 1) Facts about enlightenment?

Q: Why is there so much misinformation about enlightenment?

A: That's an interesting question. From the seeker's side, I think it is simply ignorance. The available information has increased dramatically over the past 50 years, accelerating out of sight since the Internet. But the basic ignorance is still the same. People want something for themselves (as they perceive themselves to be separate). They want to feel good and get the idea that enlightenment will make them feel permanently good!

Unfortunately, from the teachers' side, many seem to see this as an opportunity in the commercial sense and travel about the world making easy money. Whether this is their primary aim is beside the point – many no doubt genuinely believe what they say and may even feel they are providing some sort of service. (This is less easy to argue in the case of the neos since they deny the very existence of others – what are *they* doing?) But the genuine teachers have always been there and the genuine seeker will eventually find their way to one – it is usually that way round. Such teachers do not usually travel or ask for money.

But I haven't actually answered your question directly. I think the answer is probably that 'enlightenment' is perceived as being a desirable thing, and lots of people want to impress or make money by claiming to know something about it (even when they don't).

Q.105 On experiences, enlightenment and contentment

Q: So far as I understand, Advaita teaches one final enlightenment, after which there is nothing to do. To reach this enlightenment, one must remove ignorance.

Some teachers from other traditions say that we can begin cultivation only after we realize the truth.

For instance, when I was seventeen, I was meditating one day, and as I stepped out onto my backyard, I suddenly realized that my body is not me and cannot be enlightened, my mind is not me and cannot be enlightened, and awareness never changes and cannot be enlightened. Then I realized there was no one to be enlightened. And then for the next three days, I felt a deep contentment. But then after the three days, I returned to the frustrations of normal life.

Now according to some teachers (or so I understand them), no matter how many spiritual experiences (like the above) I have, I cannot achieve enlightenment unless I devote every single moment of my life to purifying my mind (from attachments and aversions). Some say I cannot achieve enlightenment unless there is total surrender from my ego.

I wonder, if I study Advaita only a few hours a day, but remain attached to sensual experiences and false conceptions for the rest of the day, will the accumulated effort of studying eventually wear away my ignorance?

When you studied Advaita, did you make a conscious effort to purify your mind and live as the Presence (in the words of Eckhart Tolle and Adyashanti)? Or did you put your total faith in the liberating power of Advaita philosophy and scriptures (instead of momentary, everyday cultivation)?

A: Advaita teaches that there is 'enlightenment' (after which one may be referred to as a j~nAnI, i.e. one who knows the truth) and then there are the 'fruits of enlightenment' – jIvanmukti – which bring the 'benefits' of peace of mind etc. For someone who is fully prepared mentally prior to enlightenment (as per Shankara's sAdhana chatuShTaya sampatti), the fruits accompany enlightenment. For those who were not fully prepared, further nididhyAsana is required. Note that mental preparation and practices such as meditation do not in themselves bring about enlightenment – for that, only Self-knowledge is effective. But the preparation makes it more likely that teaching will be heard and recognized when it is given. Those who have had no preparation at all cannot even become a j~nAnI.

As noted elsewhere, no amount of 'spiritual experience' will ever bring about enlightenment; only Self-knowledge can do this. This knowledge is gained ideally from a qualified teacher but may also come from reading or talking with others. Coming to the final understanding is almost certainly gradual, although that final understanding is itself binary – you have either realized the truth or you haven't.

As regards your point about studying for a few hours a day and wallowing in sensual experience for the rest of the day (I know you didn't phrase it quite like this – I am exaggerating to make the point): this suggests that you do not yet have mumukShutva. It has been stated elsewhere that, in order fully to qualify as a seeker, you should want enlightenment more than anything else in the world. You should have recognized that worldly pleasures are never going to bring lasting happiness. These aspects are all part of the mental preparation – cultivating vairAgya (dispassion) and viveka (discrimination). So the answer to your question is that this partial commitment will still be effective in 'wearing away' your ignorance – but it will take a lot longer (possibly lifetimes longer, says the traditional teaching).

Q.106 Liberation and enlightenment

Q: In an earlier answer on your website you state that *"Enlightenment is of the mind; the Self-knowledge that destroys the Self-ignorance takes place in the mind"*.

It may be that I am confusing absolute and relative realities, but are you implying that there exists a state of Self-ignorance which needs to be replaced by a state of Self-knowledge? And that this is a mental process occurring over time?

If Brahman is All, would that not include all apparent 'states'? Is not apparent 'Self-ignorance' also an expression of Oneness? Would not any attempt to move from one state to another (or indeed the statement that there are two states) be an expression of dualistic thinking?

I agree that the concept of 'enlightenment' is of the mind, which results in an apparent 'seeker'. Are you of the opinion that we are all 'liberated' but as yet don't know it ... and that through some sort of teaching, we can attain to this knowledge?

If the ultimate state of Awareness is our present state of Awareness, there is clearly no way to cause or produce that which is already the case. And even if we could, the result would be finite and dual. As Eckhart stated, if we imagine God can be found in a particular state of consciousness, then when that state slips from us, so God slips with it.

A: You are right – this is the sort of confusion of paramArtha and vyavahAra that often occurs when speaking about enlightenment. At the level of vyavahAra, which is where all of this discussion takes place between (apparently) separate persons, Self-ignorance is the normal condition of most minds. With the benefit of good teaching, this may be supplanted (in the mind) by Self-knowledge. When this occurs (in time), we say that the person has become 'enlightened'.

You are also right that 'Self-ignorance' is "also an expression of Oneness". Since there is only Brahman, this must necessarily be so – from the pAramArthika standpoint. But this does not preclude changes of state at the level of vyavahAra. It simply depends upon where you 'take your stand'. Advaita 'encompasses' dvaita. Apparent duality is simply misperceived non-duality.

You ask: *"Are you of the opinion that we are all 'liberated' but as yet don't know it ... and that through some sort of teaching, we can attain to this knowledge?"* This is a confusion of terms again – hence the difficulty. Yes, we are already free – i.e. we cannot be 'liberated' but no, most people are not already 'enlightened'. Accordingly, it is perfectly meaningful that Self-knowledge can be taught and can lead to enlightenment. Enlightenment is the mental realization that we are already free!

Q.115 Was Ramesh enlightened? (Part 2)

Q (continued from Q.114): You don't say it directly, but I guess the answer to my question whether Ramesh was a genuine 'enlightened' teacher, is a 'no'. But somehow I respect his honesty. Contrary to many other teachers he didn't claim to be enlightened in any traditional or mystical sense. He acknowledged that it's all just a concept, and that he was centered in his mind/ego, just like (most) other people.

Lots of teachers out there seem to believe they are enlightened. How can I know whether it's for real or not? Isn't it perfectly possible for someone to believe, beyond any doubt, that he/she is enlightened, when in fact it's only the mind playing its games? Are there any objective criteria to determine whether a person is enlightened such as, for example, constant awareness during deep sleep?

A: I appreciated that this question was behind the others but did not wish explicitly to answer it! The fact of the matter is that, no, there is no objective criterion for determining whether or not a teacher is enlightened. And ideas such as constant awareness in sleep are just that – ideas.

But enlightenment is not a concept. Enlightenment equates to Self-knowledge, and the 'final' Self-knowledge is an event in the mind of a person. Outwardly, everything remains the same. That person continues to (apparently) act in the world just as before. The difference is that it is now known by that 'person' (who now knows that he is not the person) that there is only the non-dual reality, despite all the appearance to the contrary. There is no problem in admitting enlightenment, providing that the person(s) to whom it is admitted understands what is being said.

You can pretend to be enlightened, it is true, but knowing with irrevocable certainty is not the same as believing or pretending. The mind is the means but not the end. Once enlightened, the mind is said to take on the form of the non-dual reality. There is no question of playing any more. So the answer to your specific question is that Ramesh may well have been enlightened. How he behaved or what he said is not necessarily a guide – only he knew for sure! See other questions for specific details on the concept of pratibandha-s (obstacles or impediments in the mind remaining after enlightenment because of inadequate prior mental preparation).

Q.160 'Partial' versus 'complete' enlightenment

Q: The following is quoted from your website

"I would have to say that, when Self-knowledge has completely removed the Self-ignorance in the mind of the seeker, there IS permanent enlightenment. It is then known directly that there is only the Self. That knowledge never fades. It is not an experience and not a state. The seeking ceases because it is now known, in the mind, that 'I am That'".

My own experience is that I have realized that 'I am that' and the mental chatter, which I used to think was my whole world, was seen to be something that happens regardless of a 'me'. But there are times when I am so engrossed in the mental chatter that it seems that that is all there is, so it seems that the realizing of the absolute Self is intermittent. I know that the absolute Self is always there, never changing, but the little self isn't always aware of this fact.

So it seems that full Self-realization is *"when Self-knowledge has completely removed the Self-ignorance"* whereas in my own case it has only partially removed Self-ignorance. The teachers I have spoken with on this matter have said that I may notice a gradual extension of periods of, let's say, the mind being aware that it isn't 'it'. So my question is about permanent enlightenment: is remembering this truth all that one can do to convert the 'partial' into the 'complete' enlightenment?

A: If you still have doubts of any sort, then there has not yet been akhaNDAkAra vRRitti (http://www.advaita.org.uk/discourses/teachers/knowingself_durga.htm). If there is no longer any doubt in your mind whatsoever about the truth of non-duality, then you are really talking about the distinction between j~nAna and j~nAna phalam. There are a few questions on this topic already. If one is fully mentally prepared prior to enlightenment (http://www.advaita.org.uk/discourses/definitions/sAdhana_chatuShTaya.htm), then as soon as there is enlightenment, one automatically also gets the benefits such as security, peaceful mind, absence of fear etc. In the case of those who were not fully prepared, however, there will be knowledge of the truth but no immediate fruits. In this case, one should continue with the nididhyAsana practice. This means such things as reading scriptures, listening to good teachers etc. and generally meditating on the knowledge which has been gained. This is my own situation, too, and the principal way in which I am doing my nididhyAsana is writing books (and answering questions)!

Q.168 If one person is enlightened, why not everyone?

Q: If there are not two things then it cannot be possible for one man to reach God before any other. When we do awaken, we must awaken all at once, because there is only one of us.

A: This is not the case. It is like saying that, when one person dies, everyone will die. Or it would mean that sages such as Shankara and Ramana Maharshi were not enlightened. It is a confusion of the absolute reality with the empirical. As enlightenment is an event in time in the mind of a jIva, it does not affect any other jIva. For some excellent observations on all of this, read about the pot-space versus total-space metaphor used by Gaudapada in his Mandukya kArikA II.3-9.

Q: I would say that, once a person has reached this enlightenment, they also see that we are all there already. Some of us just don't know it. There is no journey, for there is no place to go. Isn't this the knowledge that exists within each of us?

What you are saying about time is my point, exactly. Once we have stepped out of time, then we see that all time has passed because it was not real anyway. It may only appear from our Earthly domain that we are awakening in parts, and this is because of this illusion of time but, once we have woken, then the truth is otherwise.

I think, in a manner of speaking, that when a person dies for the last time (that is even to say there could be a last time, if all time occurs at once) then yes, once the transition from time is achieved, it could be said that all have died. We are all born at once and we all die at once. How can this not be so if all time is one moment? Are we all not one another; past, present and future?

A: As I said, you should read some presentations on this topic, such as the one I mentioned. In that metaphor, the 'awakening' relates to the pot (i.e. the mind), not the pot-space (i.e. the Atman), which is always only total-space. The pot (i.e. body of the person) only seemingly separates out a 'part' of the total space. The pot is born and dies but the space is unaffected. The pot is subject to time; the space is not. There is one total-space but lots of pots. 'Enlightenment' of one pot does not affect the others.

So, yes, some of what you say is correct: there is no *real* journey to be made; we are already the non-dual reality (the pot space is already the total space). People are never 'absolutely real' and enlightenment is realizing all of this. But the realization is in a single mind (a single pot), so that this understanding unfortunately does not impact directly on the understanding of another mind. This knowledge belongs to the pot and, while some have it, most do not. There is only 'seeming' duality but the appearance of duality continues after enlightenment (the sun still appears to rise even though we know this is an appearance caused by the rotation of the earth). Time continues at the relative level for all jIva-s, enlightened or not. It is only true to say that there is no time, space and causation with respect to absolute reality. 'We' as separate persons never 'step out of time'.

Q: This is what I meant when I was saying that I am sure I am not using the proper terminology. When I am speaking of 'reaching God', I am speaking of the next step after enlightenment, I suppose; the only *real* state to achieve; the goal; the step that occurs at the end of all lives.

I do appreciate your helping me to differentiate. We, as separate persons, do not step out of time but once time has been transcended then there will be no separate persons. Once it does happen it will have always been.

A: This is where you start to diverge from what we have been saying. There is no 'next step' with respect to the apparent person in the world. (There isn't even a first step with respect to who-we-really-are in reality.) Realizing that there is no person, that we are already perfect and complete, is the goal for the one who still believes himself to be a person. The idea of 'reaching God' is for the person still seemingly trapped in duality. At the end of 'our life', nothing at all happens to Consciousness. When the pot breaks, the pot-space is unaffected because the pot-space never existed. The space is not in the pot; it is the pot that is in the space. Consciousness is not in the body; it is the body that is in Consciousness.

Q: As I have read more about Advaita I have seen that this is a truth that lies within all of us if it lies within any of us. I have always said that if any one of us will see Heaven then we must all see it because we are not separate. If any one of us is to know true peace and truly experience Heaven then we must all experience it because the truth of Heaven is without the chaos of human emotion and it cannot be had as long as any part of God believes itself to be in Hell.

It cannot be possible for any one person to experience the true reality and be one with God and also still believe he is a person. In reality we are *all* one with God and this is the only reality and it is now. It could not be possible for some of us to be one while others are not. Those who are not 'enlightened' may not yet see this but those are also the same who do not see any truth, or very little.

A: If I can return to the pot-space and total-space metaphor. The individual pots (the actual material) correspond to individual persons (body-minds).

Suppose that pot A is not realized. He thinks that 'who-I-really-am' is the space inside me (equivalent to my 'soul' or whatever you want to call it). He thinks that, when he dies, his space will merge with God or go to some heavenly space or be reborn inside another pot. Or perhaps he thinks that, when he breaks (the body dies), his space will disintegrate and exist no more.

Pot B is enlightened. He knows that, in reality, there is only total-space and that who-he-really-is *is* that total-space. Each pot actually exists in total-space. Each pot does not really have pot-space inside of it. He knows that when he breaks, all that will happen is that the clay of the pot will return to the ground but he, the total-space, will be entirely unaffected.

But B's knowing of the truth is an aspect of B's pot (his mind). This does not affect A's pot and A still does not know it (unless B becomes a teacher-pot and explains the discovered truth to others).

So, the bottom line is that the pot-spaces of *all* pots are really total-space, whether or not they know this. Total-space is all there is. But most pots do not realize this. When one pot is enlightened, other pots are not automatically enlightened. Hope this is now clear.

Q.177 Dissolution of beliefs

Q: Is it the case that Self-realization comes about as a result of the dissolution of all beliefs? Without any belief, where is your individual identity? Through understanding, you discard all beliefs one by one until the very last one, whatever that might be. Following this dissolution, what you are left with is the absolute. The dictionary definition (Merriam Webster) gives: "Belief: *a state or habit of mind in which trust or confidence is placed in some person or thing*".

A: No – it is Self-ignorance that must be dispelled. Of course, in doing so, (false) beliefs will naturally go away but this is not the emphasis. In a sense, a belief is simply a strongly held opinion so is always open to change when better/more persuasive ideas come along. As your dictionary definition points out, it is akin to faith. Knowledge is beyond influence by opinion.

Q: How can you know your 'self'? That which you know cannot be your 'self'.

A: Yes, you are sort of right. You cannot know the Self in any objective sense, since I am that which illumines knower, known and means of knowing. But I am self-luminous, self-evident. I do not need a means of knowledge in order to be known, just as the sun does not need another source of light in order to be seen. You just need to remove any obstacles, such as clouds etc. (which are themselves only seen because of the sun).

Q.194 A question about the enlightened 'person'

Q: I have looked at your definition of 'enlightenment' at your website and I completely agree with your words here:

http://www.advaita.org.uk/discourses/enlightenment/enlightenment_not.htm

On the other hand, I have maybe (even intentionally) used the word 'enlightenment' in an absolute sense meaning the same as 'oneness' or 'one'.

I would like to ask you about what you say below:

"Jean Klein *(who was essentially a direct-path teacher) said:* "Liberation does not concern the person, for liberation is freedom from the person". *Tony Parsons (who is a Neo-Advaitin teacher) says:* "There is no such thing as an 'enlightened person'. No person has ever been 'enlightened'". *Jean Klein is correct to the extent that he uses the word 'liberation'; Tony Parsons is wrong since he uses the word 'enlightened'. N.B. Remember the definition of person given earlier. It is the jIva who gains enlightenment, and it takes place in the mind as was explained"*. (Note that this is a quote from the book 'Enlightenment: The Path Through The Jungle'.)

The sentence from Jean Klein seems quite clear. The seeing of the non-solid, unstable and unreal nature of the 'person' is liberation. Liberation happens from the person. It does not happen to the person. This seems very clear.

Now what about the statement of Tony Parsons? If the 'person' is only an illusion that appears in oneness, then would it not be correct to say that a person never becomes enlightened?

The 'person', the illusion of course, is oneness – that is clear. Therefore, in my maybe (wrong) usage, I would say the 'person' is 'enlightenment', is oneness. But it cannot become enlightened. It can only be seen through as being an appearance.

Or do you mean that, from the viewpoint of the person, the person can become enlightened? But this can only seem so when looking from the viewpoint of the person. It seems as if a person has become enlightened, but actually oneness has lost one more illusory belief in a 'person'. Only the 'person' can see another 'person' as being or becoming enlightened. In truth, both personas are just an appearance. In that light I could understand the sense of your critique on Tony's statement.

A: I understand what you are saying here and I do agree that I ought to have expanded a bit on the statement you quote.

The word 'liberation' is actually a bit misleading in the Jean Klein statement. To liberate means to make free. 'Who-I-really-am', Brahman, is *already* free. 'Who-I-think-I-am' does not really exist. However, at the level of empirical reality, the person and the world *do* exist. Once Self-knowledge (enlightenment) is gained, it is known that the person that I thought myself to be is only name and form of the non-dual Brahman. But the person does not thereby disappear. The name and form remains as before, up until death of the body-mind; it is simply that it is now known not to be a separately existing 'object'. So it is not really true to say that 'liberation is freedom from the person'. What he really means is that enlightenment is the realization that I am already free and that I never was a 'person'.

The second aspect comes back to the definition of enlightenment that I gave: *Enlightenment is the event in the mind of a person when it is realized that I am already free and that I never was a 'person'*. So it is certainly meaningful, from the standpoint of empirical reality, to talk about an 'enlightened person'. Tony has to accept that there are people – after all, he holds meetings and advertises for people to come to them. These people are (usually) not enlightened. If they were, they wouldn't attend his meetings!

I think your problem (apart from my lack of clarity) is in confusing absolute reality with the empirical appearance. This is the source of most misunderstandings in Advaita. All teaching takes place in duality, necessarily, yet endeavors to discuss non-duality. In absolute reality, there are no persons and the Self is ever-free. In empirical reality, there are people, some of whom are attempting to become enlightened.

Q.205 Can one lose enlightenment?

Q: I have a question about your key definition of enlightenment. I understand what you have said about the mind realizing the 'Truth' but what worries me is that the mind by nature is fickle. Is it not possible that later in time it forgets the Truth and enlightenment is reversed?

A: Enlightenment itself is irreversible. However it is true that, since the enlightened one remains functioning in the world, it is possible to get attached again and for the knowledge to recede into the background. This depends upon the degree to which the mind was 'prepared' prior to enlightenment – the distinction between the j~nAnI and the jIvanmukta – see questions 105 and 161.

Q: I read the questions 105 and 161 but something in me is not convinced. If, as you say, enlightenment itself is irreversible then how is it possible for the mind to get attached again? Irreversible means that which cannot go back. Also, if the mind can be attached again after enlightenment, then no one alive can be said to be truly enlightened because their mind is still around and could get attached again at any time until their last breath.

I once asked this question of my grandfather who has been a student of the Vedas all his life and is perhaps enlightened himself. He said that when enlightenment happens the mind gets dissolved in the universal consciousness. Then I specifically asked him, can the mind come back again? He said, "No".

Thus what I think is, if the mind can come back at a later date then it never got dissolved in the first place. Thus what we thought to be enlightenment was in reality just an experience, perhaps a glimpse into reality, such as I myself experienced 4 years ago.

What do you think?

A: True Self-knowledge (equals enlightenment), once gained, is never lost. However, if the mind was not fully prepared before this happened (i.e. sAdhana chatuShTaya sampatti), then it will still be prone to old habits. So, if one is not continually vigilant until such time as nididhyAsana brings about jIvanmukti, then there is the clear danger of following desires etc. so that the knowledge not lost, but 'pushed into the background' so to speak.

The mind does not 'dissolve' on enlightenment – otherwise a j~nAnI would no longer be able to function in the world. If you want to read literally hundreds of pages of discussion on this topic, see the archives of Advaitin Egroup from around mid-Jan to end Feb 2009. There were two or three who held your opinion but they were overwhelmed by all of the moderators and others presenting many quotations from the scriptures and Shankara. A j~nAnI does have a mind and body and does continue to interact with the world, despite knowing that everything is mithyA and there is only Brahman.

Q.221 Liberation, rebirth, and Self-knowledge

Q: If given the choice between liberation from rebirth, and rebirth with Self-knowledge, which should one choose?

A: You cannot have Self-knowledge without also knowing that I was never born in the first place, in which case where is the question of death or rebirth? Who-you-really-are has, in any case, always been free and unlimited. Where is the question of 'gaining' freedom? You are effectively asking 'can one choose to gain knowledge and still be ignorant?'

Q: What then is meant by ultimate mokSha? I thought that this meant the merging of the jIva into Brahman, just as the river merges into the ocean. Once merged, how can an individual continue to experience or have any knowledge? Is it like being in deep sleep but without any awakening, because there is no longer any 'one' to wake up?

A: Self-ignorance is the belief that one is a limited individual, subject to saMsAra. The truth is that who-you-really-are is never this, i.e. it is not a matter of gaining release from saMsAra; it is a matter of realizing that you never were subject to it in the first place. It is effectively the subtle body that goes from birth to birth so that, as long as you remain identified with this, it appears that you also are reborn. Enlightenment is simply recognizing this truth and realizing that who-you-really-are is Brahman. Subsequently, the body-mind with which you were identified continues until death of that body and that subtle body is then not reborn again.

There is no 'merging', either at the time of enlightenment or at the time of death of the body, because you were never separate to begin with. It is not that you are a 'part' of Brahman – you *are* Brahman. Think of the pot-space 'merging' with the total space when the pot breaks – nothing really happens to the space.

As far as 'experience' or 'knowledge' post-enlightenment is

concerned, the normal body-mind activities continue until death of the body. The only difference is that the Self-knowledge that 'I am not the body-mind' and 'I am Brahman' is now irrevocably in place.

Q.222 People who are enlightened but claim they are not

Q: It seems not uncommon to encounter seekers who clearly know, without a shadow of a doubt, that the world is mithyA; that Brahman is all there is and that they themselves are Brahman. But they refuse to admit that they are enlightened because 'something is missing' (while often not being able to clearly pinpoint what that something is). Some of these may even have spent many years doing sAdhana chatuShTaya sampatti [SCS]. And yet there are others who have never practiced, who *do* claim to be enlightened. Is it possible that both are enlightened but that the personality of the former is such that they need more work before they are prepared to admit it?

A: What you say about not 'claiming enlightenment' is very familiar. Basically, since the mind does continue post-enlightenment, the person is still susceptible to the habitual ways in which the mind works, including such things as false humility! Also, there is undoubtedly a very strong feeling/belief in most seekers (prior to enlightenment) that something will be clearly experienced, that one will instantly move from a position of doubt to one of absolute certainty, and so on. It is not like this. The shravaNa-manana-nididhyAsana process is one of acquiring all the knowledge – clearing all the doubts – consolidating and changing one's behavior accordingly. The 'enlightenment' comes after the manana stage but the 'fruits' of enlightenment – j~nAna phalam – do not come until during/after nididhyAsana, unless one was totally mentally prepared to begin with (fully acquired sAdhana chatuShTaya sampatti).

So, yes, I agree entirely with your assessment. And I think that perhaps the majority of 'enlightened' people, certainly in the west, are in this position because the incentive to work fully for SCS is not there. We do not have the discipline. Especially, knowing that it is Self-Knowledge that brings enlightenment, we do not want to spend years doing karma yoga. I am a typical example of this! I was with SES (the School of Economic Science in the UK) for many years, doing all the exercises and meditating etc. but felt I was not 'getting anywhere' so left. I still believe leaving was the right thing to do but I was clearly not an uttama adhikArI (highest qualified seeker) when I left!

Q: I have heard that it is possible for a madhyama adhikArI (middling qualified seeker) to be a jIvanmukta. Is that true?

I would say no, because Swami Paramarthananda equates the word jIvanmukti with j~nAna phalam. I would say that a madhyama adhikArI can be enlightened but not have j~nAna phalam. And it follows that both the one without practice and the conscientious one who has practiced, can both be enlightened, irrespective of whether they openly admit it.

As Swamiji puts it, in this position one continues to do nididhyAsana until such time as the sense of pUrNatvam (completeness, unlimitedness) is clear. Also, Swami P says that it is impossible to become enlightened without some SCS. But, of course, one may naturally have some without having done years of karma yoga (tradition would say that you acquired it in a previous life).

Q: It is also said that, without shabda pramANa [scriptures as a source of knowledge through listening to a qualified teacher], there is no possibility for liberation. This must have been the position of Shankara. Yet there are many liberated ones who never even knew about Hindu scriptures and many more who never read them. What is your position regarding this?

A: I think the key word here is 'shabda', which Monier Williams gives as 'scriptural or verbal testimony'. The point is that we already 'experience' the Self, in that we already are the

Self – we are already complete and unlimited. We just don't know it. Accordingly, we need someone or something to tell us – in such a way as to convince us. In Advaita, the 'telling' source to which all refer as ultimate authority is shruti. This is the way the sampradAya method operates. But there are obviously other valid sources – the Tao Te Ching springs to mind – and enlightened people from other traditions will be able to pass on the pointers as they see them. The ultimate truth cannot be spoken of directly but there are many indirect ways to point people in the right direction. This is the 'many paths up the mountain' metaphor. But this does not mean that one can avoid the climb! There are no helicopters in gaining enlightenment, as Neo-Advaitin teachers would have us believe!

Q.236a Enlightenment

Q: How can you judge whether a teacher is realized? On your site you state that Greg Goode is a 'self-realized teacher of Advaita'. Why do you think this? Would you say the same for Francis Lucille?

A: There is no objective way of determining whether someone else is or not enlightened. Having understood what enlightenment is, the only way to make a subjective judgment is to listen to or read what they say and use discrimination to ascertain whether they truly understand what they are talking about. In the case of Greg and Francis, I have discussed many topics with the former and listened to the latter and my view is that both are enlightened.

Q: I am half-way through 'Enlightenment: The Path Through The Jungle' and have a few questions:

1. Points 42/43/123 (in the book): "... shabda is unique in communicating knowledge about the Atman ... scriptures are regarded as the only source of knowledge about the Self ... if one does not study scripture, true knowledge does not arise even in millions of years".

If this is true, how is it possible that enlightened people such as Ramana, Anandamayi Ma, various Direct Path/Neo-Advaita people, etc. were enlightened *without* having been exposed to shabda? Please explain the exact means of knowledge (pramANa) they used to attain enlightenment?

A: The point about knowing/experiencing reality is that this is already the reality (how could it not be?). We even 'experience' the Self/non-duality every night in deep sleep. So we cannot say that all of this is alien. It is the very nature of our Self, always. The problem is one of Self-ignorance. Pre-existing ideas in the mind cover over the truth and cause us to misperceive the reality, thinking that it is dualistic.

To counteract this ignorance and misperception, Self-knowledge has to arise. This is most unlikely to do so 'of its own accord' – it hasn't done so for all of our life to date (and all our previous lives, if you believe in reincarnation). So, the natural way that it can be 'prompted' is by input from others. The 'others' who are able to give us this input are the Self-realized sages who are able to explain the truth, based upon our presently misconceived beliefs. The scriptures contain proven techniques for doing this and good teachers make use of these. These techniques have been validated over thousands of years. This is why they are uniquely valuable.

Of course, this does not directly answer your question. The reasonable answer would be that, although the vast majority of people need explanations, reasoned arguments etc., there are always the rare exceptions who, for whatever reason, make the intuitive leap on their own and then subsequently find validation for their experience in the scriptures. This, I suggest, was the case with Ramana. The strictly traditional view is that Ramana (and such like people) would have been exposed to the teaching and scriptures in previous lives and come close to enlightenment in their immediately preceding lifetime.

2. Points 50/301-304: "Use of means of knowledge automatically removes Self-ignorance ... one does have limited ability to choose actions to influence the quality of the mind, which is more conducive for enlightenment ... no cause, no effect ... etc.".

Q:

A. You essentially say, in many places, that there *is* a cause for enlightenment?

B. However, you seem to imply that I, an apparent jIva, can directly/indirectly cause my own enlightenment?

C. I always thought there are three factors enabling enlightenment: 1. Qualified Student; 2. Qualified Teacher; 3. Ishvara's grace. Is this correct? In the book, you seem to ignore factor 3. Why?

A:

A. Yes – there is a cause for enlightenment.

B. I wouldn't say that one can cause one's own enlightenment. All that I can do is optimize the conditions. This means firstly, preparing the mind (sAdhana chatuShTaya sampatti) and secondly, pursuing the Self-knowledge, ideally with the help of a qualified teacher. If I do this assiduously, then enlightenment must follow eventually (though not necessarily in this lifetime, according to traditional teaching).

C. Pedantically, you are right. I admit that I mostly ignore Ishvara in the book for three reasons. Firstly, I believe that most Western readers are not comfortable with the concept; secondly, I do not believe it is a necessary concept; thirdly, I myself have never been very happy with it.

3. Points 74/73): "... traditional teaching literally takes us to the goal ... the hearer attains enlightenment on hearing the text for the last time ...".

Q: If this is true, can you confirm that this was the case (i.e. enlightenment occurred whilst hearing/contemplating scripture) with your own enlightenment?

A: No, I cannot confirm this. I have never claimed to be enlightened but, to the extent that I am, it has been a gradual process with no obvious 'Ah-ha' event.

4. Point 142: "... a true teacher can lead the mind of a student step by step to the direct recognition of the non-dual Self without

the text/Sanskrit".

Q: Please offer some examples of where this has actually occurred. Are there any teachers alive today on the planet, who you believe have such ability in the English language? If so, who?

A: See Q.236a earlier in the book – there is no objective indicator of enlightenment. Many modern satsang teachers claim that they are enlightened as a result of listening to their own teacher (who is or was, typically, Papaji, Nisargadatta, 'Sailor' Bob). I really wouldn't want to risk being quoted as to which modern teachers I consider to be enlightened. There would always be the implication that I considered any that I didn't mention to be not enlightened! You really should not indulge in such speculation. The overriding importance is to decide for yourself whether what is said by a particular teacher helps you to remove some Self-ignorance. If it does, then that teacher is useful; not otherwise. Only if you are able to commit yourself to long-term study with a particular teacher does it become important. Even then, as Shankara has pointed out, a good, unenlightened teacher is far better than a bad, enlightened one.

5. Point 257: 'Nor is enlightenment about a still or silent mind ... '

Q: You also spoke of meditation in the Book of One. I have practiced Samatha (Buddhist) meditation with an experienced teacher for two years *but* I just don't understand the *utility* of meditation in relation to enlightenment.

A: Meditation is extremely valuable as part of the mental preparation. Only a clear, quiet, disciplined mind is able to be optimally receptive to the teaching and able to discriminate the truth. But meditation in itself can never lead to enlightenment which, as I keep saying is not the result of any action.

Q.239 The content of enlightenment

Q: I've been mulling over a question about the content of enlightenment for a couple of months, and I was wondering if you would mind giving me some guidance. As I see it, there are three core teachings of Advaita:

1. I am not an object; I am awareness/presence/Consciousness ('you' do not exist)

2. There is only one awareness/presence/Consciousness ('only one Consciousness')

3. All that exists is awareness/presence/Consciousness ('life is a dream')

I realize that most Advaita teachers would probably object to summarizing their teachings as numbered propositions and I realize that 3 implies 1 and 2, but this sort of structure helps to make my question clear.

As I see it, Advaita teachers provide lots of pointers for proposition 1 – everything from introspective exercises, to a priori arguments that the subject can never be an object, to thought experiments about having no control over one's thoughts. However, in all of the Advaita teachings I've looked at (and I've read a number of books), I haven't seen many pointers for 2 and 3.

Is the idea that the truth of 2 and 3 (or just 3 really, if it implies 2) can be grasped only when the truth of 1 has been realized? Do the truth of 2 and 3 become apparent when, and only when, the false assumption of an independent, substantial self has been disposed of? If that's the case, then I'm still confused. How could the realization that I am only presence/awareness demonstrate that everyone else and everything else is the same presence/awareness? The realization of 1 doesn't seem (to me at least) to have any necessary connection with 2 and 3. Even if the self is an illusion, why does the world and everyone's awareness of it suddenly collapse into unity (or rather why would I suddenly understand that they have all been part of an underlying unity all along)?

A: The traditional teaching of Advaita begins by negating everything (neti, neti). I am not the objects in the world, not the body or mind. This is perhaps the first stage. This 'neti, neti' teaching comes from the Brihadaranyaka Upanishad. Yet I cannot negate my own existence. (I don't understand your statement, 'You do not exist.')

Q: From my experience, there are two notions about the self that most contemporary teachers of Advaita try to get across, one negative and one positive. The negative one is that the self is not an object ('not an independent, substantial thing', as it's often put). The positive one is that the self is simply awareness, cognizing emptiness, capacity for the world, etc. From what I understand, it is this positive notion of the self that cannot be denied, according to Advaitins. Incidentally, I think the fact that most Advaita teachers do not tease apart these two notions leads to much gratuitous confusion. For example, Tony Parsons often remarks in interviews 'I do not exist', while Bob Adamson generally begins in the classical manner by showing students that they cannot doubt that they exist (!?).

A: The second stage could be to realize that all of the supposedly separate objects in the world are only name and form; that there is really only 'one thing'. This is the vAchArambhaNa teaching from the ChAndogya upaniShad, where it is also said that sarvaM khalvidaM brahma – all this is Brahman. (I don't understand why you equate this with 'life is a dream'.)

Q: Well, I think the view is often expressed as 'life is only a dream'. For example, Randall Friend and David Carse emphasize this. By the way, I think that the view that all is Brahman is 3 rather than 2 in my numbered propositions. From my experience, 2 is found in all mystical traditions, whereas, from what I can see, 3 is found only in Eastern traditions. For example, the realization that there is only one Consciousness would be complete enlightenment for someone like Meister Eckhart, while in Advaita and, more generally in Vedanta and some traditions of Buddhism, there is also the realization that everything in the external world is simply a form/name of Consciousness.

A: The third stage might be the recognition that 'I am That'.

The mahAvAkya 'tat tvam asi' (Thou art That) is covered in the vivekachUDAmaNi (I recommend the version 'Talks on 108 selected verses' by Swami Dayananda) or vAkya vRRitti.

Q: It seems to me that 'Thou art that' is a particularization of the general claim that 'All is Brahman'. If all is Consciousness, then, of course, you and that chair over there have the same being, viz. Brahman. Thank you for the pointers to Shankara's works. I haven't read anything by him, and maybe now is the time to start!

A: Traditional Advaita does not number things in this way that you have done above. A given teacher will probably have a preferred sequence for taking texts, probably beginning with something like tattva bodha, which introduces lots of terms used in other scriptures and ending with mANDUkya upaniShad and gauDapAda's kArikA-s and maybe Shankara's bhAShya on the brahma sutra-s because these require considerable background understanding first. The mANDUkya upaniShad and gauDapAda's kArikA-s are actually probably the best for your specific concern. (You can now read my book 'A-U-M' which is a presentation of these.) The second chapter is totally concerned with the mithyAtva or non-reality of the world and the third with non-duality itself.

Q: Thanks a lot for the pointers to these sources as well. I will definitely check out the mANDUkya upaniShad and Gaudapada's commentary, another book I had been meaning to read.

A: Different people have difficulty with different aspects of what you have been describing. What is quickly obvious to one will be a sticking point for another. The bhAga tyAga lakShaNa story (see Q.345) shows how a sudden realization can bring about the 'collapse' of all our previous suppositions.

One thought that occurred while reading your reply is that the confusion between 'I do not exist' and 'I cannot doubt that I exist' is specifically attacked by Ramana's 'Who am I?' enquiry. See question 237 on the subject of 'destruction of the mind'.

You will probably enjoy the mANDUkya upaniShad and Gaudapada. One of the things that is brought out in the second chapter is that waking and dream have the same ontological status. In fact, Shankara actually says at one point that the world is not absolutely real 'because we perceive it'! You should definitely read Shankara – obviously there is no one more important in the Advaita tradition. But you should note that he is not the most readable of writers, even in a good translation. You do need someone who fully understands the points that are being made so that they can be paraphrased. If you are rich, you cannot do better than the six-volume 'Shankara Source Book' from Shanti Sadan.

Q.240 Enlightenment, meditation and mithyA

Q: I have a few questions I would like to ask you:

1. You have said previously: "I wouldn't say that one can cause one's own enlightenment. All that I can do is optimize the conditions".

Why can I (jIva) not directly cause my own enlightenment? Surely if I'm a qualified seeker, and pursuing Self-knowledge under the guidance of a qualified teacher I can, by putting effort into creating this scenario at a vyAvahArika level, cause my own enlightenment? You have admitted that you feel the concept of Ishvara is unnecessary (personally, I disagree with this); hence I don't see what other extraneous unknown factor there is in the enlightenment of a jIva, which would mean that I (the jIva) cannot cause my own enlightenment.

A: I think you are interpreting the word 'cause' too loosely, while I, perhaps, am using it too precisely. One of the key prerequisites for enlightenment is mumukShutva, which means the desire to achieve enlightenment. If this is not your most desired aim in life, you are unlikely to get it. Indeed, I think it has been said that you should want it more than life itself. So, in a sense, you could say that you are yourself the cause.

However, first of all, it could be argued that what has brought about this desire is not of your own making. It is often the case that it comes about as the result of repeatedly trying to gain happiness out of life in the usual ways and being continually thwarted, finding instead only misery. In such a case, I suggest that it is not really you being the cause!

Also, if your mind is not suitably prepared, with some degree of sAdhana chatuShTaya sampatti, then no matter how hard you try you will not be able to gain enlightenment. And, even if your mind is prepared and you really want it, it does not follow that you will automatically get it, even with the guidance of a qualified teacher. This serendipity is usually referred to as 'grace', i.e. it is often said that you only get enlightenment by the grace of God. I do agree that, having already said that I did not feel that the Ishvara teaching was absolutely necessary, this might seem to be contradictory. But that is not a problem in Advaita! Let us simply call it serendipity and leave it at that.

Finally, though, Self-knowledge comes about by the removal of Self-ignorance and, for that, external teaching is required. It is that teaching which is more reasonably the cause in my view and, indeed, you could say that this stems from the guru paramparA and thence the shruti itself. ['guru paramparA' refers to the tradition of guru – disciple, with the disciple becoming the guru for the next generation.] Ultimately, of course, the only 'cause' is the Self itself, showing itself the way – but this is to talk about the absolute from the relative level and therefore a bit of a cop out.

2. You have also said previously: 'Meditation is extremely valuable as preparation.'

Maybe I am not advanced enough a seeker to appreciate this, but why is it that I feel my meditation practice does not have as much spiritual utility (on the road to mokSha) as sitting down and reading and contemplating a book on Advaita theory? I agree, it may have utility in calming an extremely rajasic mind. But, if I already have the capacity to sit and learn (which I do to an extent), then isn't meditation a waste of time? Or are there some deeper levels of the inquiry that can *only* occur in meditation (I suspect so)?

A: The value of meditation has been shown in point 1 really. It is extremely useful in stilling the mind, and viveka only functions reliably in a still mind. So, yes, if you are naturally able to listen to teaching without continual questioning chatter going on the background of your mind, you can manage without meditation. You certainly don't use meditation directly for any 'deep inquiry'. But if there is some aspect that you don't understand, it is not impossible that dropping the conscious inquiry and meditating for a while might allow the answer to arise.

3. In your book 'Enlightenment: The Path Through The Jungle', you say: *"It is knowledge of mithyA that brings about enlightenment, not knowledge of satyam"* (Note 185). However, you then proceed later on seemingly to contradict this statement in many places, e.g.: Notes 424-5: *"If these (negating prakriyA-s) were the only techniques used, it would not be clear what it is exactly that remains after all-that-we-are-not has been negated ... accordingly positive pointers are used ..."*

But I thought that: what we are *not* (indicated by 'neti, neti' techniques) = mithyA; what we are (i.e. indicated by positive pointers) = satyam? So surely, according to Note 185, we *only* need to understand what-we-are-not (= mithyA); and then knowledge of who we are (i.e. satyam) arises spontaneously?

I hope you can see my confusion because I'm pretty sure I have missed something major here!

3. There is no contradiction here. The positive pointers that are referred to, which are used after the 'negating prakriyA-s', are also mithyA. All of the teaching is mithyA. Everything in the apparent creation is mithyA. Ultimately, everything has to be dropped, including concepts such as Advaita and Brahman until there is only silence. Who-we-are is satyam but anything that we could say or think about it is mithyA.

Q.247 'Practical realization'

Q: I've been on the non-duality 'circuit' for a couple of years, and have devoured dozens of books running the gamut from

Douglas Harding to Eckhart Tolle to Krishna Menon. In fact, I recently returned from the UK, where I attended a seminar with Tony Parsons (I've read the correspondence between the two of you – great stuff!). Presently I'm working with the 'Great Freedom' teachings of Candice O'Denver, and, if you're familiar with this group, I'd really like your 'take' on their work.

Above and beyond all this, my conundrum is simplicity itself: I'm stuck! While I have a vast intellectual or conceptual understanding of the basic principles of non-duality (including Advaita Vedanta), I seem unable to incorporate these ideas into my daily life. Whether it's Douglas Harding's 'headlessness' or Tony Parsons' 'nothing is everything', any practical, experiential realization of these concepts still elude me to a great extent.

My main focus has been the 'Neo-Advaitin' writing which you routinely eschew – and I can certainly understand why! With the possible exception of 'Great Freedom' mentioned above, I've had very little success with the implementation of these concepts in my everyday life. The 'Great Freedom' teachings recommend 'resting in short moments of awareness, repeated many times, until it becomes automatic'. At least Candice O'Denver appears bright, non-cultist, and accessible.

Dennis, I need a practical suggestion or proposed methodology that will bear fruit! I feel like the guy who has read a detailed textbook on swimming and, feeling confident and informed, jumps in the water and drowns! I could go on and on, but I'd be most receptive to any ideas you might offer.

A: I really do sympathize but you need to ask yourself what it is exactly that you are expecting – disappointment is always the result of unreasonable expectation! What do you mean by 'incorporate these ideas into your life'? There is the stage of hearing or reading the material and realizing that it must be true. Then there is the stage of clearing up any remaining doubts by asking questions, listening or reading another time. Finally there is the stage of acclimatization to the now accepted knowledge. This final stage may take the rest of your life. It is necessary for those people who were not fully mentally prepared beforehand and, until it is complete, you will not see the effects in your life (of being always at peace, never worried and so on). If this is what you mean then that is your answer. It is covered by the practices of shravaNa, manana and nididhyAsana, sAdhana chatuShTaya sampatti and the result of j~nAna phalam or jIvanmukta.

The fact is that life goes on, even after enlightenment. Enlightenment is not about results for me in this life; it is purely concerned with Self-knowledge, which brings with it the knowledge that this world, this life and this very person are all mithyA.

Q.270 The Void

Q: I am writing to you simply because there is no one other than you that I remotely know to even say anything to. Last night I flipped. No, I don't mean flipped-out in the traditional sense of the word. I went to bed and, for lack of a better word, the flip happened. Nothing had an independent reality outside of 'I Am'. I know that you know what I mean. Everything was still there, but it wasn't real. This morning it seems as though I have flopped back. A flip-flop. What are the chances of flipping again? It was kind of scary, and far beyond my wildest imagination.

A: I think it's quite usual for this sort of thing to happen while the mind is still coming to terms with what has been realized to be the truth. Don't be impatient. Remember that this realization is 'non-duality in spite of duality' – the appearance still continues.

Q: Eliminate everything, and arrive at the 'I'-thought. Eliminate the thought of 'I' and arrive at the 'I'-principle. Eliminate the principle (a concept) and arrive at the 'I' as Absolute. Eliminate the 'I' and arrive at what cannot even be thought of: a void. I don't know what to say to you. It is like Consciousness is supported by what cannot even arise as a thought in Consciousness itself. An indescribable void. Even a concept or thought of this void is only that: a concept or thought. Remove these and bam! – nothing.

On the one hand, it is absolutely useless even to speak of this; on the other (moving outward) the thought arises for a confirmation of something which appears as nothing. Either there is an unknowable support for Consciousness, or Consciousness cannot be thought of and remain Consciousness. The recent realization – that of understanding that the Knower is never changed by what is known (experienced) – seems like child's play now.

A: 'Eliminating everything' is the beginning – 'accepting everything' is the end. What is 'left' is what is here now – sarvaM khalvidaM brahma. There is no 'void'.

Q: '... accepting everything is the end.' I see that this is the same as saying that I must arrive at the firm conviction that I alone exist.

A: I would never put it like that – sounds like solipsism. There is only Brahman and you are Brahman. That takes the ego out of the equation.

Q.278 Enlightenment and the end of the universe

Q: It is said that mokSha is liberation from this material world. But isn't it true that when the mahA pralaya (final dissolution of the cosmos) occurs, mokSha is also supposed to finally break down? So in this sense, one doesn't stay liberated forever and thus mokSha is also temporary. Or is it otherwise and mokSha never breaks down? I would be grateful if you could tell me the truth.

A: Have a look at Questions 241 and 256 for answers to similar questions.

mokSha is for the person. According to traditional Advaita, once the person has realized, that person is not reborn – ever. This is because the karma that was the cause for the subtle body's rebirth comes to an end when the person dies. So, whether it is individual death or cosmic death makes no difference. For the person who has not realized, there remains unfructified saMchita saMskAra at the end of the person's life (or 'Big Crunch' of the universe) and that goes back into the unmanifest for bringing out again next time to continue its cause-effect existence.

The reality is that who you really are was never born to begin with, and will never die, irrespective of yuga-s or pralaya-s. There is only Brahman and you are That.

Q: Thanks for clarifying this confusion. Just two more things I want to ask by your permission:

1. You said that mokSha is for the person, so have we as personalities always existed or were we created (I know it's an illusion) at some point in time by Brahman's supernatural thought process?

2. Can all the personalities in this world attain liberation or does each one have different intrinsic destinies?

A: You are trying to ask 'absolute' questions from the standpoint of the relative so, in a sense, you are doomed to failure – such questions cannot be answered. In order to be able to answer any question asking about the relationship between Brahman and the world, we would have to be able to stand outside both. Since there is only Brahman, this is obviously impossible. Hence we say that such questions are anirvachanIya – we cannot ask them! Instead, we postulate mAyA, effectively 'magic' as the 'explanation' for the appearance.

The scriptures have jIva-s 'evolving' from vegetable and animal to human forms. (And 'bad' karma – papa – can send an individual back down the scale!) Read the two-part article beginning with http://www.advaita-vision.org/between-lives/ if you are interested in this subject, but do bear in mind that it is all to be rescinded in the final analysis (adhyAropa-apavAda).

Traditional Advaita teaches that the individual has limited free will – to act, not act, or act differently – in the situations that are presented as a result of maturing saMskAra (past karma). According to this, one may work to acquire sAdhana chatuShTaya sampatti, a key aspect of which is the desire to attain enlightenment. This will in turn lead to seeking out the teaching, ideally from a qualified teacher. And, through shravaNa and manana, this will eventually lead to enlightenment. This is the ultimate 'destiny' of all jIva-s.

Q.290 Enlightenment = Self-knowledge

Q: In your own experiencing of this, did you begin to notice the background was not affected even when things around you would have normally upset you? Like you no longer care or not care about the situation? Does it feel obvious and tangible? Did the background 'become' more obvious over time and study, reflection, percolating?

A: Enlightenment is not about experience; it is about Self-knowledge. Irrespective of the knowledge, experiences may be 'sharp' or 'dull'; interesting or boring. The personal characteristics and tendencies of the mind continue. One does not suddenly become loving, caring, infinitely patient or anything else – that would be an event in time and therefore not enlightenment.

Q: So what is this obvious presence-awareness that is here now and seems to be brighter as it stays with itself?

As I sit here, there is no doubt of this presence. It's not difficult to see that all that is manifest comes and goes while this presence does not change. This presence could be described as solid, though I know this is not an acceptable word. When this presence was first noticed it was just a glimpse. Then I did what many have suggested and kept returning to that sense of 'I am'. At first, it was very hard work. Now it seems that attention naturally keeps going back to this being-presence. It is brighter and more obvious. Is this presence vyavahAra?

A: That which does not come and go is the non-dual reality. It is not something objective. Nor is it something subjective. The subject-experiencer is the reflected Consciousness in the mind.

So if you are talking about something that you experience from time to time, that is not the Self. It sounds like you are talking about you, the ego (i.e. the Self identified with the body-mind), having an idea of some unchanging aspect of the phenomenal, of how you think enlightenment ought to be. In reality, you are everything all the time, whether it presently seems bright or dark as perceived through the body-mind instrument.

Q: *"The subject-experiencer is the reflected Consciousness in the mind"*. This is the sentence that has been most helpful. How many non-duality/Advaita teachers are caught in this? How do you see Self-enquiry, as Nisargadatta and Ramana Maharshi recommend, as a complement to studying the traditional way?

A: I see 'Self-enquiry' as synonymous with traditional teaching. Simply asking 'Who am I?' is not going to remove Self-ignorance. The pramANa for knowledge of the Self is shabda (scripture-guru), not pratyakSha (perception).

Q: So, Self-knowledge is knowing that all four mahAvAkya-s are true? We are not talking about inference are we? Self, reflected in the mind, must be reflected from Self.

A: Self-knowledge = Enlightenment = certainty in the mind that 'I am That' (non-dual Brahman) and that 'Everything is Brahman'. No, it is not inference – you do not use perception or inference to know that you exist. And it is like that.

Q: What is this mind that Self is reflected in? Isn't mind just thoughts?

A: Call it what you want from the standpoint of vyavahAra. Advaita calls it the subtle body or antaHkaraNa. You can devise whatever scheme you like to explain the appearance but I doubt that you will find one more logical or self-consistent than that provided by Advaita. In the end it is all mithyA.

From the standpoint of paramArtha, there is no mind; there is only Brahman.

Q.296 Emotions and enlightenment

Q: I assume that you have thought very carefully about vedAnta before taking it up wholeheartedly. Can you say that on your journey 'on the razor's edge', you benefited in any way (although there's nothing to gain at all but Self knowledge)? And even when the journey seemed long and arduous before being enlightened, did you have experiences of sattva and less and less rajas and tamas as you got closer?

Can you say for certain that you honestly know or believe that vedAnta is the path to happiness and the end of suffering, at least for yourself?

A: First of all, let me emphasize (as I have pointed out in other, similar questions) that I am not a jIvanmukta. I am still prone to the usual human failings. One does not gain the mental/emotional benefits (j~nAna phalam) unless one is fully accomplished with respect to sAdhana chatuShTaya sampatti prior to enlightenment. And I would not even claim to be enlightened unless I first established with the questioner that we understood exactly the same thing by this term.

Secondly, you should dissociate 'experiences' from both the study of Advaita and from enlightenment. Any 'feelings of peace' or 'absence of fear' etc. should be considered to be independent and irrelevant. It is certainly true that, with the eradication of Self-ignorance, you know that the essential 'you' is totally unaffected by anything; is unlimited and immortal. But the body-mind continues. Perception is via reflected Consciousness in the mind and that mind is still affected by prArabdha saMskAra. So if there were certain tendencies present before, it is quite likely that, to some degree at least, they will still be there afterwards.

So the bottom line is that, if mental/emotional benefits are your principal concerns, Advaita may not be the best route. Yoga may be a better option.

Q.303 Is enlightenment a worthwhile pursuit?

Q: Since everything conceivable in any shape or form, conceptually or otherwise, is an appearance of Consciousness/Brahman, this must mean that any form of realization is appearance too. That which is revealed (so to speak) is not an appearance and is, therefore, not subject to modification or destruction. Yet the revelation itself, since it happens via the mind, is an appearance and will surely disappear at the dissolution of the body/mind. It would be magical thinking to suppose that the realization could survive the death of the mind, faculty of recognition, memory, etc. So although our true nature is eternal, indestructible and magnificent, the realization of it is limited, fragile and feeble – and really not worth a lifetime's amount of dedication to recognize it.

A: This is a problem which worried me once, too, and someone asked a question some time ago, ostensibly about near-death experiences but effectively raising the concern that you express. See question 254.

What you say is effectively true but, from the relative standpoint, the unrealized mind reincarnates indefinitely whereas the realized mind dies with the body. So, if 'Fred' becomes enlightened, 'Fred' will not be born again. If 'Fred' lives a life of dissolution, indifferent to the feelings of others, he might come back as a cockroach! Enlightenment is the only worthwhile pursuit. There's a story in one of the Upanishads (I think), where the seeker is told that he will realize in only a thousand more lives – and he is overjoyed (that the end is in sight)! So, not only is Self-realization not 'limited, fragile and feeble'; it is final, unlimited and irrevocable.

Q: What you say would indeed be worthwhile and comforting if it were true. However, it must be true that the appearance that we call a realized mind is as equally 'unreal' as the appearance we call an unrealized mind – equally mithyA. And surely neither is of any consequence to the Self. Realized or unrealized, the Self shines in its glory. It almost seems as if realization is just a fortunate blip in the human story and nothing more significant than that – except perhaps to the fantasizing capacity of the mind.

A: You are right about the realized or unrealized mind being mithyA. But you are not the mind – you are the Self, which is satyam. Is this a problem?

Q: Well, the point is that mind is required in order to recognize that you are Self. When the mind is no more, the recognition of being the Self is no more. This is the sleight of hand that the neos are fond of. They insist that your true nature cannot be lost, that it is always the case. This is true, but the *recognition* of your true nature is *not* always so – it can and will be lost at some point. If you are saying that, since you are the Self, there can ultimately not be a problem – then seeking and realization are ultimately pointless.

A: There is a danger of going round in circles, here! From the point of view of the absolute reality, there is only the Self. There is no mind, so there is no non-recognition of true nature. There is no question of seeking or realization. Agreed?

From the point of view of the individual person, who is presently not realized, there is suffering and there is the prospect of an indefinite number of future lives of suffering also (you may not believe this, but neither do you know that it is not so). This is all the result of ignorance; of not realizing that one is the unlimited Self. The only thing that can relieve the suffering is to remove this ignorance. Removal of the ignorance also removes, at a stroke, all concerns about anything. Subsequently, I know that pain and pleasure alike do not affect who I really am. (Prior to this, you might think that this is so, but this is scarcely the same. It is the difference between having been told that putting your hand in the fire will hurt and actually burning yourself.) And, when the body dies, there is no cause-effect chain to bring about rebirth of that 'person'.

So you have to ask yourself: to whom is the 'seeking and realization ultimately pointless'? They are only relevant from the vantage point of a person and the effect for that person is to put an end to suffering in this life and to future lives.

Q: This all hangs on the notion that when a mind recognizes its true nature, all cause and effect in the appearance (where else?) will expire. Now this is hard to swallow, since apparent body/minds (realized or not) are part of an unstoppable causal chain. Of course, who-you-really-are is and was always free from conditions.

If, in a movie, a character realizes he is in fact the screen and therefore untouchable, this is still a scene in the movie – even though it paradoxically seems to point beyond the movie. Both the ignorant character and now the insightful character are equally fictitious – dream characters having dream awakenings. The screen is indifferent to these goings-on. Talk of rebirths and liberations are further scenes in the movie – dream ideas. Scenes will vanish and the screen will 'persist' without the need for realizations – realizations are purely in the realm of fiction; of appearances on the screen. As you say, we are probably going round in circles here, so I'm happy to leave it for now.

A: The world is not your personal dream. When a mind recognizes its true nature, the 'owner' of that mind knows henceforth that he/she is the actor and not the role. The play continues, with pretty well all of the other actors firmly identified with their roles.

Thinking that you realize you are the screen is not a helpful metaphor here. If you want to relate to the reincarnation theme, you might say that the realized actor ends his career with this movie, while the others go on to play more, continuing to believe that they really are the roles that they are playing.

Q: Yes, the world is not anyone's personal dream – that view would be solipsism. I use the screen metaphor to emphasize my original point: a mind that realizes that its true nature is in fact Consciousness, is a relative construction, and like all conditioned things it will be subject to dissolution – and so will its realizations.

A: So are you now convinced that enlightenment is a worthwhile pursuit or is your original viewpoint unchanged?

Q: When I hear of seekers who have been at it for over 25 years, have spent a fortune, etc., and who seem to be in a constant state of frustration, yes, I do wonder if it is worth it. After all, a liberation is a liberation in the appearance (it can have no other meaning), it will last for the duration of the body/mind. It really makes no sense to suppose that a relative reorientation of the mind (so to speak) will result in a cessation of causation. But even if it did, Dennis may 'attain' a total and irrevocable cessation, but you will arise again and again as Jack, Mary, Abdul, etc. It doesn't matter which skin you appear as, the wheel of suffering will go on.

I'm sorry if this seems somewhat pessimistic, but this is where these type of teachings seem to point. Personally I'm not so sure; what happens after the death of the organism is really a mystery. Everything we could postulate about what might happen is part of a very limited knowledge which is itself merely an appearance, a dream understanding at best.

A: Please call a halt to this discussion if you've had enough. I'm continuing only because I once shared your concern and can see that you are still pretty negative about it. (And, when others come to read this exchange, they may not be satisfied with the outcome!)

It seems that you are still ignoring the absolute reality of the situation. This is that there are no individuals to begin with; there has never been any creation. Everything is only name and form of the non-dual reality, which is limitless, perfect and complete. And 'you' are that reality. There are no problems; there is no causation. This is the 'bottom-line' of these teachings and this is what is to be 'realized' by the mind of the (apparent) person. There is no way (is there?) that this truth can be construed as 'pessimistic'.

The 'reorientation of the mind' (good way of putting it!) does not result in the cessation of causation. But the reoriented mind knows that, in reality, there *is* no causation; it is only an appearance.

The problem is only a seeming one, from the vantage point of an ignorant mind, believing that 'I' am suffering and 'I' am going to die. You are still speculating in your last paragraph. Self-knowledge means what it says: knowing without any doubt the nature of the Self. Don't get hung up about topics such as karma and reincarnation – you can throw these out if you really don't click with them. From the pAramArthika standpoint all are mithyA anyway.

Q: In a way I am being Devil's Advocate with this discussion: it is your resolute contention that enlightenment occurs in the mind, and I'm just exploring the implications and possible limitations of that premise. Excuse the repetition in what follows.

It is precisely because I am not ignoring the Absolute Reality of the situation that these conclusions have arisen. To realize that I am the Supreme Reality is to know that I am the indestructible, unlimited, stainless reality in which everything appears. This is wonderful; I am untouchable and boundless, I will persist – what joy! *But,* in this eternal Supreme Reality arises a play; the play is the realization of Supreme Reality – realization of my true nature is an appearance. What I am, is not an appearance – but the realization of it, is!

What you are in danger of doing here, Dennis, is what the neos do all the time – you are flipping to the magnificent bottom-line fact that I am the Supreme Reality and are using this fact as an argument against my reasonable assertion that the knowledge of this fact (in the mind) is an appearance and is impermanent.

To sum up:

1. Realizations, like all conditioned things, are impermanent.
2. *That* which is realized is not impermanent.

The confusion of these two statements is the crucial issue here. Enlightenment is not simply the *Being* of Supreme Reality, it is the recognition of this fact. So we are left with a rather paradoxical situation: recognition by its very nature is a mithyA recognition – enlightenment is a mithyA enlightenment. The only way out of this as far as I can see, is to recognize that it's mithyA all the way down. We can throw out *all* conclusions regarding reality – and yet reality itself is irrefutable. The 'what', 'who', 'why', etc., can only ever remain speculative.

A: I actually agree with most of your statements here – and they are very well summarized and expressed. And therefore you seem to be mostly agreeing with what I have said so that the 'Devil's Advocate' appellation is not altogether appropriate.

Firstly, you say that I am "flipping to the magnificent bottom-line fact that I am the Supreme Reality and you are using this fact as an argument against my reasonable assertion that the knowledge of this fact (in the mind) is an appearance and is impermanent". I think you will find that I have never done this – I freely admit that enlightenment is part of vyavahAra. Since it is an event in the mind (which is mithyA), how could it not be?

Secondly, I don't believe I have ever confused your two statements: "1. Realizations, like all conditioned things, are impermanent. 2. *That* which is realized is not impermanent". Again, since enlightenment is an event in the mind, and since the mind of a realized person comes to an end upon death of that body, the first statement necessarily follows. So I don't see that there is any paradox here. And realization that everything other than Brahman is mithyA is another description of enlightenment.

So my understanding is that we actually agree. It just leaves the somewhat unsatisfactorily explained fact that you seem to be rather depressed about it…

Q.328 Non-dual reality

Q: Can one ever *know* that reality is non-dual?

A: Since we are Brahman and there is only Brahman, it follows that we must already be 'experiencing' non-duality. Furthermore, because we are Brahman, we do not really need to 'gain' this knowledge; rather we have to remove the ignorance that prevents us from seeing that it is already the case. When enlightenment happens, it is direct and immediate; there is no longer any question of doubt.

We cannot 'know' Brahman in the way that we know a fact, as something objectively defined. We 'know' it by virtue of 'being' it. But, to begin with, we are ignorant of our true nature so that words are needed to 'show us the way'. Straight descriptions are not available. Even obvious concepts such as 'sweetness' cannot be described – they are known by direct experience. But if I give you some sugar and ask you to taste it, there is no longer any need to describe it; I can simply say that the quality of that taste *is* sweetness.

Brahman is not an experience in this sense but we can still use words, whose meanings we understand, to point to that which is not itself an experience. Thus, for example, we know the difference between 'real' and 'unreal' from everyday experience – the chair on which I am sitting is real and the face that I see in the pattern on the carpet is unreal. Since Brahman is the reality, it cannot be non-existent, even though we do not know it in any objective sense. Although we cannot perceive via the senses (pratyakSha) or infer it (anumAna), we can know it directly from the teaching of the guru and scriptures.

The 'right' words can trigger direct understanding because we are already Brahman. The classic example that I often tell people about is called bhAga tyAga lakShaNa and it is so expressive that it is worth reading again, even if you are already familiar with it (see Q.345).

The enlightenment 'event' (akhaNDAkAra vRRitti) is effectively a catastrophic reorientation of the mind (in the mathematical sense of course, rather than the judgmental!). As the teaching is heard, knowledge 'vRRitti-s' are acquired (mental modifications) and there may be 'mini' realizations in response to particular revelations. In the final revelation, the akhaNDAkAra vRRitti, the mind 'takes on the form' of the 'undivided' reality. The light bulb metaphor is a good one for the knowledge vRRitti-s. The removal of ignorance may be gradual but enlightenment is binary.

So the answer to the question is: Yes you can know. Gaining this knowledge is what is called 'enlightenment'. And you go about getting it by listening to the unfoldment of the scriptures by a qualified teacher, who will use the methods described in the answers to all of these questions. This is called shravaNa. Then you ask questions of your own to clarify and answer your doubts. This is called manana. Eventually, however long it may take, you will 'get it'.

The final stage of nididhyAsana is carried out by going over all of this again in your mind, reading more about it, going to talks,

experienced by modern Western seekers. As I have said elsewhere, Ramana was undoubtedly a brilliant teacher but taking this one element out of context and attempting to use it as the be-all and end-all of a path to enlightenment is simply mistaken.

There are quite a few questions on the topic of 'falling back'. What you are differentiating between is the j~nAnI (who is enlightened) and the jIvanmukta (who is established in peace/ stillness etc. all the time). The obstacles are called pratibandha-s (obstacle, hindrance, impediment, opposition, resistance). And they are there because there was insufficient mental preparation (discipline, control etc.) prior to enlightenment. So the mind is still prone to fall into old habits. If nothing is done, it is possible to 'fall back' to some degree. The solution is to continue to do nididhyAsana in the form of reading, studying, teaching or whatever; continually reminding oneself of the teaching and the truth of its conclusions.

Q.339 What is the point of enlightenment?

Q: I have seen from articles and questions on your website that Brahman cannot 'know' or 'do' anything; that it (as if) acts and knows only through the body-mind of the jIva. What I would like to know is: why would anyone want to become enlightened if this means the end of rebirth, and 'becoming' one with Brahman?

OK, this may mean the end of suffering but does it not also mean the end of enjoyment? If 'I' (even though this is only a reflection in the mind) cease to exist (when the body-mind finally ceases to exist) on the death of the enlightened person, then there is no more experiencing of any kind for me as that person, and none for the Brahman that I (as it were) become.

You will perhaps say that, as Brahman, I will still experience through all the other body-minds but this does not sound like enlightenment to me! And don't I do that already anyway since there is only Brahman? In which case what is the meaning (and point) of enlightenment?

A: There is subtle confusion of paramArtha and vyavahAra here, as I am sure you must have realized. From the perspective of absolute reality, there is only Brahman even now. What is happening is that there is an appearance of duality – the world with all its separate objects and individuals. But the appearance is only mithyA. It is not unreal but its real substrate is the non-dual Brahman. As one of these mithyA jIva-s, prior to enlightenment, because of Self-ignorance, you superimpose this dualistic image onto the non-dual reality and go through the ups and downs of saMsAra.

When this ignorance is removed as a result of shravaNa-manana, this truth is realized and you no longer believe that there is any separation (even though the senses still perceive that) – you know that everything is Brahman.

Yes, this realization is in the mind and, yes, that mind is no longer reincarnated after death. But the whole process is now redundant. From the pAramArthika standpoint, nothing has changed. Before and after, you have always been Brahman – complete, unlimited in any way. 'Nothing ever happens' (to quote Papaji, I believe).

Another way of looking at it is that, whenever you say 'I', you are constrained to a vyAvahArika view. Brahman does not say 'I'. Brahman transcends happiness and suffering, saMsAra and enlightenment. In reality, all this is Brahman. 'Experiencing' is a misunderstanding resulting from Self-ignorance. Brahman doesn't 'know'; Brahman is knowledge. Brahman doesn't 'enjoy'; Brahman is 'bliss'. Brahman is not 'aware' of anything; Brahman is Consciousness. You (as a person) never existed; you (as Brahman) always existed and always will.

Q.348 Temporary Realization

Q: Two or three years ago, I had a profound realization of the truth of Advaita which stayed with me for many months. I fear that I have lost it forever. Do you think that it can come back?

A: Once you discover that the earth rotates about its axis, giving the impression that the sun rises and sets, no one can take that knowledge away from you (unless the mind itself is damaged). If your 'profound realization' was firm knowledge and not just a strong conviction, then that knowledge would still be unshakeable. It is, however, normal to have to continue reading, studying, discussing, teaching etc., following realization if you do not want the clarity of that understanding to fade. All of this is discussed in the questions relating to sAdhana chatuShTaya sampatti and jIvanmukti.

Q.366 Self-knowledge – should we bother?

Q: At the end of the day, what does knowledge of Self give us? It does not help answer the burning question of why the appearance/dream/mAyA that we are experiencing as humans or animals exists.

(I am not clear on this one but ...) It appears that even though one attains knowledge of Self in one janma [birth], he/she can actually become a cockroach in the next due to karmic effect; i.e. we are not really liberated from the birth-death cycle.

The only benefit I do see in a janma where one attains knowledge of Self is that such a person might lead a life devoid of misery in the mind as they sail through good and bad times (although they may still experience physical pain).

A: Self-knowledge removes Self-ignorance and it is the ignorance that makes us think we are limited, unhappy, doomed to old age and death. With Self-knowledge we realize that we are not human, living in an inhospitable world; we are Brahman. The world appears as separate because of our ignorance. On gaining Self-knowledge, we realize that its substance is nothing but Brahman.

From the perspective of the ignorant person, there is rebirth (possibly as a cockroach) and we are subject to karma. With Self-knowledge, we realize that there is no person, no birth or rebirth, no death, no creation.

Q.386 Has enlightenment been 'dumbed down'?

Q: Self-Realization is a very rare occurrence – the Gita states something like 1 in a billion, and there are very few authentic, fully realized beings known to us, such as Ramana Maharshi, Nisargadatta Maharaj and a few others, (as well as the great anonymous ones). Granted, the world has changed and everything is much faster than it was, but this cannot surely apply to Self-realization. The Neo-Advaitins' awakenings or enlightenments cannot possibly be synonymous with the self-realizations of the great sages such as Ramana and Nisargadatta?

Also, the hallmark of the sages is that they have a transparent, translucent quality that emanates contentment and peace. The Neo-Advaitin teachers that I have observed do not emanate peace, instead, they come across with their body-mind personality traits/baggage as either 'manic', 'neurotic', 'depressed', 'nihilistic', etc. The talking (and so much talking at that) is coming from the mind, and not from 'mauna' [silence]. It is more like a mixture of counseling, psychotherapy and psycho-babble than pragmatic Advaitin philosophy.

So my question is: has self-realization been dumbed down and redefined by the Neo-Advaitins, or do they not claim full Self-realization, but only to be 'awakened' or 'enlightened'? Tolle comes to mind and Mooji, too – the talking never stops.

A: It is certainly the case that many are teaching who ought not to be teaching. They may or may not be enlightened but being enlightened does not qualify one to teach. Teaching is a skill – with language, inter-personal communication abilities and so on; and those have nothing to do with enlightenment. Enlightenment is an event in the mind when Self-ignorance is dispelled by Self-knowledge. It does not in itself instantly bring about stillness, peace etc., unless the mind was already 'prepared' before. This may well come about in time as what is now known is dwelt upon (nididhyAsana). [Not everyone agrees with this schema! But I subscribe to the logic given by Swami Dayananda's sampradAya.]

But, as I recall from what I have read, Nisargadatta (as an example) was not the most tranquil of characters was he?

I also do not believe that enlightenment is such a rare occurrence as some make out. I think that there are many more who simply do not make such a big deal about it, simply getting on with their 'as if' lives until the body drops, in full knowledge that it is all mithyA.

But, yes, I do agree with you – Self-realization has definitely been dumbed down and redefined by the Neo-Advaitins. More significantly, many of them have confused the whole subject, to the severe detriment of seekers.

Q.389 Enlightenment is not an experience

Q: I just have to ask your opinion on something that I experienced the other day.

I was sitting in my car reading. As I finished it I put the paper down to contemplate what I had read and just sat for a moment or two, thinking about who I am really. I had the strangest experience that I was sitting in the back of my car looking at myself sitting in the front of the car, like a totally different person was viewing this strange body in the front. I felt no real connection with the body, no fear, nothing. I was going to dismiss it as just the mind at play, as I have had similar experiences before but dismissed them as mental anxiety.

What do you think?

A: You should read my book 'Enlightenment: The Path Through The Jungle'. There is a whole section on 'what enlightenment is not' that covers this sort of thing. Here are a few relevant quotes from it:

Enlightenment is not about 'experiencing the Self' – otherwise everyone would be enlightened. It is not about experience at all, it is about Self-knowledge – the direct knowledge that you are already that which you seek. (See 25 – 97.)

Nor is enlightenment itself an experience – experiences come and go. Enlightenment is not temporary – once it happens, that is it. Consequently, if you had an experience and wonder whether you are now enlightened, you can be sure that you are not. Also, there is no need for a seeker to try to recapture a 'good' experience, thinking that it was somehow closer to enlightenment than the usual 'bad' experiences. (See 102 to 104.)

It has nothing to do with 'energy', nor is it a 'force'; it is not something 'external' that enters the person. It is not a light in any literal sense, nor does it make you less heavy in anything other than a metaphorical sense.

Physical manifestations of light, whether 'flashes' or 'blinding' do not signal enlightenment but are a sign that one may need to visit the doctor.

Similarly, 'inner voices' or 'messages from the heart' invariably arise from the mind and, irrespective of spiritual content, usually relate to the ego.

It is not an 'expansion of consciousness'; it is not 'within' us (or without). Consciousness is already everywhere and always.

Enlightenment is not about altered states of awareness. Enlightenment is not a state and Consciousness is the reality of all apparent states, in the same way that gold is the reality of rings, bangles and chains.

Feelings of ecstasy, visions of God, yogic flying, astral projections etc. have nothing to do with enlightenment. Nor do bright lights, visions, hallucinations or premonitory dreams.

Hope this effectively answers your question, although I appreciate you did not actually mention the E word.

Q.403 The enlightenment perspective

Q: If you have the time (and inclination) I would really love to get some clarification on exactly what you mean when you write *"There is still a personal self after enlightenment; it is just that it is now known not to be who I really am; it is simply a 'reflection' in the mind".*

I would tend to label what you seem to be calling 'enlightenment' as a transpersonal perspective, not a transcendent one. But words are terribly slippery and do not necessarily convey the same meaning to the recipient as they do to the sender.

For example I absolutely know (and it is far more than simply an intellectual 'knowing') that I am not 'Fred' – my personal identity, name, desires, dreams, experiences, thoughts and opinions. And yet I would hardly call myself enlightened.

My experience (and what a joke it is to phrase it like that since it is not 'my' experience at all. But that's the most convenient grammatical way to put it) is that the bliss of union arrives with the absence of 'me' altogether. Oneness arrives with 'my' departure. There have been hours and days and even weeks when the perspective of any sense of the personal self has disappeared altogether. The personal memories of Fred were there and available for use, as was the personality, but there was no shred of what I would call a 'personal self' remaining.

A: I wouldn't have thought to put it like that but yes, enlightenment *is* a 'transpersonal perspective' as opposed to transcendent. There is already only Consciousness, and you are that *already*. How could you be anything else? (There is nothing else.) So the problem of the unenlightened person is that they do not know this. To 'become enlightened' is to realize the truth of this. This is to realize that who-you-really-are is not the person or the mind. But this does not negate the *appearance* of body and mind.

So, if you 'absolutely know this', then you are enlightened. Denying that is simply giving in to mental habits of humility or whatever. (Of course, I don't suggest that you go around claiming to be enlightened; this is not the sort of statement that is appreciated by most people!)

Experiences of bliss etc. have nothing to do with enlightenment.

Q.414 Is liberation guaranteed?

Q: Is final liberation from the birth and death cycle guaranteed for everyone? Will some individuals attain liberation in 300 lifetimes, others in 300,000, but it will always be a finite time? Or is it the case that some individuals can collect worse and worse karma and as a result experience more and more suffering without end?

A: I don't really like this sort of question! Implicit in the question is the assumption that there really are individual people who undergo birth and death and rebirth. This, of course, is how it seems to be from the vantage point of the mind 'before liberation'. And traditional Advaita certainly teaches all of this in the beginning. However, the 'bottom line' of Advaita is that there never has been any creation; there are not really any jIva-s or worlds; there is not really any karma or reincarnation. So, in the end, the question is meaningless. The truth is that there is only ever Brahman or Consciousness, and Brahman ever was and ever will be; no birth or death, no heaven or hell.

This may not be the answer you were looking for but I don't want to give you an interim explanation which has to be taken back later.

Q: There is still the fear in me that my suffering will never end. It does not matter that this is only from a relative 'dreamer' perspective. When I was young and stupid, I had an obsessive compulsive disorder which 'made' me perform rituals. I had to do them in the proper sequence and time, and told myself that if I 'passed' I would be happy forever and if I not I would suffer worse and worse pain; progressive suffering forever; the worst imaginable fate.

A: What you have to understand is that you are not these ideas in your mind. In fact, you are not the mind or body. One of the most useful metaphors is to think of the mind as a 'reflector' of Consciousness, in a similar way to a mirror being a reflector of (photons of) light. Just as the sun in the mirror is not the real sun, so the consciousness in your mind is not the real Consciousness. You currently think that you are the reflection but who you really are is the Consciousness itself, which 'shines' independently of the existence of the reflection. It is only the reflection that thinks it is suffering, just as a dirty mirror might 'think' that it is not reflecting properly. You are really eternal and ever free, unaffected by anything.

Q.418 When enlightenment occurs

Q: "You cannot experience Brahman. But everything you experience is Brahman (since Brahman is all there is)".

1. Are both assertions true?

2. My understanding (based on both being true) is that you cannot experience Brahman directly, but you are always experiencing it indirectly via vyavahAra/mithyA objects. Very much like Plato's cave and Kant's phenomena/numina, you experience shadows/phenomena… not the dinge-an-sich/numina which cast the shadows.

My Advaita is rusty (shoving vyavahAra and mithyA together into vyavahAra/mithyA is probably not kosher)… but is the gist of my understanding correct?

A: That's pretty much all correct! Interchanging vyavahAra and mithyA is fine as long as you know what you are doing. But you do have to know what you are doing. After all, Brahman is not an experiencer either, and yet you are Brahman! The main thing to remember is not to mix vyavahAra and paramArtha in your thinking/discussion.

Of course, this thinking does all relate to vyavahAra – a world with separate people. The reality is that there are neither.

It doesn't matter if your recollection of the teaching gets rusty. Once you fully understand it, you can work out your own 'explanations'. And it sounds as though your understanding is pretty good!

Q: A student of James Swartz posted this:

"Self realization happens when pure awareness reflects upon the subtle body (which is reflective, like a mirror), in a clear, still mind. Then there is the thought of limitlessness/oneness. There is the apprehension that this is what you truly are in the intellect, which is the discriminating aspect of the mind. When this knowledge is assimilated fully in every aspect of one's life, the jIva/person gains mokSha ... which is the fruit of this knowledge".

I had never heard of this account of how Self-realization occurs. Does it jibe with your understanding?

A: To be pedantically correct, the jIva/person never gains mokSha because there is no person. Atman is ever free. True 'liberation' is when this already-existent fact is realized. But this is the final truth/understanding. What you say could be taken as interim understanding for the person (ahaMkAra) that is looking for a personal mokSha.

Q: So you would say this is correct:

"Self realization happens when pure awareness reflects upon the subtle body (which is reflective, like a mirror), in a clear, still mind. Then there is the thought of limitlessness/oneness. There is the apprehension that this is what you truly are in the intellect, which is the discriminating aspect of the mind".

Is the bolded part what always happens with self realization... like knowing Brahman=Atman always happens with Self knowledge? In other words, if someone were to ask you, how does Self realization happen... would it be your answer also?

A: My answer is that Self-realization occurs when Self-ignorance is removed by Self-knowledge. All the stuff about reflection in subtle body is adhyAropa-apavAda. In other words, if it helps get you there, fine, but then you drop it completely.

Q.424 Paradox of the Illusory Self

Q: I've read your wonderful book, 'Back to the Truth', and much from your website. I've learned so much from what you've offered, it's impossible to thank you enough. I do have a question that continues to arise again and again. Though simple, it's never quite answered head-on. It's hard to phrase it in a single sentence, so here goes:

Sometimes it seems that non-dual teachers are simply saying "Did you notice you're conscious? That's what you are". There are many such teachers, as I'm sure you are aware. Some, similarly, seem to say that realizing there is no person is all there is to it, everything else stays the same. Meanwhile there are very many accounts of realization that include an understanding of the nature of consciousness, of seeing the world of objects as empty or transparent, and many have said that the mark of realization is an awareness that does not go away (or seem to go away) during deep sleep. These understandings seem beyond the simple concept of 'no-self'.

So when an instructor says something like "who wants to know?" or "who wants enlightenment?" I get very frustrated. I get it that there is no person that wants to know. Maybe I don't get it enough (certainly not experientially), but just dropping the idea of a self and saying "yep I'm conscious, I'm aware" does not lead to these other powerful understandings, or deeper truths.

Body-minds that have realized 'no-self' still go on through life with a few desires and interests that they try to satisfy (Ramana Maharshi reading the news, for instance). This body-mind is interested in big Truths. So why tell me that seeing through the self, knowing that I am aware (or awareness) is enough? There seem to be other, bigger, even more interesting truths to be discovered.

So, I guess a simple way of asking my question is: Paradoxes arise from an illusory self seeking to see through itself. But they don't arise from a body-mind (or even an illusory self) seeking to understand oneness, Consciousness, the universe, etc. I assume we have to see through the self to realize the rest, but why do so many seem to ignore the rest?

A: Glad that you have found the book and website useful – always good to hear! I do notice that you refer to 'Back to the Truth' specifically. This was an attempt to express the truth through the words of many teachers, rather than specifically through my own understanding. Thus, if you want the latter, 'Book of One (2nd edition)' is the better book. I will, however, try to answer your specific question.

The 'bottom line' teaching of Advaita is best expressed by

Shankara's summary: Brahman is the truth, the world is mithyA, the jIva is none other than Brahman. 'Enlightenment' or 'Self-realization' is the irrevocable gaining of this knowledge, all doubts having been eliminated. Whether you are subsequently totally serene and blissful is not directly dependent upon this knowledge but on the mental preparation that preceded it. Your life continues. Desires and aversions continue in an attenuated form, but you are no longer perturbed too much whether or not they are met. Again, the degree of 'too much' depends upon prior preparation or continued 'devotion' to the truth.

It is the mind of the person that realizes this. It *is* the person who 'wants to know' and it *is* the person who gains enlightenment. Part of the realization is, indeed, that the person is mithyA. But that does not alter the empirical experience (c.f. you still see the sun rise, even though you know that it is actually the earth rotating).

I don't really understand your phrasing of the question about paradox. The problem is one of language. In a sense, it is language that it is the cause of all our seeming problems. It is fortunate that, through Advaita, language can also provide the solution. (Now that is a paradox!)

Q: Hearing this helps so much: "It is the mind of the person that realizes this. It is the person who 'wants to know' and it is the person who gains enlightenment". There is a similar line in your book and, when I read it, I assumed there must have been a typo or a left out word. I had heard so many times that the 'I' cannot realize itself since it's non-existent, so I couldn't believe I was reading it right. But I have always had the following thought (when hearing Neo-Advaitins say such things): If there never was a self, then all the things that we thought were a self are still there to understand the truth, even if that truth is that the person that knows is not a person. I think you are basically confirming this.

There is one very simple part of my question that you did not fully answer, largely because I garbled how I asked it. Let me try to put it another way, even though it's simple. I have read of many interactions where the seeker finally gets it when being pointed to awareness. In one case, for instance, a seeker meets John Wheeler at a satsang. Wheeler asks him two questions. First, *"Do you exist?"* then, *"Are you aware?"* The seeker is then enlightened and is even so 'done' that he then leaves the satsang. But I don't know from such stories if he means simply that he realizes that he is awareness (even if more completely than before) or if he now *also* understands what I think are essential things: that all sentient beings share a single consciousness, that consciousness does not come from brain, that there is no death. Is he now, from this simple pointing to awareness, aware during deep sleep?

Put another way, does seeing through the self simply let you know there is no self (with possible benefits, such as bliss and an easier way through life) or does it necessarily reveal Brahman, the oneness of consciousness, etc.? I mean, if the only goal is to see through the self (and life stays the same) then I could imagine being 'done', stopping seeking. But if deeper truths are necessarily a part of it, how can I not think that there is something to get that I don't have?

A: There are quite a few misunderstandings in what you say here. It may well be better for you to read 'Book of One' first and see if any questions (along the lines of what you are asking) still remain.

One particular concept usually clarifies the confusion regarding 'existence of the self (with a small 's'). It is that of chidAbhAsa – reflected Consciousness. Read these two articles on the website (http://www.advaita-vision.org/chidabhasa/) and http://www.advaita-vision.org/continuing-reflections-on-reflections/).

Understanding that you exist and are aware is *not* enlightenment! I referred to Shankara's summary. You have to understand that Consciousness is the non-dual reality, that the universe is only name and form of Consciousness and that the essential 'you' (Atman) is this same Consciousness. You must have not a shadow of a doubt that this is the case. Only then can you claim to be enlightened. Also, no-one is 'aware during deep sleep', not even Shankara! And no-one 'sees' Brahman. How could they when there is *only* Brahman?

The route to a total realization of this is usually gradual, requiring lots of interim explanations. The only reliable source is scriptural unfoldment from a qualified teacher.

Q.438 Could a computer become enlightened?

Q: Will an 'upload' be capable of giving mokSha to a computer? By 'upload' I am referring to the Science Fiction concept of scanning the contents of a human brain down to the quantum level, and then simulating that complex entity in a virtual environment. Ray Kurzweil is a key proponent who claims this will be possible sometime within the next few decades.

A: The mind is rather more than just data, and more than processing-software running on brain hardware. Although all these things are ultimately Consciousness alone, there has to be something there to reflect the light of Consciousness in order for a thing actually to become conscious. And it has to do this very well indeed before it can become Self-conscious. And it has to do it brilliantly in order to gain mokSha! I don't think uploads satisfy these criteria!

Q: I agree with your answer, but I suppose the answer will depend largely on the assumptions one makes in thinking through the problem. Can reflected Consciousness arise in a silicon-based entity? Or only carbon-based creatures like ourselves? It's actually a pretty stimulating question, and it touches on the 'hard problem' as defined by David Chalmers, etc. If you ever do get around to reading his book, he has an interesting thought experiment on the principle of organizational invariance, where neurons are one-by-one replaced with silicon equivalents. At what point does consciousness (which here would only be reflected) disappear in this process?

A: You are still assuming that consciousness relates to the gross body – replacing carbon with silicon. The mind is the 'subtle body' in Advaita. Having said that, I see no reason why there should not be silicon-based life forms associated with subtle bodies elsewhere in the universe…

Q: Good point, thanks. It makes me wonder though, if the mind is the subtle body and doesn't relate to the gross body/ brain, then why is the subtle body affected at all when the brain becomes physically damaged? I was thinking in terms of reflected Consciousness arising in the 'mirror' that consisted of gross + subtle body.

A: Good point, too. I guess the metaphor of computers does come into play here, the mind needing the hardware of the brain in order to manifest (better word than function, since it retains the autonomy of the subtle body, which is supposed to migrate to a new body after the death of the existing one).

Q.447 Realizing Brahman

Q: I know that Brahman is not an object I can find; I think of it more like the realization that I am the tenth man (you know this story I assume). But when I have this sort of realization (I have a lot of them), I can't tell whether I am realizing Brahman or something else.

One set of realizations involves a sort of inner presence that reveals itself like existence-consciousness-limitless, and I feel it as present in my heart region. It's very deep and real and it does not come and go like an experience. It gets covered up by my thoughts and emotions, but it's always there.

Another set of realizations involve a sense that the world of objects is not actually there because the objects are made of consciousness rather than matter.

So my question is:

Is Self-realization something you discover in your heart like a presence of happiness or of a consciousness that doesn't ever come and go but only seems to be obscured by thoughts? Or is self-realization the knowledge that all the objects in the world and mind are made of only consciousness, in the way that dream objects are made of dream-consciousness?

I believe that Advaita Vedanta is saying that somehow nothing exists other than consciousness and thus the objects that appear (including the mind and subtle realm) are not made of matter but rather are 'made of' consciousness. Is this correct?

A: The realization that you are the tenth* is a good metaphor, as is the example given in the bhAga-tyAga-lakShaNa story (see Q.345). It is the sudden appreciation that something is radically different from how you had previously thought it was and, moreover and quite specifically, you know that your new way of seeing things is correct. No doubt – it is now clear.

These are metaphors, however. In the case of 'Self'-realization, it is the recognition that the teaching that you have been hearing (ideally listening to a qualified teacher – i.e. shravaNa) is true, namely that reality is non-dual, that the world and who-you-thought-yourself to be are not in themselves real, that who-you-really-are is that same non-dual reality.

This inner presence that does not come and go is an aspect of it. But everyone has this to some degree. Each one of us feels that 'who-I-am' now, at whatever age, is the same 'who-I-was' when I was a child. There is an intrinsic awareness that I am not the body or mind, both of which are constantly changing. But this is not the same as realizing why this is, as in the above paragraph. Also, beware of 'feelings' – they are as much mithyA as the rest! And the idea that 'I' am in the heart is one promulgated by Ramana, though it occurs in the Upanishads. [See Q.61 for more on this.]

Objects in the world are mithyA. But this does not mean that they do not exist. Their separateness is something imposed by our minds. Their 'substance' is Consciousness; matter is Consciousness. And Consciousness certainly exists.

Have you read 'A-U-M' incidentally? Gaudapada is the original and possibly the best explicator of what Advaita is saying ultimately.

Q: Not to be melodramatic, but what you have said (*"you know that your new way of seeing things is correct. No doubt – it is now clear"*) ... I think this is the best thing I've ever heard in my life or ever will do. Clearly, you have understood my question which was basically, is self-realization something real or just an idea you can hitch yourself to out of terror and desperation! From what you say I know exactly what you mean: the recognition is that it is real.

A: Great! But just to clarify: post-enlightenment, yes, you are now clear about the teaching; you know that who-I-really-am is unaffected by any of this. In a sense, everything changes but nothing changes. You still see the world; you still function empirically as you did before. There are still desires and fears but you know that whatever happens does not really matter. The body is still susceptible to pain and will still die; but you know that 'I' am not affected by pain and 'I' will not die (I was never born). And so on… As I have said before, the extent to which you become serene and totally happy etc. is determined more by the extent that you were fully mentally prepared prior to enlightenment. Enlightenment itself is merely (!) an event in the mind.

[* Here is the story of the 'Tenth Man', as I related it in The Book of One (2nd edition):

"There is a party of ten men travelling together to a distant village in a remote and rugged area. They encounter a swollen river, which they are obliged to cross. They join hands and begin the perilous crossing but inevitably they lose their footing in the strong current and have to swim. Much later and wetter, they reassemble on the opposite bank. As each counts the number of men who have arrived, they can only find nine and conclude that one of their number has drowned.

"As they are bemoaning their loss, a monk passes by and asks them what the matter is. They explain and, quickly assessing the situation, he recognizes their mistake. He asks them to line up and, taking a stick, he hits the first man once, the second twice and so on down the line, counting out the number aloud each time. Reaching the end, he hits the

last man ten times and calls out 'ten'. What had happened, of course, is that each man had counted the others but forgotten to count himself, and so had only reached nine".]

Q.455 Physical changes on enlightenment

Q: In his book of talks called 'The New Freedom', Rajneesh (Osho) has stated that awakening disturbs the body and brain so much that a majority of people leave the body. Those who survive may suffer some severe physical deformity or inability to speak etc.

In the Gospel of Ramakrishna, Mahendranath Gupta relates how the Paramahamsa suffered on awakening. One of the changes that occurred was an enormous release of energy in the body which was unbearable. Adyashanti also states that the disturbance of the nervous system takes years to settle down. In 'The Mystique of Enlightenment', U. G. Krishnamurti has described at length the many drastic changes that took place in his body on account of awakening. In 'Nothing is Everything', a book on talks given by Nisargadatta Maharaj, the Sage is quoted as saying: *"This body is on fire. Self-knowledge has a strange quality. Sometimes it is unbearable"*.

What I want you to throw some light on, if possible, is the following:

Does awakening lead to drastic physical changes? Are they the same for all individuals or do these changes vary from person to person? Should one be deterred from attempting self-realization?

Steven Norquist, who claims to have awakened, told his audience in a 2010 talk available on the Internet that they should not seek awakening but should be 'spiritual'. One of the reasons he mentioned was the bodily changes I have referred to.

I would also be obliged if you could suggest some literature on the subject, if it exists.

A:

"Does awakening lead to drastic physical changes?" No.

"Are they the same for all individuals or do these changes vary from person to person?" It is certainly conceivable that such a significant

change in the mental outlook could bring about some bodily change but I am not aware of any authoritative records of such a thing, and it is not relevant anyway – we are not the body or mind.

"Should one be deterred from attempting self-realization?" No.

"Steven Norquist, who claims to have awakened, told his audience in a 2010 talk available on the Internet, that they should not seek awakening but should be 'spiritual'". What does this even mean?

"I would also be obliged if you could suggest some literature on the subject, if it exists". Nothing in this vein exists in traditional Advaita texts to my knowledge and I would be more than surprised if it did!

'Awakening' is not a term that I would ever use. What happens on so-called enlightenment is that the mind realizes the truth of the non-dual teaching. Obviously this affects one's mental outlook on life but otherwise, things continue pretty much as usual. There still seems to be a world and other people. It is just that one now knows that these are just forms of Brahman/Consciousness, in an analogous way to continuing to see waves and rivers etc., even knowing that all are just name and form of water.

I am surprised at your quotations. If literally true, they detract from the regard in which I hold those teachers. In the case of Osho, this is the sort of thing he might have said to insure that his audience was genuinely serious about seeking enlightenment. The 'kundalini' and 'samAdhi' to which Ramakrishna refers regarding 'awakening' have nothing to do with Advaita. Nor was U. G. Krishnamurti an Advaitin. The quotation from Nisargadatta does not necessarily mean what you suggest, especially if it is a poor translation. I don't know anything about Norquist but don't believe he was an Advaitin (or necessarily knew anything about Advaita). Lots of people speak or write about enlightenment but one thing you should know: if they make a big issue about the enlightenment 'experience', you can be pretty sure that they are not enlightened in the true sense of the word (having Self-knowledge).

Some miscellaneous observations

Q: Can you recommend any book that talks about how traditional vedAnta can improve one's life, and give deep peace as a result of j~nAna phalam?

A: I doubt that such a thing exists. You've really got this the wrong way round. vairAgya – being disinterested in one's life, good or bad – is one of the pre-requisites for enlightenment. And the phalam is a spin-off rather than the prime objective. Enlightenment brings freedom from saMsAra; our aim is to get off the treadmill altogether rather than to get cushioned seats!

Q: If all we can do is to remove the ignorance that prevents us from seeing the truth, who is removing it? If there is something that can be done, it implies that there is someone who can do it. Who is that someone if we do not really exist?

A: This is just a confusion between paramArtha and vyavahAra, between satyam and mithyA.

At the level of the world, there is a person; there is ignorance and there is the possibility of removing it so that the person can understand this teaching and realize that, in truth, there is no person, ignorance or realization, since there is, in truth, no creation at all.

No one 'removes' the ignorance exactly. The words of the guru act as a pramANa and bring about a direct realization of the truth in the mind of the seeker. Again, at the transactional level, there is someone speaking and someone listening, and words passing between them, but in reality no one is doing anything, since there are no individuals. All there is is Brahman or Consciousness if you prefer. 'Everything else' is just name and form of that Consciousness.

Summary

Enlightenment = Self-knowledge.

No experience can ever gain one Self-knowledge.

Meditation can never gain one Self-knowledge.

The only way to gain Self-knowledge is by removing Self-ignorance. And this is done by listening to explanations from a qualified teacher and asking questions to remove all doubts. It is a gradual process, even though the final realization may come suddenly, following the removal of some specific problematic misunderstanding.

As I have indicated before, any explanation for what happens to bring a jIva to realization of the truth is fine if it works. You cannot say that one explanation is true and another false. All explanations are mithyA. Nor can you say that, post 'real' enlightenment, a jIva is somehow 'established in Brahman' (or however you want to phrase this). Both prior to, and after, enlightenment (however defined), the jIva *is* Brahman, whether this is known or not. The key thing that matters to the jIva is that it is known by the mind.

A three-part essay I wrote on 'Enlightenment' can be read at http://www.advaita-vision.org/enlightenment-akhandakara/.

Enlightened Man

Q.1 Book-writing

Q: I understand that no realized man has written a book after realization. In your view is this correct? And if so, why would this be?

A: Shankara and Ramana (for example) both wrote books subsequent to realization. Whilst it is true that there is only the Self in reality and this is obviously known by the 'realized man', ignorance obscures this truth for 'other individuals'.

There will always be the need for knowledge to remove the ignorance from the 'other jIva-s' to enable them to realize that they are already the non-dual Atman. If the nature of the body-mind of the now realized man was to teach or write, existing prArabdha saMskAra will dictate that he continue to do it following realization.

Q.10 'Inappropriate' behavior

Q: From time to time, there have been reports of supposedly realized men behaving improperly towards young women or taking advantage of others with respect to monetary gain. What do you say about this?

A: So-called enlightenment is the deep realization of the truth of the teaching of Advaita. It is now known that there are no people, that every 'thing' is simply name and form of the non-dual reality. But, to some degree, these names and forms continue just the same after 'realization' as they did before, i.e. action and reaction continue according to their prior conditioning. The difference is that there is now an additional, tremendously significant factor in this cause-effect nexus, namely the knowledge that 'all there is, is Brahman'.

There is no 'I' and nothing to achieve, nothing that I could want and so on. It might be expected that this knowledge would override all of the trivial desires and fears that were present before. Accordingly, it might be thought that the so-called 'realized man' would not be affected by these in quite the same way as he might previously have been. So, in each 'individual' case, all of the various causes act as before to produce the particular actions. Whether or not the knowledge overrides the previously conditioned tendencies depends on their relative strengths. And the strength of the overriding cause depends upon the degree of 'preparation' in the form of sAdhana chatuShTaya sampatti. (See the section on 'Preparation'.)

Q.68 Destruction of the ego

Q: On page 258 of 'How to Meet Yourself' you seem to suggest that someone can come to an understanding of the truth about reality. Who is that someone? And why is it that so few have? Surely this is dependent on your upbringing and genes and, as you rightly say, we have no control over this.

From page 224 you suggest meditation as a path to removing the ego. Is it possible we might be creating the illusion of a meditator? Is it not suggested that we give up any and all paths? You continue then to suggest that religion brings about the destruction of the ego. Where in the Christian and Islamic faith is this apparent? Most religious paths and scriptures are an incomplete instruction book to enlightenment and seem to conflict with regard to explanation, understanding and expression.

Would it be better just to recognize that the ego is an expression of consciousness and can be bypassed but not destroyed? Haven't met too many enlightened people but stories about them would indicate they still had egos!

A: One general point before I answer your specific questions: Any attempt to describe the way things 'really are' is certain to fail. Each of the descriptions, metaphors, stories etc. aims to clear up particular aspects of misunderstanding and there will always be contradictions. Also, 'How to Meet Yourself' was specifically written for those knowing nothing at all about Advaita and it does not go into much detail. If you want more accurate explanations, you should go to 'The Book of One (2nd edition)'. Finally, as my own studies continued, I came across better ways of explaining things and sometimes realized that previous explanations had fallen short or possibly even misled. OK – that's the disclaimers and excuses out of the way!

Who is it who 'comes to an understanding'? It is the person, the jIva, the mind, as we normally understand these terms in vyavahAra. If circumstances in life lead us towards questioning these matters, and if our brain is genetically able to reason and comprehend the answers, then it is quite likely that we will end up on a 'path'. A good path, such as Advaita, will bring about a gradual removal of Self-ignorance. Ultimately, if circumstances are favorable (i.e. good teacher, sufficient time before the body dies etc.!) then *all* Self-ignorance will be removed and the Self will fully reveal itself as it were. The reason so few people do this is that so few genuinely want to. We are so programmed to believe that fulfillment will be found through objects, achievement etc.

It is regarding the second question that I made all of the excuses above. 'How to Meet Yourself' was written quite a few years ago and I definitely would not now use expressions such as 'destroy the ego or mind'. The purpose of meditation is rather to 'prepare' the mind, to inculcate mental discipline, stillness, discrimination etc. The book 'Enlightenment: The Path Through The Jungle' is the definitive one (from my understanding) on what enlightenment is (and is not) and the process/path for getting there.

There are in fact two aspects to enlightenment. Here is a post I made to the Advaitin group on this precise topic:

"... the distinction between j~nAna – the knowledge gained as a result of one's sAdhana through to enlightenment – and j~nAna phalam – the fruits of that knowledge in the form of peace of mind, equanimity in the face of adversity etc. Thus it is the case that one can have all the knowledge and be enlightened, yet still be subject to the sort of disturbances of mind that you describe. According to commentaries on Gaudapada's *mANDUkya kArikA (III.40-2), it all depends upon the extent of preparation (sAdhana chatuShTaya sampatti) that was done in the past. The seeker who has done none will gain neither enlightenment nor the fruit. The middling student will gain enlightenment but not the fruit. The one who was fully prepared will gain both.*

"The one who is now enlightened but does not have the peace of mind etc. (the madhyamA adhikArI *or 'middling' student) must perform nididhyAsana to recover the situation. This will convert the emotional blockage into j~nAna phalam. This practice should take the form of repeatedly listening to, reading or writing scriptures or discussion or teaching. (Alternatively, Vedantic meditation, as per Patanjali yoga, may be practiced.)"*

The meditator is not an illusion from the perspective of the person in vyavahAra. This is the perennial mistake made by the Neo-Advaitin. It is only from the perspective of the one Self that there is no person etc. The seeker does not appreciate that perspective by definition (i.e. if he did, he would not be a seeker).

It is definitely *not* suggested by traditional Advaita that we 'give up all paths'. This is again the stance of the Neo-Advaitin and is possibly the most damaging idea that there is for the seeker. If the typical seeker takes this idea on board then he is doomed. The intellectual ideas of the Neo-Advaitin will never bring about enlightenment – and the fact that such a thing as 'enlightenment' is denied meaning only adds to the confusion.

Could you point me to the passage where I suggest that religion brings about the destruction of the ego? I don't recall claiming this and can't think why I would. My stance on religions is that most have lost their way, with the original teachings having been subsumed into misguided and mythologized versions devised to prop up the political structures within the hierarchy of the time, (i.e. not a positive view!).

The ego is certainly an expression of Consciousness (as is everything). But what do you mean by ego? It is best to use the term ahaMkAra, so that everyone knows what is being discussed. To the extent that we define ego as a 'mistaken identification of the non-dual Self with something in the mithyA world', then the ego does naturally disappear with enlightenment, because it is then known that 'I am Brahman' and not the body/mind/role etc. But, as noted above, such things as desires, preferences, fears etc. may still arise, according to how much preparation was done in the early stages. In that case, there would still effectively be an ego, although most certainly an attenuated one.

Q.72 Life-style of an 'enlightened' person

Q: What should be the life-style of an 'enlightened' person in today's world?

A: In reality, nothing changes when 'someone' becomes enlightened – before there was the non-dual Brahman; after there is the non-dual Brahman. From the standpoint of the relative world, what has happened is that Self-knowledge has arisen in the mind of the now-enlightened person so that he or she now *knows* that everything is Brahman.

From the standpoint of another person, it will outwardly appear that nothing has happened, except that the enlightened person's behavior is likely to change. I say 'likely' because the extent to which this happens is somewhat dependent upon the mental preparation that this person underwent prior to the enlightenment. Such things as mental equanimity are likely to increase post-enlightenment. The person's behavior to others is likely to be different – more sympathetic, loving etc. – because it is now known that these 'others' are in fact one's own Self.

Desires etc. are likely still to arise but whether these are satisfied or not will no longer be important. And so on ... The person's working, social life etc. may well continue as before, since there is no reason to try to change anything when all is known to be perfect (and changeless) in reality, but then again it may not. For example, perhaps the person had a natural inclination to teach, which had been suppressed and, since there are now no ambitions etc., he may give up his materialistic lifestyle and devote it to others. Who knows?

Q: A personal question if I may ask: Having this knowledge or understanding, how does your day to day living happen? Meaning: are you serious, playful, easy-going, stressed, etc.; and do you look at things as funny, comical, silly, absurd, ridiculous, insane, much ado about nothing?

A: I no longer worry about the 'big' issues in life. But my particular nature – likes and dislikes – remains. And this means that I still do not feel comfortable in certain situations, such as with large groups of people, or with small children for example. And my biggest problem – impatience – is still quite active! It is certainly true that I see how people identify with, and assign tremendous importance to, things that really do not matter. How I feel about this varies according to situation and mental state, as it does with everyone. Having spent a lifetime being predominantly 'serious' in thought and outlook, this is still the principal trait.

Maintaining the website, writing books, answering all these questions etc. is all part of my nididhyAsana.

Q.74 More on life after enlightenment

Q: I have just finished reading your book ('Back to the Truth') and found it a noble and mature work.

I note that in the 'Teaching Method' section you say you come from the Traditional perspective and looked into Direct & Neo before eventually returning to Traditional. I come from the Direct perspective because that was what resonated with me. I have read one book on the Neo perspective which I found invalid. I have also read the bhakti essays on your website which were interesting. I see bhakti not as worship, reciting mantras, singing, dancing, a descent into sentimentality or anything like that but as in devotion to the work of integration. Do I now need to go to the Traditional methods, I don't know?

What happens when we no longer identify with who we take ourselves to be (and this is not a case of switching identity to another conceptualized sense of self)? How do we live as we did before, playing our roles as before, if that now seems ridiculous? For example, a child in a kindergarten might find that, although she still looks the same on the outside, has now discovered that it's no longer necessary to play with toys, enacting little dramas etc. Is she supposed to just carry on playing, whilst not identifying with it, until the scenery changes? Surely you only carry on doing it whilst you believe it's true?

A: If you still have doubts or uncertainties, you are still lacking some aspect of Self-knowledge. The surest way of gaining this is traditional teaching. However if, as seems to be the case, you already understand, and know to be true, most of this stuff, then it may be that reading more, seeing some reputable teacher, discussion etc. will be sufficient.

Once the Self-ignorance is gone (or, if you prefer, when you are 'enlightened'), life carries on much as before outwardly. Yes, you now know that all is Brahman, that there is no created world etc. but the body still exists (as name and form) and prArabdha karma is not wiped out (if it were, the body would come to an end there and then). So it just carries on and, knowing that you are not doing any of this, you can just watch and enjoy. It's not ridiculous; you are just fulfilling your role in the play.

Q.110 Experience of dying

Q: What is the difference in the experience of dying between one who has realized and one who has not?

A: Interesting question! However, the answer has to be: how would anyone ever know?

If someone actually dies, they are no longer able to tell us. If they just have a 'near death experience', they don't actually die so all we have is a description of what is seen/felt as the brain starts to close down and is flooded with unusual hormone combinations (perhaps). So, all that we can usefully talk about is the attitude to dying. Here, the situation is much more clear-cut.

The ordinary person believes that 'who-they-really-are' dies. They may believe that this will be total annihilation or perhaps they think that they will go to heaven or hell or perhaps be reborn in another body. Whichever is the case, the death-event will almost certainly be something to fear above all else. The realized person, on the other hand, knows that only the body-mind dies, while 'who-they-really-are' is totally unaffected. The metaphor of a pot breaking is often used – the space that was thought to be 'contained' within the pot remains totally unaffected – it was always the case that the pot was in space, not the other way round.

Q.123 Does nothing matter?

Q: I read so much on websites and in books saying that nothing matters.

From the level of Brahman, the relative level has no meaning. Let's say I become enlightened or realized, will there be any concern for apparent others, or will I turn my head and not care? From all I've read I know there is no 'I' with a head to turn, but does Brahman care? What is the unconditional love that is spoken of so much if not Brahman? I want to care, even if the 'I' is false, and therefore the 'want' is false.

A: Once enlightened, a person knows that there are no others in reality. But he/she also knows that this was not appreciated before and is not appreciated now by the vast numbers of seeming others. Accordingly, it is natural for there to be compassion/love for these seeming others and this has been seen to be the case for all jIvanmukta-s.

You should also be careful not to anthropomorphize Brahman. Brahman is the non-dual reality; there is nothing other than Brahman to 'care about' and it is not meaningful to speak of Brahman 'caring' anyway. It is you, the person, who becomes 'enlightened' and 'cares' in this empirical but mithyA world.

Q.161 Teachers and saMskAra-s

Q: Many teachers seem to imply that the ego will disappear simply by ignoring or denying it. But if the innate tendencies or saMskAra-s have not been completely eradicated, a teacher cannot call himself 'enlightened'. A tree whose branches have been cut grows again. So long as the roots of the tree remain unimpaired, the tree will continue to grow. Unless the saMskAra-s are totally destroyed by j~nAna, they will automatically attract rebirth at the appropriate time.

A: Of course, what you say is what is taught by the traditional teaching at a particular point – and very useful it has proven to be for many seekers for centuries. To the extent that it 'fits' with one's upbringing, culture, education etc., it will continue to be invaluable for providing provisional answers for seekers until such time as they are ready for more appropriate pointers to the absolute truth.

In the West, many seekers do not have any affinity for ideas such as reincarnation or divine beings wielding powers of creation and destruction. Since the ultimate truth is that none of these are absolutely real, it may be counter-productive to try to impose such ideas upon them. Teachers in the West generally do not make use of them and I do not believe that you can say that is unacceptable.

Your main point seems to relate to the difference between enlightenment and j~nAna phalam (jIvanmukti). See Q.68 for details.

The key point with respect to what you are saying here is that not having j~nAna phalam need not impact on a teacher's ability. Indeed, Shankara has pointed out that a skilled and knowledgeable teacher who is not even enlightened is preferable to an enlightened one who is lacking teaching skills. Someone who is both a skilled teacher and enlightened would still be an excellent teacher even if still suffering occasional mental problems as a result of insufficient preparation.

Q.184 Functioning post-enlightenment

Q: I've just read your enlightening article in Watkins magazine. Your statement that speech and thought are dualistic came as a bit of a blow. It implies that someone who has attained enlightenment will naturally retire from work and an active life.

My question is this: Is enlightenment a state that can only exist in between periods of thinking (necessary for the planning and execution of tasks) and as such cannot be a continuous state?

A: The life of a saMnyAsin may have been appropriate in ancient India but it is certainly not appropriate to modern Western society. And there is no reason why one should resort to it.

Enlightenment is the event in the mind after which the truth is known about the nature of reality but the appearance does not change. The apparent world does not disappear. The j~nAnI still functions in the world, though knowing that all is mithyA and that no one is doing anything in reality. And, if he travels, he still has to look up the times of the trains/planes and organize his time so as to catch them. And so on – the appearance continues and the enlightened and unenlightened alike continue to be a part of that appearance. So enlightenment and planning are not 'mutually exclusive'. Enlightenment itself is part of the appearance – the Self is already free.

As to your specific question, enlightenment is not a state, continuous or otherwise. As noted above, it is simply an event in time. Before it, the mind thinks 'I am a person'; after, it knows 'there never were any people; there is only Brahman'. Before, it thinks that the world is real; after it knows that the world is mithyA.

Q: Your reply is very clear, but I am still confused about 'the mind' in your reply. If I understand correctly then, before enlightenment, the person's mind formulates and executes plans to fulfill its desires e.g. survival. In doing so, it interacts with other 'people' with the intention of achieving that desired outcome. It has to take account of other people's agendas, misinterpretations, judgment, gossip, etc. where those people can affect the outcome. If, after enlightenment, the mind still makes plans e.g. for the body to survive, it must still carry out these interactions with a view to achieve the desired outcome. So what's different?

My other questions are:

1. If there is no 'person', who generates the desire to survive? (The desire that gives rise to the plan/action e.g. for which catching the train/plane is required etc.)

2. If (dualistic) speech and thought have to happen to put the plan into action (to catch trains planes etc. to fulfill the desire), then how can speech and thought emerge from an enlightened mind?

3. If enlightenment is binary, why does practice need to continue? What more could be achieved if it's already happened?

I suspect that these are rather puerile questions. I'm finding this really difficult. I am so fed up of 'me'. I thought I was at the 'Who cares' stage some years ago (re: Ramesh Balsekar), but clearly not.

I've recently read the 'Big Mind, Big heart' Neo book. The Big Mind process gets me to the same place as the 'Who am I?'

meditation – infinite, impersonal, comfortable and totally safe space. The Big Heart gets me to this all encompassing love that has been quite a familiar feeling in my life. However, I don't feel that either of these conveys the sense that no people exist or that life is a dream.

A: You are right. The mind functions in the same way after enlightenment as it did before. The crucial difference is that, before, the mind believed that all this was real whereas, after, it knows that it is all mithyA. This makes all the difference! Traditional Advaita explains this by saying that the prArabdha karma that effectively brought this body into existence has still to be used up, even though this person, since now enlightened, will not incur any new karma.

Regarding your subsequent questions:

1. Desires and fears are just thoughts. No one generates them; they simply arise as a result of the particular circumstances and the particular nature of that body-mind; it is simply a cause-effect nexus.

2. As already noted, the enlightened mind still operates according to the nature of minds in general so there is no problem about thinking, planning or speaking etc.

3. Practice may need to continue in order to gain j~nAna phalam – the 'fruits of enlightenment'. See Q.160.

The questions are not puerile. Indeed, if a question such as these is causing you problems, you must ask it no matter how silly you feel it to be. The only truly silly question is that one that goes unasked. I don't know the book to which you refer but it is worth remembering that no practice will ever bring about enlightenment, and feelings such as spaciousness, all-encompassing love or whatever, are not enlightenment.

Q.253 Behavior of the guru

Q: I have been reading 'Stripping the Gurus: Sex, Violence, Abuse and Enlightenment' by Geoffrey D. Falk and this suggests that many teachers were unprincipled or worse regarding their disciples. The bibliography is quite impressive: Ramana Maharshi, Dalai Lama, Yogananda, Sivananda, Ramakrishna, Vivekananda... This is really too much for me.

A: I've not heard of it before but it doesn't surprise me all that much.

There are two points, I think. First is that there will always be cults and individuals who are intent on talking advantage of seekers who do not know any better. You just have to do your research before getting involved.

Secondly, though, you need to be very aware of the distinction between a j~nAnI and a jIvanmukta. One can be Self-realized yet still be subject to mental suffering, still indulge in bad habits, etc. This will occur when there was insufficient preparation (sAdhana chatuShTaya sampatti) prior to enlightenment. The remedy is continuing nididhyAsana. This need not affect one's ability to teach. Indeed, even someone who is not yet enlightened may be a good teacher if they know the scriptures and have learned the various methods from a sampradAya. Of course, someone who is enlightened as well will be even better.

This does mean that a seeker has to be alert to the potential dangers and there is always the possibility of scandal in the extreme, as happened with Ramesh a few years ago.

What the 'seeker community' fails to appreciate is that the teacher, too, is a person from the vyAvahArika standpoint. Of course, he is the Self in reality (and knows this if he is enlightened). But so is the seeker (although he does not know it). And the teacher still functions as a person for the remainder of their life. The extent to which this person's behavior tallies with the seeker's notion of how it ought to be will depend, as I said above, on the state of the teacher's mind – better prepared means purer and less likely to behave in any way 'antisocially'!

Q.264b Behavior of an enlightened person

Q: In 'The Book of One', you said an enlightened master can have 'unenlightening' traits and you quote from Osho and seem to regard him as enlightened in your book. But if his later actions 'caused' others to 'sin' (encouraging free sex, even with children) does this mean Osho was never enlightened but only close to enlightenment? Dr. David Hawkins (considered enlightened by many) claimed Osho 'fell' from a high consciousness to a low one.

A: As I have answered more fully in questions from others, one can be enlightened (a 'j~nAnI'), without also being a jIvanmukta. Such a one could indeed behave in ways deemed not to be representative of how we think that someone enlightened ought to behave. Osho is almost certainly a good example of this. Such a person might be a very good teacher, but seekers obviously need to be wary of being seduced into inappropriate behavior themselves. Such people are often also charismatic and can exert tremendous influence over the vulnerable.

Coincidentally, I have just written to a friend earlier today on the subject of Osho. Here is what I said:

"There are certainly many who denounce him as fraudulent, dangerous, manipulative, exhibitionist, narcissistic, etc. And his life and lifestyle tend to support this. And one could reasonably claim that there is 'no smoke without fire'. However, much of what has been written along these lines has been written without the benefit of any familiarity with his teaching. Also, if you investigate into the lives of a number of well-known teachers, you can unearth the unsavory without too much difficulty. Most of those, however, were not so much in the public eye as Osho became. Even so, you have the reported indiscretions of someone who was as respected as Ramesh Balsekar and even Vivekananda. You might be interested in a book called 'Stripping the Gurus', which denounces many, including Osho.

"However, I tend to accept that one can be a j~nAnI yet still suffer from bad habits! And I tend to be more interested in what someone teaches rather than what they do when they are not teaching. I agree

that one cannot simply ignore that, and there may well come a point where one cannot reconcile someone's behavior with what they purport to teach. But, regarding someone like Osho, we have little to go on apart from, on the one hand, scurrilous reports (often apocryphal and usually at least second hand) about the way he behaved and, on the other, the many books of his talks and discourses. Have you read any? 'The Mustard Seed, a discourse on the Gospel According to St. Thomas', is one I would particularly recommend. Read it and then see if you are still happy to denounce him. I think you will be very surprised. It is readable, entertaining but also extremely perceptive and informative.

"Incidentally, I am currently reading a book due for publication later in the year probably, called Three Dangerous Magi, about Crowley, Gurdjieff and Osho. It is written by someone who spent several years with Osho – Philip Mistlberger – and whose book A Natural Awakening I highly recommend". [Note: book since published.]

Q: When you say a j~nAnI, do you mean an enlightened person who may have 'bad' habits? Does a j~nAnI suffer from his 'bad' influence and, after physical death, does he come back as another person to 'pay' for his 'misdeeds'? But if he is enlightened, there is no reincarnation for him?

I was reading the kaThopaniShad – it says that the intellect cannot attain the Self but I know that only the intellect (which you call 'mind' in your book, 'Enlightenment: The Path Through The Jungle') can gain knowledge if the Self dispels ignorance (this is what Chinmaya taught me). Am I misreading anything here?

A: Someone who has realized the Self but is not a jIvanmukta may indeed still suffer to some degree but they also know that it is not their real Self that is suffering, only the body-mind. If the mind was insufficiently prepared, it will still be subject to desires and fears, and satisfaction or denial of these will cause some discomfort. But a j~nAnI does not incur AgAmin saMskAra so that, once the prArabdha is exhausted (in this life), there is no rebirth. The existing saMskAra that had not yet matured is 'burnt up' on enlightenment.

The intellect or mind does not 'attain' anything. But it is the mind of the person that gains the Self-knowledge that who-I-really-am was, is and always will be free.

Q: Is it more realistic to strive for spiritual purification by becoming a j~nAnI rather than a jIvanmukti? I am finding it challenging to seek! Firstly, after deciding to seek, my health has turned worse and it seems the ego does not want this path and is 'using' the body to react. Also, I am losing interest in life and hobbies, which is scary as I had clinical depression and did not want to worsen anything.

A: The best way is to combine shravaNa (listening to the teachings with a good teacher) with spiritual practices. If one does this, then it is possible to become a j~nAnI and a jIvanmukta simultaneously. This is the ideal. It is certainly natural that, as one becomes more involved with this serious work, one loses interest in the mundane aspects of life. It is the natural progression of more worthwhile desires supplanting the more trivial. Don't get hung up about the ego – it would only be the ego doing that after all!

The best text that I am aware of describing the state/condition of the realized man is jIvan-mukti-viveka by Swami VidyAraNya. There is a translation by Swami Mokshadananda published by Advaita Ashrama. The Gita also has various bits talking about this (refers to the 'perfected' man as sthitapraj~na). See II. 54 – 72; V 18-21, 24-26; VI 29-32; XII 13-20; XIV 22-26.

Q.295 Does a j~nAnI still see the world?

Q: When someone who is enlightened perceives an object (e.g. a cup), what do they think? Do they think that the cup is mithyA and, therefore, not real in an ultimate sense (i.e. neti neti)? Or do they think that what they perceive is Brahman in the form of a cup?

From my understanding both of these perspectives are correct, however, I was wondering what ends up being the initial or dominant viewpoint that someone who is enlightened has, when perceiving the world day to day. What got me thinking about this was that I noticed that Swami Rama Tirtha, when touring the US, used to open each of his lectures with a statement like, *"My own Self in the form of ladies and gentlemen"*, or *"The Infinite One in the form of ladies and gentlemen"*. Assuming that he was indeed enlightened it seems that when he perceived the world he 'saw' Brahman. Contrast this with someone who instead focuses on the fact that objects are mithyA and thinks 'neti neti' when perceiving something.

A: I cannot speak for everyone (!) but the key point is that everything still looks the same. Someone who is enlightened still sees cups and enjoys coffee, despite knowing that in reality there is only Brahman. Or, if you like, what they see is a cup; what they know is Brahman. A teacher may make statements such as you mention in order to alert the listener to the topic of the discussion but obviously he still sees the audience – otherwise it would not really be possible to give the talk!

Q.324 Enjoying Being Brahman

Q1: When I had steady awareness that I was Brahman, I used to enjoy the Thoughts that all indeed was Brahman. Since I progressed to the simply I AM I am not enjoying the earlier feelings of thinking everything as Brahman. Is it that the state of being in simply I AM is absolute absence of any thought whatsoever?

Q2: How to overcome the sleep state to be in constant awareness of 'Who am I?' Please some practical hints!

Regarding my second point I intended to know more about the Fourth State in which the Saints wait to consume all their Prarabdha. How is this state practiced and what are the skills of it?

Please shed some light on how do the realized but unpracticed people live in their day to life while all the time immersed in their truest identity. My readings tell me just to let things happen without worrying at all how they happen. Is it this way?

A : In reality, there is only Brahman. In reality, there is nothing more to say.

At the empirical level, there is the individual 'I', which is a reflection of Brahman (for the sake of talking about it). The individual 'I' experiences and has thoughts and feelings. In this respect, it is meaningless to differentiate between "awareness of Brahman" and "simply I AM" – both are the individual mind thinking/feeling/experiencing. Any differences between what you perceive as being these two states is not of any relevance. There is no 'progress' here.

What do you mean by 'progress', anyway? You were always Brahman and always will be. All you can say is that once you did not realize this and then (hopefully) you did (or will). The only meaningful 'progress' is the removal of Self-ignorance. Afterwards thoughts, feelings and experiencing continue as before; the difference is that you now know that you are Brahman regardless of the nature of those thoughts etc. There is no attachment or threat in any of them because you know that they cannot touch you.

The deep sleep state is simply deep-sleep, without any awareness of self or the outside world, for the enlightened and unenlightened alike. It is rest for body and mind. Mind being inactive, there is no experience or awareness for anyone. On awakening, the individual continues in his or her state of Self-ignorance or Self-knowledge. There is nothing to be done here. All that has to be done is to purify the mind and gain Self-knowledge!

What the Mandukya Upanishad calls 'the fourth' (turIya) is not a state. It is the non-dual reality itself. Upon enlightenment, we know that who-we-really-are does not act. Consequently, no further karma is accrued. Because the prArabdha karma is that which brought about this (apparent) embodiment, it continues to play out until the body dies. This is so regardless of whether one is enlightened or not.

So there is no 'fourth state', nothing to be practiced and no skills. Simply purify the mind as per sAdhana chatuShTaya sampatti and then gain Self-knowledge through listening to the scriptures unfolded by a qualified teacher.

Nature of Self

Q.80 Is 'I am' the content?

Q: Is this sense of Being inert? This sense of 'I AM' that Nisargadatta and others say to stay with. I AM 'seems' like the ground. What we are and what we are looking for. But isn't this also content? Is 'being' just more content? I'm not sure of my question. 'Being' seems as transient as any other content. Can the other be without content? Awareness and I AM may be one but so is any other content.

A: 'I' am that in which everything apparently arises, exists and to which it returns. 'I' am that which is unchanging. In fact, everything is simply name and form of that same non-dual reality that 'I am'.

'Being', 'I AM', 'ground', 'content' – all these are mithyA concepts. If ideas such as these lead you to the realization of the non-dual reality, then they serve a useful purpose. Otherwise, I suggest you drop them – they only lead to the mind expending energy trying to make sense of them!

Q.86 How can I be Brahman yet not know Brahman?

Q: If I (mind-body) cannot access Brahman (because Brahman is beyond any concept, and thus, beyond me, mind-body), how can I (mind-body) ever *be* that Brahman? At Neo-Advaita meetings we were told that we *are* that (Brahman). But who are 'we'? Mind-body?

The same question can be posed a different way:

If I (mind-body) am not Brahman and cannot ever know Brahman, why bother with the teaching?

If I (mind-body) am already Brahman but somehow still cannot know myself (Brahman), that simply sounds ridiculous!

If I am *not* the mind-body but still somehow (?) cannot know

Brahman, then who am I? I can surely observe how thoughts are arising and going away; hence I'm *not* those thoughts. But nevertheless I still do not feel myself as Brahman.

If I am *not* mind-body and already Brahman, then where is the difference between the teaching and non-teaching?

A: You are not a body or mind. Whatever you are aware of, you can be sure that you are not that. You cannot be an object of any kind – you are the ultimate subject. This is the reason why you cannot point to 'I' or give it any attributes.

Your words indicate that you believe yourself to be a body-mind. You are Brahman, so that you are like the eye that cannot see itself. It is understandable that you find the concept difficult to 'take on board'. This is why there is a need for teachers and a proven methodology for explaining everything. It is true that this teaching cannot 'describe' Brahman either, but what it can do is give you pointers to the truth, stories and metaphors that enable you ultimately to come to a realization of the truth for yourself. The problem with Neo-Advaita is that it simply *tells* you that there is no person, no path etc., only Brahman, none of which actually helps you to come to this understanding.

You also say that it is difficult to understand how you can be Brahman without knowing it. The problem is that dualistic knowledge – knower, knowing, known – takes place in the mind, and the mind does not know that you are Brahman (until you are enlightened, of course)! The process of gaining Self-knowledge, eliminating Self-ignorance, takes place in the mind and it is there that realization takes place when all of the ignorance has been dispelled. Without the benefit of proper teaching to enable this process, you will remain ignorant despite the fact that you are already Brahman.

Q.87 Pairs of opposites

Q: If Brahman is absolute truth, consciousness and bliss, is it valid to conclude that unhappiness is due to eternal bliss being covered over by ignorance; that it is mithyA, and does not have an existence independent from bliss? Could we also say the same about other pairs of opposites – good/evil, truth/untruth, eternity/transience etc.? Is it the case that evil is the absence of good and does not have an independent existence apart from good? I realize that 'good' and 'evil' are mental constructs but could you please provide some illustrations which would appeal to someone on the Way of Knowledge?

A: The word Ananda, used as a 'description' of Brahman is confusing. A much better word to use is anantam – unlimited. Happiness (of any degree, from mild to ecstatic) arises from and is the nature of the Self. The value of the word is in pointing us to the Self as the source of happiness.

Everything in vyavahAra is mithyA, including the world itself and the ignorance (mAyA) that apparently creates it. All of the pairs of opposites continue to appear until such time as investigation reveals that none of them exist separate from Brahman. Ultimately, you cannot describe anything in the universe as good/bad, true/false etc. because there is no 'thing' there to describe; every apparent thing is only name and form of the non-dual substrate – Brahman.

Of course, the pairs of opposites continue to be very relevant to the person who does not know this. For him or her, the world is very real, along with all of its injustices and unhappiness. And they continue to exist in empirical reality for the person who does know the truth; it is just that he/she knows they are mithyA and is not affected by them in the way that the ignorant person is. For example, the body is still subject to illness and pain but there is no longer mental 'suffering' as a result of these, since the mind knows that who-I-really-am is not the body or mind.

It is worth noting, too, that the 'descriptions' of Brahman (such as truth, consciousness, bliss) are only relevant in vyavahAra. Swami Paramarthananda uses the metaphor of night and day. It is meaningful to speak about these while we are living on the earth (i.e. vyavahAra) but they would become meaningless if we lived on the sun itself (paramArtha).

Q.99 On the existence of Consciousness

Q: When I consider the difference between small 'c' consciousness and big 'C' Consciousness, I feel/understand consciousness, understood as an integral part (mutually arising) with its contents, but when I try to find a pulse for Consciousness, it all seems to look like revelation which is altogether unsatisfying. Is Consciousness offered as Truth, an all-encompassing One from which all else arises and is its emanations, but simply non-existent unless it is? (There is an experience without duration that either is or is not.)

A: Your question is couched in an extremely intellectual manner – are you a philosopher by any chance? The point is that you cannot investigate Consciousness (or think about it or reason about it) because you, the subject, *are* that Consciousness. Whatever tools you used, whatever you discovered, it would be 'you, the subject' discovering it, whereas whatever you discovered would be objective.

The best way to appreciate the problem is to think in terms of the differentiation between paramArtha and vyavahAra (there are lots of questions which depend upon this understanding – see the section on 'Appearance' in particular). All of any investigation, including the language in which you attempted to describe any 'findings' would all be part of the relative reality, vyavahAra. You can never make an investigation in paramArtha because that is the non-dual reality – there is no separate subject and an object to be investigated. If you can accept that, then all that needs to be said is that 'Consciousness', as I and most other Advaitins use the term, is another name for that non-dual reality.

On the other hand, 'consciousness' with a small 'c' is used to refer to the apparent individual awareness of things. Other apparent individuals may not be aware of the same things. This 'small' consciousness is best thought of as a 'reflection' of the 'big'

Consciousness in the mind of the individual. And everything, including minds and individuals is actually just name and form of that non-dual Consciousness.

Q.157 Sense of 'being'

Q: Using metaphors: Is this strong sense of 'being' only a reflection of the absolute? I.e. the moon in the bucket of water is not the moon itself. Using the pot and clay as a metaphor, is the 'being' of the pot only the clay manifesting as pot? Could we say that the pot is Atman, and clay is Brahman, and that therefore 'All' is Brahman?

What I seem to feel is that this strong sense of 'being' is a temporary manifestation. When 'I' goes, all goes (deep sleep example). Of course I knew this 25 years ago but only as conventional knowledge.

I love the metaphor of the Zen monk carrying a bucket of water and there is a reflection of the moon dancing in the ripples. The bottom falls out of the bucket of water and the reflection disappears. The Moon is not affected.

A: The 'I am' certainty is not a reflection; it is the reality. It is the belief (in the mind that 'I am X') which is the reflection. Similarly, the pot thinking that it is a pot is the mistake; realizing that it is the clay is the reality. But I don't like that metaphor used in this context. The best one is the wave-water metaphor. Thinking that I am a wave and therefore a part of the ocean is being stuck at the jIva – Ishvara level. The full realization is that I am water, just as the ocean is water. If you want to differentiate for clarity: The ocean equates to Ishvara; wave equates to the jIva. But the reality is that Ishvara is Brahman + mAyA; jIva is Atman + avidyA and Atman = Brahman, of course.

Another metaphor, used in the Mandukya Upanishad is pot and space. There appears to be a 'pot space' – a space associated with the pot. But if the pot is moved or broken, the space is entirely unaffected and realized to have been only seemingly limited by the boundary of the pot.

'I' never go – not even in deep sleep. What happens there is that the mind goes so that all that it 'projects' goes with it, leaving the subject without an object (the bottom falls out of the bucket).

I must say that I used to wonder why the scriptures use two words – Atman *and* Brahman. I always thought it would be far less confusing if they only ever used one. I think it is because most people come to an understanding of Advaita through the bhakti approach, i.e. most start off believing in a separate God, and in themselves as real enduring entities. Since I never had this 'problem', I never really found the need to differentiate.

Q.167 Am 'I' the 'sense of I'?

Q: The sense of 'I' cannot be detached from the other perceived objects 'floating in consciousness' because it is itself a part of consciousness. Waking up from deep sleep, for example, gives birth to the sense of 'I' together with everything else. It simply sticks to the perceived all the time. How can it be separated from the perceived? It is impossible. During deep sleep there is no sense of 'I' at all but your real nature is still there, with or without the sense of 'I'. So the identification with the 'I' is in my opinion also mAyA.

In other words, the sense of 'I' is also perceived and as the perceived cannot be the perceiver (which is your real nature), the 'I' is not your real nature. Your real nature therefore possesses no sense at all. All senses can only exist in the domain of consciousness. Do you agree?

A: Atman is not a 'part' of consciousness. Atman is Brahman and that is all there is.

As soon as you start talking about 'witnessing' 'objects' (including the sense of 'I'), you are in duality – vyavahAra. You can try to bring the two together by talking about there being no separation between 'I' and the 'perceived' but this is ultimately only an attempt to rationalize the ineffable and must necessarily fail.

I would argue that the sense of 'I' is *not* perceived. Who would perceive this? The sense of 'I' is a priori and sat. Everything else is only mithyA.

Q: In deep sleep there is no sense of 'I'. Waking up, the sense of 'I' comes out with everything else (like in a dream). So my question is: Is it true that the sense of 'I' is perceived by that entity (our true nature) which is 'I-less' and is alone present in deep sleep? Is that the entity which is perceiving knowledge, ignorance and, at the end, the sense of 'I' too?

A: When we (the jIva) are in deep sleep, the mind is inactive so that we do not 'know' anything. But the Atman is not affected; it is 'state-less'. In deep-sleep, we directly experience our true nature of sat-chit-Ananda but all that we know, when we wake up and the mind functions once more is that 'I slept well'.

I think the problem you are having is in your use of the word 'I'. Do you see that you are in danger of an 'ad infinitum' problem? Who is it who has 'the sense of I'? If you say that 'I' have the sense of 'I', then who is it that has the sense of *that* 'I'? The 'real I' is self-evident (you do not need a light in order to see another light).

The point is that all of this perceiving and thinking is in vyavahAra and 'I = Brahman' is an (the) ultimate truth. Consciousness (turIya) is the only reality; waking, dream and deep-sleep are apparent states that 'take place' within that. You cannot say that the 'true I' is only present in deep sleep. It is *always* present (since that is all there is). But the mind is reactivated in dream and waking and the apparently separate world appears once again.

There is obviously a lot of teaching around this one topic. My book 'A-U-M' deals with all of this so I do suggest that you read that if you want all of the fine detail!

Q.190 'Waking consciousness' and Brahman

Q: I understand that 'waking consciousness' is not Brahman. Does it mean we are completely ignorant of our true nature in the waking state? What is the relation between this 'waking consciousness' and Brahman?

Is 'waking consciousness' the reflection of Brahman or is it Brahman itself limited by the mind (antaHkaraNa)?

Why is Brahman referred to as 'pure' consciousness? What does 'pure' mean here?

In Sri Ramana Maharshi's path of self-enquiry, I understand the method is to find the source of 'I'/Ego. Who should do this? Intellect (buddhi) or Ego (ahaMkAra) itself?

A: As is so often the case with these questions, you have to think carefully about the standpoint from which you are asking them.

From the standpoint of absolute reality, there is only Brahman. So you cannot say that waking consciousness is *not* Brahman. On the other hand, from the standpoint of empirical reality, no 'thing' is absolutely real. The world, the 'person', ego, thoughts, objects and everything else is mithyA, which means that they are only name and form imposed upon the non-dual substratum, Brahman. Any 'explanation' that anyone gives you about all of this is provisional only. If it helps you to move forward towards a full realization of the truth, then it is useful; if it does not then it isn't useful.

In the waking state, the absolute Consciousness (Brahman, turIya) is associated with gross name and form. At the individual level, this is called the waker; at the cosmic level, it becomes the gross objects of the universe. The (subtle) mind may be ignorant of the true nature of reality or, in the case of an enlightened person, it will have recognized the truth. This does not mean that the world will no longer appear for the realized man, just that he now knows it to be not other than Brahman, his own self.

In reality, since there is always only Brahman; Brahman can never be limited. Since there is ignorance of this fact in the mind of the unenlightened, it *seems* as though Brahman is limited. There have been volumes written about the nature of ignorance (avidyA at the level of the individual, mAyA at the cosmic level) so I would not even attempt to summarize this. However Shankara has said that, since there is only Brahman, then Brahman 'has to be' the locus of avidyA. But this should all be seen as mithyA.

Again, since there is only Brahman, I also am That. Who-I-really-am is Brahman ... always, whether I know it or not. But, whilst in the thrall of this ignorance, I believe I am a body or mind, separate from all other things and people. And it is from this apparently limited position that Ramana's self-enquiry begins. Both investigation and enlightenment relate to the mind. ahaMkAra is better thought of as the process by which we identify with body, mind, role etc. There is a concept in Advaita, called chidAbhAsa, whereby 'pure' consciousness (i.e. Brahman) is said to be 'reflected' in the mind and this reflection may also be equated with ego or a 'false sense of I'. This 'explains' how it is that some people always seem to be calm and able to discriminate etc. whereas others are confused, quick to anger and so on. It is compared to moonlight being reflected from the surface of still or agitated water. But, again, if you find it useful to think of it in this way, do so, otherwise don't bother.

Q.214 On the concept of 'Beingness'

Q: The idea or concept of 'Beingness': I have been reading a great deal on this idea that Beingness is perhaps the closest word or concept in terms of knowing who you are as God. I agree that enlightenment is gaining Self-knowledge so as to eradicate the ignorance of who you are in terms of the false 'self/identity'. So my question is: can you define Beingness in light of enlightenment and how to arrive at it?

Westerners are strongly hung up on 'doing' as opposed to the Easterners' 'being.' Somehow I think that the universe or God is about balancing these two but knowing that you are not the 'doer'. It occurred to me that the 'doer' is 'Beingness'. Maybe *that* is the question? What is the difference, in the light of knowing yourself as God, between doing and being?

A: I'm afraid I have great antipathy to words like 'beingness', 'knowingness' and other such 'waffly' words, whose meaning never seems to be defined by the author. It is true that, ultimately, one cannot talk about the non-dual reality (because it is non-dual) but this is no excuse for sloppy language.

One can say that who-I-really-am exists, is conscious and is unlimited and that 'everything else' has only seemingly separate existence; that it is only name and form of that same reality that I am. Such statements, even though they may seem counter-intuitive, at least 'mean' something!

Having said that, your question "can you define Beingness in light of enlightenment and how to arrive at it?" leaves me a bit cold, I'm afraid. You can define any word to mean whatever you like but you have to ask whether, in the end, it actually helps you to make any progress in understanding.

With regard to your subsidiary question, "how to arrive at enlightenment", the answer is that enlightenment is the same as acquiring Self-knowledge. For that, mere words or definitions are not enough. You need to have your Self-ignorant concepts undermined and replaced by reasoned understanding about the nature of the Self and the seeming world. The traditional source of this knowledge is the Upanishads and later works and, because they are so old and difficult to understand, you really need someone who *does* understand them to interpret them for you.

I wouldn't worry too much about the apparent conflict between doing and being. It is true that who-you-really-are simply *is*, whilst it is only matter that apparently 'does'. But, even after enlightenment, the 'person' will continue to (seemingly) act for the rest of the life of that body-mind. The difference is that the enlightened person knows that this is all a 'show' and what is real remains unchanged and unchanging.

Q.298 I am not the reflection

Q: As I sit here, the whole of the waking state appears in this illumination that I am, reflected in mind. This isn't some awesome moment described by Jeff Foster featured in one of the recent bimonthly newsletters, although that has happened many times. In fact, some annoyance came and went because I cannot write what I want to say. This is more like a slow, subtle dawning. I can also see clearly that dreaming is a state that comes and goes in this illumination. Deep sleep is another state that comes and goes but there isn't any reflection in mind; however, without doubt, the Self is there.

A: Not sure what you are asking here. But what you are is 'in and through' the three states of waking, dreaming and deep sleep, but 'free' of them all.

Gaudapada describes turIya as prapa~nchopashamaM, which means 'negation (ama) of the experience (pash) of all plurality of the universe', i.e. the three 'universes' (prapa~ncha) of the three states of Consciousness. turIya is free from these prapa~ncha-s. pashamaM means rahita, free from (upashama means cessation, stopping, becoming quiet).

Q: Is this feeling that I exist, that I know that I am, what Ramana calls the I-thought?

A: Maybe this quotation from the second edition of Book of One will help:

"According to Ramesh Balsekar, Consciousness could be described in a hierarchical way as follows. The starting point is Consciousness 'at rest', without any attributes or qualities – nirguNa Brahman or 'Unconditioned Consciousness'. Then there is Consciousness 'in movement', functioning as the Witness or 'Conditioned Consciousness'. As soon as there is the thought 'I am', this becomes 'embodied' Consciousness. Finally, this becomes identified with the body-mind and is the 'attached' Consciousness – the jIva. The process of enlightenment is to remove the identification and return to the witness and ultimately the unconditioned Brahman".

Q: So it is this pure witness that is reflected in the mind, then it becomes 'conscious in movement', which is manifested as mithyA? The way I see it is that this pure witness is always there in the mithyA. Seeing this makes all the difference – seeing the rope that was once seen as a snake.

A: Still sounds a bit confused. Pure Consciousness reflected in the mind is the sense of the individual 'I' – it is called chidAbhAsa [false appearance or reflection (AbhAsa) of Consciousness (chit)]. Brahman is 'sat' – existence-reality. Anything other than Brahman is mithyA. (Of course, in reality, there *isn't* anything other than Brahman – that is the point.) The idea of a 'witness' is still an idea, albeit a rarefied one. Since there is only Brahman, there isn't anything (else) to be witnessed. So even the witness is mithyA, ultimately.

Q.304 How did 'I' come to deceive itself?

Q: How did 'I', the all knowing, all loving, all powerful, the absolute & infinite blissful, one without a second, come to deceive itself, and place itself in this illusion of illusions? How or why did the Ultimate Reality have this come to pass?

A: The spirit of your question is unanswerable – it is effectively asking why there is Self-ignorance and this is said to be anirvachanIya – inexplicable. From the standpoint of absolute reality, of course, there is no deception because there is no creation; and there is no illusion because there are no persons to be deluded. There is only Brahman – satyam j~nAnam anantam as the taittirIya upaniShad says, limitless consciousness. It is only from the perspective of this apparently limited entity, the mind of the person, that there seems to be a problem. Once the truth is realized, it is also seen that there is no problem because everything is Brahman – sarvaM khalvidam brahma.

Q.310 Self and the body-mind

Q: In order to determine that awareness is my true self and that my true self is not my 'I' concept, I've been looking into the 'I' concept. It is not my mind, because I can say 'my mind'. It is not my body, because I can say 'my body', but could it be the mind-body complex? Most would say no, because the mind and body are plural and the self cannot be plural. However, I'm confused because I don't see it this way. I see the mind and body as acting as one, which means that the 'I' could possibly be it. It is difficult to determine where the mind begins and the body ends, and vice versa, so I see them as one, like the Yin Yang symbol. How do I know that the true self is not the 'I' concept that arises within me? Is it because I can make the 'I' concept the object of awareness, thus it cannot be the subject?

My other concern is Maya. It seems that Maya is the only 'thing' that stands in the way of us and higher Brahman. Higher Brahman is attributeless and without cause and effect. Lower Brahman, where we experience a personal God, is where we experience cause and effect as a consequence of Maya – am I right so far? The point I want to get to is that surely if there was no Maya, we would be living a life in the higher Brahman? So, essentially, this life that I am experiencing, where one moment seems separate from another, is the higher Brahman, but would seem otherwise because of Maya? Is that right? If not, would you please correct my thinking?

A: I don't follow your logic in the first part. Why can't you say 'my' body-mind? And how could the true Self be any concept? A concept by definition is an idea which occurs within the mind. Basically, anything that I can perceive or conceptualize cannot be 'me' because I am doing the perceiving or conceptualizing and am therefore separate from that.

In the second part, mAyA is a way of explaining how it is that there appears to be duality. But the world itself is mithyA, and this includes mAyA and Ishvara. 'Living life in higher Brahman' has no meaning. There is only Brahman – there is no 'you' separate from Brahman to live a life anywhere.

So, yes, you are effectively right in saying that the life you are experiencing is the 'higher' Brahman. It doesn't seem so because of your avidyA – your 'personal' Self-ignorance if you like. Even those who are enlightened still perceive duality (because mAyA applies at the macrocosmic level), but they know that the world is really Brahman only (because their 'personal' ignorance has been eliminated).

Q: I think it might just be a problem with language. Think about it like this. When I have, for example, an apple, I say 'my apple'. The word 'my' refers to me, the 'I', the apparent self. The statement makes clear that the apple belongs to me, hence it is 'my' apple. When I say 'my body', this implies that the body is separate or different from the self that it belongs to. It's the same with 'my mind', which seems to say that the mind belongs to this 'my', making it separate from the apparent self. So my question is: what can be seen as the self when we say 'my mind-body'? It might actually be a Buddhist way of examining the self, which is different from the Advaita examination using subject and object.

To another point: what would existence be if I could turn off all my senses, so I didn't see the world, hear the world, touch the world etc.? I suppose we would just be aware of mind?

I'm confused about something: it's said that anything you can objectify is not the self, but yet there are some sources, like the Upanishads, that say *everything* is the Self. Would you explain this? How can this PC be the Self if I can objectify it?

Last week I spent quite a long time looking through your question and answer pages feeling quite overwhelmed by the amount of questions there were, wondering whether there was any way out of it all. To an extent, questions help, but they go on and on. What if I choose to stop asking questions? The paradox is that I don't need to keep asking questions, but I do at the same time because it gets me to a point where I give up asking questions? I guess there is no point even in saying 'how can I keep my mind clear', since there is no 'I' that possesses a will, volition, to keep the mind clear. That my mind is full of questions is not something under my control, right, since there is no person to have control ... is any of that correct?

A: Yes, I think you are right – it is a language problem. Basically, I think that use of the term body-mind is simply an indication that one has been thinking about these things and considering the possibility that maybe 'I' am different from that/those. (Of course, one might also have realized that this is, in fact, the case.)

Regarding 'turning off the senses', there have been quite a few scientific studies on sensory deprivation that look at this. But you could regard deep-sleep as 'maximum' turning off and the Self is still there, in and through all states of Consciousness.

The position regarding 'objectification' is that duality of experience is intrinsic to vyavahAra. Traditional teaching begins with this, since it is our fundamental experience, and 'negates' the world: 'I am not that – neti, neti'. As our understanding progresses, we come to realize that we are not the perceiving body-mind either and that everything 'arises' within the Consciousness that I am. Ultimately, it is realized that every seeming separate thing is only name and form of that same Consciousness. Thus the final understanding is that everything is Brahman and I am Brahman.

Regarding asking questions, you initially find that these seem to go on forever. You hear a little more and immediately some new questions come. It seems as though this might be an exponential process. But it isn't. As time goes on and your understanding grows, questions arise with ever-decreasing frequency until there comes a time when there are no more. But it is a natural process. Read about shravaNa, manana, nididhyAsana and it should become clear – don't stop asking questions!

Q.317 Self 'knowing' the Self

Q: Nisargadatta Maharaj (especially in his later books) emphasizes that the 'I am' or Consciousness is not the final Reality which he calls Parabrahman or Awareness. He goes on to state that Awareness is 'unaware of itself'. However, others such as Francis Lucille and Rupert Spira seem to disagree. Francis Lucille, for example, specifically states that Awareness (in the sense Nisargadatta means) is aware of itself as itself.

I am not exactly clear what Nisargadatta meant. It could be

interpreted as the Final Reality being essentially almost a nihilistic eternal stupor rather than the more appealing (at least to this body/mind) sat-chit-Ananda. I rather suspect not, and that he was merely indicating the essential non-duality of reality perhaps along the lines of Ramana Maharshi's comment: *"Although (the Self) is consciousness, since there is nothing for it to know or to make itself known to, it is said to be different from the sentient and the insentient"*.

Nevertheless it perplexes me that, if Awareness is not aware of itself as itself as Nisargadatta suggests, then do we not have the situation whereby an enlightened sage such as Ramana Maharshi is (before his 'death') not only aware as the Self but conscious thereof and in a better position, so to speak, than 'final reality', which is not so aware?

A: Nisargadatta, for some reason I have never understood, uses the words 'awareness' and 'consciousness' in the opposite sense to most other teachers – and causes much confusion as a result! But the question of Brahman not 'being aware of itself' is often raised and discussed. The point is that any awareness 'of', or knowledge 'of' in the usual sense of these words would be dualistic and therefore contradict the teaching of non-duality.

Consciousness, when it manifests in the human mind, is said to do so in the nature of a reflection, using the metaphor of Consciousness as the sun, and the mind as a mirror. So now we have come down from the absolute reality to the relative, where duality is fine.

The question itself is inevitably posed from a dualistic standpoint and, of course, any answer has to be given in duality and can only *point* towards the absolute. It is not really meaningful to speak of Consciousness being aware of itself (or not) in reality, because in reality there is *only* Consciousness. Knowledge and existence – without limit – are the nature of non-dual Consciousness. But it is Consciousness that enables you to know that you exist, and you would still know this in a sensory deprivation tank.

That you exist is what you would say is 'self-evident'. So, yes, you have to say that the Self is evident to the Self or 'knows itself'. But you also have to keep in mind that you are trying to understand the ineffable. And it is beyond the mind! As Sri Poonja said: *"The Self will always be a mystery because there can never be anything apart from it to comprehend it, analyze it or understand it"*.

Sureshvara's 'naiShkarmya siddhi' has this to say (3.47-49): *"Because the Self is of the form of constant awareness, it requires no second means of knowledge to reveal it; because it is without sound or other attributes it is beyond the sphere of doubt. The Self cannot be known through the empirical means of knowledge such as perception, etc., which are but phlegm coughed up by the thirst for life. Indeed, it is not a possible object of empirical cognition, since it is the innermost Self and since it exists for its own sake. One cannot see with sight that which is self-revealed. The visible is limited, external and has form, but the self-revealed is infinite, internal and formless"* (Realization of the Absolute, translation by A. J. Alston, Shanti Sadan, 1959. ISBN 0-85424-021-7.).

There is also a discussion of this topic in upadesha sAhasrI – the one prakaraNa grantha agreed by all authorities as having been written by Shankara. This is in the prose section of the book around 2.90 up to the end of section 2. He says that knowing the knower would lead to infinite regress and also the knower cannot be separate from himself; the knower's knowledge relates to knowable objects only.

And of course the jIva cannot ever know the Self in any objective manner, nor be 'all-knowing' etc., as is Ishvara. The jIva *is* the Self, functioning through a body-mind but remains effectively limited by that body-mind in life, even if its name is Ramana Maharshi.

Q.402 Witness versus jIva

Q: Please correct my logic below:

- The 'negating' (neti, neti) is actually done by the not-Self (intellect, jIva).

- The things negated are not-Self (body, senses, mind/intellect, jIva itself?).
- The witness cannot be negated because it precedes the objects of negation and the act of negation.
- The witness itself cannot negate but it is because of it that misidentification and negation are possible.
- The knowledge that 'I am That which cannot be negated' is in the intellect, which is not-Self, and therefore unreal.
- Once that knowledge takes place, then there are no further thoughts such as 'I am an individual, so and so, this/that'. And I know that I never was.
- Although the knowledge is in the intellect, it is as if the Self regains knowledge of itself. This individual 'being' just became sentient due to my reflection in it?
- It is 'me' that is reflected in all apparent individuals?

A: That is mostly correct. But I think that you are using the word 'witness' to mean 'Consciousness' or 'Brahman' because of your point that it is because of the witness that negation is possible. If that is correct, then your third statement is true. But if you mean 'witness' in the sense that I (and tradition) use the term, then your third statement is false.

To avoid confusion, you have to differentiate 1. the jIva who acts and enjoys etc., 2. the witness that simply observes and does nothing, 3. Brahman or Consciousness that is the non-dual reality.

The 'witness' also has to be negated intellectually, since the act of witnessing has to take place through the body-mind-intellect, which is not who you really are. And the Self-knowledge also takes place in the intellect – it is the jIva who gains Self-knowledge. 'Self-knowledge' doesn't apply to the Self (Brahman), which is never anything other than Brahman. And Brahman does not 'know' this in the sense that this word implies – to 'know' something requires seeming duality and an intellect.

The theory that 'I' am the only jIva (that I am Brahman that is 'imagining this world and all the jIva-s), so that it is 'me' that is 'reflected in all apparent individuals, is called eka-jIva-vAda (one-jIva-theory). It follows logically from the vAchArambhaNa verses in the Chandogya Upanishad that have been discussed in answer to Q.73. This theory (that we effectively create the world around us by separating the non-dual reality into forms and giving then names) is called dRRiShTi-sRRiShTi-vAda – the theory that I 'perceive' and then 'create'. It is another intermediate theory (see adhyAropa-apavAda), which has to be dropped in the end when we accept ajAti-vAda – there never has been any creation.

The eka-jIva-vAda theory is one that gained prominence post-Shankara – there is no evidence that Shankara himself ever promoted it. Ramana Maharshi is also associated with dRRiShTi-sRRiShTi-vAda. Appendix 7 of my book 'A-U-M' discusses eka-jIva-vAda. Basically, the answer to your question is: if you find it helpful, accept it as a temporary explanation; otherwise ignore it.

This particular question shows how important it is to use correct terminology!

Q.429 Discussion on 'I am That'

Q: I have a couple of questions about 'I Am That'. As I understand it, this essentially says: Atman = Brahman. So the 'I' is not the ahaMkAra 'I', rather the Atman 'I'.

1. Did I get that right?

2. When one begins to reflect upon 'I Am That', is one expected to feel the 'I' as the ahaMkAra I? And then move, gradually, towards realizing the 'I' is in fact Atman?

3. The reason I ask 2 is because I have a great deal of difficulty 'feeling' my 'ahaMkAra I'. It just doesn't 'compute' with me. Does this brain/body sense things, have feelings, emotions, thoughts; am I aware of external and internal things? Yes! All the time. But are these sensations, feelings, thoughts, etc. = ahaMkAra 'I-me'? No. They're just... stuff that happens, electrochemical dances in a brain in a skull in a body that is identified as 'Fred'. Is this a problem –

that I can't consciously/directly feel my 'ahaMkAra I'? That when I look for it I see mithyA, nothing of essential substance? Could my not being able to directly experience my 'ahaMkAra I' be a stumbling block?

A: Perhaps the first thing to recognize is the paramArtha-vyavahAra distinction. Speaking from the pAramArthika 'viewpoint' there is only Brahman, i.e. no 'I' or 'That'. Everything within vyavahAra is mithyA.

So let's now talk vyavahAra! When you say tat tvam asi, you are saying that you are Ishvara; 'who you really are' is not the body-mind but the all-knowing, all-powerful, limitless creator of the universe. The mind – antaHkaraNa – consists of manas, buddhi, chitta and ahaMkAra. So when it is said that you are not the mind, it is also implicit that you are not the ahaMkAra either.

When it is said that Atman is Brahman, that of course is true. Everything is Brahman – sarvaM khalvidam brahma. But what does it mean? A good metaphor is the wave-ocean-water one. The wave is name and form of water; the ocean is name and form of water. Both wave and ocean are mithyA; water is the only satyam. Wave is part of the ocean and cannot exist in isolation from it. Similarly, the jIva is the mithyA aspect of Brahman from the vyaShTi or individual aspect; Ishvara is the mithyA aspect of Brahman from the samaShTi or universal aspect. The reality of the jIva is Atman; the reality of Ishvara is Brahman. And Atman is Brahman.

If by 'reflect upon' 'I am That', you mean nididhyAsana, this entails that you already have no doubt about the truth of what I have said. You have already done the shravaNa of hearing all of this explained. And you have done the manana of asking 'what the hell does it all mean?' and you have had all your questions answered so that you have no further doubts. The nididhyAsana is then the reflection, re-reading, discussion and so on until the truth is firmly fixed in your mind.

None of this has anything to do with 'feeling' or 'moving' or indeed 'doing' anything. Trying to 'feel' the ahaMkAra shows that you have still not understood these things. The Atman does not do anything. 'Doing' relates to the mithyA aspects only. As the Gita puts it, "The one who is together, who knows the truth, thinks, 'I do not do anything at all,' even while seeing, hearing, touching, smelling, eating, walking, sleeping, breathing, talking, releasing, grasping, opening and closing the eyes, (the person) knowing (full well that) the organs are engaged in their objects". (V.8-9) It is all just movement of names and forms.

So, yes, you sum it up quite nicely when you say: "They're just ... stuff that happens, electrochemical dances in a brain in a skull in a body that is identified as Fred". And, no, it is not a problem! Again, as you say, all that you see is mithyA. But the essential (ultimate) observer is not mithyA; it is Atman. After you have fully understood this intellectually, then you just have to sort out the business of witnessing and reflected consciousness (http://www.advaita-vision.org/chidabhasa/ and http://www.advaita-vision.org/continuing-reflections-on-reflections/ and discussion at http://www.advaita-vision.org/discussion-on-chidabhasa/).

Q.453 Consciousness is happiness?

Q: I have just read your book 'How to meet yourself'. I am not sure if I understand what you mean when you say that "Consciousness is happiness" and that "I am happiness". Since everything is an appearance within consciousness, wouldn't happiness be just that? Why would we equate consciousness to happiness?

A: Before answering the question, it would be useful to note the difference between Consciousness and consciousness. Consciousness with as capital 'C' is used throughout in all of these answers to refer to Brahman, the non-dual reality. The mind is conscious because Consciousness is reflected by the mind. The body and mind are both inert in themselves. It is important not to confuse these terms.

The actual paragraph is:

"Fourthly, it would not be meaningful to talk about Consciousness

being happy or unhappy. Being complete and without limitations of any sort, it is more appropriate to say that Consciousness is *happiness. This, then, is an aspect of my true nature. Since I am Consciousness, there is nothing that I need, nothing to be achieved, nowhere to which I have to get. I am already perfect and complete – I am happiness".*

So I effectively agree with you, saying that "it would not be meaningful...". The problem with trying to say anything at all about the ultimate reality is that you cannot. Any descriptive term is extremely partial and also excludes its opposite. In the end, you have to follow Wittgenstein's dictum: 'Whereof we cannot speak, thereof we should remain silent.'

It also depends upon how you define the word 'happiness'. 'Perfect and complete' seems not too bad a definition!

A general point however is that, if you want a good explanation of what Advaita is all about, 'How to Meet Yourself' is not such a good book. It was intended to stimulate readers looking for happiness, meaning etc. to investigate Advaita and maybe gain some real mumukShutva – intense desire to gain Self-knowledge. If you want a more 'accurate' explanation of all this, a better book to read is the second edition of 'Book of One'.

Q: Is this understanding directly about what we truly are, and are not? Does all of this actually come down to that specific understanding of true identity? Or, is it a more 'full' understanding of the scientific facts of life, the cycles, the elements, etc.?

Please help clarify!

A: The scriptures from which the teaching of Advaita derives cover all these aspects. But the point is that only the Self is truly real; everything else depends upon the Self for its seeming reality. Much of the 'scientific' description will seem archaic to the modern mind. For example, only five elements are described (space, air, fire, water, earth). But this is ultimately irrelevant anyway and does not detract from the essential presentation and unfoldment of the nature of 'life, the universe and everything'. Rather the opposite – the relative simplicity makes it easier to avoid getting bogged down in irrelevancies. Aspects relating to human behavior, motivation, spiritual practices and so on are timeless, anyway.

Q: So at the end of the day, *everything* is pointing to That!? And *all* of the stories and explanations and removing of ignorance is also to ultimately get to That?

If so, this really helps and takes so much effort and struggle away from trying to figure everything out!

A: Shankara's précis of the message of Advaita is: 'Brahman is the reality; the world is mithyA; the jIva is non-different from Brahman' and you could say that the entire message of the scriptures is contained in the mahAvAkya 'tat tvam asi' – you are That. So yes, it is all very simple. But you do not need to be told that it is also contradictory to everything we experience and most of what everyone else tells us. So ideally you *do* need a teacher to explain it all step by step and answer your questions. Simply reading the scriptures is extremely unlikely to bring you Self-knowledge, even if you can read Sanskrit!

Reality

According to Vladimir Nabokov, 'reality' is one of the few words that mean nothing without quotation marks. One imagines that what he means is that a particular state of affairs does not mean the same thing to all people. What is considered to be significant and meaningful to one person might not even be noticed by someone else. Advaita does not use the word in this way. Whatever the 'appearance' might be, and however someone might interpret what they apprehend, Advaita says that the reality is always non-dual. Call this non-dual reality whatever you like (I use the words 'Brahman' or 'Consciousness' throughout these answers), the reality remains the same. The form may change; the name certainly changes; the reality never changes.

Q.102 How did we become ignorant?

Q: It is said that the "true goal of a man's life is to discover one's true nature, i.e. Atman which is Brahman". If Man's true nature is divine, how did he become ignorant in the first place? How did we become ignorant of our true nature? Being truly a divine and perfect soul, should we not have remained that way? What happened to our divine nature?

A: This is one of those questions that are ultimately unanswerable. Ignorance is said by Advaita to be anAdi – beginningless. And who is it who is ignorant? Clearly the jIva – but then the jIva does not exist as an entity separate from Brahman so that this means that Brahman is ignorant – which is clearly nonsensical (there is nothing other than Brahman, so the concept has no meaning).

Swami Paramarthananda tells a story about a game he used to play as a child. [See Q.443 for full story quoted in 'Book of One'.] They would take a child into a room that was entirely empty and then place pillows about the room and stand the child up against one wall. He was told to memorize the positions of the pillows and then they blindfolded him. He was then told that he had to cross the room to the other wall without touching any of the pillows. The other children then watched as he very carefully edged his way forward. Whenever they laughed, he would retreat and move sideways before trying again. Eventually he reached the other wall and was allowed to remove the blindfold. He then discovered, of course, that all of the pillows had been removed before he began and that he had been moving across an empty floor trying to avoid non-existent objects.

And he says that mokSha is like this. As seekers, we make our way through life trying to avoid all the pitfalls of Self-ignorance and arrive at the other wall of Self-knowledge and enlightenment. But when we attain enlightenment, we realize that there never were any obstacles to begin with. In a sense, the ignorance was non-existent – you are That already.

Q.131 Is there room for individuality in Brahman?

Q: Does Brahman have 'room' for the spark of unique individuality that is in all living organisms: humans, animals, plants, stones, ideas? Or is all this precious individuality forever lost in the oneness?

A: So-called 'individuality' is related to the attributes and not the essence. In vyavahAra, each person, creature or object has its own individual characteristics. There is no question of 'losing' this, only of recognizing that this individuality is only apparent; the ever-changing, now beautiful, now ugly but always only the seeming surface characteristic of what is always one reality. It is the outwardly differing manifestation of the inner unity. Since all is always That, how could there not be room for it?

Q: My question concerns the ring of gold analogy for the changelessness of Brahman.

I understand from the analogy that the ring is mithyA and the gold is Brahman. The implication being that 'change' as we perceive it is only at the apparent level while the substance (Brahman) remains unchanged. Is it then correct to say that Brahman does indeed change but only in form? I believe the answer is 'no' since the Upanishads clearly state that Brahman is changeless. That said, the fact remains that although I don't perceive an object's substance/essence (i.e. Brahman) my senses do gather information that results in thoughts leading to the experience of change in the world of objects. But if Brahman doesn't change even at the level of 'form' then I don't know how to rationalize changeless Brahman with the experience of a changing world.

Can you point me in the right direction on this one?

A: This is one of those 'mixing levels' questions. The changeless Brahman refers to paramArtha; the changing world refers to vyavahAra. Brahman is never amenable to objectification in any way, is attributeless and without name or form. The world is intrinsically dualistic; ever changing and *only* name and form. So Brahman doesn't change. The apparently changing appearance of duality is the result of adhyAsa – superimposing some mental image upon what is actually there. as in seeing a snake instead of a rope.

In the end all of this is part of the adhyAropa-apavAda teaching of Advaita. First read Chapter 6 of the Chandogya Upanishad with Shankara's commentary to learn all about vAchArambhaNa (generating a seeming reality as a result of giving 'names' to the 'forms' that we see) and then read the Mandukya Upanishad with Gaudapada's kArikA-s and Shankara's commentary to learn about ajAti vAda (the knowledge that there has never been any 'birth' or creation).

You have to understand the distinction between paramArtha and vyavahAra. In reality, there is only Consciousness. But there appears to be a separate world and, as far as day to day experience is concerned, we treat this as though it were real. The world is an *empirical* reality, not an absolute one. mithyA means that it is not real in itself but relies upon some real substrate for its apparently separate existence. A metaphor that is used is gold and ornaments. A (gold) ring appears to be a separate entity but the ring has no real existence; it is only name and form of gold. It is the gold that is 'satyam'; the ring is only 'mithyA'. Take the gold away and the ring ceases to exist. Similarly, the world is mithyA; the reality is Consciousness.

All of this explanation, all words and concepts are also mithyA. Their purpose is only to lead your mind to make the intuitive leap to understanding – and that is 'enlightenment'.

Q.209 Consciousness is not the final reality

Q: To deepen my understanding of Advaita Vedanta I am reading your excellent book: 'Back to the Truth – 5000 years of Advaita'. But I am a little puzzled when reading Chapter 6 – 'Who I Really Am', the section describing the Self. In subsection 'Even Consciousness is not the Final Reality', you reference Nisargadatta Maharaj and (primary) Robert Powell to state that Consciousness is not the final

Reality.

A: Advaita is a progressive teaching, gauged (by the teacher) to the current level of understanding of the student. Many things are taught by traditional teachers in the early stages that are later supplanted by more sophisticated explanations, as the seeker's understanding grows. Nisargadatta is not a traditional teacher. His style of teaching tends to work by shaking up and breaking down all of our preconceived notions of the way things are. Thus it is that he does not go through all of these early stages, trying instead to go straight to the final truth. Indeed, in his later works, what he says is often so 'uncompromising' that it is difficult to understand at all unless you have been reading/learning/studying for many years.

What is said in the section to which you refer is an attempt to point towards this 'final truth'. Since reality is non-dual and there is, from that absolute standpoint, no creation at all, everything has to go in that final analysis. Most Upanishads are concerned with various aspects of the earlier stages of teaching and you do not find these ultimately radical statements in most places. The best known of the sources where you do is the Gaudapada kArikA, which is a commentary on the Mandukya Upanishad and almost has equivalent status. Here you have statements such as: "*There is no dissolution, no origination, none in bondage, none possessed of the means of liberation, none desirous of liberation, and none liberated. This is the ultimate truth*" (2.32) and "*No kind of jIva is ever born nor is there any cause for any such birth. The ultimate truth is that nothing whatsoever is born" (4.71).*

The Mandukya Upanishad, in the 7th mantra, itself come closest to describing the nature of absolute reality:

chaturthaM manyante nAntaHpraj~naM – the fourth (chaturtha) (i.e. turIya or Brahman) is not that which thinks itself to be (manyante) the internal, subtle world (antaHpraj~na), i.e. not the dreamer, taijasa;

na bahiShpraj~naM – nor the external, gross world of objects (bahis means 'outside'), i.e. not the waker, vishva;

na ubhayataHpraj~naM – nor both (ubhaya), i.e. not some intermediate state;

na praj~nAnaghanaM – and not that which is a (compact) mass of (ghana) consciousness (i.e. not the deep-sleep state, in which the mind is resolved and there is consciousness which is 'conscious of nothing');

na praj~naM – neither simply 'consciousness', awareness or sentience;

na apraj~naM – nor unconsciousness, unawareness or insentience.

adRRiShTam – (it is) unseen (by any of the senses) [dRRiShTi means, seen, perceived, visible, apparent]; also means 'beyond the five j~nAnendriya-s [sense organs];

avyavahAryam – nothing to do with 'worldly' things [vyavahArya is to do with common practice, ordinary life, conduct, behavior etc. i.e. transactions within vyavahAra];

agrAhyam – beyond understanding [grAhya means to be perceived, recognized or understood]; also means beyond the five karmendriya-s [organs of action] – [grahaNa literally means to catch, where the organs of action are involved in catching but is used in the sense of comprehension.]

alakShaNam – without any characteristics [lakShaNa is a mark or sign or, more commonly in Advaita, a pointer] also translated as 'un-inferable';

achintyam – inconceivable, beyond thought;

avyapadeshyam – indefinable;

ekAtmapratyayasAraM – its essence (sAra) is certainly (pratyaya) the same as (eka) Atman;

prapa~nchopashamaM – negation (ama) of the experience (pash) of all plurality of the universe (prapa~ncha);

shAntaM – peace, tranquility;

shivam – favorable, propitious, auspicious;

advaitaM – non-dual;

sa Atma – that is the Self;
savij~neyaH – that is to be understood.

The upshot of this is that no word can ever describe the nature of reality and, indeed, anything that we predicate of it cannot be true. Even to speak of it as 'Consciousness' or 'non-dual' or 'Brahman' has to be, in the final analysis, merely an attempt to understand it with our feeble mind.

Q: Surely "even Consciousness is not the Final Reality" is itself a piece of knowledge and there cannot be any knowledge without a conscious entity behind it or without Consciousness itself being there behind it.

A: Of course, all that you say is correct. The point is, however, that all of this is vyAvahArika knowledge, even though it is according to shruti. Knowledge, in our usually understood sense of the word could have no meaning in a pAramArthika sense. Similarly, Consciousness – Brahman has neither parts nor attributes; neither name nor form. This was my point in answer to the original question.

Q.468 Gaining knowledge of the real

Q: How can the unreal (i.e. mithyA scriptures) bring about knowledge of the real? If the relative plane is irredeemably mithyA then how can the individual seeker transcend it? There can be no bridge between the absolute and the relative plane.

A: Isn't this analogous to asking 'how can the dreamer wake up?'? 'vyAvahArika speak' is for the sake of convenience only, while we are in the midst of the delusion. In reality, there *is* no individual just as, from the vantage point of the waker, there is no dreamer. So there is no question of transcendence – the seeker already *is* the real, nondual Brahman. There is no bridge because there is no need of a bridge – there are not two places.

Q: All those words that you use – illusion/delusion, real/unreal – are drawn from your experience on the everyday plane. Have you any rational grounds for the transference of these polar concepts to a plane which is beyond experience. If you haven't, are you not open to the charge that what you are making is a counter-intuitive assertion that is wholly a matter of faith?

By the way is the flight to such assertions about illusion not the basis for the mAyA vAdin sneer? In any case the immediate appeal to the mAyA doctrine is not the recourse of Shankara particularly in Upadesha Sahasri and brahma sutra bhAShya. From an examination of the nature of knowledge and knowing we are led to a view that suggests unrestricted being and consciousness.

A: Yes, you are right! I don't take back anything that I said but, to avoid confusion, would add the words 'according to the teaching of Advaita'.

I think the point is that the 'bottom line' of Advaita is not derivable via reason. Shankara says that scripture is the only means for knowing that Brahman is the reality (Brihadaranyaka Upanishad bhAShya IV.iv.20) You are right in assuming that the initial step is one of faith. But I don't see this as faith in the derogatory sense that is often used when talking about, say, fundamentalist Christians. It is faith in the sense of 'trusting in the words of those who have shown themselves to be trustworthy'. The prompting for that 'bottom line' comes from shruti and guru and we then subject what they say to reason and experience until the moment comes when we are certain that what they have said is true. That is mokSha and then, providing we have also gained understanding of the techniques of shruti and guru, we are in the position to give prompting to others.

I think there are adequate rational grounds for believing this process to work.

Having said all that, I still don't like your words 'plane which is beyond experience'. There is no such plane. It is rather a case of seeing that the way we used to look at the world (assuming separation) was wrong and that what we have been seeing all along is simply name and form of one unchanging reality. When we realize that the mirage is not water but only refraction of light over a hot surface, there is no change in our basic perception, even though our response will now be different. It is simply that we see the situation in a totally new way, realizing that the previous way was a mistake.

Also I don't think I mentioned mAyA, did I? mAyA is just as much mithyA as the world that we claim as the 'caused appearance'. It is all just an interim teaching until we can see the full picture.

Q: If all there were to this path were faith and a handful of analogies, a pamphlet would cover it all and we could all go home to tea. However, it is not even as though it would be a great saving of mental energy, banana leaves and paper. If you read Chapter II of Upadesha Sahasri, you will find that the disciple questions the assertion of the teacher and requires that the knots of Vedic wisdom be teased apart and the line of coherent rational explication of the concepts of identity and awareness be made clear.

A: Quite so, but the fact remains that the bare assertions – 'all there is is Brahman', 'you are That', etc. – are not *derivable* by reason. We use reason to show that such statements are not incompatible with experience; indeed they are found ultimately to explain everything. But they begin life as un-provable propositions. That is the point.

Q: Shankara uses or appears to use the rational argument known as the Intelligent Design argument in his rebuttal of the Sankhya theory of pradhAna (brahma sutra bhAShya (II.ii.1)). He claims that the insentient pradhAna as the basis of all manifestation is not adequate to the manifest design shown by creation. Instead we ought to believe that pradhAna is under the control of some intelligent agent.

At the end of brahma sutra bhAShya (II.ii.2), the causal argument for the existence of God comes into play:

"Similarly it is but logical that God who is all-pervasive, the Self of all, omniscient and, omnipotent, should be the impeller of all, even though He is himself free from any tendency to act.

"Objection: Since God is one (without a second) and there is nothing else to be impelled, the impeller-ship itself is a fiction.

"Vedantin: No, for it has been said again and again that God can be the impeller because of an illusory association with name and form conjured up by ignorance. Hence the existence of such tendency becomes a possibility only if omniscient God be accepted as the cause (of creation), but not so on the assumption of something insentient as the cause".

A: I thought our discussion concerned making the intellectual leap from vyavahAra to paramArtha. You seem now to have diversified into talking about God and creation, which is firmly at the level of vyavahAra – and I don't really want to go there. Shankara's points that you quote relate to saguNa Brahman, Ishvara and not to the absolute reality. Although interesting (of course), all such ideas have ultimately to be rejected in the recognition of there being no creation at all.

In the context of (what I understood to be) our original discussion, although arguments such as Intelligent Design can be made to justify a belief in a creator-god, they have no relevance to arguing a nondual reality. ajAtivAda is, I suggest, not something that would reasonably be intuited, since it contradicts all of our experience.

Q.259 Describing Brahman

Q: According to Advaita, Brahman has been described as sat-chit-Ananda meaning truth-infinite being-bliss as its characteristics. But Adi Shankara has said that Brahman is nirguNa (having no qualities or characteristics). Don't they contradict each other?

A: Brahman cannot be described at all, since language is necessarily dualistic. So the words that are used are actually 'pointers' rather than descriptors or attributes. One way of looking at it is to say that Brahman is not the opposite of the word used as the pointer. Thus, Brahman is not 'limited', not 'unreal', etc. If you want a more detailed explanation, something like Swami Dayananda's Talks on 108 verses of vivekachUDAmaNi is brilliant.

See the website for more on that. Ultimately, anything at all that you say about Brahman is mithyA only, even that it is 'non-dual'. This is why some teachers resort to silence when asked such a question!

Q: Thanks for your kind guidance but I cannot understand the two lines written by you:

1. Brahman cannot be described at all, since language is necessarily dualistic.

2. Ultimately, anything at all that you say about Brahman is mithyA only, even that it is 'non-dual'.

According to these lines, Advaita philosophy can never be understood, owing to the above reasons, thus rendering the whole philosophy false. It will be a great help if you could give an elaborate explanation.

A: Everything in the empirical realm is mithyA, including Advaita philosophy. But mithyA does not mean false. It means that it is only name and form of the non-dual Brahman. Advaita works by saying what reality is not and pointing towards 'what is' as best as it is able, given the nature of language. And its efficacy has been proven over thousands of years. As a (not very good) metaphor, Newtonian physics does not provide an accurate description of motion but it still works pretty well at the macro level, at below-light speeds. Furthermore, you need to understand Newton before you can move on to Einstein and quantum mechanics.

Another metaphor that might help is that you know that your body is warmed when you stand in the sun but, if you have never studied science, you may not understand precisely how this happens. You have direct knowledge of the warmth of your body, whereas previously you might have felt cold. Sort of similarly, you can 'know' Brahman because who-you-really-are *is* Brahman.

See the other questions on this topic for further explanation or read 'Book of One' or 'A-U-M' for detailed discussion.

Q.336 Reality of the World

Q: I understand the Advaita Vedanta teaching – that we are what is perceiving, the Consciousness in which the world, including our body-minds, appear. And that it is mAyA that makes us think we are a separate self. I can see this as one logical explanation of our experience. As many teachers say, there is nothing in our experience that can prove to us that there is a 'real' world out there, since everything has to arise in consciousness.

It seems to me that an alternative, plausible explanation of our experience, is that there is a world which this body-mind experiences. However, even in this model, it is clear to me that there is no separation – that everything is inter-dependent, and that we are simply conditioned beings, programmed by our genetics and environment, and under the illusion that we are somehow separate from the world. But the truth is that we are just chemicals/molecules/energy quanta, the essence of which is the same in all things. As Krishnamurti used to say, you are the world and the world is you. This also seems to be more in line with the Buddhist emptiness/dependent origination explanations.

So the question is, do you find one model of reality more 'provable'/plausible above the other? I presume you will say the Advaita model, but why not the above alternative model I sketched out? I know that both end up at similar conclusions – that the ego is illusory and there is no separation, but it would be interesting to know if one is 'truer' than the other.

A: There are whole books written on this topic and half-a-dozen (at least) differing theories regarding the creation of the world. All suffer from deficiencies and often contradict one another.

Your 'alternative, plausible explanation' sounds like the Charvaka's (materialist) view. You say that 'the truth is that we are just chemicals/molecules/energy quanta'. Is the salt on your table aware of the sugar? The missing, and quite inexplicable factor (by materialists/scientists) is consciousness. Unless you can explain this, you have no viable theory.

The mAyA explanation is also deficient in the final analysis. According to Advaita, there are not two things, so we cannot have Brahman *and* mAyA. And Brahman cannot 'do' anything (and could have no desire to do it anyway). So, such explanations can only ever be interim, 'explaining' the seeming world at the level of that world. In the end, you have to accept that there is no creation and that everything is just name and form of Brahman.

There is an interesting refutation of Buddhism in Shankara's bhAShya on the Brihadaranyaka Upanishad (IV.iii.7). The Buddhist is arguing that there is nothing other than consciousness, which is 'self-luminous', like a lamp which illuminates itself as well as the objects around it. But Shankara says that the lamp needs consciousness to 'reveal' it. For something to be 'revealed', it must be possible for it to be present or absent to the revealer. Since the lamp cannot be absent from itself, it cannot be its own revealer. The bottom line of this is that consciousness is distinct from its objects. In other words, realism, not idealism. (Of course, the 'objects' are mithyA, so this does not pose any threat to Advaita.) [Ref. Vol. III of Karl Potter's 'Encyclopedia of Indian Philosophies' for this discussion.]

See also Q.64.

Q: How do we really know that everything, i.e. energy, matter, elements, the body, etc. is Consciousness and not separate from it?

A: Every 'thing' is dependent upon (or is just name and form of) something more fundamental for its existence. This goes 'all the way down' and does not stop until it hits Consciousness. (Read the 'story' which describes this at http://www.advaita.org.uk/discourses/definitions/advaita.htm.)

If there were something that no one has ever been aware of, no one is aware of, and no one ever will be aware of, could it be said to exist? The clay-clay pot, gold-gold-ornament metaphors are helpful for contemplating this sort of question.

Q.393 Idealism or Realism?

Q: Advaita often uses certain language and metaphors, and these can often come across as sort of a 'subjective idealism plus'. Where subjective idealism argues that the 'outside world' is a completely nonexistent illusion produced in a mind, Advaita sometimes seems to say yes, that's true – only behind that mind that imagines the world is Consciousness witnessing the mind, which is 'projected' onto Consciousness by the mysterious mAyA. In other words, Berkeley was right, only he didn't go far enough. This leaves Advaita sounding like total solipsism, blended with hard-line idealism. Consciousness, some sort of unimaginable void incapable of anything, is having a mind and a world 'imagined onto it' by mAyA, which despite the incapability of Consciousness to do anything is still a 'power' of that Consciousness. (Of course, this is very much a conceptualization, taking these metaphors too literally and looking at these terms and concepts through a very Westernized lens. But this is often the way some teachings sound!)

But in addition to the talk of all things being total illusion, I will also hear that Advaita is realist – that the universe is not an hallucination; that it is, in one sense, 'actually there'; and that it is in comparison to the changeless pAramArthika viewpoint that vyavahAra is 'unreal'. This position makes much more sense to me than imagining the universe to be some sort of magic trick.

Now, I recognize that these explanations – both of them – are attempts to 'point' at truth, and not a tidy description of truth itself. Ultimately, there is only Brahman; there are no 'illusory things' and no 'real things'. But I'm far from truly grasping that yet, so I suppose my question is: which of these descriptions more accurately reflects the nature and relation of vyavahAra and paramArtha? Or are both illustrations only as useful as what they can communicate to a student? Or am I just getting way too caught up in concepts here?

A: Advaita is a 'flexible' teaching rather than a hard philosophy, and a good teacher (which means a sampradAya teacher) will aim to explain things at the current level of understanding of the seeker. The scriptures, from which the teaching derives, themselves contain superficially conflicting ideas for the same reason. The mechanism is called adhyAropa-apavAda, which I am sure you will be aware of given your clearly very knowledgeable background.

Thus it is that *all* of the teaching, whatever it may be, is rescinded in the final analysis. This is because it is intrinsically impossible to talk about the ultimate reality. Shankara was notable amongst the main teachers in that he was willing to go further even than the scriptures in providing 'explanations' to help get across the message and the concept of mAyA was one such device.

There are certainly parallels between Advaita and Berkeley. You may have come across Greg Goode, a teacher of Direct Path Advaita (with Buddhist leanings). Berkeley was one of Greg's specializations and he believes that Berkeley actually wrote a final book which does go much further towards Advaita. Unfortunately, this book has been lost.

The solipsism idea is treated in Advaita by the concept of 'one jIva' – eka jIva vAda – and there are some (post Shankara) philosophers who advocate this. Dr. Ramesam Vemuri posted a series of articles on this (http://www.advaita-vision.org/eka-jiva-vada-i-am-alone/). And I submitted a further post, which was a question and answer discussion with Dr. K. Sadananda, the AchArya at Washington Chinmaya Mission (http://www.advaita-vision.org/more-on-ekajiva-vada/). Sadananda concludes that neither the 'one jIva' nor the 'many jIva' notions makes any sense since the very concept of a jIva is mistaken to begin with.

If you want the other side of the story, the series by Chittaranjan Naik on 'A Realist View of Advaita' can be read at my website (http://www.advaita.org.uk/discourses/chittaranjan/realist_chittaranjan.htm). There are ten parts + a bibliography.

The 'bottom line' has to be that neither view 'accurately reflects the nature and relation of vyavahAra and paramArtha'. They are merely attempts to point the way towards understanding. As you put it: "both illustrations are only as useful as what they can communicate to a student". Perhaps the most useful concept is that provided by Gaudapada – the notion of ajAti vAda – there has never been any creation; nothing has ever been born. When you have climbed up, you throw away the ladder, as Wittgenstein put it!

(From Q.385, which was not posted because the rest of the question would not be of interest to others.)

You are never going to be able to 'explain' the appearance in terms of the real. The various suggestions, imputing reasons to Brahman, are just interim explanations to satisfy the ignorant. They all have to be taken back eventually. Brahman is beyond time, space and causality, without attributes of any sort, indescribable, unthinkable. For lots more detail, read 'A-U-M: Awakening to Reality'. This is effectively a commentary on the Mandukya Upanishad and Gaudapada kArikA-s with Shankara's bhAShya, which aims to provide a reasoned explanation of the nature of reality.

Q.406 Multiverse

Q: Although understanding that there is only one true Self, can we not imagine multiple parallel consciousness-es of multiple Self's? Are there any categorical arguments against such a thing existing? If Brahman came 'of itself' (anAdi, beginningless), could there not equally be many anAdi Brahmans? I know that this doesn't help in calming our brains at all, but it does challenge the non dual core concept, doesn't it?

A: There is only Consciousness, which is non-dual. There are not subject(s) and object(s). You can imagine whatever you like but imagination is not reality. The multiverse is the realm of cosmologists trying to make sense of perceived things. But perceived things are mithyA. Even the perceiver is mithyA. It would not matter if there *were* multiple universes, they would all still be mithyA.

In kArikA-s 2.20 – 28, Gaudapada derides some 36 different, then current, theories of the nature of reality and concludes: *"All these ideas are nothing but imaginations in Atman. In Consciousness, there is neither creation, nor sustenance, nor destruction – all are mAyA".*

Q.425 Truth and reality

Q: As I see it, Truth (with a capital T) is a human concept and, like all concepts, is not real (except in our minds). 'What is' is simply 'what is'... period; end of story (literally).

Advaita Vedanta seems to say that Truth (Brahman) is real, that it is in fact the only reality.

Are the two assertions above incompatible? (I have the feeling that, ultimately, they're not, because the Truth I'm talking about is a concept and Brahman is not.) If they are, is my take that 'Truth is a human concept and therefore not real' a deep obstacle (perhaps even a show-stopper) to my studying Advaita?

A: It is not possible to talk about Brahman/reality because it is non-dual and without attributes (see Q.328). You need to accept and appreciate this. But of course, as part of the process of removing Self-ignorance from the mind, we do need to 'as if' talk about it. And we do this via pointers, negation and so on. All of these are concepts and have to be dropped *in the end*. But, in the interim, we make use of them without worrying about the fact that they are mithyA.

The other point is that words are very slippery things and different people can understand different things. The word 'sat' can certainly mean both 'reality' and 'truth' (as well as 'existence'). Whether or not you regard these as synonyms may cause you a problem of the sort you describe. But the word 'reality' is as much a concept as the word 'truth'! These are the sort of things that twentieth century Western philosophers argued about. Don't worry about it! Gain Self-knowledge and you can then happily drop all the concepts, or simply use them as appropriate when you want to talk to someone who doesn't have Self-knowledge!

Summary

Q.443 A 'simple summary of Advaita'

Q: Based on your own search and discoveries over many years, and the writing of all of the books and blogs, if you had to summarize everything – the truth of life – what would you say?

A: Not sure what you are looking for here. My 'personal' view is surely not important and I could scarcely find any better summary than Shankara's. Anyway, I spent an hour thinking about it (while washing up and vacuuming) and here is my one line summary:

The form does not matter – it is the substance that is important.

Q: How do we know that energy/matter is Consciousness and not just what it seems to be – energy/matter? And why does it make any difference? Can't Consciousness just be what it is by itself and simply aware?

A: Energy and matter are both objects of experience. They are transient and finite, changing one into the other and ultimately ending in absolute zero (temperature). Consciousness is the non-dual, unchanging, eternal and infinite reality.

It does not matter from the standpoint of absolute reality. It does not even matter to most jIva-s, since they just get on with the usual pleasure-seeking aims. It matters to one who is seeking Self-knowledge.

Consciousness *does* 'just be what it is' (there is nothing else) but is not 'aware' in the usual meaning of the word, since there is nothing else of which to be aware.

Q: I completely stopped reading and listening to stuff about all of this a few days ago, and my mind basically 'forgot', if you will, the teachings and all of the 'knowledge'. So there's no doubt that it was in the mind as knowledge or information. But the one and only thing, that was very firm and clear, was simply the fact of Consciousness or Existence, all by itself with no 'knowledge' or information and pointers, etc.; so it seems that *being* it is completely different from just *knowing* about it.

And, as Consciousness, it's not important to know about anything or have knowledge of the way everything works or is, in the body and universe. So I guess what I'm saying, and asking for your thoughts on, is that all of the knowledge in the mind effectively went, and left what I would say is 'really real'. It reminded me of a quote by Nisargadatta Maharaj when he said that anything you can remember or forget is not it. And this seems to be what I'm realizing and really seeing as the case here ...

A: A number of points arise in response to what you say here:

1. Not reading/listening/thinking about something does not equate to not having the knowledge. You know tons of stuff that you never think about; it comes to mind only when relevant but that does not mean it is not there.

2. Existence/Consciousness has always been the case and always will be (sat, chit and anantam). You have always been Brahman. Brahman is all there ever is. So what is different? Why do you say that this is now 'firm and clear'?

3. All 'knowledge' that can be spoken or thought about is ultimately mithyA. But, the reason that we fail to recognize the fact of sat-chit is that we are ignorant. We are immersed in duality and never question its seeming reality. No amount of experiencing the world will bring about understanding of the truth. Only knowledge about self and world, transmitted by someone who already knows, can bring this about. Only knowledge can remove ignorance.

4. Maybe what you are really concerned about here is the meaning of speaking about Brahman as 'knowledge'. This stems from the statement 'satyam j~nAnam anantam brahma' in the Taittiriya Upanishad (2.1.1). And there is a huge 'discussion' following this in Shankara's bhAShya. I have been reading some of this myself but I would not want to attempt to summarize. Do you have A. J. Alston's 'Shankara Source Books'? If not, they are brilliant and well-worth buying. Volume 1, 'Shankara on the Absolute' contains a whole section on "Texts on the Absolute as

'Reality, Knowledge, Infinity'" And this could well answer your concerns. Alternatively, Swami Dayananda's commentary on the Taittiriya has many pages on this single phrase, but it is very 'Sanskrit-heavy' and would require quite a lot of effort to read (and even more to follow!).

Q: Great responses, very clear. I think that my problem is with the whole 'knowledge' thing. I always felt or sensed that Consciousness was and is something *other than* the mind and intellect, and therefore has nothing to do with the mind-intellect or knowledge. Also, that the mind is the problem, so 'getting out of it' is the whole key! So, why knowledge?

A: Everything is Consciousness. So, although Consciousness is not mind-intellect, mind-intellect is Consciousness. Just like saying that the ring and bangle are gold but gold is neither ring nor bangle.

The mind *is* the problem; you are right. But it is also the solution. The reason that we believe that we are not already 'free', perfect and complete is not that this is untrue. Since there is only Brahman, we must already *be* Brahman. The reason is that we do not *know* this. So the only solution is to gain that knowledge and remove the ignorance of the already-existent fact.

I had a further thought on the 'Brahman being knowledge' question. I mention in my books, several times I think, that I always had a problem with Ishvara in the teaching of Advaita. But, if you think rather in terms of paramArtha-vyavahAra or, more appropriately when it comes to this topic, in terms of nirguNa-saguNa, then it becomes rather obvious.

Just think of the complexity and wonder of this apparent creation. Think of the science, from general physics and chemistry down to detailed specialties – the vast, incomprehensible intricacy of interacting laws, known and unknown. How does this all operate? There are clearly areas that we are not yet even aware of, where interactions take place according to principles not yet understood. Where *is* all of the 'knowledge' that enables this universe to exist? Even though it is all, ultimately, mithyA, the appearance is consistent at the gross empirical level. Just as the dream *is* the mind in the final analysis, so the universe has to be Brahman. Of course, this way of looking at it might lead one to conclude that Brahman *has* the knowledge rather than *is* the knowledge. But if you already accept that there is *only* Brahman…

Q: It comes back to the simplicity of it all being only one 'thing' – Consciousness!

So to keep the analogy, it's like the ring thinking it's a separate thing or self. And then simply realizing that it's not what it thinks, that it's really gold?

At that point, there is no separate self or thing, so therefore, there's really no free will and choice, and that's where Ishvara comes in as the doer and creator, and all that can happen at the 'ring' level is watching or seeing what happens moment by moment; which would make it quite fun and exciting actually, as well as meaning that there is no suffering or misery ...

A: What you say is ok up to a point. 'Enlightenment' is analogous to the ring realizing that it is actually gold. But there is no 'at that point'. The 'ring' has always only been gold. There never has been a separate self. So there never is any 'free will' in reality.

But the realization of all this does not alter the appearance; what changes is our understanding. It still seems as though there is a separate world out there; that we perceive, think, act and enjoy. But we now know that this is all just an appearance. There still appears to be a body, and it still gets old, pains develop and it eventually stops working and returns to dust. But it is now known that all of that is inert matter only. I-Brahman 'animate' it for a while. I perceive it but am not affected by all of those changes. So, although I 'feel' the pain through the brain's equipment, there is no 'suffering' because I know that it is not happening to who-I-really-am.

Q: Ahhhhh!! I see, yes!

So every bit of stress, fear, worry, anxiety, hate, violence, depression, wars, misery and suffering that we see every day is simply and only because people think in their minds that they're a 'ring'?

And enlightenment is like going behind the scenes of a magic show and seeing how the trick really works?

A: It is pretty much like that, although that does not reduce the suffering of those who are still unenlightened.

I like the story of Swami Paramarthananda that I quoted in Book of One:

"Of course, once this awakening has taken place, it is realized that the seeming person, mind and knowledge were all part of the mistaken view and that before, during and after, there was only the Self and no actual person to 'become enlightened'.

"Swami Paramarthananda tells a story about a game he used to play as a child. They would take a child into a room that was entirely empty and then would place pillows about the room and stand the child up against one wall. He was told to memorize the positions of the pillows and then they blindfolded him. He was then told that he had to cross the room to the other wall without touching any of the pillows. The other children then watched as he very carefully edged his way forward. Whenever they laughed, he would retreat and move sideways before trying again. Eventually he reached the other wall and was allowed to remove the blindfold. He then discovered that all of the pillows had been removed before he began and that he had been moving across an empty floor trying to avoid non-existent objects.

"And he says that mokSha is like this. As seekers, we make our way through life trying to avoid all the pitfalls of Self-ignorance and arrive at the other wall of Self-knowledge and enlightenment. But when we attain enlightenment, we realize that there never were any obstacles to begin with. In a sense, the ignorance was non-existent – tat tvam asi already".

Q: LOL ... it's pretty amazing! And thank you, I am getting this clearly!

So like the snake, it's all just an appearance and once realized and known, the stress-fear-worry-anxiety-etc. go away and one is left with 'what is' and the sense of self and doership are gone, and a 'letting go' happens. Is this where Ishvara comes in as that which is doing it all?

And if this is all the case, it really doesn't matter what happens or not, it doesn't affect me in the slightest ...

A: That's right! The fact that the appearance remains is attributed to Ishvara as the intelligent/material cause of the world, in the same way that we are the intelligent/material cause of our dreams. But of course Ishvara, too, is mithyA in the final analysis.

Q: One final question for now:

Since we *are* Consciousness and that's all there is, does that mean we would have free will and choice to do what we want, or the opposite – 'thy will be done' and it's all up to Ishvara?

A: At the level of paramArtha, there are no jIva-s so there is no question of free will. Consciousness is not a doer or enjoyer so there is also no question of free will.

At the level of vyavahAra, karma apparently operates so free will is relevant. Ishvara is responsible for 'administering' the laws of the universe (which includes ensuring that karmaphala is received – and villains get their come-uppance in this life or the next)...

Q: So once this is really known and understood, that's it!? It seems like it's really an 'aha' thing like finding the necklace around your neck ...

A: Once this is *really* known, that is it. But it is not something that anyone could expect to suddenly realize (like finding the necklace). Someone has to tell you – and initially you will probably not believe them!

Q: So to get the words correct here: mithyA or the appearance exists, but it's not real? Or just not what it seems to appear as? Or is the appearance an illusion entirely like the snake on rope?

A: mithyA does not mean 'unreal' or 'illusory'; it means that its reality is 'borrowed'. The ring is not real in itself but is clearly not an illusion; it is simply name and form of gold. The world is, if you like, name and form of Brahman.

Q: So in the end, consciousness is all there is; is everything. And that's the simplicity of it!

Could you say this knowledge is the great secret of life? Or is there actually something they call this knowledge in the Scriptures?

A: It is simple; all the mahAvAkya-s (important sayings) in the Upanishads *are* simple. The problem is that they are counter-intuitive and most people will simply reject them.

Some teachers make a careful distinction between 'knowledge' and 'wisdom' and I guess that really one ought to use Sanskrit again and call this knowledge 'j~nAna'. The tripurA rahasya has this to say:

155. Therefore the appearance of a thing and its utility do not determine the reality of a thing or otherwise. All knowledge is secondary and unreliable. There is no doubt about it.

156-159. The greatest of all delusions is the conviction that knowledge is not a delusion. A hallucination holds the field in the interval antecedent to correct knowledge, in the same way as it does when we mistake a shining mother-of-pearl for a piece of silver. So also the mistake of the reality of the universe persists until primary and basic Self-knowledge is realized. This false sense is universal, like the blue color of the sky, and it will end simultaneously with the realization of Pure Intelligence.

Q: Reading that made me think that even the saying 'Consciousness is all there is' is not true. The word Consciousness is not true. *All of it* is mithyA. The word Consciousness is not even what it really is ... amazing but very strange too that we make all of this up and yet we can still 'understand' and 'get it'!

A: Exactly! You cannot say anything at all about reality. Language only functions with respect to ideas and percepts – which are only forms. And all forms are mithyA. It is not so much that you 'understand' it or 'get' it. You *are* it essentially. Hence the term 'realize'.

Q: satyam and mithyA really explain or point to a lot! The whole thing really ...

A: Yes! Hence Shankara's introduction to his commentary on the brahmasUtra. And the generally accepted 'summary-in-a-sentence' of Advaita: brahma satyam, jaganmithyA, jIvo brahmaiva nAparaH.

Q: So then is mithyA or the appearance just 'play' as some say, or a 'passing show', or a dream?

A: No. Ideas such as lIlA, or anything relating to Brahman 'doing' something, are just concepts to help the seeker on the way to understanding and have to be dropped later (adhyAropa-apavAda). There is *only* Brahman.

Q: So *any* idea or explanation is ultimately nonsense really, and Brahman doesn't do anything. And does Brahman 'non-experientially witness' anything?

A: There is nothing other than Brahman. How could Brahman 'witness'? This is a transitive verb and requires an object.

Q: So the methodology takes you to the fact that all there is is Brahman, and with that, the concepts of satyam/mithyA. And then ... even *that* is at the level of mithyA. Is this correct understanding?

A: The 'message' of Advaita is that 'all there is, is Brahman' and 'I am That'. The rest really follows from these two statements. (Although, of course, the essence of this is repeated many times in different forms throughout the scriptures.)

Q: So there's no need to 'abide' as Consciousness/Awareness, or anything else, since everything already is what it is, as it is, and that would all be a 'doing' or 'experiencing' of some sort. So the only possibility, if you will, is Knowledge or Understanding?

A: You have no choice but to 'abide' as Consciousness, since that is what you are. There is nothing to do or experience. As you say, what is needed to understand or 'realize' this and that is where Self-knowledge comes into it, which you gain from the teaching of Advaita.

Q: So all of this talk and teaching and scriptures and studying and practices and everything that is done, is to 'get to' or 'finally arrive' if-you-will at this utter simple fact that all there is is

Consciousness or Brahman, and I am that! Why all the volumes of books and all this Brahmasutra for that simple fact and realization?

The real 'truth' or fact, is that there's absolutely nothing to do, acquire, achieve or understand, *only* something to realize!

A: What has to be done by the seeker is to remove his/her ignorance so that the truth about the nature of reality is realized: brahma satyam, jaganmithyA, jIvo brahmaiva nAparaH. The 'doing' of the jIva is whatever is necessary to arrive at this realization. This entails sAdhana chatuShTaya sampatti followed by shravaNa and manana. But, yes, in the end it could not be simpler!

If we assume that reality is non-dual, then it is a fact of life that this reality cannot be amenable to definition or objectification of any kind, for the simple reason that this would require subject-object duality. This is not a deficiency in the teaching of Advaita. Indeed, the Brihadaranyaka Upanishad specifically utilizes its teaching of 'neti, neti' to state what Brahman is *not*, the idea being that reality is whatever 'is left' when everything (else) has been negated. Shankara says (Br. U. 4.4.20) that *"the scriptures do not enjoin that identity with Brahman should be established, but that the false identification with things should stop"*.

The 'conclusion' of Advaita (brahma satyam, jagat mithyA, jIva brahmaiva nAparaH) is not an obvious one, not even intuitive. It has to be approached obliquely. There are many metaphors, stories etc. in the scriptures to help in this, but the scriptures are in Sanskrit (because that was the written language of the times) and overly concise (because the material had to be memorized in the early days, in order to pass on from teacher to disciple). This is why a qualified teacher is needed; it is not a means for retaining exclusivity!

Finally, Advaita is available for anyone who genuinely wants to follow that path – and always has been. Brahmins stand for an attitude of mind dominated by sattva and a clear, controlled mind is a prerequisite for attending to the teacher. Minds enmeshed in tamas (shUdra) or rajas (kShatriya) will be unable to concentrate sufficiently. Similarly, saMnyAsa represents a mind that has effectively renounced the usual worldly pursuits (i.e. desires) and has mumukShutva. Shankara says (Br. U. 3.5.1) that *"this monasticism is a part of Self-knowledge because it is the renunciation of desires which contradict Self-knowledge, and are within the province of ignorance"*.

Q: So you mean to tell me that *all* of the volumes of books and books and books and scriptures come down to the *one simple thing* that all there is is Brahman or Consciousness?!

All of the talking and praying and practicing etc. is simply provisional to get to *that*?!

A: That's about it! sarvaM khalvidam brahma – All this, verily, is Brahman. Plus, of course, tat tvam asi – you are That. The thing is that, without 'all of the talking, praying, practicing etc.', you would never believe it…

Author biography

Educated to degree-level in Chemistry, he has worked for most of his life in computing. Since 2000, he has devoted his life to writing. He completed a philosophical/ecological thriller in 1999 (extensively revised in 2007-8) and a book on Earned Value metrics in March 2001. His first book on Advaita, 'The Book of One', was published in 2003. This was extensively revised and republished in 2010.

An introductory book on Sanskrit 'The Spiritual Seeker's Essential Guide to Sanskrit' was published in India in 2005. His book 'How to Meet Yourself', published in 2007, was aimed at the non-specialist reader and addresses the fundamental topics of meaning and purpose in one's life and the nature of happiness.

His major book on Advaita, also published in 2007, was entitled 'Back to the Truth'. This is a systematic treatment of Advaita which, by using examples from many sources, helps the reader to differentiate between approaches and teachers. It compares the scriptures of traditional Advaita with the words of contemporary Sages and with the modern 'nothing to be done' teaching of neo-Advaita.

'Enlightenment: the Path through the Jungle' was published in 2008. This aimed clearly to define the term enlightenment and dispel the many myths about it propagated by new-age books on the subject. It endeavored to set down the proven methods, passed down for over a thousand years in the traditional teaching of the subject and contrast these with Western approaches, demonstrating in the process that only the traditional methods are likely to bring about enlightenment. 'Advaita Made Easy', published in 2012, aims to summarize the essentials of the subject in a short, easily assimilable form. 'Sanskrit for Seekers' (2014) gives the reader just enough understanding of the language to be able to use a Sanskrit dictionary. 'A-U-M: Awakening to Reality', published Autumn 2015, is a presentation for the modern reader of the Mandukya Upanishad and Gaudapada kArikA-s. 'Time for the Wind' is a novel, an ecological thriller which also gives an insight into Advaita philosophy as part of the plot. It was published in December 2015.

Dennis maintains the most popular website on Advaita at www.advaita.org.uk. There is an integrated blogging facility at www.advaita-vision.org. You may also browse a portfolio of his photographs (a lifetime hobby) at http://dwaite1.500px.com/.

Books by Dennis Waite

Advaita Made Easy, Jul 2012

Advaita provides answers to all of the difficult questions!

A-U-M: Awakening to Reality, Sep 2015

Know the truth: There is neither death nor birth; no creation; no multiplicity; nothing apart from Consciousness.

Enlightenment: the path through the jungle, Aug 2008

What is Enlightenment? What is it not? Which teaching methods will get you there… and which will not?

The Book of One (2nd Edition), Apr 2010

The Book of One is a comprehensive, articulate guide along the spiritual path of Advaita, the one (not two) philosophy that explains life, the universe and all existence.

Back to the Truth: 5000 years of Advaita Feb 2007

Demysifies this ancient, non-dualist philosophy from India

How to Meet Yourself… and find true happiness, Feb 2007

Explains what you are not, so that you can understand who you really are and, ultimately, come to the conclusion that you are already happy now!

Sanskrit for Seekers, May 2014
For travelers in the foreign land of spiritual literature.

Time for the Wind, Dec 2015
Mankind meets its karmic retribution – but is it 'real'? (A SF novel – an 'ecological thriller', not primarily about Advaita.)

Western Philosophy Made Easy, Jul 2018
What can Western Philosophy tell us about purpose and meaning in our lives?

Appendix 1 – ITRANS

All that this appendix will attempt to do is to explain to you how to pronounce the Sanskrit words used in this book. They have been written (italicized in brackets after what is usually a poor attempt to render the word phonetically in English) in what is called transliterated form, using the ITRANS scheme. Avinash Chopde devised this scheme for use on the Internet. His software, and details about the system, may be downloaded from his website, https://www.aczoom.com/itrans. There already existed at least one widely used scheme for rendering Sanskrit letters in a 'Romanized' way. However, since this used symbols called macrons (lines above letters) and dots above and below letters, it was quite unsuitable for computer keyboards with basic letters and the normal fonts provided with word processors. Accordingly, this scheme uses only the usual letters of our alphabet, together with the occasional special character such as the tilde ~.

[Note that there is no attempt in this short summary to indicate how stress or accents are applied to words within, for example, a Sanskrit verse in the Upanishads. This is entirely outside the scope of this book (and my knowledge). For some indication of what is involved here, see https://en.wikipedia.org/wiki/Vedic_accent.]

General

Sanskrit is an extremely interesting language. It is amazingly logical. There are lots of rules but, once you have learnt them, there are none of the tiresome exceptions found in most languages (I think that is genuinely *none*!). Also, once you have learned how to pronounce a letter, it is *always* pronounced in that way. Unfortunately, simply learning the letters is not sufficient to enable you to look up words in the dictionary. Letter combinations can look quite different from the same letters on their own. Also words found in the scriptures usually consist of combinations of many separate words and, when words join, they often change. An example that you will have seen in the book is *sachchidAnanda*. If you did not know this word, you would have to know the rules of these combinations in order to be able to work out that the separate words of which this consists – *sat, chit* and *Ananda* – in order to be able to look them up. You can see that, when a word ending in t combines with one beginning with ch, the t also changes to a ch. And the t at the end of chit becomes a d. Accordingly, you will not find this word in the dictionary under 'sach' but just after 'sat'. This particular word is present in its complete form because it is in such common usage but infrequent combinations will not themselves be listed and you have to break them down into the individual words to find out the meaning. (This is known as euphony or *saMdhi*.)

Finally, it is interesting to note in passing that there is a close parallel between the structure of the language and the Advaita-related myth of the creation. Indeed, some schools of thought, notably in the North of India and Kashmir, believe that the universe was 'spoken' into existence. Though this 'primordial' language is beyond ordinary sound, Sanskrit is its earthly manifestation as it were and embodies many of the 'universal principles'. The language itself is believed to embody the truth of the unity of the Self. Since pure Advaita tells us that there is effectively no such thing as creation, the value of discussing these ideas is ultimately academic. Such studies can help prepare the mind to acknowledge those truths that remain forever beyond its grasp but they can also prove a hindrance. They have more appeal to those whose nature is inclined towards *bhakti yoga* rather than *j~nAna*.

The entire language evolves in an almost mathematical way from a fundamental sound. The laws governing the way that words are constructed, and the grammar used to join them, are strict. It is amazing that the language, though the most ancient known and no longer in general use, remains true to its original form and someone learning it now would be able to communicate perfectly well with someone speaking the language thousands of years ago.

Regarding pronunciation

In the brief exposition below, a guide to sounding of each letter is given by reference to an English word and character, where a similar sound may be heard. For more definitive guidance it is necessary actually to hear someone sounding the letters and words. Obviously this is not possible in written material. Two on-line videos have been suggested to me. These are helpful, although having listened to some of each I found that I disagreed with some aspects of both! (The problem here is that I was taught by the School of Economic Science in the UK and they are very pedantic and demanding. They follow strict, logical rules for formulation rather than allowing actual Indian pronunciation to guide them for example.) On the assumption that some readers may find these helpful, however – and certainly better than nothing at all – the references are:

https://vimeo.com/57042409 and https://www.youtube.com/watch?v=-wTDvmElnlM.

The five basic vowels

The first letter of the alphabet forms the fundamental sound from which all others are derived simply by moving the tongue and lips. It is made by opening the mouth wide and letting the vocal chords operate. The sound which emerges sounds like a cross between the short 'a' in cat and 'u' in but. It is written as *'a'* in ITRANS but the correct letter in the proper script, called *devanAgarI* (meaning city of the gods), is:

A *a*

This is the first letter of the alphabet and the first vowel or, to use its correct term, *svara,* meaning sound. I will not show the Devanagari for any of the other letters for the reasons already discussed above.

If the back of the tongue is now raised slightly towards the back of the roof of the mouth, keeping the front of the tongue down against the back of the lower teeth, and the same short movement of the vocal cord is made, a slightly different sound emerges. This sounds a bit like the short 'i' in bit. It is written as *i* in ITRANS.

The next two vowels seem strange to Westerners but follow the logic of the development. The underlying sound for both of these is the *i* sound just covered but the tip of the tongue is first moved further forward in the mouth. If you raise the tip of the tongue until it is almost touching the roof of the mouth and then, make the 'i' sound as before, the next vowel sound emerges. Modern students often actually flick the tongue downwards as the sound is made so that the result sounds something like 'ri' in the word rip, though the rolling 'r' beginning is not clearly enunciated because the tongue never actually touched the roof of the mouth. However, strictly speaking this pronunciation is not correct. It is written *RRi* in ITRANS (or, in old releases, *R^i*).

This procedure is repeated but now the tip of the tongue moves further forward still, to just behind the front teeth, before the 'i' is sounded. Again, modern speakers often flick the tongue up towards the roof and down so that the sound that actually comes out is 'lri'. Again, not strictly correct but it hardly matters since there is only one word in the language that uses this letter! It is written *LLi* in ITRANS (or, in old releases, *L^i*).

Continuing the development, the emphasis finally shifts to the lips (labial position), having begun in the throat (guttural position), moved to at the back of the mouth (palatal), then to the roof of the mouth (cerebral) and then the teeth (dental). If a circle is formed of the lips but without any tension and the basic sound is made, a short 'oo' sound comes out as in soot or cut. This is the last of the simple vowels, written *u*.

These five vowels with their characteristic mouth positions effectively head up the five main groups of consonants. Consonants all effectively still sound the basic 'a' but 'stop' it from coming out in that simple way by varying the position of the tongue and lips in the way dictated by the vowel at the head of the group.

The long vowels

The basic five vowels above are all *short* vowels – *hrasva*. This means that, when pronounced, the sound is made as short as possible whilst still being distinguishable – really quite short! Each of these vowels *can* be sounded long. The length is actually very precise. If the short form is treated as one beat, then the long form should be two beats. The long form is called *dIrgha*. In ITRANS, the vowel is shown as long either by putting two of them, as with the *ii* in *diirgha* or by capitalizing it thus: – *dIrgha*. The latter form has been used as standard in this book. [Note that 'length' of the sound is called mAtra in Sanskrit and this is usually translated as 'measure'. The short vowel is 1 mAtra and the long is 2.]

When the vowels become long, the pronunciation naturally changes slightly, too. Thus, the short *a* becomes *aa* or *A* and sounds like the 'a' in calm. The short *i* becomes *ii* or *I* and sounds like the double 'ee' sound in words like sleep. The short *RRi* becomes *RRI* (or *R^I* in old releases of ITRANS). Here there is no option of having two small i's. The *dIrgha* vowel is sounded as for the *hrasva* form but with the ending 'ee' instead of 'i'. Similarly, the short *LLi* becomes *LLI* (or *L^I* in the old releases of ITRANS) but, since there are no words at all known to contain it, this hardly seems to matter! Finally, short *u* becomes long *uu* or *U* and sounds like the double 'oo' in root.

The vowels can be sounded for longer than two beats, in which case they are called *pluta* – prolonged. In this case they are written with a number '3' below and just to the right of the letter, both in *devanAgarI* and in the Romanized version. This form cannot be represented in ITRANS.

The compound vowels

Now, if the sound *a* is made and continues to sound while the mouth is slowly closed, the sound made before the lips come together is *u*. If these two sounds are made together or, more practically speaking, if the sound corresponding to the mid-point between these two is made, the sound that emerges is *o* (as in 'boat'). This new letter is called a compound vowel. Similarly, when *a* combines with *i*, it forms the compound vowel *e*. If you sound a prolonged a_3, and then raise the back of the tongue towards the *i* position, but stop before you get there, you should hear the *e* sound. It's a bit like the 'a' in 'late' but not as open as we would pronounce this. If, after making the above sound for *e*, you relax the tongue back towards the *a* position but again stop before you get there, there is another sound formed as a compound between *a* and *e* which sounds like the 'ie' in 'pie'. It is written *ai*.

In a similar way to that described above, if the mouth moves from the *a* (open-mouthed) position to the *o* (partially closed) position but stops half-way, there is a sound similar to 'ow' in 'brown'. This is written *au* in ITRANS.

These, then are the fourteen vowels but there are two final letters to be added to complete the group of sixteen, so-called *mAtRRikA*. They are not really part of the alphabet but act as modifications to a preceding vowel. (Note that, because of this, if they are sounded as letters in their own right, they assume an 'a' before rather than after.)

The first of these is called an *anusvAra*. It is written as *M* and causes the preceding vowel to be sounded through the nose. The precise nasal sound is determined by the consonant that follows it, in that it uses the mouth position of the consonant so that the effect is something like the nasal consonant (*anunAsika*) described below.

The other special letter, not really part of the alphabet, also modifies the sound of the preceding vowel, is written *H* and it has the effect of adding a brief, breathing out, 'unvoiced' sound after the vowel. It is as though there were a word beginning with 'h' immediately following and you start to sound it as soon as you finish the preceding letter (i.e. without changing the mouth position) but stop before the word itself starts to sound. It is called a *visarga.*

So, to recap, the 16 vowels, or *mAtRRikA,* are as follows:

a A i I u U RRi RRI LLi LLI e o ai au aM aH

The first group of consonants (guttural)

The Sanskrit term for consonants is *vya~njana,* meaning a 'decoration' (of the basic vowel sound). Twenty-five of these are grouped in five sets of five 'underneath' the five basic vowels described above. They are formed by positioning the mouth (tongue or lips) in such a way as to 'stop' the sound of the vowel in some way. The first group uses the mouth position of the *a* sound for decorating. This all takes place at the back of the mouth where it becomes the throat – the 'guttural' position.

Strictly speaking it is not possible to pronounce a consonant on its own. It is in itself only a positioning of the mouth to 'stop' the sound made by a vowel. Accordingly, when speaking the alphabet, the sound of *a* is used by default after each letter. The first consonant of this group is written *k,* sounded (with *a*) 'ka' as in cat.

Clearly this consonant could occur at the end of the word (as 'k' in 'rack' for example). In this case it would have an additional mark underneath the Devanagari character, called a 'halant', which means 'don't make any vowel sound after this'. In ITRANS, this used to be written *k.h* – *.h* after any consonant in ITRANS means that it is followed by a halant and 'a' is not sounded after it. In fact, it is no longer necessary in ITRANS to do this – if the letter is written on its own, a halant is inserted automatically when it is converted to Devanagari.

The second consonant in the guttural group is written *kh.* Its pronunciation is much like the preceding one but with the addition of a slight breathy sound caused by actually letting out some air immediately following the 'k' sound. It is often sounded as though it were 'k-h' in an imaginary word 'k-hat' but there is much too much emphasis in this – it is really more subtle. Consonants such as *k* are said to be 'with little breath' (*alpaprANa*) while ones like *kh* are 'with much breath' (*mahAprANa*).

The third in this group is written *g*, sounded 'g' as in gap (*alpaprANa*). The fourth is written *gh* and, like 'kh' is *mahAprANa* and sounds like 'gh' in doghouse.

The final consonant in this group is the first of the type mentioned briefly above – *anunAsika*, meaning that the sound is made through the nose. It is written *~N*. There are four n-related sounds; hence the need for the tilde and capitalization. It has the sound of 'ng' made at the back of the throat and sounding through the nose, like 'sing' but with the ending further back in the throat like someone being strangled rather than singing!

The second group of consonants (palatal)

This second group forms the sounds in the back part of the mouth but not the throat. Based on the *i* vowel, these use the back of the tongue and the rear of the mouth; they are called 'palatal'. They follow the same pattern as the previous group (as do all five of these groups of consonants, you will be pleased to know!) in that the first and third members are *alpaprANa*, the second and fourth are *mahAprANa*, and the fifth is *anunAsika*. The first, then is written *ch* and is sounded like the 'cha' in chap but, whereas English pronounces this by using the *front* of the tongue near the *front* of the roof of the mouth, Sanskrit uses the *rear* parts.

The second character is written *Ch* (or *chh* in older versions). Since I have already said that the pattern of the first group is repeated in the others, you might guess that this is sounded pretty much like *ch* but with some added breath – and you would be right! Just remember not to make it too pronounced so that it comes out like 'ch-ha' and it should be fine.

The third is written *j* and pronounced more or less as would expect, like the 'ja' in 'jam' spoken as far back in the mouth as you can without injuring yourself. It uses minimum breath again as for all in this third 'row' of the main consonants. The fourth is written *jh* and you can work out now how it should sound – like 'j-ha' but not too much so.

The final letter in this group the second of the *anunAsika* characters (the 'n' type sounds made through the nose). It is written *~n* and has a sort of 'ny' sound, as in canyon. However, whereas the latter is made by the front of the tongue at the front of the mouth, you have to try to make this sound with the back of the tongue at the rear of the mouth.

The third group of consonants (cerebral)

This third group has now moved the mouth position another step forward so that the tip of the tongue is used, pointing up to the roof of the mouth. To construct the main consonants, the tongue actually touches the roof. It is called the cerebral position. The first is written *T.* All of this third, (middle) group are written as capital letters to differentiate them from the fourth group. (In the Romanized transliteration, the letters have a dot beneath them.) *T* is pronounced as the 't' in tub but instead of having the tongue forward of the roof of the mouth, put it right up to the roof as you say it. That should have been spoken 'with only a small breath' as usual (*alpaprANa*). The second letter is the same but with more breath as you make the sound (*mahAprANa*), a bit like 'po-<u>th</u>-ole' (pothole). It is written *Th.*

The next is written *D* and pronounced like 'd' in dot but, as before, with the tip of the tongue right up in the roof of the mouth. The fourth letter sounds the same as the third but with more breath (e.g. go-dh-ead) and is written *Dh*. The last in the group is another 'na' sound but with the tongue in the roof of the mouth. Written, as you already know, *N*.

The fourth group of consonants (dental)

This group of consonants are sounded just behind the teeth and called, unsurprisingly, dental. The first is *t*. It is sounded just like our t, as in 'tip'. Then comes the equivalent letter, but with more breath (*mahAprANa*), *th*, as in 'carthorse'. Next is *d* as in 'dog' and the breathy equivalent *dh*, as in 'redhead'. Finally, in this group, is the one sounded through the nose (*anunAsika*) *n*, as in ...er 'nose'.

The fifth group of consonants (labial)

And so, at last, the final group of the main consonants sounded at the lips and called labial. The first is *p* just like our p, as in 'put'. Then comes the corresponding breathy *ph*, as in uphill. Next is *b*, as in 'bad' and the *mahAprANa bh*, as in 'clubhouse'. And finally the *anunAsika* in this group is *m*, as in 'man'.

Table of basic consonants

The table of the five groups of consonants, with the corresponding vowel shown in Column 1 for reference, is as shown below:

Guttural	***a***	*k*	*kh*	*g*	*gh*	*~N*
Palatal	***i***	*ch*	*Ch*	*j*	*jh*	*~n*
Cerebral	***RRi***	*T*	*Th*	*D*	*Dh*	*N*
Dental	***LLi***	*t*	*th*	*d*	*dh*	*n*
Labial	***u***	*p*	*ph*	*b*	*bh*	*m*

The semi-vowels

There are two small groups of letters left. The first of these is the group of four so-called 'semi-vowels'. They are formed by combining the four main vowels other than 'a' with 'a'. Thus, if you sound *i* and then immediately move to the *a* sound, what emerges sounds like 'ya' and this is the first semi-vowel or *antaHsth***A:** – *y* as in 'yap'. If you sound *RRi* and move to *a*, you get *r* as in 'rap'. If you sound *LLi* and move to *a*, you get *l* as in 'lap'. Finally, if you sound *u* and move to *a*, you get the sound *'w'* as in 'wag', though in Sanskrit this is denoted by the letter 'v'. Note that Americans seem to prefer to ignore this logical derivation and pronounce it as 'va' in 'van'. Since it is somewhat illogical to write it as beginning with

a 'v' while sounding it as a 'w', I suppose both sides of the Atlantic have a case.

The sibilants

Almost last of all, there are three sibilants or sss-sounds. (A sibilant is called *UShman* in Sanskrit.) These are in the palatal, cerebral and dental positions. (In theory there are also ones in the other two positions but these are so rare that they are usually ignored.) In the palatal position, there is *sh* sounded by making a shh sound in that mouth position; it comes out like the ending of a soft German 'ich' with the default *a* ending of course. The second, in the cerebral position, is *Sh* (or *shh* in older releases) made by sounding 'sha' with the tongue up to the roof of the mouth. Finally is the dental *s*, sounding like the normal 's' in 'sand'.

h

This leaves the last letter in the alphabet, *h*, sounding, as you would expect, as 'h' in 'hat'. It is sometimes considered to be another sibilant and is also called *UShman*, which literally means 'heated'.

The complete alphabet

The order of the alphabet, if you want to look up a word in the dictionary, is pretty much the order used here in introducing the letters. The 16 *mAtRRikA* are at the beginning, followed by the basic consonants – guttural, palatal, cerebral, dental and labial. Then come the 4 semi-vowels (*antaHsthA*) and the three sibilants and finally *h*.

a, A, i, I, u, U, RRi, RRI, LLi, LLI, e, o, ai, au, aM, aH,

k, kh, g, gh, ~N, ch, CH, j, jh, ~n, T, Th, D, Dh, N, t, th, d, dh, n, p, ph, b, bh, m

y, r, l, v, sh, Sh, s, h

Further study

As you will certainly have realized by now, in order to learn how to sound these correctly, you really need to listen to someone who knows – try the two on-line videos referenced earlier. But, for recognizing key words, listening to and reading about traditional Advaita, it doesn't matter too much if you do not know the correct pronunciation – and you certainly do not need to learn the language in any depth.

We are unused to making full use of our mouth and tongue in speaking and, since Sanskrit makes almost scientific use, we will find much of it peculiar and initially uncomfortable. If you want a more thorough introduction, my book 'Sanskrit for Seekers' (Ref. 78) expands upon this to give you a more thorough grounding but without going into too much detail. Its aim is to teach you the rudiments of Sanskrit in order to enable you to read the script, pronounce words and look them up in a dictionary.

Glossary – Sanskrit terminology

Each word is presented in the following format:

Typical English Spelling (*ITRANS representation*, Devanagari Script) – meaning.

Words appear in order of the English (Roman) alphabet, not the Sanskrit alphabet.

(This section is based upon the Glossary in Ref. 63.)

a (*a*, अ) – as a prefix to another word, it changes it into the negative. E.g. vidya – knowledge, avidya – ignorance.

acharya (*AchArya*, आचार्य) – a spiritual guide or teacher. See Shankaracharya.

achintya (*achintya*, अचिन्त्य) – inconceivable or beyond thought.

adhikari (*adhikArin* or *adhikArI*, अधिकारिन् or अधिकारी) – a seeker who is mentally prepared (see *chatuShTaya sampatti*) and therefore ready to receive the final teaching from the guru; literally 'possessing authority, entitled to, fit for.'

adhisthana (*adhiShThAna*, अधिष्ठान) – substratum; literally basis, support, that upon which something rests.

adhyaropa (*adhyAropa*, अध्यारोप) – erroneously attributing one thing to another. **(*adhyAropa-apavAda*, अध्यारोप अपवाद)** – One of the principal methods of teaching Advaita, whereby an attribute is applied to Brahman initially (and erroneously – hence *adhyAropa*) but is later taken back, once the point has been understood. *apavAda* means denial or contradiction.

adhyasa (*adhyAsa*, अध्यास) – used to refer to the 'mistake' that we make when we 'superimpose' a false appearance upon the reality or mix up the real and the unreal. The classical example is when we see a snake instead of a rope, which is used as a metaphor for seeing the world of objects instead of the reality of the Self. This concept is fundamental to Advaita and Shankara devotes a separate section to it at the beginning of his commentary on the Brahmasutra.

adhyaya (*adhyAya*, अध्याय) – lesson, lecture or chapter.

adrishta (*adRRiShTa*, अदृष्ट) – unseen (this stands for not being accessible to any of the senses).

Advaita (Advaita, अद्वैत) – not (*a*) two (*dvaita*); non-dual philosophy. Note that a capital 'A' has been used throughout in the English fashion of a proper noun. (Adjective – *advitIya* – unique, without a second.)

agamin (*AgAmin*, आगामिन्) – That type of sanskara which is generated in reaction to current situations and which will not bear fruit until sometime in the future. It literally means 'impending,' 'approaching' or 'coming.' Also called *kriyamANa*, which means 'being done.' See prarabdha, sanchita, sanskara.

agocara (*agochara*, अगोचर) – (literally) imperceptible by the senses but treated as anything that is unavailable to any *pramANa* other than *shabda* (i.e. scriptures).

agrahya (*agrAhya*, अग्राह्य) – ungraspable (i.e. inaccessible to the organs of action).

aham (*aham*, अहम्) – I am.

aham vritti (*aham vRRitti*, अहम् वृत्ति) – the thought 'I am' as opposed to thoughts about objects, feelings etc. – idam vritti. See vritti.

ahankara (*ahaMkAra*, अहंकार) – the making, kara (*kAra*), of the utterance 'I,' aham (*aham*) – this is the equivalent of what we would call the 'ego' but specifically refers to the identification or attachment of our true Self with something else, usually the body or mind but can be much more specific e.g. I am a teacher, I am a woman. It is one of the 'organs' of the mind in classical Advaita – see antakarana.

ahimsa (*ahiMsA*, अहिंसा) – not injuring anything (one of the yama-s).

aikya (*aikya*, ऐक्य) – unity, oneness; in Advaita specifically the identity of *Atman* and *Brahman*.

aja (*aja*, अज) – unborn.

ajati (*ajAti*, अजाति) – *a* – no or not; *jAti* – creation; the principle that the world and everything in it, including these mind-body appearances were never created or 'brought into existence'. Most clearly stated by Gaudapada in his karika on the Mandukya Upanishad. *jAta* is the adjective, meaning born, brought into existence. The theory that there has never been any creation is called either *ajAta vAda* or *ajAti vAda*.

ajnana (*aj~nAna*, अज्ञान) – (spiritual) ignorance. See jnana. An *aj~nAnI* is one who is not enlightened, i.e. still (spiritually) ignorant.

akasha (*AkAsha*, आकाश) – space, ether or sky; one of the five elements in the Upanishads, the subtle fluid supposed to pervade the universe. Associated with sound and hearing.

akhaNDAkAra vRRitti (अखण्डाकार वृत्ति) – the mental 'occurrence' which effectively causes enlightenment. This is the vRRitti (thought) in the form of (AkAra) the formless or undivided (akhaNDa).

akshara (*akShara*, अक्षर) – imperishable, unchangeable.

alakshana (*alakShaNa*, अलक्षण) – without any characteristics.

amurta (*amUrta*, अमूर्त) – unmanifest, formless, shapeless.

anadi (*anAdi*, अनादि) – without any beginning, often used to refer to 'ignorance'.

ananda (*Ananda*, आनन्द) – 'true' happiness; usually called 'bliss' to differentiate it from the transient variety that always alternates with pain or misery. It is an aspect of our true nature and is often combined with the other elements of our real nature – sat and chit – into a single word, satchidananda. Note that this is one of those words where you really have to get the capitalization of the word correct if you are using ITRANS. The word 'Ananda' means happiness, joy etc. but the word 'ananda' means joyless, cheerless. This is simply because the capital 'A' splits into 'a-a'. So the word 'Ananda' is really 'a-ananda', which means 'NOT ananda'. See sat, chit and satchidananda.

ananta (*ananta*, अनन्त) – eternal, without end.

anatman (*anAtman,* अनात्मन्) – something other than spirit or soul (not Self or Atman); perceptible world. See Atman.

anirvachaniya (*anirvachanIya,* अनिर्वचनीय) – not able to be categorized; literally: unutterable, indescribable, not to be mentioned. Used to describe nature of reality etc.

anitya (*anitya,* अनित्य) – transient. Also **anityatva (*anityatva,* अनित्यत्व)** – transient or limited existence (mortality).

antakarana (*antaHkaraNa,* अन्तःकरण) – used to refer to the overall 'organ' of mind; the seat of thought and feeling. It derives from *antar* – within, interior – and *karaNa,* which means 'instrument' or sense-organ (an alternative for indriya). It consists of a number of separate functions – see manas, buddhi, chitta and ahankara.

anubhava (*anubhAva,* अनुभाव) – perception, understanding, experience; knowledge derived from personal observation. Intuition as (opposed to reasoning – *yukti*).

anubhuti (*anubhUti,* अनुभूति) – knowledge gained by means of the *pramANa*-s.

anugraha (*anugraha,* अनुग्रह) – grace; literally showing favor or kindness, conferring benefits.

anumana (*anumAna,* अनुमान) – inference (in logic); one of the 6 means of obtaining knowledge. See pramana.

anupalabdhi (*anupalabdhi,* अनुपलब्धि) – non-perception, non-recognition; one of the 6 means of obtaining knowledge. See pramana.

aparoksha (*apArokSha,* अपारोक्ष) – immediate (relating to gaining of knowledge, i.e. does not require application of reason).

aparokshanubhuti (*apArokShAnubhUti,* अपारोक्षानुभूति) – one of the works attributed to Shankara. The word means 'knowledge acquired directly by one of the valid *pramANa*-s.'

apaurusheya (*apauruSheya,* अपौरुषेय) – literally 'not coming from men'; used to refer to the shruti – scriptural texts passed on verbatim from generation to generation since their original observation by realized sages. See shruti.

artha (*artha*, अर्थ) – acquisition of wealth. One of the four *puruShArtha*-s. See purushartha.

asat (*asat*, असत्) – non-existent. See sat.

asatkarya vada (*asatkArya vAda*, असत्कार्य वाद) – the doctrine which denies that the effect pre-exists in the cause (usually in reference to the creation).

ashrama (*Ashrama*, आश्रम) – generic term for one of the four 'stages' in the life of a Hindu brahmin, viz. *brahmacharya, gRRihastha, saMnyAsa, vanaprastha.*

astika (*Astika*, आस्तिक) – literally 'there is or exists'; used to refer to one who believes in the existence of God or, more specifically, one who defers to the authority of the Vedas. See nastika, veda.

atma (*Atma*, आत्म) – see Atman.

atmabodha (*Atmabodha*, आत्मबोध) – knowledge of Self or supreme spirit; a book attributed to Shankara.

Atman (*Atman*, आत्मन्) – the Self. Usually used to refer to one's true (individual) nature or consciousness but Advaita tells us that there is no such thing as an 'individual' and that this Atman is the same as the universal Consciousness, Brahman. see also jiva.

atmavicara (*AtmavichAra*, आत्मविचार) – *vicAra* in this context means reflection or examination upon the *Atman*, the Self. See Atman.

avarana (*AvaraNa*, आवरण) – the veiling power of maya. In the rope-snake metaphor, this prevents us from seeing the reality of the rope. See maya, vikshepa.

avastha (*avasthA*, अवस्था) – state; literally 'to stay, abide, exist, remain or continue doing (anything).' In Advaita, it is most frequently encountered as *avasthA traya* – the three states of waking, dreaming and deep-sleep.

avidya (*avidyA*, अविद्या) – ignorance (in a spiritual sense) i.e. that which prevents us from realizing the Self. See also maya.

avyakta (*avyakta*, अव्यक्त) – unmanifest, imperceptible, invisible; the universal spirit (paramAtman).

bandha or bandhana (*bandha* or *bandhana*, बन्ध or बन्धन) – bondage, attachment to the world.

(*bhAga tyAga lakShaNa*, भाग त्याग लक्षण) – a technique used by the scriptures to point to aspects that cannot be explained directly in words. The oneness that is pointed to (*lakShaNa*) is understood by 'giving up' (*tyAga*) the contradictory parts (*bhAga*). An example would be in the apparent contradiction of the *jIva* being 'created' while *Ishvara* is the 'creator.' Both are given up in order to recognize their identity as *Brahman*.

Bhagavad (*bhagavat*, भगवत्) – holy; prosperous, happy; illustrious, divine. In the context of Bhagavad Gita, it refers to the God, Krishna and Bhagavad Gita means Krishna's Song (the *t* changes to a *d* when the words join). See below.

Bhagavad Gita (*bhagavadgItA*, भगवद्गीता) – the scriptural text forming part of the Hindu epic, the Mahabarata. It is a dialogue between Krishna, the charioteer/God, representing the Self and the warrior Arjuna, representing you and me, on the battlefield of Kurukshetra prior to the commencement of battle. The scripture is regarded as smriti. See Bhagavad, smriti.

bhakta (*bhakta*, भक्त) – one who practices bhakti yoga. See bhakti yoga.

bhakti (*bhakti*, भक्ति) yoga – devotion or worship as a means to enlightenment. See also karma and jnana.

bhashya (*bhAShya*, भाष्य) – explanatory work, exposition or commentary on some other scriptural document. Thus Shankara, for example, has written bhashyas on a number of Upanishads, the Bhagavad Gita and the Brahmasutra.

bhavana (*bhAvana*, भावन) – reflection, contemplation.

Brahma (*brahma*, ब्रह्म) – God as the creator of the universe in Hindu mythology (the others are Vishnu, *viShNu*, the preserver and Shiva, *shiva*, the destroyer). N.B. Not to be confused with Brahman!

brahmacharya (*brahmacharya*, ब्रह्मचर्य) – the first stage of the traditional Hindu spiritual path, in which the Brahman begins his life as an unmarried, religious and chaste student. (*charya* means 'due observance of all rites and customs'.) One of the five *yama*-s in Raja yoga. See also grihasta, sanyasa, vanaprastha.

Brahman (Brahman, ब्रह्मन्) – the universal Self, Absolute or God. There is only Brahman. It derives from the Sanskrit root *bRRih,* meaning to grow great or strong and could be thought of as the adjective 'big' made into a noun, implying that which is greater than anything. See also Atman, Brahma, jiva, jivatman, paramatman. (Note that 'Brahman' has been used throughout – i.e. with a capital 'B' – in accordance with English capitalization of proper nouns.)

Brahmana (*Brahmana,* ब्राह्मण) – an aspirant; a member of the first of the traditional four castes in India (also called Brahmin); alternatively a portion of the Vedas, containing information relating to the use of mantras and hymns in sacrifices.

Brahma Sutra (*brahmasUtra,* ब्रह्मसूत्र) – a book (in sutra form, which is terse verse!) by Vyasa. This book is the best known of the third accepted source of knowledge (nyaya prasthana). Effectively, it attempts to summarize the Upanishads. It has been extensively commented on by the three main philosophical branches of Indian thought, dvaita, Advaita and vishishtAdvaita, and the proponents of each claim that it substantiates their beliefs. Shankara has commented on it and provided extensive arguments against any interpretation other than that of Advaita. See bhashya, nyaya prasthana, sruti, smriti.

brahmavidya (*brahmavidyA,* ब्रह्मविद्या) – knowledge of the one Self. (Also *brahmavitva,* with someone with this knowledge being called a *brahmavit.*) See Brahman.

Brihadaranyaka (*bRRihadAraNyaka,* बृहदारण्यकफ – one of the major Upanishads (and possibly the oldest). The word derives from *bRRihat* – great, large, wide, tall etc. and *Aranyaka* – produced in (or relating to) a forest. See Upanishad.

buddhi (*buddhi,* बुद्धि) – the organ of mind responsible for discrimination and judgment, perhaps nearest equated to the intellect in Western usage. See also, ahankara, antakarana, manas and chitta.

Chandogya (*chhAndogya,* छान्दोग्य) – one of the major Upanishads. See Upanishad.

Charvaka (*chArvAka,* चार्वाक) – materialist philosopher or a follower of him.

chatushtaya sampatti (*chatuShTaya sampatti,* चतुष्टय सम्पत्ति) – the fourfold pre-requisites specified by Shankara as needed by a seeker before he can achieve Self-realization. *chatuShTaya* means 'fourfold'; *sampatti* means success or accomplishment. See sadhana, vairagya, viveka, mumukshutvam.

chetana (*chetana,* चेतन) – consciousness, intelligence etc.

chidabhasa (*chidAbhAsa,* चिदाभास) – false appearance or reflection (*AbhAsa*) of consciousness (*chit*) – i.e. the ego.

chit (*chit,* चित्) – pure thought or Consciousness. See ananda, sat, satchidananda.

chitta (*chitta,* चित्त) – the organ (part) of mind responsible for memory. See antakarana, ahankara, buddhi, manas.

dama (*dama,* दम) – self-restraint but understood as control over the senses; one of the six qualities that form part of Shankara's chatushtaya sampatti. See chatushtaya sampatti, *shamAdi shhaTka sampatti*.

deva (*deva,* देव) – (pl. noun) the gods; (adj.) heavenly, divine.

Devanagari (*devanAgarI,* देवनागरी) – the script used in Sanskrit representation. The word literally means 'city of the Gods' (deva – gods; nAgara – belonging or relating to a town or city).

dharma (*dharma,* धर्म) – customary practice, conduct, duty, justice and morality. One of the four *puruShArtha*-s. The favored meaning of most traditional teachers is, however, 'nature, character, essential quality,' which they often translate as 'essence.' Our own dharma (*svadharma*) is what we ought to do with our lives in order to dissolve our accumulation of sanskara. See sanskara, karma.

dhyana (*dhyAna,* ध्यान) – meditation, usually in the sense of the mechanical act using a mantra as opposed to *nididhyAsana*.

drg-drsya-viveka (***dRRigdRRishya viveka,* दृग्दृश्य विवेक**) – 'Discrimination between the Seer and the Seen' – a work attributed to Shankara. *dRRik* is the seer or perceiver and *dRRishya* that which is seen or which can be objectified.

drishti-srishti-vada (***dRRiShTisRRiShTivAda,* दृष्टिसृष्टिवाद**) – the theory that our mistaken view of the world arises from a mental image (based on memory and sense data) superimposed upon the reality. *dRRiShTi* means 'seeing'; *sRRiShTi* means 'creation'; *vAda* means 'thesis' or 'doctrine.' See also adhyasa, ajati, srishti-drishti-vada.

drishya (***dRRishya,* दृश्य**) – visible; seen; i.e. objects of experience.

dukha (***duHkha,* दुःख**) – pain, sorrow, trouble.

dvaita (***dvaita,* द्वैत**) – duality, philosophy of dualism; belief that God and the Atman are separate entities. Madhva is the scholar most often associated with this philosophy.

dvesha (***dveSha,* द्वेष**) – hatred, dislike.

eka-jiva-vada (***eka-jIva-vAda,* एक-जीव-वाद**) – theory that there is only one *jIva* who 'imagines' the world.

Gaudapada (***gauDapAda,* गौडपाद**) – The author of the commentary (karika) on the Mandukya Upanishad. He is said to have been the teacher of Shankara's teacher. See karika, Mandukya, Upanishad.

gita (***gIta,* गीत**) – a sacred song or poem but more usually refers to philosophical or religious doctrines in verse form (*gIta* means 'sung'). The most famous are the Bhagavad Gita and Astavakra Gita. If the word is used on its own, it will be referring to the former. See Bhagavad, Astavakra.

grihasta (***gRRihastha,* गृहस्थ**) – this is the second stage of the traditional Hindu spiritual path, called the period of the householder, in which the Brahman performs the duties of master of the house and father of a family. See also brahmacharya, grihasta, sanyasa, vanaprastha.

guna (***guNa,* गुण**) – According to classical Advaita, creation is made up of three 'qualities,' sattva, rajas and tamas. Everything –

matter, thoughts, feelings – is 'made up of' these three in varying degrees and it is the relative proportions that determine the nature of the thing in question. See sattwa, rajas and tamas for more details.

guru (*guru*, गुरु) – literally 'heavy'; used to refer to one's elders or a person of reverence but more commonly in the West to indicate one's spiritual teacher.

hiranyagarbha (*hiraNyagarbha*, हिरण्यगर्भ) – the known subtle (*sUkShma*) universe; macrocosmic form of *taijasa*. (Literally 'golden womb' or 'egg'.)

iccha (*ichChA*, इच्छा) – wish, desire, inclination.

Isha Upanishad (*IshopaniShad*, ईशोपनिषद्) – also known as the Isavasya Upanishad, because its first verse begins: OM IshA vAsyamidam{\m+} sarvaM. IshAvAsya means 'pervaded by the lord.'

Isvara (*Ishvara*, ईश्वर) – the Lord; creator of the phenomenal universe. See saguna Brahman.

jada (*jaDa*,जड) – inert, lifeless.

jagat (*jagat*,जगत!) – the world (earth), mankind etc.

jagrat (*jAgrat*, जाग्रत्) – the waking state of consciousness. The 'waker ego' is called vishva. See also, sushupti, svapna, turiya.

janma (*janma*, जन्म) – birth.

japa (*japa*,जप) – the simple repetition of a mantra; usually associated with the initial stage of meditation. See mantra.

jati (*jAti*, जाति) – birth, the form of existence (as man, animal etc.); genus or species.

jiva (*jIva*, जीव) – the identification of the Atman with a body and mind; sometimes spoken of as 'the embodied Atman.' See Atman.

jivanmukta (*jIvanmukta*, जीवन्मुक्त) – someone liberated (in this life) from all future births. In other words, self-realized. (*mukta* is the adjective – liberated; *mukti* is the noun – liberation.)

jivatman (*jIvAtman*, जीवात्मन्) – another word for Atman, to emphasize that we are referring to the *Atman* in this embodied state, as opposed to the *paramAtman*, the 'supreme Self.' In the Sri Dakshinamurti Stotram of Shankara, *jIvatman* is equated with Consciousness and *paramAtman* with Existence. (All are, of course, equivalent.) See Atman.

jnana (*j~nAna*, ज्ञान) yoga – yoga based on the acquisition of true knowledge (j~nAna means 'knowledge') i.e. knowledge of the Self as opposed to mere information about the world of appearances. See also bhakti, karma.

jnana kanda (*j~nAna kANDa*, ज्ञान काण्ड) – those sections of the Vedas concerned with knowledge, i.e. the Upanishads.

jnana phalam (j~nAna phalam, ज्ञान्) – the 'fruit' or benefits of gaining Self-knowledge.

jnani or jnanin (*j~nAnI* or *j~nAnin*, ज्ञानी खर ज्ञानिन्) – one who practices jnana yoga. (*j~nAnin* is the *prAtipadika*; *j~nAnI* is the nominative singular *pada*.) See jnana yoga.

kama (*kAma*, काम) – desire, longing; one of the four *puruShArtha*-s. Not to be confused with karma. Shankara differentiates this from *rAga*: *rAga* is attachment to something one already has whereas *kAma* is wanting something one doesn't have. See purushartha.

kanda (*kANDa*, काण्ड) – part or section, division of a work or book, especially relating to the Vedas.

karana (*karaNa*, करण) – 'instrument' in the context of causality. *karaNa kAraNa* – instrumental cause. (The first 'a' is short.)

karana (*kAraNa*, कारण) – cause (noun) as in *nimitta kAraNa* or causal (adj.) as in *kAraNa sharIra*. Literally 'a cause (in philosophy i.e. that which is invariably antecedent to some product).' (The first 'a' is long.)

karika (*kArikA*, कारिका) – (strictly speaking) a concise philosophical statement in verse. The most well known is that by Gaudapada on the Mandukya Upanishad. (Not to be confused with *karika*, which is an elephant!) See Gaudapada, Mandukya, Upanishad.

karma (*karma*, कर्म) – literally 'action' but generally used to refer to the 'law' whereby actions carried out now will have their lawful effects in the future (and this may be in future lives). Note that karma yoga is something different – see below. See also sanskara.

karmakanda (*karmakANDa*, कर्मकाण्ड) – that portion of the Vedas relating to ceremonial acts, the rituals we should follow, sacrificial rites and so on.

karmaphala (*karmaphala*, कर्मफल) – the fruit (*phala*) of action; i.e. the result or consequence of our actions.

karma yoga (*karma yoga*, कर्म योग) – the practice of acting in such a way as not to incur karma, by carrying out 'right' actions, not 'good' or 'bad' ones. As explained in the Bhagavad Gita, it is the first phase of spiritual 'seeking', gaining the mental pre-requisites for beginning j~nAna yoga, namely sAdhana chatuShTaya sampatti. See bhakti, karma, jnana.

karya (*kArya*, कार्य) – effect or result.

Katha Upanishad (*kaThopaniShad*, कठोपनिषद्) – one of the 108+ Upanishads and one of the 10 major ones. *kaTha* was a sage and founder of a branch of the Yajur Veda. See Upanishad.

Kena Upanishad (*kenopaniShad*, केनोपनिषद्) – one of the 108+ Upanishads and another one of the 10 major ones. *kena* means 'whence?' ('how?,' 'why?' etc.) and is the first word of this Upanishad. See Upanishad.

khalvidam (*khalvidam*, खल्विदम्) – in the statement sarvam kahlvidam brahma – all this is verily Brahman. *khalu* means 'indeed, verily,' *idam* is 'this' (neutral pronoun).

kosha (*kosha*, कोश) – literally 'sheath' as in the scabbard of a sword; one of the five layers of identification that cover up our true nature.

krodha (*krodha*,क्रोध) – anger, passion.

kshanika vada (*kShaNika vAda*, क्षणिक वाद) – theory that Consciousness is 'momentary', arising and disappearing in each moment. This is the belief of the Yogachara or *vij~nAna vAda* Buddhist.

lakshana (*lakShaNa*, लक्षण) – pointer; indicating or expressing indirectly; accurate description or definition.

laukika (*laukika,* लौकिक) – worldly, belonging to or occurring in ordinary life. *laukika anumAna* is inference by scientific reasoning, based on observation.

laya (*laya,* लय) – literally 'dissolution' (and the last stage in the cycle of creation, preservation and destruction of the universe).

lila (*lIlA,* लीला) – literally 'play,' 'amusement' or 'pastime'; the idea that the apparent creation is a diversion for a creator – a means for Him to enjoy Himself. He plays all the parts in such a way that they are ignorant of their real nature and believe themselves separate.

loka (*loka,* लोक) – world, universe, sky or heaven etc. (adjective laukika).

Madhva (*madhva,* मध्व) – founder of the school of dvaita philosophy.

mahavakyas (*mahAvAkya,* महावाक्य) – *maha* means 'great'; *vAkya* means 'speech, saying or statement.' The four 'great sayings' from the Vedas are: – 'Consciousness is Brahman,' 'That thou art,' 'This Self is Brahman' and 'I am Brahman.'

manana (*manana,* मनन) – reflecting upon what has been heard (shravana). This is the second stage of the classical spiritual path, to remove any doubts about the knowledge that has been received via shravana. See also samshaya, shravana, nididhyasana.

manas (*manas,* मनस्) – the 'organ' of mind acting as intermediary between the senses and the intellect (buddhi) on the way in and the intellect and the organs of action on the way out. These are its primary functions and 'thinking' ought to consist only of the processing of data on behalf of the intellect. Unfortunately, it usually tries to take on the role of the intellect itself and this is when thinking becomes a problem. See ahankara, antakarana, buddhi and chitta.

Mandukya (*mANDUkya,* माण्डूक्य) – One of the major Upanishads and possibly the single most important, when considered in conjunction with the karika written by Gaudapada. (In many versions of this Upanishad, there is no distinction made between the original and the additions made by Gaudapada and there is some argument over which is which.) See Gaudapada, karika, Upanishad.

manonasha (*manonAsha*, मनोनाश) – literally 'death of the mind'; the idea being that the mind is the cause of our seeing duality and we gain enlightenment by putting an end to this. The intended meaning is only figurative.

mantra (*mantra*, मन्त्र) – a group of words (or sometimes only one or more syllables), traditionally having some mystical significance, being in many religions an actual 'name of God' or a short prayer. Often used in meditation (always in Transcendental Meditation). See japa.

maya (*mAyA*, माया) – literally 'magic' or 'witchcraft,' often personified in Hindu mythology. The 'force' used to explain how it is that we come to be deceived into believing that there is a creation with separate objects and living creatures etc. See also avarana and vikshepa.

mimamsa (*mImAMsA*, मीमांसा) – profound thought, reflection, examination. See purvamimamsa, utteramimamsa.

mithya (*mithyA*, मिथ्या) – dependent reality; literally 'incorrectly' or 'improperly,' used in the sense of 'false, untrue.' It is, however, more frequently used in the sense of 'depending upon something else for its existence.' It is ascribed to objects etc., meaning that these are not altogether unreal but not strictly real either i.e. they are our imposition of name and form upon the undifferentiated Self. See adhyasa.

moksha (*mokSha*, मोक्ष) – liberation, enlightenment, Self-realization; one of the four *puruShArtha*-s. mokSha literally means 'liberation'; 'enlightenment' is when the mind gains Self-knowledge. But the essence of the enlightenment is the realization that we are already free so, in that sense, the words are synonymous.

mumukshu (*mumukShu*, मुमुक्षु) – one for whom the desires to achieve enlightenment is the predominant goal in life; a seeker.

mumukshutva (*mumukShutva,* मुमुक्षुत्व) – the desire to achieve enlightenment, to the exclusion of all other desires. See sadhana, chatushtaya sampatti.

Mundaka Upanishad (*muNDakopaniShad,* मुण्डकोपनिषद्) – Another one of the 108+ Upanishads and also one of the 10 major ones – but not to be confused with the Mandukya. *muNDa* means 'having a shaved head' and the Upanishad is so called because everyone who comprehends its sacred doctrine is 'shorn,' i.e. liberated from all error. See Upanishad.

naimittika (*naimittika,* नैमित्तिक) – occasional, special. *naimittika karma* are those occasional duties that we have to perform, such as helping a neighbor who has helped one in the past.

Naiyayika (*naiyAyika,* नैयायिक) – a follower of the *nyAya* philosophy.

nama-rupa (*nAma-rUpa,* नामरूप) – name and form.

nara (*nara,* नर) – man, humanity; see *vaishvAnara.*

nasha (*nAsha,* नाश) – loss, destruction, annihilation, death.

nastika (*nAstika,* नास्तिक) – atheist, unbeliever; usually refers to one who does not recognise the authority of the Vedas.

neti (*neti,* नेति) – not this (*na* – not; *iti* – this). From the Brihadaranyaka Upanishad (2.3.6). Used by the intellect whenever it is thought that the Self might be some 'thing' observed e.g. body, mind etc. The Self cannot be anything that is seen, thought or known. See Brihadaranyaka, Upanishad.

nididhyasana (*nididhyAsana,* निदिध्यासन) – meditating upon the essence of what has now been intellectually understood until there is total conviction. The third stage of the classical spiritual path. See also shravana and manana. It is to be understood as 'right apprehension' (*vij~nAna*) rather than simply mechanical as *dhyAna* might be construed.

nidra (*nidrA,* निद्रा) – sleep – the 'individual' power of *mAyA.*

nigraha (*nigraha,* निग्रह) – restraint, control.

nimitta (*nimitta,* निमित्त) – literally the 'instrumental or efficient cause' but normally used (*nimitta kAraNa*) as meaning the latter, which is also referred to as 'intelligent cause'.

nirguna (*nirguNa*, निर्गुण) – 'without qualities'; usually referring to Brahman and meaning that it is beyond any description or thought. Since there is only Brahman, any word would imply limitation or duality. See Brahman, saguna, Isvara.

nirupadhika (*nirupAdhika*, निरुपाधिक) – without attributes or qualities. *nirupAdhika adhyAsa* is superimposition as of the snake on the rope, as opposed to *sopAdhika adhyAsa* e.g. the sunrise, which is still seen even when the mistake is realized.

nirvikalpa (*nirvikalpa*, निर्विकल्प) – (referring to samadhi) 'without' doubts about one's identity with the one Self. See savikalpa, samadhi, vikalpa.

nirvishesha (*nirvisheSha*, निर्विशेष) – making or showing no difference. *nirvisheShaNa* – attributeless.

nishkama (*niShkAma*, निष्काम) – desireless, disinterested. *niShkAma karma* is so-called 'right action,' performed in response to the need, neither selfishly nor unselfishly – it generates no *saMskAra*.

nishtha (*niShTha*, निष्ठ) – committed or devoted to; having a basis or grounding in. *niShThA* is the noun, meaning firmness, steadiness, devotion.

nitya (*nitya*, नित्य) – eternal. It also means 'ordinary, usual, necessary, obligatory.' It is used in this latter sense in connection with action. *nitya karma* are those daily duties that we have to perform, such as looking after one's children.

nivritti (*nivRRitti*, निवृत्ति) – giving up, abstaining, renouncing (esp. of desires in the path to enlightenment – *nivRRitti mArga*).

nyaya (*nyAya*, न्याय) – logical argument; literally, 'that into which a thing goes back,' a 'standard' or 'rule'; one of the 6 classical Indian philosophical systems, whose principal exponent was Gautama in the 3rd Century BC. So called because the system 'goes into' all physical and metaphysical subjects in a very logical manner.

nyaya prasthana (*nyAya prasthAna*, न्याय प्रस्थान) – refers to logical and inferential material based upon the Vedas, of which the most well known is the Brahmasutra of Vyasa (*nyAya* can also mean method, axiom, logical argument etc.). See pramana, prasthana-traya, smriti, sruti.

omkara (*omkAra*, ओम्कार) – the syllable OM.

pada (*pAda*, पाद) – quarter, i.e. one of the 'three states + *turIya*'.

Panchadashi (*pa~nchadashI*, पञ्चदशी) – literally means 'fifteen' because it has this many chapters – a book written by Vidyaranya (*vidyAraNya*), based upon the Upanishads. It discusses many Advaitic truths and uses some original metaphors to illustrate the concepts.

papa (*pApa*, पाप) – literally 'bad' or 'wicked' but used in the sense of the 'sin' that accrues (according to the theory of karma) from performing 'bad' actions, i.e. those done with a selfish motive. See also punya.

parama (*parama*, परम) – chief, highest, most prominent, best etc.

paramartha (noun), (*paramArtha*, परमार्थ);

paramarthika (adj.), (*pAramArthika* (adj.), पारमार्थिक – the highest truth or reality; the noumenal as opposed to the phenomenal world of appearances (vyavaharika). See pratibhasika and vyavaharika.

paramatman (*paramAtman*, परमात्मन्) – usually translated as the 'supreme Self' as opposed to the Atman in the embodied state, the jivatman. Swami Dayananda insists that it actually means 'limitless' in the sense of not limited by time or place and therefore changeless (Ref. 58). See Atman.

parampara (*paramparA*, परम्परा) – literally 'proceeding from one to another'; 'guru parampara' refers to the tradition of guru – disciple, with the disciple becoming the guru for the next generation. See also sampradaya.

parinama (*pariNAma*, परिणाम) – literally 'change, transformation into'; encountered in the context of a material cause in which the effect is a transformation from its cause as opposed to simply distinguishable from, e.g. butter made from milk as opposed to cloth made from cotton.

parinama vada (*pariNAma vAda*, परिणाम वाद) – the doctrine of creation as proposed by *sAMkhya* philosophy.

paroksha (*pArokSha*, पारोक्ष) – remote, mysterious, invisible, hidden (also *pArokShya*); opposite of *pratyakSha*.

Patanjali (*pata~njali*, पतञ्जलि) – philosopher, writer of the 'Yoga Sutras' and responsible for *aShTA~Nga* or *rAja yoga*.

phala (*phala*, फल) – fruit; often used in the context of the consequences that necessarily follow as a result of action. See *karmaphala*.

pradhana (*pradhAna*, प्रधान) – primary nature or matter (belief of *sAMkhya* philosophy).

prajna (*praj~nA*, प्रज्ञा) – (verb) to know or understand, find out, perceive or learn; (noun) wisdom, intelligence, knowledge. Not to be confused with *prAj~na* below.

prajna (*prAj~na*, प्राज्ञ) – the 'deep-sleep ego' in the deep-sleep state of consciousness, sushupti. Literally, 'wise, clever' (adj.) or 'a wise man' or 'intelligence dependent on individuality.' See also vishva, taijasa.

prajnana (*praj~nAna*, प्रज्ञान) – consciousness.

pralaya (*pralaya*, प्रलय) – the destruction of the world at the end of a kalpa. See kalpa.

prakarana (*prakaraNa*, प्रकरण) – subject, topic, treatise etc. but especially opening chapter or prologue.

prakarana grantha (*prakaraNa grantha*, प्रकरण ग्रन्थ) – this is the term used to refer to authoritative commentaries on the scripture but which are not part of the *prasthAna traya*. It is frequently used with respect to the works attributed to Shankara such as *upadesha sAhasrI*, *vivekachUDAmaNi* etc. The word *grantha* literally means 'tying or stringing together' though can itself mean composition or treatise.

prakriti (*prakRRiti*, प्रकृति) – literally the original or natural form or condition of anything; generally used to refer to what we would call 'nature.'

prakriya (*prakriyA*, प्रक्रिया) – a methodology of teaching; literally a chapter (esp. the introductory chapter of a work).

pralaya (*pralaya*, प्रलय) – dissolution, destruction, annihilation, specifically relating to the universe at the end of a *kalpa*.

pramana (*pramANa*, प्रमाण) – valid means for acquiring knowledge. There are 6 of these in Vedanta: – perception (*pratyakSha*), inference (*anumAna*), scriptural or verbal testimony (*shabda* or *Agama shruti*), analogy (*upamAna*), presumption (*arthApatti*) and non-apprehension (*anupalabdhi*). The first three are the major ones referred to by Shankara.

prameya (*prameya*, प्रमेय) – the object of knowledge obtained via a *pramANa*; also 'thing to be proven' or 'topic to be discussed.'

prana (*prANa*, प्राण) – literally the 'breath of life'; the vital force in the body with which we identify in the 'vital sheath.'

pranayama (*prANayAma*, प्रानयाम) – usually understood to mean control of breathing in advanced yoga techniques or as a prelude to meditation. According to Swami Chinmayananda, however, it does not mean this but relates to the five 'departments' of active life as described in the chapter on Spiritual Practices.

prapanchopashamam (*prapa~nchopashamam*, प्रपञ्चोपशमम्) – negation (*ama*) of the experience (*pash*) of the universe (*prapa~ncha*). This confirms the status of the world as *mithyA* or *vaitathya* and thereby negates it.

prarabdha (*prArabdha*, प्रारब्ध) – This literally means 'begun' or 'undertaken.' It is the fruit of all of our past action that is now having its effect. This is one of the three types of sanskara. See agamin, sanchita, sanskara. Also, there are three types of prArabdha karma – *ichChA*, *anichChA* and *parechChA* (personally desired, without desire and due to others' desire).

prasthana-traya (*prasthAna traya*, प्रस्थान त्रय) – *prasthAna* means 'system' or 'course' in the sense of a journey; *traya* just means 'threefold.' It refers to the three sources of knowledge of the Self (*shabda*), nyaya prasthana, sruti and smriti. See nyaya prasthana, shabda, sruti, smriti.

pratibhasa (noun) (*pratibhAsa*, प्रतिभास);
pratibhasika (adj.) (*prAtibhAsika*, प्रातिभासिक) – appearing or occurring to the mind, existing only in appearance, an illusion. See paramartha, vyavahara.
pratibimba (*pratibimba*, प्रतिबिम्ब) – a reflection. In logic, *bimba* is the object itself, with the *pratibimba* being the counterpart with which it is compared.
pratibimba-vada (*pratibimba vAda*,प्रतिबिम्ब वाद) – the theory that the jiva is a reflection of the Atman, similar to a the reflection of an object in a mirror.
pratyaksha (*pratyakSha*, प्रत्यक्ष) – 'present before the eyes, clear, distinct etc.' but particularly 'direct perception or apprehension' as a valid source of knowledge. Opposite of *pArokSha*, hidden. See pramana.
pravritti (*pravRRitti*, प्रवृत्ति) – active life, following one's desires (*pravRRitti mArga* as opposed to the path to enlightenment – *nivRRitti mArga*).
punya (*puNya*, पुण्य) – literally 'good' or 'virtuous'; used to refer to the 'reward' that accrues to us (according to the theory of karma) through the performing of unselfish actions. See also papa.
purna (*pUrNa*, पूर्ण) – full, complete, satisfied, perfect.
purusha (*puruSha*, पुरुष) – person (usually male), spirit.
purushartha (*puruShArtha*, पुरुषार्थ) – The general meaning of this term is 'any object of human pursuit' but it is used here in the sense of human (i.e. self) effort to overcome 'fate,' the fruit of one's past actions. The four classical pursuits are kAma, artha, dharma and mokSha. *puruShArtha-labha* is fulfillment of those pursuits. See karma, sanskara.
purvapaksha (*pUrvapakSha*, पूर्वपक्ष) – objection; view of the 'opponent' in a philosophical discussion. A common technique used in philosophical presentations.
Purva mimamsa, (*pUrva mImAMsA*, पूर्व मीमांसा) – the philosophical system based upon the first part of the Vedas and attributed

free, and yet continue to fall back into the conundrum of no longer feeling this freedom? Moments of complete freedom… knowing that it's not my business to 'do' life, not even to attempt to not 'do' life… and yet slowly fall back into the habit?

A: Enlightenment is not an experience; nor is it the 'nature of existence'. It is true that you are already free; it is also true that you apparently do not yet realize this. 'Not being enlightened' is simply the mind's not appreciating that you are already free. 'Becoming enlightened' is simply the gaining of the knowledge (in the mind) that you are already free. The 'I' that is already free is the 'I' that you are – it is Brahman.

You cannot really talk about a 'source' of ignorance but you are right that it is the removal of this ignorance that has to be achieved. It is only knowledge that will remove it since only knowledge is opposed to ignorance. So it is perfectly legitimate to talk about the 'acquisition of Self-knowledge' – you don't yet have it (otherwise you would know that you are Brahman) so you need to get it. You get it from the scriptures by way of a teacher.

Speaking of 'seeing how things are' is a 'new-agey' or Neo-Advaitin concept. You don't achieve this by 'disregarding things that can be seen'. The things that can be seen are seen because they are in front of you. They are all forms of the non-dual Brahman. Seeing them as separate is part of the ignorance. But, once the ignorance is removed, you still see them; it is just that you now know them to be none other than Brahman – your Self. Seeing blackness or a void, or conversely seeing bright lights or flashes, has nothing to do with enlightenment but indicates malfunctioning of the eyes.

Basically, what you are describing is not true enquiry. The path to Self-knowledge is via shravaNa, manana and nididhyAsana. I'm sure that the attitude that you are describing is very common, and represents a misdirection brought about by latching on to Ramana's 'Who am I?'. I do wonder sometimes whether this single, oft-quoted mantra is the principal cause of most of the problems discussing and writing about it. This consolidates the knowledge and the mind becomes serene in that knowledge, unaffected by the travails of life. Then you are termed a jIvanmukta – one who is 'liberated while living'.

(You can read my essay on enlightenment at http://www.advaita-vision.org/enlightenment-akhandakara/.)

Q.333 Incomplete Enlightenment

Q: As I understand it, the sense of 'I' (distinguished from the ultimate I/Self) is the source of ignorance. Ignorance leads to the fear, which inspires us to attempt to find enlightenment. The attempt to find enlightenment is the delusion that there is something to gain. The teachings tell us that 'enlightenment' is the nature of existence.

What needs to happen is the destruction/removal of ignorance, rather than the acquisition of anything. I already feel as if I have approached the 'screen' upon which phenomena occur. By practicing 'neti neti', I attempt to see what always is, which is a temporary attempt to disregard things that can be seen. Once this happens, there is the inference of blankness/darkness/all-inclusiveness/voidness. And once this practice of 'neti neti' is over, I begin to see things come of themselves, from little sparks… flakes of concepts… to their blooming as a climax of a concept. The climax wanes and the concept disappears of itself just as it arose.

A short time after this attempt at enquiry, the ease I had with reality fades. The sense that reality is not okay begins to gradually return. It feels as if I missed something from this experience. At other times, I feel as if perhaps this effort is part of the problem. Maybe the enquiry is meant to be a last ditch attempt to notice the fallacy of trying to 'do' something, or even the attempt to try to do nothing.

Is this the realization? That effort is resistance? That surrender to this fact is the best that we can do?

How does it happen that one can know 'in the mind' that one is to Jaimini. Mainly concerned with enquiring into the nature of dharma or right action. See mimamsa, uttaramimamsa.

raga (*rAga*, राग) – any feeling or passion but especially vehement desire; interest in, attachment. Shankara differentiates this from *kAma*: *rAga* is attachment to something one already has whereas *kAma* is wanting something one doesn't have. *rAga-dveSha* is love-hatred.

rajas (*rajas*, रजस्) – the second of the three guna. Associated with animals and activity, emotions, desire, selfishness and passion. Adjective – rajassic (Eng.); *rAjasa* or *rAjasika* (Sansk.) See guna.

Ramanuja (*rAmAnuja*, रामानुज) – founder of the *vishiShTAdvaita* school of philosophy.

rishi (*RRiShi*, ऋषि) – author or singer of sacred Vedic hymns but now more generally used to refer to a saint or Sage.

rupa (*rUpa*, रूप) – form, outward appearance.

sadhaka (*sAdhaka*, साधक) – a seeker or, more pedantically, a worshipper.

sadhana (*sAdhana*, साधन) – literally 'leading straight to a goal'; refers to the spiritual disciplines followed as part of a 'path' toward Self-realization. See also chatushtaya sampatti.

sadhu (*sAdhu*, साधु) – a sage, saint, holy man; literally leading straight to the goal, hitting the mark.

saguna (*saguNa*, सगुण) – 'with qualities.' The term is usually used to refer to Brahman personified as the creator, Iswara, to symbolise the most spiritual aspect of the world of appearances. See Brahman, Isvara, nirguna.

sahaja sthiti (*sahaja sthiti*, सहज स्थिति) – Once Self-realisation has been attained, there is full and lasting knowledge of the Self. '*sahaja*' means 'state' but this stage of samadhi is not a state – it is our true nature. It is permanent (*sthiti* meaning 'steady' or 'remaining'), unlike the earlier stages of samadhi. See nirvikalpa, samadhi, savikalpa, vikalpa.

sakshin (*sAkShIn*, साक्षिन) – a witness, the ego or subject as opposed to the object (also *sAkshi*).

sakshibhava (*sAkshibhAva*, साक्शिभाव) – being or becoming (*bhAva*) a 'witness' (*sAkshin*).

samadhana (*samAdhAna*, समाधान) – contemplation, profound meditation; more usually translated as concentration; one of the 'six qualities' that form part of Shankara's chatushtaya sampatti. See chatushtaya sampatti, *shamAdi shhaTka sampatti*.

samadhi (*samAdhi*, समाधि) – the state of total peace and stillness achieved during deep meditation. Several 'stages' are defined – see vikalpa, savikalpa samadhi, nirvikalpa samadhi and sahaja sthiti.

samashti (*samaShTi*, समष्टि) – totality, as opposed to *vyaShTi*, the individual.

sambandha (*sambandha*, सम्बन्ध) – relationship, literally 'union, association, conjunction.'

samkhya (*sAMkhya*, सांख्य) – one of the three main divisions of Hindu philosophy and one of the six darshanas; attributed to Kapila.

sampradaya (*sampradAya*, सम्प्रदाय) – the tradition or established doctrine of teaching from master to pupil through the ages. See also parampara.

samsara (*saMsAra*, संसार) – the continual cycle of death and rebirth, transmigration etc. to which we are supposedly subject in the phenomenal world until we become enlightened and escape. *saMsArin* – one who is bound to the cycle of birth and death.

samshaya (*saMshaya*, संशय) – uncertainty, irresolution, hesitation or doubt. See manana.

samuchchaya vada (samuchchaya vAda, समुच्चय वाद) – the belief that karma yoga is needed, as well as j~nAna yoga, in order to attain enlightenment. (The word samuchchaya means 'combination'). The idea is refuted by Shankara.

sanchita (*saMchita*, संचित) – one of the three types of sanskara, literally meaning 'collected' or 'piled up.' That sanskara, which has been accumulated from past action but has still not manifest. See agamin, prarabdha, sanskara.

sanga (*sa~Nga,* सङ्ग) – assembly, association, company. See satsanga.

sanskara (*saMskAra,* संस्कार) – Whenever an action is performed with the desire for a specific result (whether for oneself or another), sanskara is created for that person. These accumulate and determine the situations with which we will be presented in the future and will influence the scope of future actions. There are three 'types' – agamin, sanchita and prarabdha. The accumulation of sanskara (sanchita) dictates the tendencies that we have to act in a particular way (vasanas). This is all part of the mechanism of karma. See agamin, karma, prarabdha, sanchita and karma.

sanyasa (*saMnyAsa,* संन्यास) – the final stage of the traditional Hindu spiritual path; involves complete renunciation. The word literally means 'putting or throwing down, laying aside'; i.e. becoming a professional ascetic. One who does so is called a sanyasin (*saMnyAsin*). See also brahmacharya, grihasta, vanaprastha.

sarvajna (*sarvaj~na,* सर्वज्ञ) – all knowing (of Ishvara).

sat (*sat,* st!) – existence, reality, truth (to mention a few). See also ananda, chit, satchitananda.

satchitananda (*sat-chit-Ananda* or *sachchidAnanda,* सच्चिदानन्द) – the oft used word to describe our true nature, in so far as this can be put into words (which it can't). It translates as being-consciousness-bliss but see the separate bits for more detail.

satkarya vada (*satkArya vAda,* सत्कार्य वाद) – the doctrine of the effect actually pre-existing in the cause (usually in reference to the creation).

satsanga (*satsa~Nga,* सत्सङ्ग) – association with the good; keeping 'good company'; most commonly used now to refer to a group of people gathered together to discuss (Advaita) philosophy.

sattva (*sattva,* सत्त्व) – the highest of the three guna. Associated with stillness, peace, truth, wisdom, unselfishness and spirituality, representing the highest aspirations of man. Adjective – sattwic (Eng.); *sAttva* or *sAttvika* (Sansk.). See guna.

satya (*satya*, सत्य) – true, real. *satyam* – truth. Also one of the *yama*-s – truthfulness, sincerity.

savikalpa (*savikalpa*, सविकल्प) – (referring to samadhi) still 'with' doubts about one's identity with the one Self. See nirvikalpa, samadhi, vikalpa.

shabda (*shabda*, शब्द) – scriptural or verbal testimony. See pramana, nyaya prasthana, prasthana-traya, sruti, smRRiti

shama (*shama*, शम) – literally tranquillity, absence of passion but more usually translated as mental discipline or self-control; one of the *shamAdi shhaTka sampatti* or 'six qualities' that form part of Shankara's chatushtaya sampatti. See chatushtaya sampatti, *shamAdi shhaTka sampatti*.

(*shamAdi ShaTka sampatti*, शमादि षट्क सम्पत्ति) – the six qualities that form part of Shankara's chatushtaya sampatti. These are *shama, dama, uparati, titikShA, samAdhAna* and *shraddhA*.

Shankara (*shaMkara*, शंकर) – 8th Century Indian philosopher responsible for firmly establishing the principles of Advaita. Though he died at an early age (32?), he commented on a number of major Upanishads, the Bhagavad Gita and the Brahmasutra, as well as being attributed as the author of a number of famous works, such as Atmabodha, Bhaja Govindam and Vivekachudamani.

Shankaracharya (*shaMkarAchArya*, शंकराचार्य) – The title given to one of the four teachers (see acharya) following the tradition in India established by Shankara (see Shankara). He set up four positions, North, South, East and West, to be held by realized men, who would take on the role of teacher and could be consulted by anyone having problems or questions of a spiritual nature.

shanti (*shAnti*, शान्ति) – peace, tranquility.

sharira (*sharIra*, शरीर) – one's body (divided into gross, subtle and causal aspects); literally 'that which is easily destroyed or dissolved.'

shastra (*shAstra*, शास्त्र) – order, teaching, instruction; any sacred book or composition that has divine authority.

shastriya anumana (*shAstrIya anumAna*, शास्त्रीय अनुमान) – inference based upon the material contained in the scriptures.

shishya (*shiShya*, शिष्य) – pupil, scholar, disciple.

shraddha (*shraddhA*, श्रद्धा) – faith, trust or belief (in the absence of direct personal experience); the student needs this initially with respect to what he is told by the guru or reads in the scriptures; one of the 'six qualities' that form part of Shankara's chatushtaya sampatti. See chatushtaya sampatti, *shamAdi shhaTka sampatti*.

shravana (*shravaNa*, श्रवण) – hearing the truth from a sage or reading about it in such works as the Upanishads; first of the three key stages in the classical spiritual path. See also manana, nididhyasana.

shrotriya (*shrotriya*, श्रोत्रिय) – someone (usually a *Brahmana*) who is well-versed in the scriptures.

shruti (*shruti*, श्रुति) – refers to the Vedas, incorporating the Upanishads. Literally means 'hearing' and refers to the belief that the books contain orally transmitted, sacred wisdom from the dawn of time. See nyaya prasthana, pramana, smriti.

shunya (*shunya*, शुन्य) – literally 'empty' or 'void'. This is associated with the beliefs of the *mAdhyamika* branch of Mahayana Buddhists.

siddha (*siddha*, सिद्ध) – literally 'accomplished' or 'perfected'; used to refer to one who has practiced Yoga for many years and acquired special powers.

siddhanta (*siddhAnta*, सिद्धान्त) – final end or purpose; conclusion of an argument.

smriti (*smRRiti*, स्मृति) – refers to material 'remembered' and subsequently written down. In practice, it refers to books of law (in the sense of guidance for living) which were written and based upon the knowledge in the Vedas, i.e. the so-called *dharma-shAstra*-s – Manu, Yajnavalkya, Parashara. In the context of nyaya prasthana, it is used to refer to just one of these books – the Bhagavad Gita. See pramana, nyaya prasthana, sruti.

sopadhika (***sopAdhika,* सोपाधिक**) – *nirupAdhika adhyAsa* is superimposition as of the snake on the rope, as opposed to *sopAdhika adhyAsa* e.g. the sunrise, which is still seen even when the mistake is realized.

sri (***shrI,* श्री**) – used as a title, c.f. 'reverend,' to signify an eminent person. May also be used in a similar manner to refer to revered objects or works of scripture, for example.

srishti (***sRRiShTi,* सृष्टि**) – creation.

srishti-drishti-vada (***sRRiShTidRRiShTivAda,* सृष्टिदृष्टिवाद**) – the theory that the world is separate from ourselves, having been created (by God or big-bang) and evolving independently of ourselves, i.e. the 'common sense' view of things. See also adhyasa, ajati, drishti-srishti-vada.

sthula (***sthUla,* स्थूल**) – large, thick, coarse, dense; the gross body (*sthUla sharIra*).

sukha (***sukha,* सुख**) – comfortable, happy, prosperous etc. *sukham* – pleasure, happiness.

sukshma (***sUkShma,* सूक्ष्म**) – subtle, as in the subtle body – *sUkShma sharIra*.

sushupti (***suShupti,* सुषुप्ति**) – the deep-sleep state of consciousness. The 'sleeper ego' is called prajna. See also jagrat, svapna, turiya.

sutra (***sUtra,* सूत्र**) – an especially abbreviated verse in which the fewest possible words are used to convey the message (literally 'thread').

sva (***sva,* स्व**) – one's own.

svabhava (***svabhAva,* स्वभाव**) – one's natural disposition.

svadharma (***svadharma,* स्वधर्म**) – one's own dharma. See dharma.

svapna (***svapna,* स्वप्न**) – the dream state of consciousness. The 'dreamer ego' is called taijasa. See also, jagrat, sushupti, turiya.

svarga (***svarga,*** स्वर्ग) – heaven.

svarupa (***svarUpa,* स्वरूप**) – one's own character or nature and, e.g. *svarUpAnanda* – one's own Ananda (limitless bliss).

svatapramanya vada (svataHprAmANyavAda, स्वतःप्रामाण्यवाद) – the theory of the 'self validity of knowledge', i.e. not needing to validate knowledge acquired from one pramANa by another.

taijasa (*taijasa*, तैजस) – the 'dreamer ego' in the dream state of consciousness, svapna. See also visva, prajna.

Taittiriya (*taittirIya*, तैत्तिरीय) – one of the principal Upanishads. (*taittirIya* was one of the schools of the Yajur Veda.)

tamas (*tamas*, तमस्) – the 'lowest' of the three guna. Associated with matter and carrying characteristics such as inertia, laziness, heedlessness and death. It literally means 'darkness' or 'gloom.' Adjective – tamasic (Eng.); *tAmasa* or *tAmasika* (Sansk.). See guna.

tarka (*tarka*, तर्क) – reasoning, speculation, philosophical system or doctrine.

tarkika (*tArkika*, तार्किक) – logician or philosopher.

tatastha (*taTastha*, तटस्थ) – a property distinct from the nature of the body and yet that by which it is known. An example would be telling someone that the house they are referring to in the street ahead is the one with the crow on the chimney. The house is what the listener is interested in but the crow is a *taTastha lakShaNa*, i.e. that by which it is known.

titiksha (*titikShA*, तितिक्षा) – forbearance or patience; one of the 'six qualities' that form part of Shankara's *chatuShTaya sampatti*. See chatushtaya sampatti, *shamAdi shhaTka sampatti*.

trikalatita (*trikAlAtIta*, त्रिकालातीत) – that which transcends past, present and future (describing the Self).

tucha (*tuchCha*, तुच्छ) – completely unreal, e.g. son of a barren woman.

turiya (*turIya*, तुरीय) – the 'fourth' state of consciousness (turiya means 'fourth'). In fact, some (e.g. Sri Atmananda Krishna Menon) define it rather as the background against which the other states (waking, dream and deep-sleep) take place. In this latter case, it is also our true nature. (If defined merely as the highest 'state' then our true nature is called turiyatita.)

upadana (*upAdAna*, उपादान) – literally 'the act of taking for oneself'; used to refer to the 'material cause' in logic (*upAdAna karaNa*).

upadesha (*upadesha*, उपदेश) – instruction or teaching.

upadesha sahasri (*upadesha sAhasrI*, उपदेश साहस्री) – 'A Thousand Teachings' – book attributed to Shankara (with more certainty than most). *sAhasrika* means 'consisting of a thousand.'

upadhi (*upAdhi*, उपाधि) – Literally, this means something that is put in place of another thing; a substitute, phantom or disguise. In Vedanta, it is commonly referred to as a 'limitation' or 'limiting adjunct' i.e. one of the 'identifications' made by *ahaMkAra* that prevents us from realizing the Self.

upanishad (*upaniShad*, उपनिषद्) – one of the (108+) books forming part (usually the end) of one of the four Vedas. The parts of the word mean: to sit (*Shad*) near a master (*upa*) at his feet (*ni*), so that the idea is that we sit at the feet of a master to listen to his words. Monier-Williams (Ref. 5) states that, 'according to native authorities, upanishad means 'setting at rest ignorance by revealing the knowledge of the supreme spirit.' See Vedanta.

uparama (*uparama*, उपरम) – see uparati.

uparati (*uparati*, उपरति) – desisting from sensual enjoyment; 'revelling' in that which is 'near' i.e. one's own Self; also translated as following one's dharma or duty; one of the 'six qualities' that form part of Shankara's chatushtaya sampatti. See chatushtaya sampatti, *shamAdi shhaTka sampatti.*

upasana (*upAsana*, उपासन) – worship, homage, waiting upon; literally the act of sitting or being near to; sometimes used in the sense of 'meditation.'

uttama (*uttama*, उत्तम) – uppermost, excellent, highest.

Uttara mimamsa (*uttara mImAMsA*, उत्तर मीमांसा) – the Vedanta philosophy, based on the latter (uttara) part of the Vedas rather than the earlier (purva). Its founder was Badarayana, who authored the Brahmasutra. There are three main schools – dvaita, Advaita and vishishtAdvaita. See Brahmasutra, mimamsa, purvamimamsa, veda.

vacharambhana (*vAchArambhaNa*, वाचारम्भण) – depending on mere words or some merely verbal difference. From the Chandogya

Upanishad 6.1.4 – 6. (These sutras explain how we effectively create the world by notionally separating out forms and giving them names.)

Vachaspati (*vAchaspati,* वाचस्पति) – name of one of the two schools of Advaita, after the philosopher *vAchaspati mishra*. It is also called the *bhAmati* school. The other school is the *vivaraNa* school.

vada (*vAda,* वाद) – speech, proposition, discourse, argument, discussion, explanation or exposition (of scriptures etc.).

vairagya (*vairAgya,* वैराग्य) – detachment or dispassion; indifference to the pleasure that result from success or the disappointment that result from failure. Literally to be 'deprived of' (*vai*) 'passion or desire' (*rAga*). See sadhana, chatushtaya sampatti.

vaishvanara (*vaishvAnara,* वैश्वानर) – the gross physical condition, or waking state of man (more usually known as *vishva*). Brahman 'located in' the bodily form. Literally means 'relating to or belonging to all men, universal.'

vaishya (*vaishya,* वैश्य) – a working man, trader or farmer – the third of the traditional four castes in India.

vanaprastha (*vanaprastha,* वनप्रस्थ) – the third stage of the traditional Hindu spiritual path, in which the Brahman retires from life and becomes a 'forest dweller,' living as a hermit. Traditionally speaking, 'a properly initiated *dvija* or twice-born.' See also brahmacharya, grihasta, sanyasa, vanaprastha.

vasana (*vAsanA,* वासना) – literally 'desiring' or 'wishing' – latent behavioural tendency in one's nature brought about through past action (karma) and the sanskara that resulted from this. See karma, sanskara.

Vasishta (*vAsiShTha,* वासिष्ठ) – eponymous sage of the 'Yoga Vasishta' one of the classical works of Advaita.

vastu (*vastu,* वस्तु) – a thing that exists, object, subject matter. Strictly speaking, there is only one vastu – Atman. Everything else is incidental – it comes and goes. Only Consciousness is always there, intrinsic.

vastu-tantra (*vastu-tantra*, वस्तुतन्त्र) – objective, dependent on things.

veda (*veda*, वेद) – knowledge, but the word is normally only used to refer to one of the four Vedas (see Vedanta) and vidya is used for knowledge per se. See vidya.

Vedanta (*vedAnta*, वेदान्त) – literally 'end' or 'culmination' (*anta*) of knowledge (*veda*) but veda in this context refers to the four Vedas, the Hindu equivalents of the Christian bible (called Rig, *RRig* Veda; Sama, *sama* Veda; Atharva, *atharva* Veda; Yajur, *yajur* Veda). Traditionally, the last part of the vedas (i.e. 'end') is devoted to the Upanishads. See upanishad.

vichara (*vichAra*, विचार) – consideration, reflection, deliberation, investigation. *vichAra mArga* is translated as 'Direct Path,'

vidya (*vidyA*, विद्या) – knowledge, science, learning, philosophy. *Atma-vidyA* or *brahma-vidyA* is knowledge of the Self.

vijnana (*vij~nAna*, विज्ञान) – discerning, understanding, comprehending; 'right apprehension' in the case of *nididhyAsana* as opposed to *dhyAna*. *vij~nAna vAda* is the philosophical theory of Idealism, held by the Yogachara Buddhists.

vikalpa (*vikalpa*, विकल्प) – doubt, uncertainty or indecision; division or manifoldness.

vikara (*vikAra*, विकार) – transformation, modification, change of form or nature. Also *vikAratva* – the state of change; and *vikAravat* – undergoing changes.

vikshepa (*vikShepa*, विक्षेप) – the 'projecting' power of *mAyA*. In the rope-snake metaphor, this superimposes the image of the snake upon the rope. See avarana, maya.

vilakshana (*vilakShaNa*, विलक्षण) –differing from; not possible to define exactly; one definition of *mithyA* is *sad-asad-vilakShaNa*.

virat (*virAT*, विराट्) – objective, gross, physical universe; macrocosmic form of *vishva*.

vishaya (*viShaya*, विषय) – object of sensory perception; any subject or topic; the subject of an argument. The word *viSha* from which it derives means 'poison' or 'venom.

vishesha (*visheSha,* विशेष) – literally 'distinction' or 'difference between'; particular or specific. The Vaisheshika philosophy believes that the material universe is made up of nine substances, each of which is 'essentially different' from any other. See Vaisheshika.

visheshya (*visheShya,* विशेष्य) – noun; that which is to be distinguished (from something else).

vishishtAdvaita (*vishiShTAdvaita,* विशिष्टाद्वैत) – qualified non-dualism; belief that God and the Atman are distinct but not separate. Ramanuja is the scholar most often associated with this philosophy. See Advaita, dvaita.

vishva (*vishva,* विश्व) – the 'waker ego' in the waking state of consciousness, jagrat. Also sometimes referred to as *vaishvAnara*. See also taijasa, prajna.

vivarana (*vivaraNa,* विवरण) – literally 'explanation' or 'interpretation'; name of one of the two schools of Advaita. The other school is the *vAcaspati or bhAmati* school.

vivarta (*vivarta,* विवर्त) – an apparent or illusory form; unreality caused by avidya.

vivarta vada (*vivarta vAda,* विवर्त वाद) – the theory that the world is only an apparent projection of Ishvara (i.e. an illusion); apparent transformation only; manifestation not creation.

viveka (*viveka,* विवेक) – discrimination; the function of buddhi, having the ability to differentiate between the unreal and the real. See sadhana, chatushtaya sampatti.

Vivekachudamani (*vivekachUDAmaNi,* विवेकचूडामणि) – the title of a book attributed to Shankara. *chUDAmaNi* is the name given to the jewel worn on top of the head. An English version of the book is called 'The Crest Jewel of Discrimination.'

vritti (*vRRitti,* वृत्ति) – in the context of Vedanta, this means a mental disposition. In general, it can mean a mode of conduct or behaviour, character or disposition, business or profession etc. See aham vritti and idam vritti.

vyashti (*vyaShTi,* व्यष्टि) – the individual or 'individuality' as opposed to the totality, *samaShTi*.

vyavahara (noun) (*vyavahAra*, व्यवहार);

vyavaharika (adj.), (*vyAvahArika*, व्यावहारिक) – the 'relative,' 'practical,' or phenomenal world of appearances; the normal world in which we live and which we usually believe to be real; as opposed to *pAramArthika* (reality) and *prAtibhAsika* (illusory). See paramarthika and pratibhasika.

yoga (*yoga*, योग) – literally 'joining' or 'attaching' (our word 'yoke' derives from this). It is used generally to refer to any system whose aim is to 'join' our 'individual self' back to the 'universal Self.' The Yoga system pedantically refers to that specified by Patanjali. See bhakti, jnana, karma.

Yogachara (*yogAchAra*, योगाचार) – branch of Hinayana Buddhism; also known as *vij~nAna vAda*.

yukti (*yukti*, युक्ति) – reasoning, argument, induction, deduction (as opposed to intuition – *anubhava*).

Index

Recent bestsellers from MANTRA BOOKS are:

The Way Things Are

A Living Approach to Buddhism

Lama Ole Nydahl

An introduction to the teachings of the Buddha, and how to make use of these teachings in everyday life.

Paperback: 978-1-84694-042-2 ebook: 978-1-78099-845-9

Back to the Truth

5000 Years of Advaita

Dennis Waite

A demystifying guide to Advaita for both those new to, and those familiar with this ancient, non-dualist philosophy from India.

Paperback: 978-1-90504-761-1 ebook: 978-184694-624-0

Shinto: A Celebration of Life

Aidan Rankin

Introducing a gentle but powerful spiritual pathway reconnecting humanity with Great Nature and affirming all aspects of life.

Paperback: 978-1-84694-438-3 ebook: 978-1-84694-738-4

In the Light of Meditation

Mike George

A comprehensive introduction to the practice of meditation and the spiritual principles behind it. A 10 lesson meditation programme with CD and internet support.

Paperback: 978-1-90381-661-5

The Less Dust the More Trust

Participating in The Shamatha Project, Meditation and Science

Adeline van Waning, MD PhD

The inside-story of a woman participating in frontline meditation research, exploring the interfaces of mind-practice, science and psychology.

Paperback: 978-1-78099-948-7 ebook: 978-1-78279-657-2

I Know How To Live, I Know How To Die

The Teachings of Dadi Janki: A warm, radical, and life-affirming view of who we are, where we come from, and what time is calling us to do

Neville Hodgkinson

Life and death are explored in the context of frontier science and deep soul awareness.

Paperback: 978-1-78535-013-9 ebook: 978-1-78535-014-6

Living Jainism

An Ethical Science

Aidan Rankin, Kanti V. Mardia

A radical new perspective on science rooted in intuitive awareness and deductive reasoning.

Paperback: 978-1-78099-912-8 ebook: 978-1-78099-911-1

A Path of Joy

Popping into Freedom

Paramananda Ishaya

A simple and joyful path to spiritual enlightenment.

Paperback: 978-1-78279-323-6 ebook: 978-1-78279-322-9

Ordinary Women, Extraordinary Wisdom

The Feminine Face of Awakening

Rita Marie Robinson

A collection of intimate conversations with female spiritual teachers who live like ordinary women, but are engaged with their true natures.

Paperback: 978-1-84694-068-2 ebook: 978-1-78099-908-1

The Way of Nothing

Nothing in the Way

Paramananda Ishaya

A fresh and light-hearted exploration of the amazing reality of nothingness.

Paperback: 978-1-78279-307-6 ebook: 978-1-78099-840-4

Readers of ebooks can buy or view any of these bestsellers by clicking on the live link in the title. Most titles are published in paperback and as an ebook. Paperbacks are available in traditional bookshops. Both print and ebook formats are available online.

Find more titles and sign up to our readers' newsletter at http://www.johnhuntpublishing.com/mind-body-spirit.
Follow us on Facebook at https://www.facebook.com/OBooks and Twitter at https://twitter.com/obooks.

www.ingramcontent.com/pod-product-compliance
Lightning Source LLC
LaVergne TN
LVHW040257220826
846147LV00009B/49

9781789042207